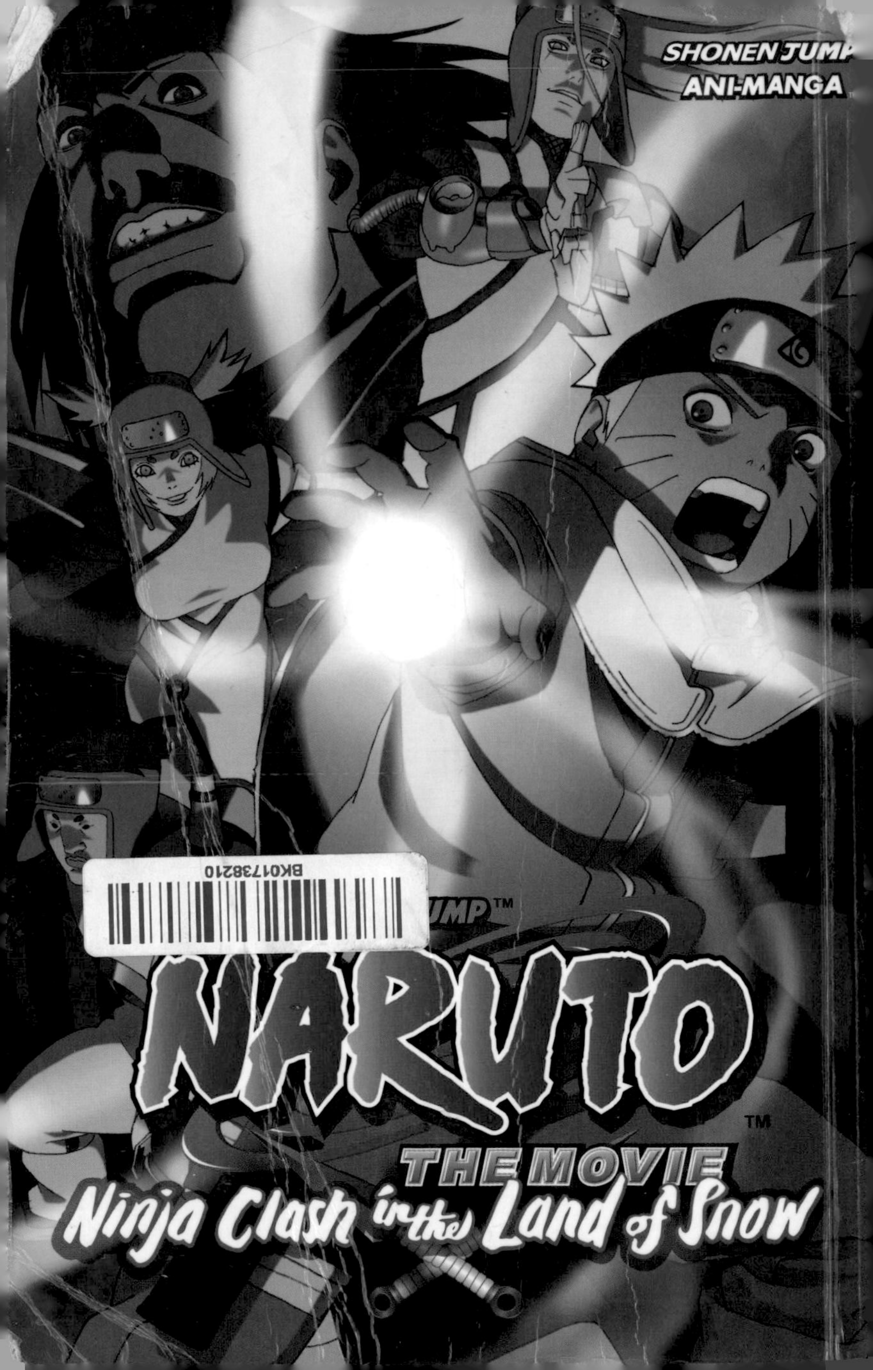
SHONEN JUMP
ANI-MANGA
JUMP™
NARUTO™
THE MOVIE
Ninja Clash in the Land of Snow

SHONEN JUMP™

NARUTO™

THE MOVIE

Ninja Clash in the Land of Snow

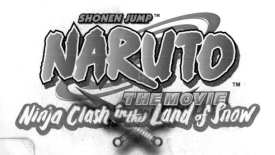

SHONEN JUMP™

NARUTO™
THE MOVIE
Ninja Clash in the Land of Snow

Original Story and Art by Masashi Kishimoto

English Adaptation/Annie Blacklock
Touch-up Art & Lettering/Rina Mapa
Design/Sean Lee
Editor/Carol Fox

Editor in Chief, Books/Alvin Lu
Editor in Chief, Magazines/Marc Weidenbaum
VP of Publishing Licensing/Rika Inouye
VP of Sales/Gonzalo Ferreyra
Sr. VP of Marketing/Liza Coppola
Publisher/Hyoe Narita

GEKIJOBAN NARUTO – DAIKATSUGEKI! YUKIHIME
NINPOCHO DATTEBAYO! – © 2002 MASASHI KISHIMOTO
© NMP 2004. All rights reserved. First published in Japan in
2004 by SHUEISHA Inc., Tokyo. English translation rights in the
United States of America and Canada
arranged by SHUEISHA Inc.

Printed in China

Published by VIZ Media, LLC
P.O. Box 77010
San Francisco, CA 94107

10 9 8 7 6 5 4 3 2 1
First printing, October 2007

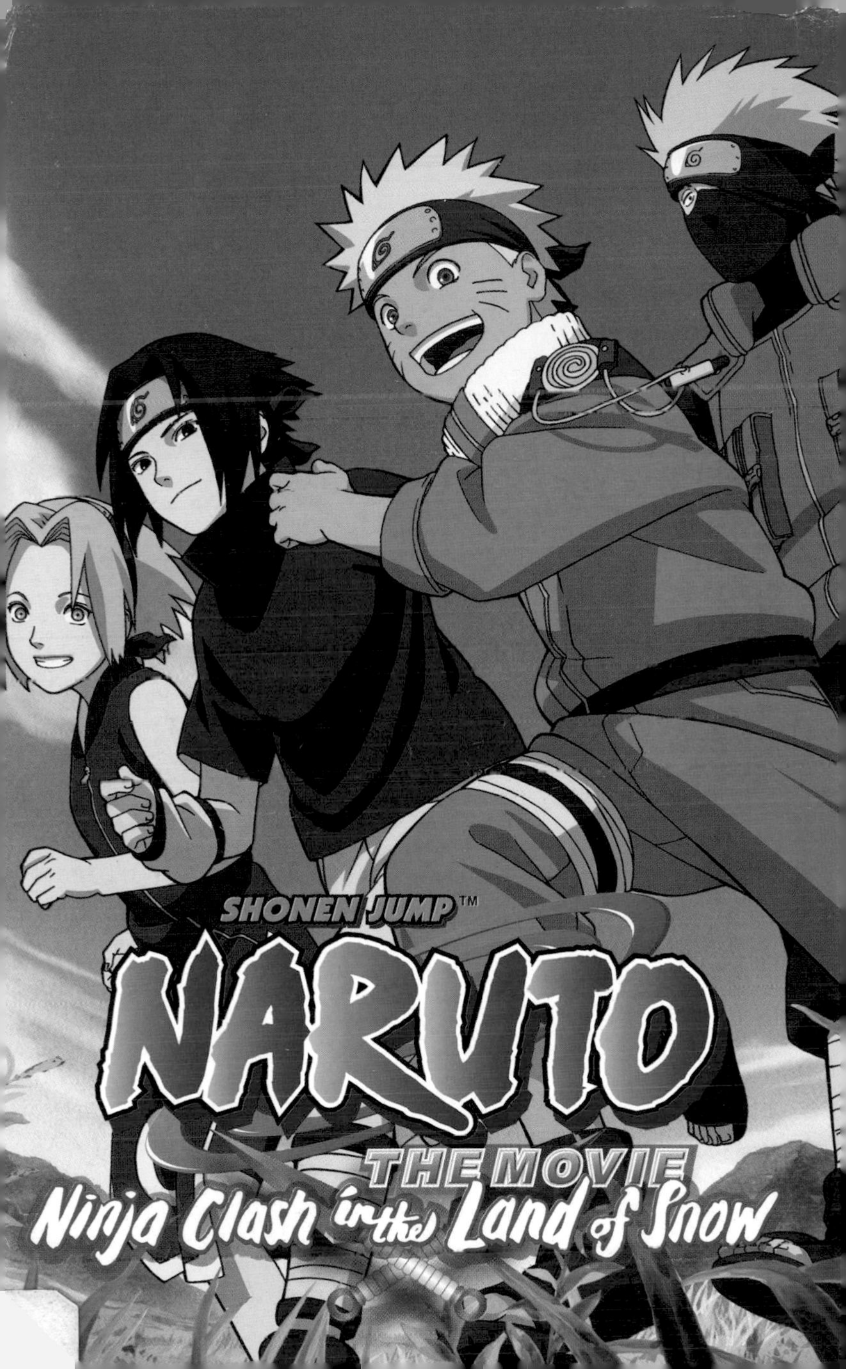
SHONEN JUMP™
NARUTO
THE MOVIE
Ninja Clash in the Land of Snow

Prologue

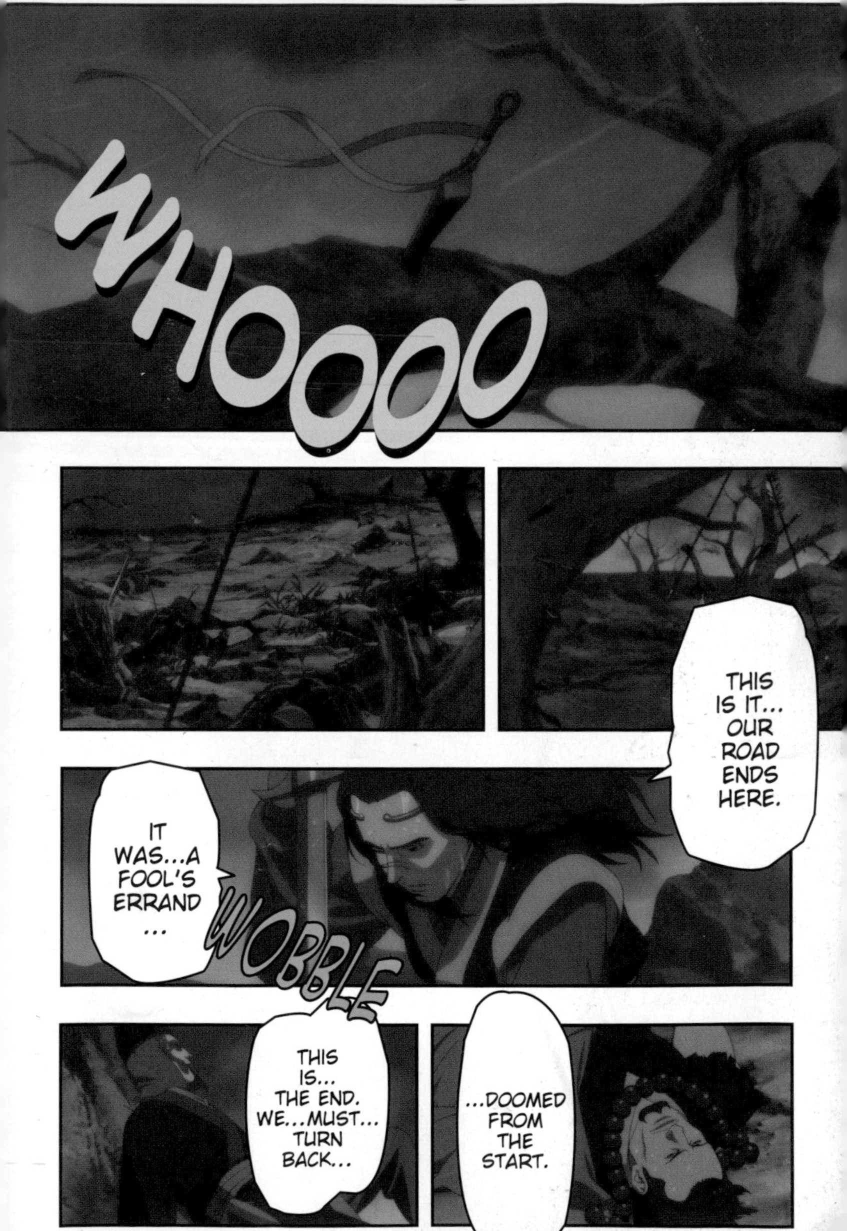
WHOOOO
THIS IS IT... OUR ROAD ENDS HERE.
IT WAS...A FOOL'S ERRAND ...
WOBBLE
...DOOMED FROM THE START.
THIS IS... THE END. WE...MUST... TURN BACK...

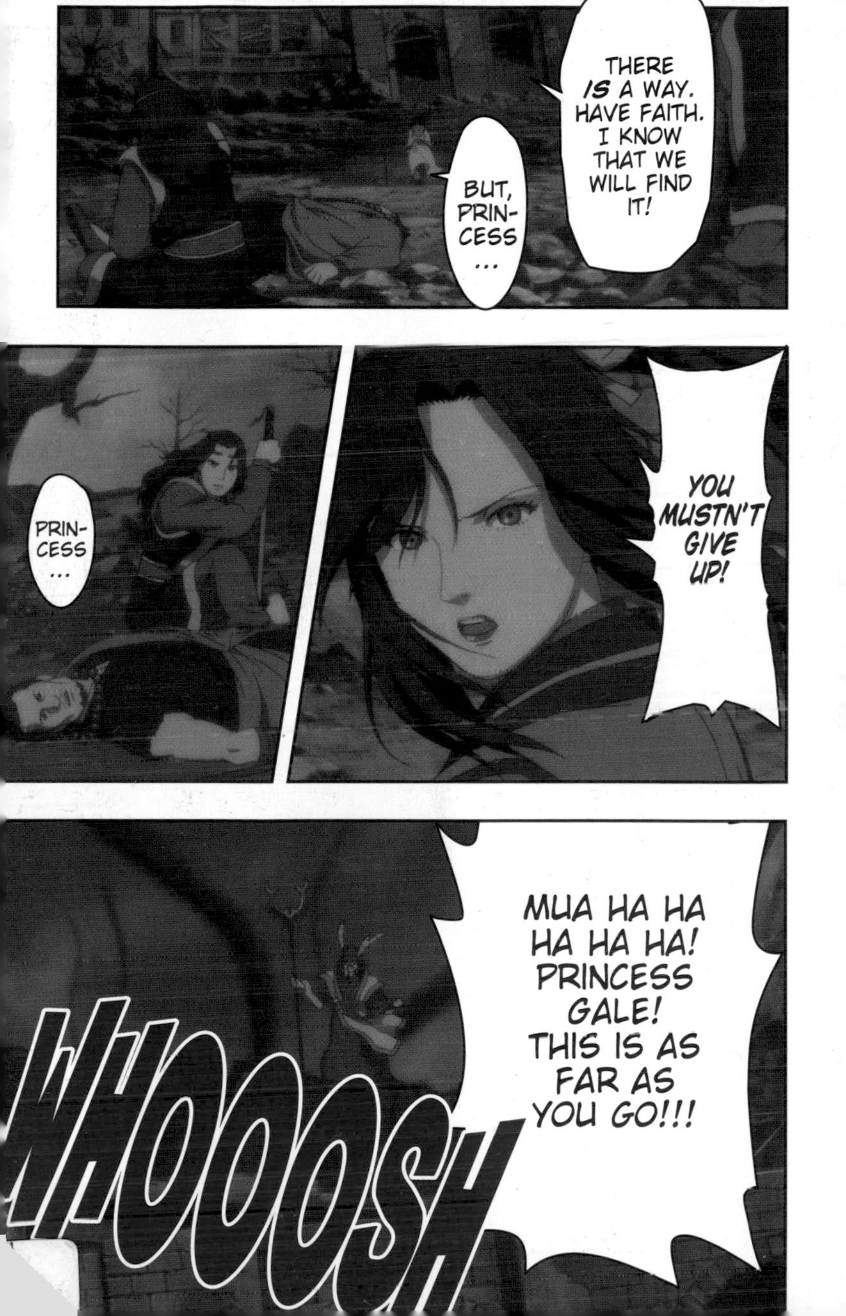
THERE *IS* A WAY. HAVE FAITH. I KNOW THAT WE WILL FIND IT!
BUT, PRINCESS...
YOU MUSTN'T GIVE UP!
PRINCESS...
MUA HA HA HA HA HA! PRINCESS GALE! THIS IS AS FAR AS YOU GO!!!
WHOOOSH

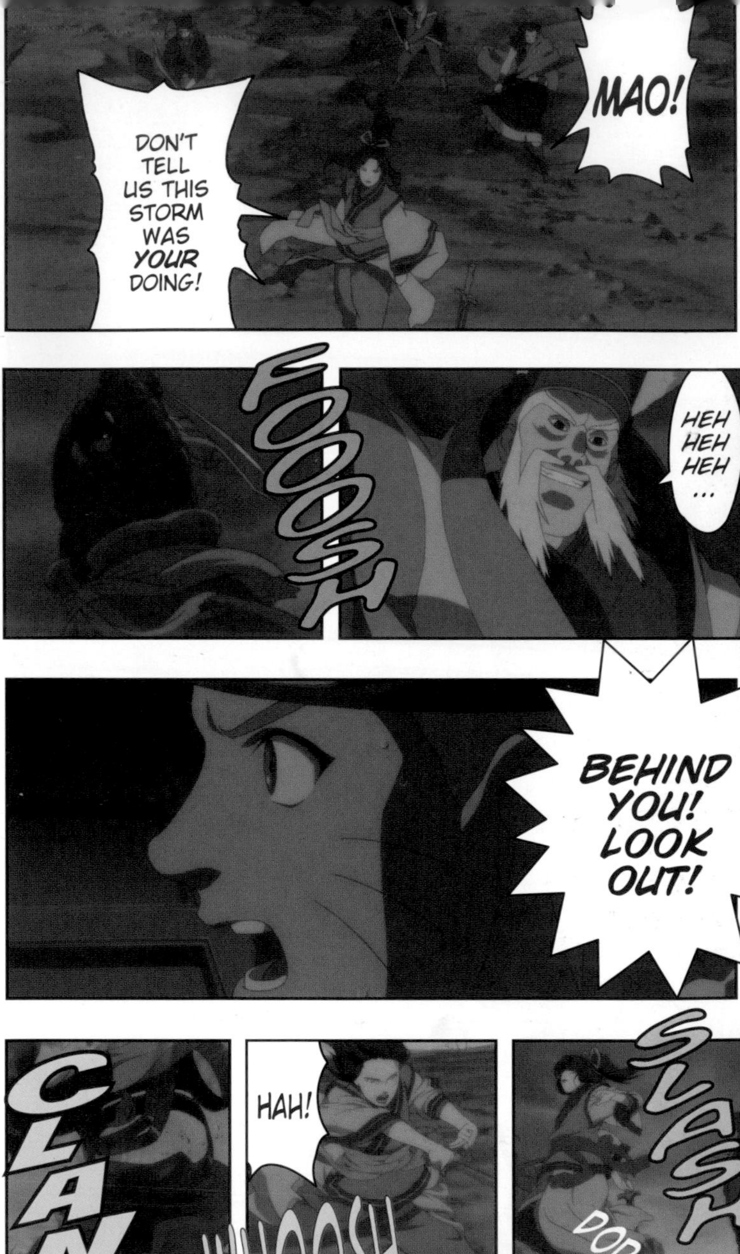
MAO!
DON'T TELL US THIS STORM WAS *YOUR* DOING!
HEH HEH HEH ...
FOOOSH
BEHIND YOU! LOOK OUT!
SLASH
DODGE
HAH!
WHOOSH
CLANG

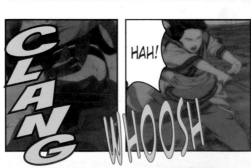

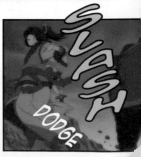

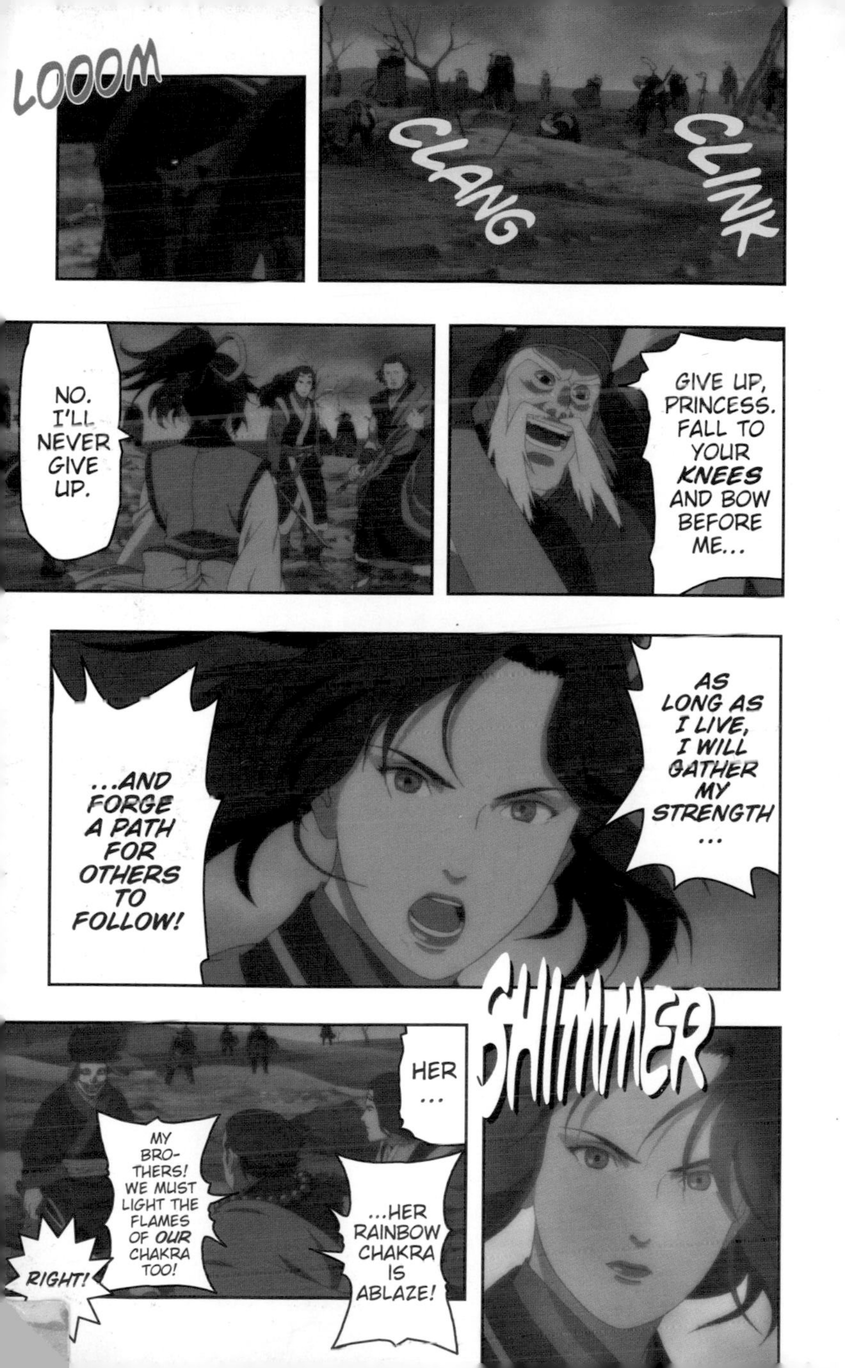
CLINK
CLANG
LOOOM
GIVE UP, PRINCESS. FALL TO YOUR KNEES AND BOW BEFORE ME...
NO. I'LL NEVER GIVE UP.
AS LONG AS I LIVE, I WILL GATHER MY STRENGTH...
...AND FORGE A PATH FOR OTHERS TO FOLLOW!
SHIMMER
HER...
...HER RAINBOW CHAKRA IS ABLAZE!
MY BROTHERS! WE MUST LIGHT THE FLAMES OF OUR CHAKRA TOO!
RIGHT!

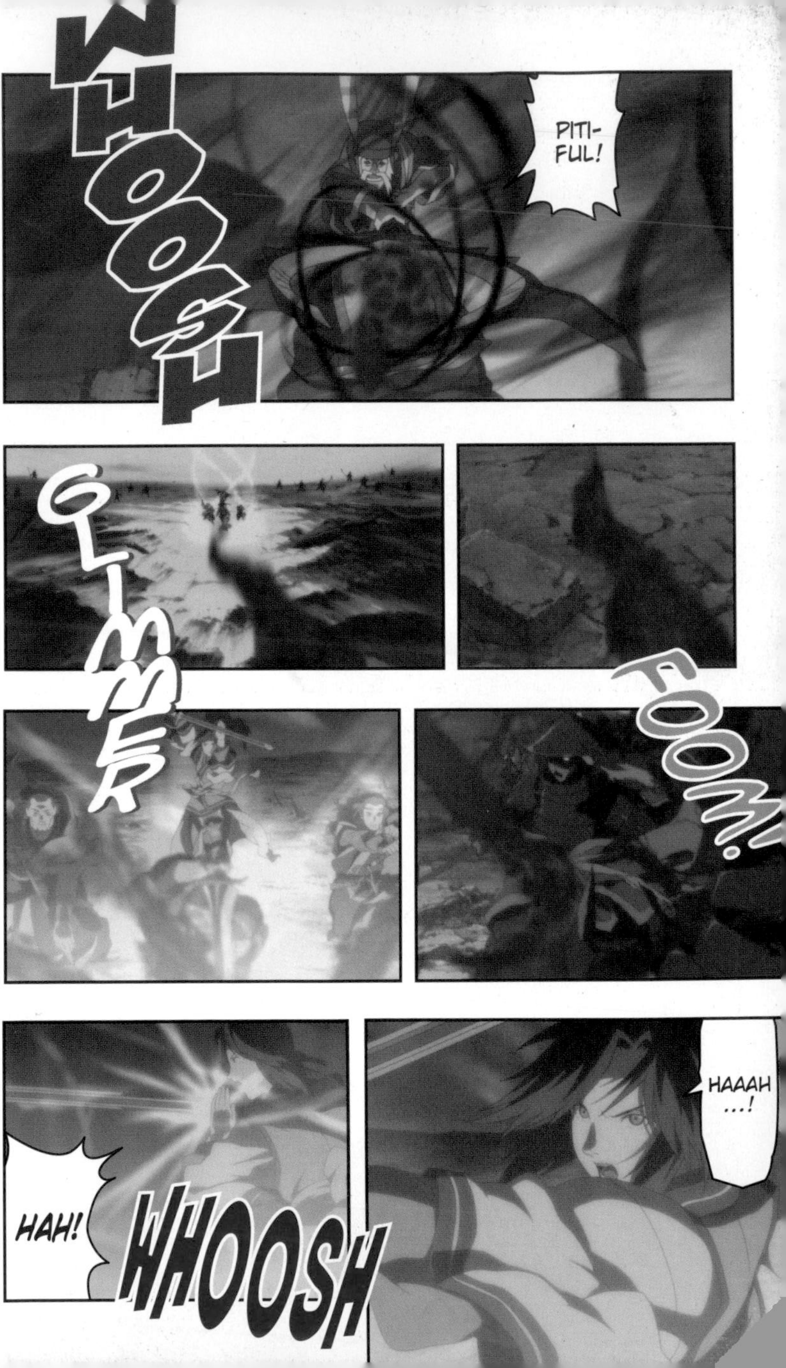
PITI-
FUL!
WHOOSH
GLIMMER
FOOM!
HAAAH
...!
HAH!
WHOOSH

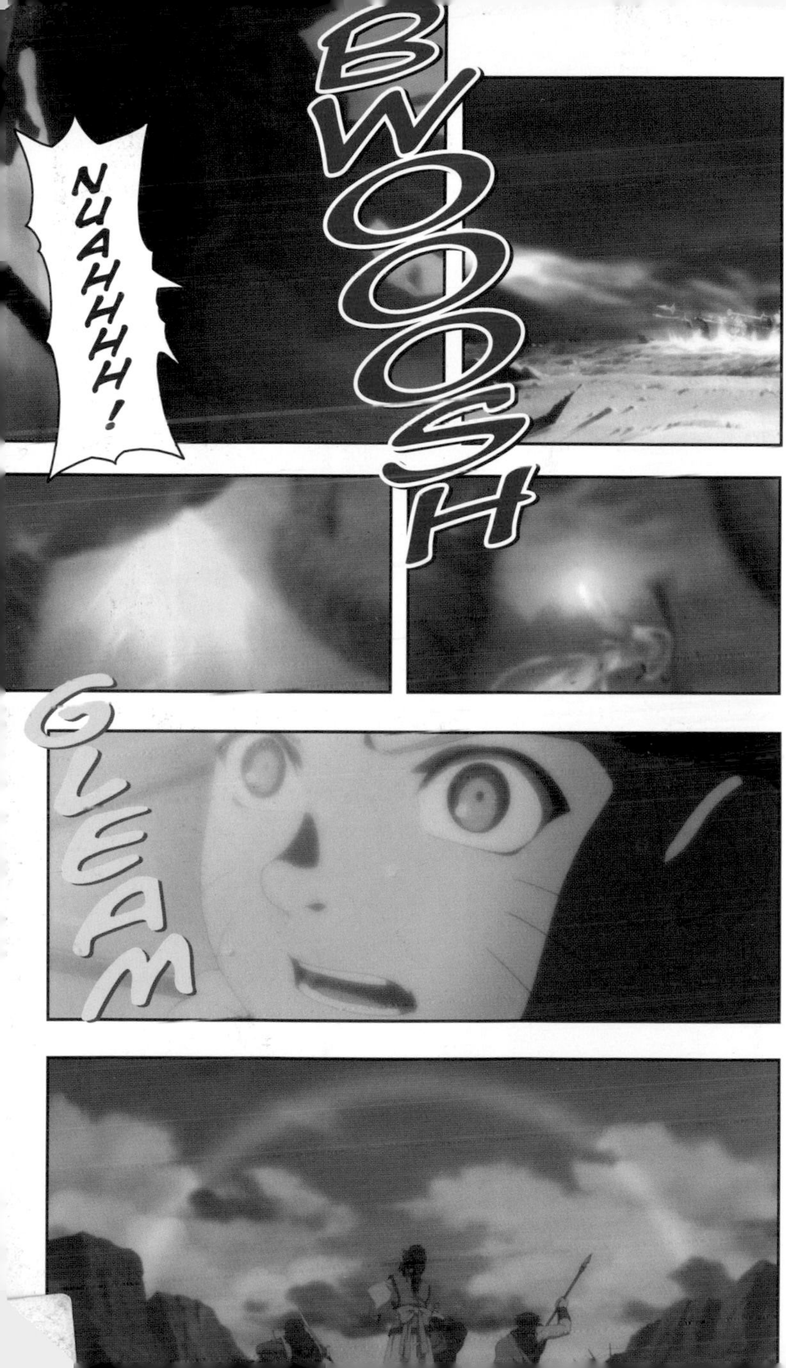
BWOOOSH
NUAHHHH!
GLEAM

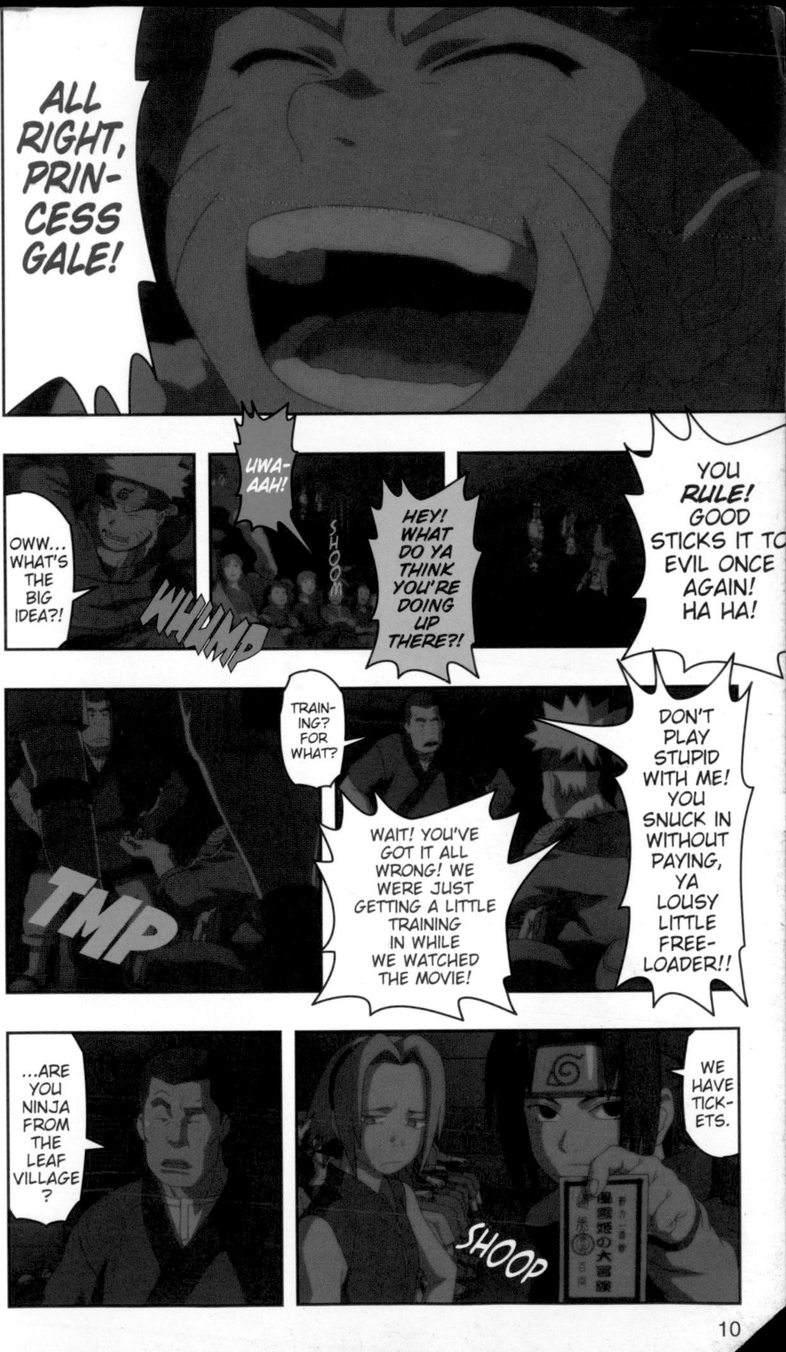
ALL RIGHT, PRINCESS GALE!
YOU RULE! GOOD STICKS IT TO EVIL ONCE AGAIN! HA HA!
UWA-AAH!
SHOOM
HEY! WHAT DO YA THINK YOU'RE DOING UP THERE?!
OWW... WHAT'S THE BIG IDEA?!
WHUMP
DON'T PLAY STUPID WITH ME! YOU SNUCK IN WITHOUT PAYING, YA LOUSY LITTLE FREE-LOADER!!
WAIT! YOU'VE GOT IT ALL WRONG! WE WERE JUST GETTING A LITTLE TRAINING IN WHILE WE WATCHED THE MOVIE!
TRAIN-ING? FOR WHAT?
TMP
WE HAVE TICK-ETS.
SHOOP
...ARE YOU NINJA FROM THE LEAF VILLAGE?

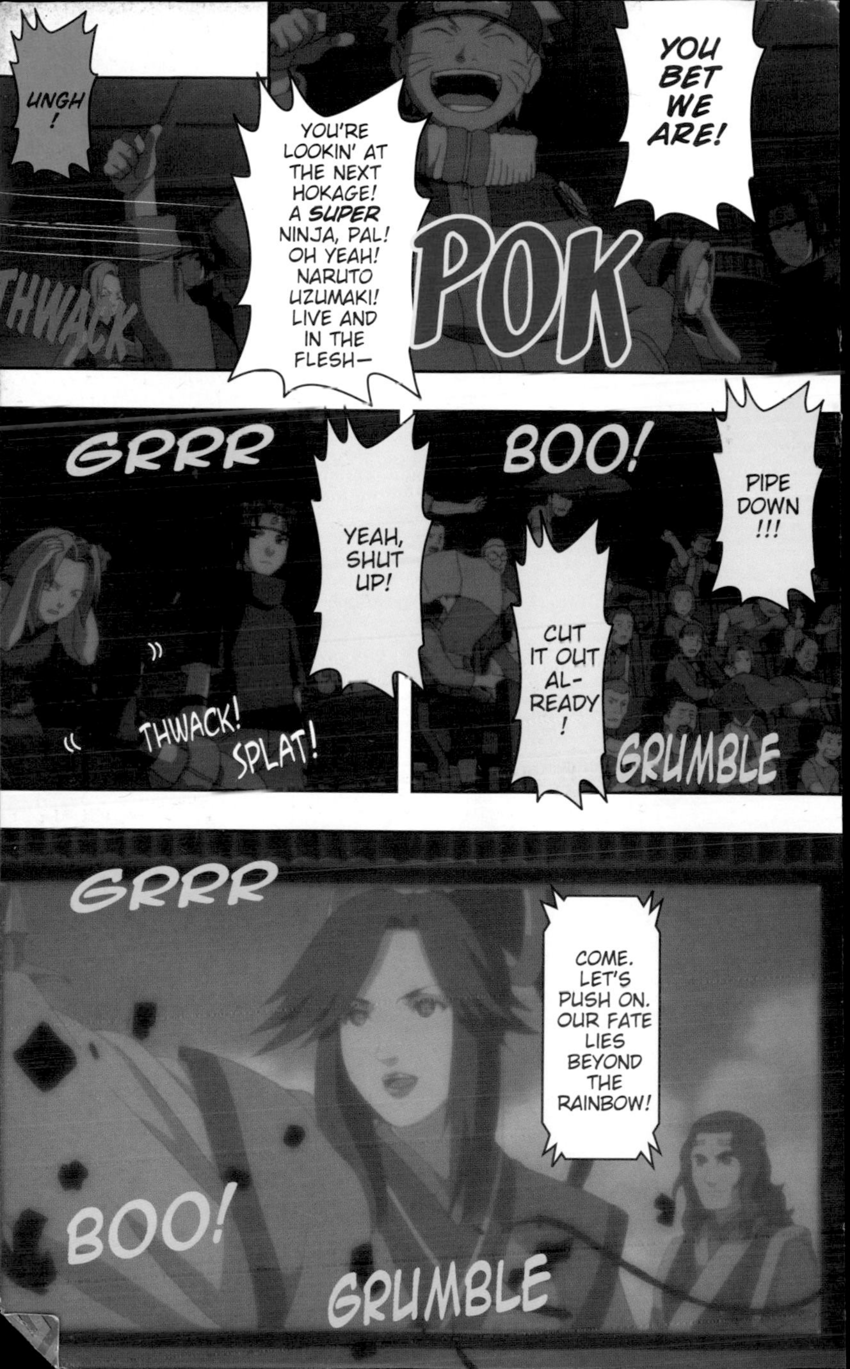
YOU BET WE ARE!
YOU'RE LOOKIN' AT THE NEXT HOKAGE! A SUPER NINJA, PAL! OH YEAH! NARUTO UZUMAKI! LIVE AND IN THE FLESH—
POK
UNGH!
THWACK
PIPE DOWN!!!
BOO!
CUT IT OUT AL-READY!
GRUMBLE
YEAH, SHUT UP!
GRRR
THWACK!
SPLAT!
COME. LET'S PUSH ON. OUR FATE LIES BEYOND THE RAINBOW!
GRRR
BOO!
GRUMBLE

Main Characters

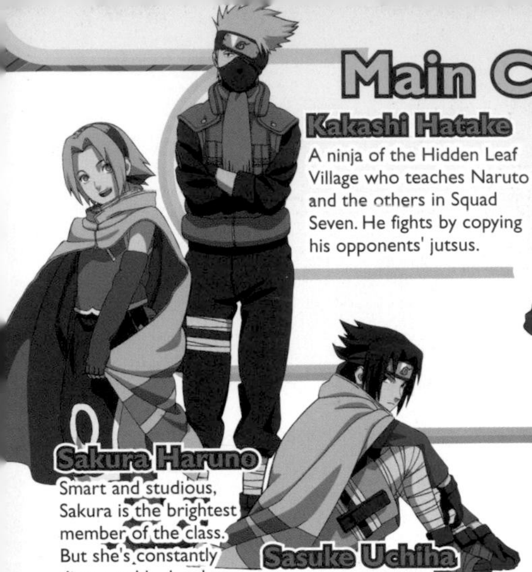

Kakashi Hatake

A ninja of the Hidden Leaf Village who teaches Naruto and the others in Squad Seven. He fights by copying his opponents' jutsus.

Sakura Haruno

Smart and studious, Sakura is the brightest member of the class. But she's constantly distracted by her huge crush on Sasuke.

Sasuke Uchiha

The top ninja in his class, Sasuke is the heir to the prestigious Uchiha clan. His pedigree gives him impressive natural-born talent...not to mention a huge chip on his shoulder.

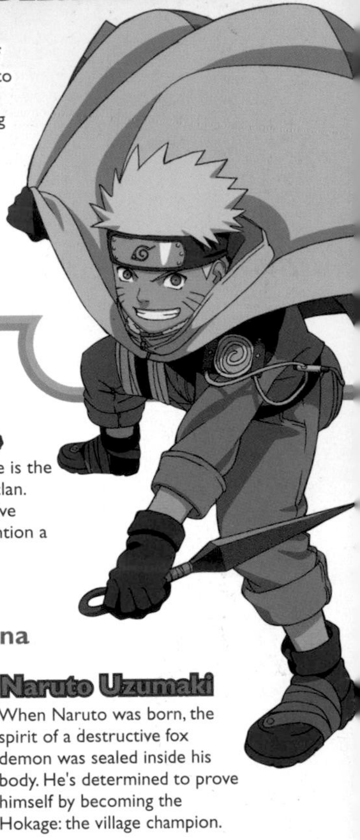

Naruto Uzumaki

When Naruto was born, the spirit of a destructive fox demon was sealed inside his body. He's determined to prove himself by becoming the Hokage: the village champion.

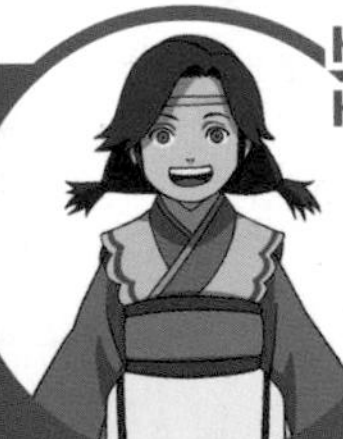

Koyuki Kazahana

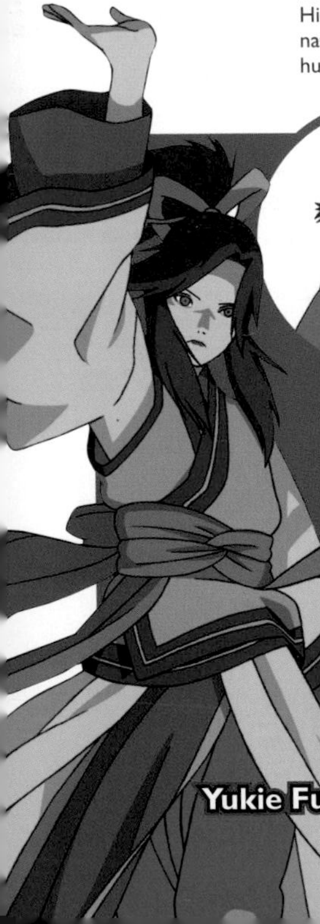

Yukie Fujikaze

A well-known actress in the Land of Fire. Her performances are top notch, but her aspirations don't spill over into her character. She seems haunted by some big event in the past…

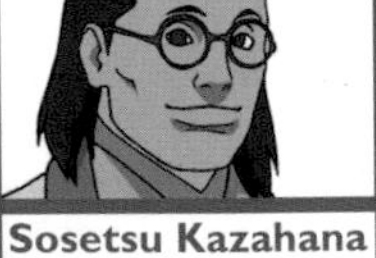

Sosetsu Kazahana

Ruler of the Land of Snow, Sosetsu was a peaceful, gadget-loving man...until he lost his life in the coup ten years ago.

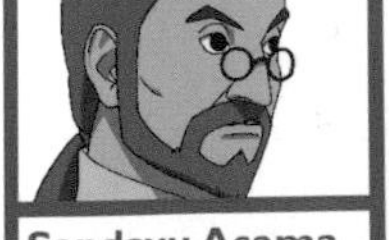

Sandayu Asama

Manager of the actress Yukie Fujikaze. He suffers much abuse from the self-centered Yukie.

The three members of the Snow Ninja team

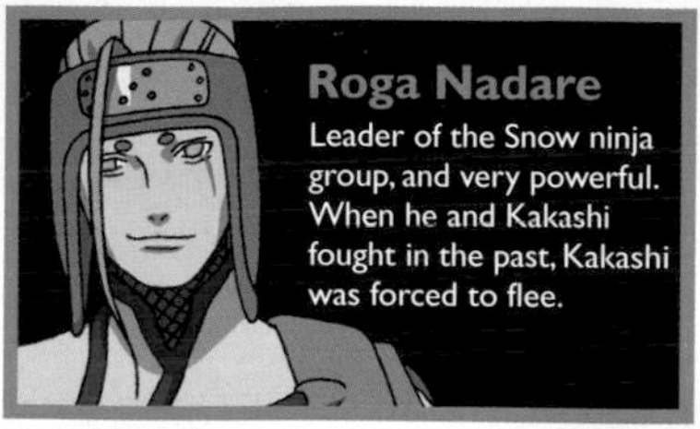

Roga Nadare
Leader of the Snow ninja group, and very powerful. When he and Kakashi fought in the past, Kakashi was forced to flee.

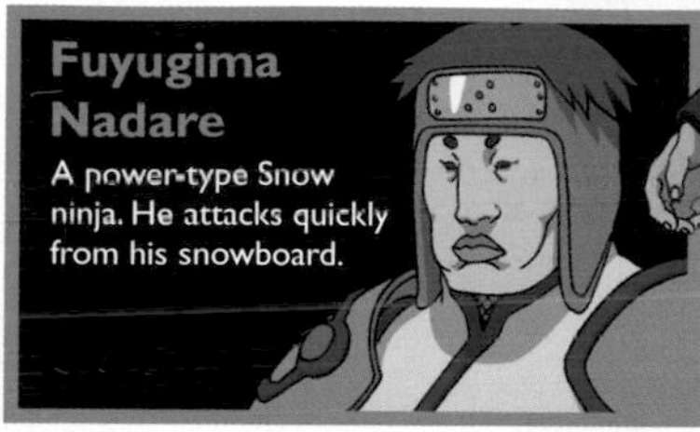

Fuyugima Nadare
A power-type Snow ninja. He attacks quickly from his snowboard.

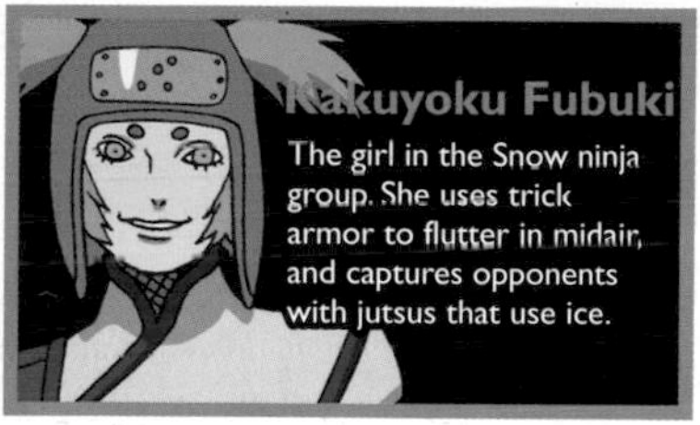

Kakuyoku Fubuki
The girl in the Snow ninja group. She uses trick armor to flutter in midair, and captures opponents with jutsus that use ice.

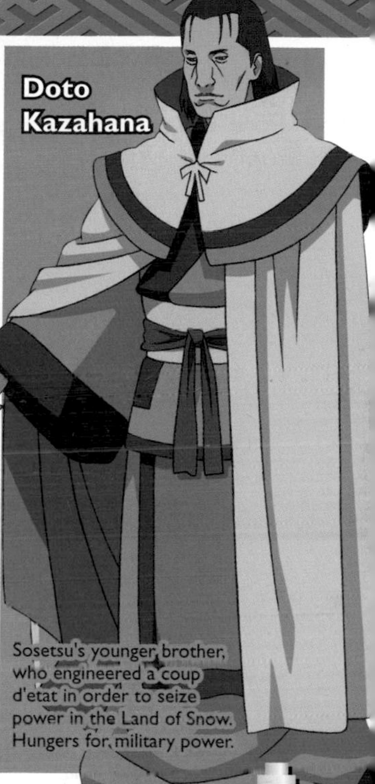

Doto Kazahana
Sosetsu's younger brother, who engineered a coup d'etat in order to seize power in the Land of Snow. Hungers for military power.

The Story of Naruto

Naruto Uzumaki, former problem child of the Ninja Academy in the Hidden Leaf Village, is now training hard to reach his goal of becoming Hokage: the village's number one ninja! His school grades put him at the bottom of the class, but through cooperation with the school, he was still able to become a ninja. Now with his teammates Sasuke and Sakura and his teacher Kakashi, he spends every day in training, tackling the toughest missions. Naruto may have become a ninja, but the road to becoming Hokage is a long one!

Our story begins when Naruto and his crew are instructed to see a certain movie as preparation for their next mission. It seems like a simple enough task...but they're about to become involved in a dastardly plot that could shake an entire country to its core!

SHONEN JUMP™

NARUTO™ THE MOVIE Ninja Clash in the Land of Snow

ANI-MANGA™

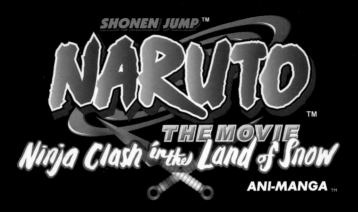

Contents

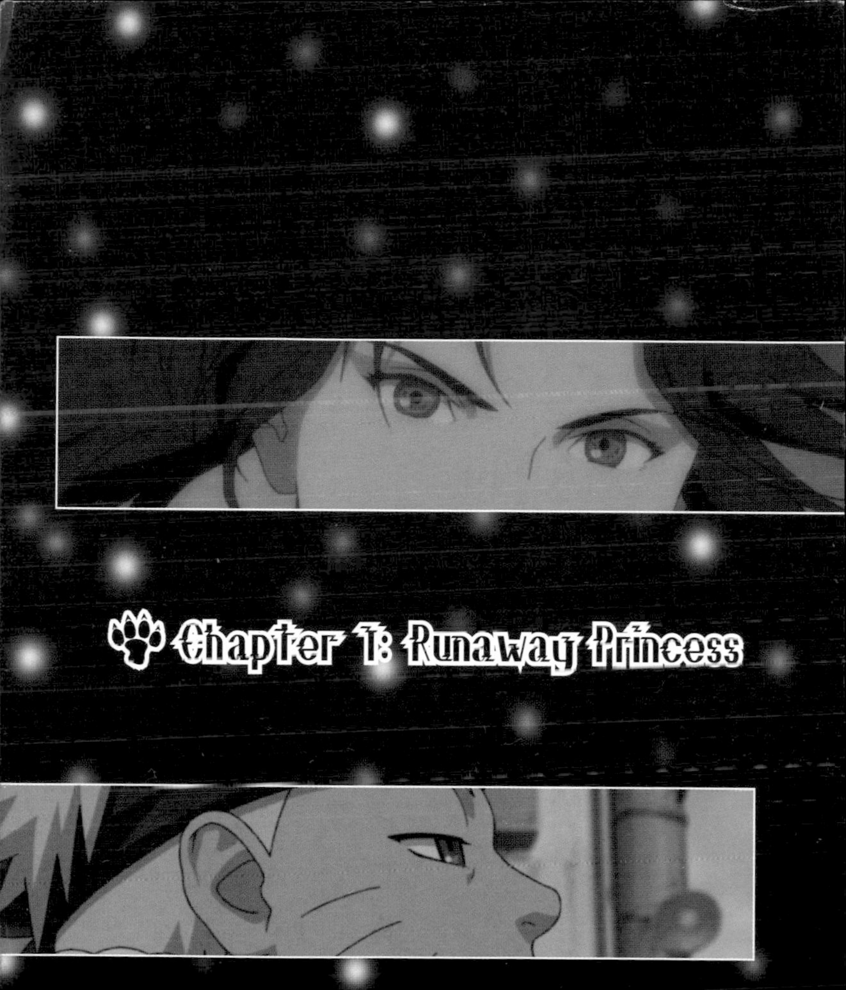
Chapter 1: Runaway Princess

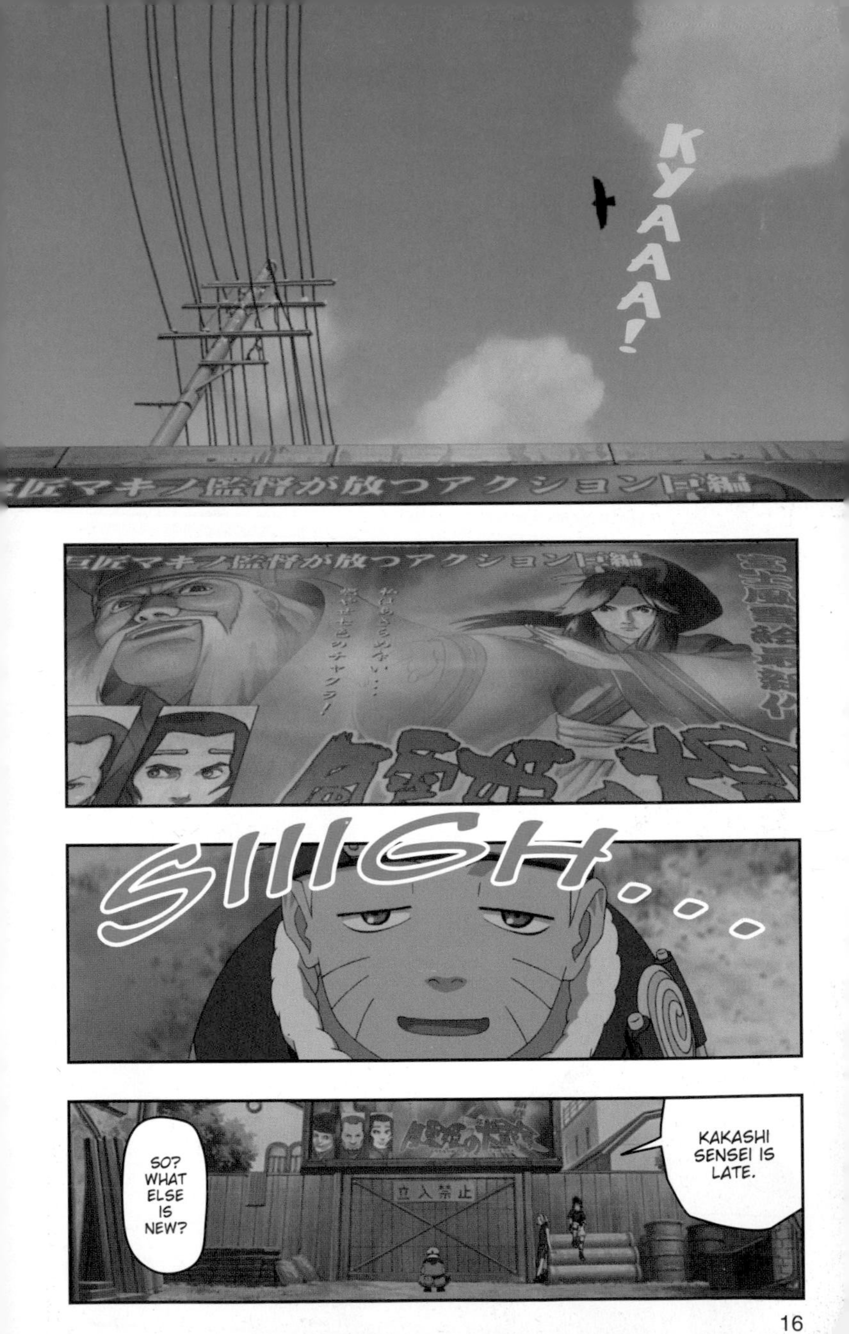
KYAAA!
巨匠マキノ監督が放つアクション巨編
SIIGH...
KAKASHI SENSEI IS LATE.
SO? WHAT ELSE IS NEW?
立入禁止

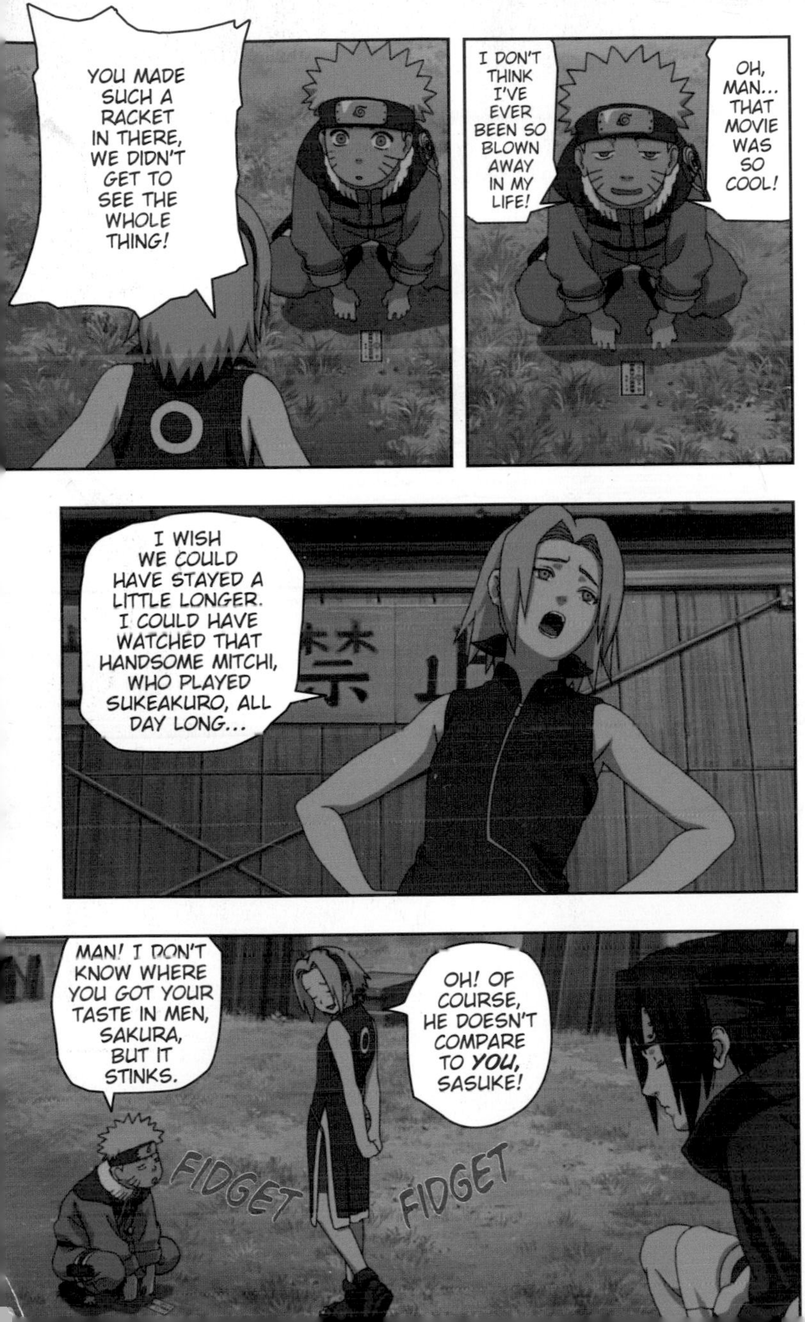

OH, MAN... THAT MOVIE WAS SO COOL!
I DON'T THINK I'VE EVER BEEN SO BLOWN AWAY IN MY LIFE!
YOU MADE SUCH A RACKET IN THERE, WE DIDN'T GET TO SEE THE WHOLE THING!
I WISH WE COULD HAVE STAYED A LITTLE LONGER. I COULD HAVE WATCHED THAT HANDSOME MITCHI, WHO PLAYED SUKEAKURO, ALL DAY LONG...
MAN! I DON'T KNOW WHERE YOU GOT YOUR TASTE IN MEN, SAKURA, BUT IT STINKS.
OH! OF COURSE, HE DOESN'T COMPARE TO *YOU*, SASUKE!
FIDGET
FIDGET

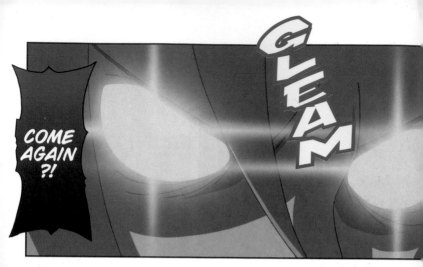

GLEAM

COME AGAIN ?!

DROOP

S/I/GH

GOOD!

I-I'M SORRY, WHAT WAS THE QUES- TION?

S/I/GH

I WONDER IF THERE'S ANYONE LIKE *HER* OUT THERE...I MEAN, WHERE'S *MY* PRINCESS GALE, Y'KNOW?

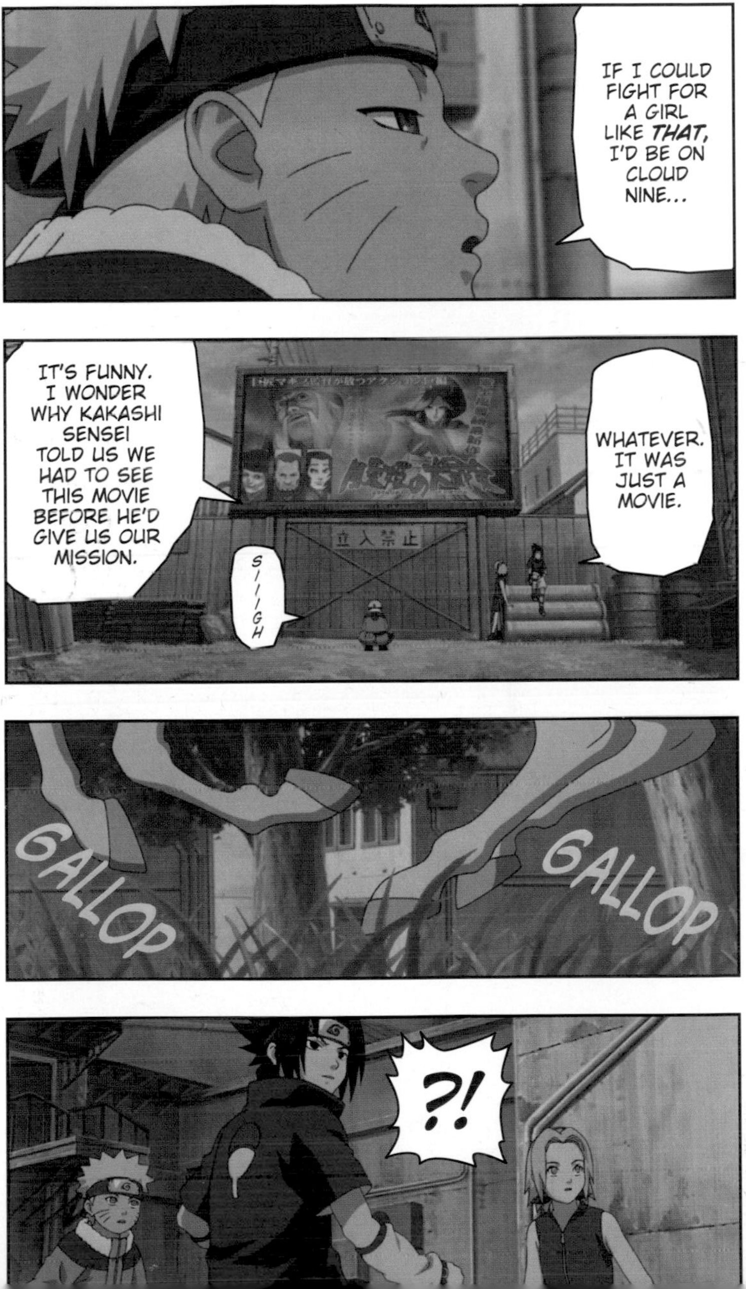
IF I COULD FIGHT FOR A GIRL LIKE ***THAT,*** I'D BE ON CLOUD NINE...
WHATEVER. IT WAS JUST A MOVIE.
IT'S FUNNY. I WONDER WHY KAKASHI SENSEI TOLD US WE HAD TO SEE THIS MOVIE BEFORE HE'D GIVE US OUR MISSION.
立入禁止
SIIIGH
GALLOP
GALLOP
?!

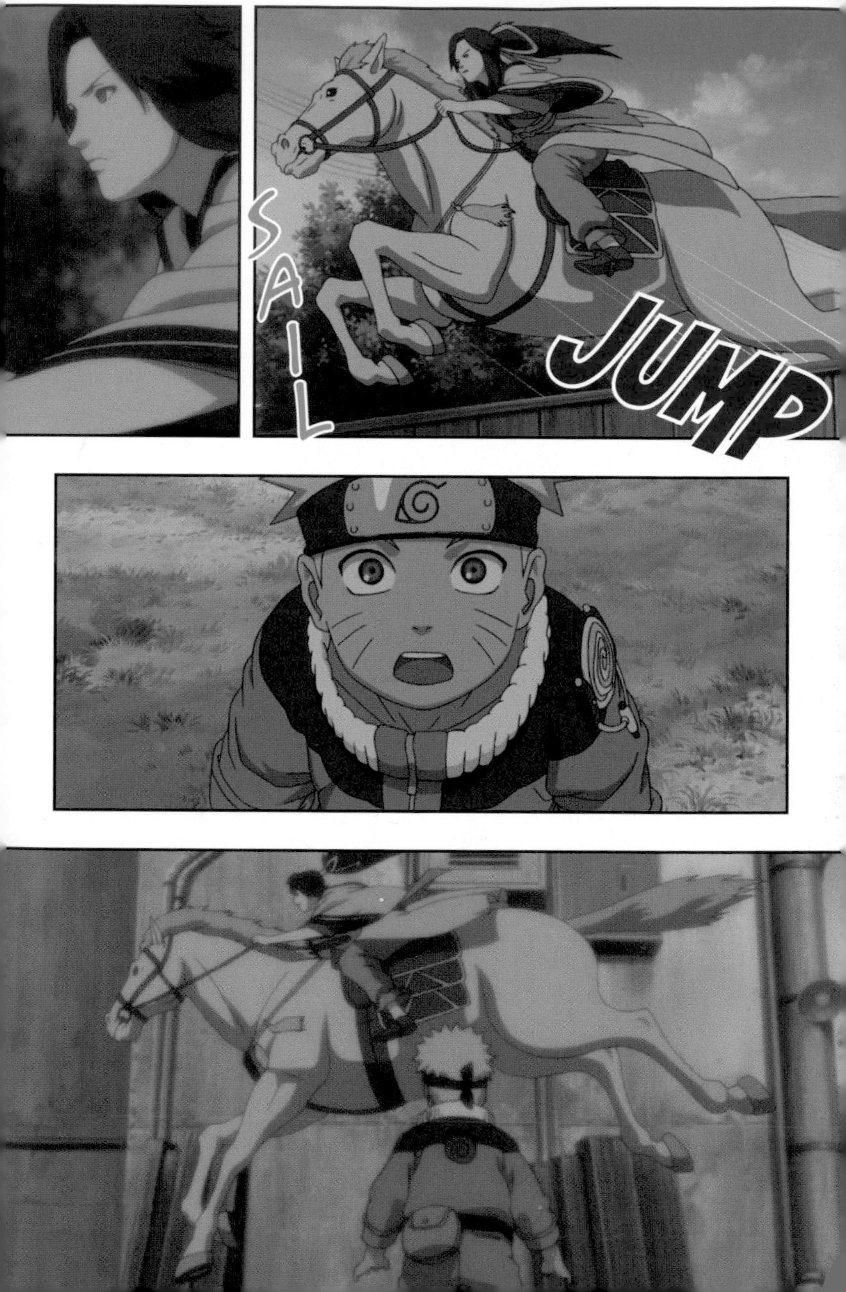
SAIL
JUMP

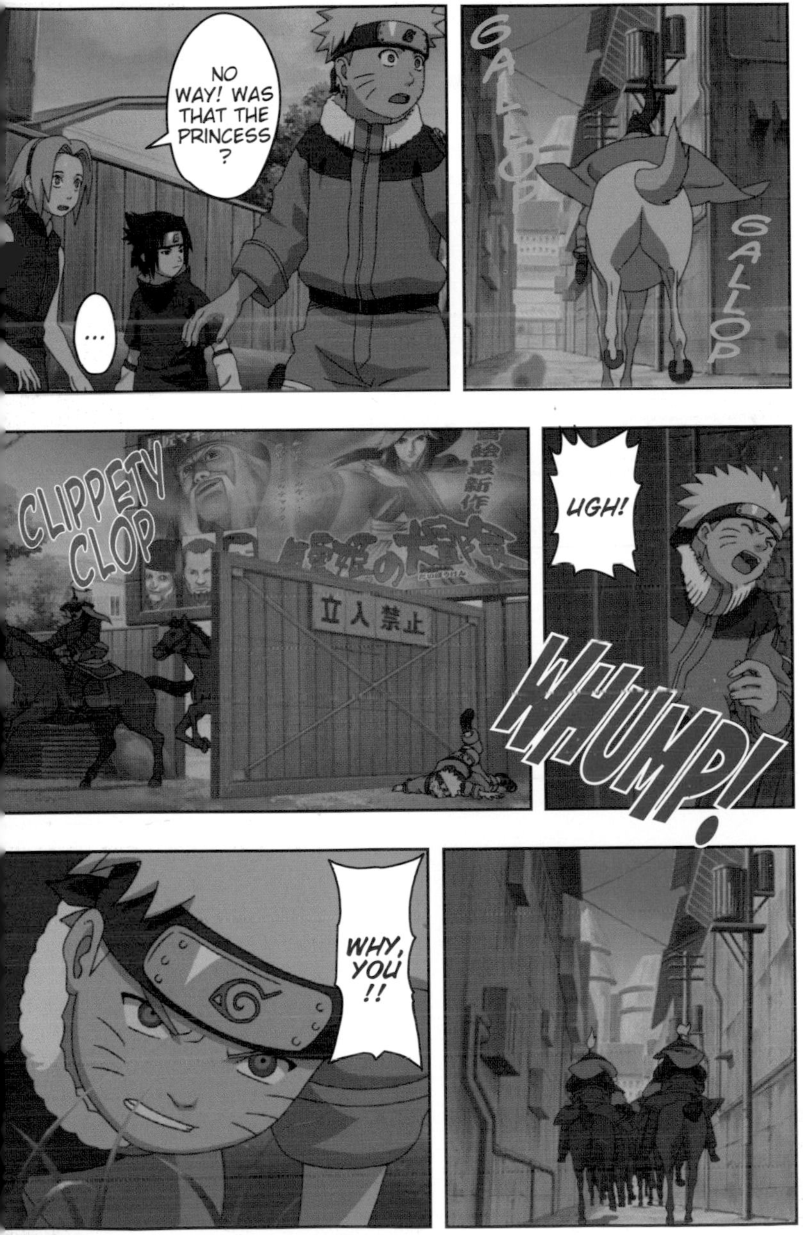
GALLOP
GALLOP
NO WAY! WAS THAT THE PRINCESS ?
...
UGH!
WHUMP!
CLIPPETY CLOP
立入禁止
WHY, YOU!!

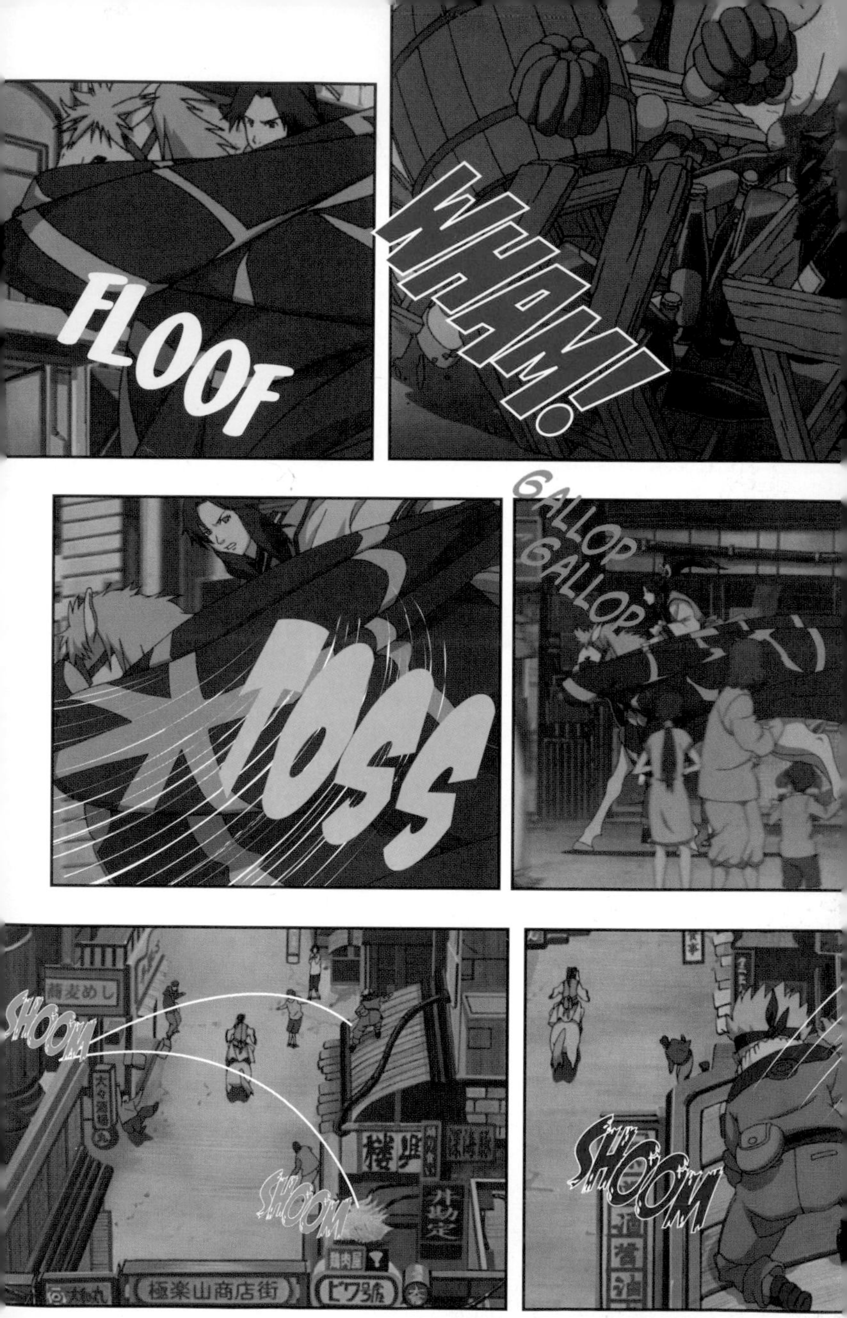
WHAM!
FLOOF
GALLOP GALLOP GALLOP
TOSS
SHOOM
SHOOM
SHOOM

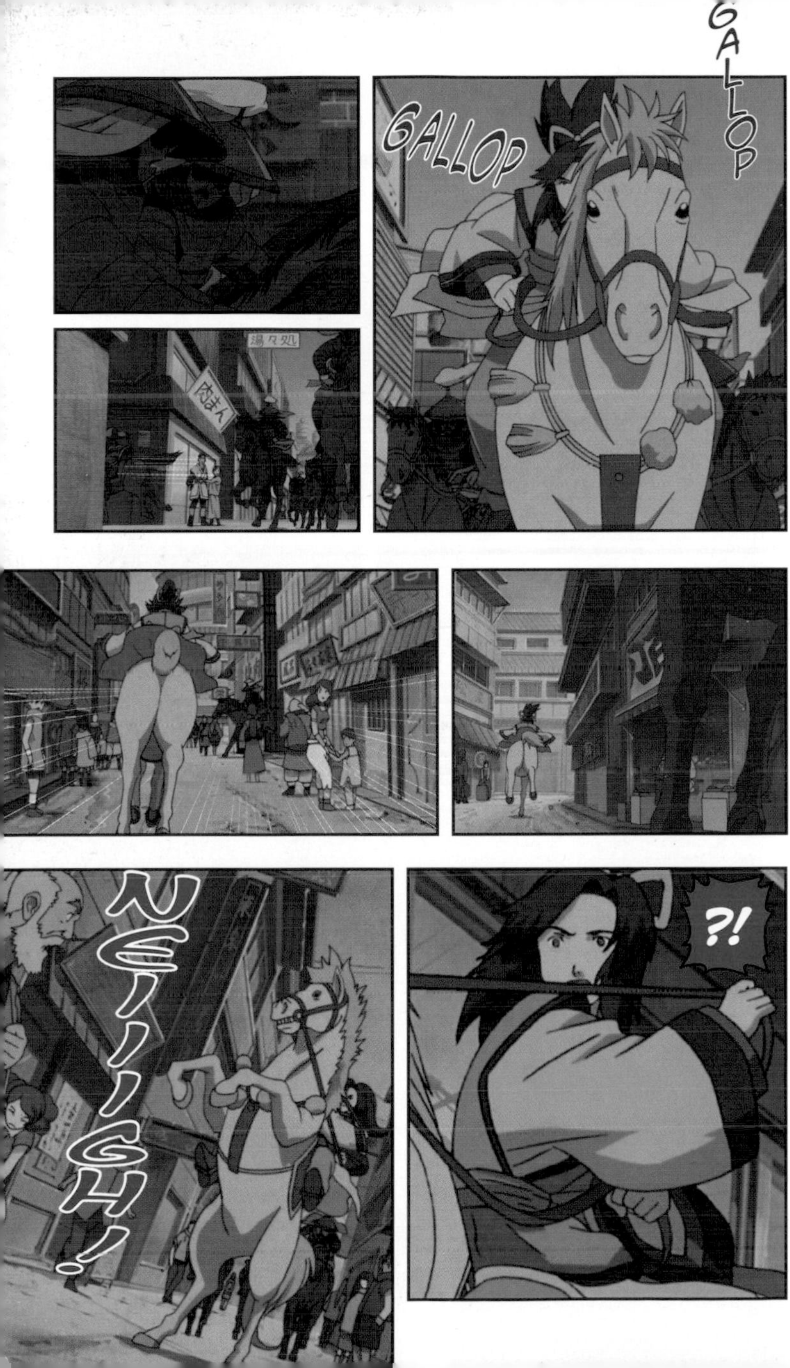
GALLOP
GALLOP
?!
NEIIIGH!

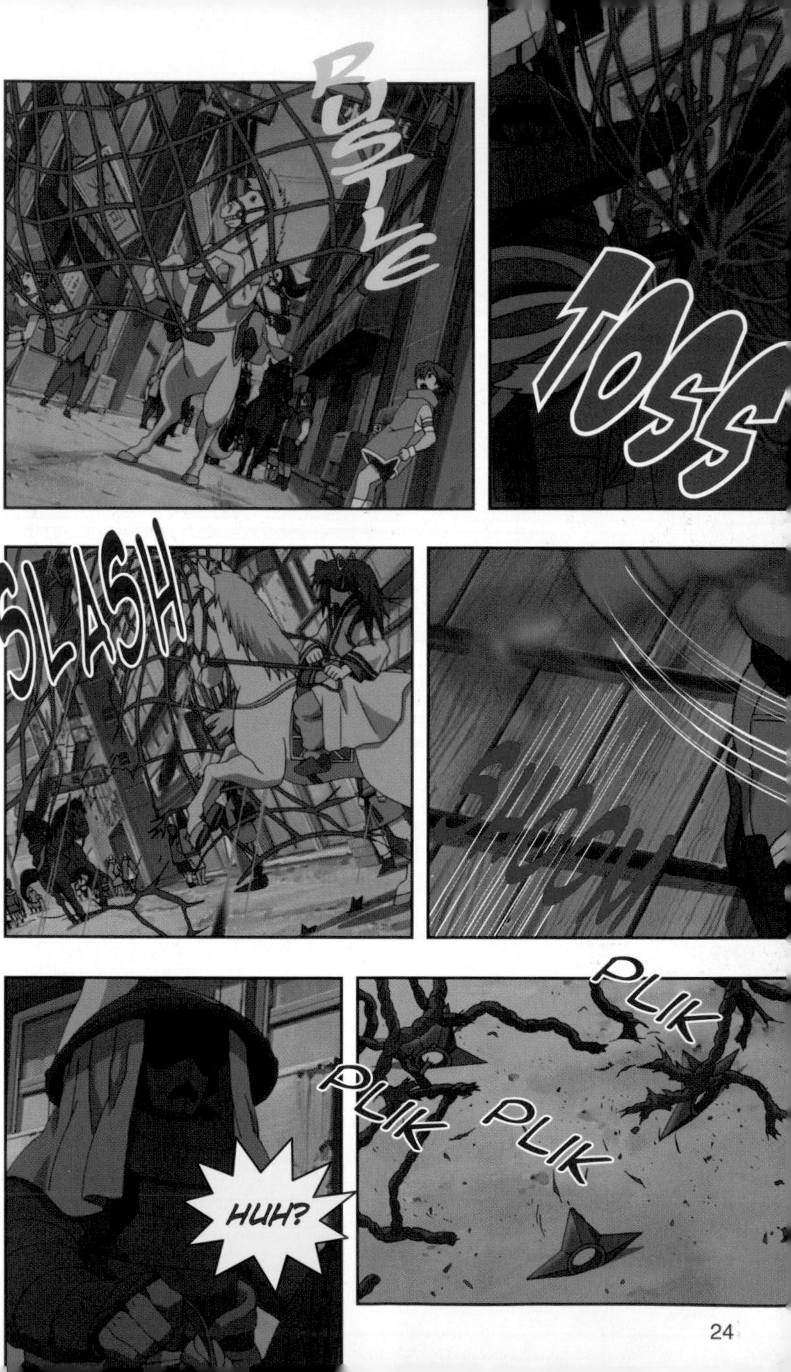
TOSS
RUSTLE
SHOOM
SLASH
PLIK
PLIK
PLIK
PLIK
HUH?

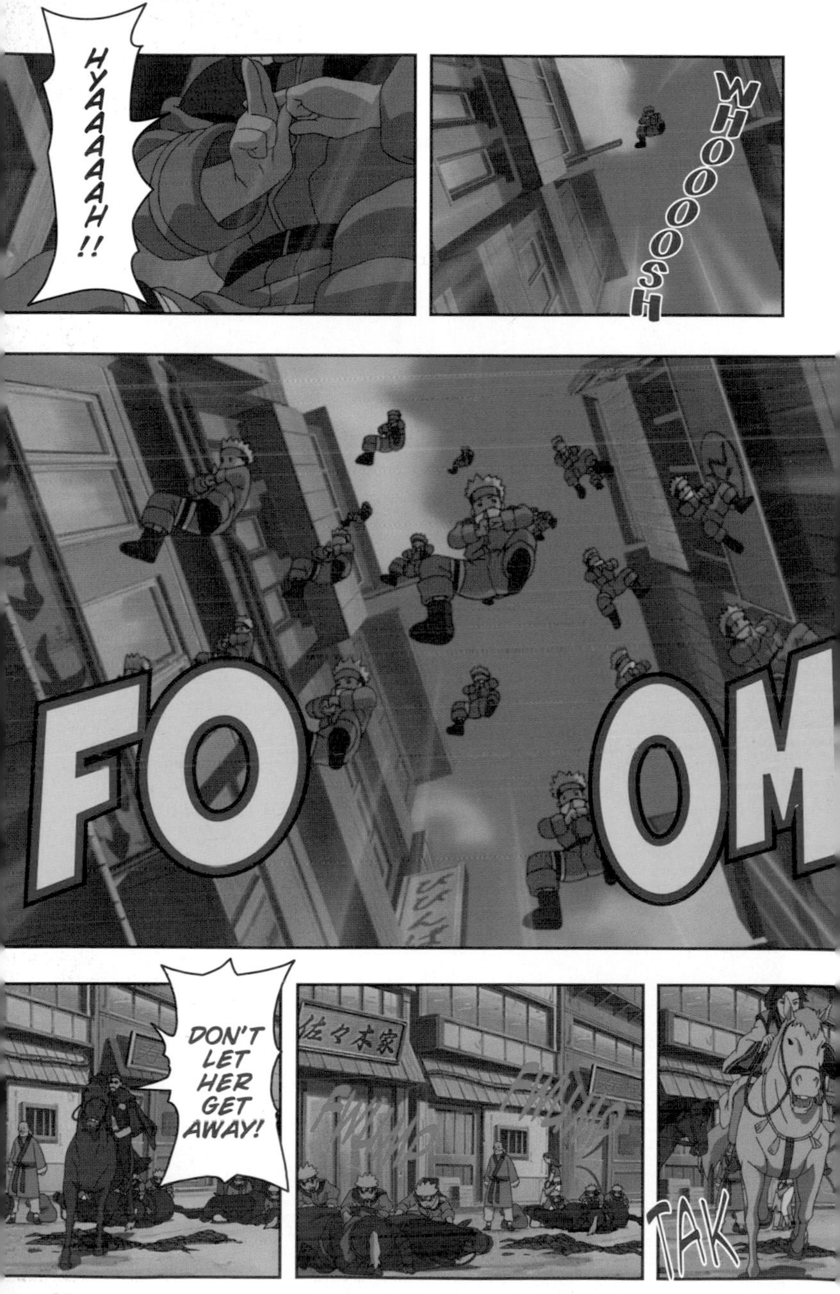
WHOOOOSH
HYAAAAAH!!
FOOM
TAK
DON'T LET HER GET AWAY!

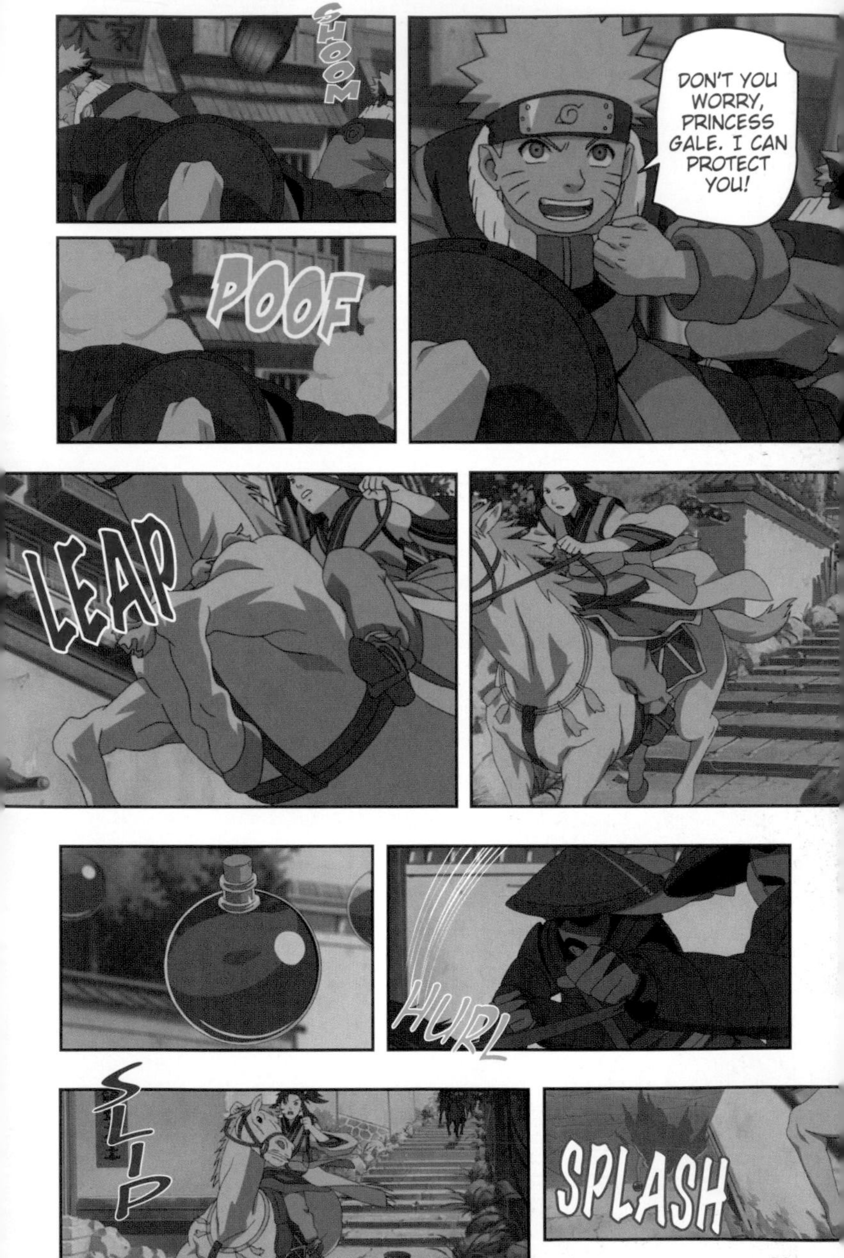
DON'T YOU WORRY, PRINCESS GALE. I CAN PROTECT YOU!
SHOOM
POOF
LEAP
HURL
SPLASH
SLIP

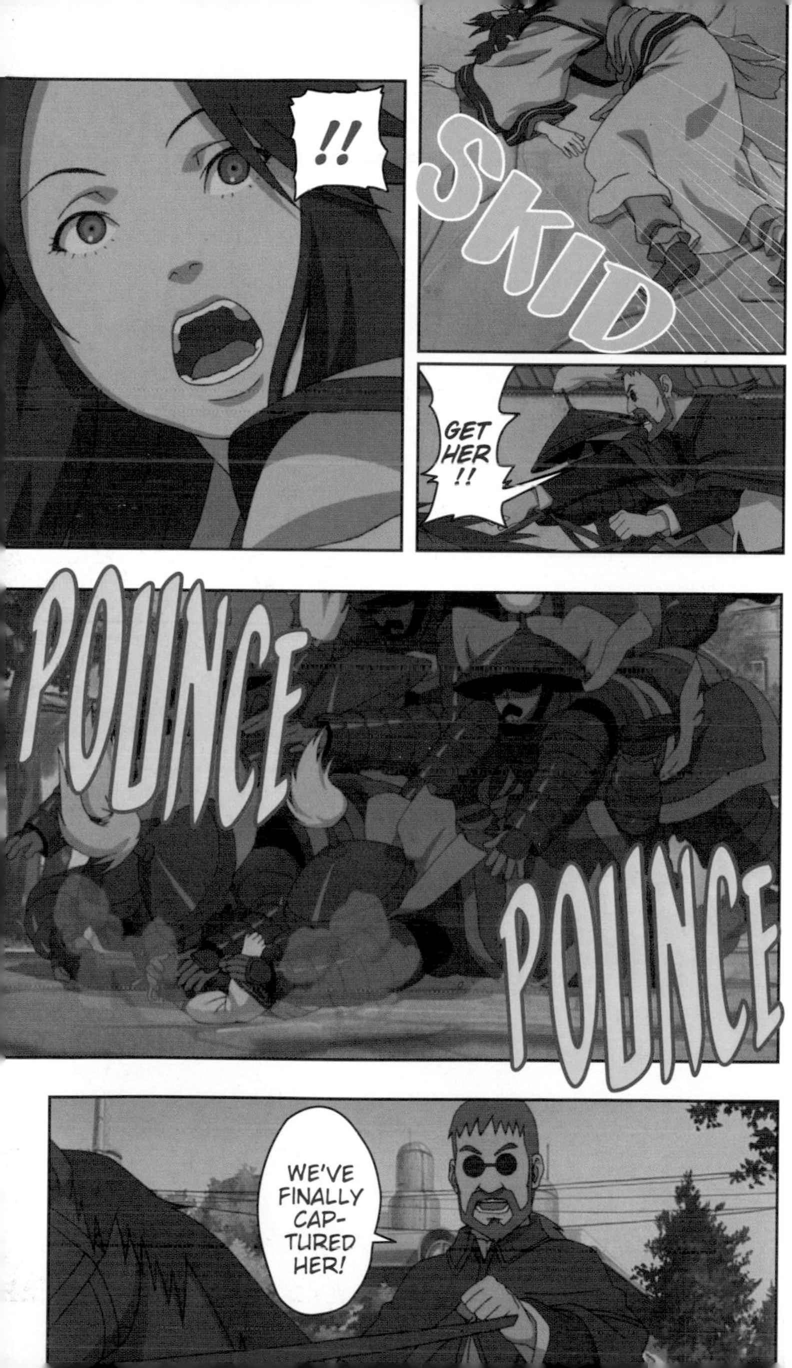
SKID
GET HER !!
!!
POUNCE
POUNCE
WE'VE FINALLY CAP-TURED HER!

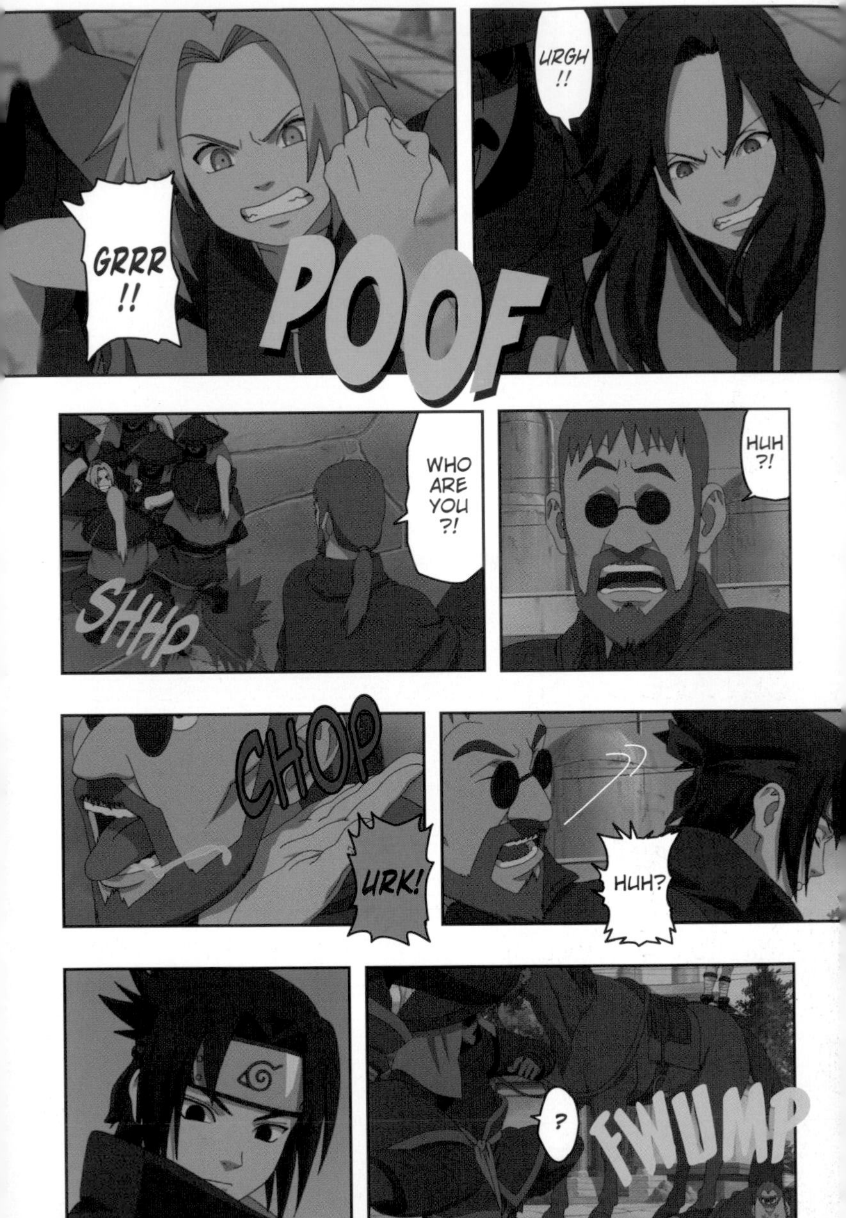
URGH !!
GRRR !!
POOF
HUH ?!
WHO ARE YOU ?!
SHHP
HUH?
CHOP
URK!
?
FWUMP

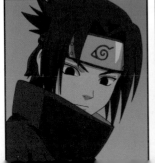

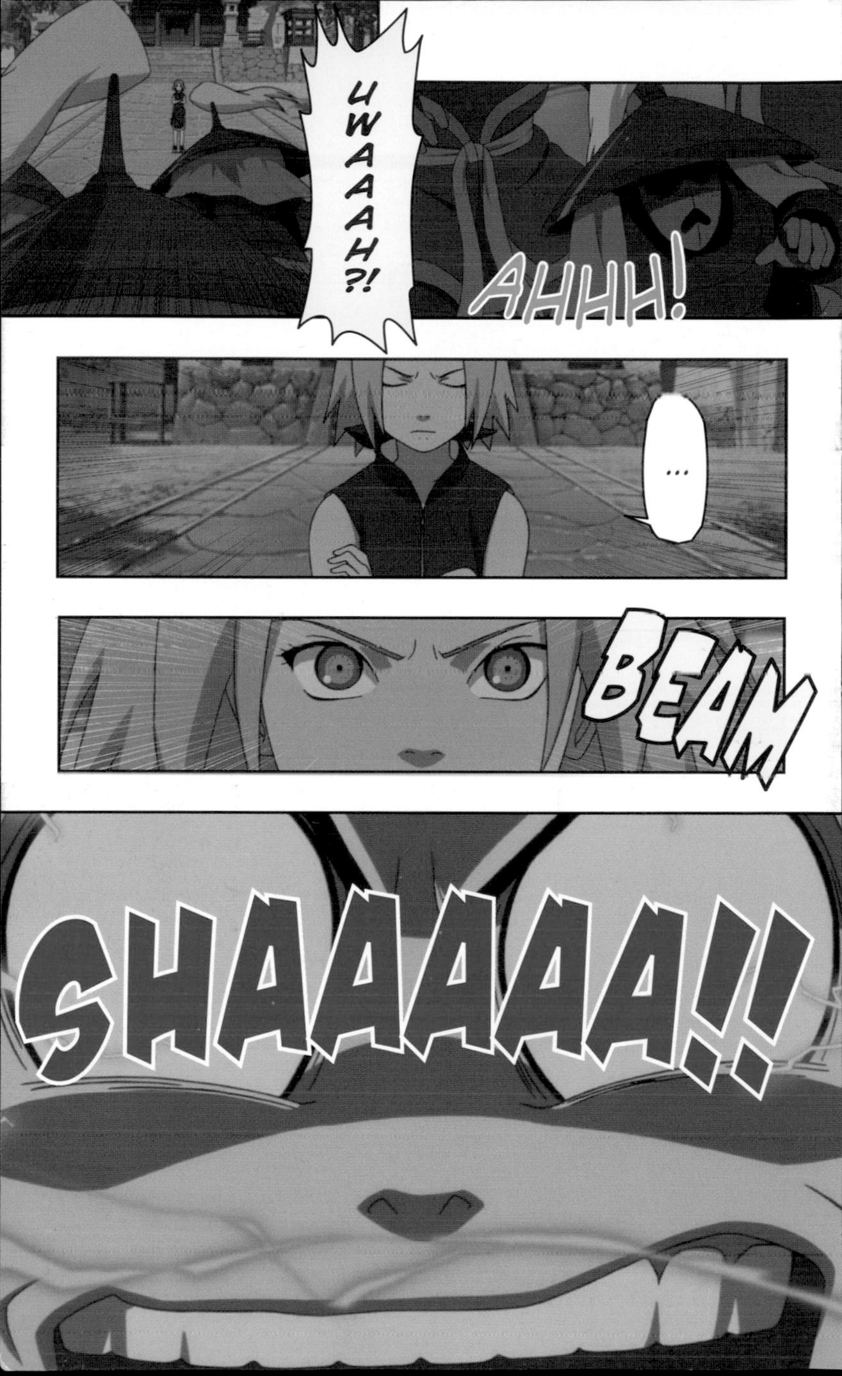
AHHH!
UWAAAAH?!
...
BEAM
SHAAAAA!!

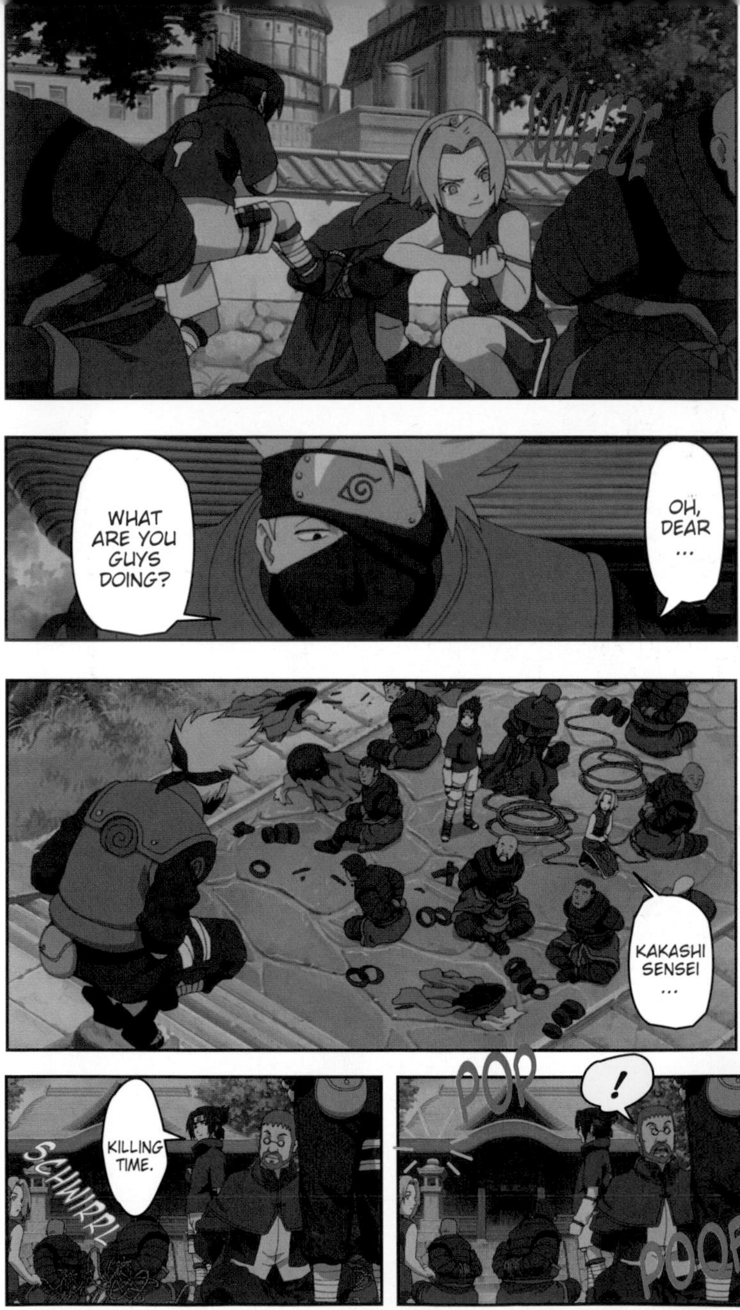
SQUEEZE
OH, DEAR...
WHAT ARE YOU GUYS DOING?
KAKASHI SENSEI...
POP
!
POOF
KILLING TIME.
SCHWIRRL

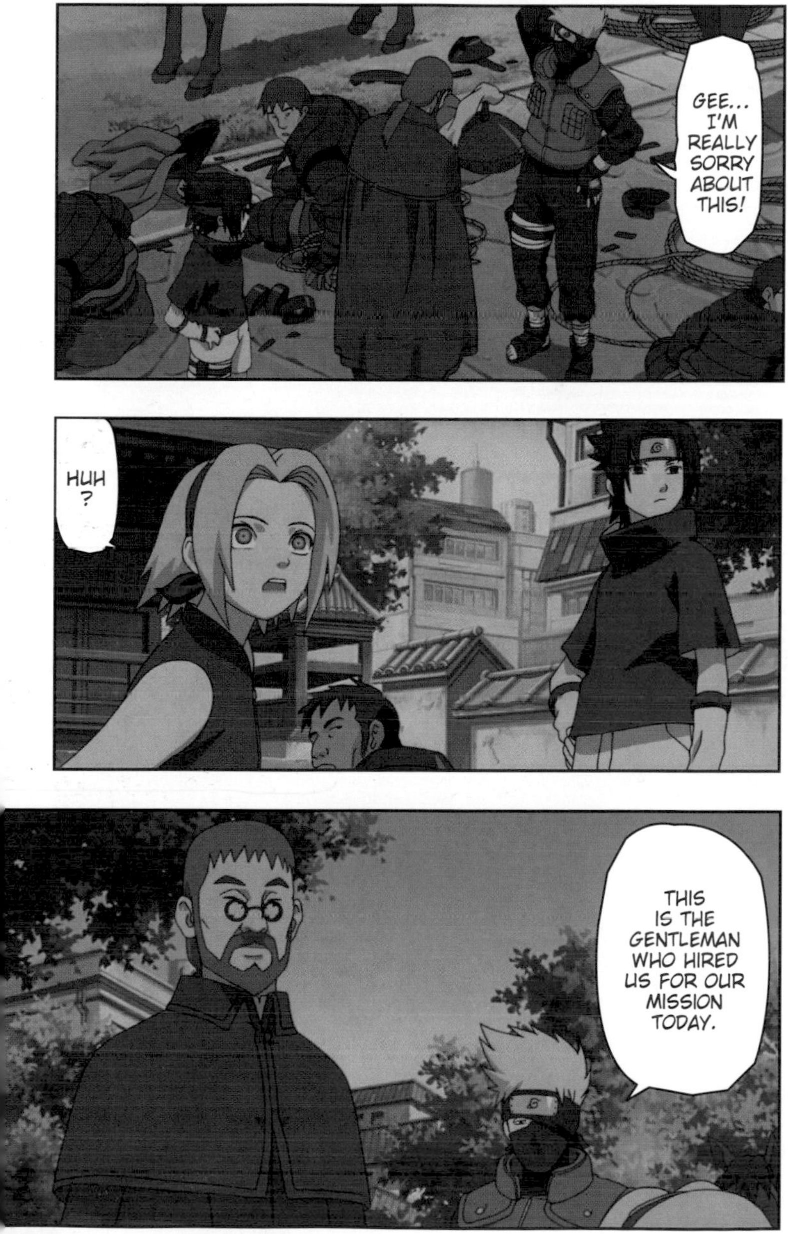
GEE... I'M REALLY SORRY ABOUT THIS!
HUH?
THIS IS THE GENTLEMAN WHO HIRED US FOR OUR MISSION TODAY.

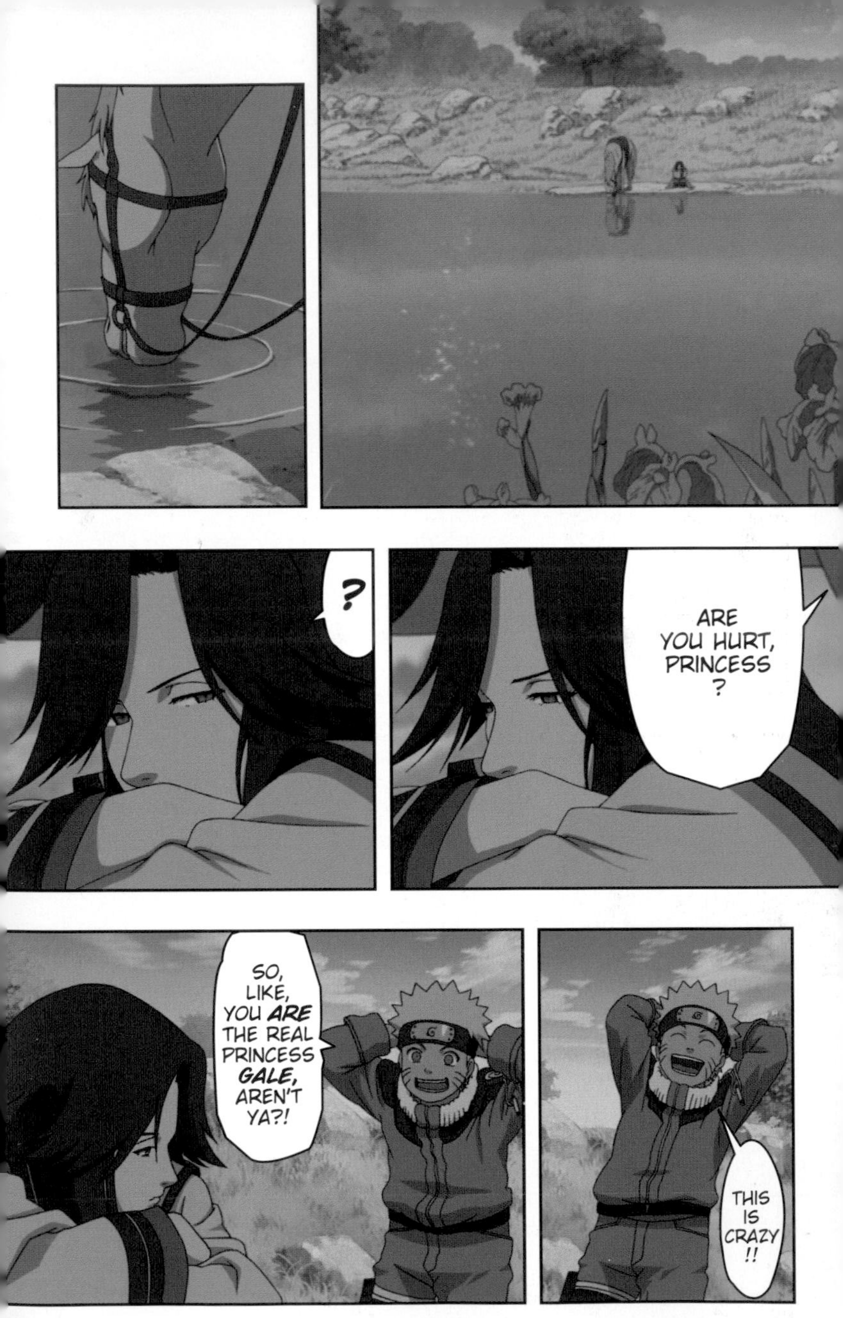
ARE YOU HURT, PRINCESS?
?
THIS IS CRAZY!!
SO, LIKE, YOU **ARE** THE REAL PRINCESS **GALE,** AREN'T YA?!

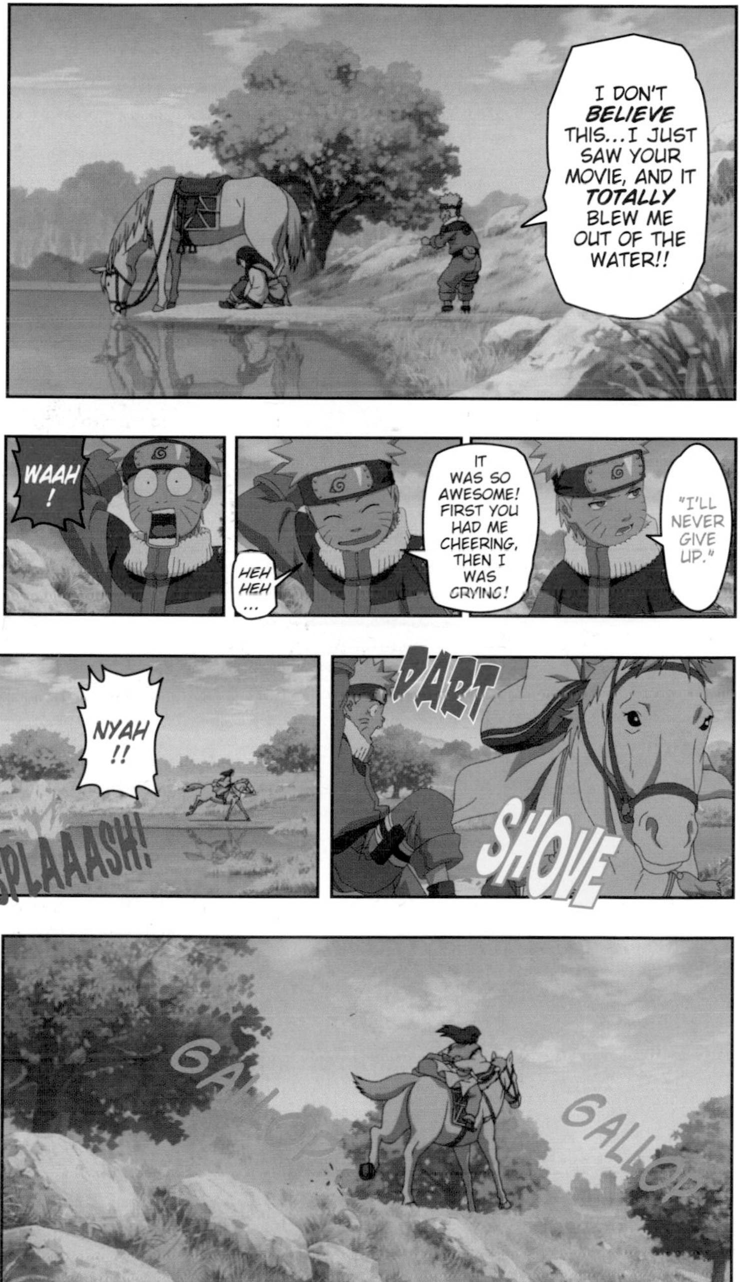

I DON'T **BELIEVE** THIS...I JUST SAW YOUR MOVIE, AND IT **TOTALLY** BLEW ME OUT OF THE WATER!!
"I'LL NEVER GIVE UP."
IT WAS SO AWESOME! FIRST YOU HAD ME CHEERING, THEN I WAS CRYING!
HEH HEH ...
WAAH!
DART
SHOVE
NYAH!!
SPLAAASH!
GALLOP
GALLOP

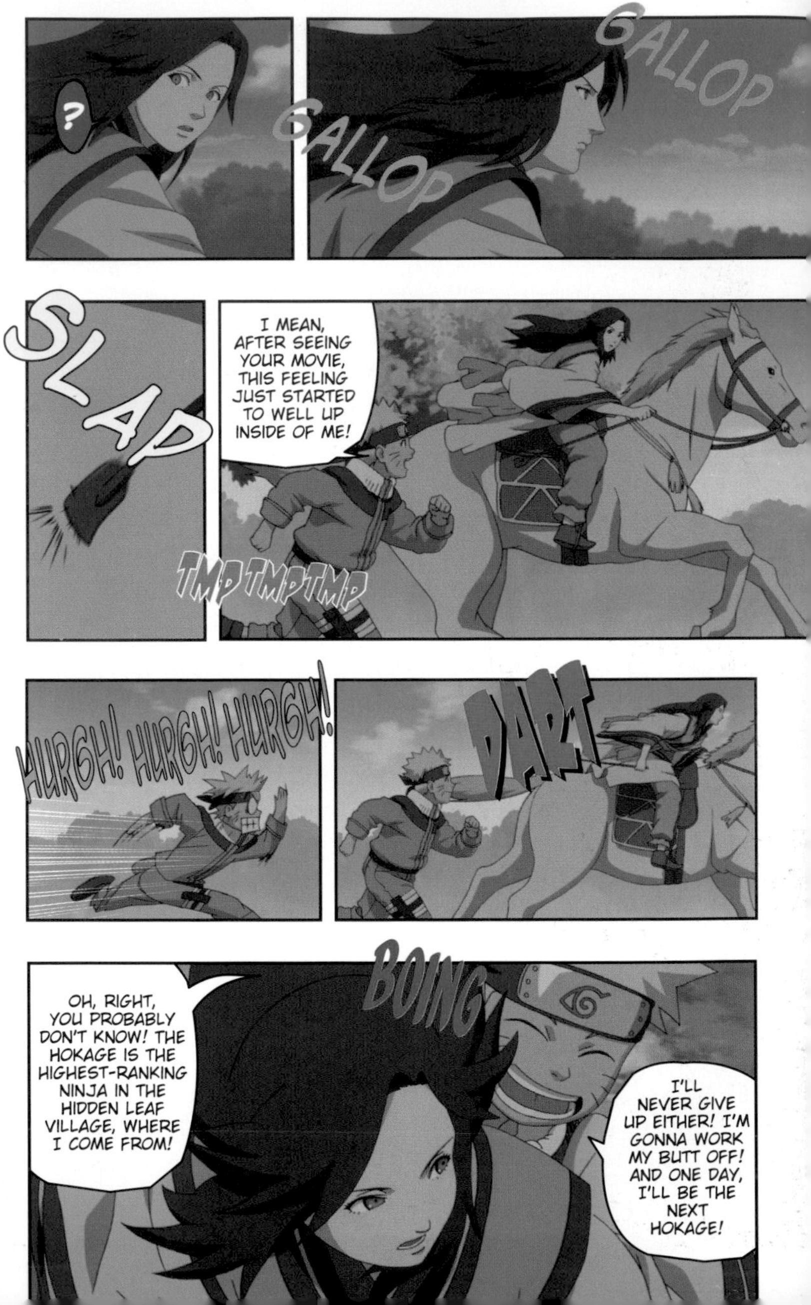
GALLOP
GALLOP
?
I MEAN, AFTER SEEING YOUR MOVIE, THIS FEELING JUST STARTED TO WELL UP INSIDE OF ME!
TMP TMPTMP
SLAP
DART
HURGH! HURGH! HURGH!
BOING
I'LL NEVER GIVE UP EITHER! I'M GONNA WORK MY BUTT OFF! AND ONE DAY, I'LL BE THE NEXT HOKAGE!
OH, RIGHT, YOU PROBABLY DON'T KNOW! THE HOKAGE IS THE HIGHEST-RANKING NINJA IN THE HIDDEN LEAF VILLAGE, WHERE I COME FROM!

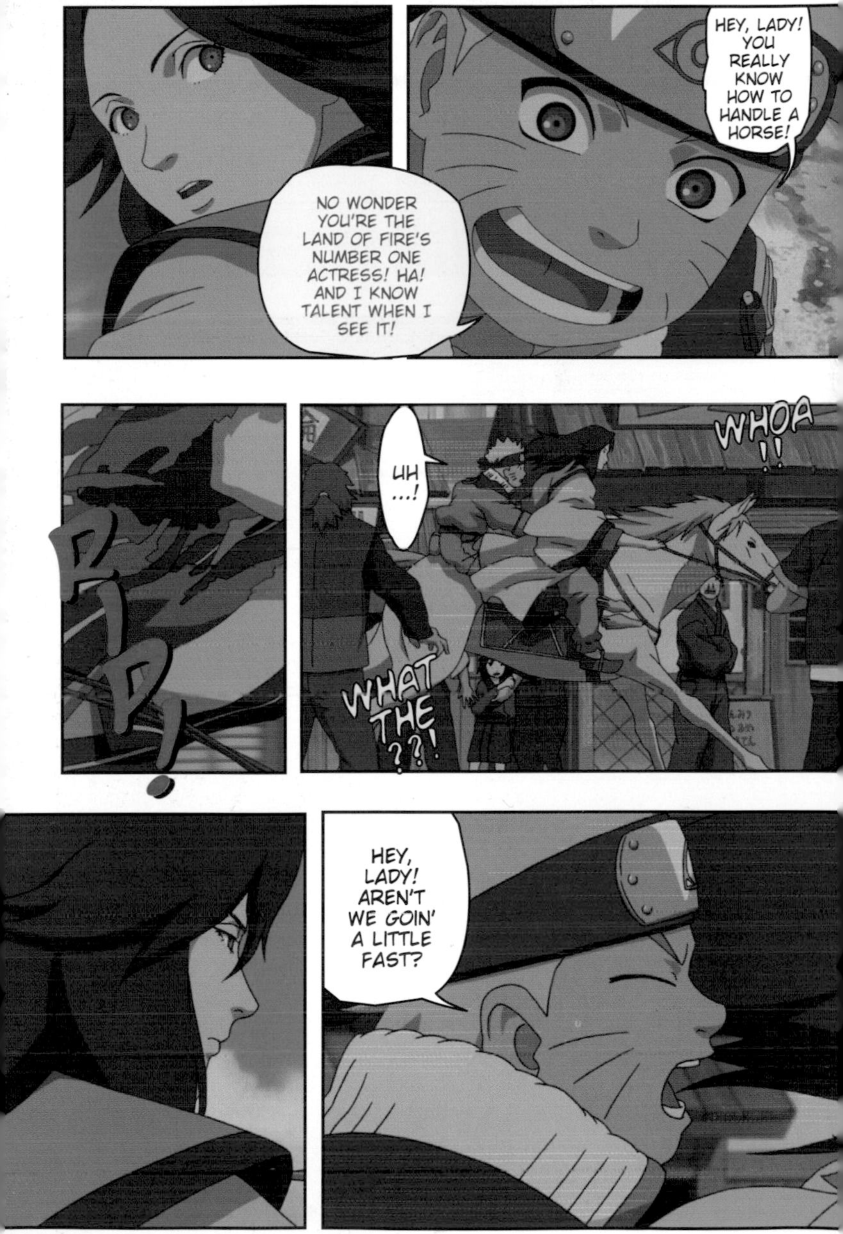
HEY, LADY! YOU REALLY KNOW HOW TO HANDLE A HORSE!
NO WONDER YOU'RE THE LAND OF FIRE'S NUMBER ONE ACTRESS! HA! AND I KNOW TALENT WHEN I SEE IT!
WHOA!!
UH...!
WHAT THE ??!
RIP!
HEY, LADY! AREN'T WE GOIN' A LITTLE FAST?

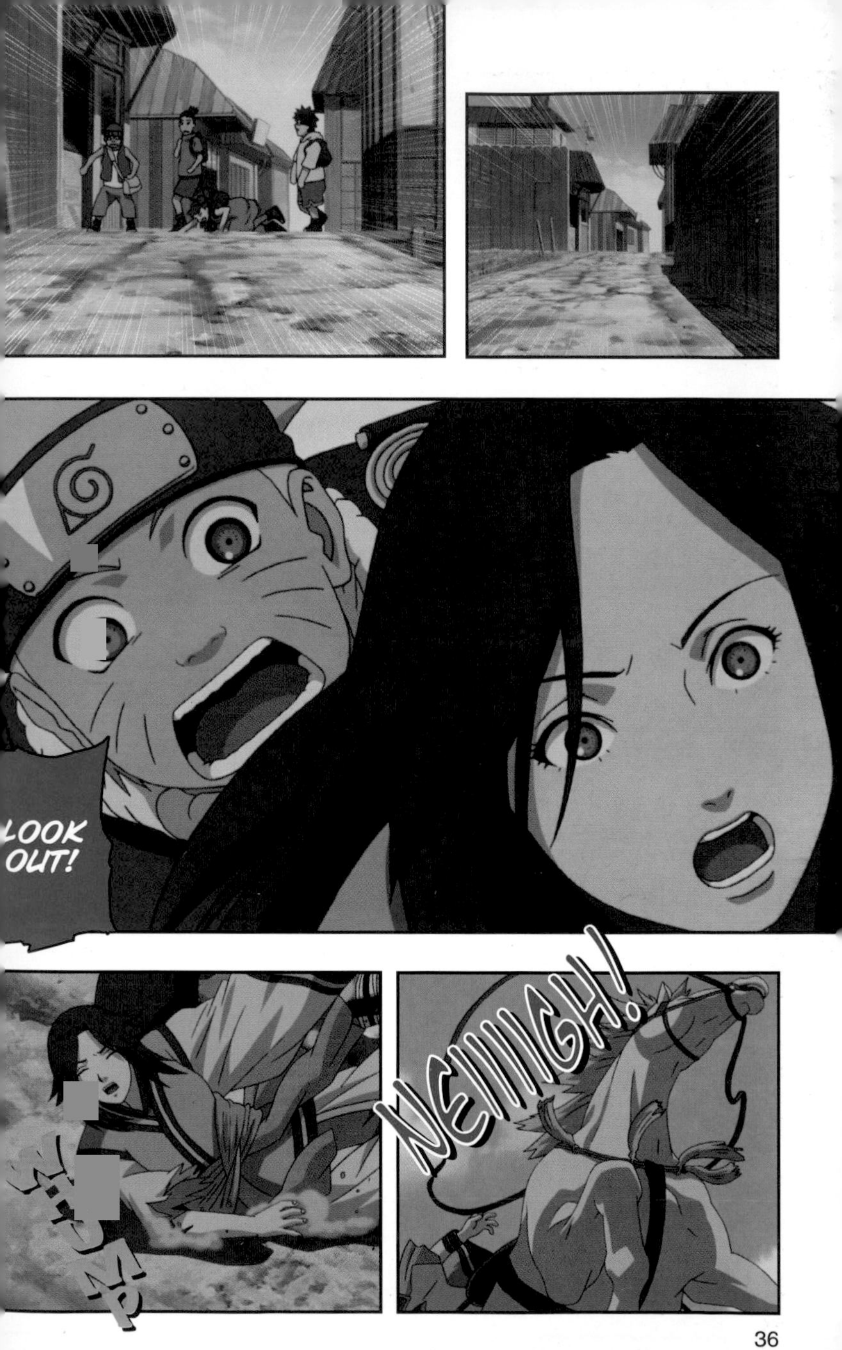
LOOK OUT!
NEIIIGH!

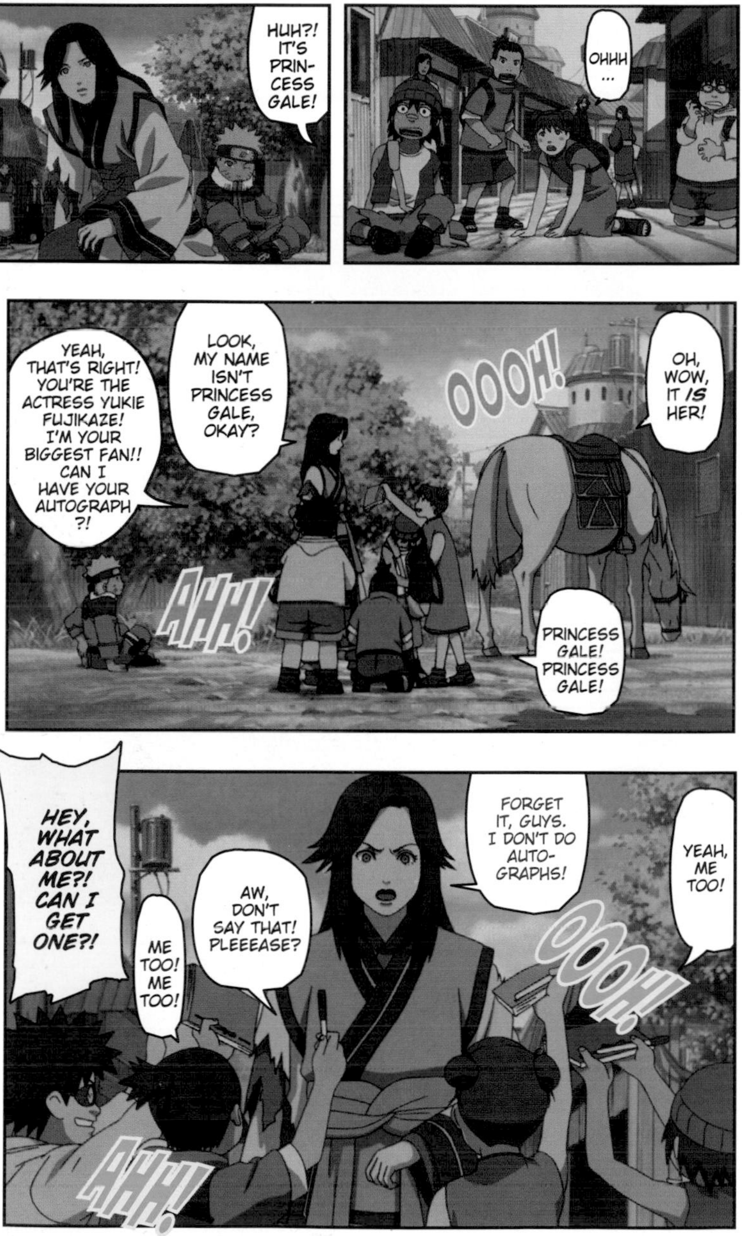
OHHH ...
HUH?! IT'S PRIN-CESS GALE!
OH, WOW, IT *IS* HER!
OOOH!
LOOK, MY NAME ISN'T PRINCESS GALE, OKAY?
YEAH, THAT'S RIGHT! YOU'RE THE ACTRESS YUKIE FUJIKAZE! I'M YOUR BIGGEST FAN!! CAN I HAVE YOUR AUTOGRAPH ?!
PRINCESS GALE! PRINCESS GALE!
AHH!
YEAH, ME TOO!
FORGET IT, GUYS. I DON'T DO AUTO-GRAPHS!
OOOH!
AW, DON'T SAY THAT! PLEEEASE?
ME TOO! ME TOO!
HEY, WHAT ABOUT ME?! CAN I GET ONE?!
AHH!

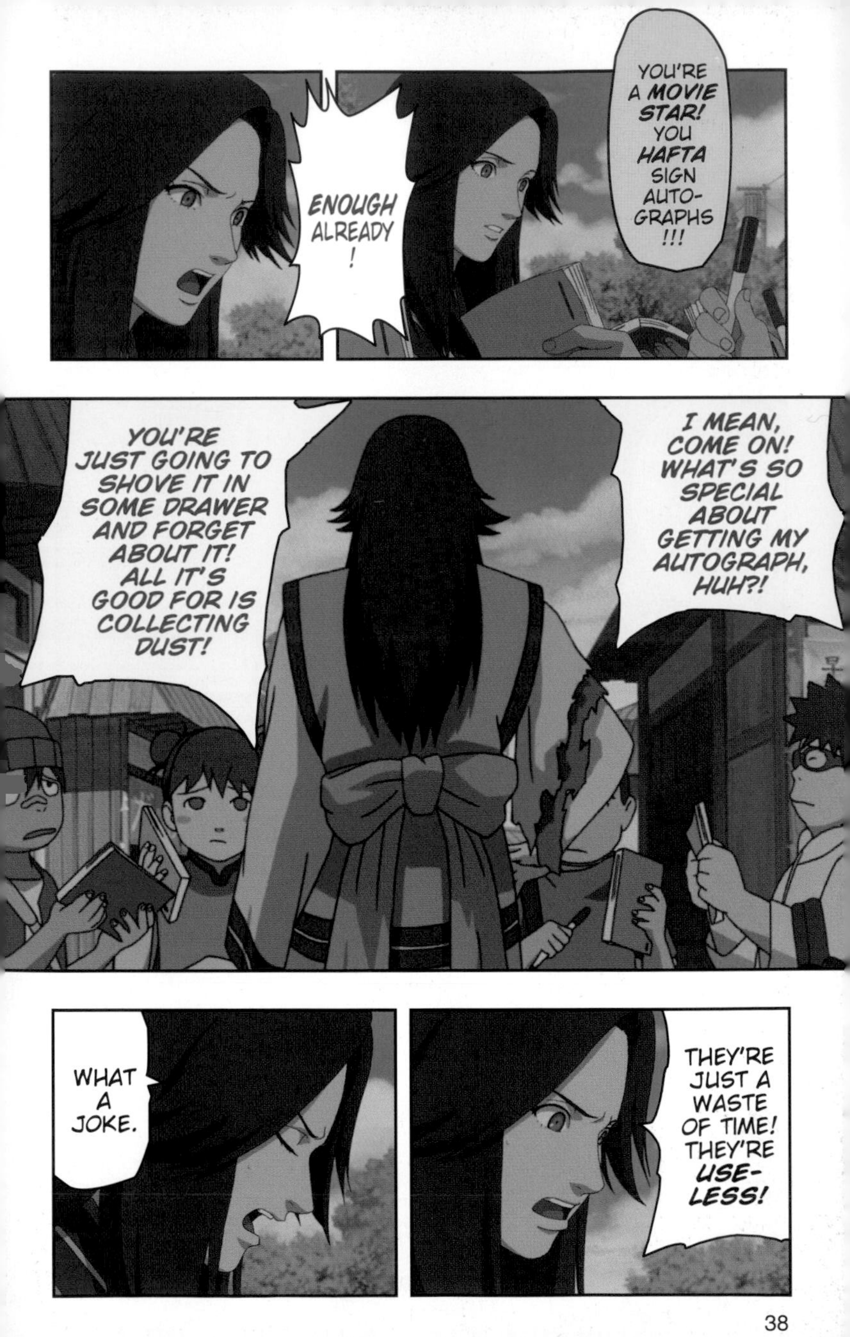
YOU'RE A MOVIE STAR! YOU HAFTA SIGN AUTO-GRAPHS!!!
ENOUGH ALREADY!
I MEAN, COME ON! WHAT'S SO SPECIAL ABOUT GETTING MY AUTOGRAPH, HUH?!
YOU'RE JUST GOING TO SHOVE IT IN SOME DRAWER AND FORGET ABOUT IT! ALL IT'S GOOD FOR IS COLLECTING DUST!
THEY'RE JUST A WASTE OF TIME! THEY'RE USE-LESS!
WHAT A JOKE.

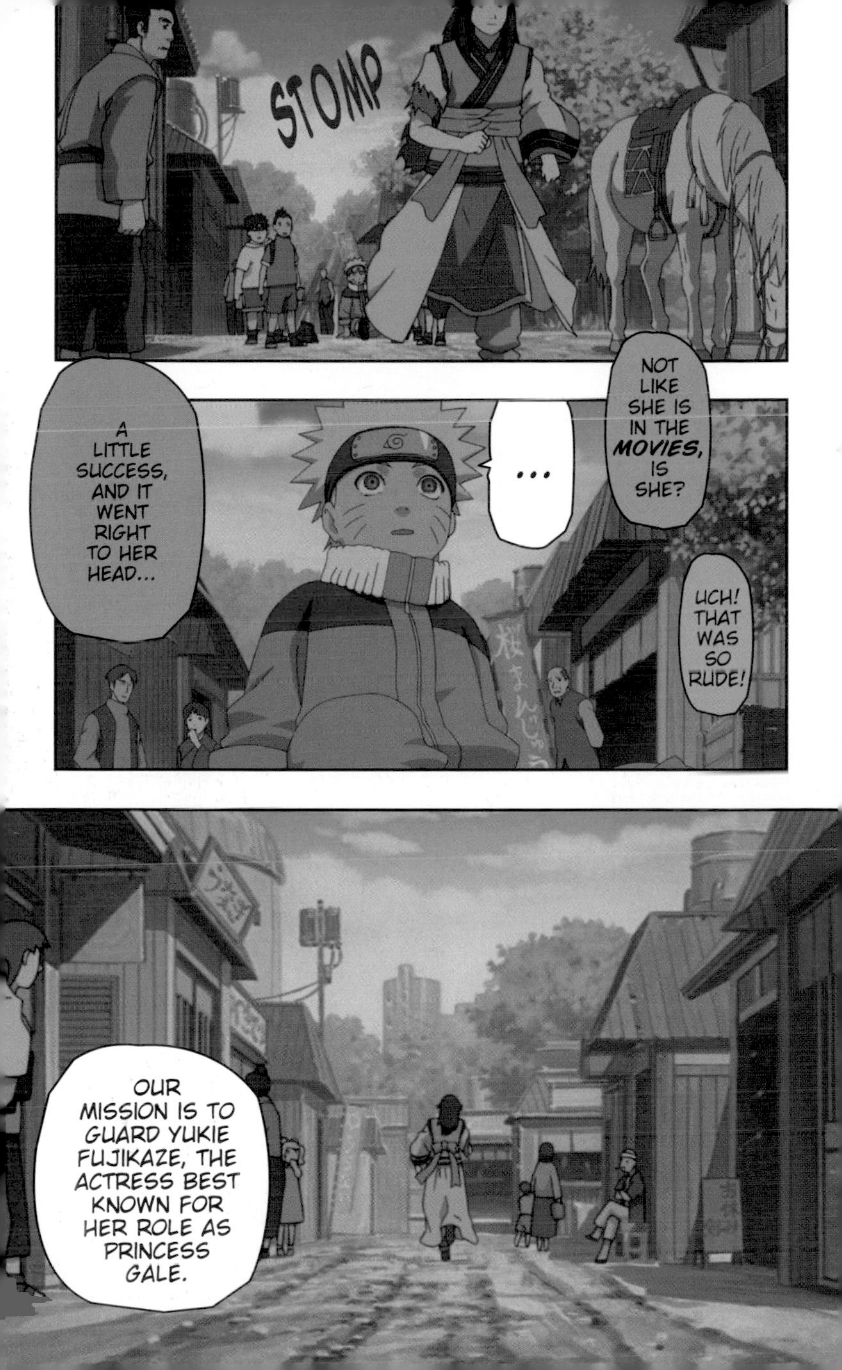
STOMP
NOT LIKE SHE IS IN THE MOVIES, IS SHE?
...
UCH! THAT WAS SO RUDE!
A LITTLE SUCCESS, AND IT WENT RIGHT TO HER HEAD...
OUR MISSION IS TO GUARD YUKIE FUJIKAZE, THE ACTRESS BEST KNOWN FOR HER ROLE AS PRINCESS GALE.

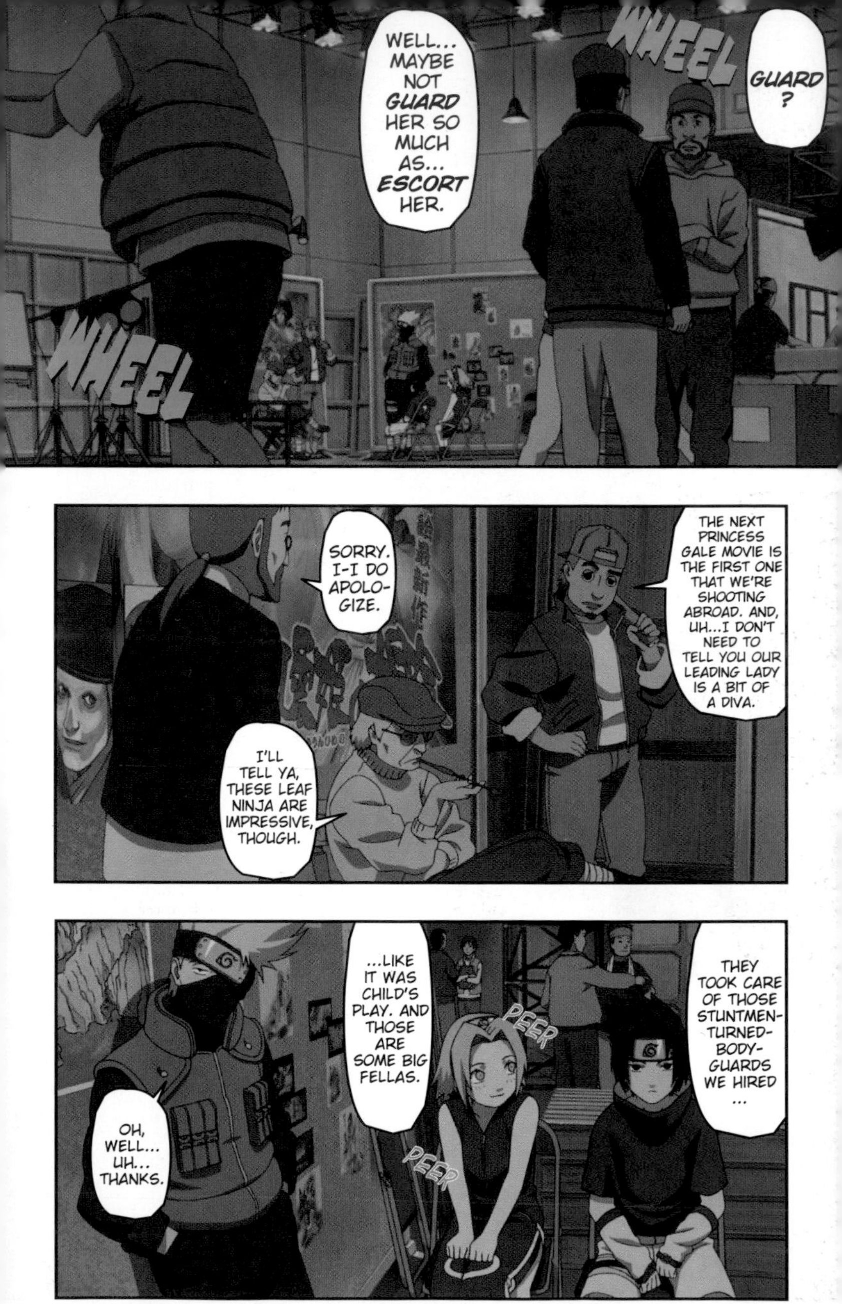
WHEEL
GUARD?
WELL... MAYBE NOT GUARD HER SO MUCH AS... ESCORT HER.
WHEEL
THE NEXT PRINCESS GALE MOVIE IS THE FIRST ONE THAT WE'RE SHOOTING ABROAD. AND, UH...I DON'T NEED TO TELL YOU OUR LEADING LADY IS A BIT OF A DIVA.
SORRY. I-I DO APOLOGIZE.
I'LL TELL YA, THESE LEAF NINJA ARE IMPRESSIVE, THOUGH.
THEY TOOK CARE OF THOSE STUNTMEN-TURNED-BODYGUARDS WE HIRED...
...LIKE IT WAS CHILD'S PLAY. AND THOSE ARE SOME BIG FELLAS.
PEER
PEER
OH, WELL... UH... THANKS.

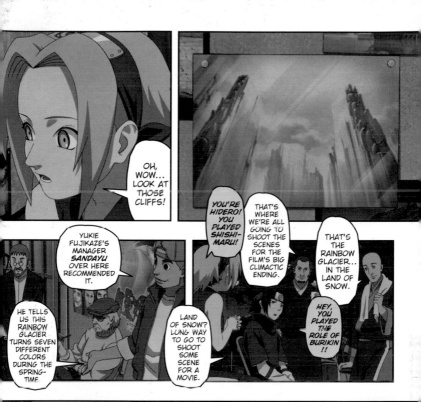

OH, WOW... LOOK AT THOSE CLIFFS!
THAT'S THE RAINBOW GLACIER... IN THE LAND OF SNOW.
THAT'S WHERE WE'RE ALL GOING TO SHOOT THE SCENES FOR THE FILM'S BIG CLIMACTIC ENDING.
YOU'RE HIDERO! YOU PLAYED SHISHI-MARU!
HEY, YOU PLAYED THE ROLE OF BURIKIN!!
LAND OF SNOW? LONG WAY TO GO TO SHOOT SOME SCENE FOR A MOVIE.
YUKIE FUJIKAZE'S MANAGER ***SANDAYU*** OVER HERE RECOMMENDED IT.
HE TELLS US THIS RAINBOW GLACIER TURNS SEVEN DIFFERENT COLORS DURING THE SPRING-TIME.
NO. THAT'S JUST AN OLD LEGEND. THE TRUTH IS, THERE ISN'T ANY SPRING IN THE LAND OF SNOW.
WHAT, NOT EVER?
DOES THAT MEAN IT'S WINTER ALL YEAR LONG?
MM-HMM. YOU GOT IT.

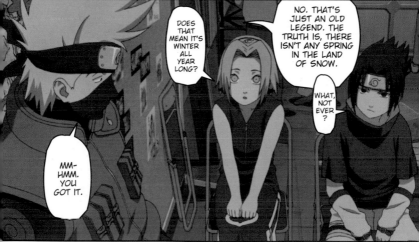

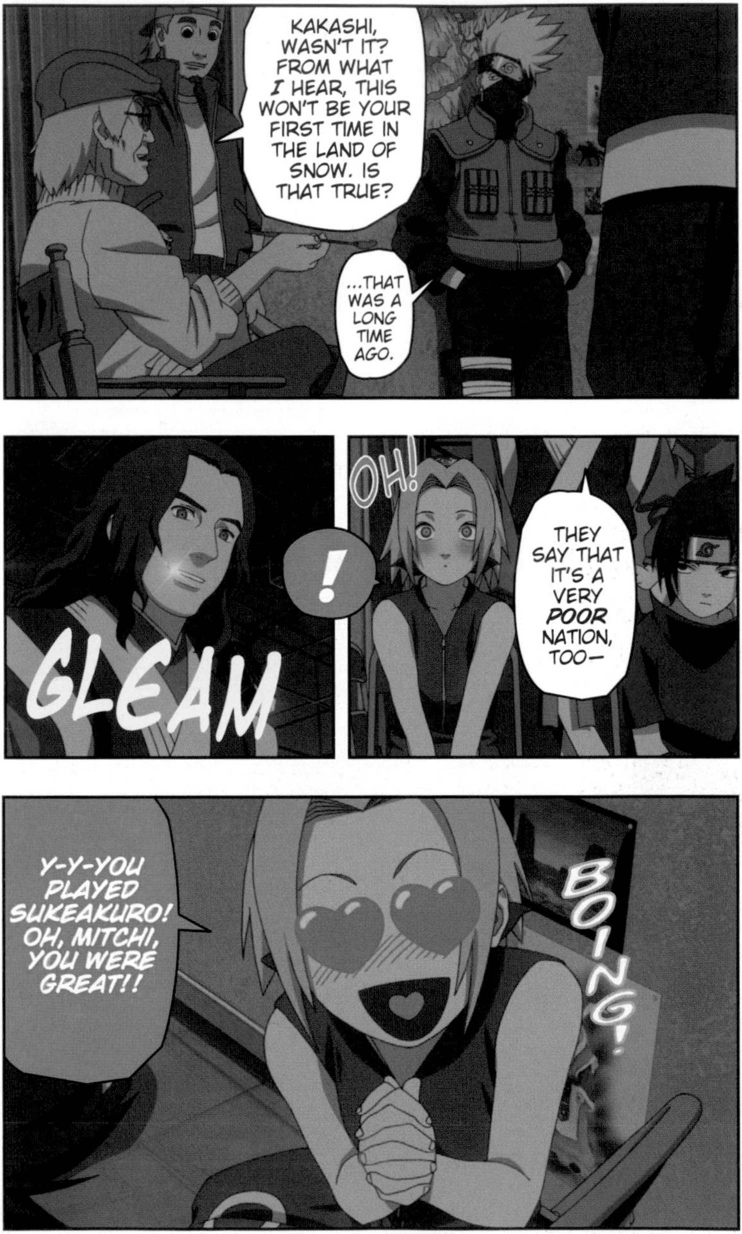

KAKASHI, WASN'T IT? FROM WHAT *I* HEAR, THIS WON'T BE YOUR FIRST TIME IN THE LAND OF SNOW. IS THAT TRUE?
...THAT WAS A LONG TIME AGO.
OH!
THEY SAY THAT IT'S A VERY **POOR** NATION, TOO—
!
GLEAM
Y-Y-YOU PLAYED SUKEAKURO! OH, MITCHI, YOU WERE GREAT!!
BOING!

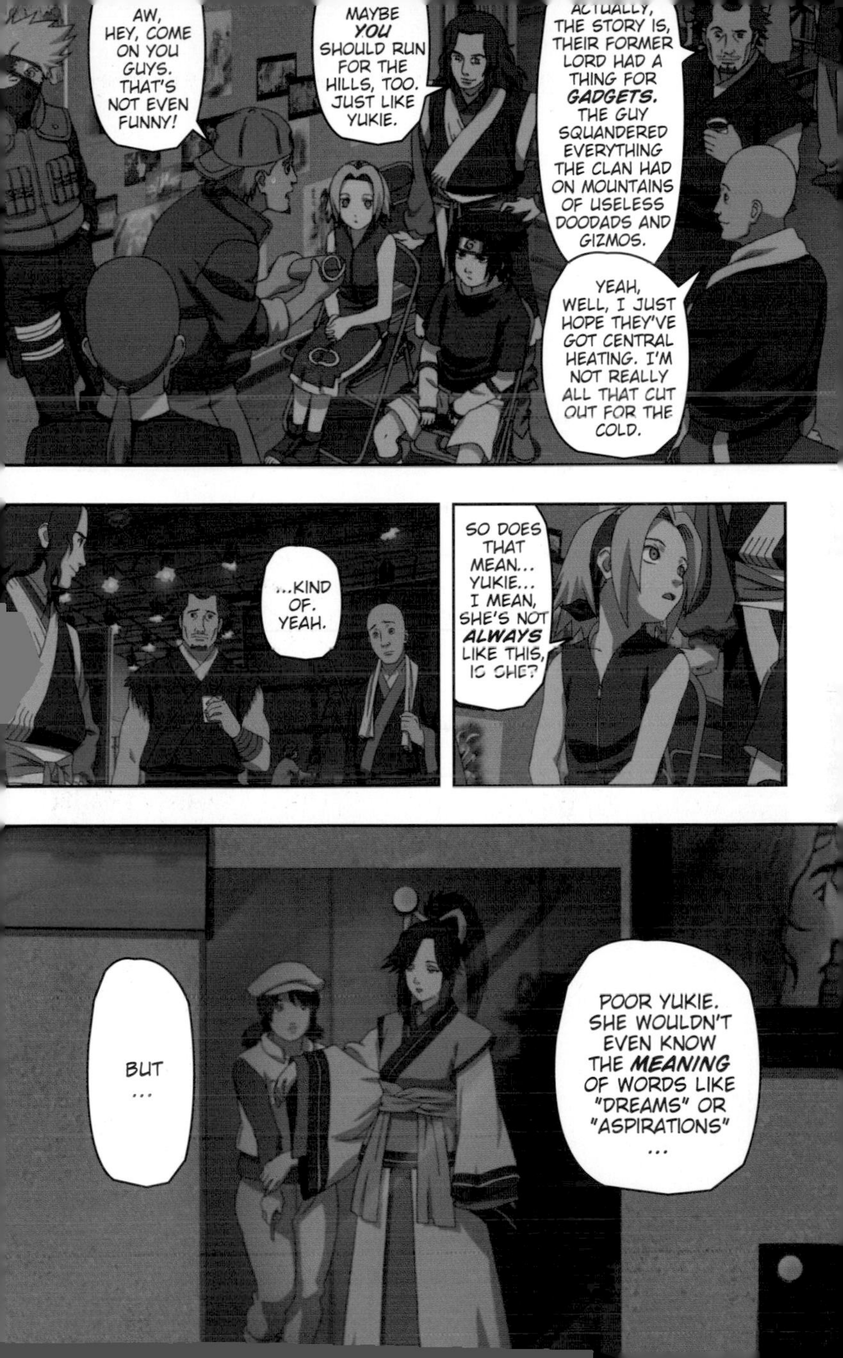
ACTUALLY, THE STORY IS, THEIR FORMER LORD HAD A THING FOR **GADGETS.** THE GUY SQUANDERED EVERYTHING THE CLAN HAD ON MOUNTAINS OF USELESS DOODADS AND GIZMOS.
YEAH, WELL, I JUST HOPE THEY'VE GOT CENTRAL HEATING. I'M NOT REALLY ALL THAT CUT OUT FOR THE COLD.
MAYBE ***YOU*** SHOULD RUN FOR THE HILLS, TOO. JUST LIKE YUKIE.
AW, HEY, COME ON YOU GUYS. THAT'S NOT EVEN FUNNY!
SO DOES THAT MEAN... YUKIE... I MEAN, SHE'S NOT ***ALWAYS*** LIKE THIS, IS SHE?
...KIND OF. YEAH.
POOR YUKIE. SHE WOULDN'T EVEN KNOW THE ***MEANING*** OF WORDS LIKE "DREAMS" OR "ASPIRATIONS" ...
BUT ...

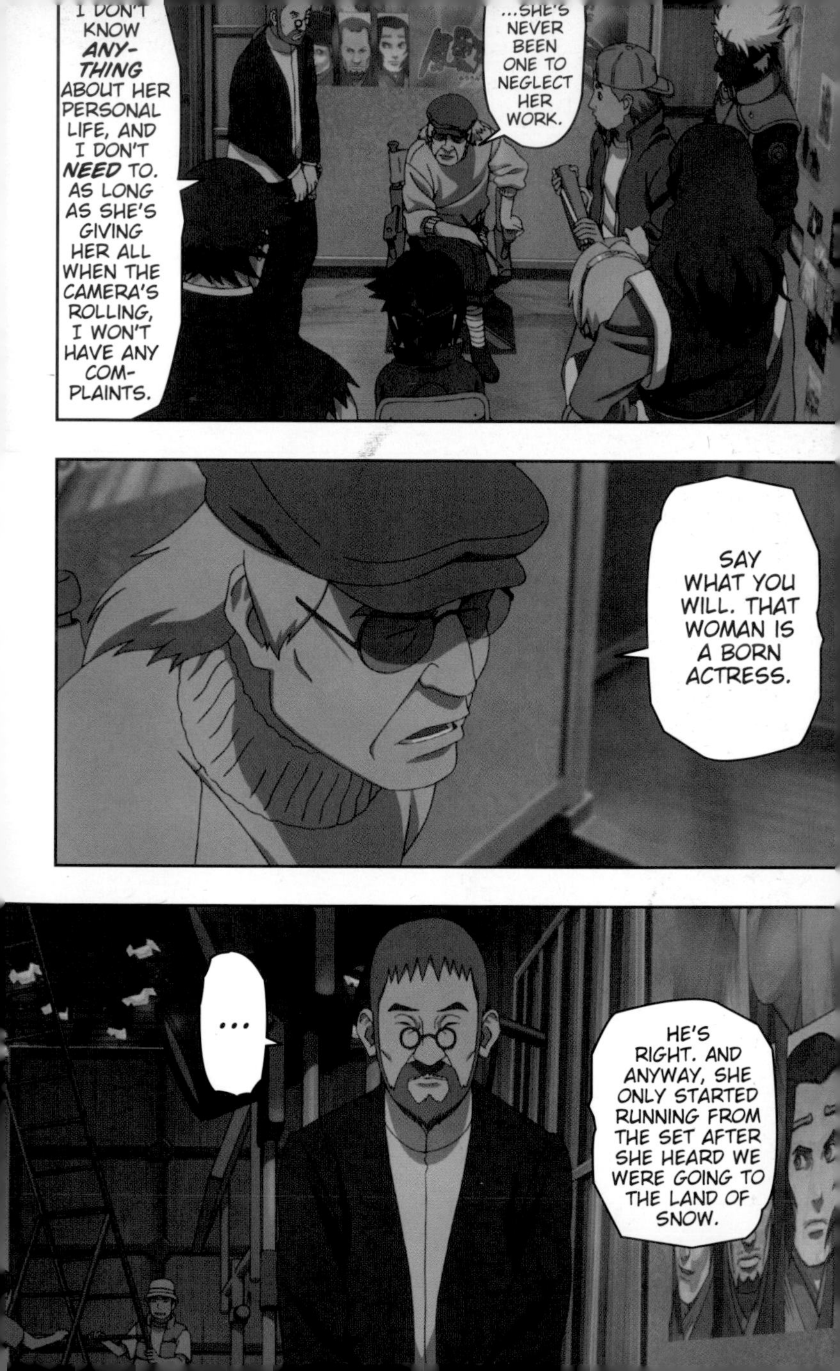
...SHE'S NEVER BEEN ONE TO NEGLECT HER WORK.
I DON'T KNOW ANYTHING ABOUT HER PERSONAL LIFE, AND I DON'T NEED TO. AS LONG AS SHE'S GIVING HER ALL WHEN THE CAMERA'S ROLLING, I WON'T HAVE ANY COMPLAINTS.
SAY WHAT YOU WILL. THAT WOMAN IS A BORN ACTRESS.
HE'S RIGHT. AND ANYWAY, SHE ONLY STARTED RUNNING FROM THE SET AFTER SHE HEARD WE WERE GOING TO THE LAND OF SNOW.
...

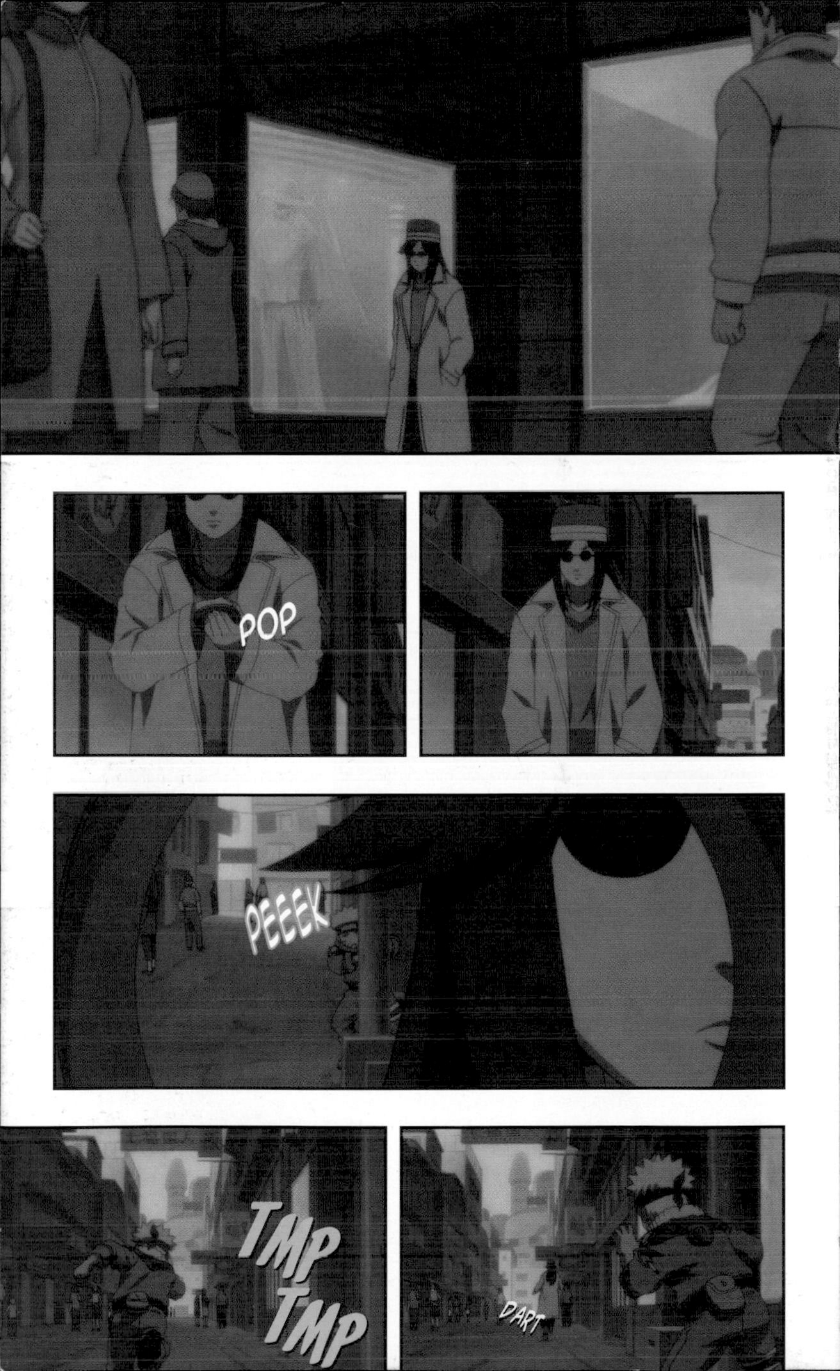
POP
PEEEK
DART
TMP
TMP

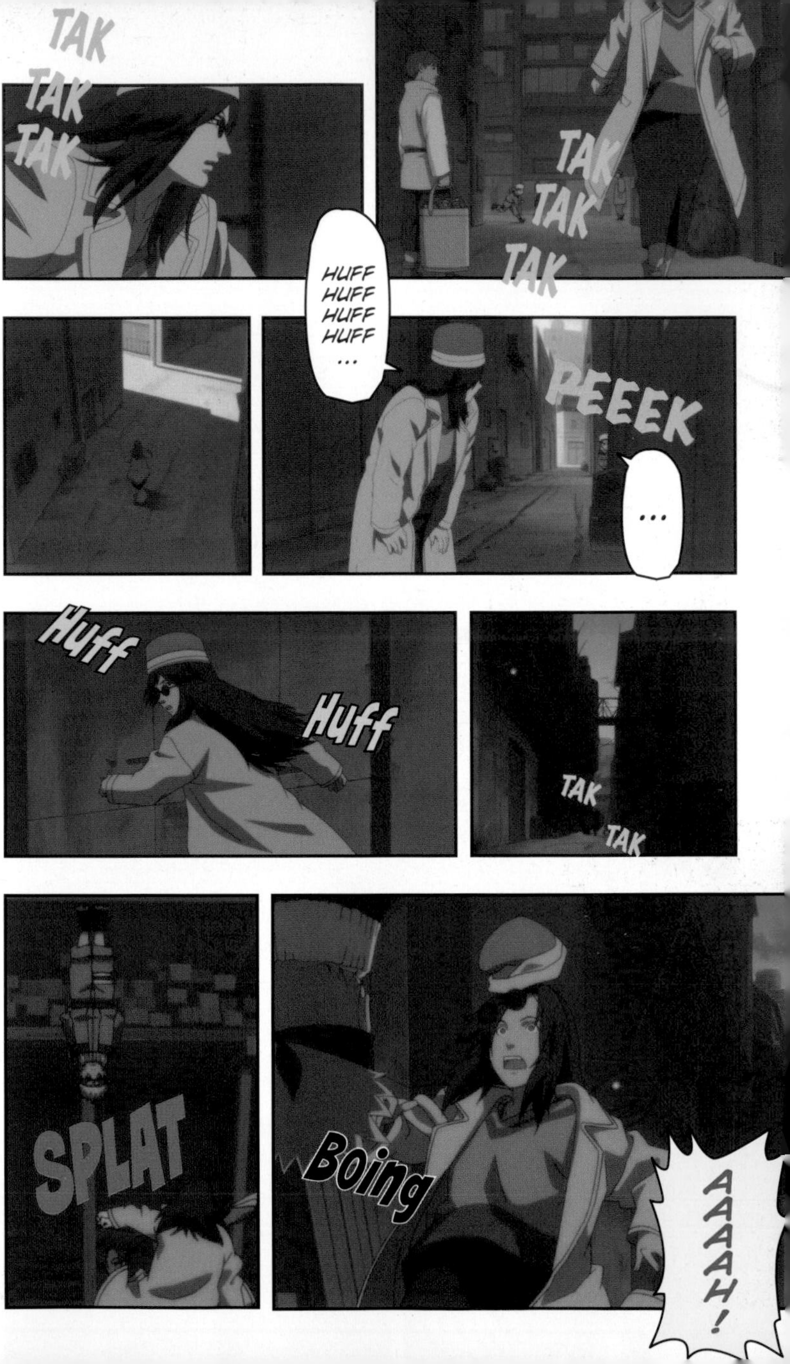
TAK
TAK
TAK
TAK
TAK
TAK
HUFF HUFF HUFF HUFF ...
PEEEK
...
TAK
TAK
Huff
Huff
Boing
AAAAH!
SPLAT

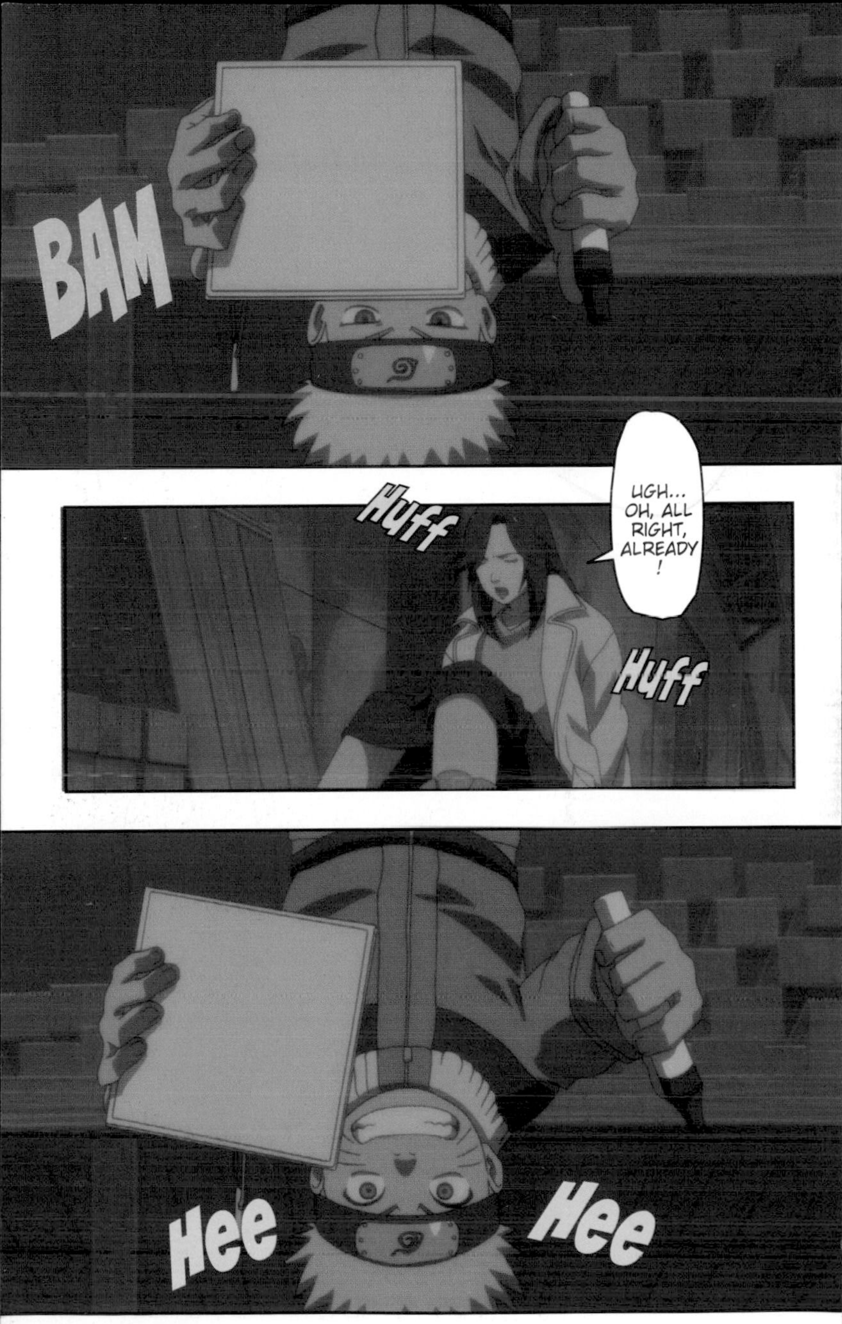
BAM
UGH... OH, ALL RIGHT, ALREADY!
Huff
Huff
Hee
Hee

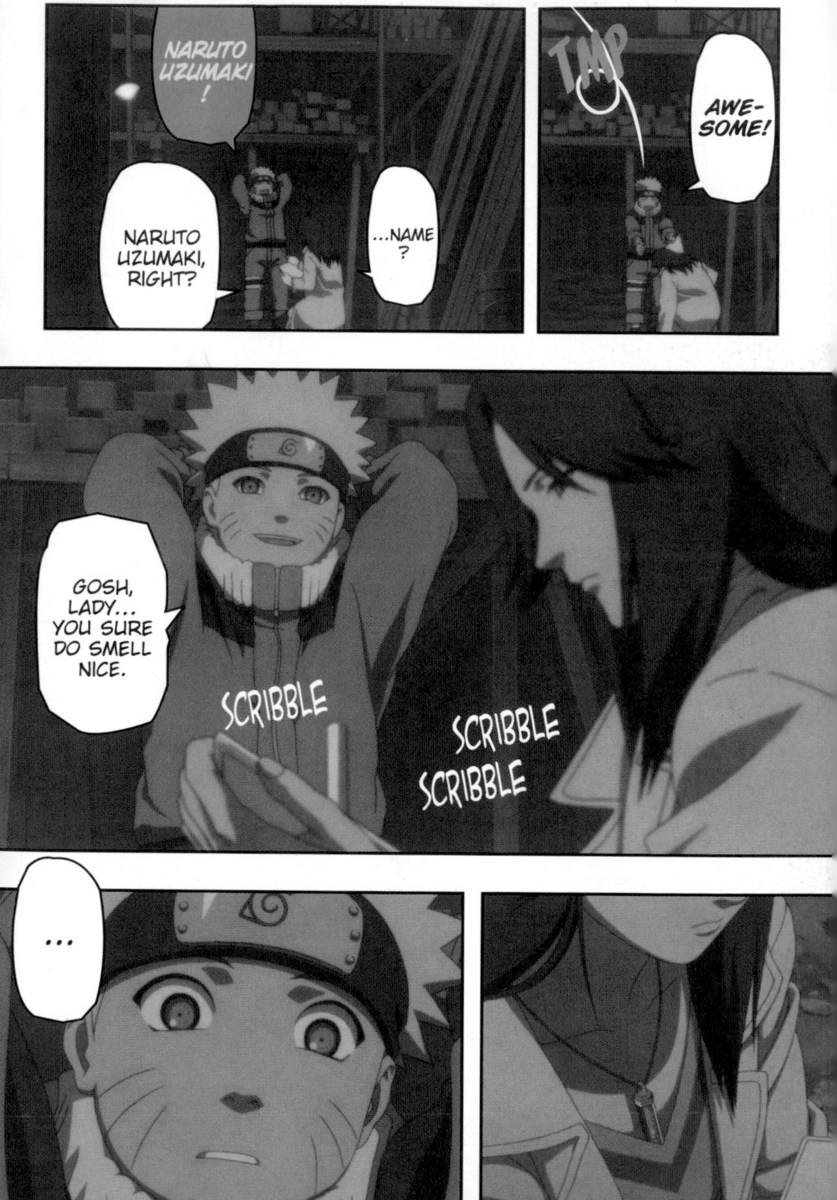

TMP
AWE-SOME!
NARUTO UZUMAKI!
...NAME?
NARUTO UZUMAKI, RIGHT?
SCRIBBLE
SCRIBBLE
GOSH, LADY... YOU SURE DO SMELL NICE.
SCRIBBLE
...

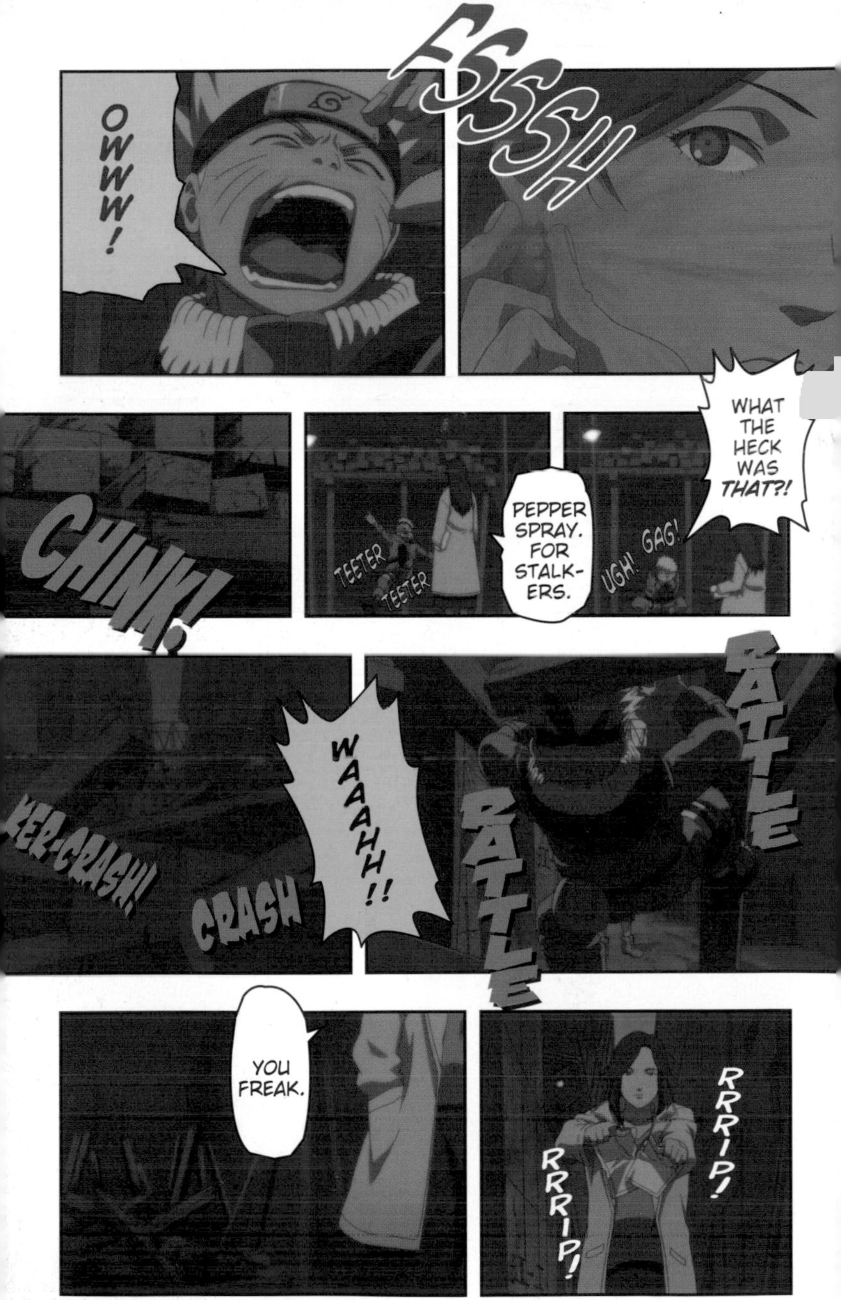
FSSSH
OWWW!
WHAT THE HECK WAS THAT?!
UGH! GAG!
PEPPER SPRAY. FOR STALKERS.
TEETER TEETER
CHINK!
RATTLE
RATTLE
WAAAHH!!
CRASH
KER-CRASH!
RRRIP!
RRRIP!
YOU FREAK.

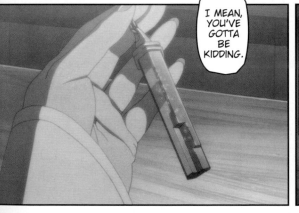

I MEAN, YOU'VE GOTTA BE KIDDING.

CLINK

WHO'D WANNA GO TO THE LAND OF SNOW?

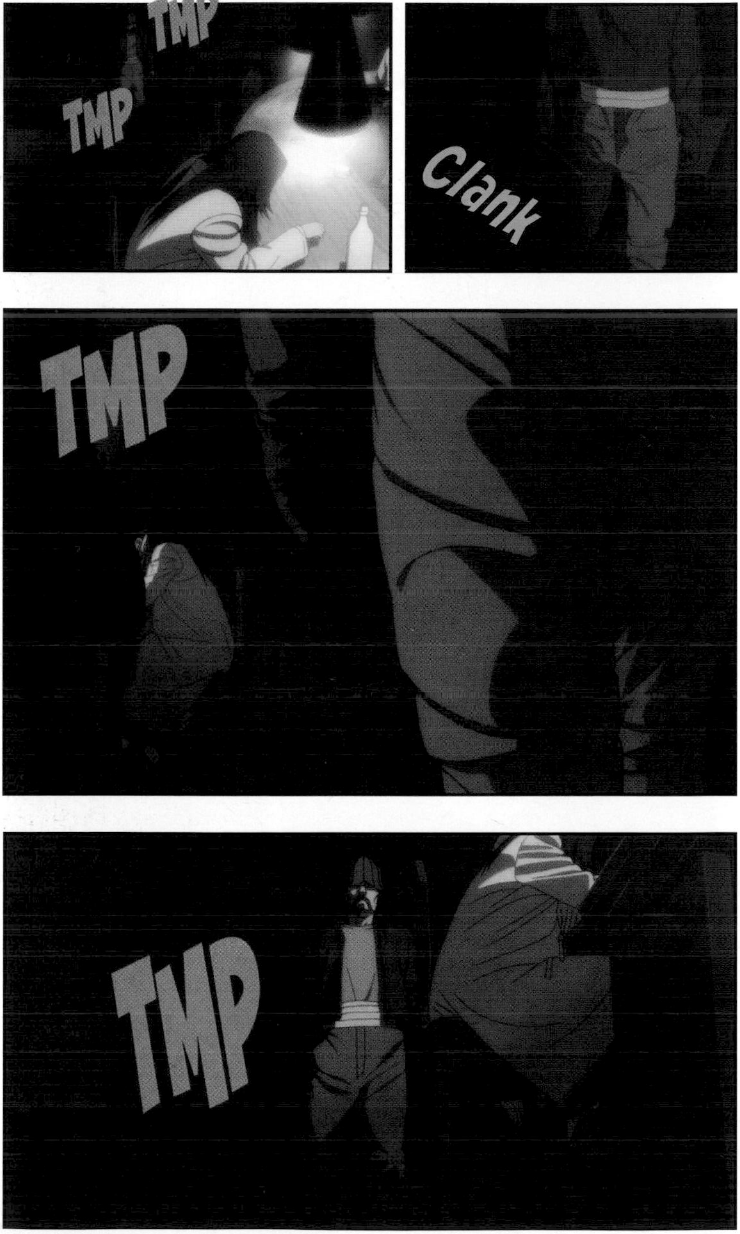
Clank
TMP
TMP
TMP
TMP

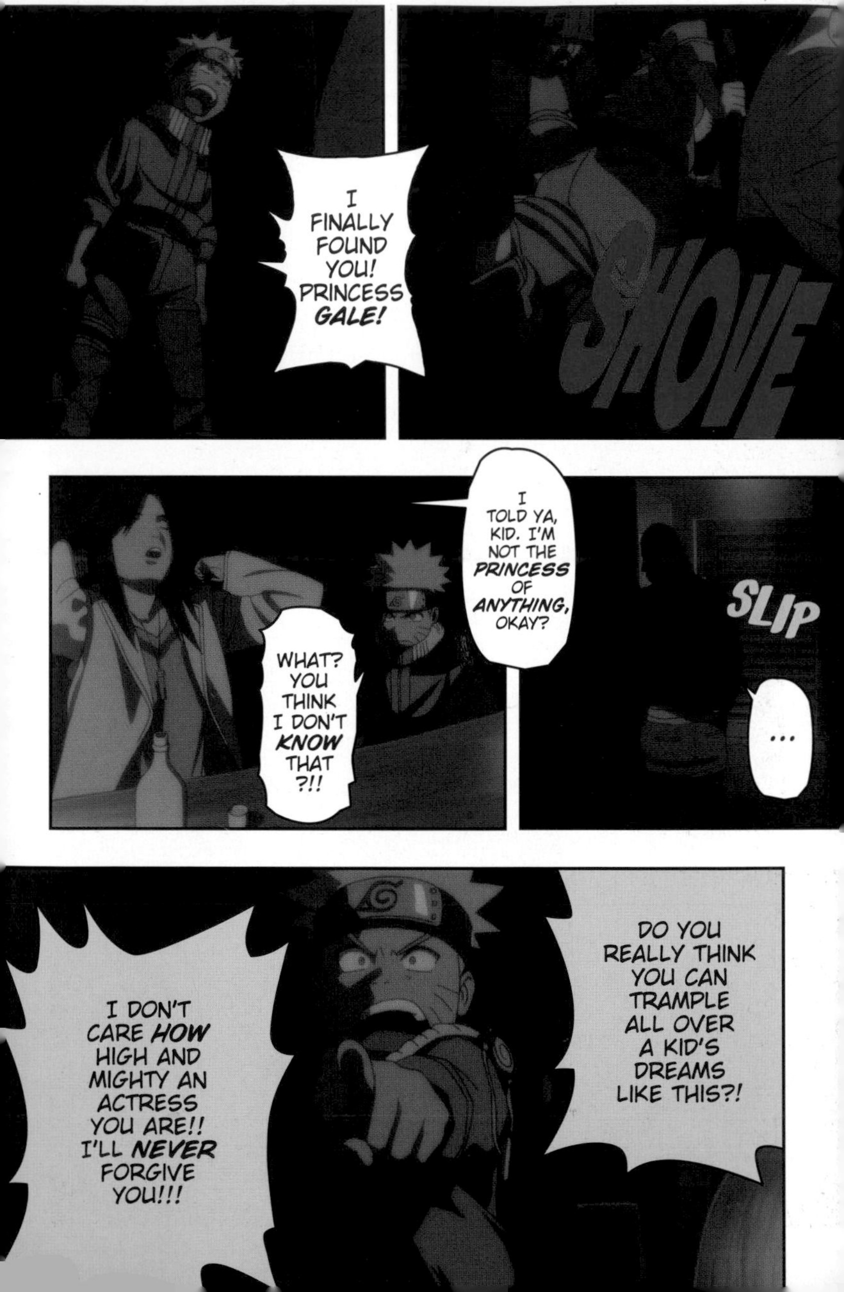
SHOVE
I FINALLY FOUND YOU! PRINCESS GALE!
SLIP
...
I TOLD YA, KID. I'M NOT THE PRINCESS OF ANYTHING, OKAY?
WHAT? YOU THINK I DON'T KNOW THAT?!!
DO YOU REALLY THINK YOU CAN TRAMPLE ALL OVER A KID'S DREAMS LIKE THIS?!
I DON'T CARE HOW HIGH AND MIGHTY AN ACTRESS YOU ARE!! I'LL NEVER FORGIVE YOU!!!

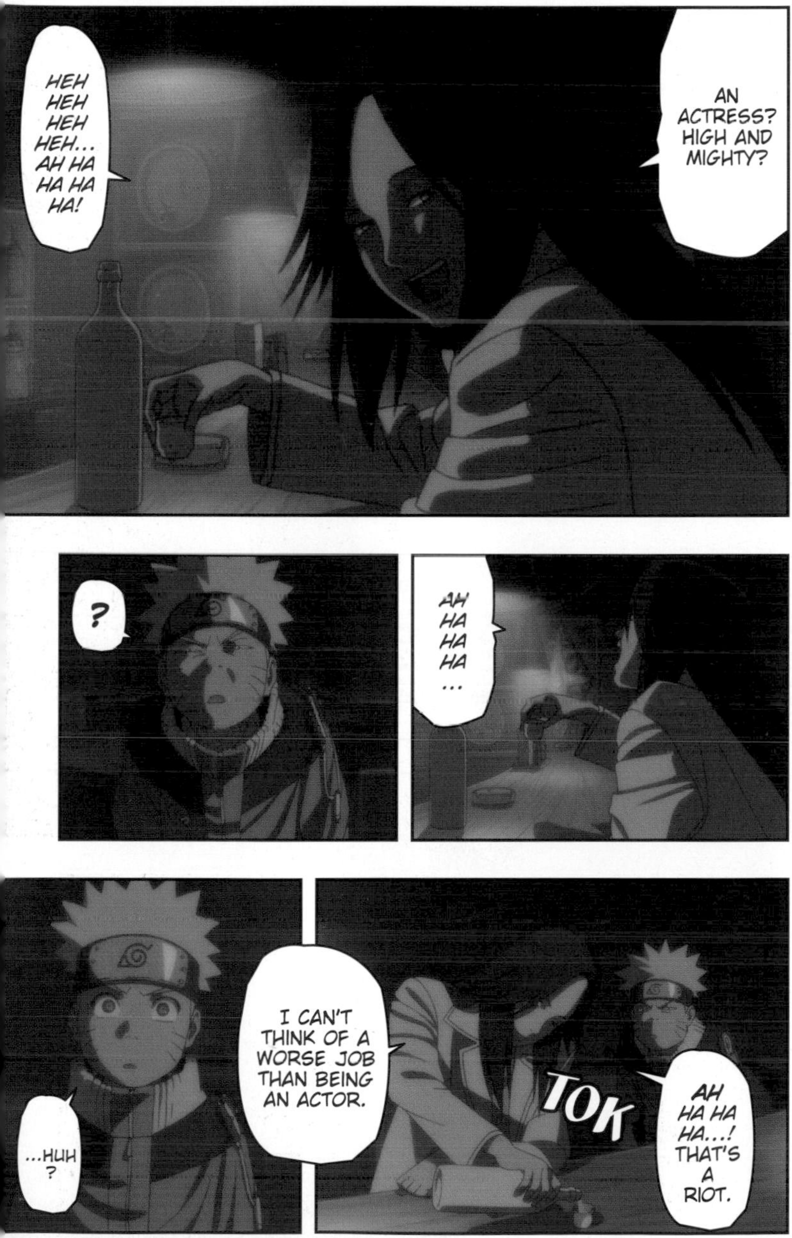

AN ACTRESS? HIGH AND MIGHTY?
HEH HEH HEH HEH... AH HA HA HA HA!
AH HA HA HA ...
?
AH HA HA HA...! THAT'S A RIOT.
TOK
I CAN'T THINK OF A WORSE JOB THAN BEING AN ACTOR.
...HUH?

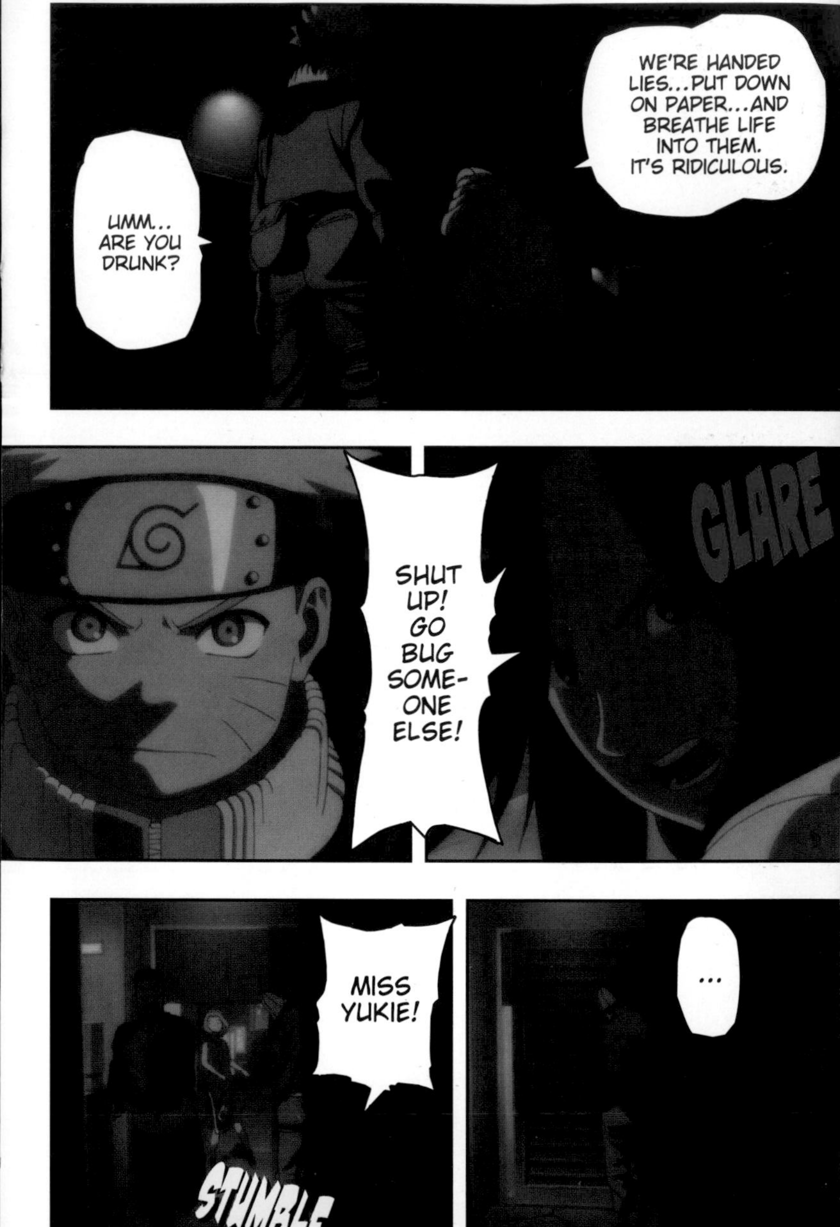
WE'RE HANDED LIES...PUT DOWN ON PAPER...AND BREATHE LIFE INTO THEM. IT'S RIDICULOUS.
UMM... ARE YOU DRUNK?
GLARE
SHUT UP! GO BUG SOME-ONE ELSE!
...
MISS YUKIE!
STUMBLE

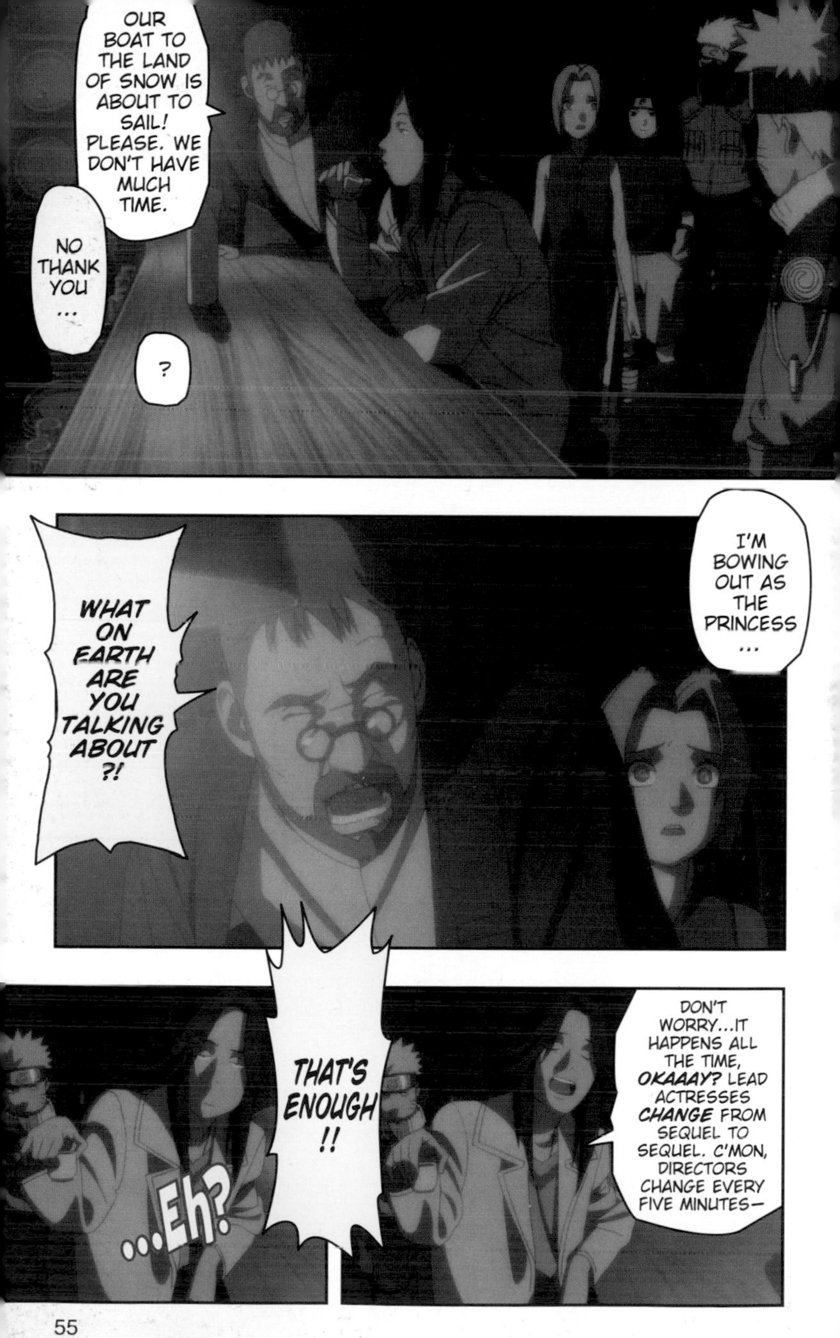
OUR BOAT TO THE LAND OF SNOW IS ABOUT TO SAIL! PLEASE. WE DON'T HAVE MUCH TIME.
NO THANK YOU ...
?
I'M BOWING OUT AS THE PRINCESS ...
WHAT ON EARTH ARE YOU TALKING ABOUT ?!
DON'T WORRY...IT HAPPENS ALL THE TIME, OKAAAY? LEAD ACTRESSES CHANGE FROM SEQUEL TO SEQUEL. C'MON, DIRECTORS CHANGE EVERY FIVE MINUTES—
THAT'S ENOUGH !!
...Eh?

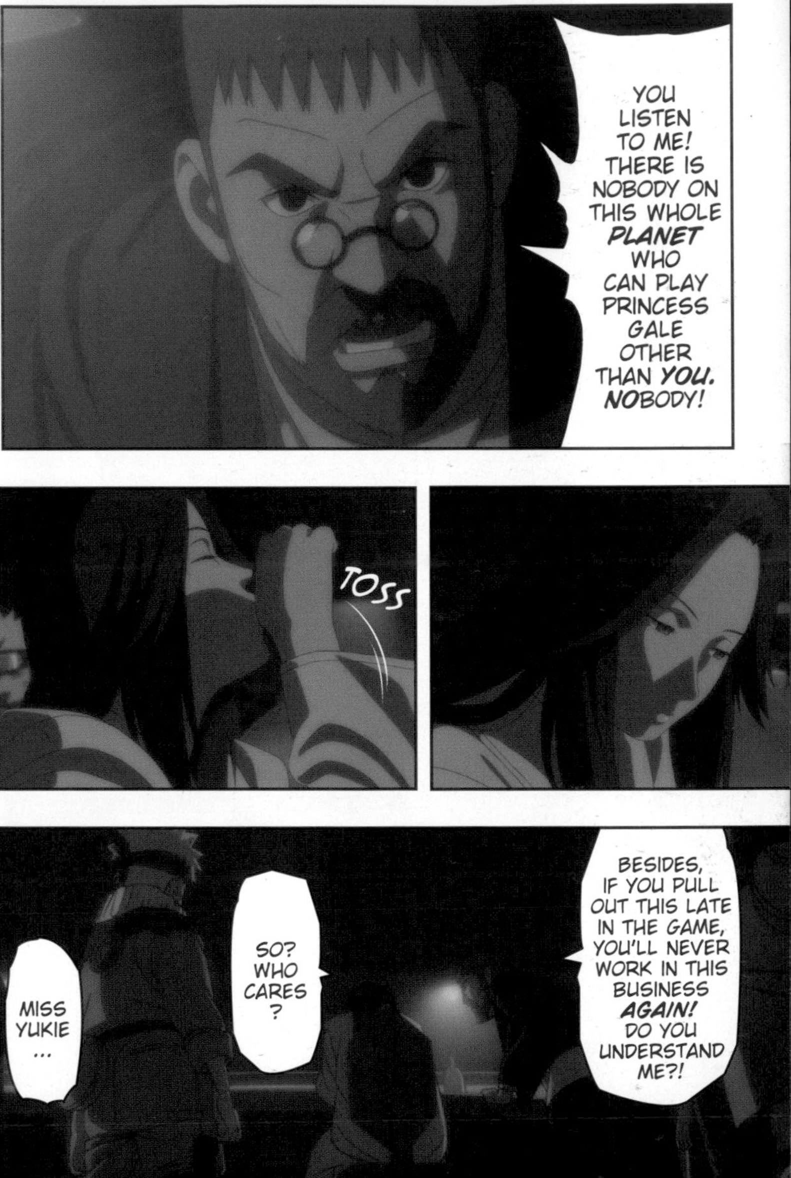
YOU LISTEN TO ME! THERE IS NOBODY ON THIS WHOLE ***PLANET*** WHO CAN PLAY PRINCESS GALE OTHER THAN ***YOU. NO***BODY!
TOSS
BESIDES, IF YOU PULL OUT THIS LATE IN THE GAME, YOU'LL NEVER WORK IN THIS BUSINESS ***AGAIN!*** DO YOU UNDERSTAND ME?!
SO? WHO CARES?
MISS YUKIE...

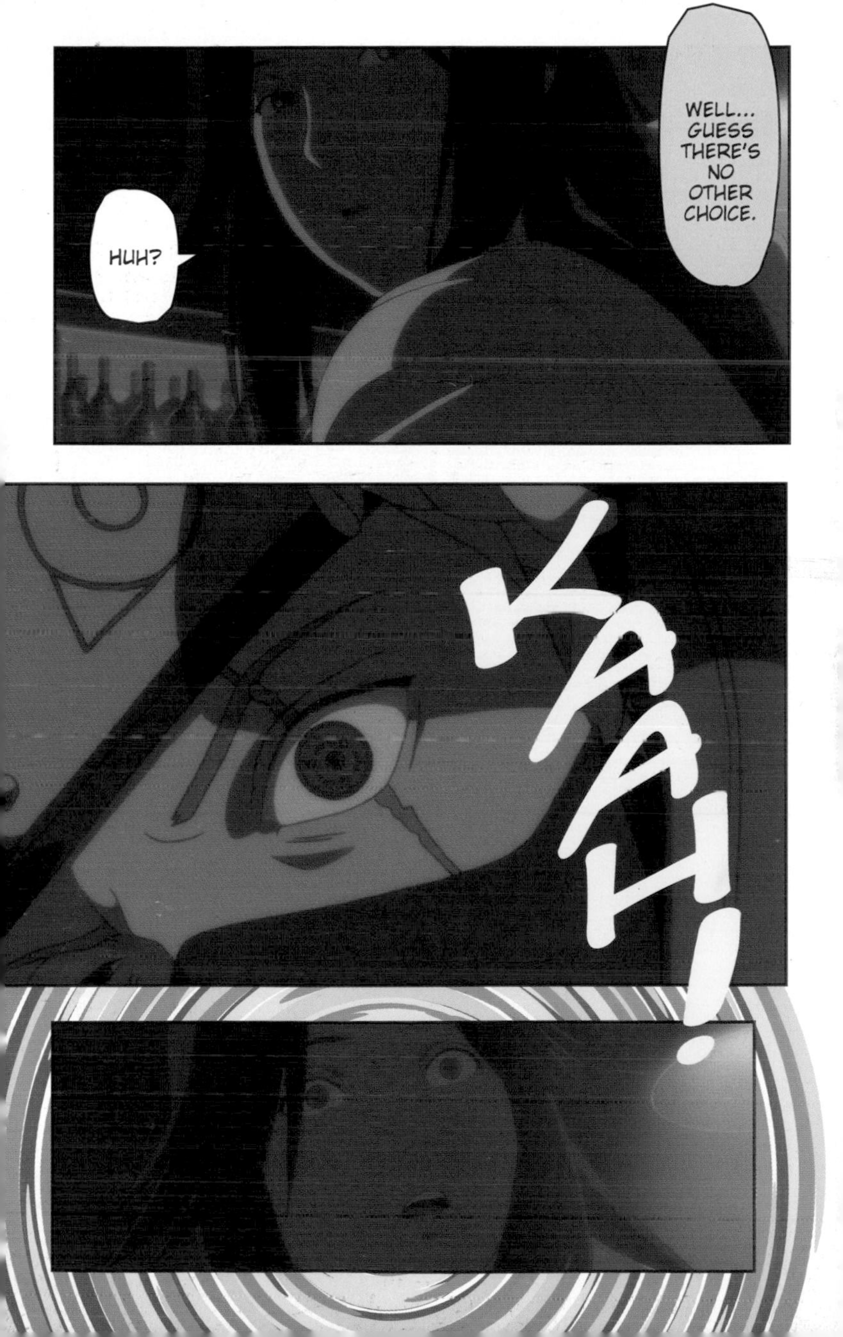
WELL... GUESS THERE'S NO OTHER CHOICE.
HUH?
KAAAH!

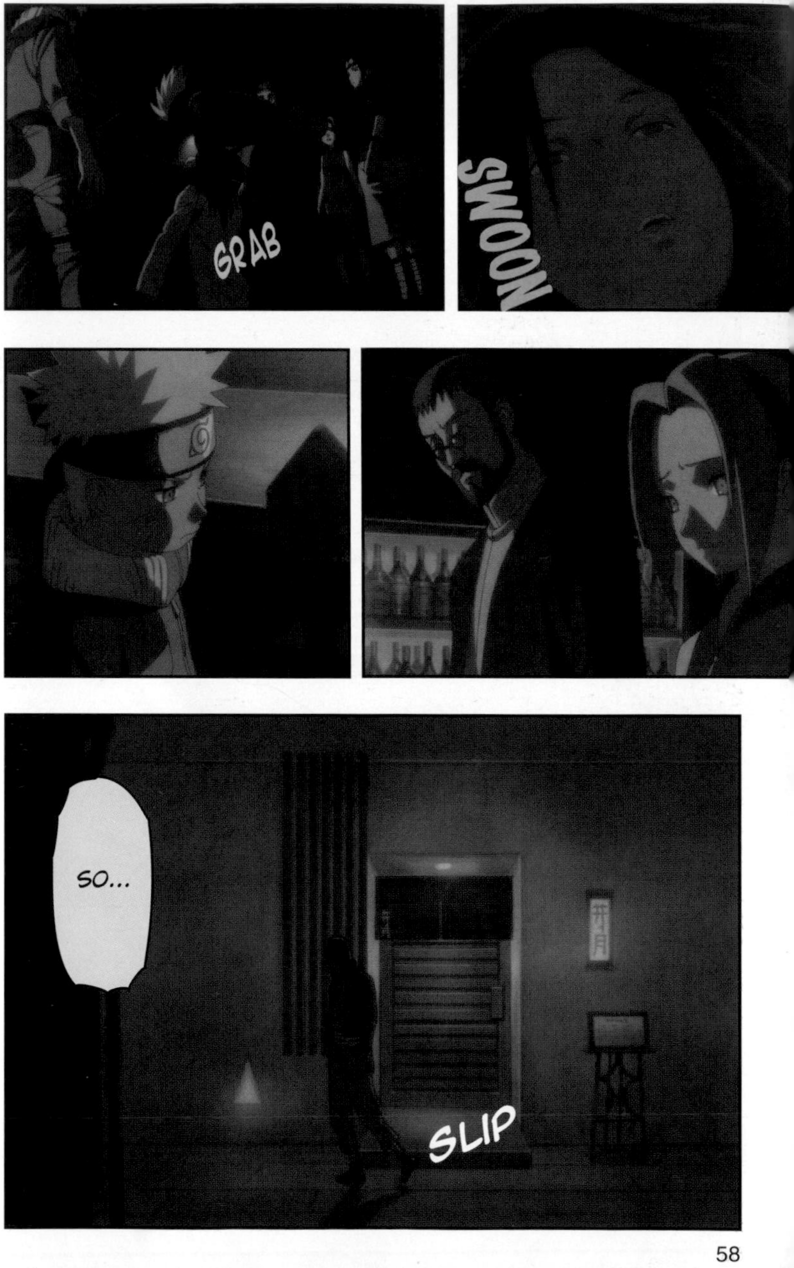
SWOON
GRAB
SO...
SLIP

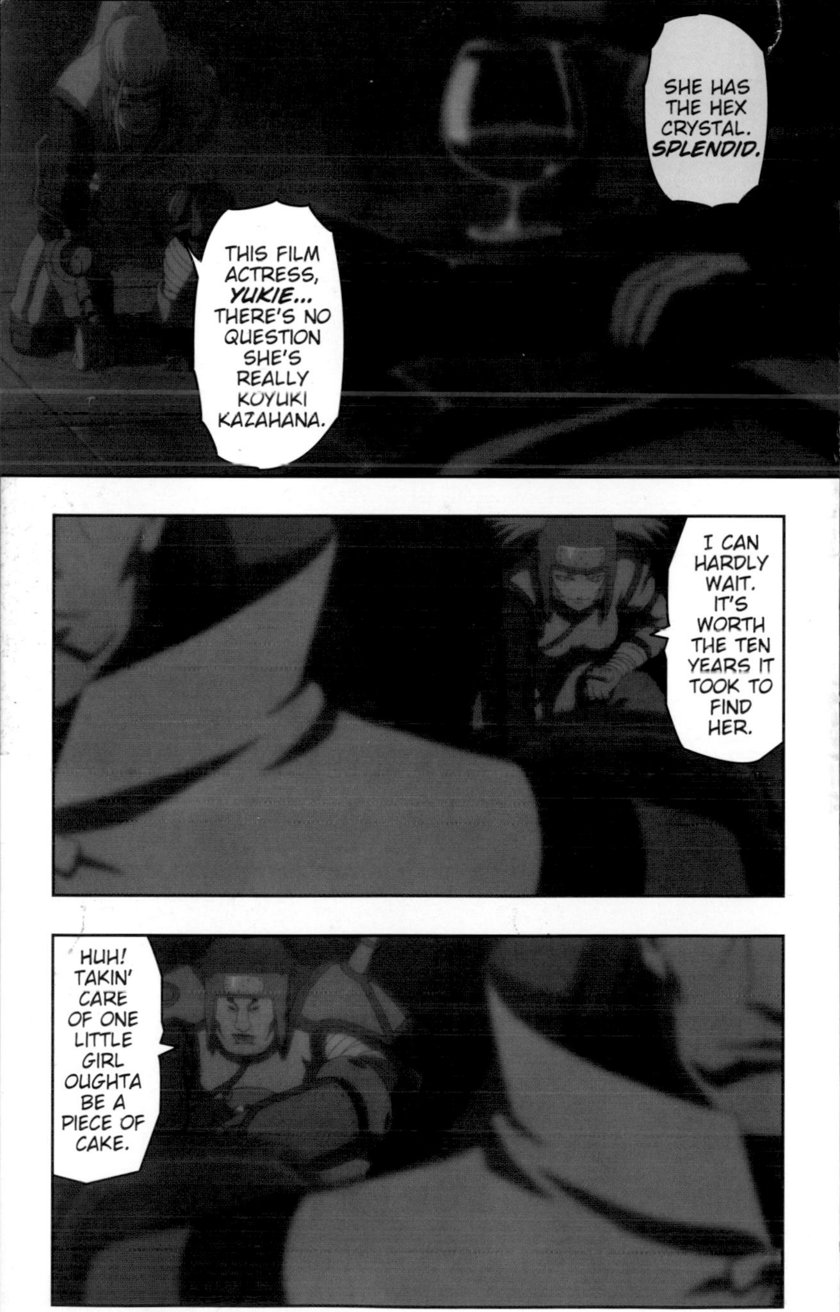
SHE HAS THE HEX CRYSTAL. SPLENDID.
THIS FILM ACTRESS, YUKIE... THERE'S NO QUESTION SHE'S REALLY KOYUKI KAZAHANA.
I CAN HARDLY WAIT. IT'S WORTH THE TEN YEARS IT TOOK TO FIND HER.
HUH! TAKIN' CARE OF ONE LITTLE GIRL OUGHTA BE A PIECE OF CAKE.

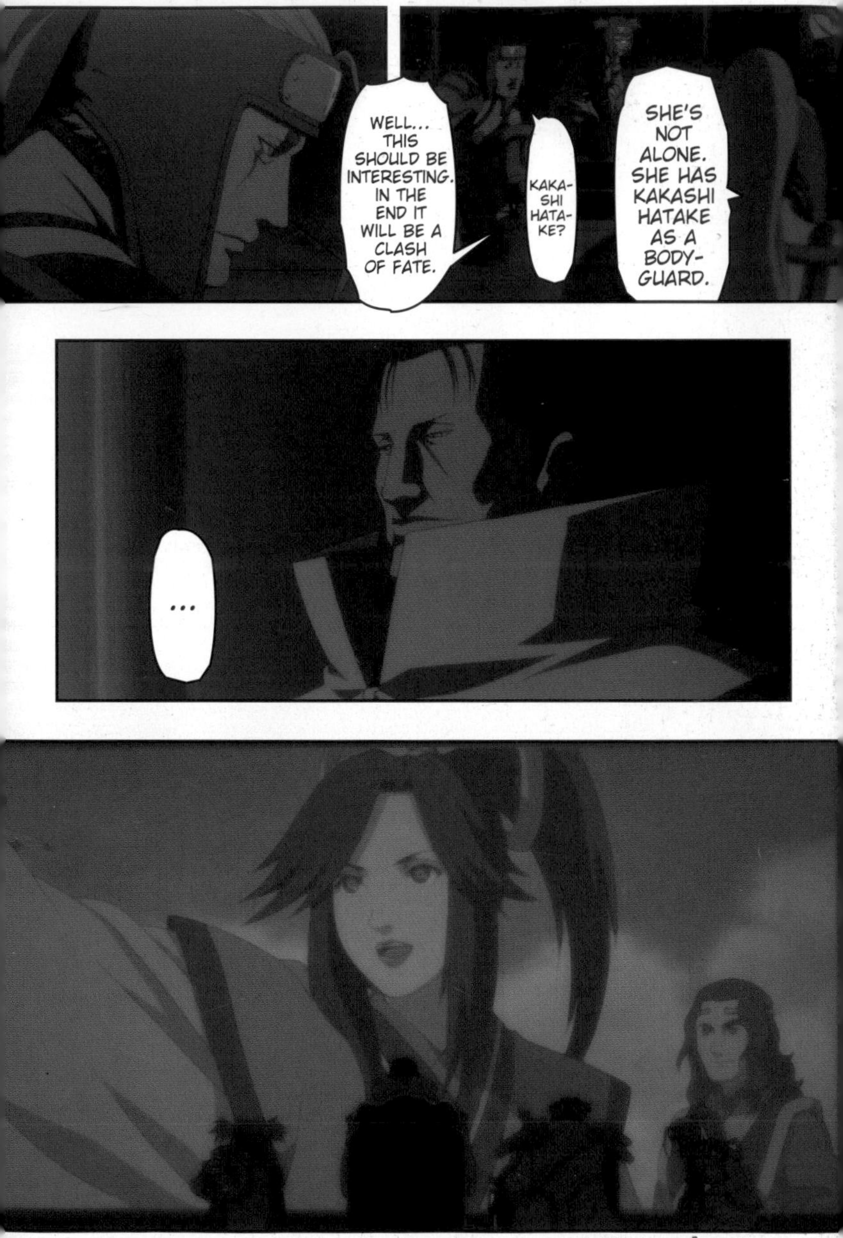
SHE'S NOT ALONE. SHE HAS KAKASHI HATAKE AS A BODY-GUARD.
KAKA-SHI HATA-KE?
WELL... THIS SHOULD BE INTERESTING. IN THE END IT WILL BE A CLASH OF FATE.
...

🐾 Chapter 2: Attack of the Snow Ninja

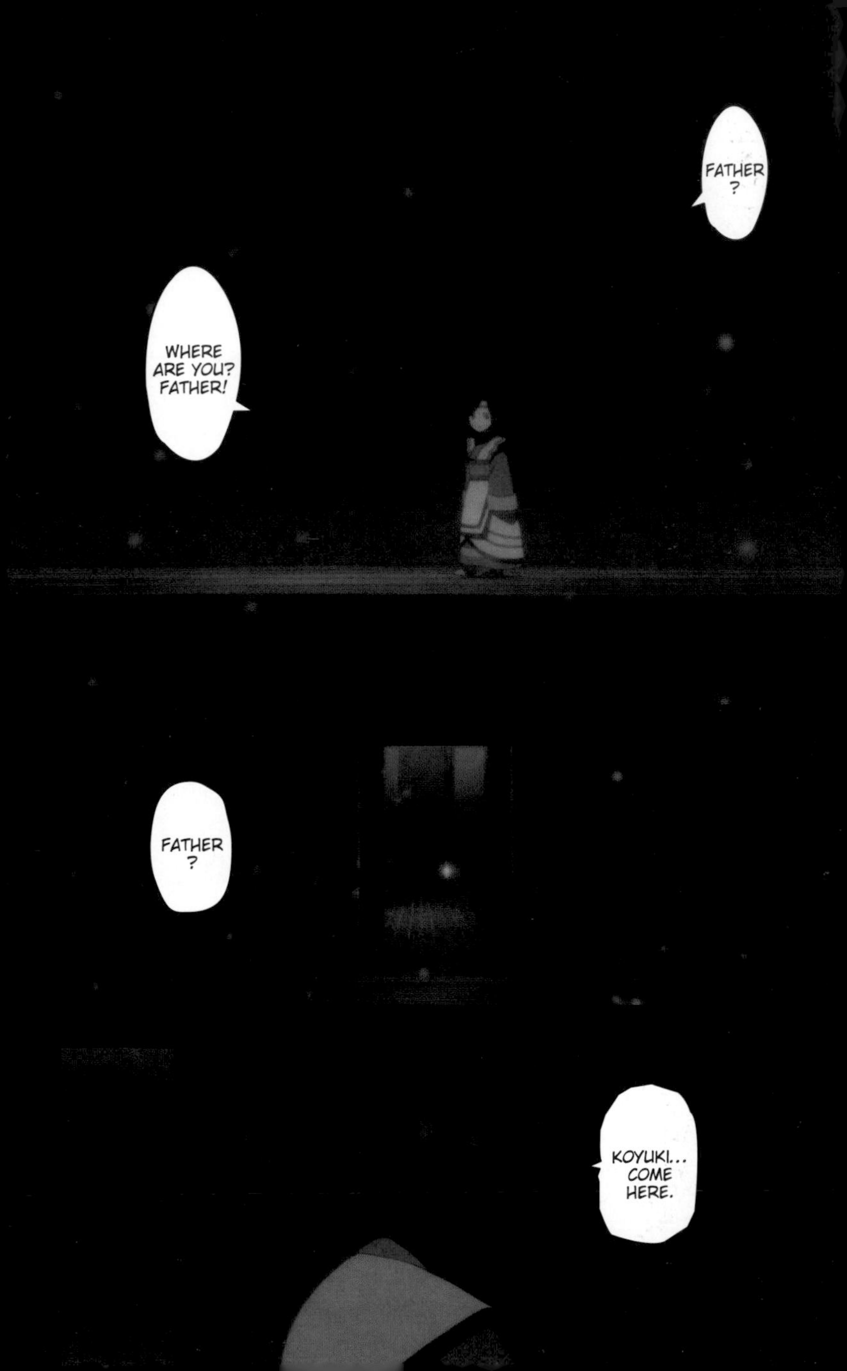
FATHER ?
WHERE ARE YOU? FATHER!
FATHER ?
KOYUKI... COME HERE.

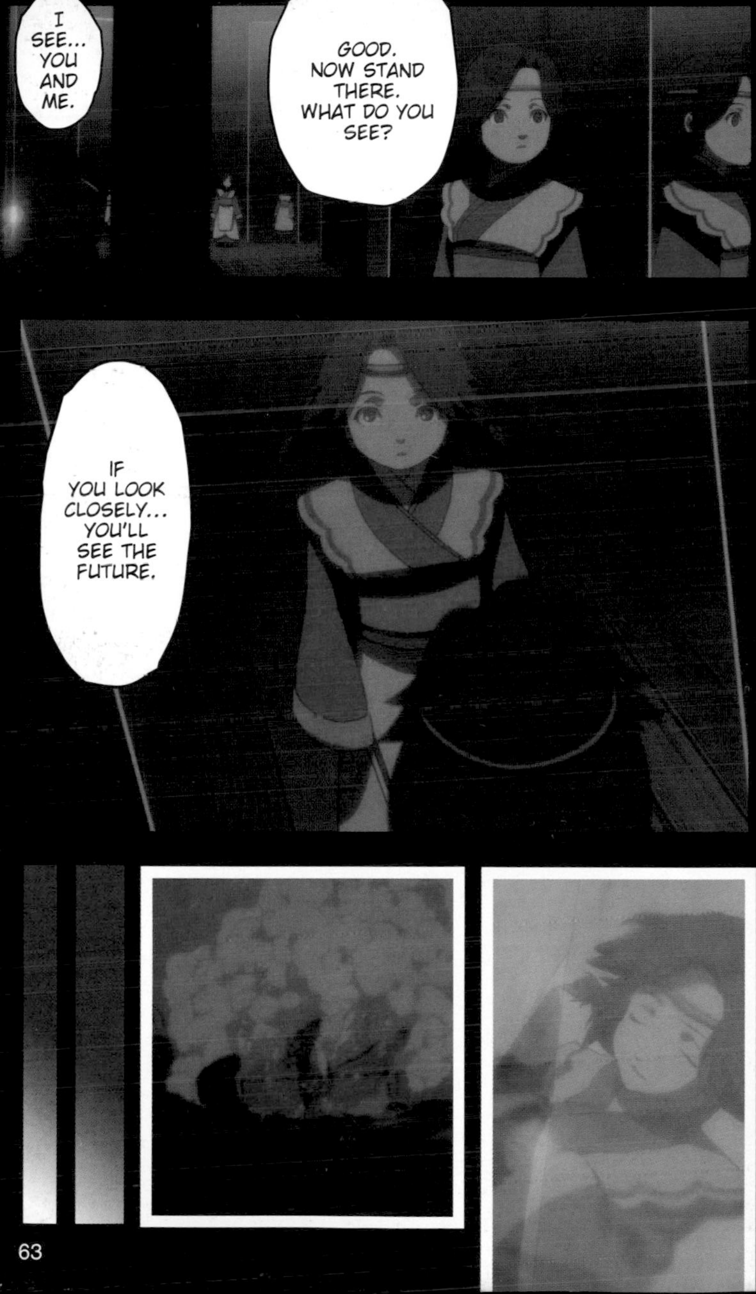
GOOD. NOW STAND THERE. WHAT DO YOU SEE?
I SEE... YOU AND ME.
IF YOU LOOK CLOSELY... YOU'LL SEE THE FUTURE.

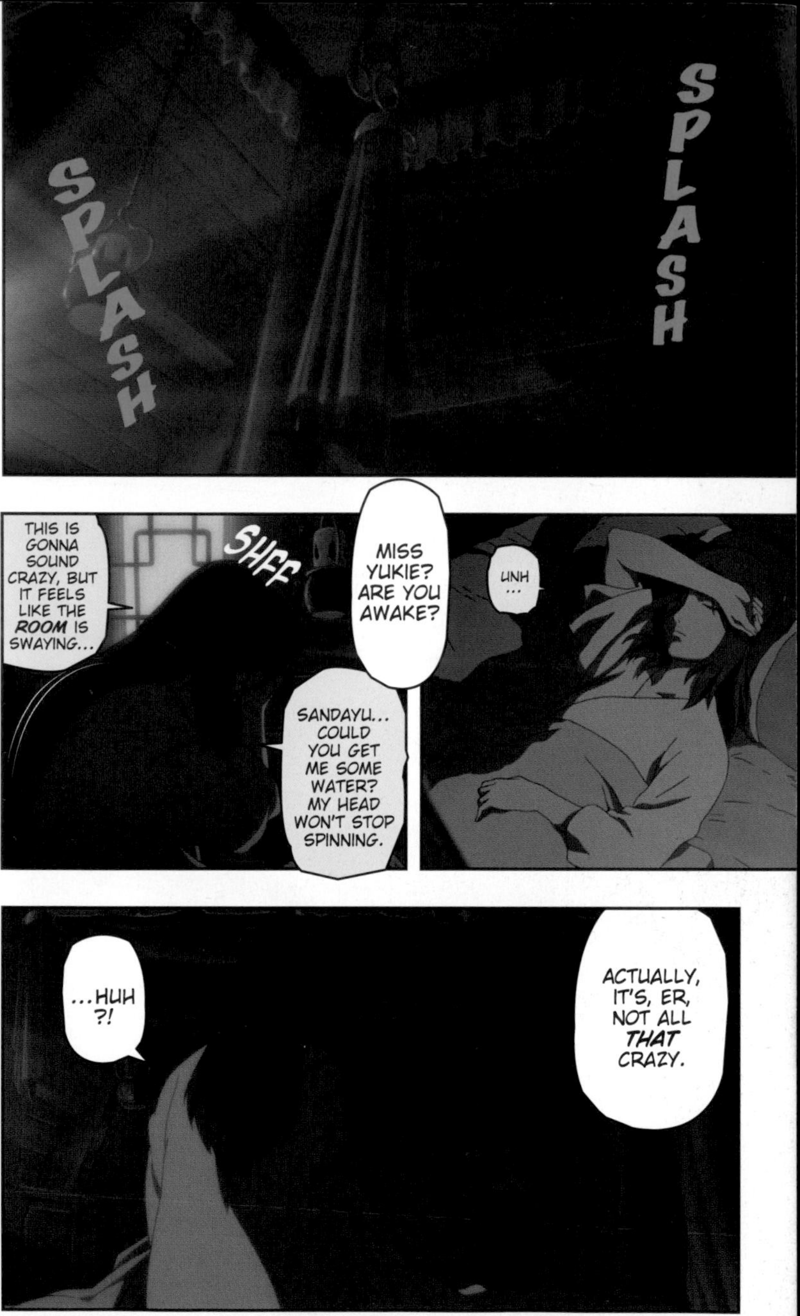

SPLASH
SPLASH
MISS YUKIE? ARE YOU AWAKE?
UNH...
SHFF
SANDAYU... COULD YOU GET ME SOME WATER? MY HEAD WON'T STOP SPINNING.
THIS IS GONNA SOUND CRAZY, BUT IT FEELS LIKE THE *ROOM* IS SWAYING...
ACTUALLY, IT'S, ER, NOT ALL *THAT* CRAZY.
...HUH ?!

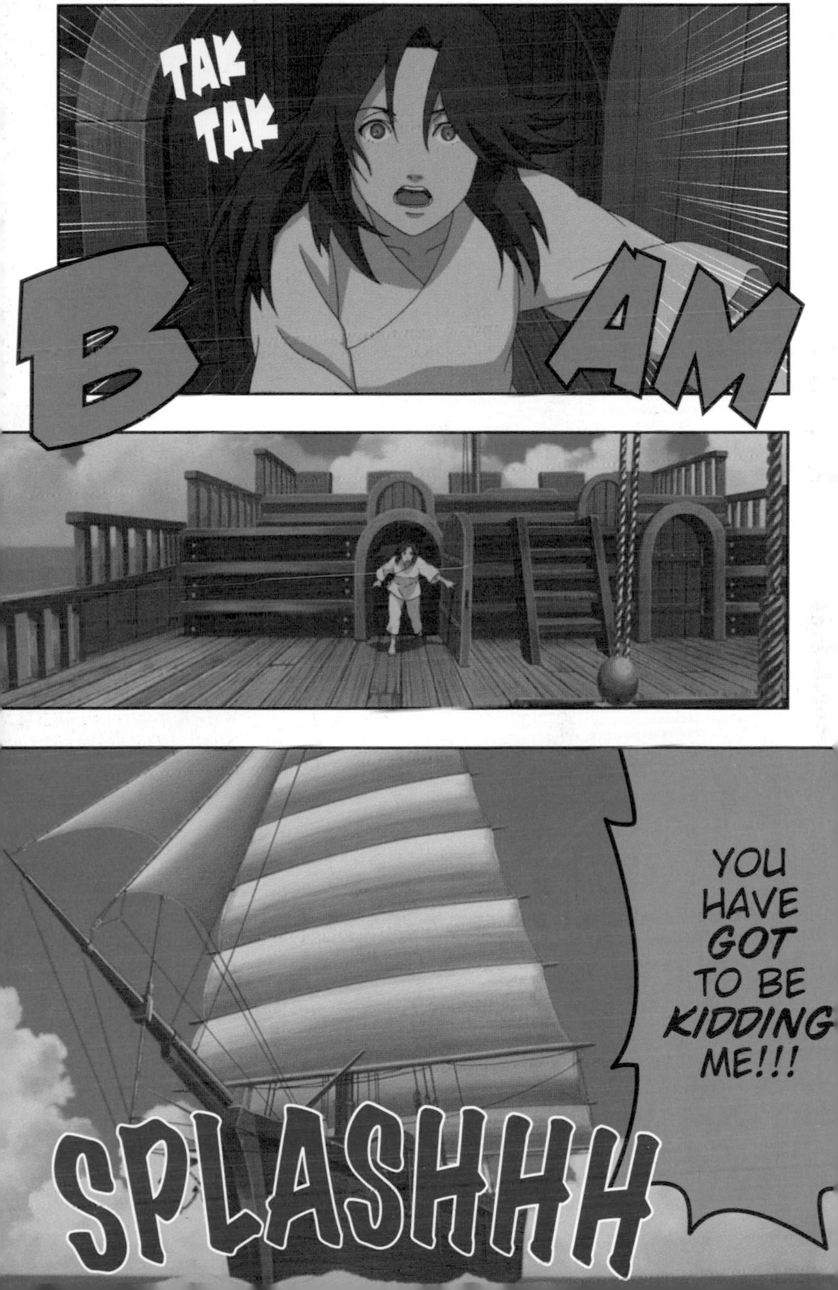
TAK TAK
BAM
YOU HAVE GOT TO BE KIDDING ME!!!
SPLASHHH

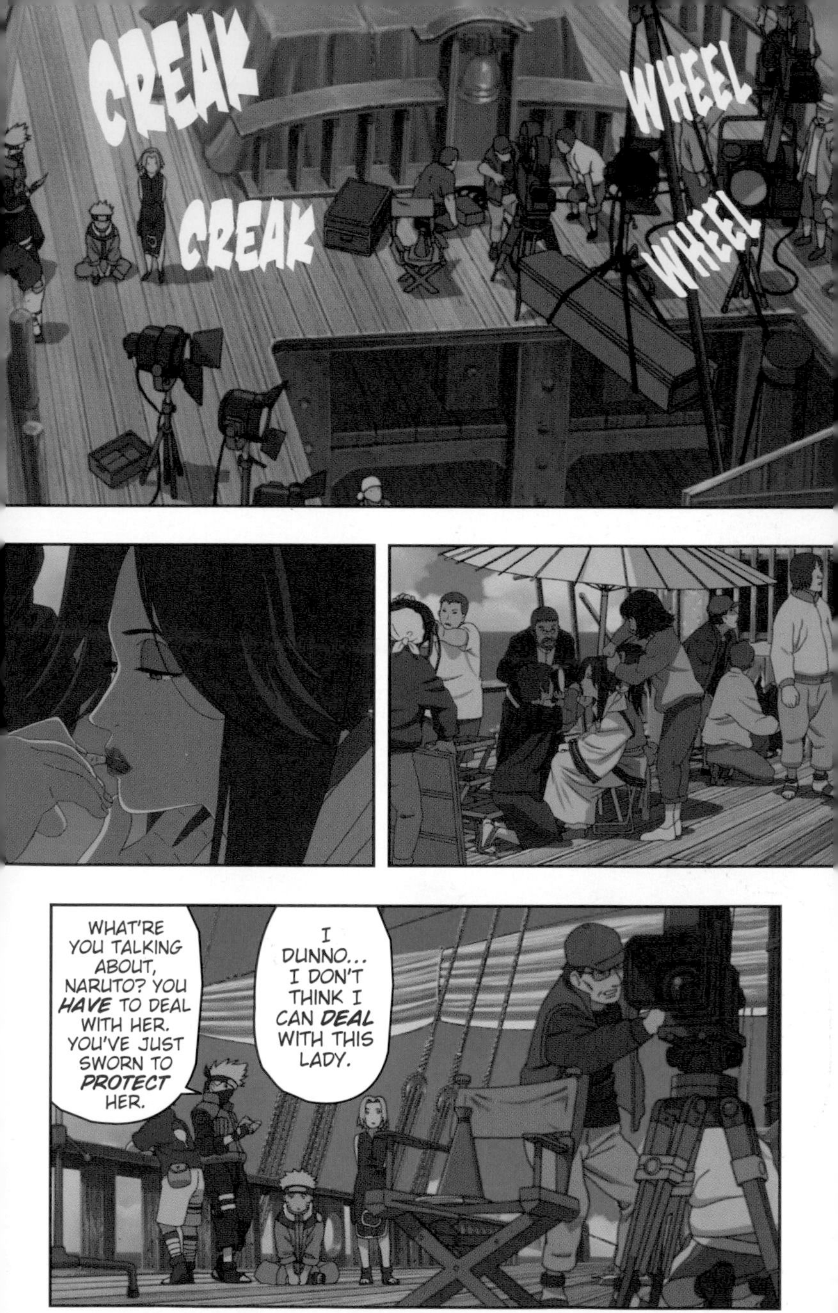
WHEEL
WHEEL
CREAK
CREAK
I DUNNO... I DON'T THINK I CAN DEAL WITH THIS LADY.
WHAT'RE YOU TALKING ABOUT, NARUTO? YOU HAVE TO DEAL WITH HER. YOU'VE JUST SWORN TO PROTECT HER.

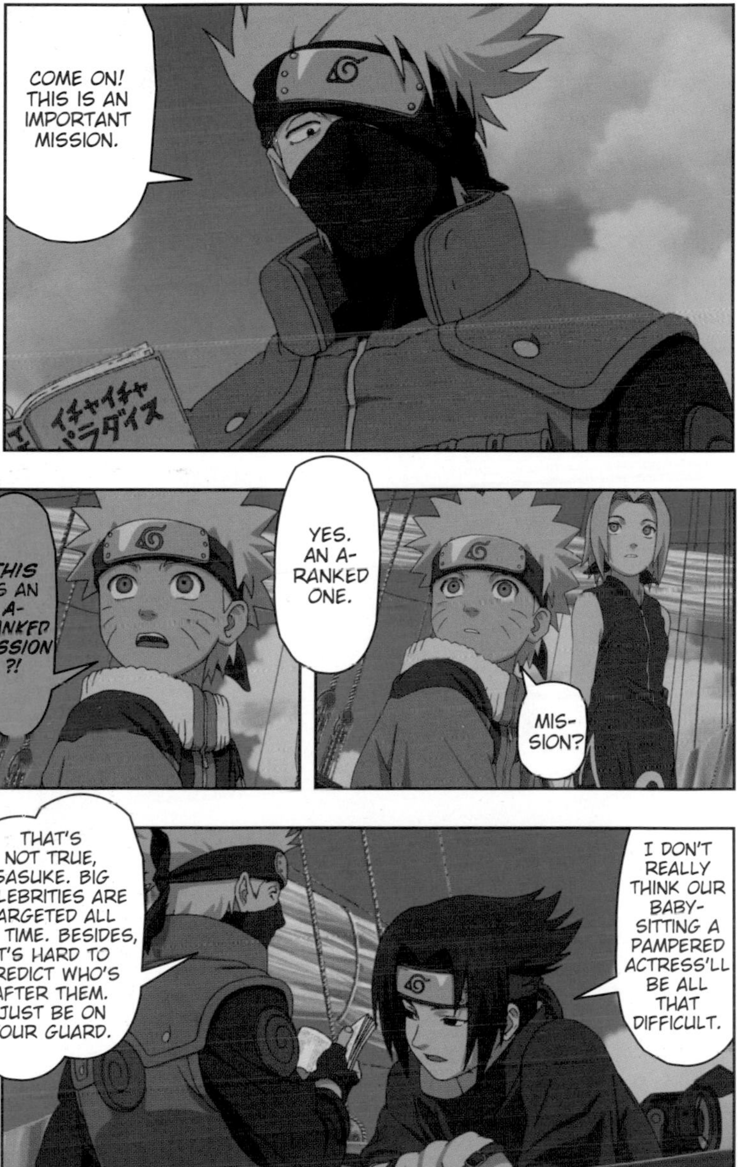
COME ON! THIS IS AN IMPORTANT MISSION.
イチャイチャパラダイス
MIS-SION?
YES. AN A-RANKED ONE.
THIS IS AN *A-RANKED MISSION*?!
I DON'T REALLY THINK OUR BABY-SITTING A PAMPERED ACTRESS'LL BE ALL THAT DIFFICULT.
THAT'S NOT TRUE, SASUKE. BIG CELEBRITIES ARE TARGETED ALL THE TIME. BESIDES, IT'S HARD TO PREDICT WHO'S AFTER THEM. JUST BE ON YOUR GUARD.

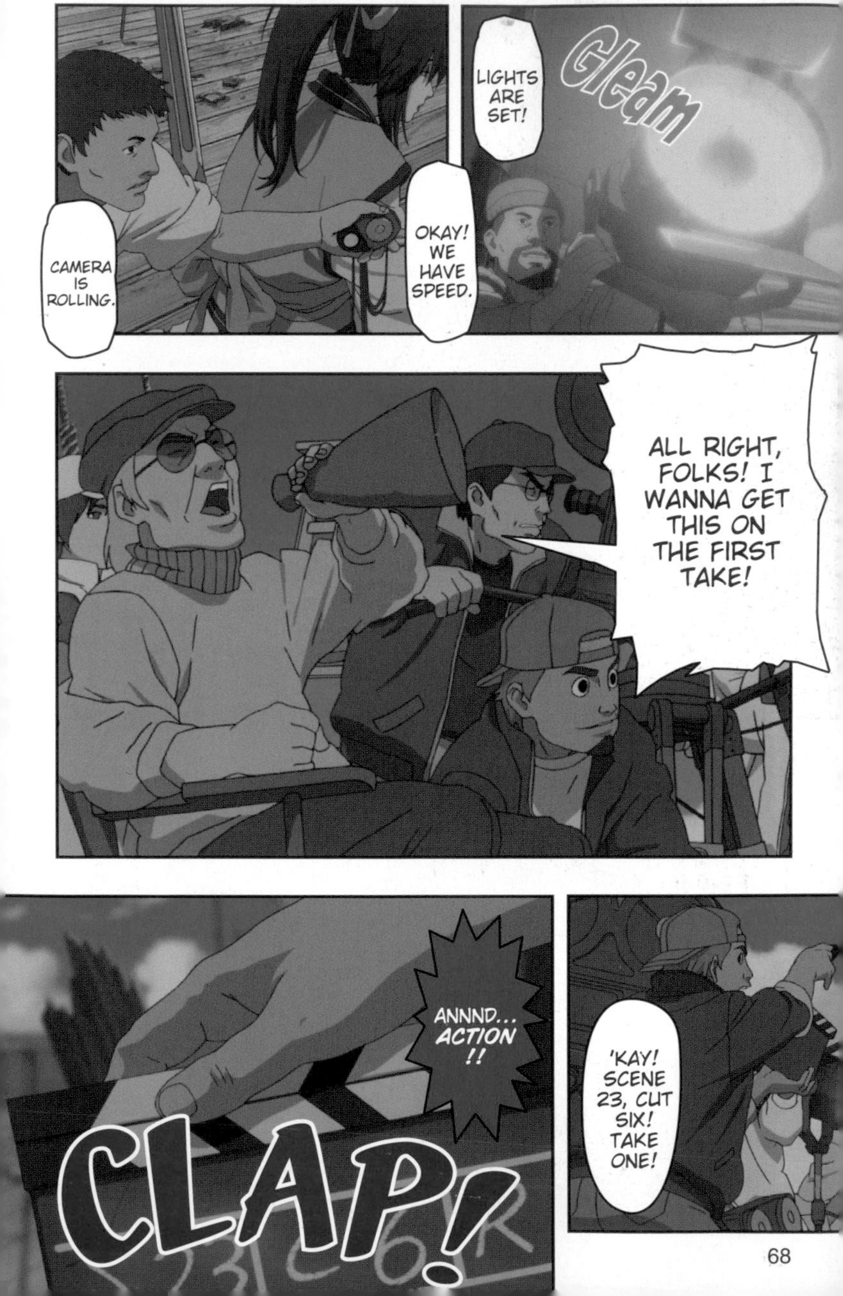
LIGHTS ARE SET!
Gleam
OKAY! WE HAVE SPEED.
CAMERA IS ROLLING.
ALL RIGHT, FOLKS! I WANNA GET THIS ON THE FIRST TAKE!
'KAY! SCENE 23, CUT SIX! TAKE ONE!
ANNND... ACTION!!
CLAP!

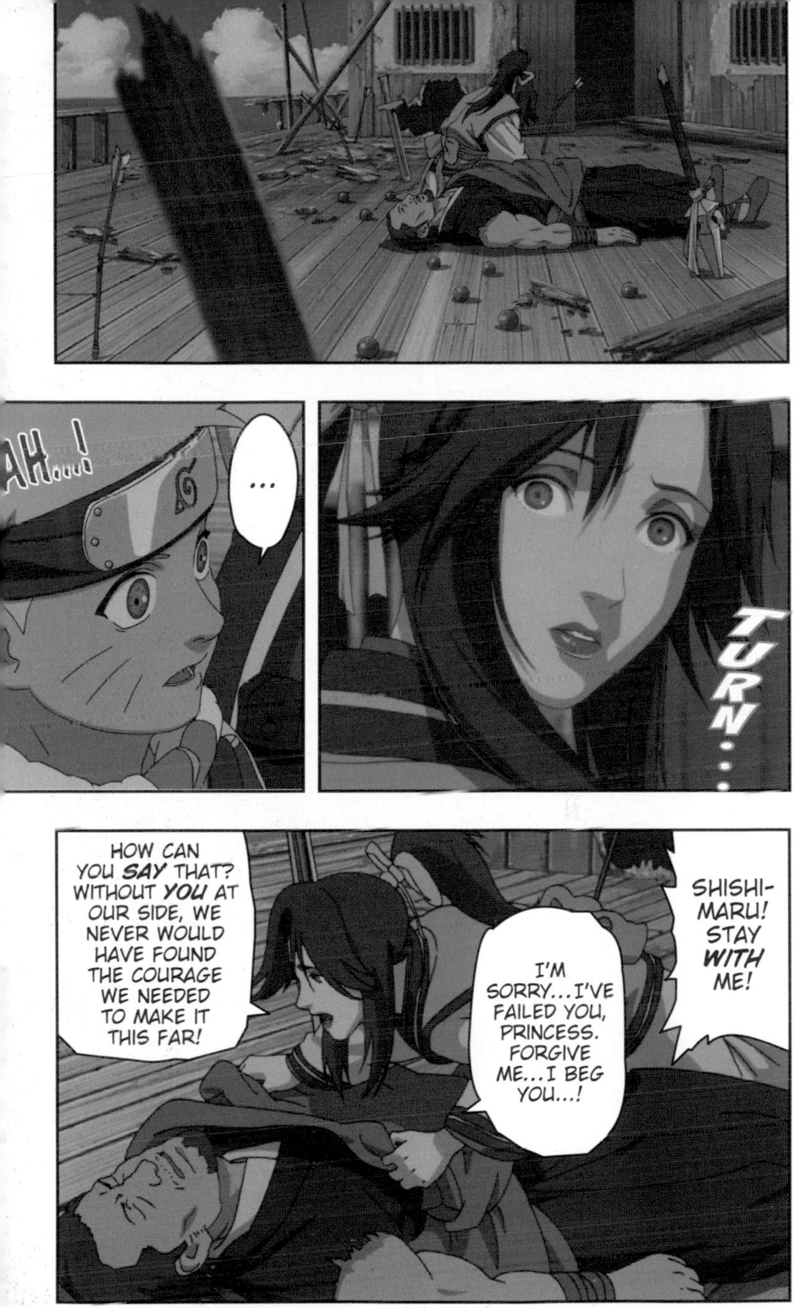
TURN...
AH...!
...
SHISHI-MARU! STAY WITH ME!
I'M SORRY...I'VE FAILED YOU, PRINCESS. FORGIVE ME...I BEG YOU...!
HOW CAN YOU SAY THAT? WITHOUT YOU AT OUR SIDE, WE NEVER WOULD HAVE FOUND THE COURAGE WE NEEDED TO MAKE IT THIS FAR!

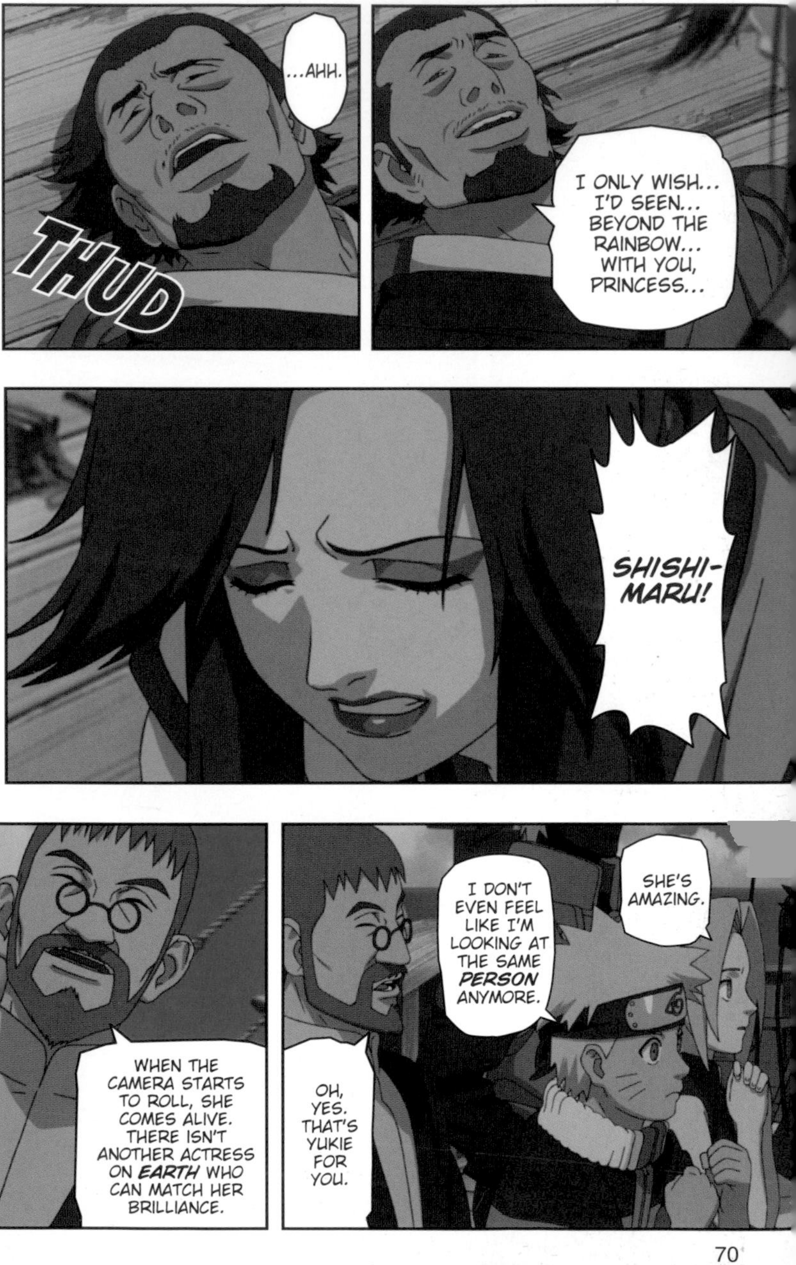
I ONLY WISH... I'D SEEN... BEYOND THE RAINBOW... WITH YOU, PRINCESS...
...AHH.
THUD
SHISHI-MARU!
SHE'S AMAZING.
I DON'T EVEN FEEL LIKE I'M LOOKING AT THE SAME PERSON ANYMORE.
OH, YES. THAT'S YUKIE FOR YOU.
WHEN THE CAMERA STARTS TO ROLL, SHE COMES ALIVE. THERE ISN'T ANOTHER ACTRESS ON EARTH WHO CAN MATCH HER BRILLIANCE.

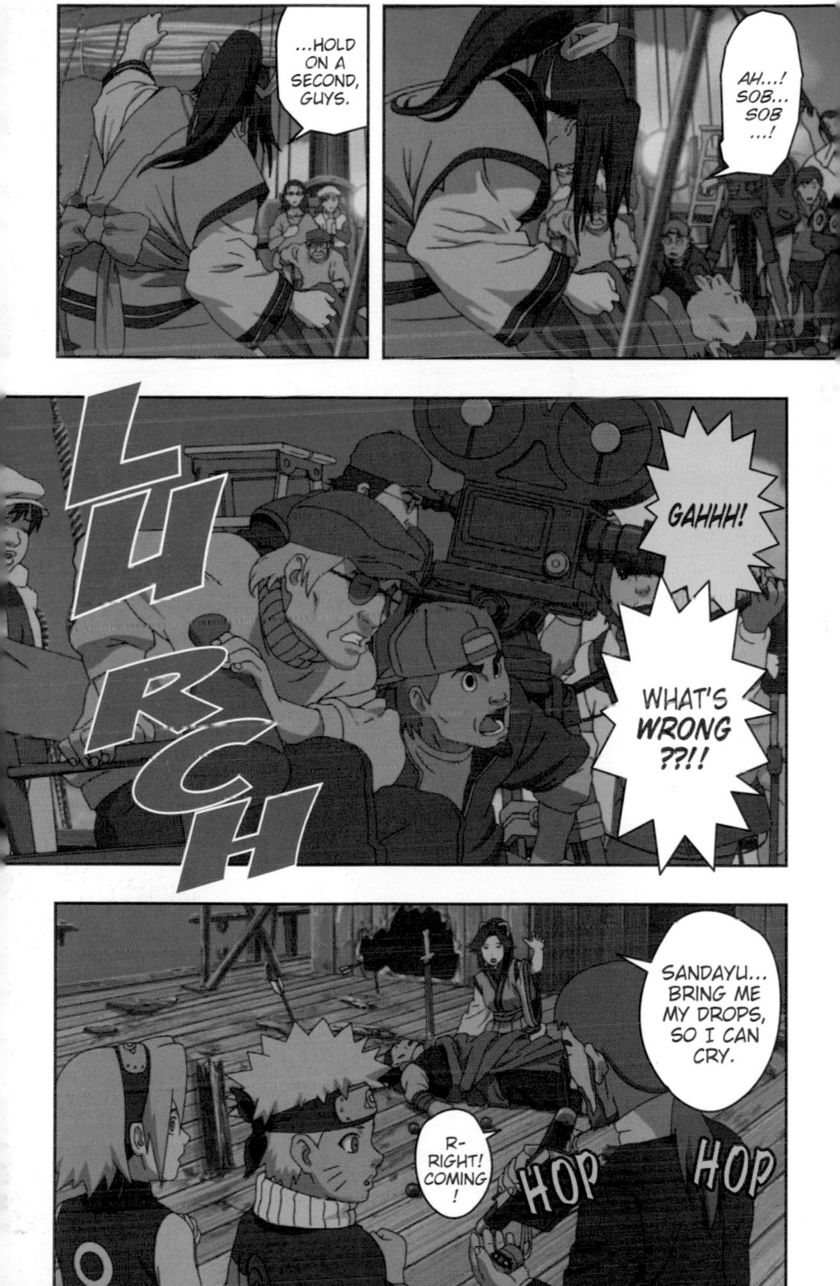
AH...! SOB... SOB ...!
...HOLD ON A SECOND, GUYS.
GAHHH!
WHAT'S WRONG ??!!
LURCH
SANDAYU... BRING ME MY DROPS, SO I CAN CRY.
HOP
HOP
R-RIGHT! COMING !

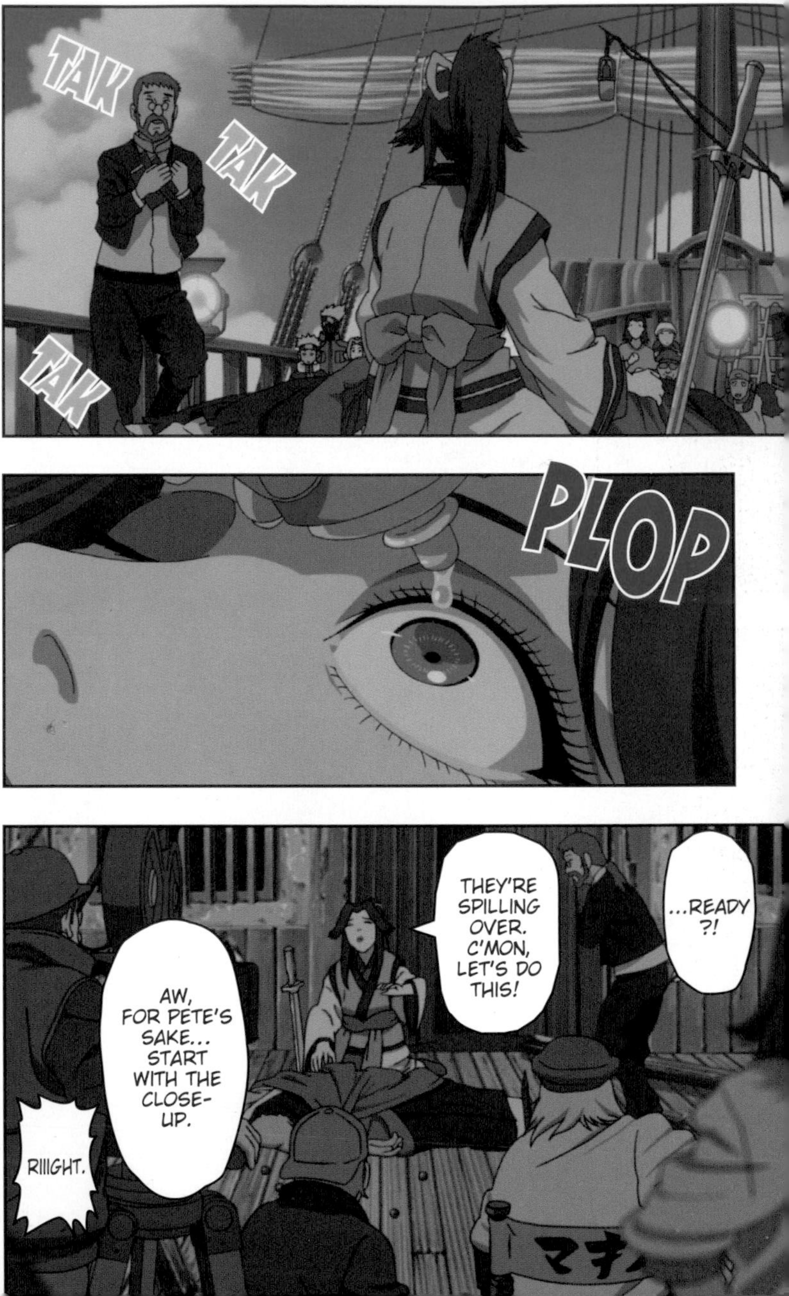
TAK
TAK
TAK
PLOP
...READY?!
THEY'RE SPILLING OVER. C'MON, LET'S DO THIS!
AW, FOR PETE'S SAKE... START WITH THE CLOSE-UP.
RIIIGHT.

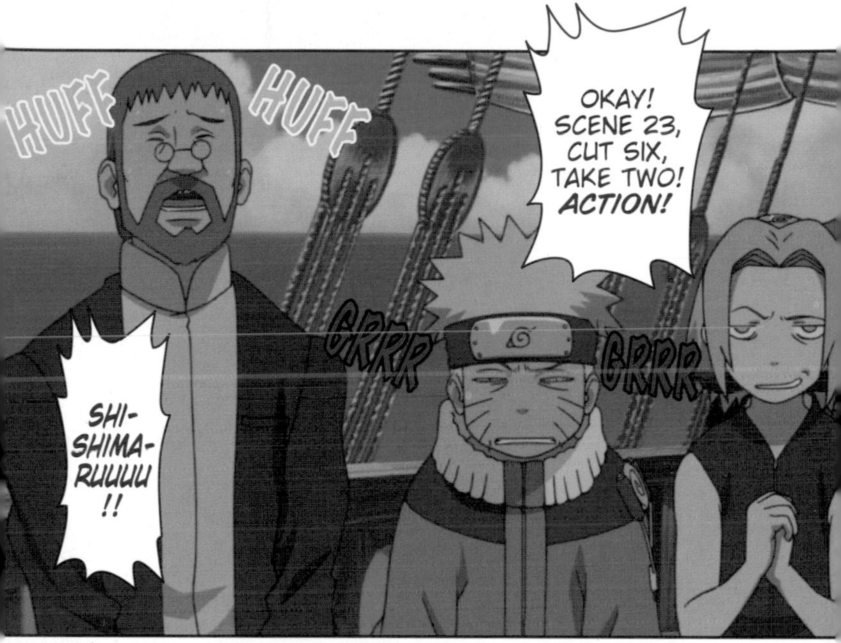
OKAY! SCENE 23, CUT SIX, TAKE TWO! ACTION!
HUFF HUFF
GRRR GRRR
SHI- SHIMA- RUUUU !!

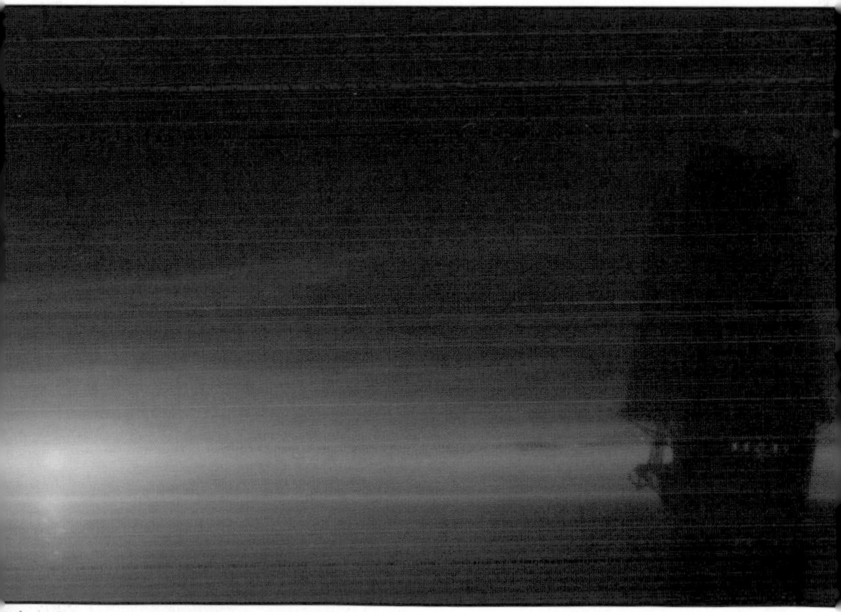

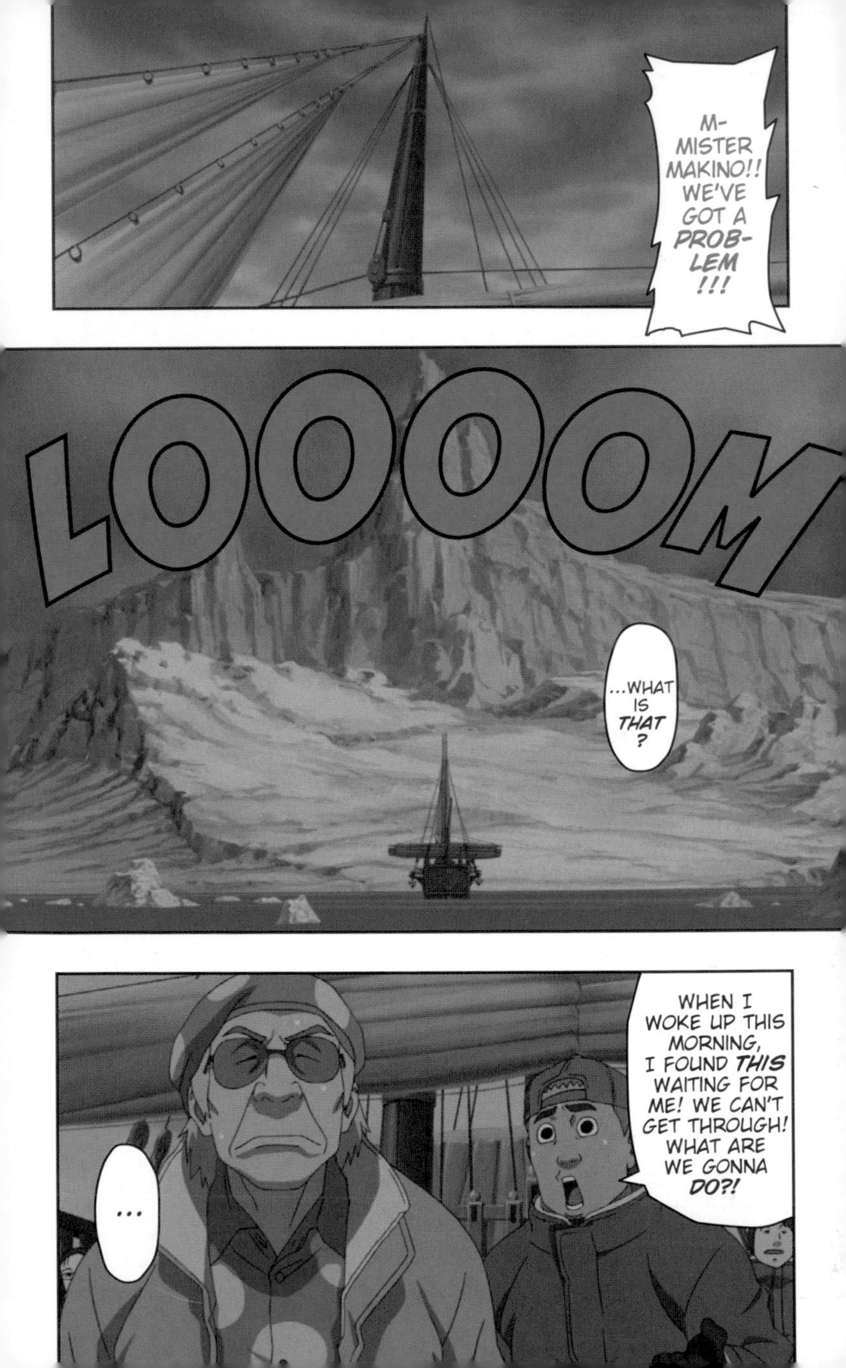
M-MISTER MAKINO!! WE'VE GOT A PROB-LEM!!!
LOOOOM
...WHAT IS THAT?
WHEN I WOKE UP THIS MORNING, I FOUND THIS WAITING FOR ME! WE CAN'T GET THROUGH! WHAT ARE WE GONNA DO?!
...

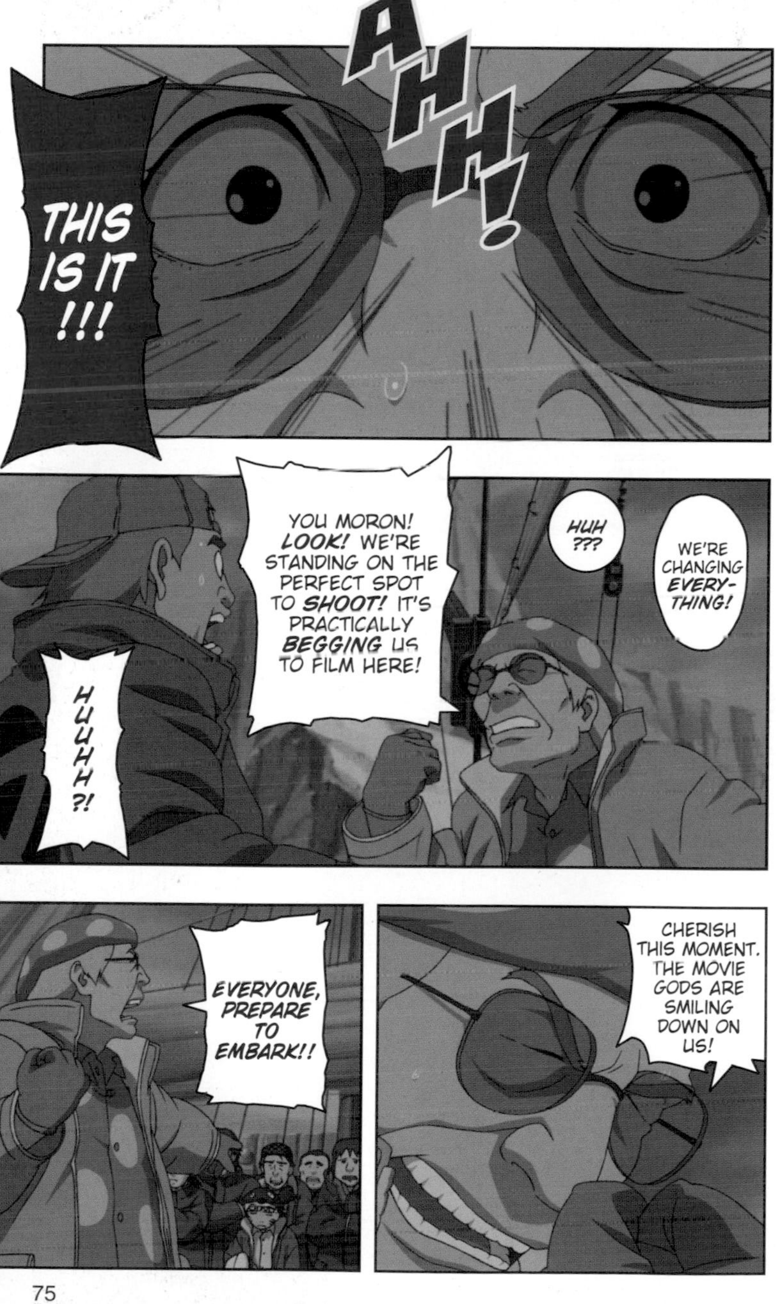
AHH!
THIS IS IT!!!
WE'RE CHANGING EVERYTHING!
HUH???
YOU MORON! LOOK! WE'RE STANDING ON THE PERFECT SPOT TO SHOOT! IT'S PRACTICALLY BEGGING US TO FILM HERE!
HUUHH?!
CHERISH THIS MOMENT. THE MOVIE GODS ARE SMILING DOWN ON US!
EVERYONE, PREPARE TO EMBARK!!

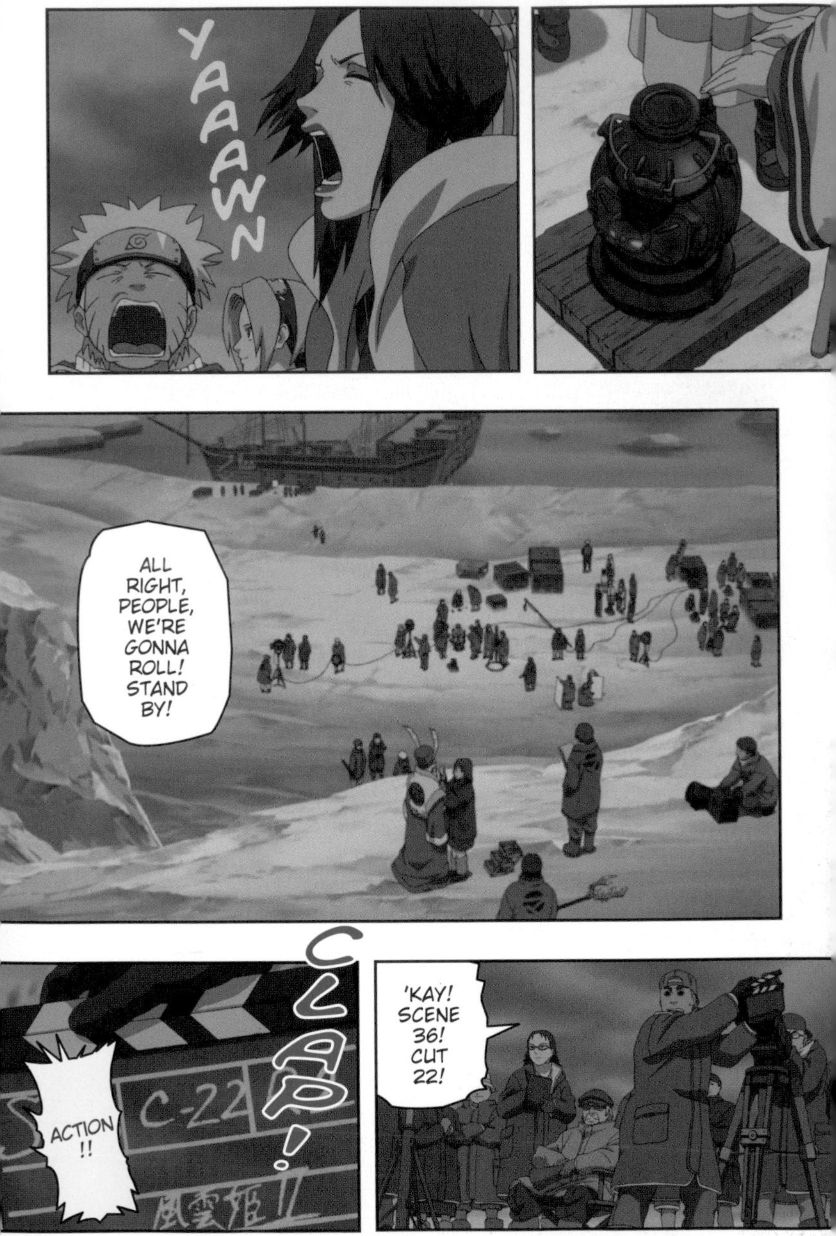
YAAAWN
ALL RIGHT, PEOPLE, WE'RE GONNA ROLL! STAND BY!
'KAY! SCENE 36! CUT 22!
CLAP!
C-22
風雲姫 II
ACTION!!

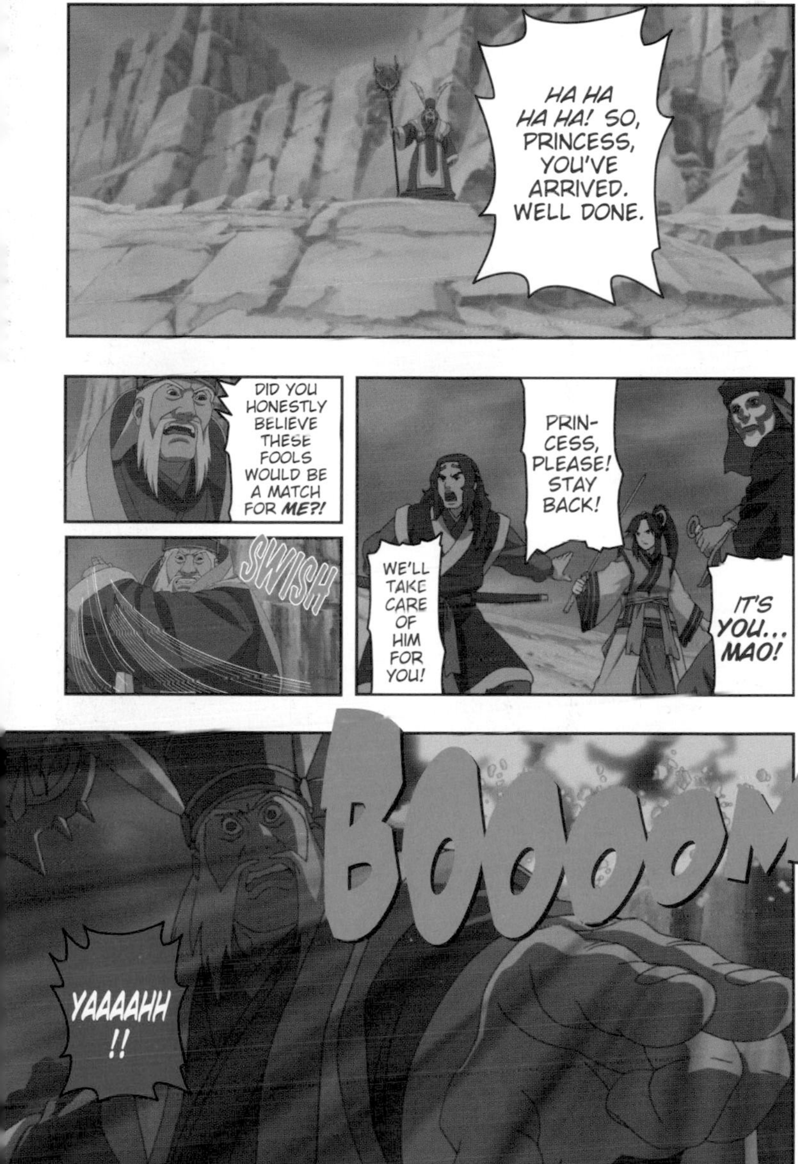

HA HA HA HA! SO, PRINCESS, YOU'VE ARRIVED. WELL DONE.
PRIN-CESS, PLEASE! STAY BACK!
WE'LL TAKE CARE OF HIM FOR YOU!
IT'S YOU... MAO!
DID YOU HONESTLY BELIEVE THESE FOOLS WOULD BE A MATCH FOR ME?!
SWISH
BOOOOM
YAAAAHH !!

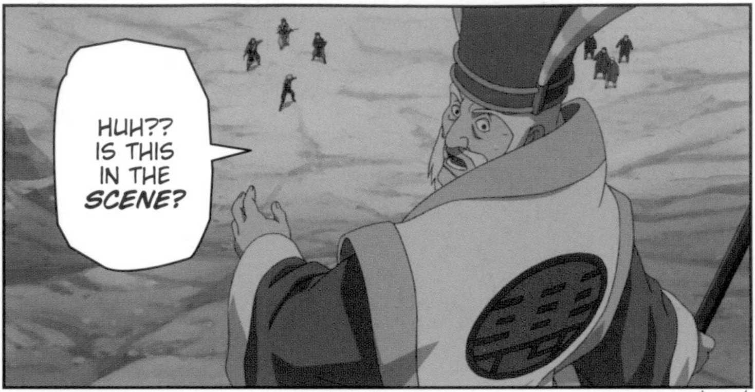
HUH?? IS THIS IN THE *SCENE?*

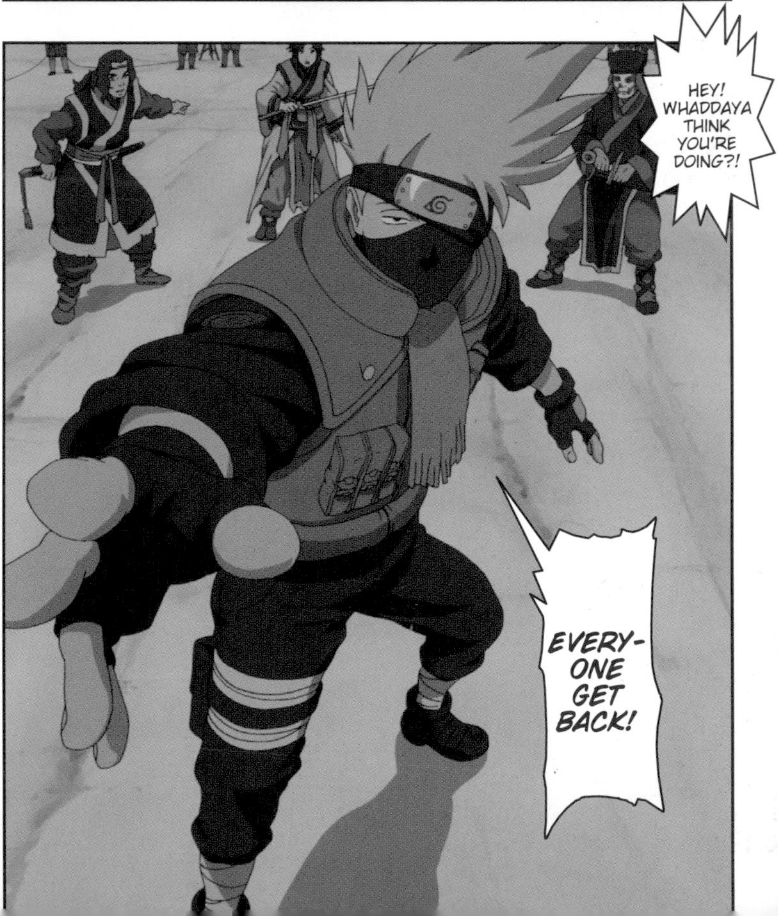
HEY! WHADDAYA THINK YOU'RE DOING?!
EVERY-ONE GET BACK!

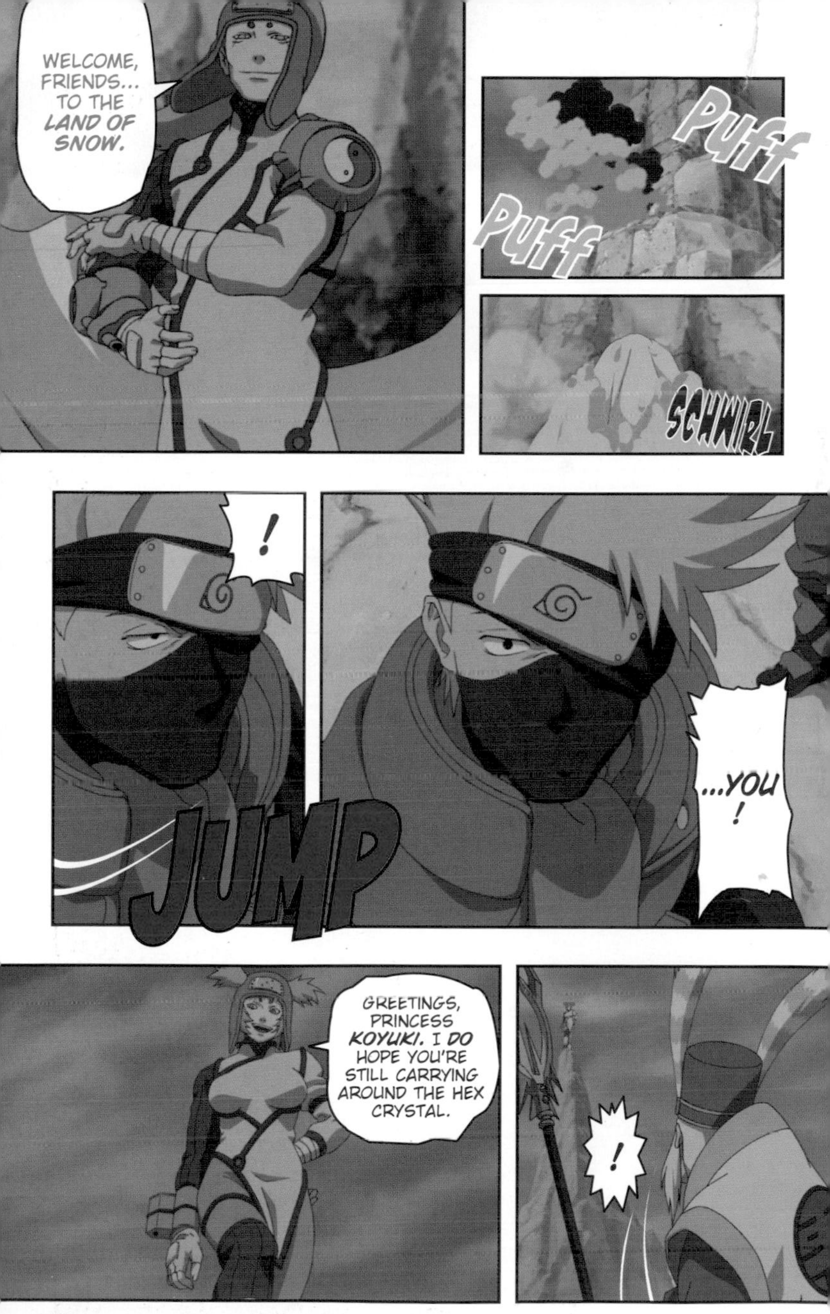
Puff
Puff
SCHWIRL
WELCOME, FRIENDS... TO THE LAND OF SNOW.
...YOU !
!
JUMP
!
GREETINGS, PRINCESS KOYUKI. I DO HOPE YOU'RE STILL CARRYING AROUND THE HEX CRYSTAL.

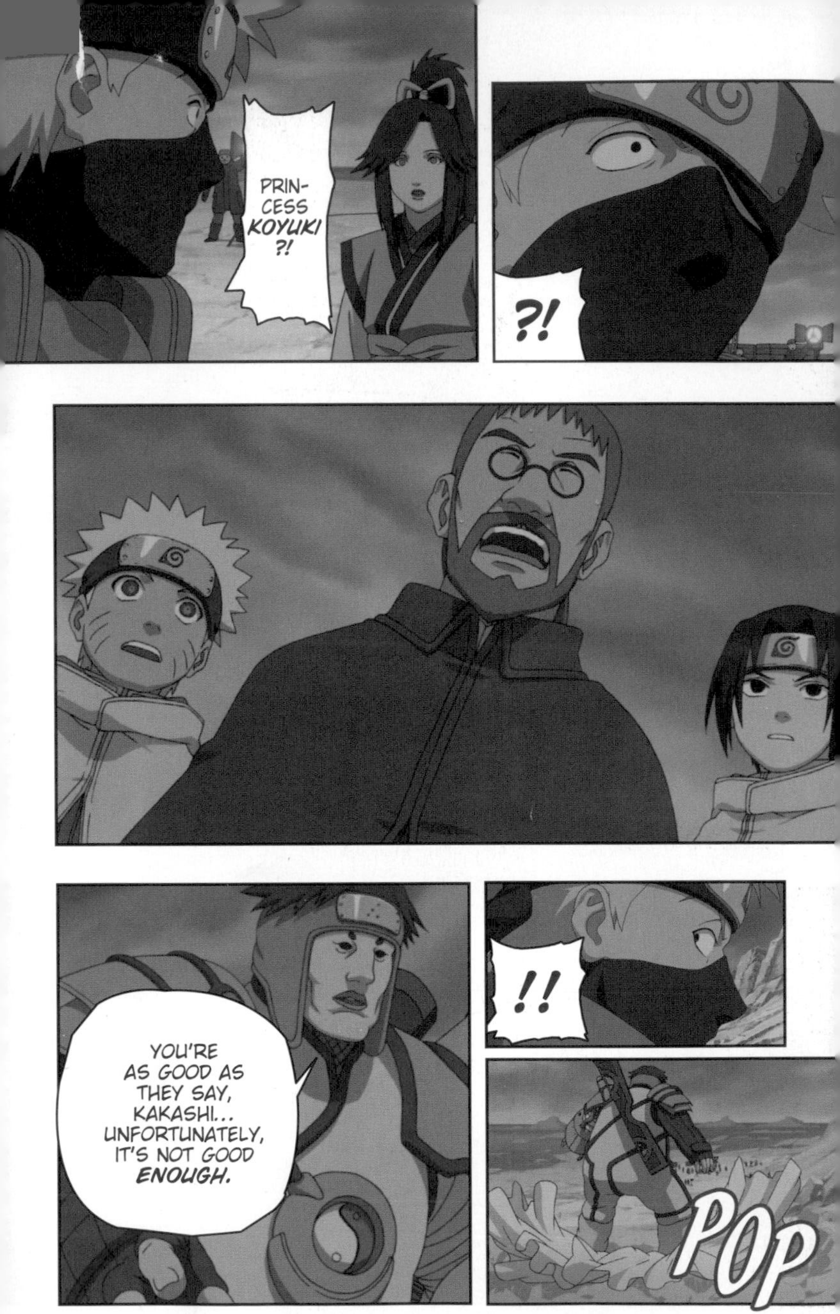
?!
PRIN-CESS KOYUKI ?!
!!
POP
YOU'RE AS GOOD AS THEY SAY, KAKASHI... UNFORTUNATELY, IT'S NOT GOOD ENOUGH.

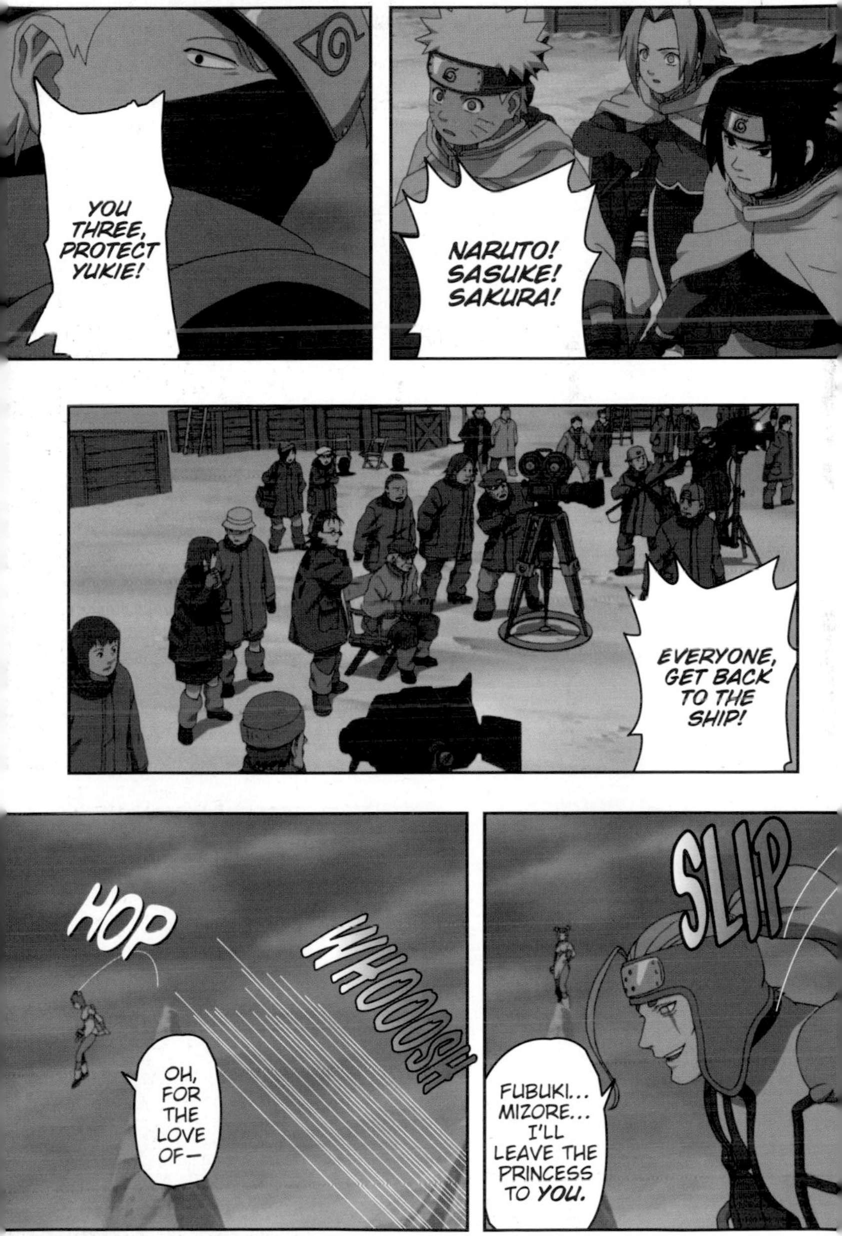
NARUTO! SASUKE! SAKURA!
YOU THREE, PROTECT YUKIE!
EVERYONE, GET BACK TO THE SHIP!
SLIP
FUBUKI... MIZORE... I'LL LEAVE THE PRINCESS TO YOU.
WHOOOSH
HOP
OH, FOR THE LOVE OF—

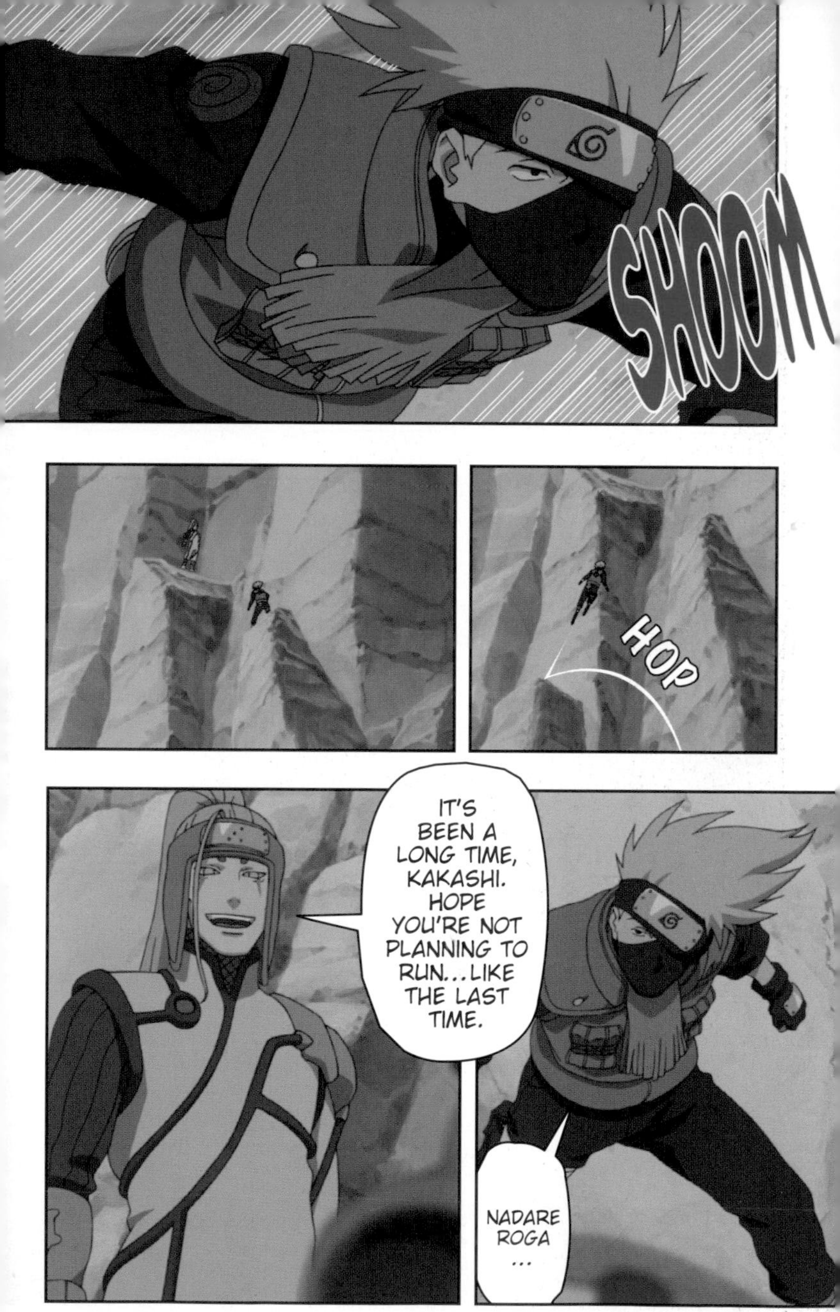
SHOOM
HOP
NADARE ROGA ...
IT'S BEEN A LONG TIME, KAKASHI. HOPE YOU'RE NOT PLANNING TO RUN...LIKE THE LAST TIME.

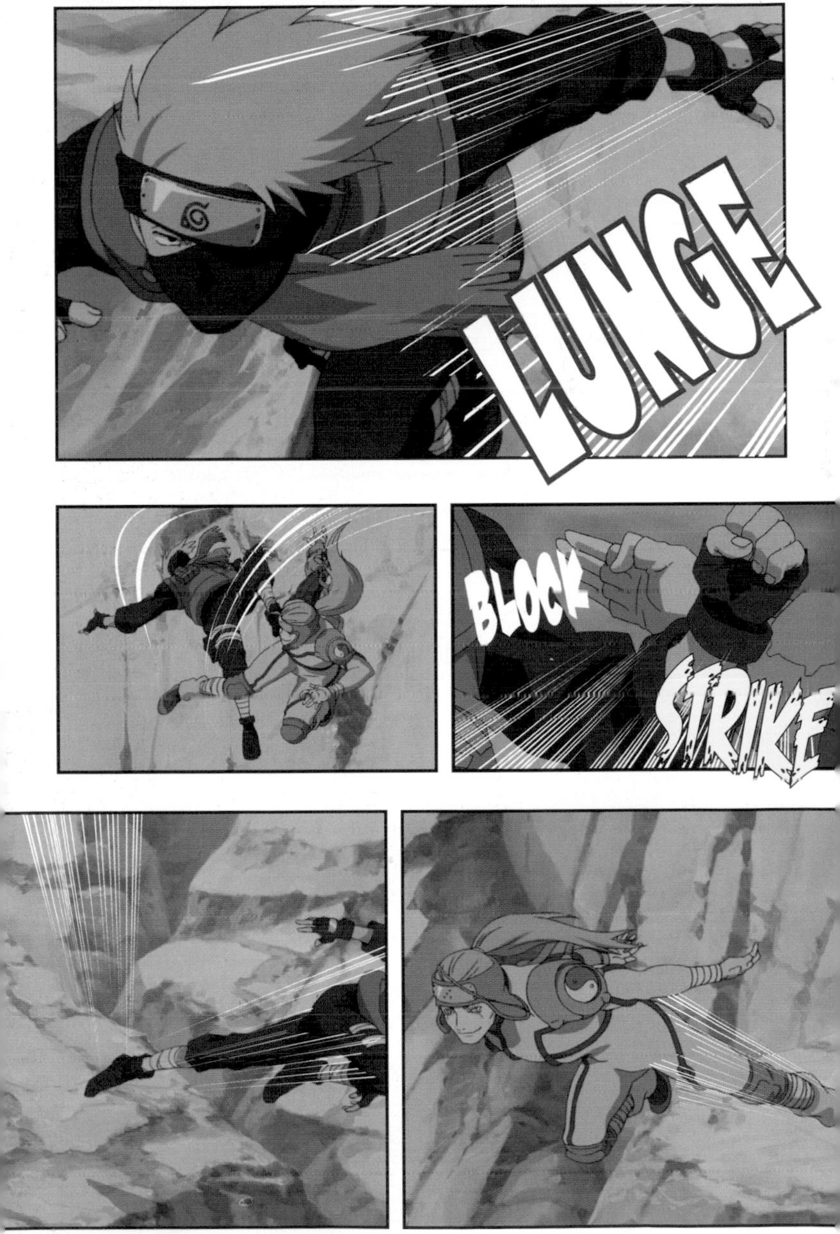
LUNGE
BLOCK
STRIKE

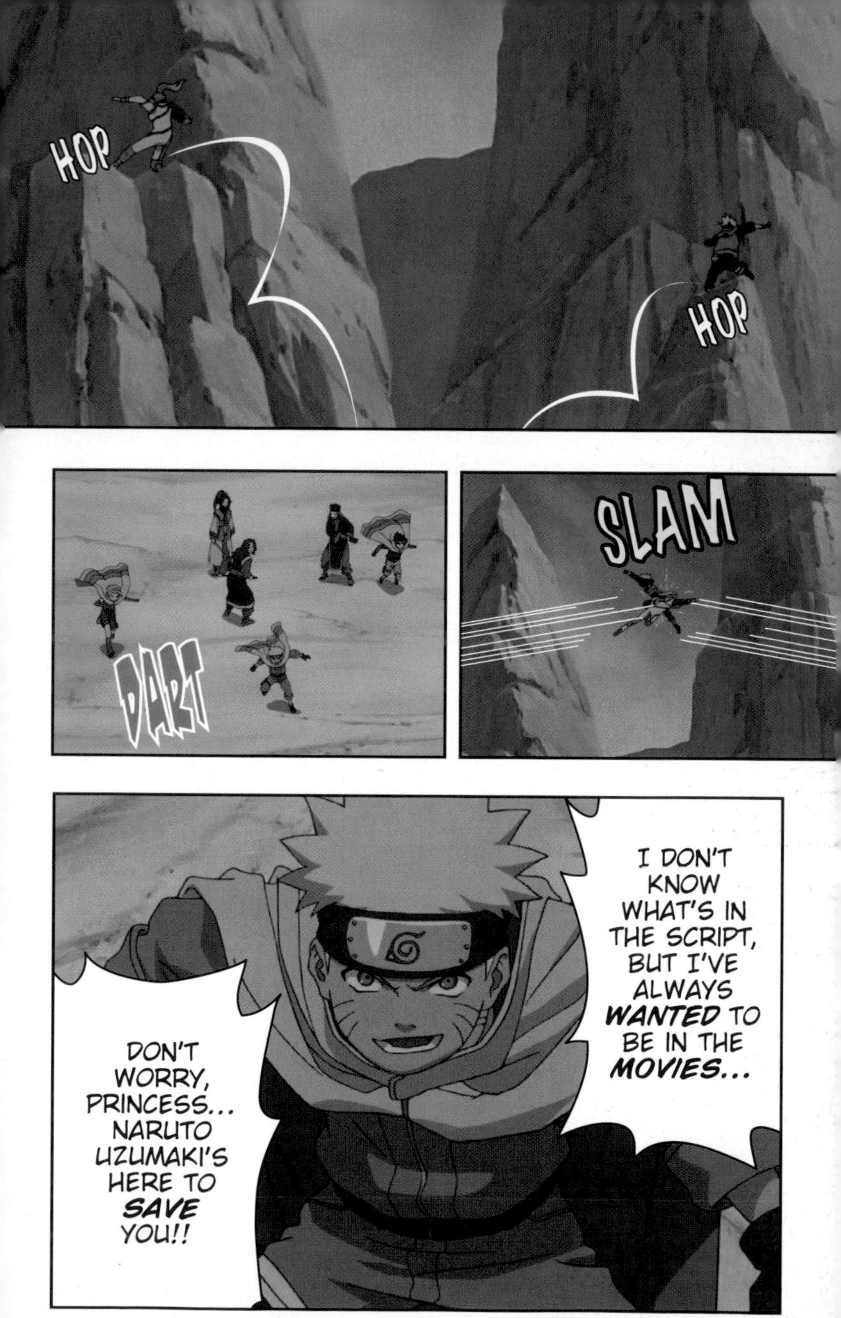
HOP
HOP
SLAM
DART
I DON'T KNOW WHAT'S IN THE SCRIPT, BUT I'VE ALWAYS **WANTED** TO BE IN THE **MOVIES...**
DON'T WORRY, PRINCESS... NARUTO UZUMAKI'S HERE TO **SAVE** YOU!!

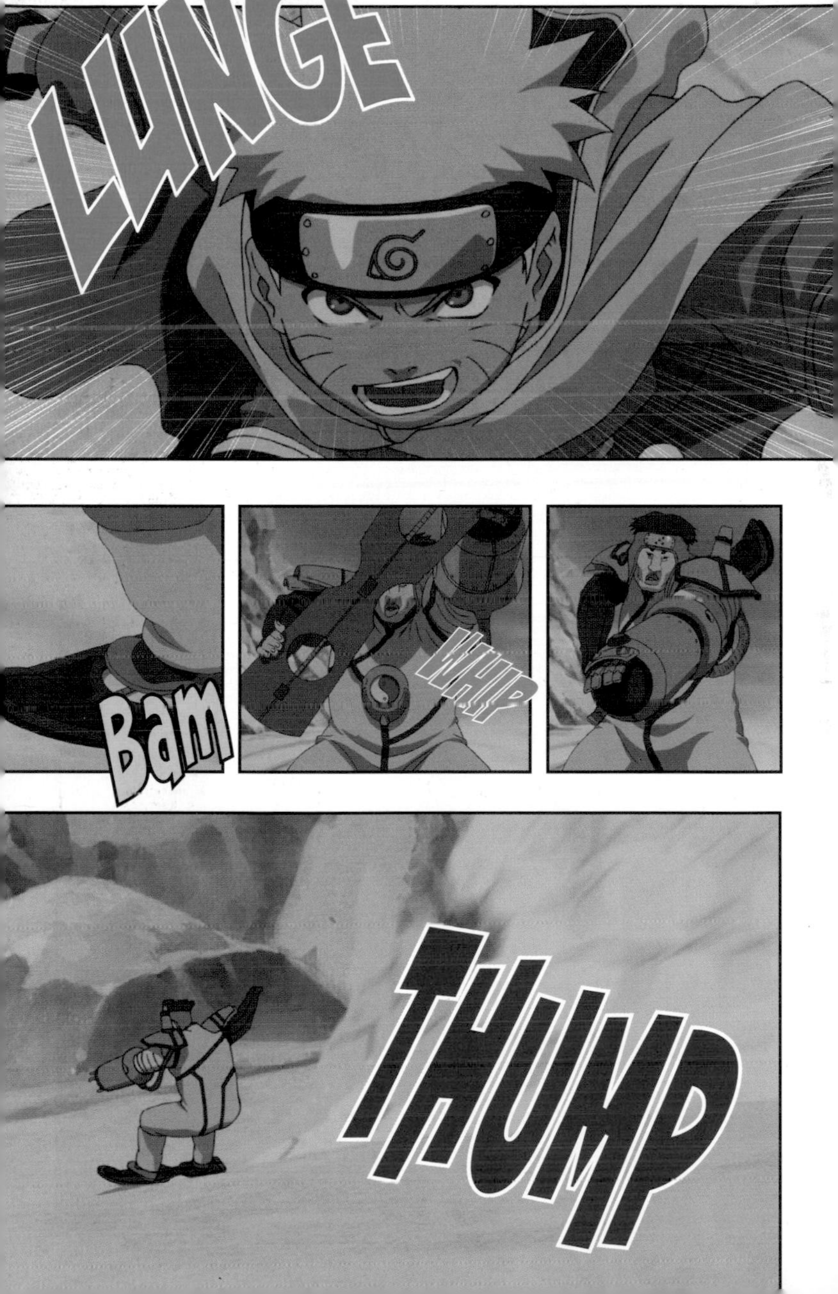
LUNGE
WHIP
Bam
THUMP

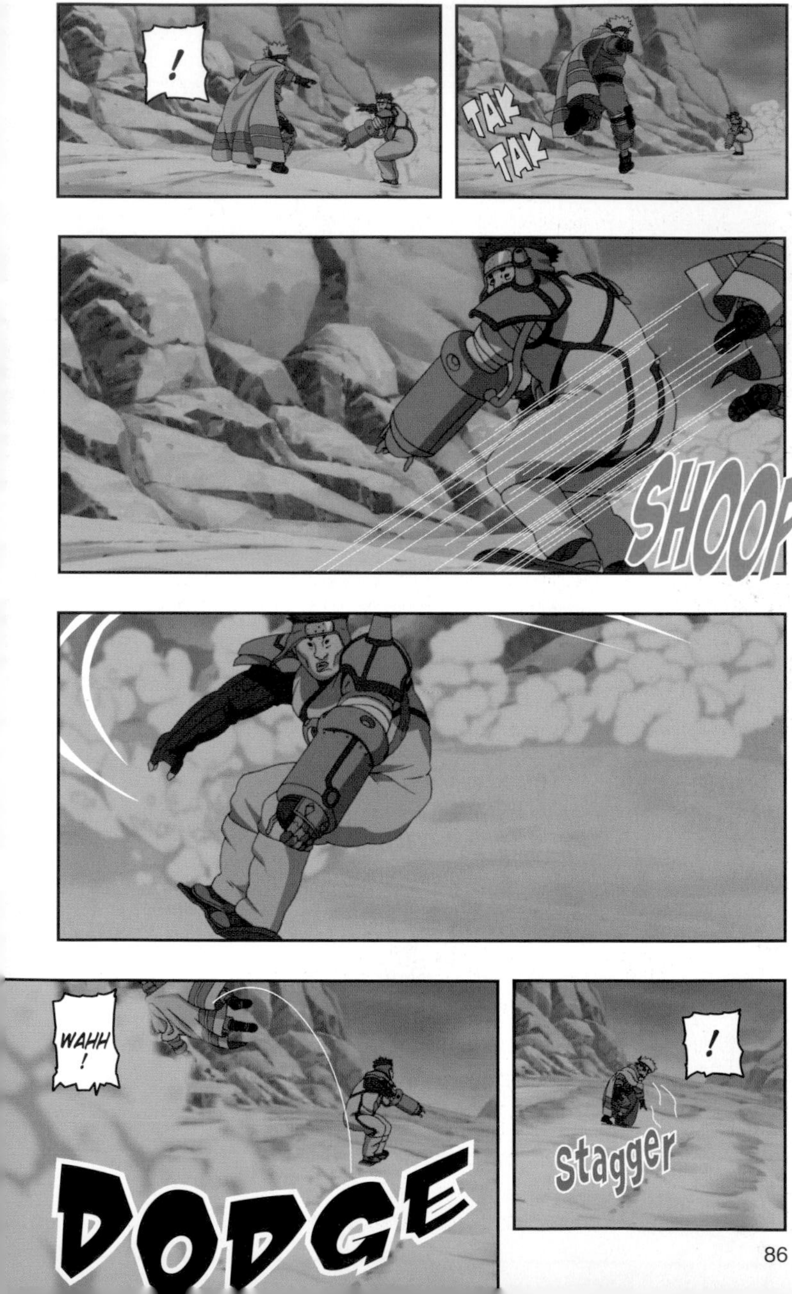
TAK
TAK
!
SHOOP
!
Stagger
WAHH!
DODGE

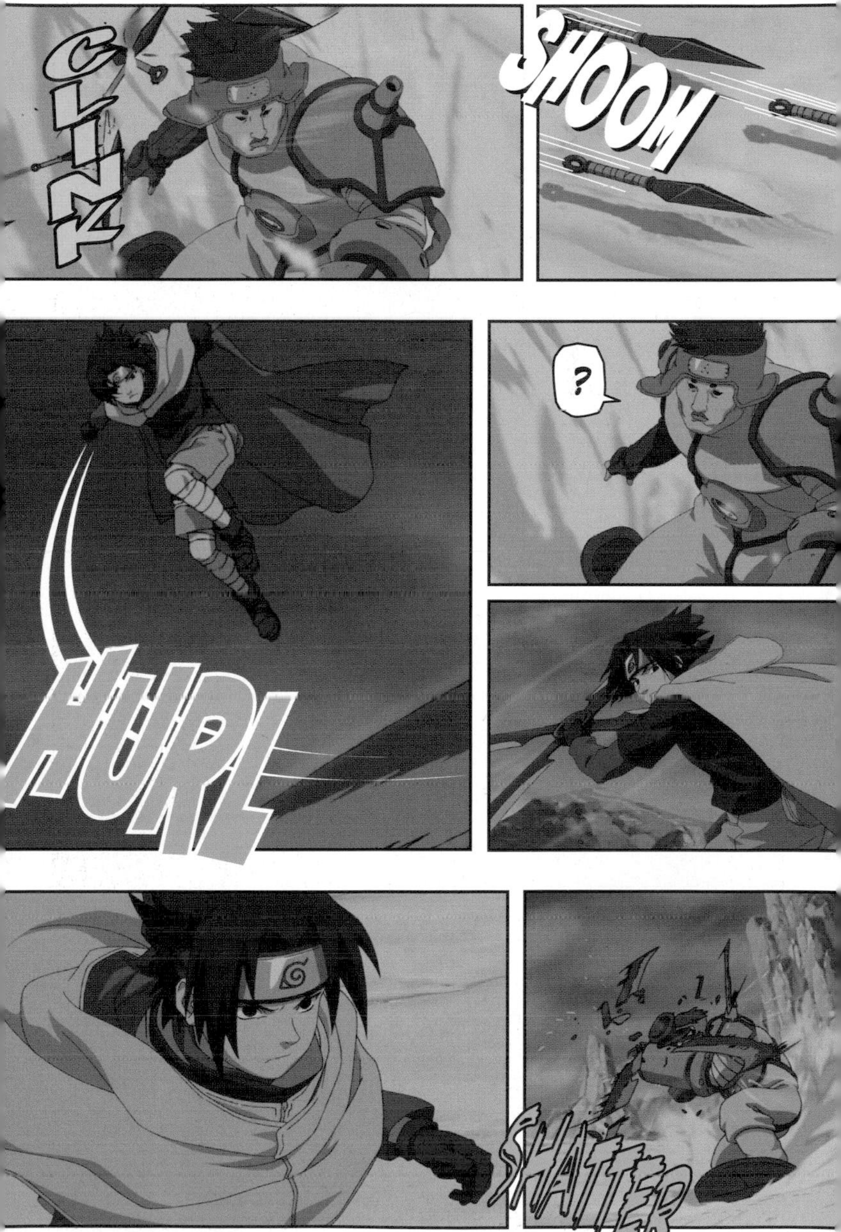
SHOOM
CLINK
?
HURL
SHATTER

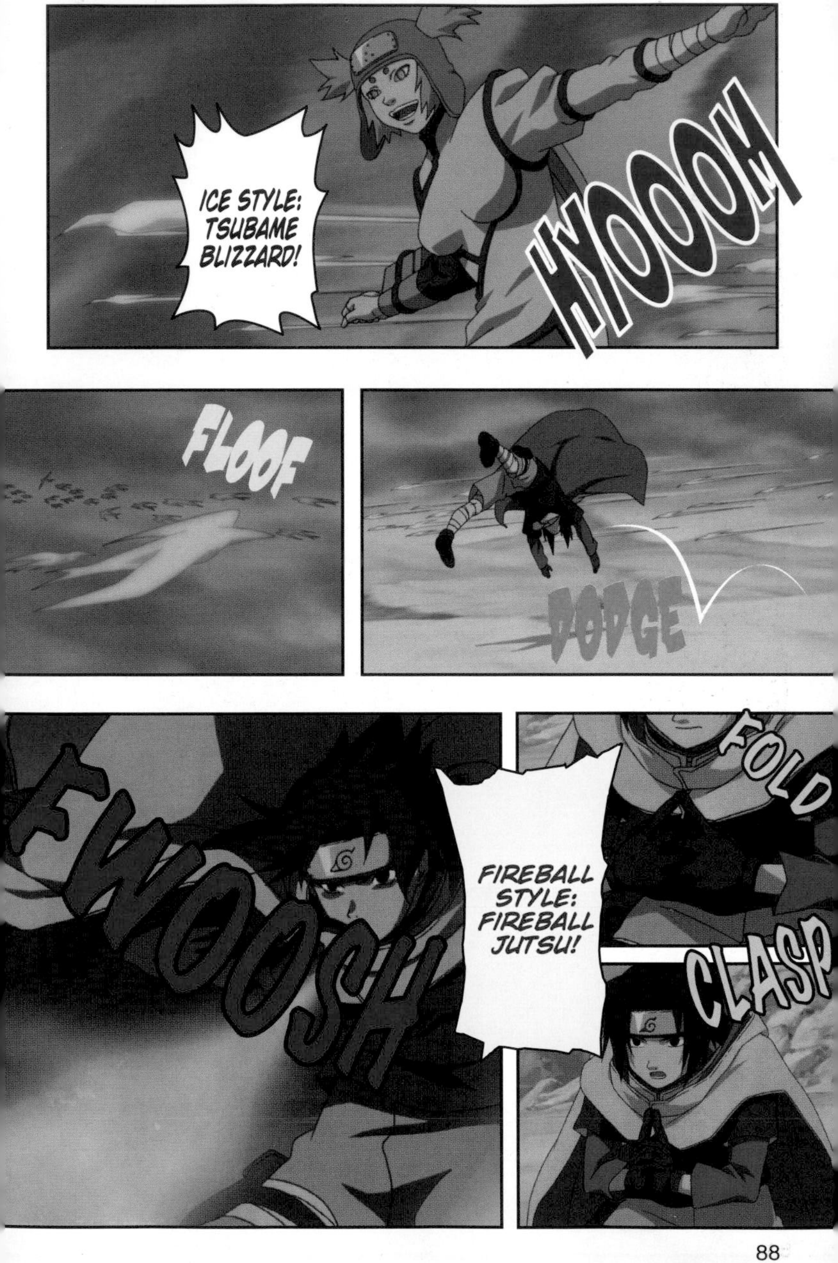
ICE STYLE: TSUBAME BLIZZARD!
HYOOOM
DODGE
FLOOF
FOLD
CLASP
FIREBALL STYLE: FIREBALL JUTSU!
FWOOSH

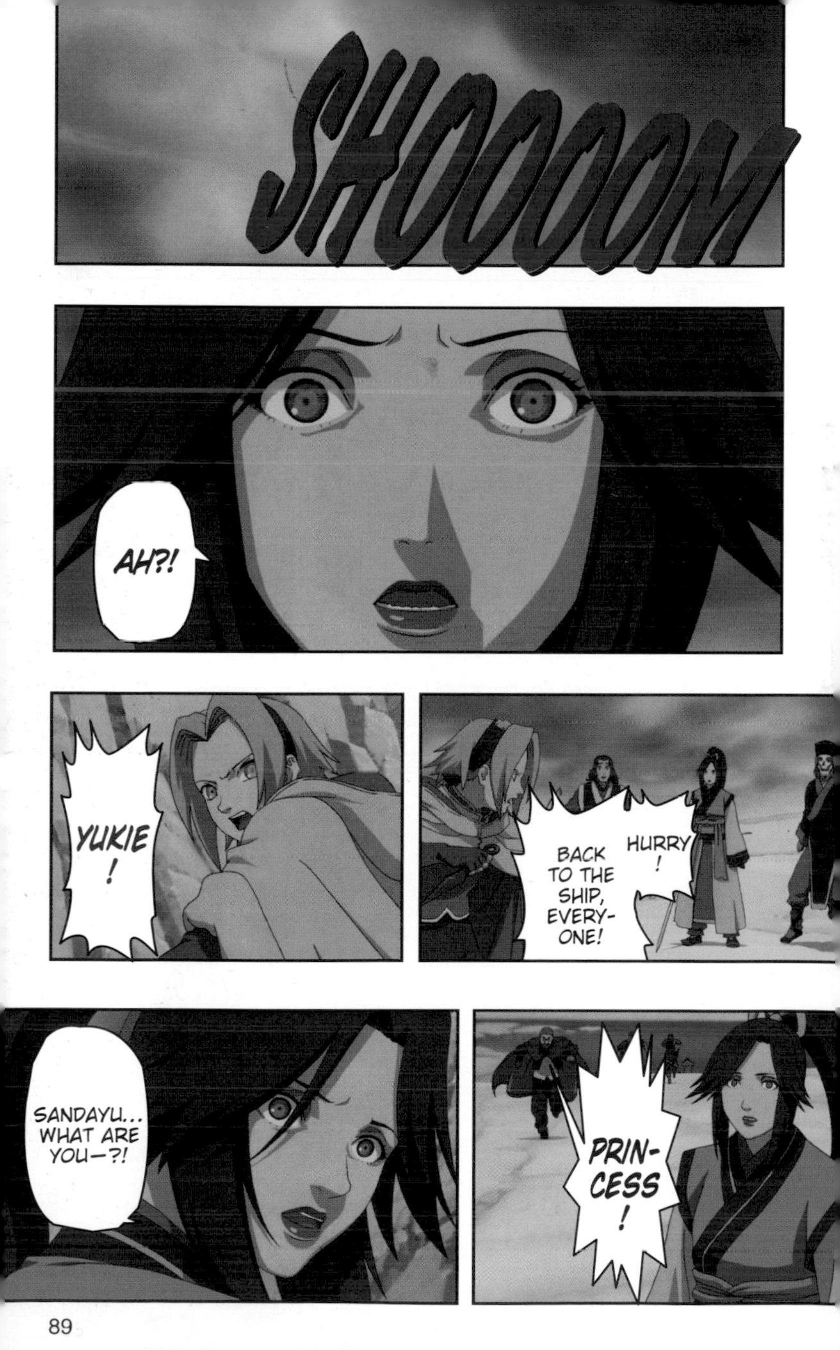
SHOOOOOM
AH?!
HURRY!
BACK TO THE SHIP, EVERYONE!
YUKIE!
PRIN-CESS!
SANDAYU... WHAT ARE YOU—?!

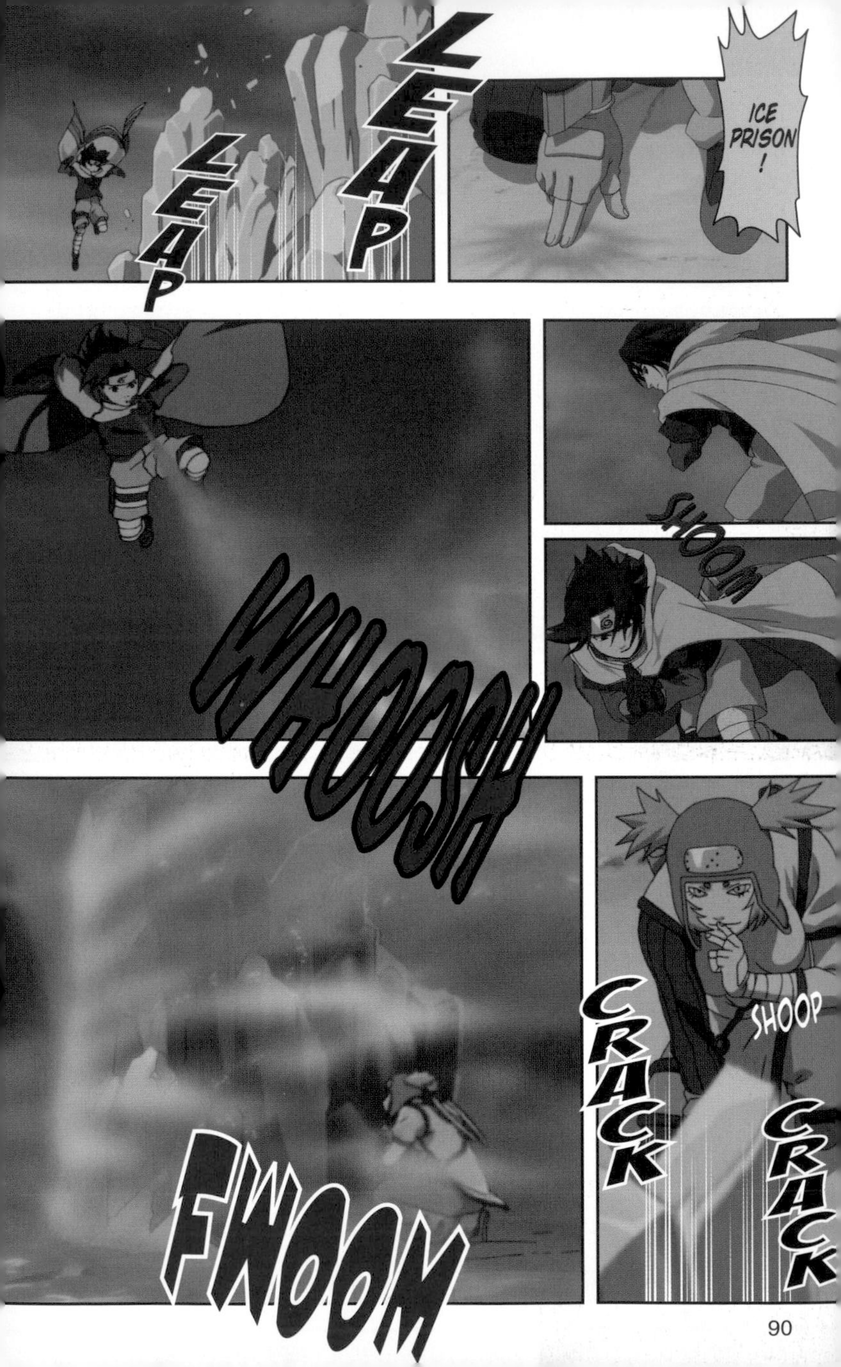
ICE PRISON!
LEAP
LEAP
SHOOM
WHOOSH
SHOOP
CRACK
CRACK
FWHOOM

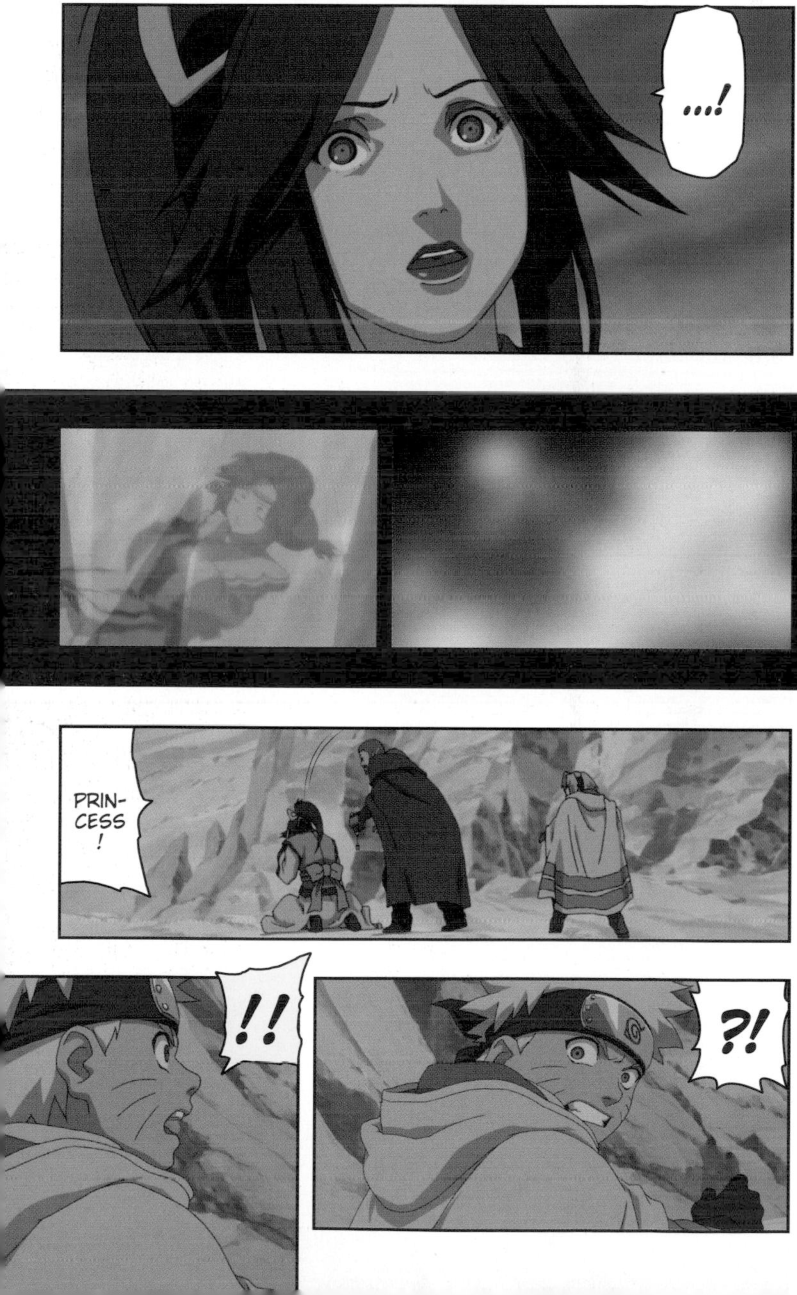
...!
PRIN-CESS!
?!
!!

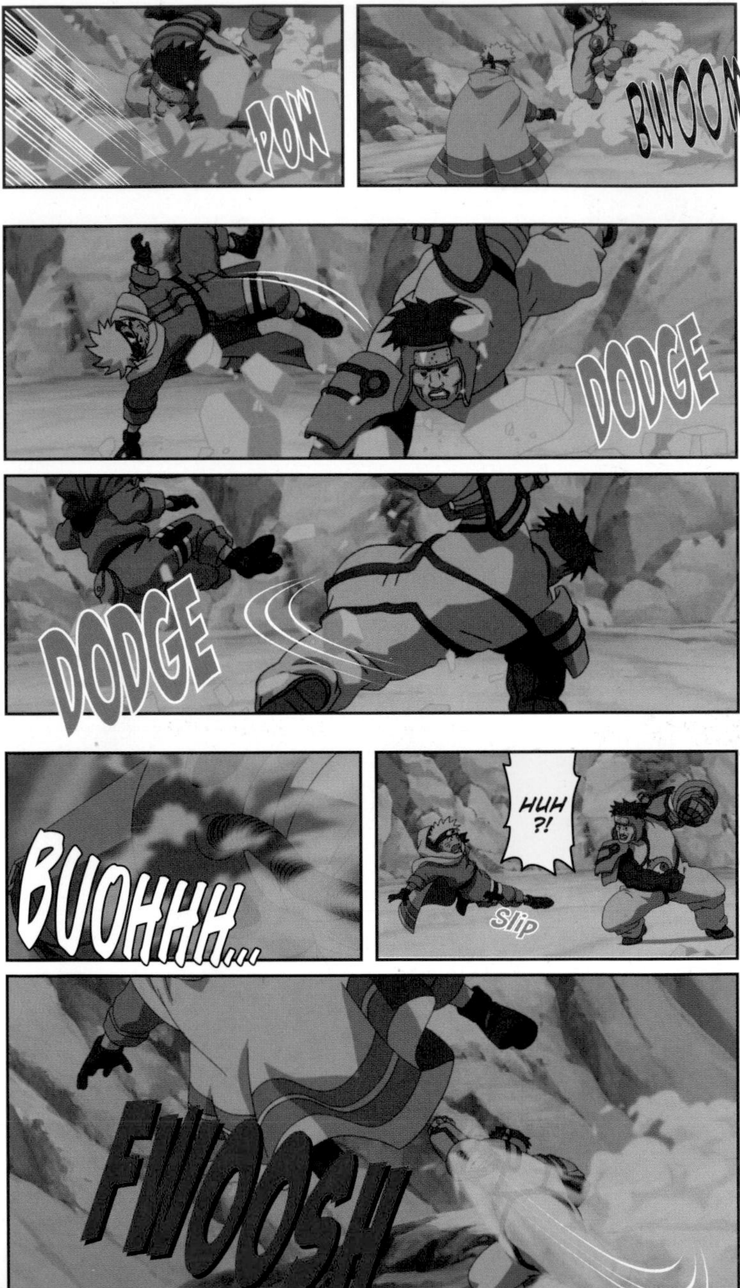
BWOOM
POW
DODGE
DODGE
HUH?!
Slip
BUOHHH...
FWOOSH

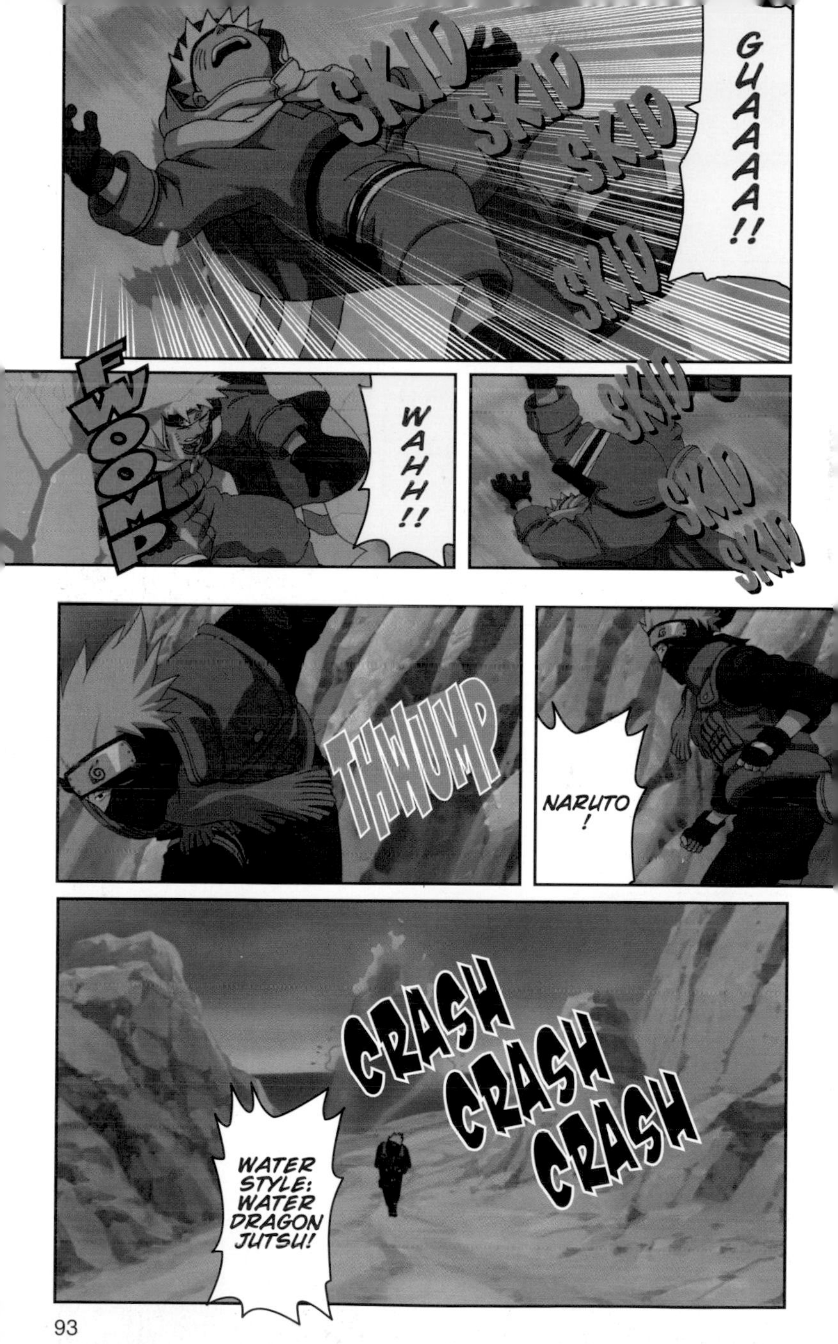
GUAAAAA!!
SKID SKID SKID SKID
SKID SKID SKID
WAHH!!
FWOOMP
NARUTO!
THWUMP
CRASH CRASH CRASH
WATER STYLE: WATER DRAGON JUTSU!

WHOOOSH

!!

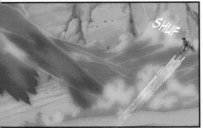

SHUF

Brrmm

KEEP THE
CAMERA
ROLLING,
EVEN IF IT
KILLS YOU!
SHOW 'EM
THE RESOLVE
OF THE
CINEMA-
TOGRAPHER!

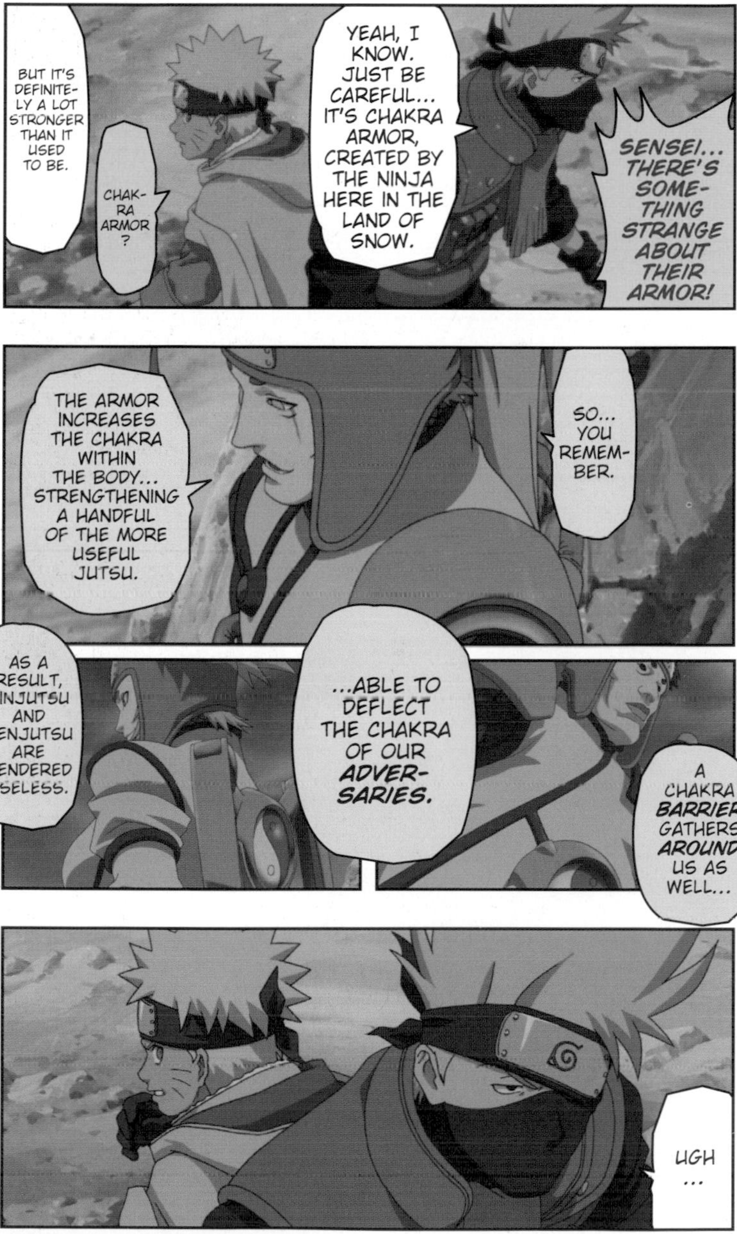
SENSEI... THERE'S SOMETHING STRANGE ABOUT THEIR ARMOR!
YEAH, I KNOW. JUST BE CAREFUL... IT'S CHAKRA ARMOR, CREATED BY THE NINJA HERE IN THE LAND OF SNOW.
CHAKRA ARMOR?
BUT IT'S DEFINITELY A LOT STRONGER THAN IT USED TO BE.
SO... YOU REMEMBER.
THE ARMOR INCREASES THE CHAKRA WITHIN THE BODY... STRENGTHENING A HANDFUL OF THE MORE USEFUL JUTSU.
A CHAKRA **BARRIER** GATHERS **AROUND** US AS WELL...
...ABLE TO DEFLECT THE CHAKRA OF OUR ***ADVERSARIES.***
AS A RESULT, NINJUTSU AND GENJUTSU ARE RENDERED USELESS.
UGH...

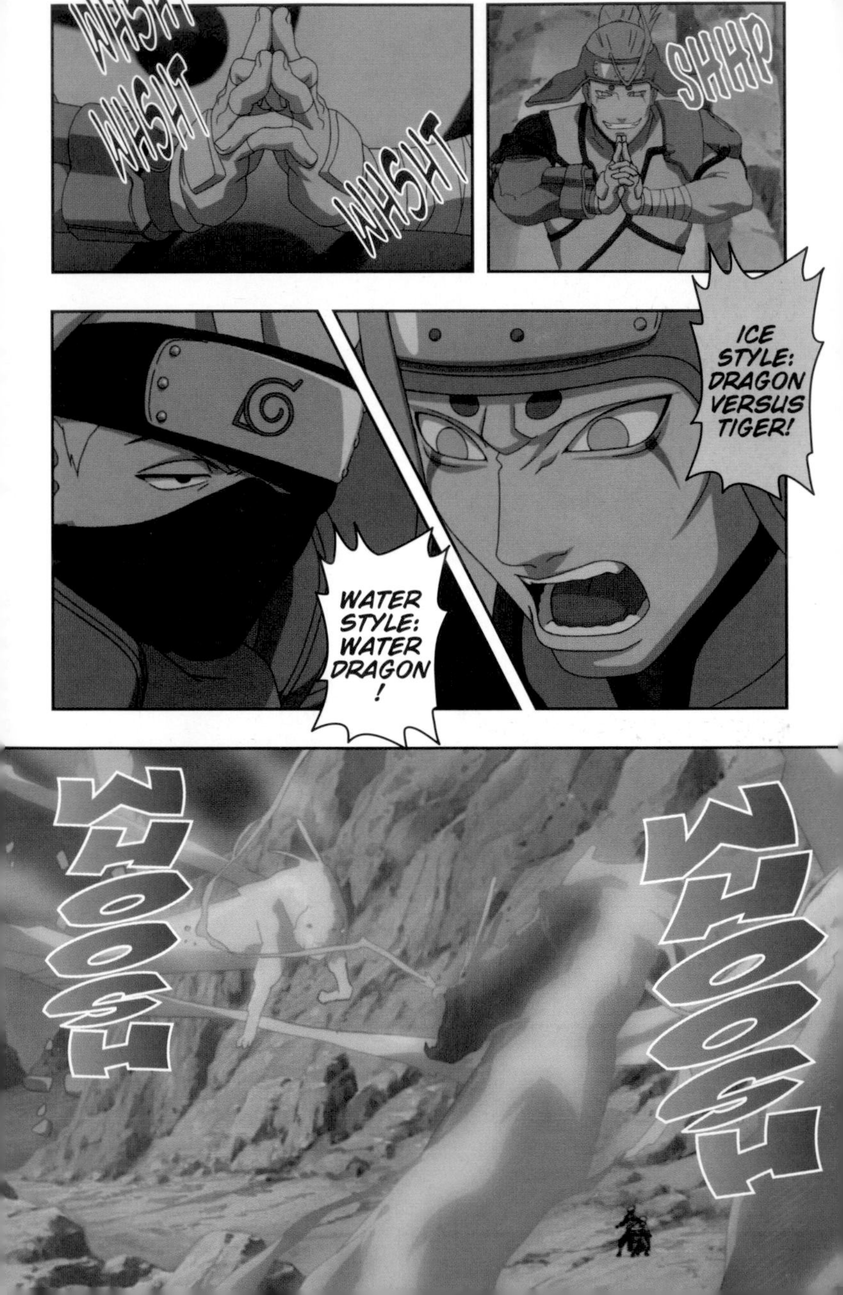
SHHP
WHSHT
WHSHT
WHSHT
ICE STYLE: DRAGON VERSUS TIGER!
WATER STYLE: WATER DRAGON!
WHOOSH
WHOOSH

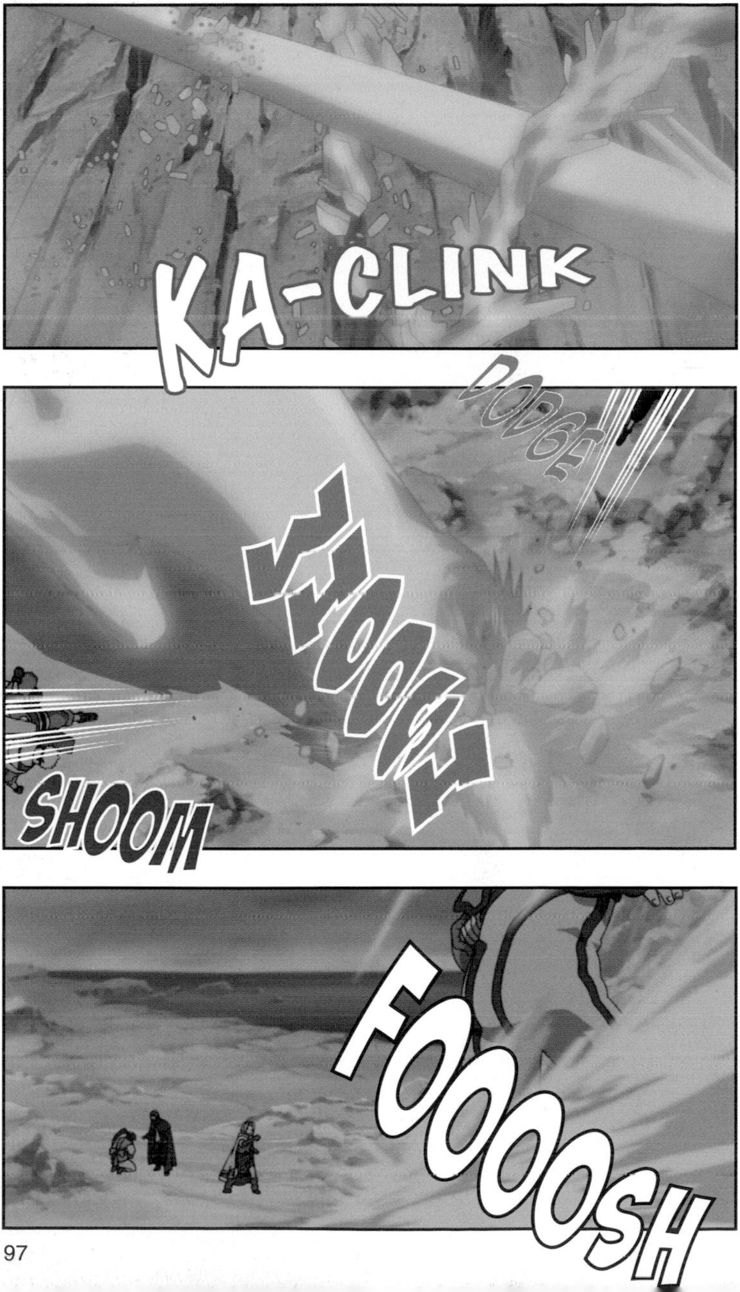
KA-CLINK
DODGE
SHOOM
FOOOOSH

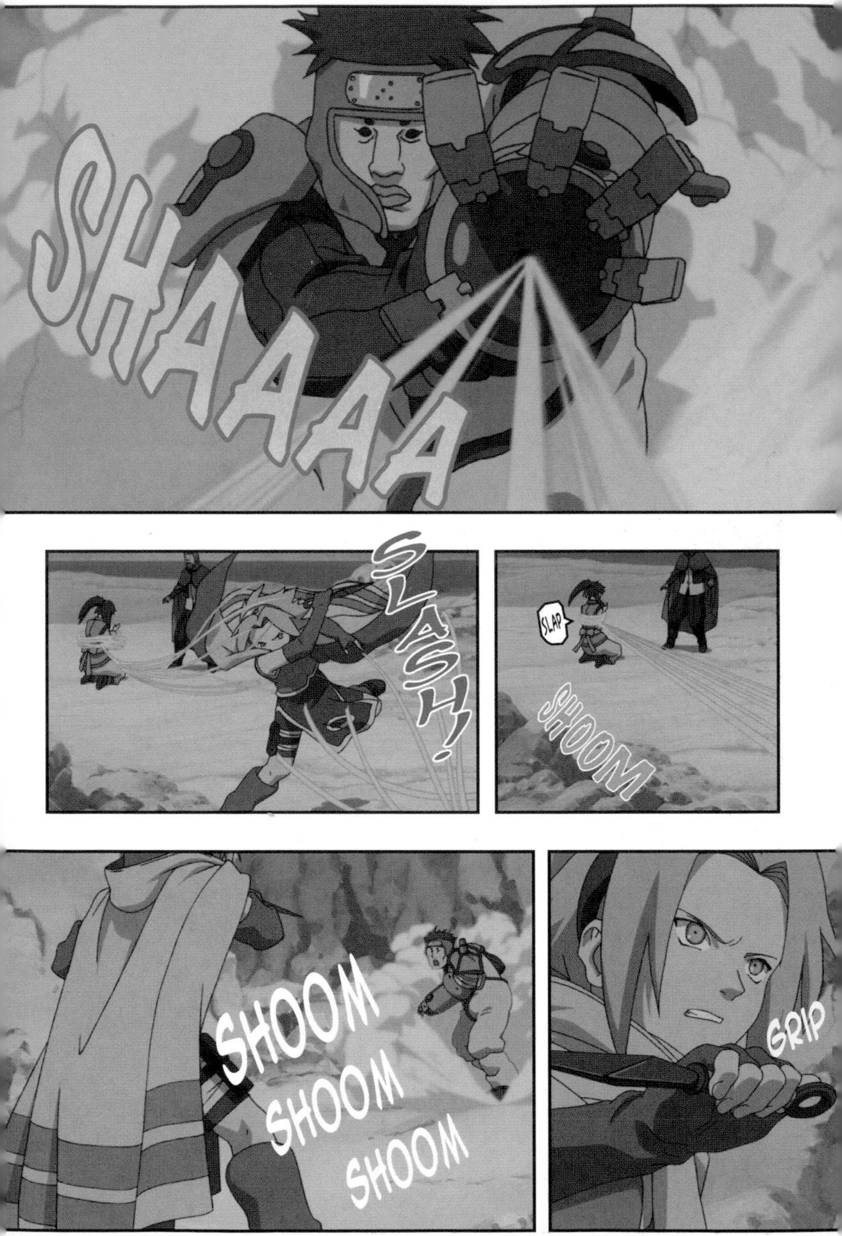
SHAAAAA
SLAP
SHOOM
SLASH!
GRIP
SHOOM
SHOOM
SHOOM

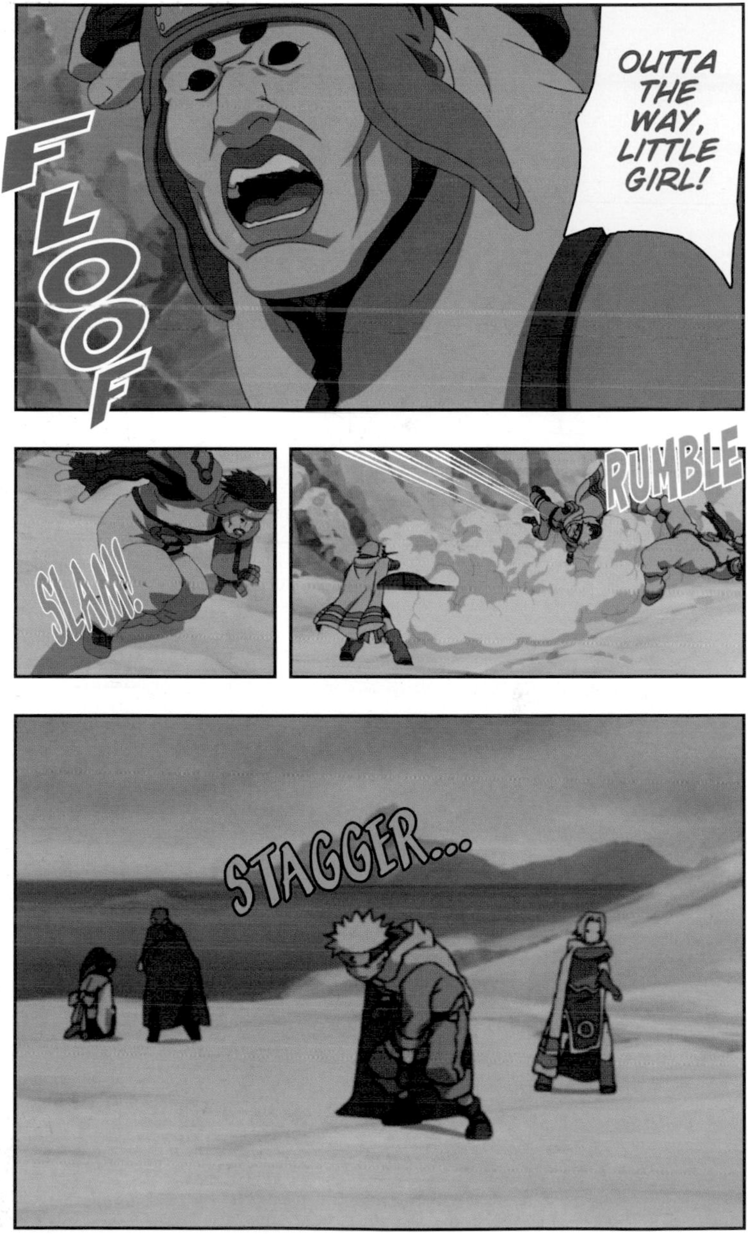
OUTTA THE WAY, LITTLE GIRL!
FLOOF
RUMBLE
SLAM!
STAGGER...

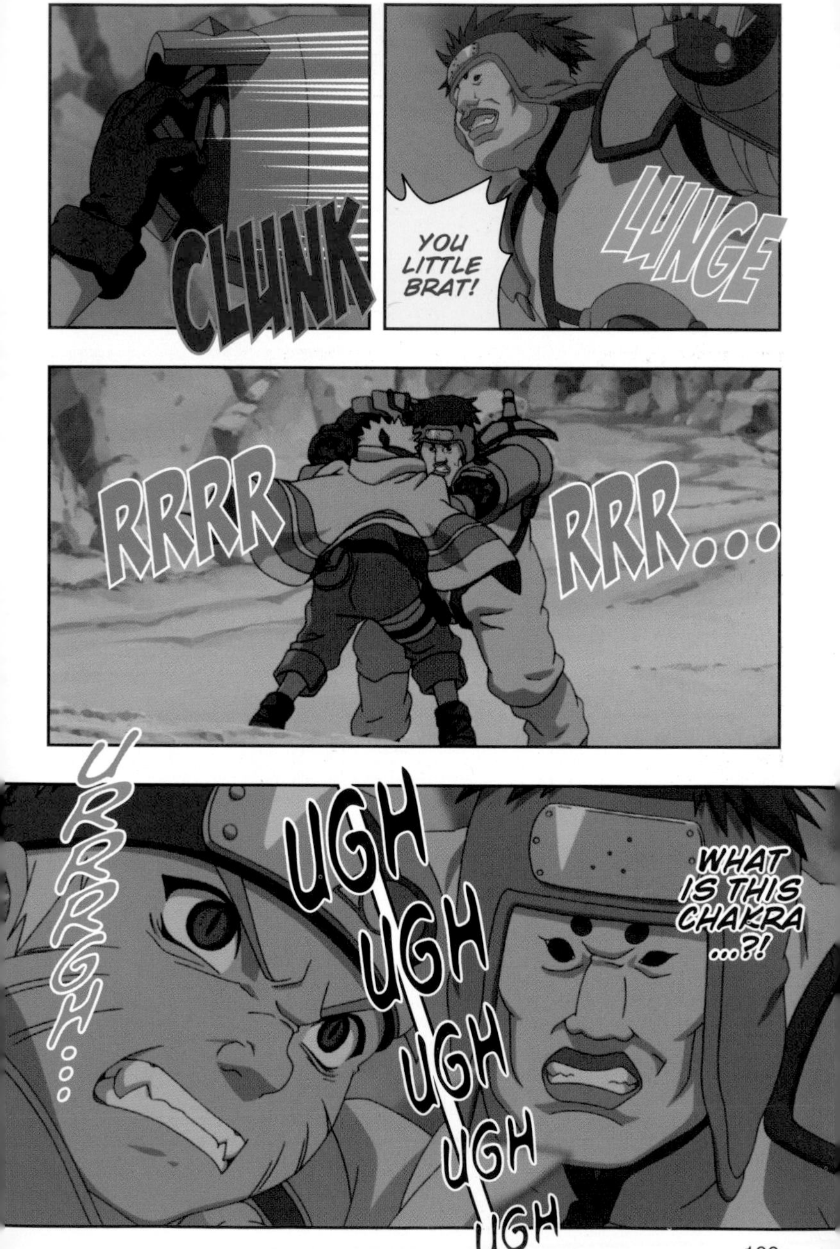
YOU LITTLE BRAT!
LUNGE
CLUNK
RRRR
RRR...
WHAT IS THIS CHAKRA...?!
UGH UGH UGH UGH UGH UGH
URRRGH...

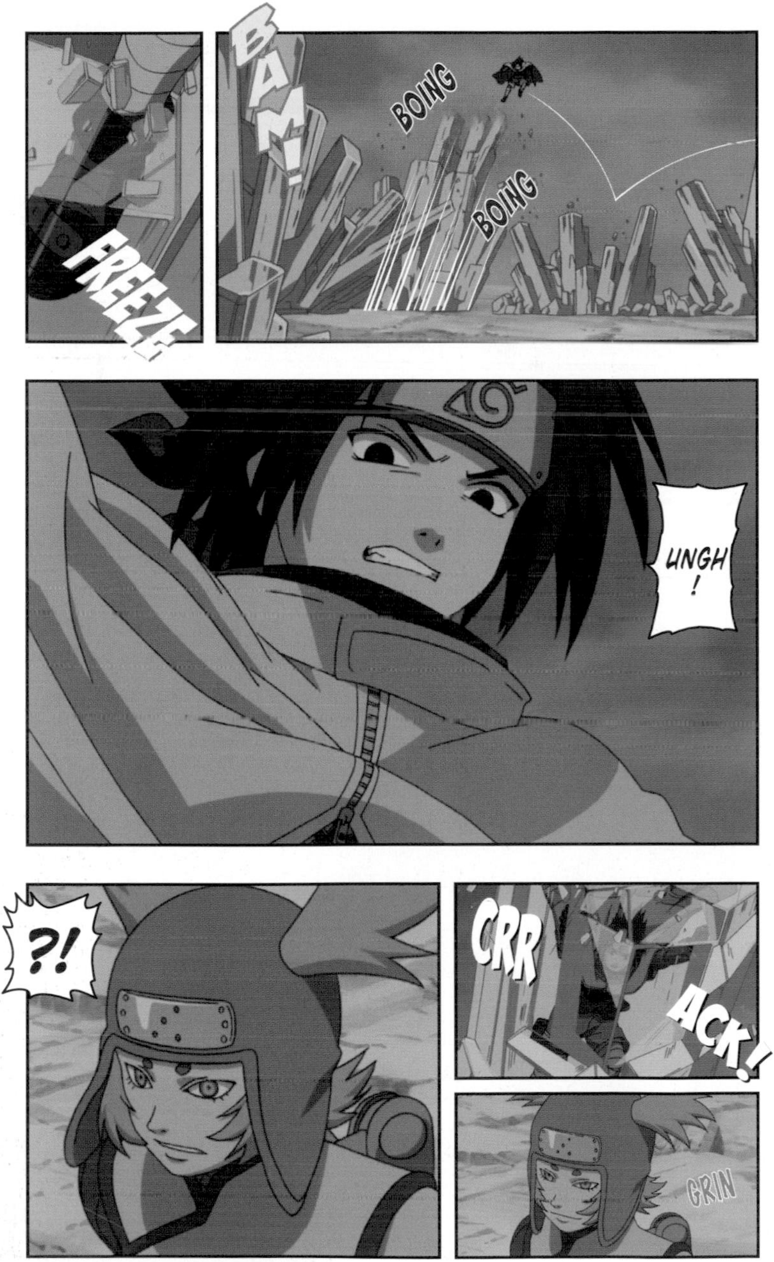
BAM!
BOING
BOING
FREEZE
UNGH!
CRRACK!
GRIN
?!

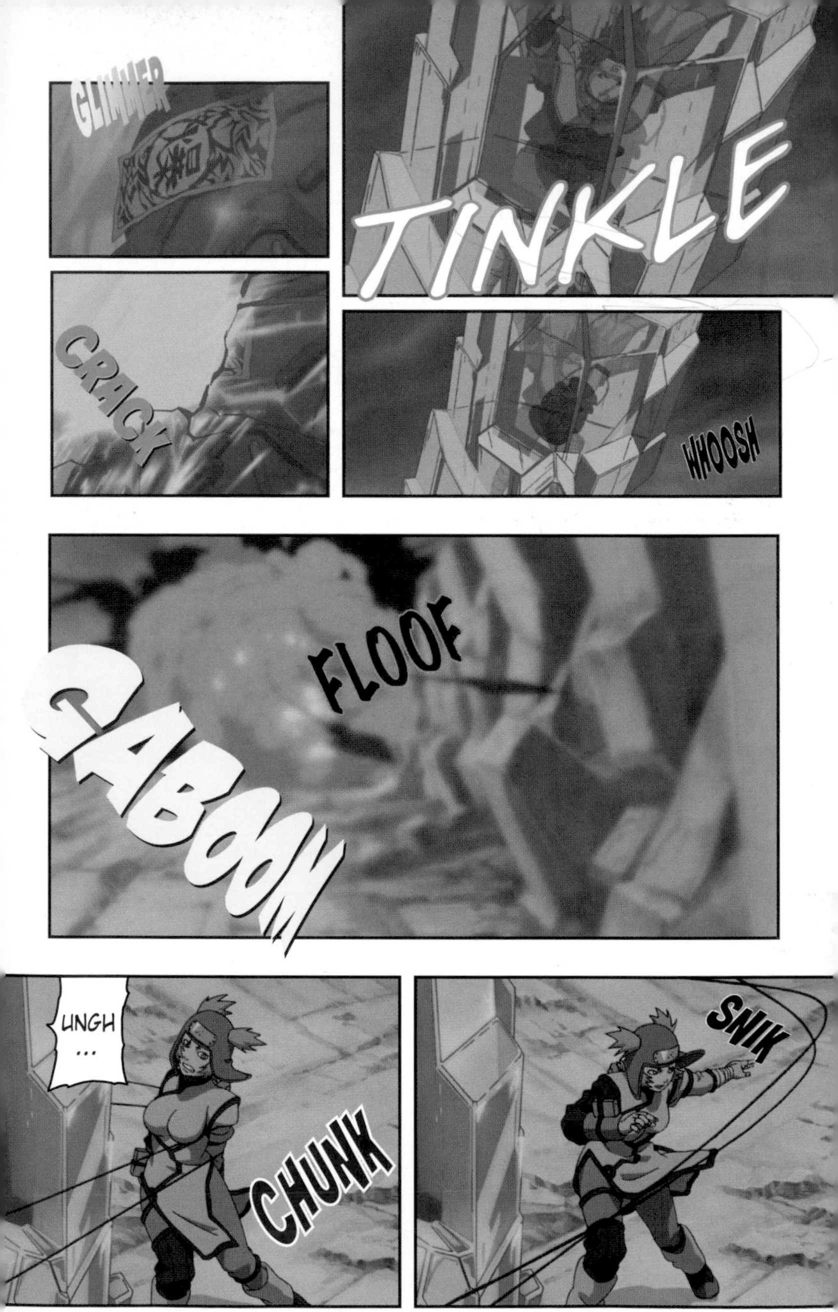
TINKLE
GLIMMER
WHOOSH
CRACK
FLOOF
GABOOM
SNIK
UNGH ...
CHUNK

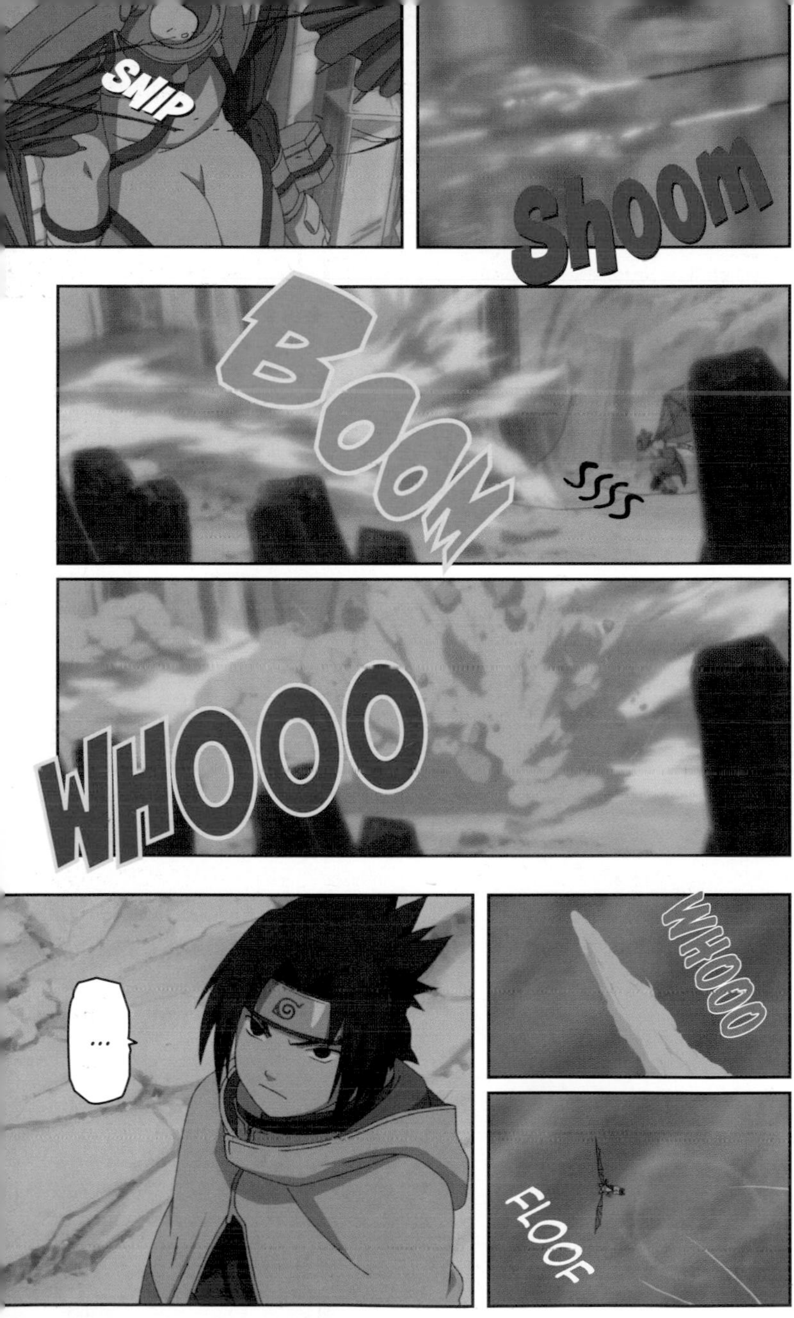
Shoom
SNIP
BOOM
SSSS
WHOOO
WHOOO
FLOOF
...

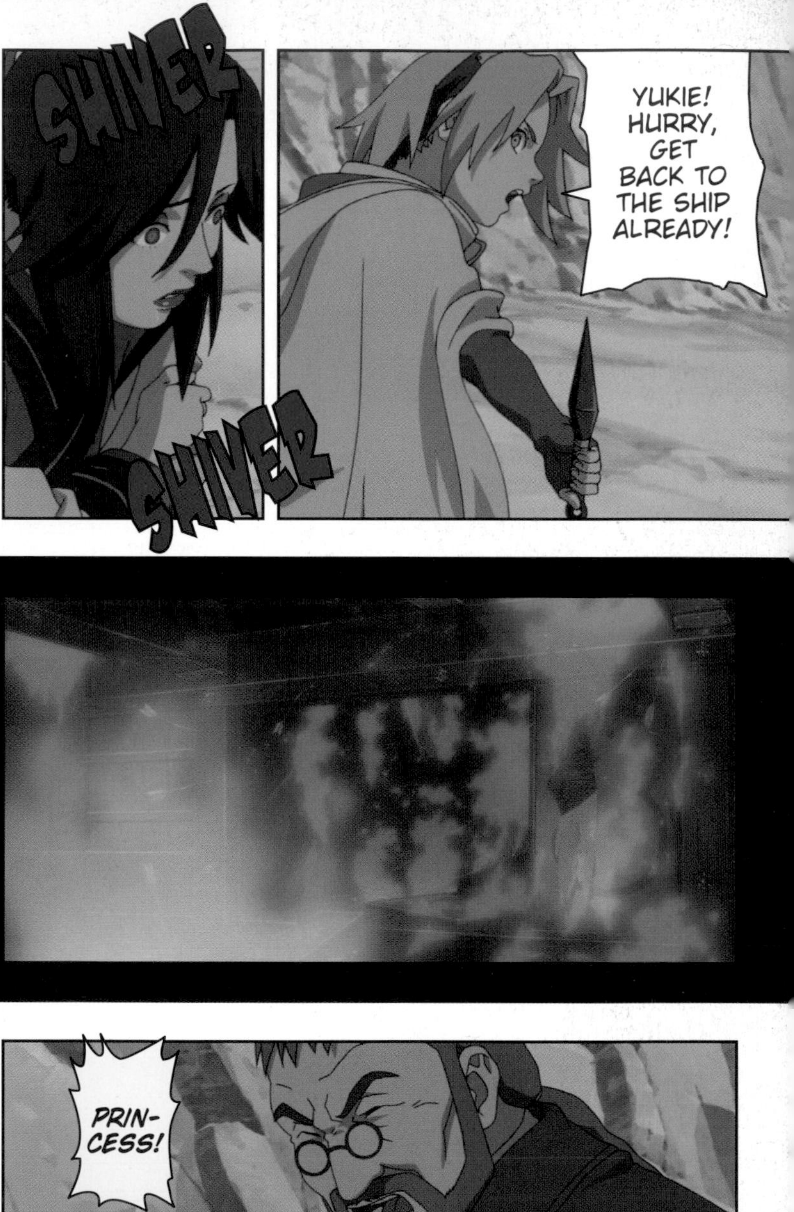
YUKIE! HURRY, GET BACK TO THE SHIP ALREADY!
SHIVER
SHIVER
PRIN-CESS!

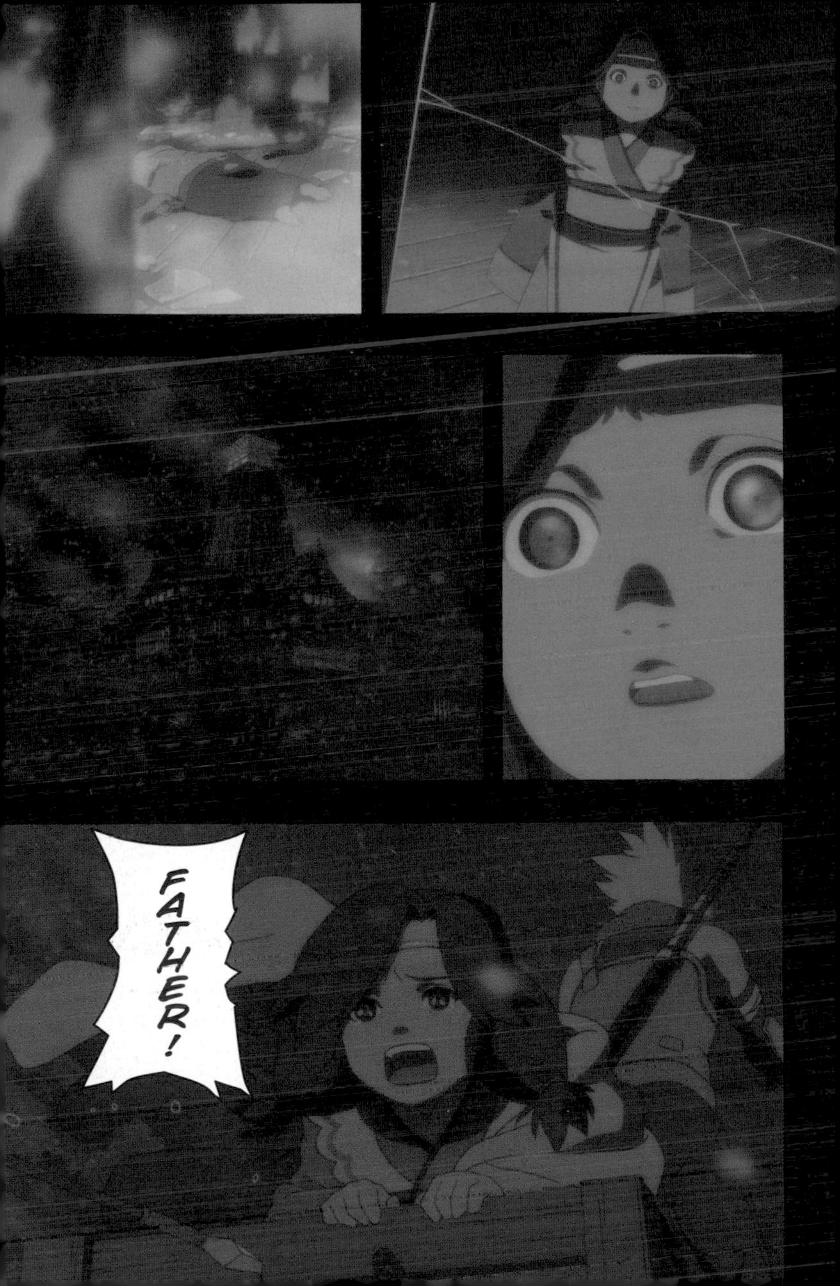
FATHER!

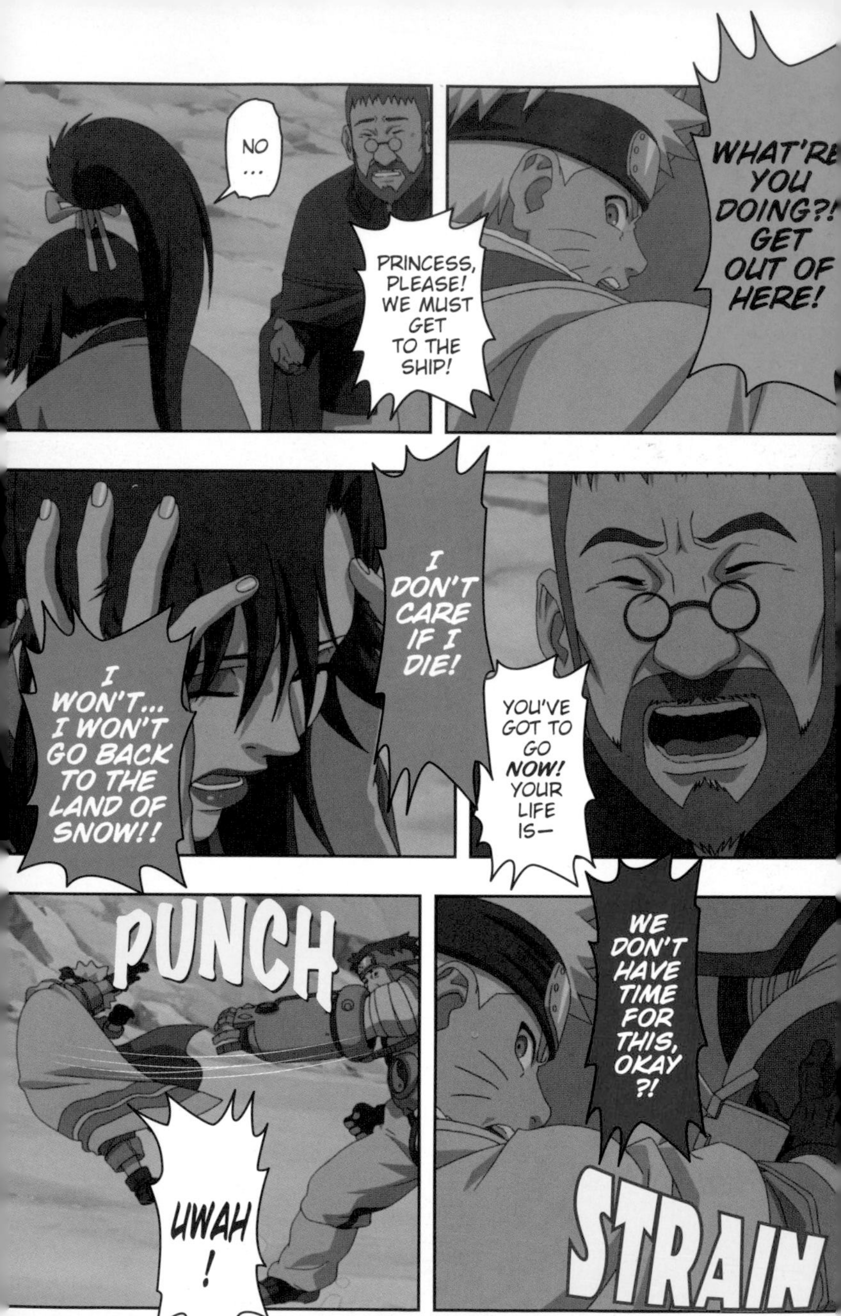
WHAT'RE YOU DOING?! GET OUT OF HERE!
PRINCESS, PLEASE! WE MUST GET TO THE SHIP!
NO ...
YOU'VE GOT TO GO *NOW!* YOUR LIFE IS—
I DON'T CARE IF I DIE!
I WON'T... I WON'T GO BACK TO THE LAND OF SNOW!!
WE DON'T HAVE TIME FOR THIS, OKAY ?!
STRAIN
PUNCH
UWAH !

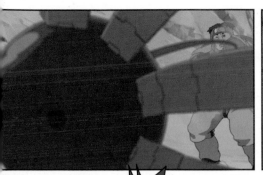

RRRMM

AHH!

GRAB

DART

TCH!

SQUEEZE

BOO OM

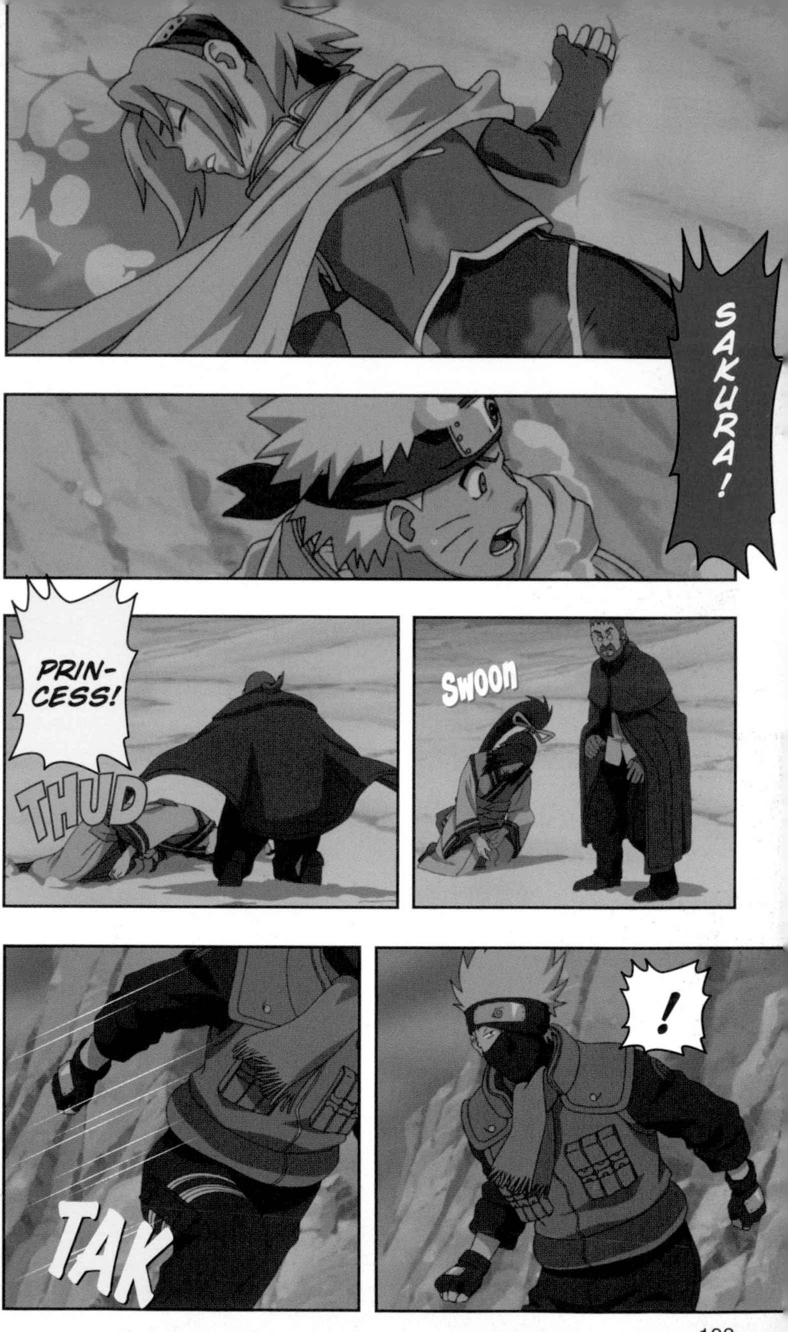
SAKURA!
Swoon
PRIN-CESS!
THUD
!
TAK

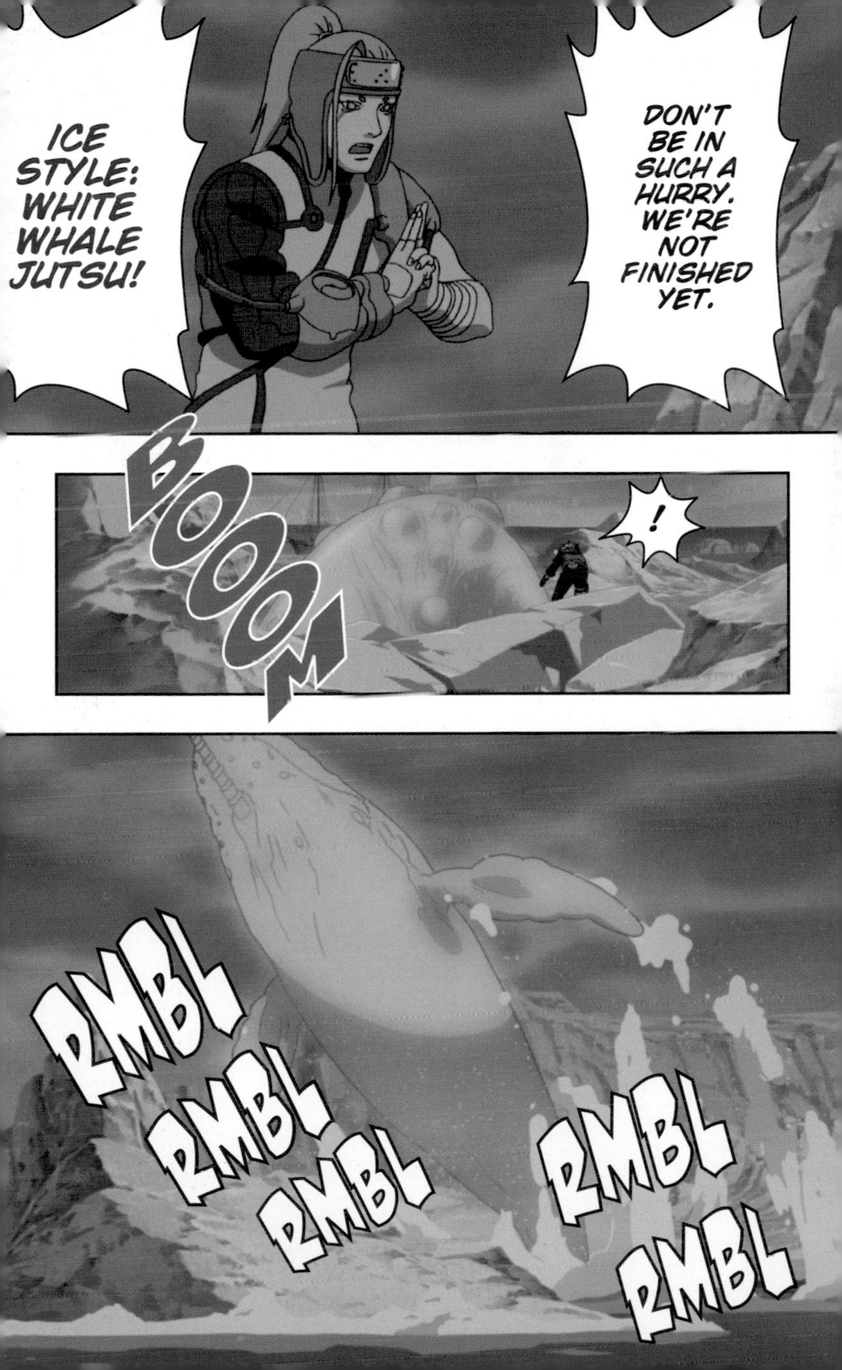
DON'T BE IN SUCH A HURRY. WE'RE NOT FINISHED YET.
ICE STYLE: WHITE WHALE JUTSU!
BOOOOM
!
RMBL RMBL RMBL
RMBL RMBL RMBL

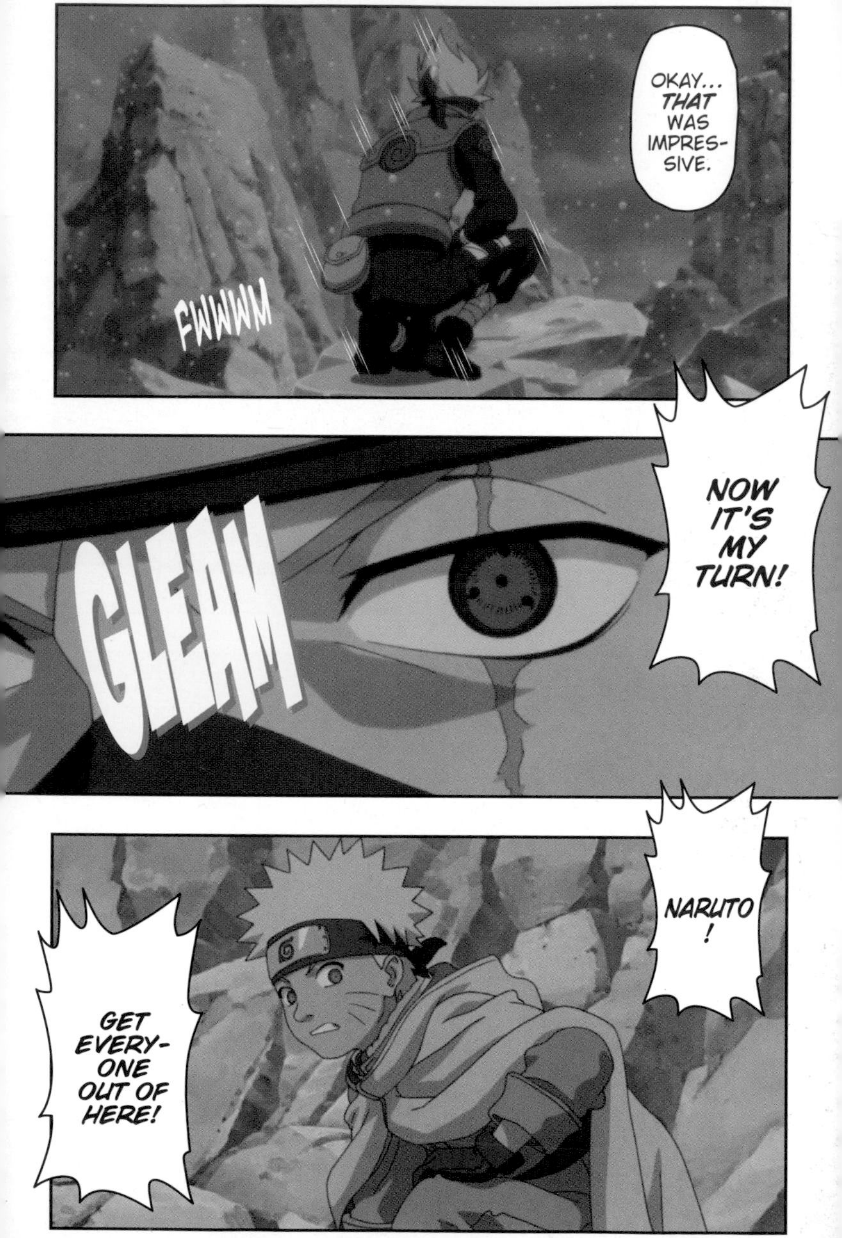
OKAY... THAT WAS IMPRES-SIVE.
FWWWM
NOW IT'S MY TURN!
GLEAM
NARUTO!
GET EVERY-ONE OUT OF HERE!

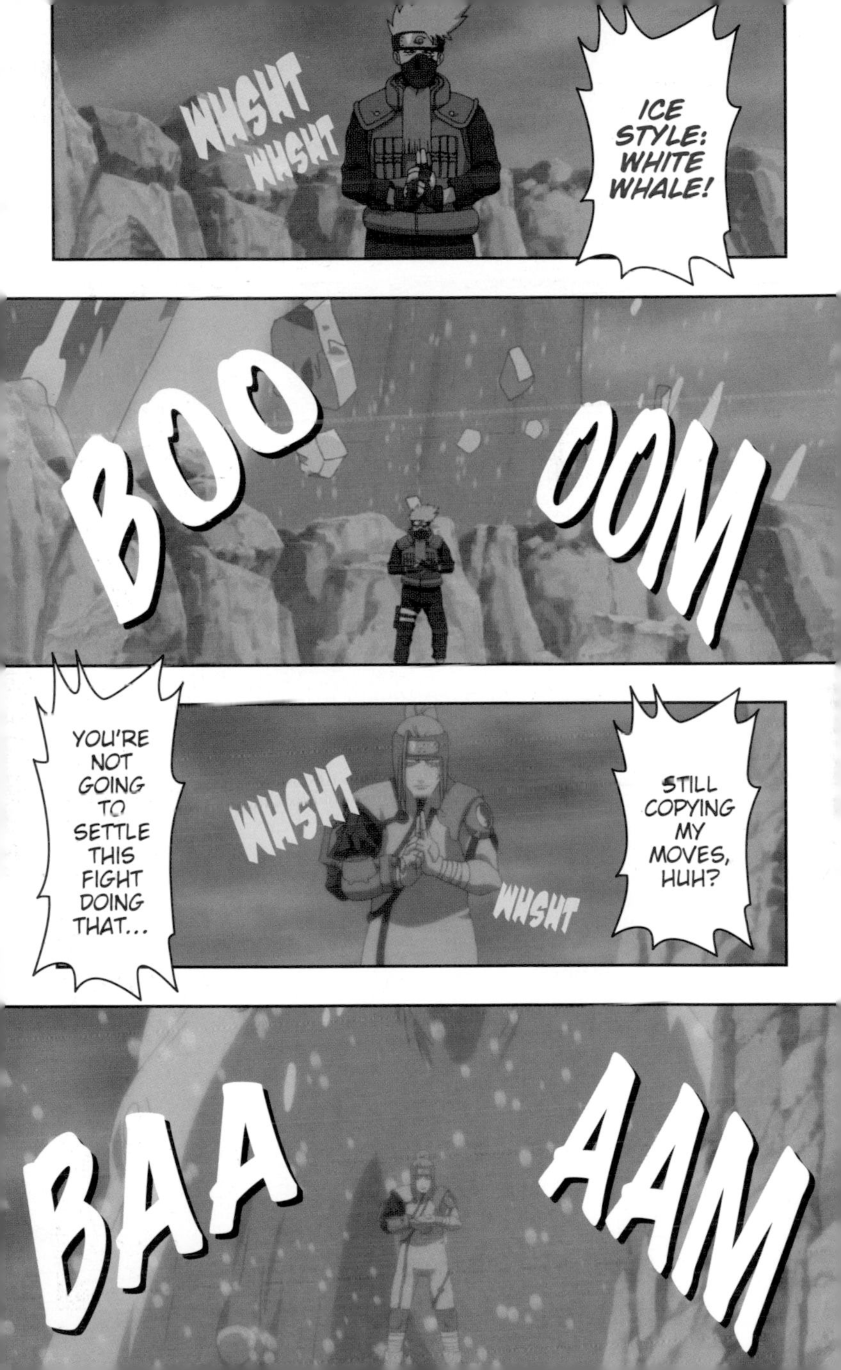
ICE STYLE: WHITE WHALE!
WHSHT WHSHT
BOO OOM
STILL COPYING MY MOVES, HUH?
WHSHT
WHSHT
YOU'RE NOT GOING TO SETTLE THIS FIGHT DOING THAT...
BAA AAM

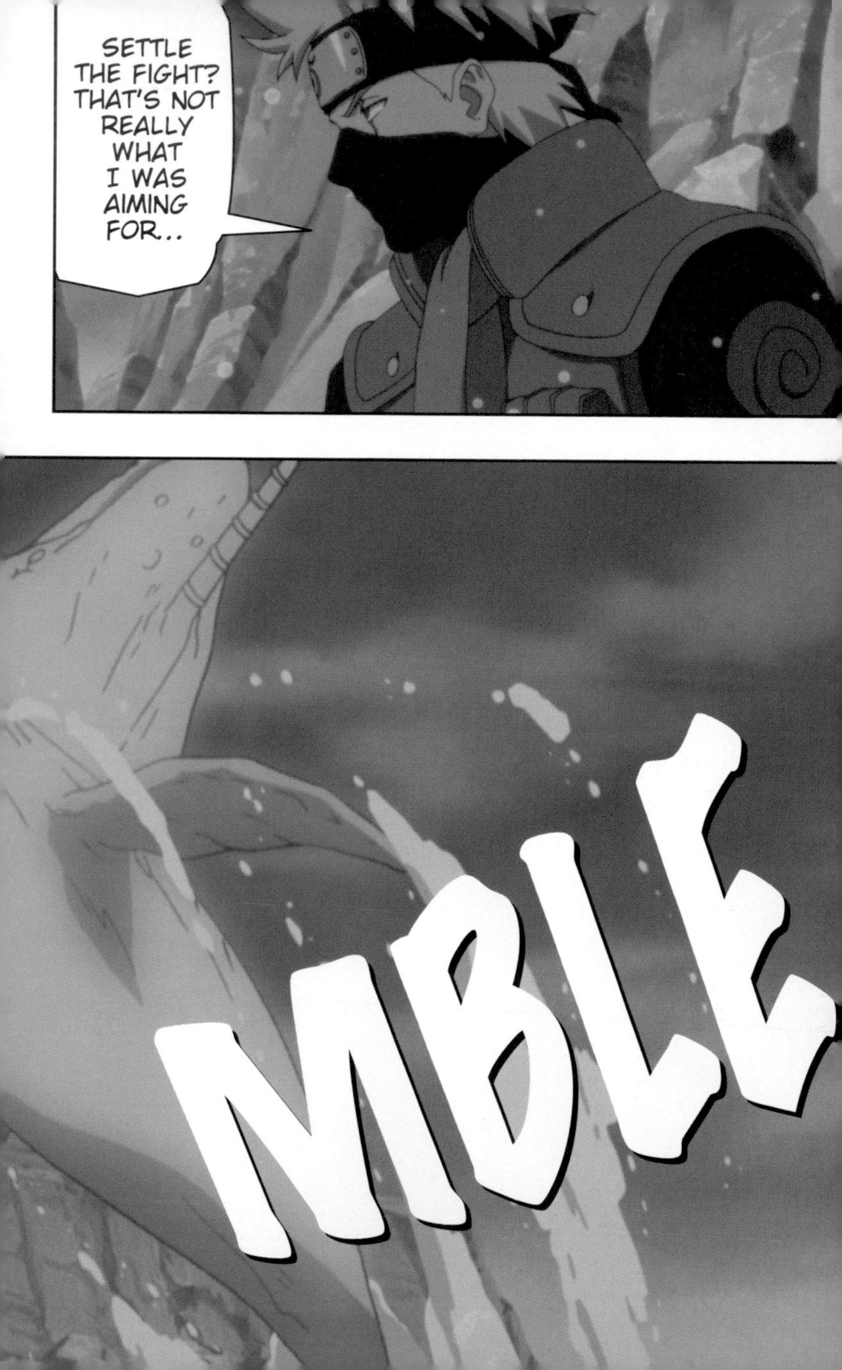
SETTLE THE FIGHT? THAT'S NOT REALLY WHAT I WAS AIMING FOR...
MBLE

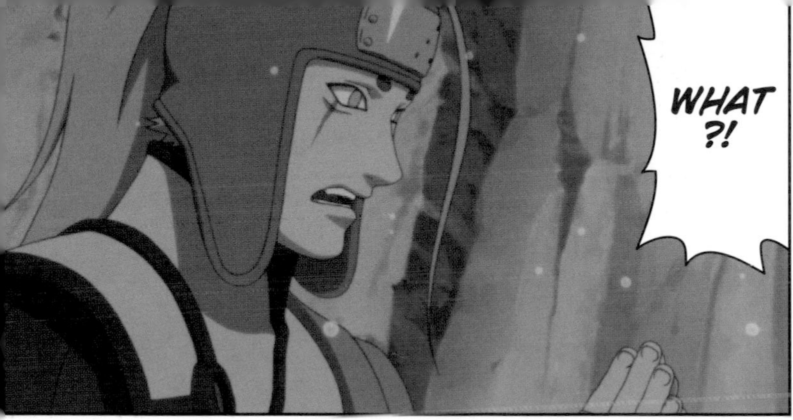
WHAT ?!
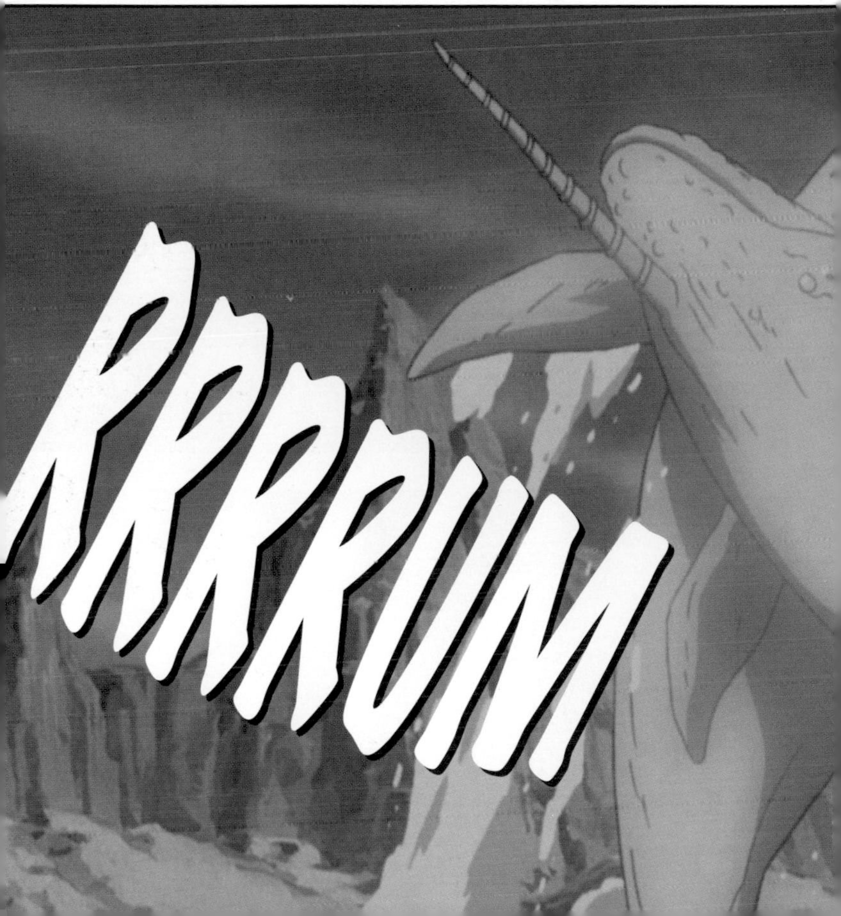
RRRRUM

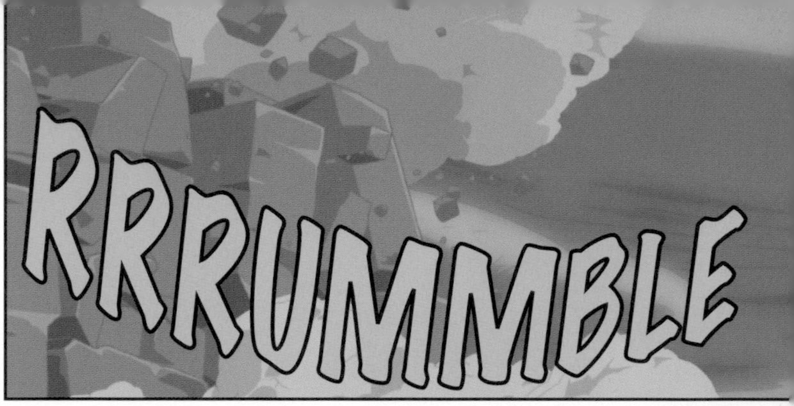
RRRUMMBLE

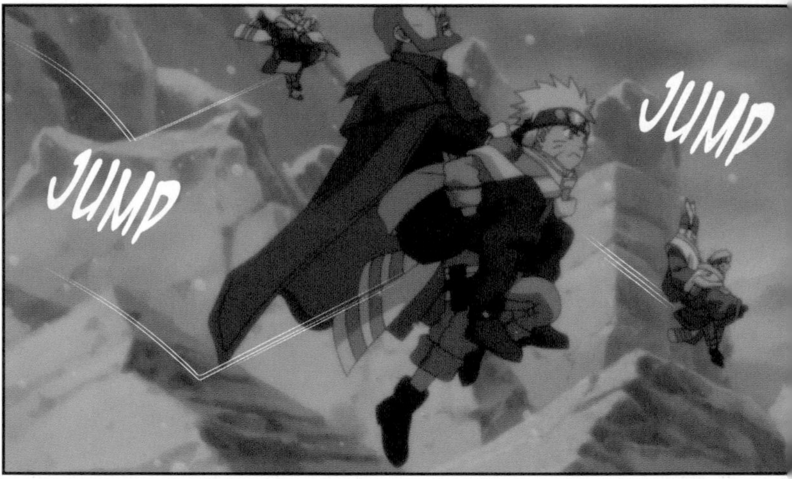
JUMP
JUMP

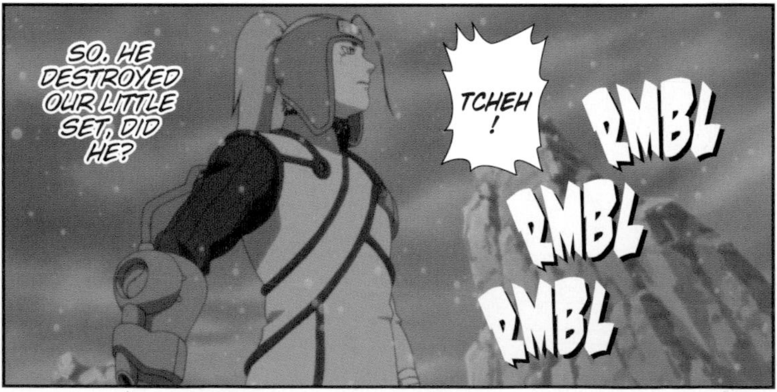
TCHEH!
RMBL
RMBL
RMBL
SO. HE DESTROYED OUR LITTLE SET, DID HE?

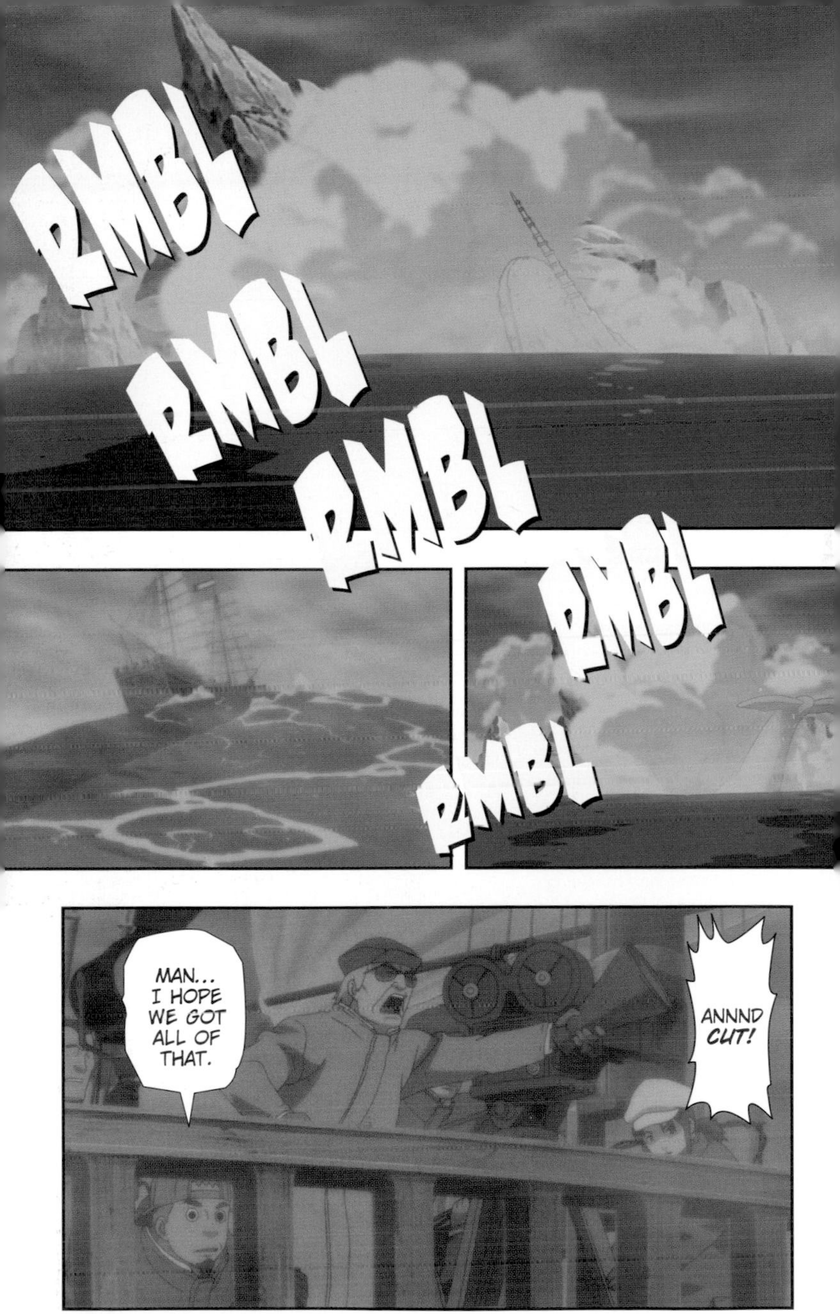
RMBL
RMBL
RMBL
RMBL
RMBL
ANNND CUT!
MAN... I HOPE WE GOT ALL OF THAT.

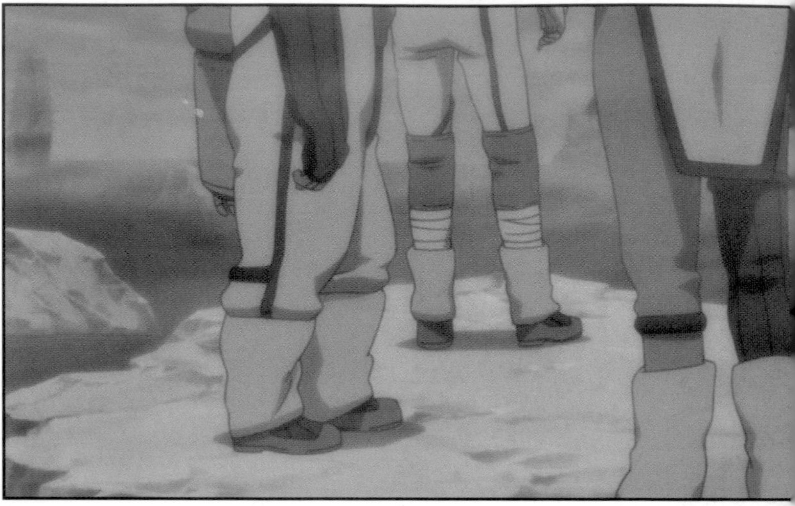

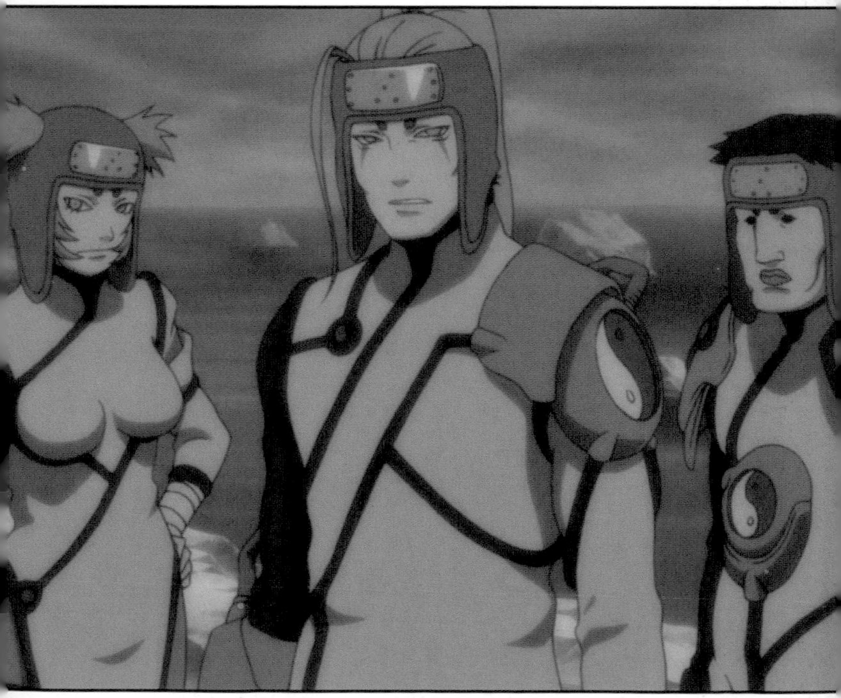

Chapter 3: Unbreakable Heart

TEN YEARS... IT'S BEEN A LONG TIME.

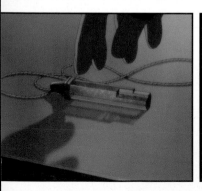

THE SHIP PULLED INTO DOCK A MOMENT AGO.

CREAK

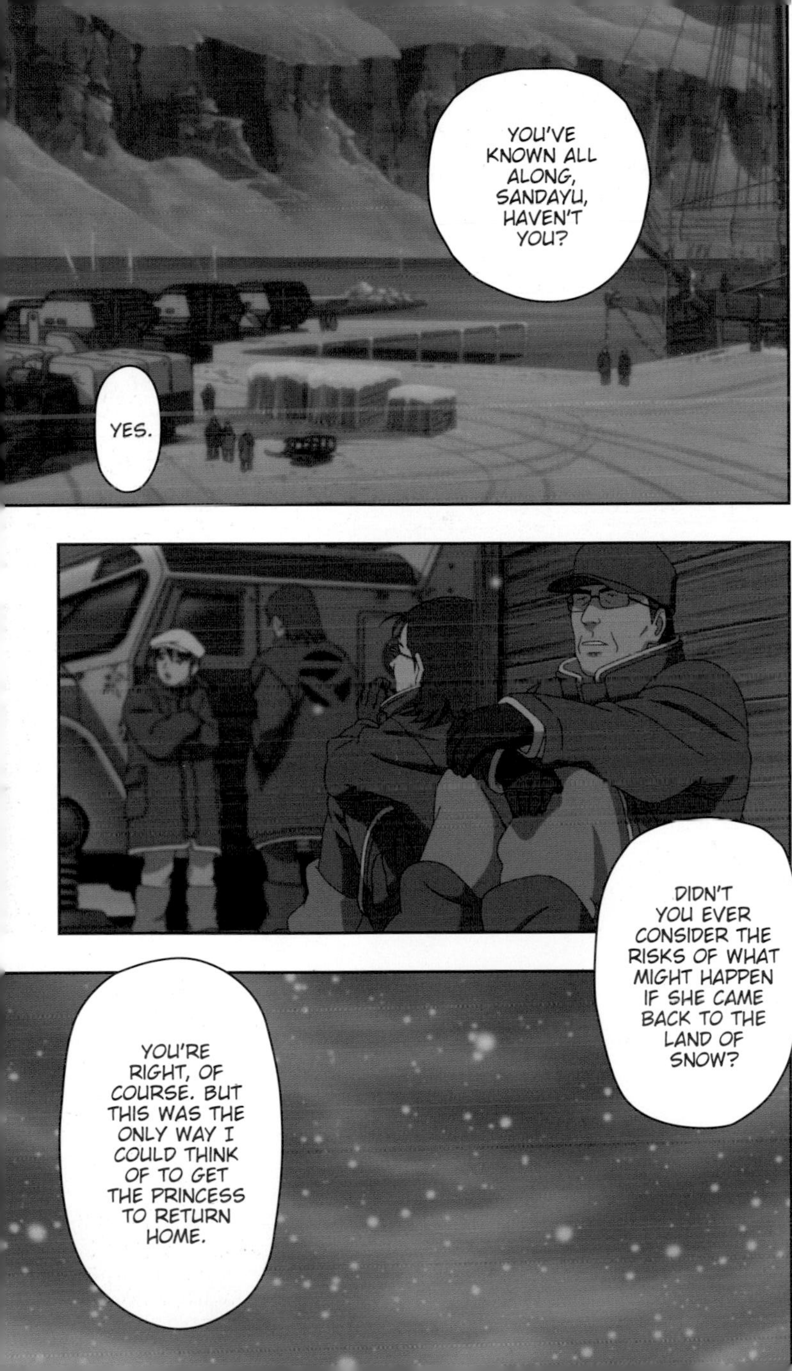
YOU'VE KNOWN ALL ALONG, SANDAYU, HAVEN'T YOU?
YES.
DIDN'T YOU EVER CONSIDER THE RISKS OF WHAT MIGHT HAPPEN IF SHE CAME BACK TO THE LAND OF SNOW?
YOU'RE RIGHT, OF COURSE. BUT THIS WAS THE ONLY WAY I COULD THINK OF TO GET THE PRINCESS TO RETURN HOME.

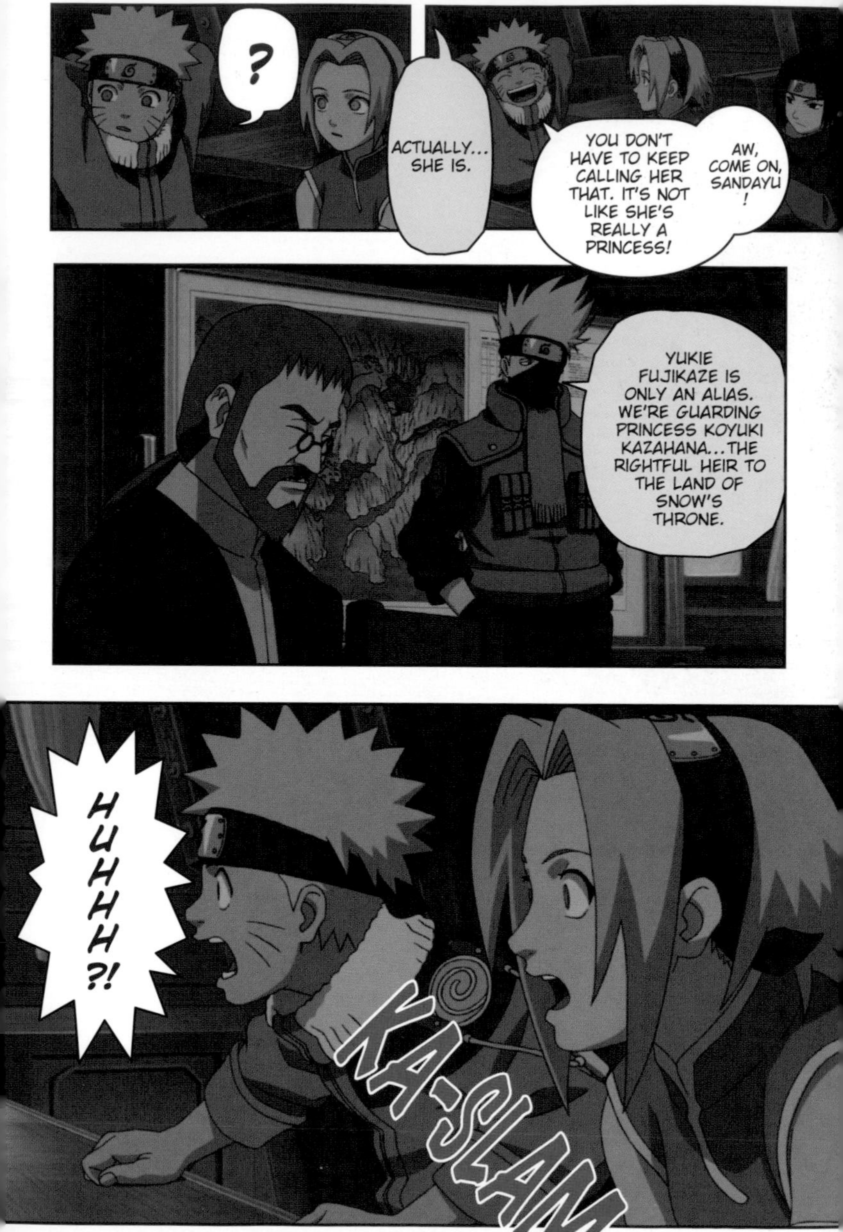
AW, COME ON, SANDAYU!
YOU DON'T HAVE TO KEEP CALLING HER THAT. IT'S NOT LIKE SHE'S REALLY A PRINCESS!
ACTUALLY... SHE IS.
?
YUKIE FUJIKAZE IS ONLY AN ALIAS. WE'RE GUARDING PRINCESS KOYUKI KAZAHANA...THE RIGHTFUL HEIR TO THE LAND OF SNOW'S THRONE.
KA-SLAM
HUHHH?!

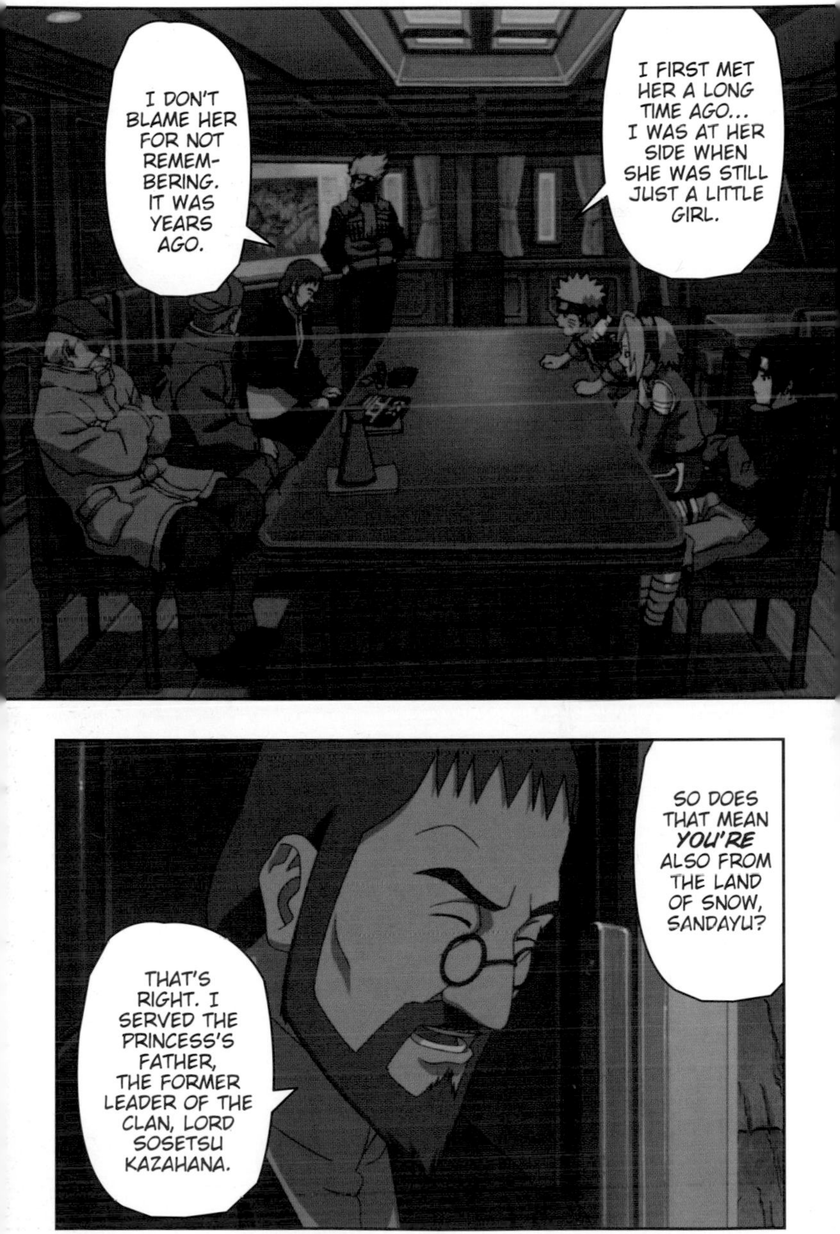
I FIRST MET HER A LONG TIME AGO... I WAS AT HER SIDE WHEN SHE WAS STILL JUST A LITTLE GIRL.
I DON'T BLAME HER FOR NOT REMEM-BERING. IT WAS YEARS AGO.
SO DOES THAT MEAN ***YOU'RE*** ALSO FROM THE LAND OF SNOW, SANDAYU?
THAT'S RIGHT. I SERVED THE PRINCESS'S FATHER, THE FORMER LEADER OF THE CLAN, LORD SOSETSU KAZAHANA.

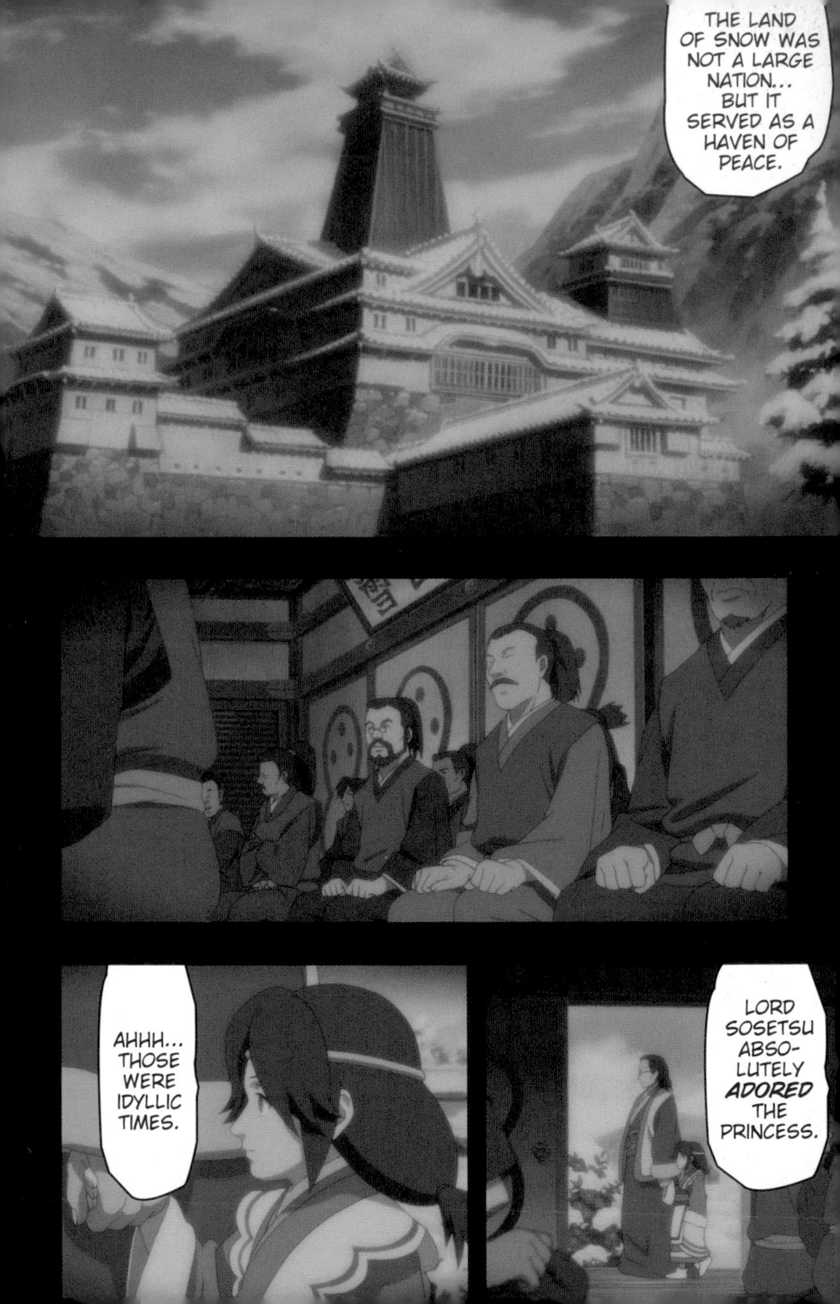
THE LAND OF SNOW WAS NOT A LARGE NATION... BUT IT SERVED AS A HAVEN OF PEACE.
LORD SOSETSU ABSO-LUTELY ***ADORED*** THE PRINCESS.
AHHH... THOSE WERE IDYLLIC TIMES.

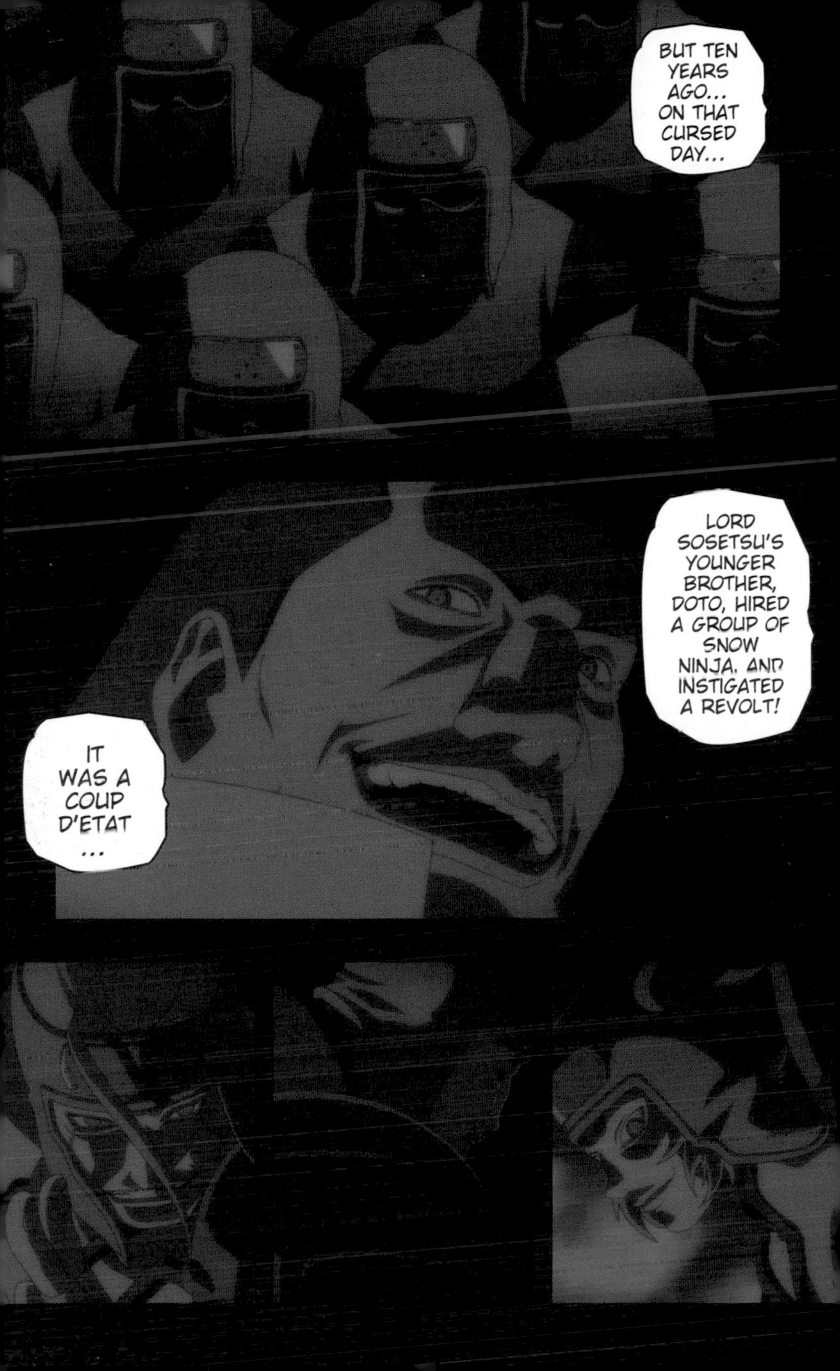
BUT TEN YEARS AGO... ON THAT CURSED DAY...
LORD SOSETSU'S YOUNGER BROTHER, DOTO, HIRED A GROUP OF SNOW NINJA, AND INSTIGATED A REVOLT!
IT WAS A COUP D'ETAT ...

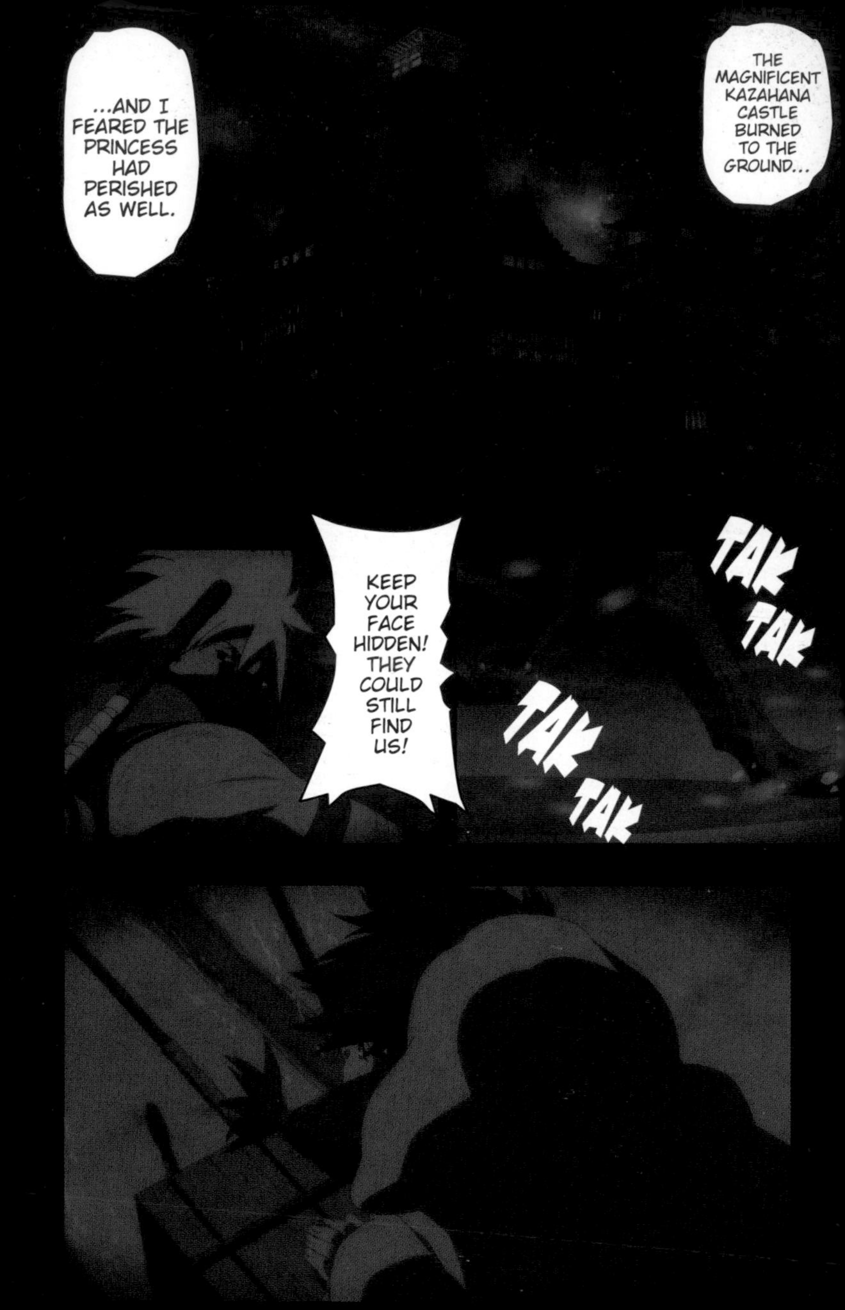
THE MAGNIFICENT KAZAHANA CASTLE BURNED TO THE GROUND...
...AND I FEARED THE PRINCESS HAD PERISHED AS WELL.
TAK TAK
KEEP YOUR FACE HIDDEN! THEY COULD STILL FIND US!
TAK TAK

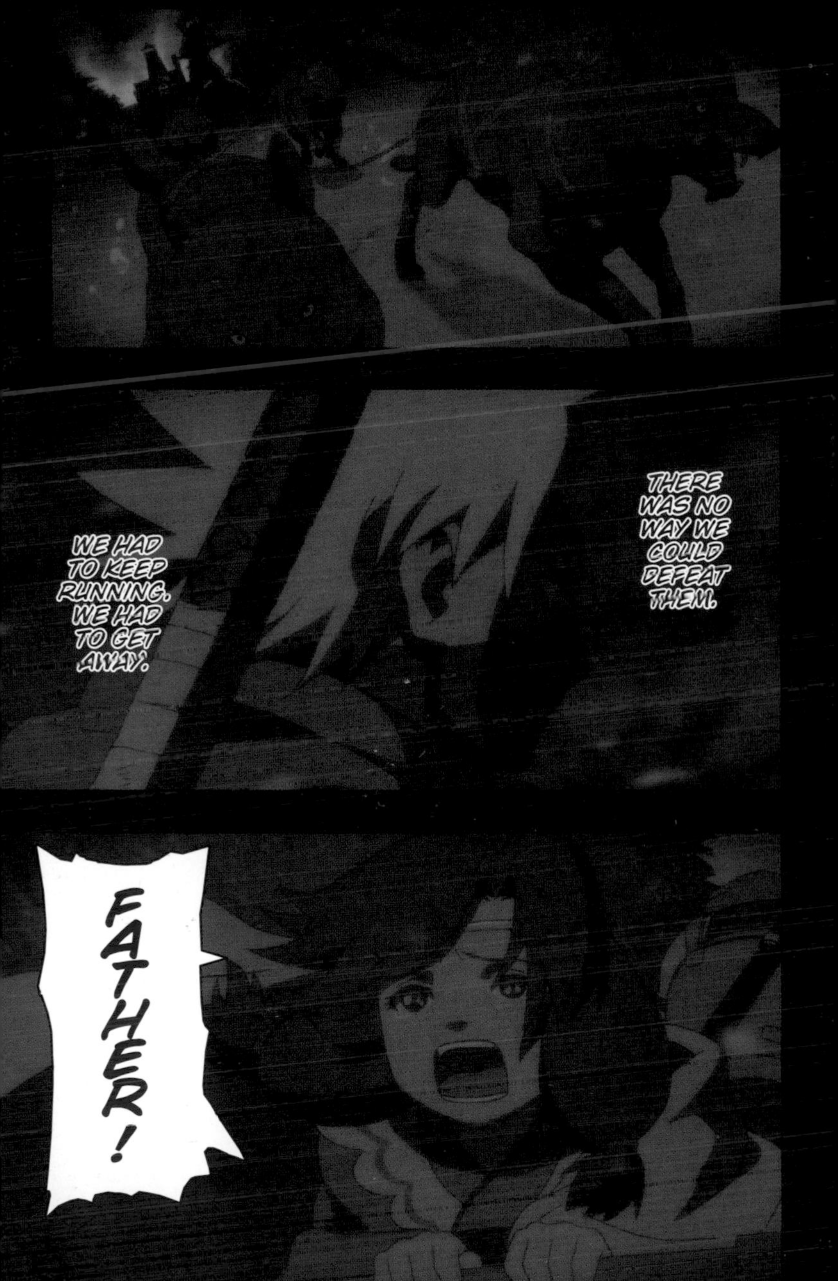
THERE WAS NO WAY WE COULD DEFEAT THEM.
WE HAD TO KEEP RUNNING. WE HAD TO GET AWAY.
FATHER!

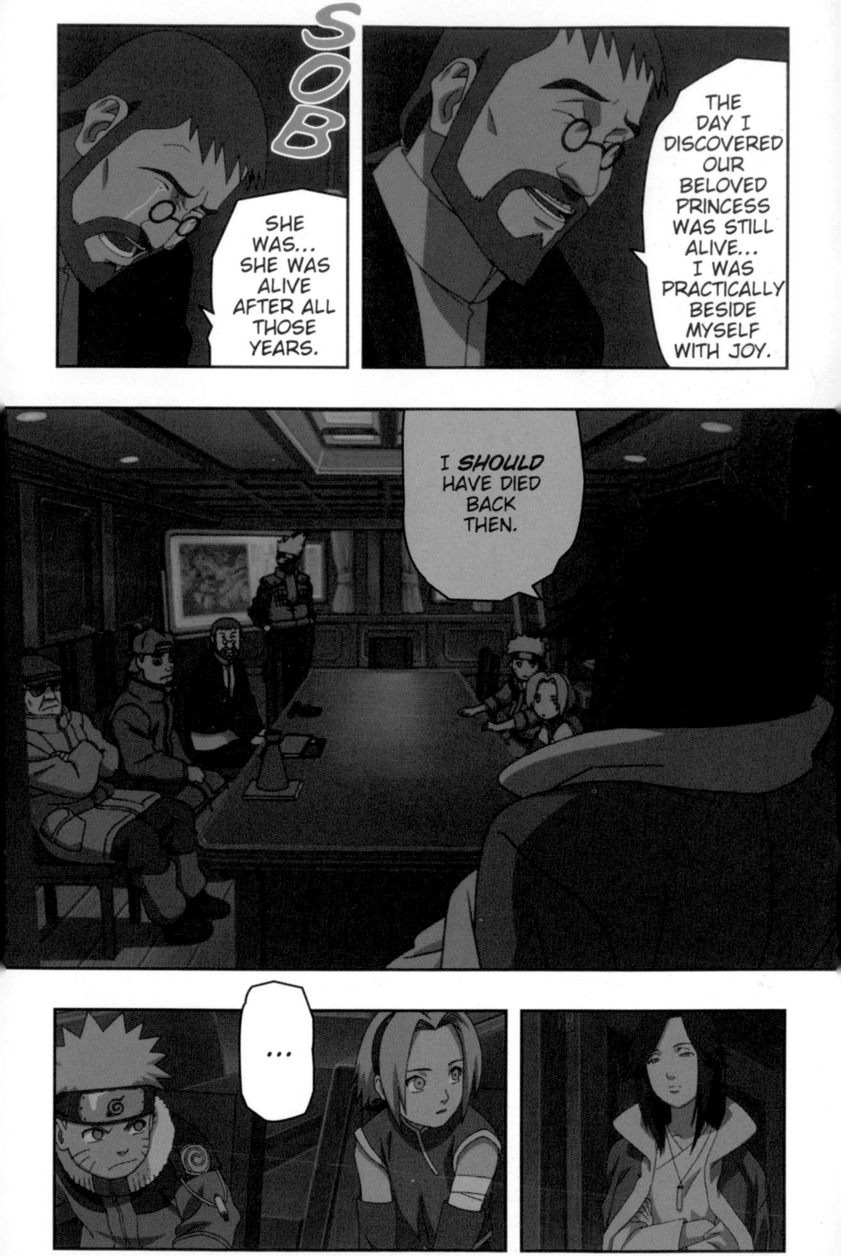
THE DAY I DISCOVERED OUR BELOVED PRINCESS WAS STILL ALIVE... I WAS PRACTICALLY BESIDE MYSELF WITH JOY.
SOB
SHE WAS... SHE WAS ALIVE AFTER ALL THOSE YEARS.
I *SHOULD* HAVE DIED BACK THEN.
...

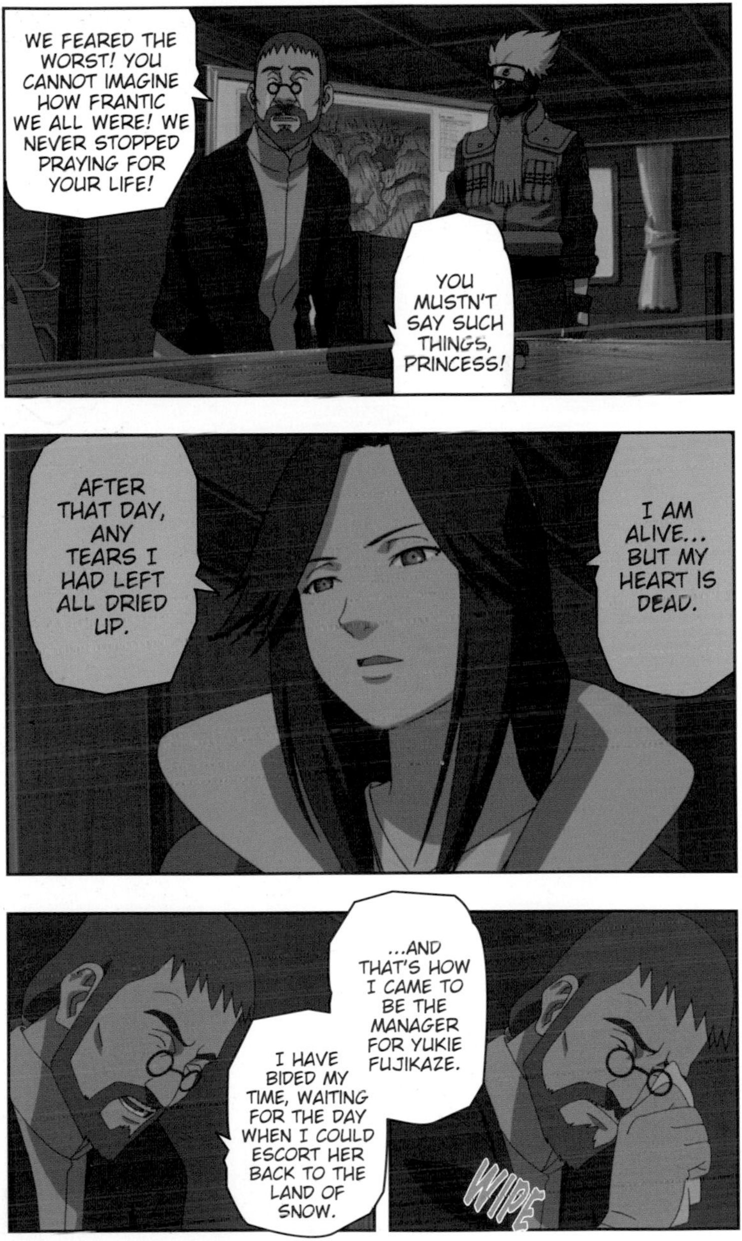
YOU MUSTN'T SAY SUCH THINGS, PRINCESS!
WE FEARED THE WORST! YOU CANNOT IMAGINE HOW FRANTIC WE ALL WERE! WE NEVER STOPPED PRAYING FOR YOUR LIFE!
I AM ALIVE... BUT MY HEART IS DEAD.
AFTER THAT DAY, ANY TEARS I HAD LEFT ALL DRIED UP.
...AND THAT'S HOW I CAME TO BE THE MANAGER FOR YUKIE FUJIKAZE.
I HAVE BIDED MY TIME, WAITING FOR THE DAY WHEN I COULD ESCORT HER BACK TO THE LAND OF SNOW.
WIPE

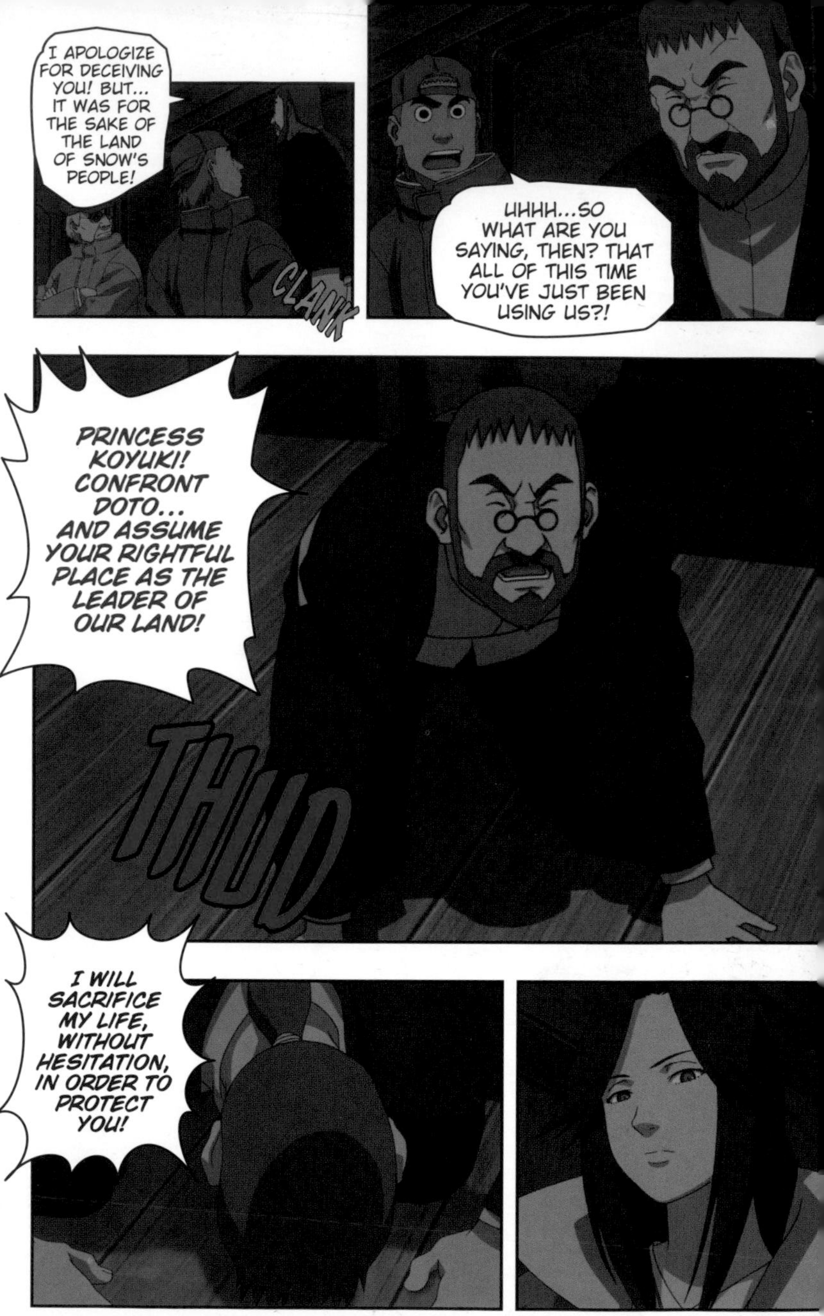
UHHH...SO WHAT ARE YOU SAYING, THEN? THAT ALL OF THIS TIME YOU'VE JUST BEEN USING US?!
I APOLOGIZE FOR DECEIVING YOU! BUT... IT WAS FOR THE SAKE OF THE LAND OF SNOW'S PEOPLE!
CLANK
PRINCESS KOYUKI! CONFRONT DOTO... AND ASSUME YOUR RIGHTFUL PLACE AS THE LEADER OF OUR LAND!
THUD
I WILL SACRIFICE MY LIFE, WITHOUT HESITATION, IN ORDER TO PROTECT YOU!

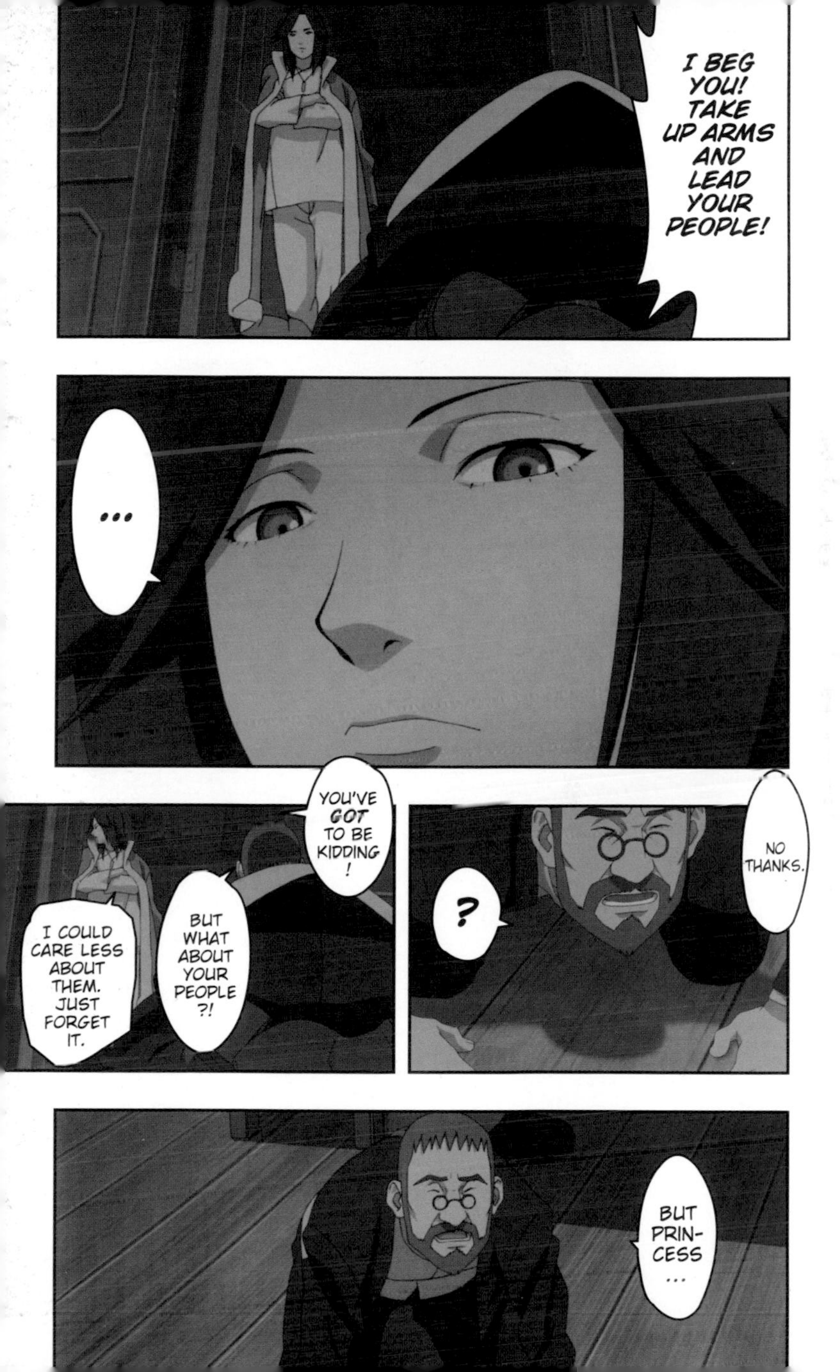
I BEG YOU! TAKE UP ARMS AND LEAD YOUR PEOPLE!
...
NO THANKS.
?
YOU'VE GOT TO BE KIDDING!
BUT WHAT ABOUT YOUR PEOPLE?!
I COULD CARE LESS ABOUT THEM. JUST FORGET IT.
BUT PRINCESS...

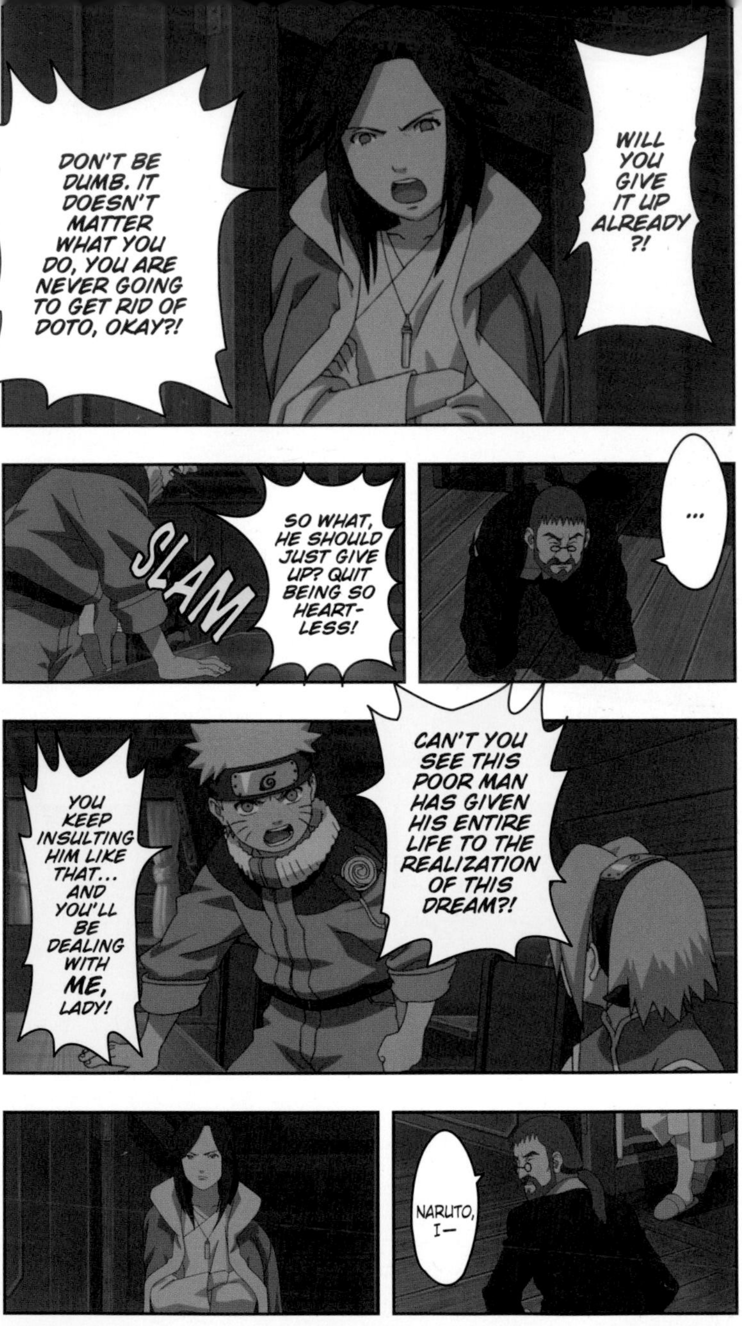
WILL YOU GIVE IT UP ALREADY?!
DON'T BE DUMB. IT DOESN'T MATTER WHAT YOU DO, YOU ARE NEVER GOING TO GET RID OF DOTO, OKAY?!
...
SO WHAT, HE SHOULD JUST GIVE UP? QUIT BEING SO HEART-LESS!
SLAM
CAN'T YOU SEE THIS POOR MAN HAS GIVEN HIS ENTIRE LIFE TO THE REALIZATION OF THIS DREAM?!
YOU KEEP INSULTING HIM LIKE THAT... AND YOU'LL BE DEALING WITH ME, LADY!
NARUTO, I—

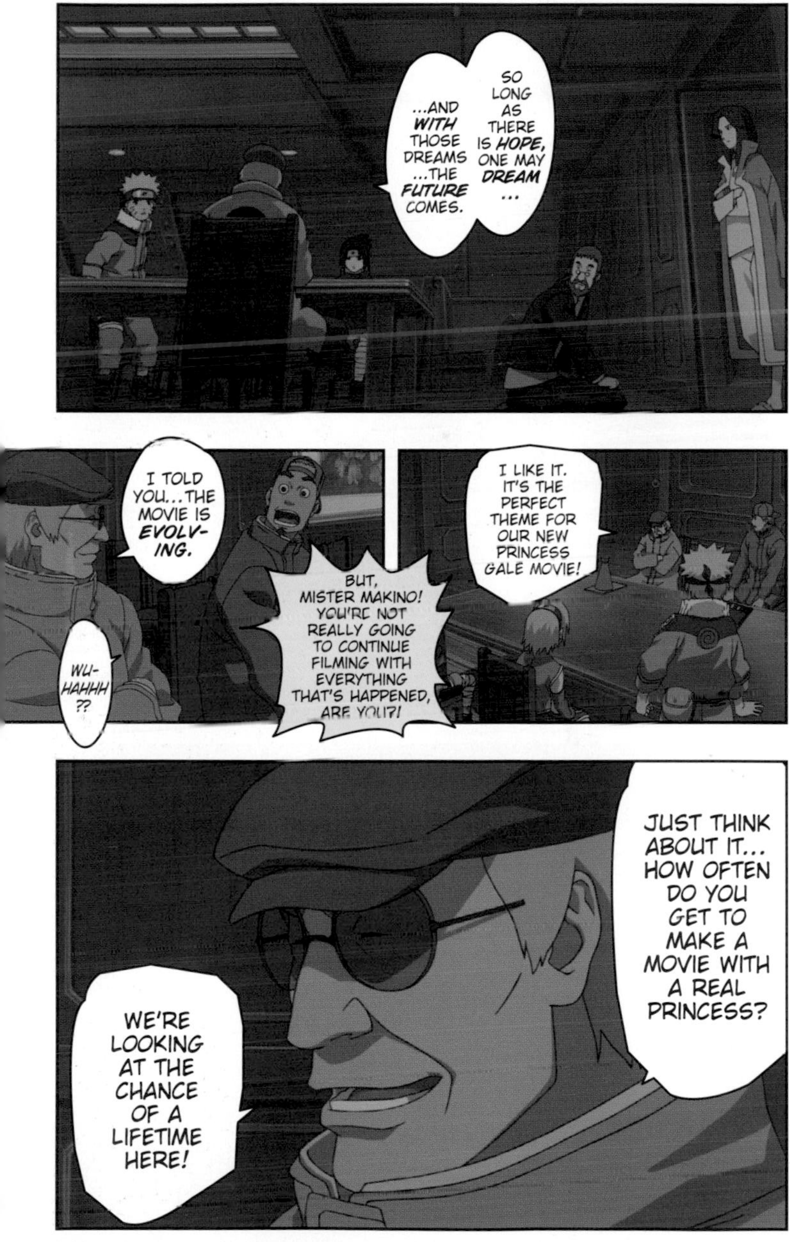
SO LONG AS THERE IS HOPE, ONE MAY DREAM...
...AND WITH THOSE DREAMS ...THE FUTURE COMES.
I LIKE IT. IT'S THE PERFECT THEME FOR OUR NEW PRINCESS GALE MOVIE!
BUT, MISTER MAKINO! YOU'RE NOT REALLY GOING TO CONTINUE FILMING WITH EVERYTHING THAT'S HAPPENED, ARE YOU?!
I TOLD YOU...THE MOVIE IS EVOLVING.
WU-HAHHH??
JUST THINK ABOUT IT... HOW OFTEN DO YOU GET TO MAKE A MOVIE WITH A REAL PRINCESS?
WE'RE LOOKING AT THE CHANCE OF A LIFETIME HERE!

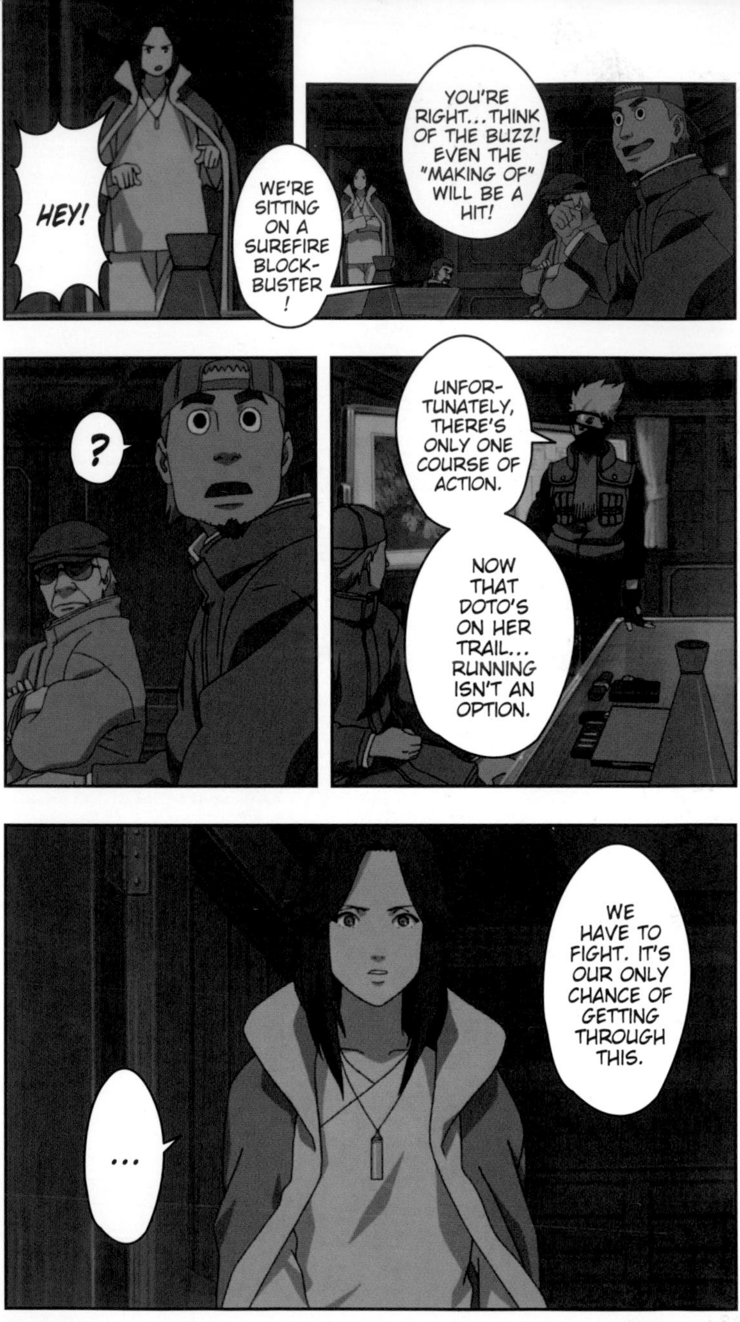
YOU'RE RIGHT...THINK OF THE BUZZ! EVEN THE "MAKING OF" WILL BE A HIT!
WE'RE SITTING ON A SUREFIRE BLOCK-BUSTER!
HEY!
UNFOR-TUNATELY, THERE'S ONLY ONE COURSE OF ACTION.
NOW THAT DOTO'S ON HER TRAIL... RUNNING ISN'T AN OPTION.
?
WE HAVE TO FIGHT. IT'S OUR ONLY CHANCE OF GETTING THROUGH THIS.
...

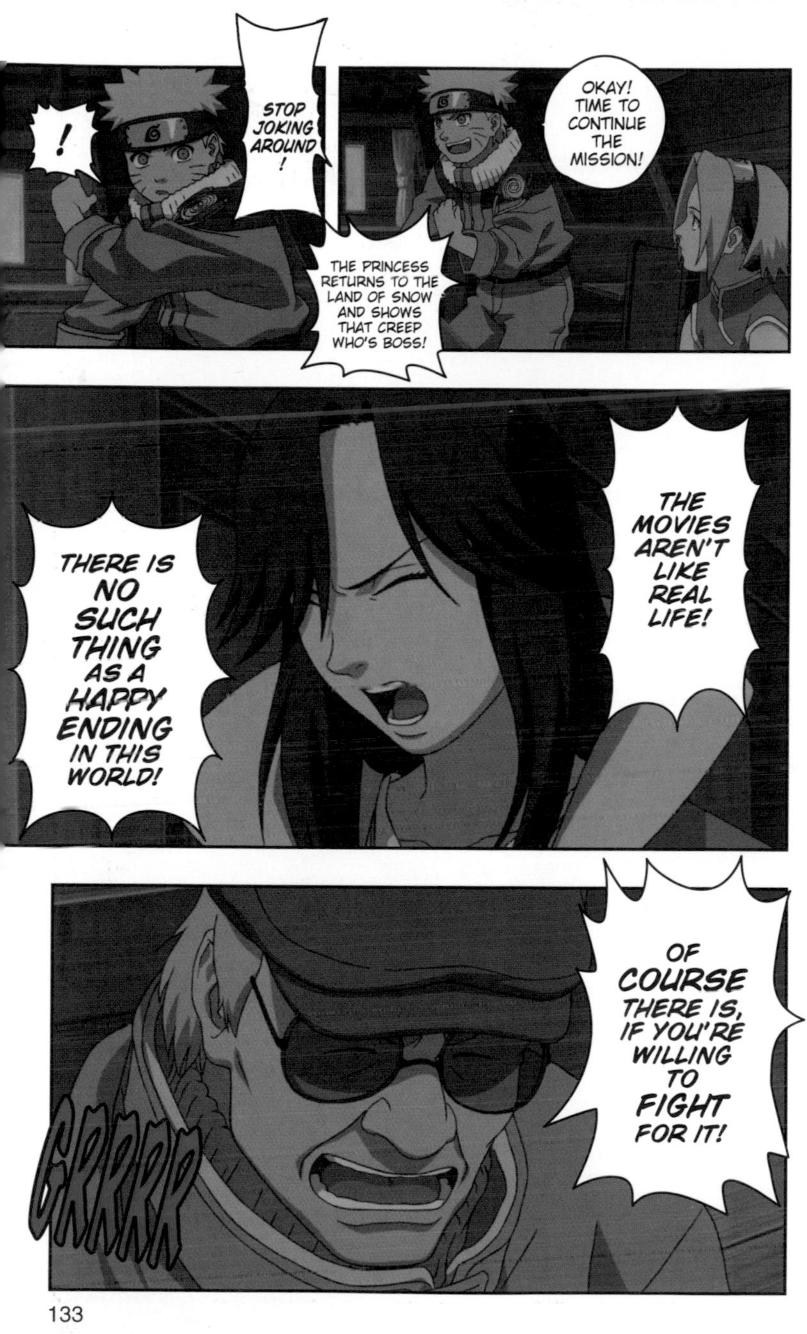
OKAY! TIME TO CONTINUE THE MISSION!
THE PRINCESS RETURNS TO THE LAND OF SNOW AND SHOWS THAT CREEP WHO'S BOSS!
STOP JOKING AROUND!
!
THE MOVIES AREN'T LIKE REAL LIFE!
THERE IS NO SUCH THING AS A HAPPY ENDING IN THIS WORLD!
OF COURSE THERE IS, IF YOU'RE WILLING TO FIGHT FOR IT!
GRRRR

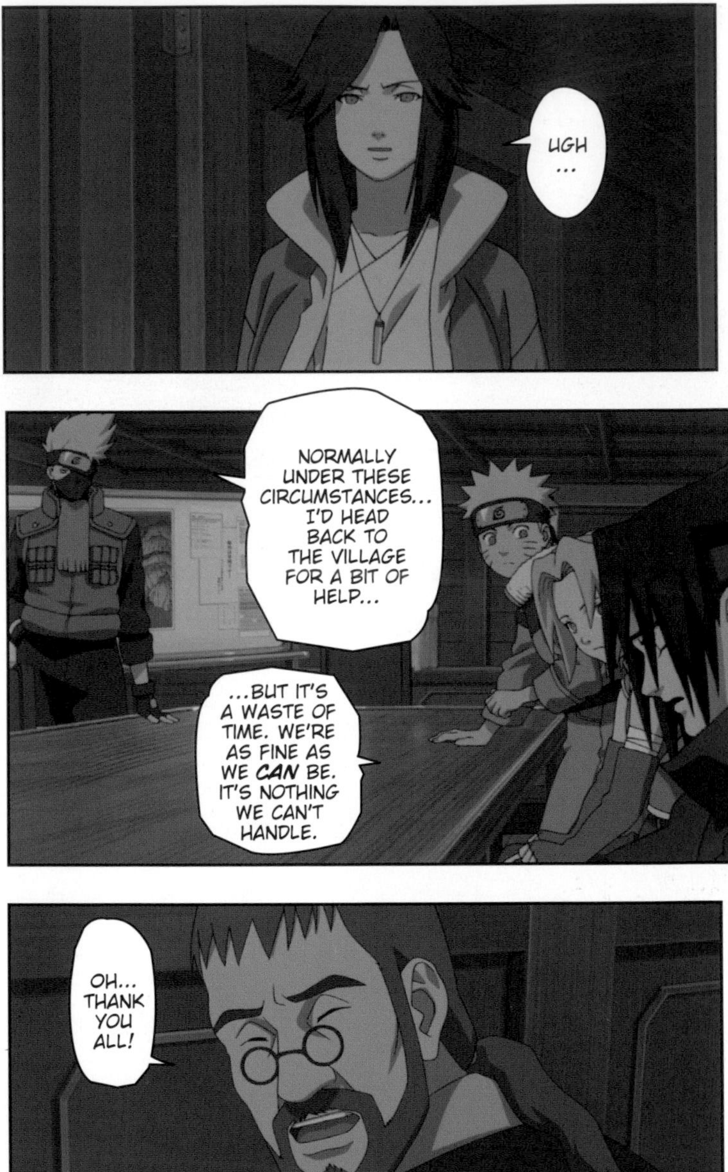
UGH ...
NORMALLY UNDER THESE CIRCUMSTANCES... I'D HEAD BACK TO THE VILLAGE FOR A BIT OF HELP...
...BUT IT'S A WASTE OF TIME. WE'RE AS FINE AS WE CAN BE. IT'S NOTHING WE CAN'T HANDLE.
OH... THANK YOU ALL!

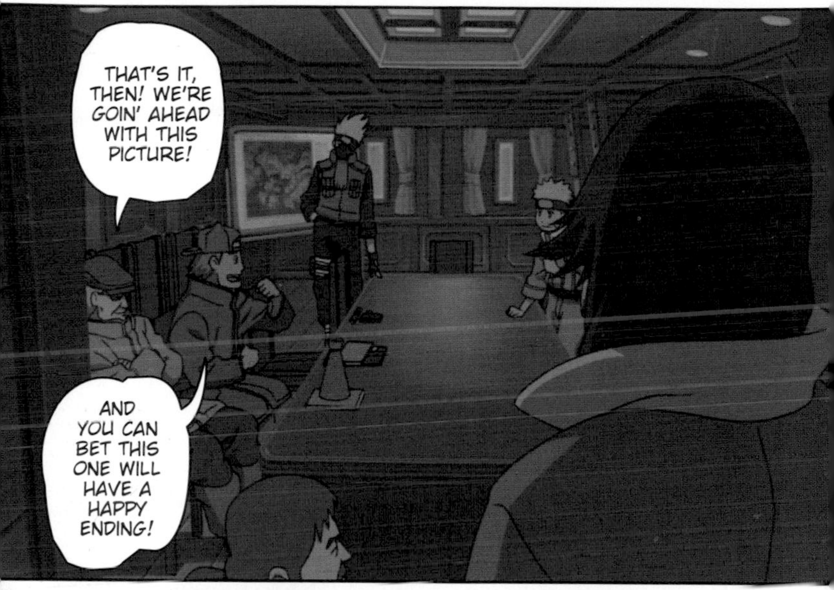
THAT'S IT, THEN! WE'RE GOIN' AHEAD WITH THIS PICTURE!
AND YOU CAN BET THIS ONE WILL HAVE A HAPPY ENDING!

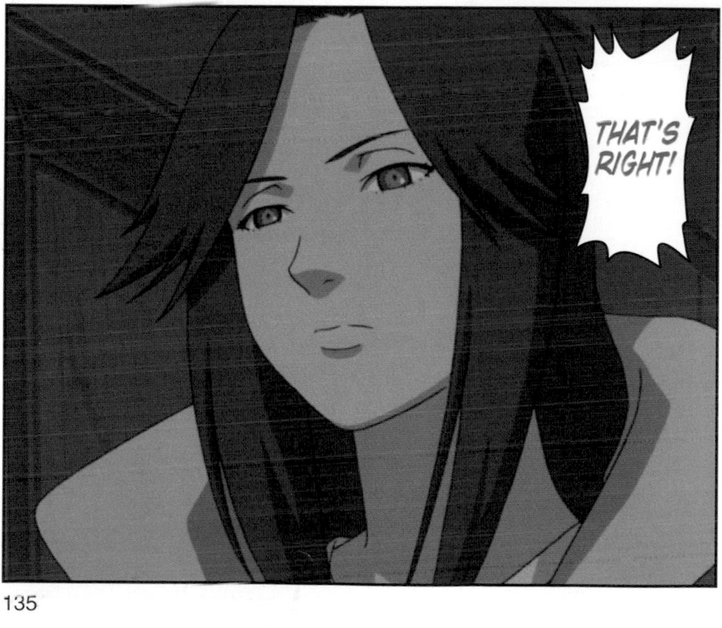
THAT'S RIGHT!

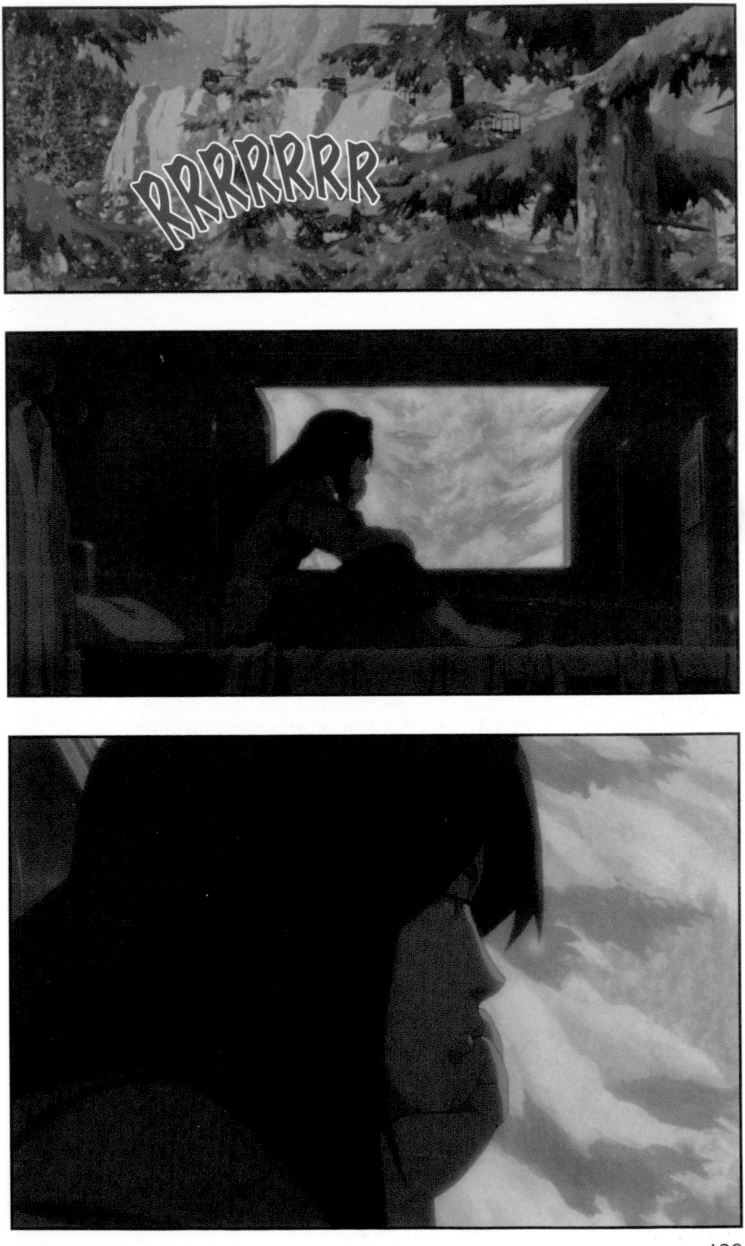
RRRRRRR

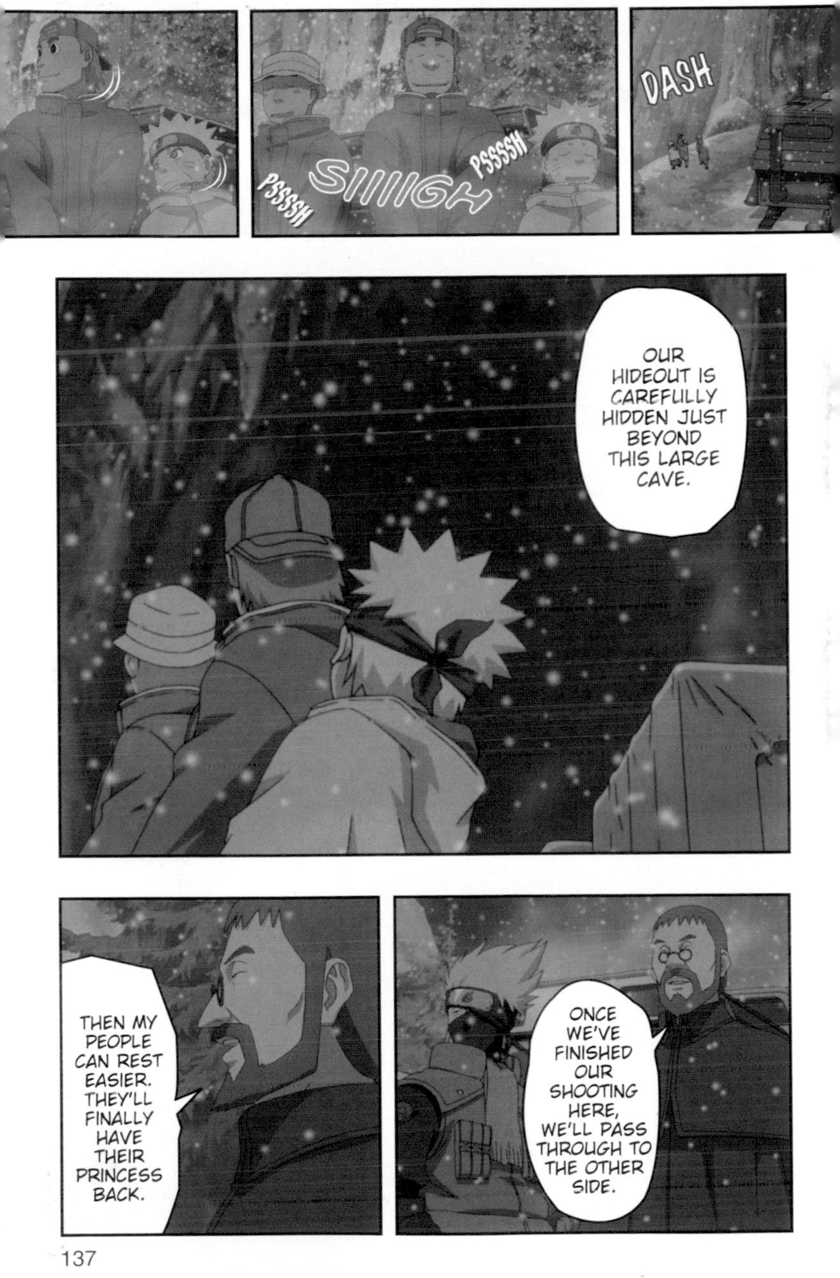
DASH
PSSSSH
SIIIGH
PSSSSH
OUR HIDEOUT IS CAREFULLY HIDDEN JUST BEYOND THIS LARGE CAVE.
ONCE WE'VE FINISHED OUR SHOOTING HERE, WE'LL PASS THROUGH TO THE OTHER SIDE.
THEN MY PEOPLE CAN REST EASIER. THEY'LL FINALLY HAVE THEIR PRINCESS BACK.

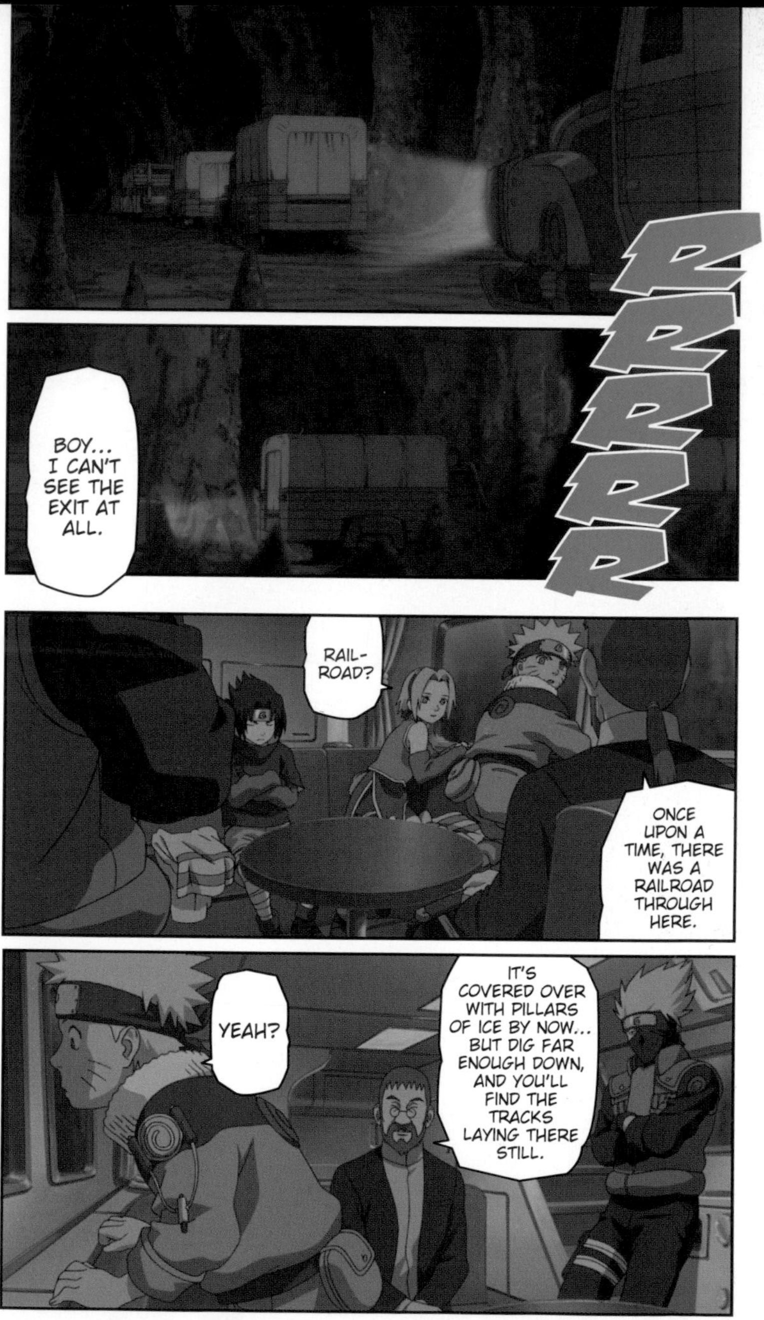
RRRRR
BOY... I CAN'T SEE THE EXIT AT ALL.
ONCE UPON A TIME, THERE WAS A RAILROAD THROUGH HERE.
RAIL-ROAD?
IT'S COVERED OVER WITH PILLARS OF ICE BY NOW... BUT DIG FAR ENOUGH DOWN, AND YOU'LL FIND THE TRACKS LAYING THERE STILL.
YEAH?

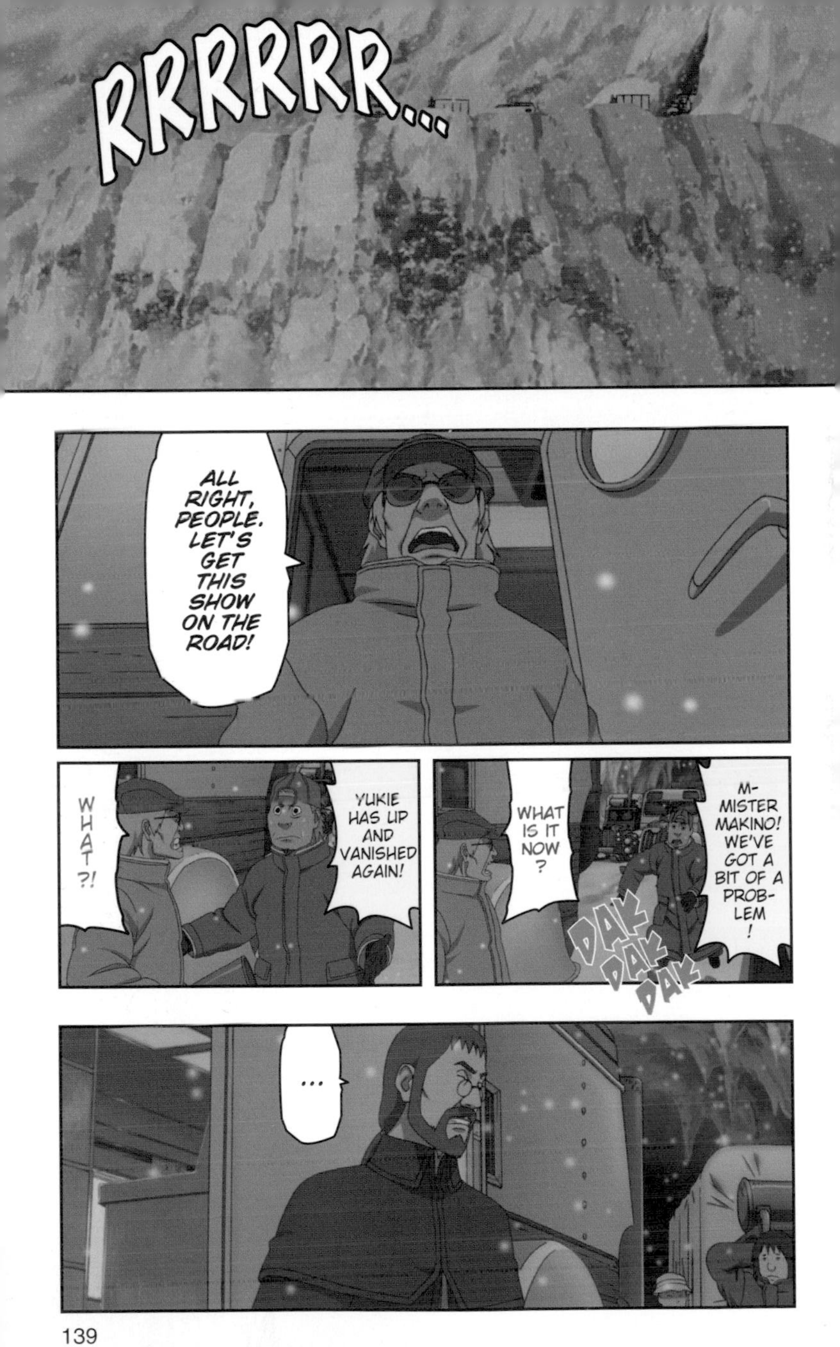
RRRRRR...
ALL RIGHT, PEOPLE. LET'S GET THIS SHOW ON THE ROAD!
M-MISTER MAKINO! WE'VE GOT A BIT OF A PROB-LEM!
WHAT IS IT NOW?
DAK DAK DAK
YUKIE HAS UP AND VANISHED AGAIN!
WHAT?!
...

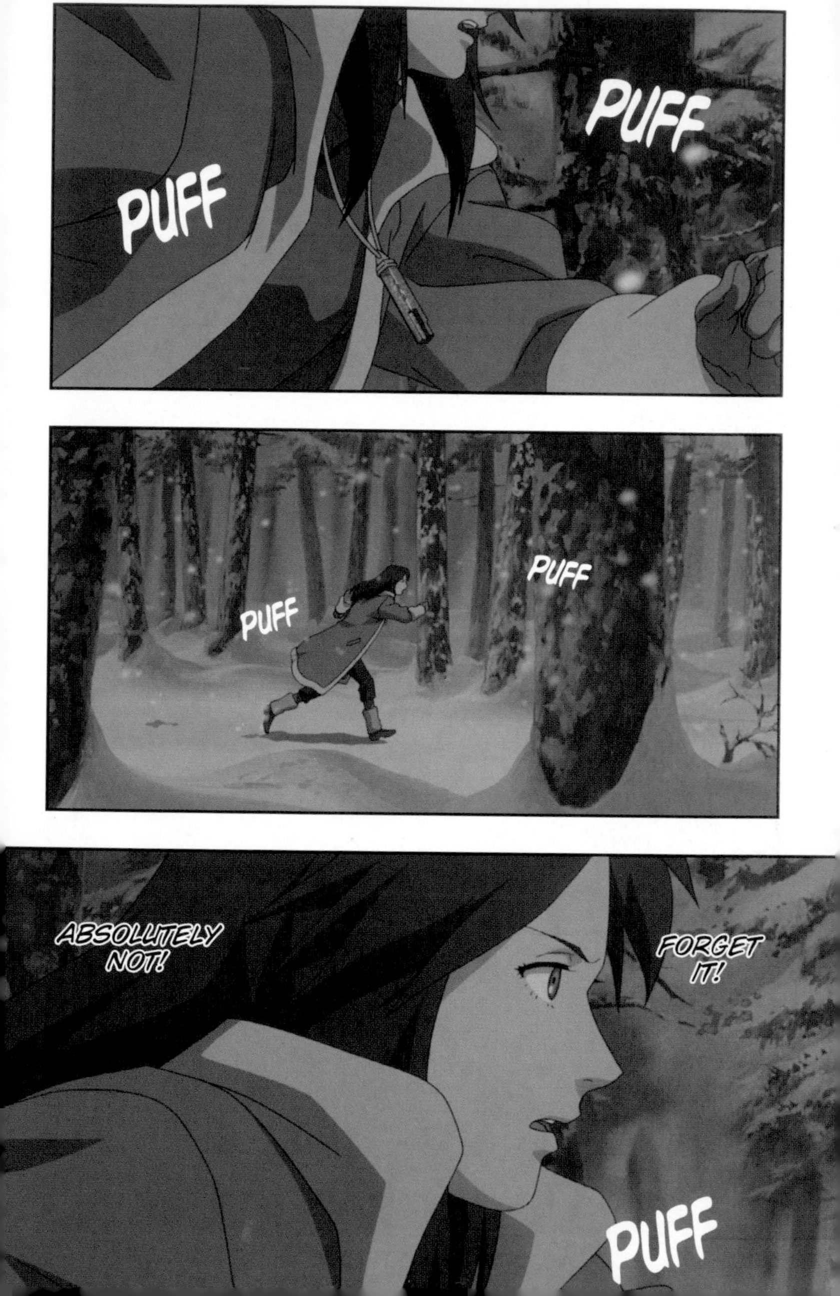
PUFF
PUFF
PUFF
PUFF
FORGET IT!
ABSOLUTELY NOT!
PUFF

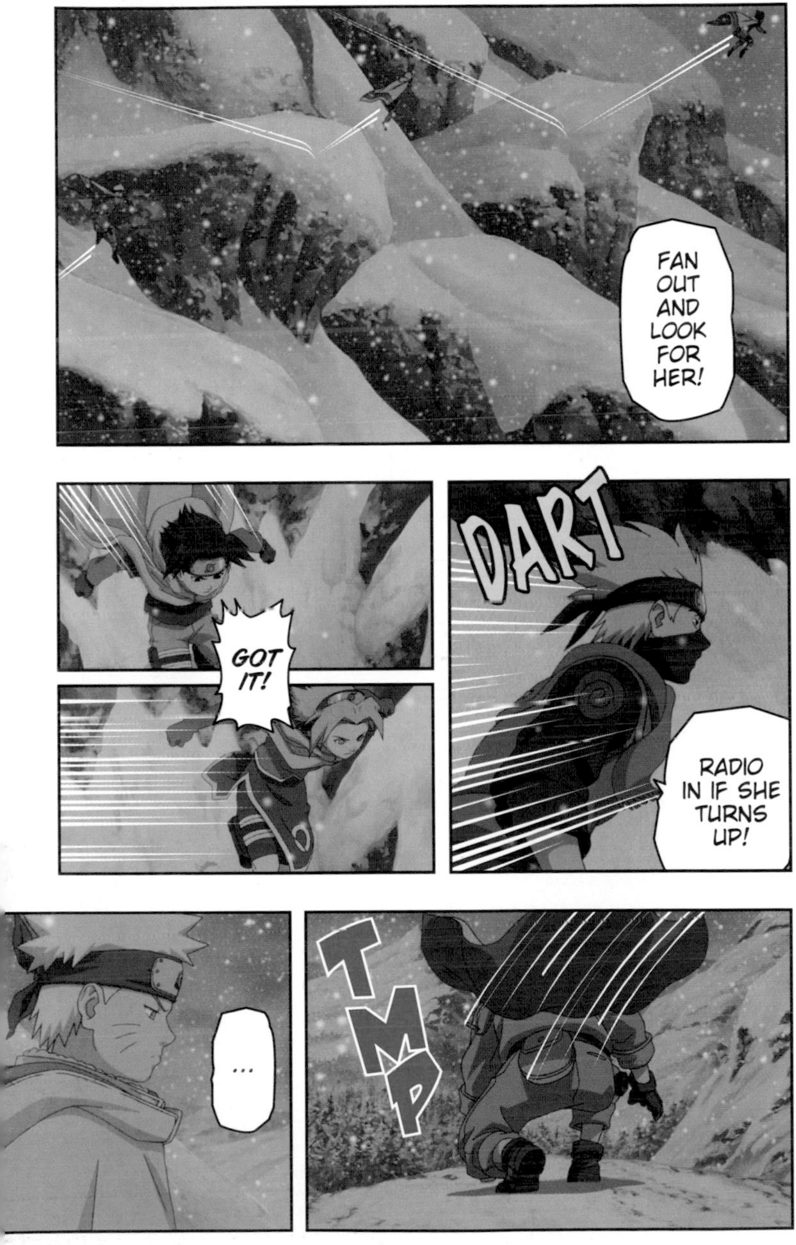
FAN OUT AND LOOK FOR HER!
DART
RADIO IN IF SHE TURNS UP!
GOT IT!
TMP
...

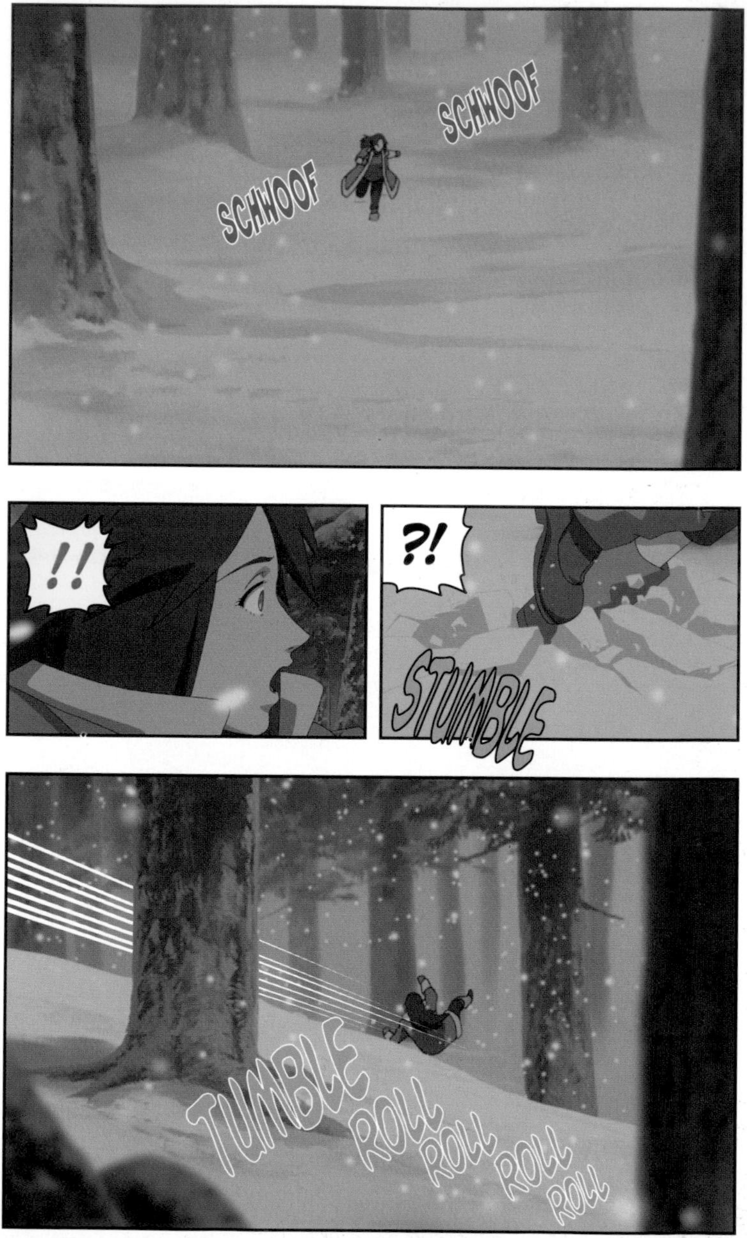
SCHWOOF
SCHWOOF
?!
STUMBLE
!!
TUMBLE
ROLL
ROLL
ROLL
ROLL

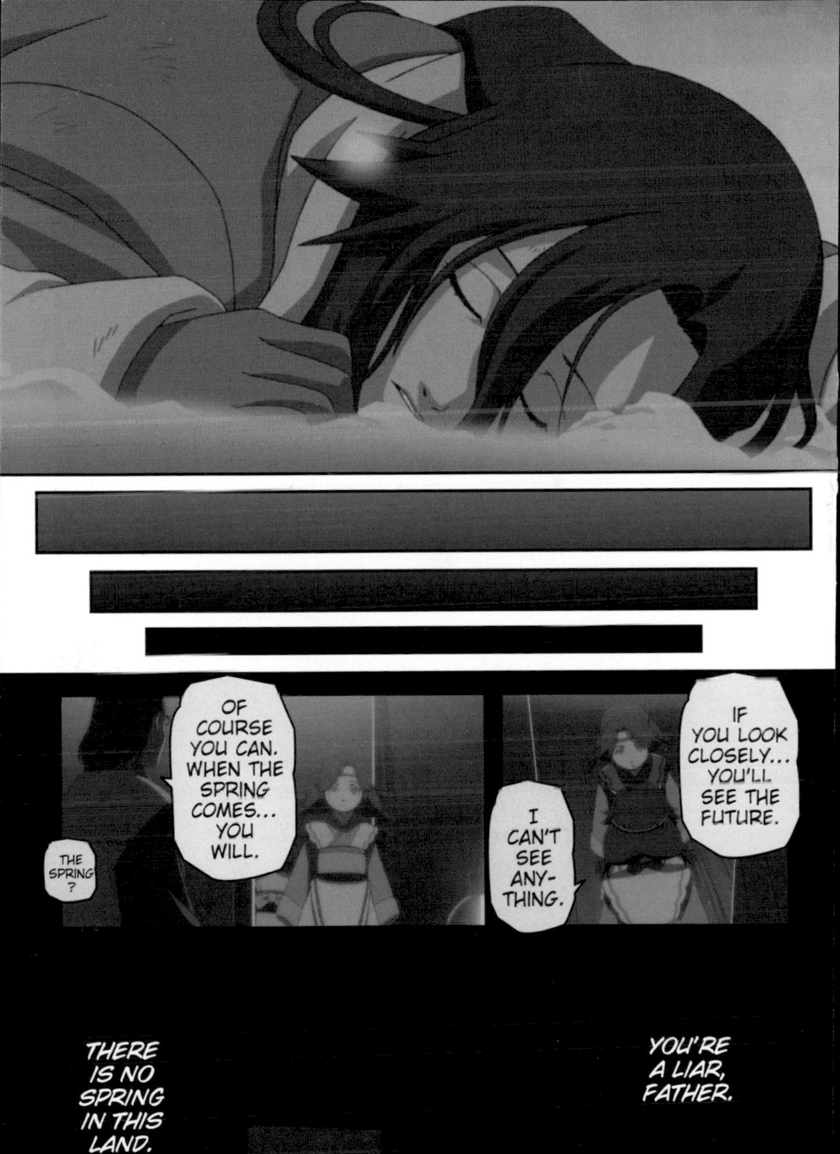
IF YOU LOOK CLOSELY... YOU'LL SEE THE FUTURE.
I CAN'T SEE ANY-THING.
OF COURSE YOU CAN. WHEN THE SPRING COMES... YOU WILL.
THE SPRING?
YOU'RE A LIAR, FATHER.
THERE IS NO SPRING IN THIS LAND.

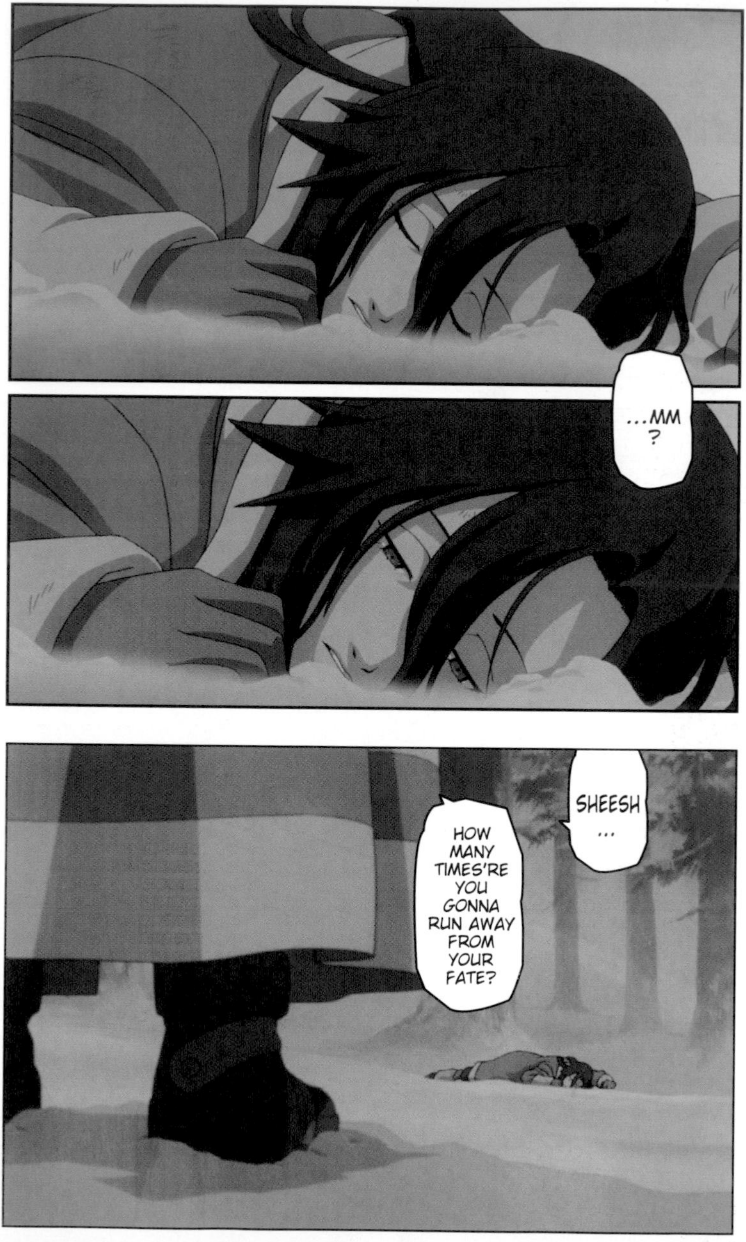
...MM ?
SHEESH ...
HOW MANY TIMES'RE YOU GONNA RUN AWAY FROM YOUR FATE?

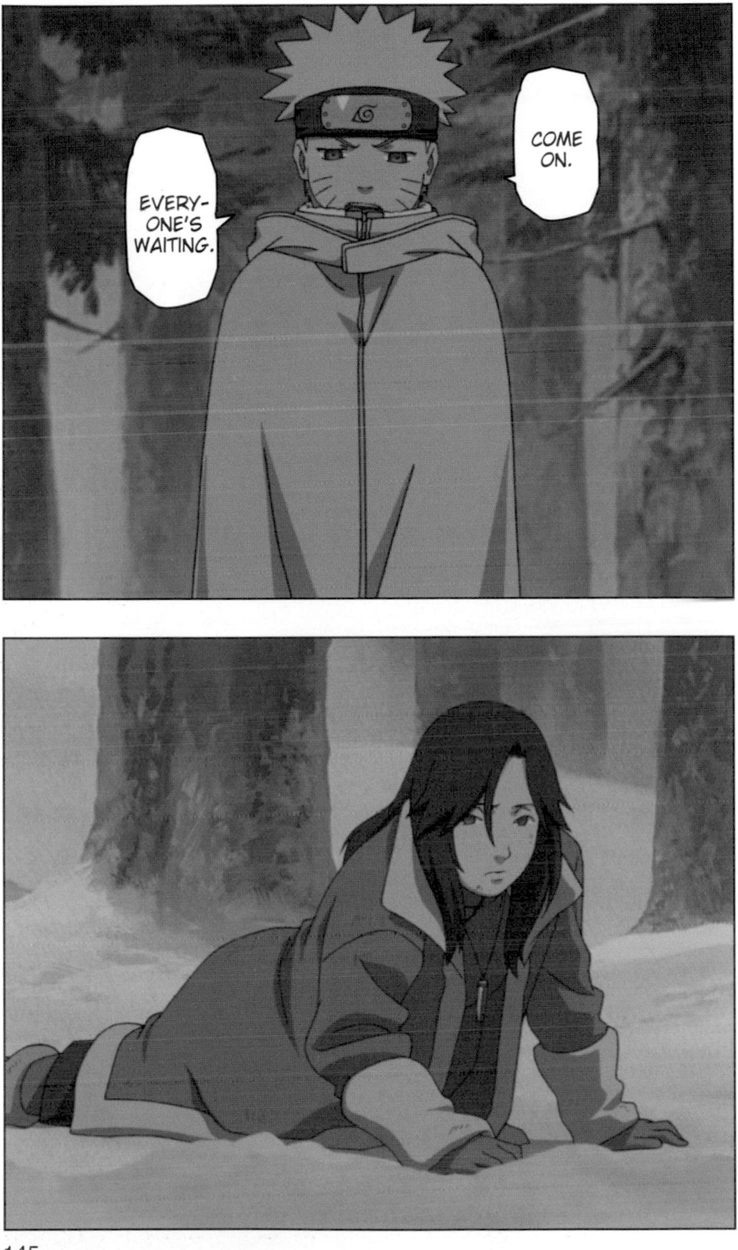
COME ON.
EVERY-ONE'S WAITING.

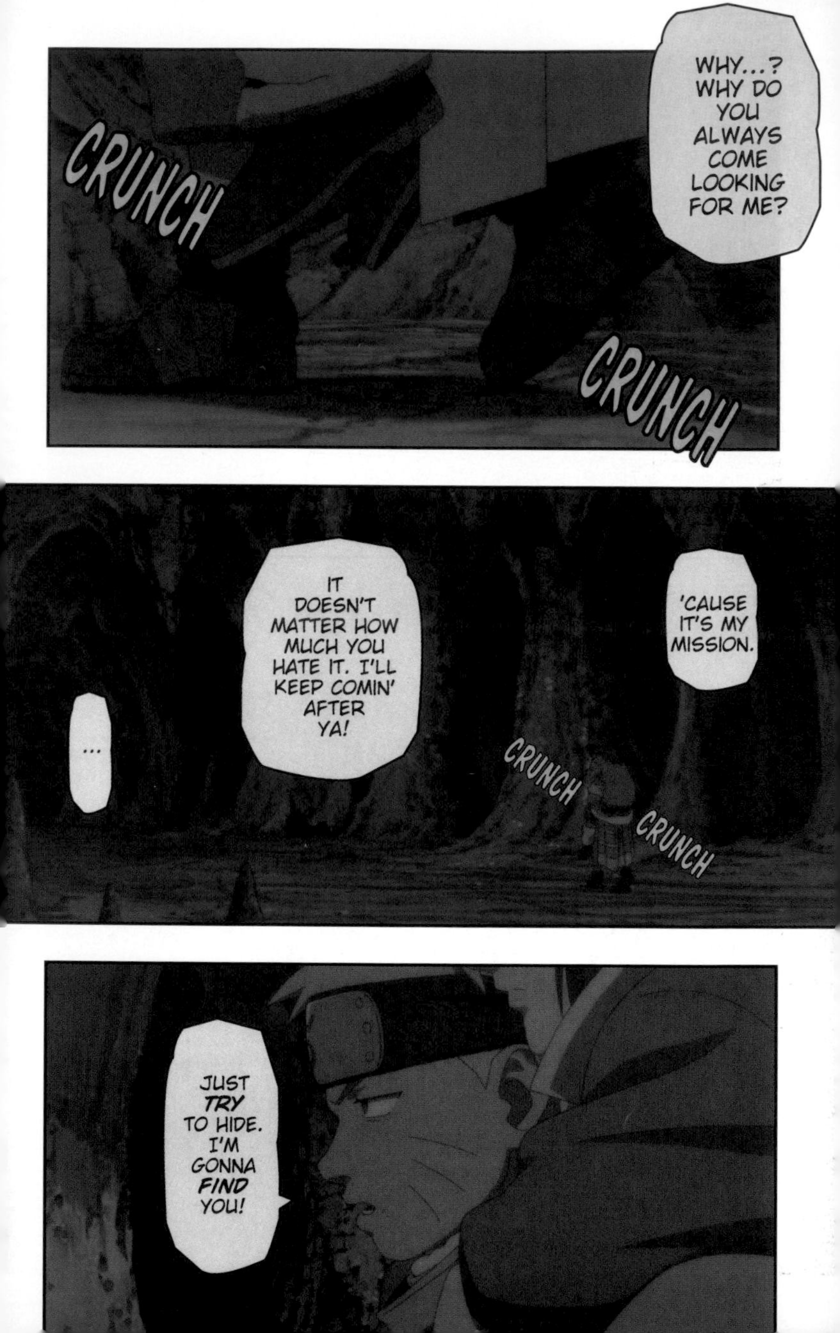
WHY...? WHY DO YOU ALWAYS COME LOOKING FOR ME?
CRUNCH
CRUNCH
'CAUSE IT'S MY MISSION.
IT DOESN'T MATTER HOW MUCH YOU HATE IT. I'LL KEEP COMIN' AFTER YA!
CRUNCH
CRUNCH
...
JUST *TRY* TO HIDE. I'M GONNA *FIND* YOU!

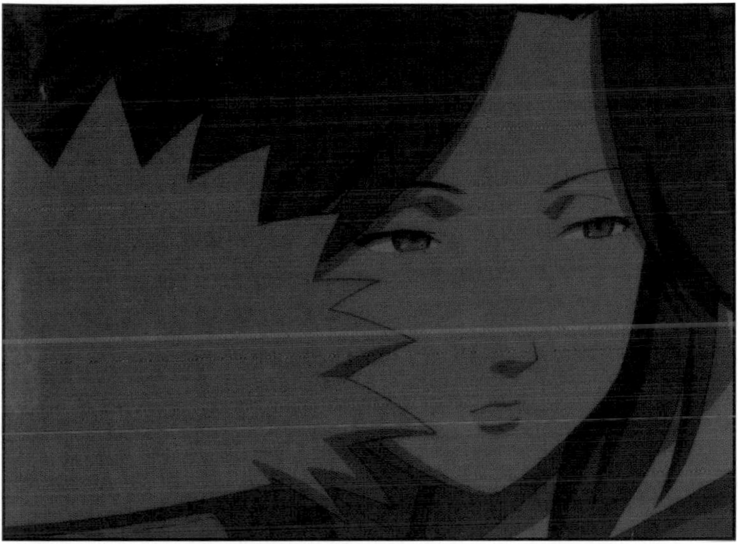

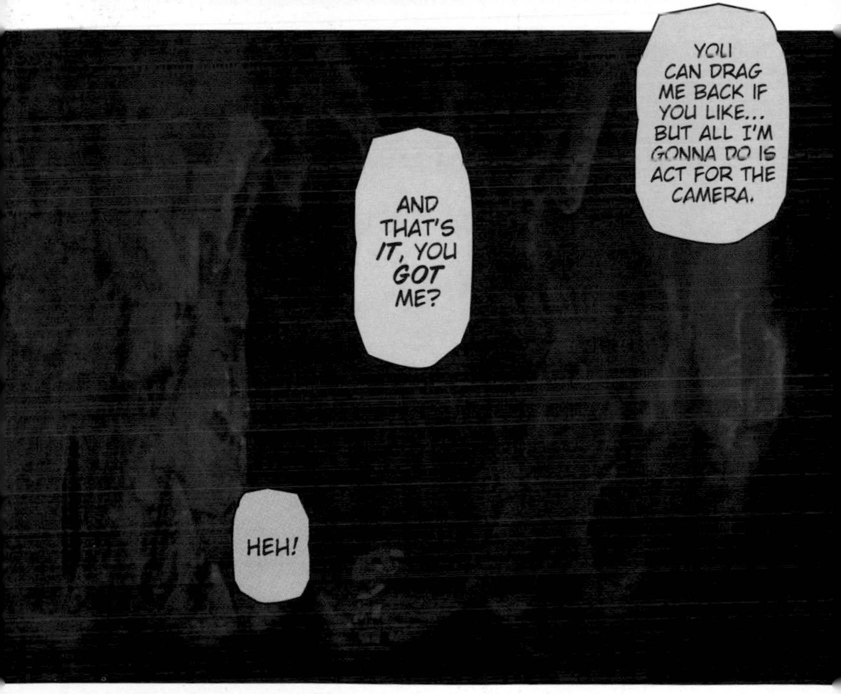
YOU CAN DRAG ME BACK IF YOU LIKE... BUT ALL I'M GONNA DO IS ACT FOR THE CAMERA.
AND THAT'S *IT*, YOU ***GOT*** ME?
HEH!

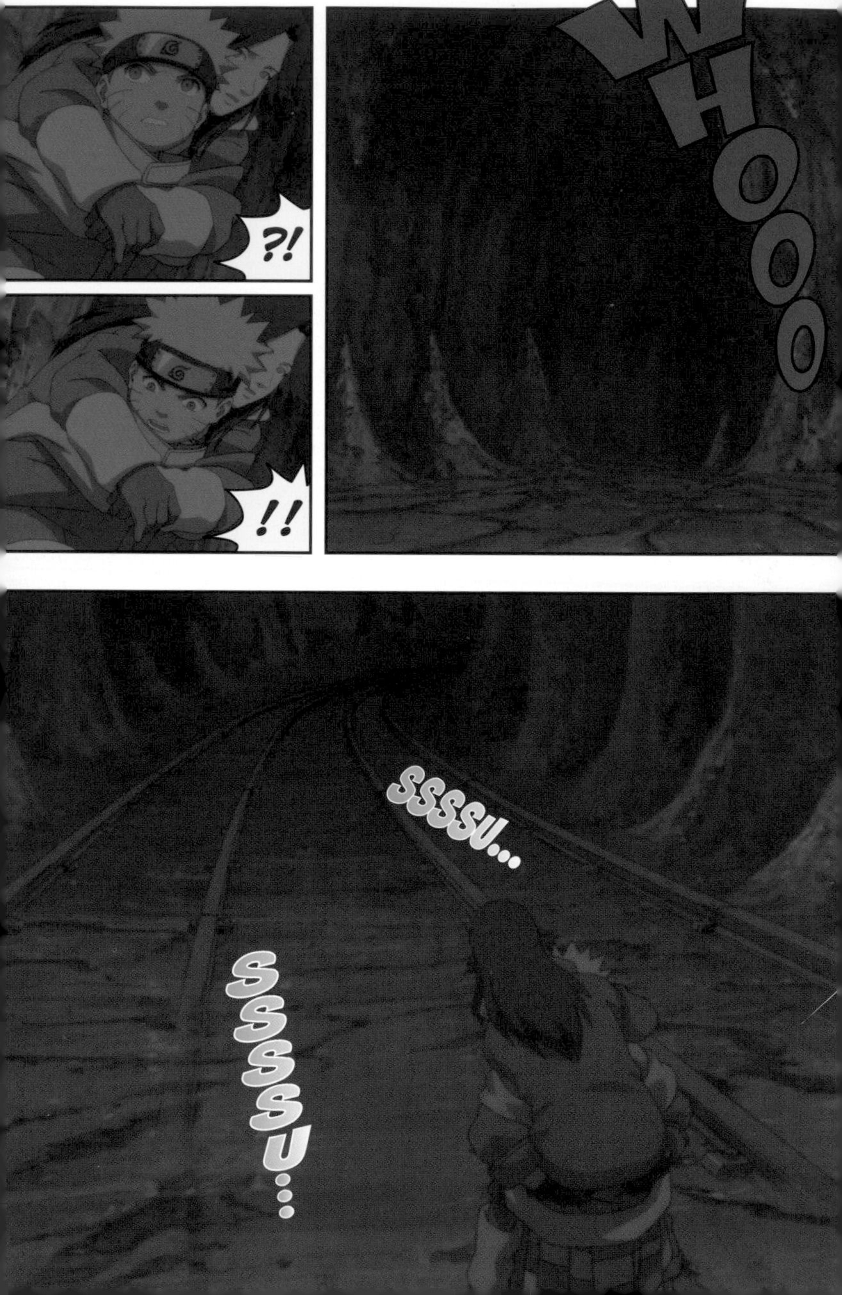
WHOOOO
?!
!!
SSSSU...
SSSSU...

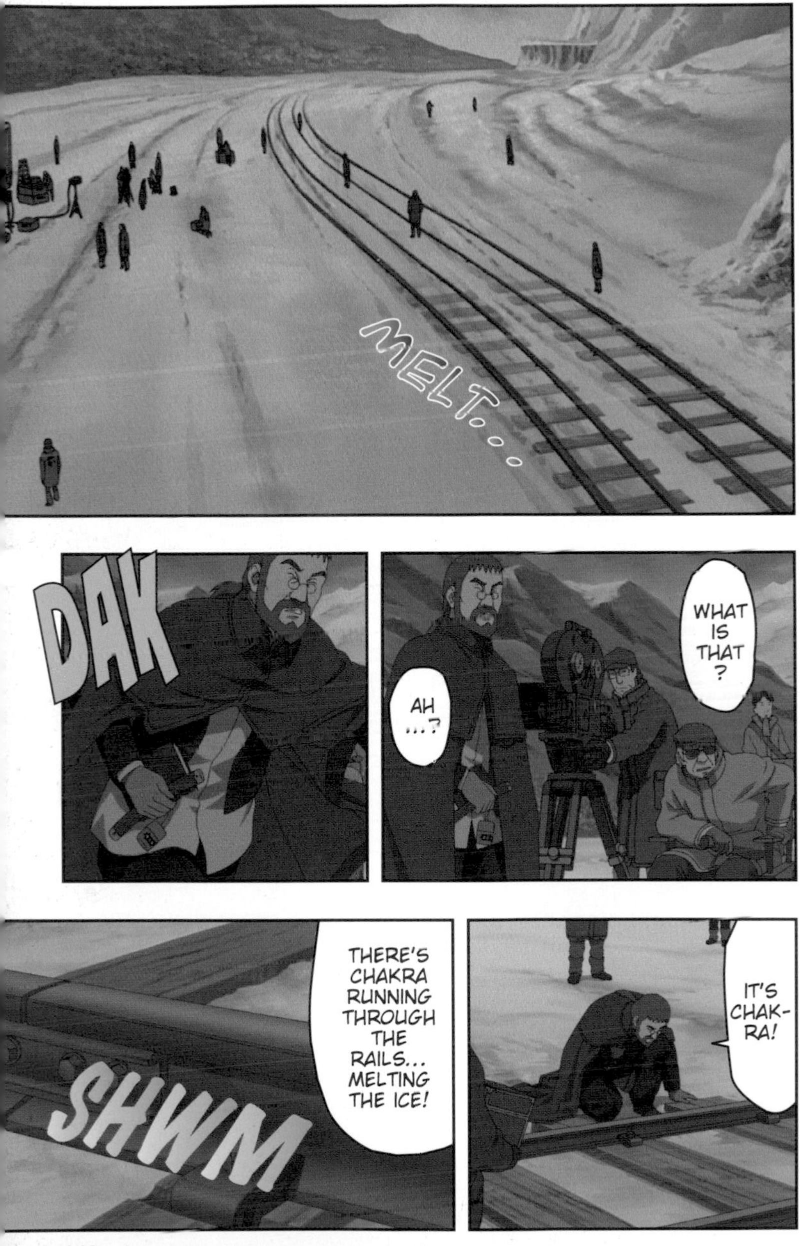
MELT...
WHAT IS THAT?
AH...?
DAK
IT'S CHAK-RA!
THERE'S CHAKRA RUNNING THROUGH THE RAILS... MELTING THE ICE!
SHWM

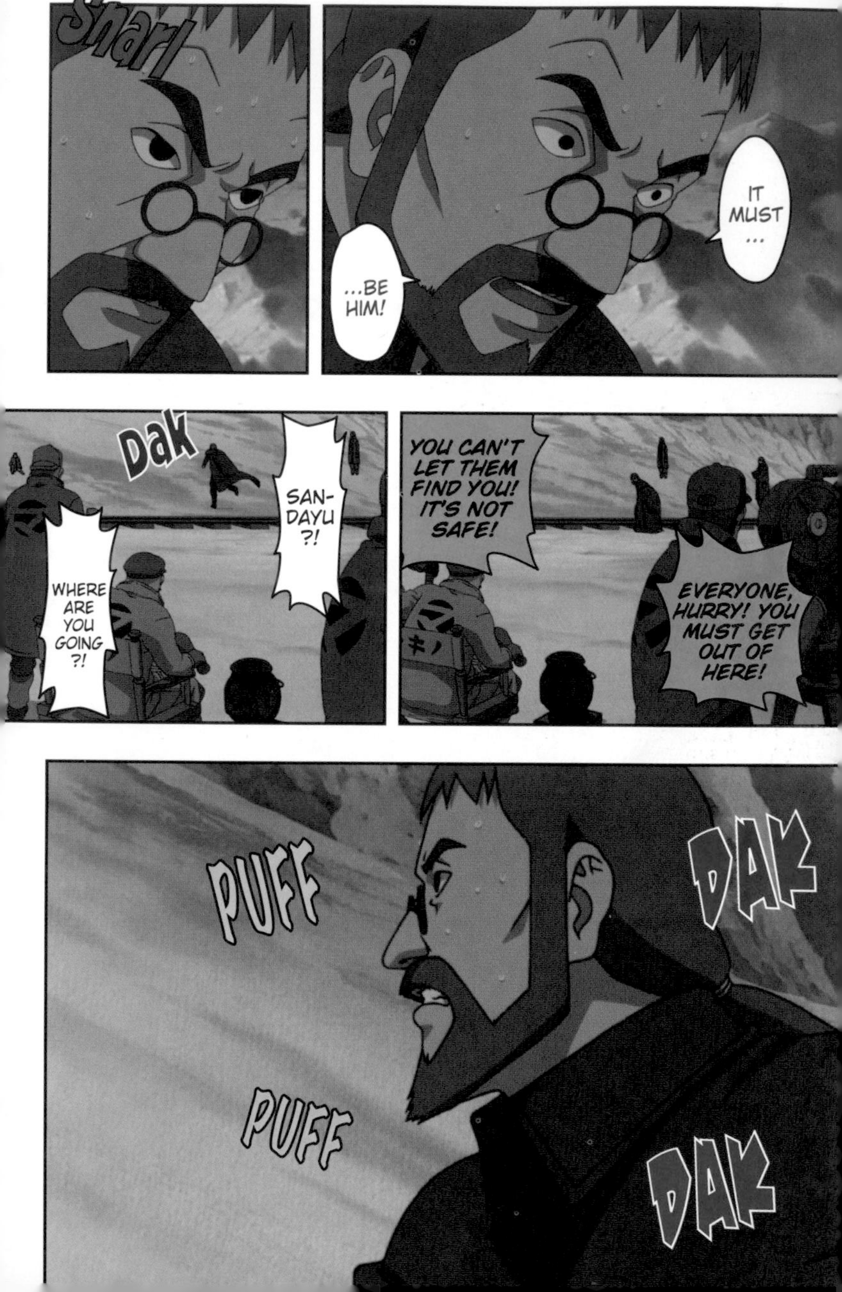
IT MUST ...
...BE HIM!
Snarl
YOU CAN'T LET THEM FIND YOU! IT'S NOT SAFE!
EVERYONE, HURRY! YOU MUST GET OUT OF HERE!
SAN-DAYU ?!
Dak
WHERE ARE YOU GOING ?!
DAK
PUFF
PUFF
DAK

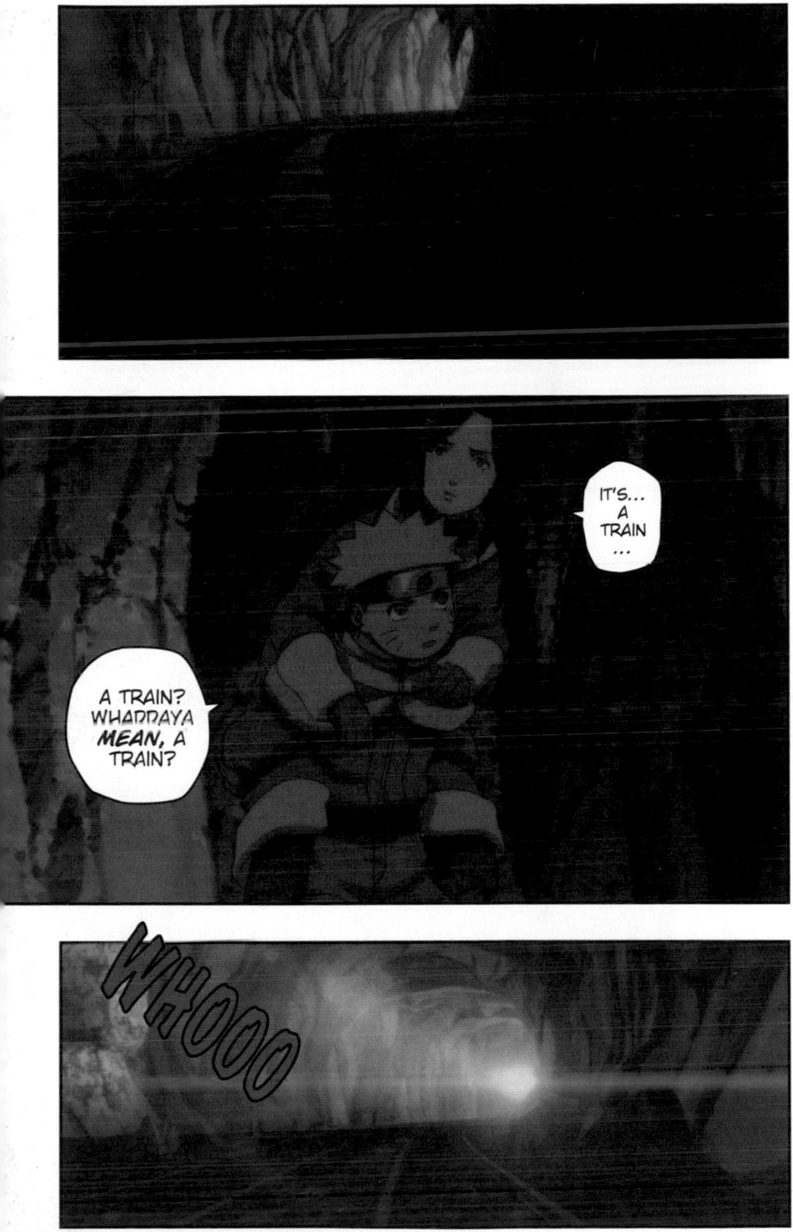
IT'S... A TRAIN ...
A TRAIN? WHADDAYA MEAN, A TRAIN?
WHOOO

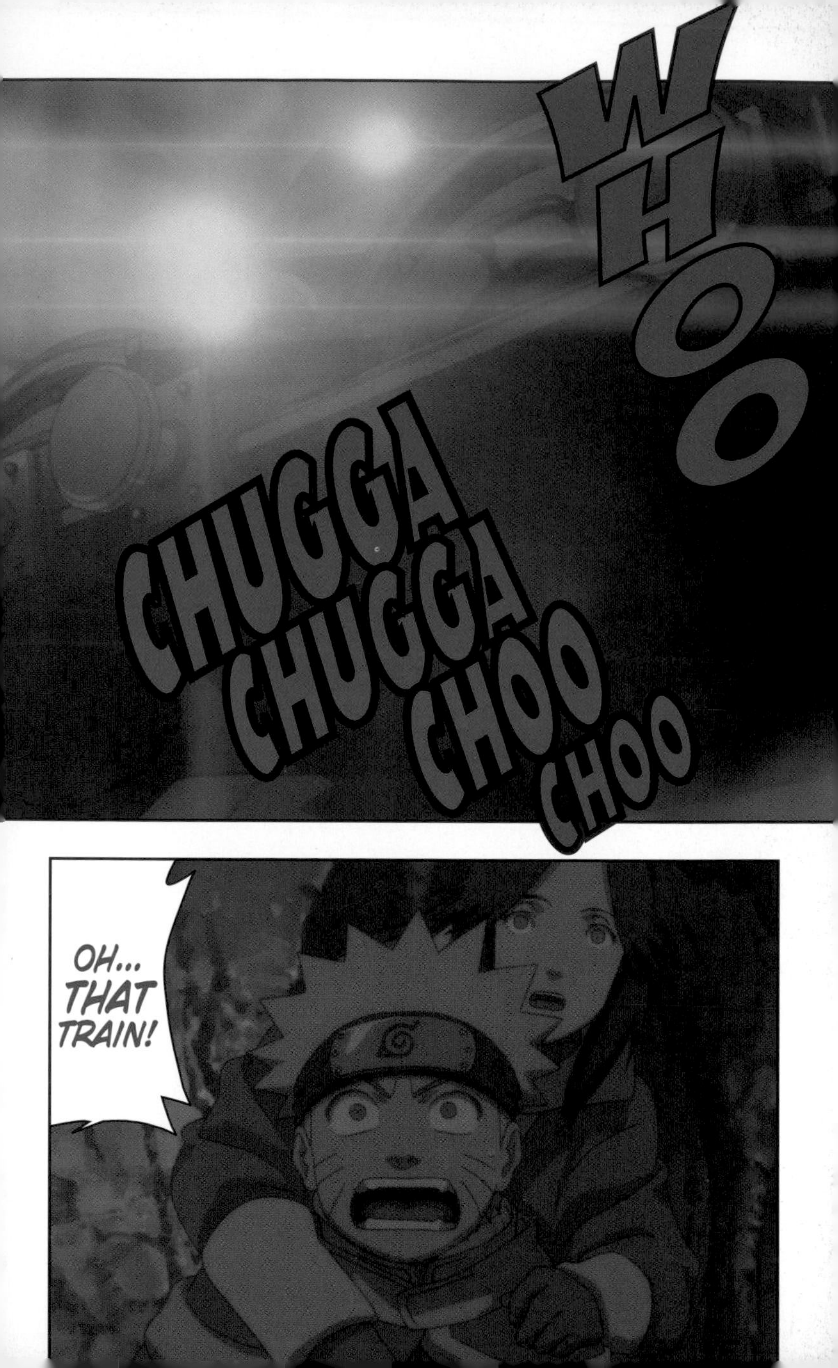
WHOO
CHUGGA CHUGGA CHOO CHOO
OH... THAT TRAIN!

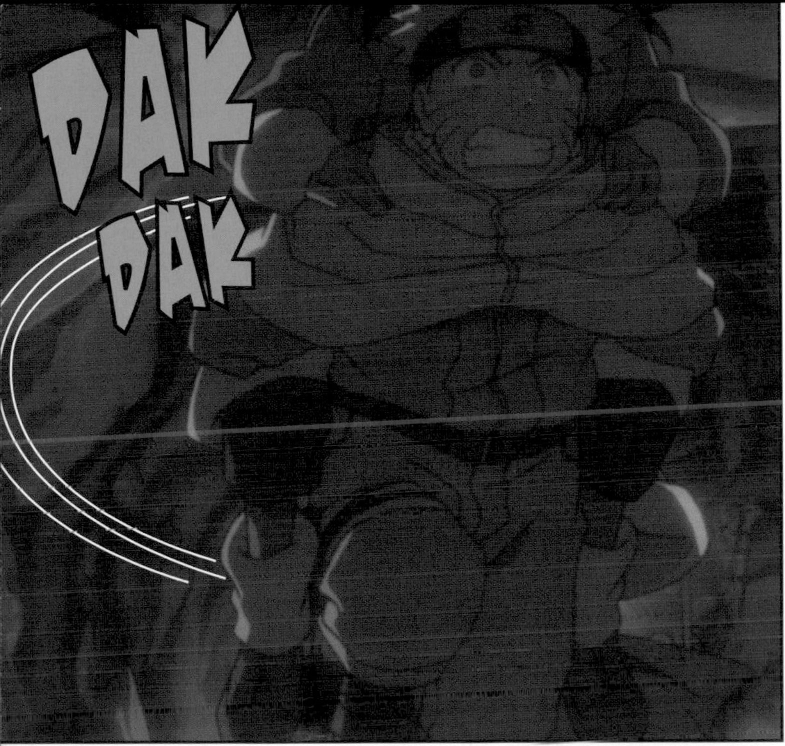
DAK
DAK
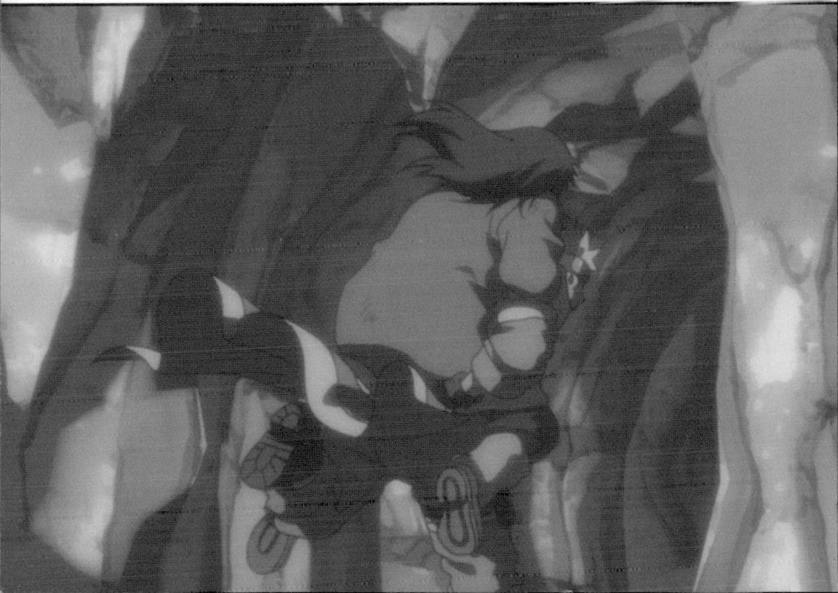

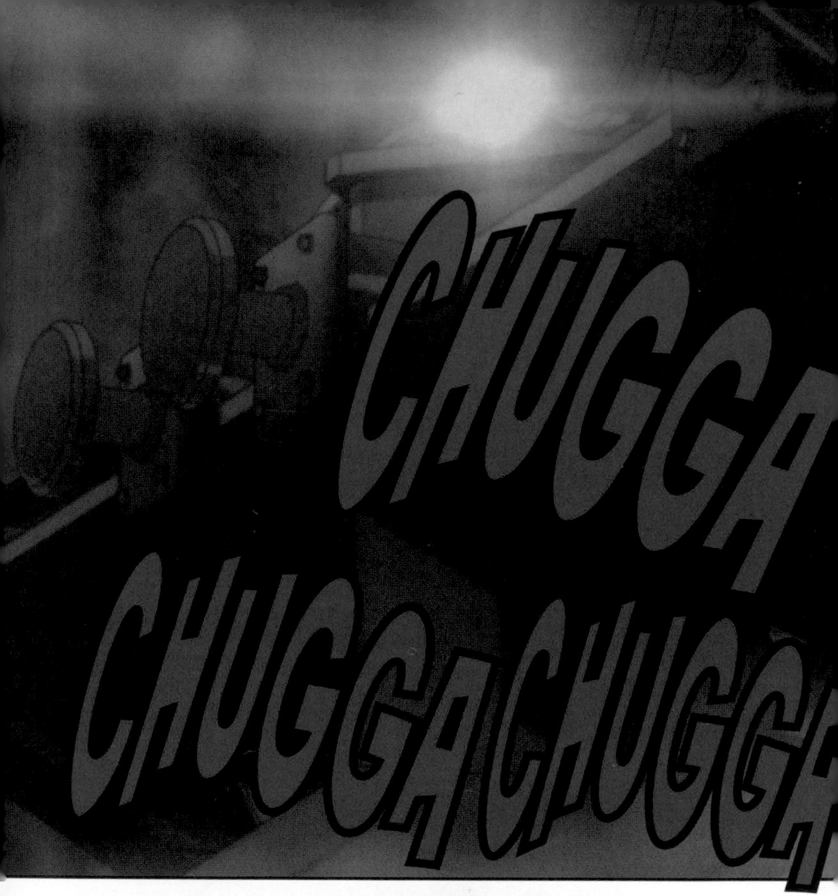
CHUGGA
CHUGGA CHUGGA

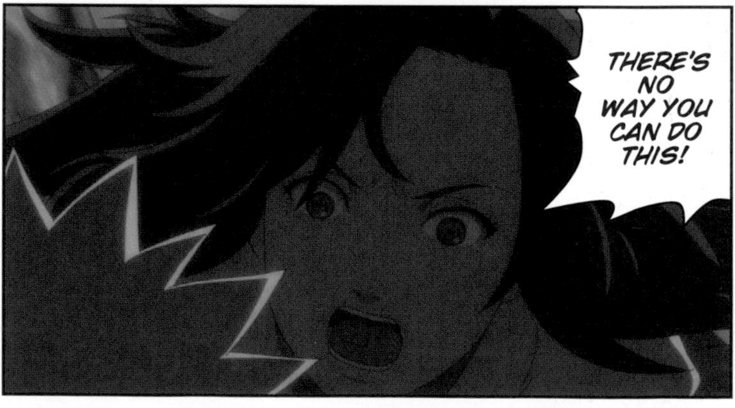
THERE'S NO WAY YOU CAN DO THIS!

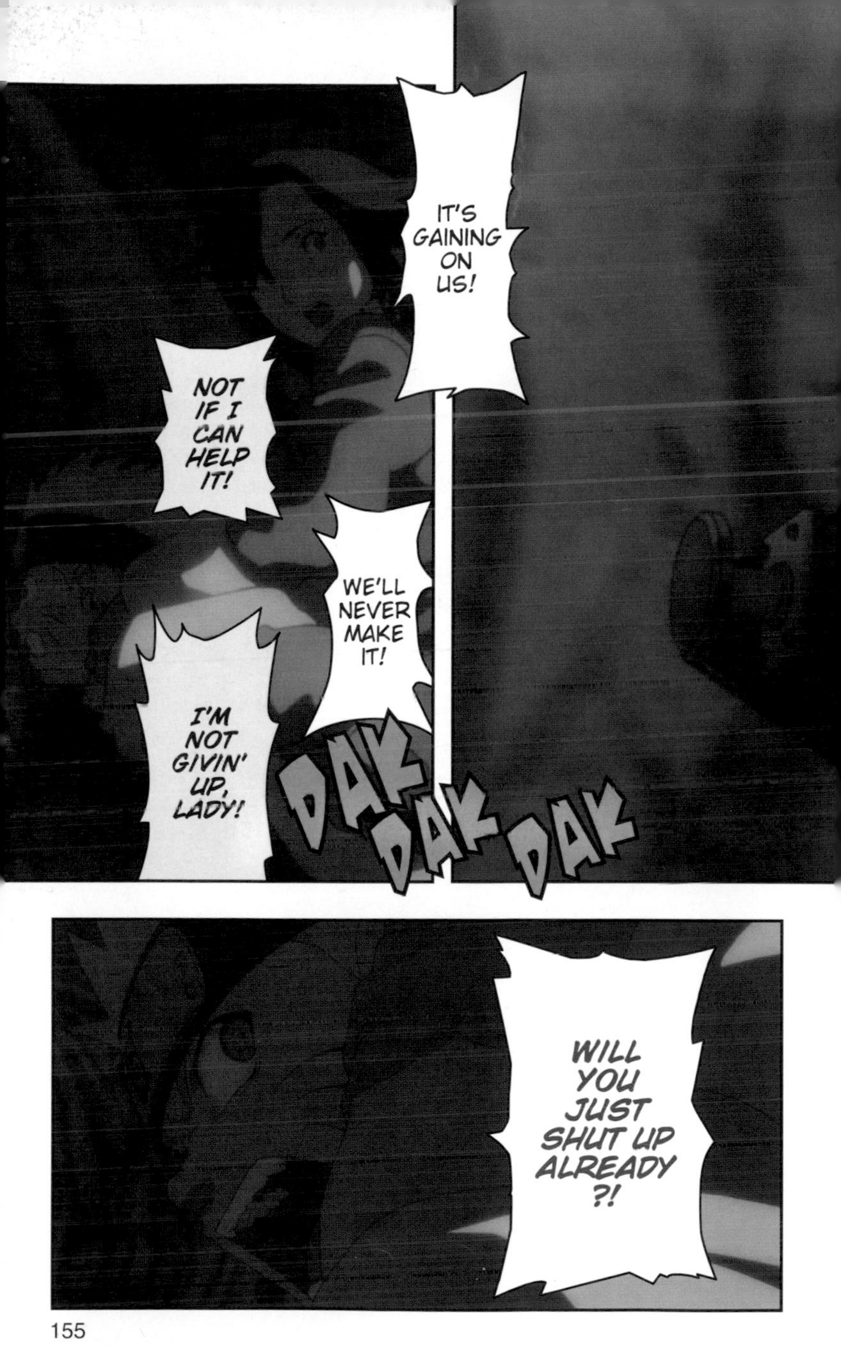
IT'S GAINING ON US!
NOT IF I CAN HELP IT!
WE'LL NEVER MAKE IT!
I'M NOT GIVIN' UP, LADY!
DAK DAK DAK
WILL YOU JUST SHUT UP ALREADY?!

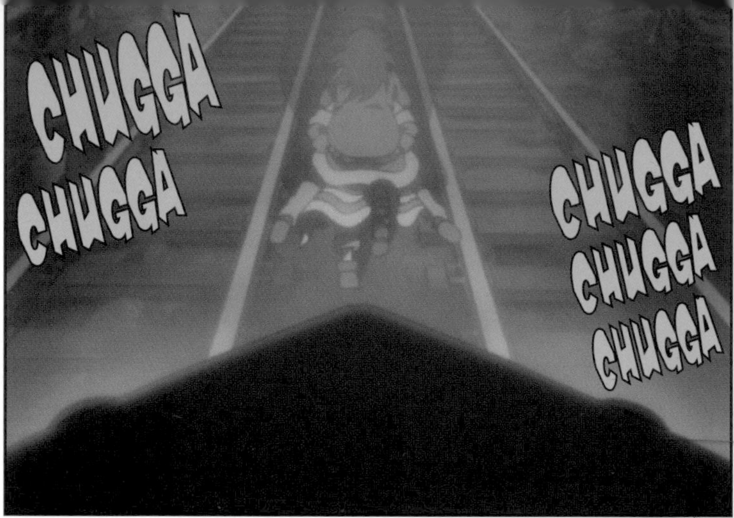
CHUGGA CHUGGA CHUGGA
CHUGGA CHUGGA
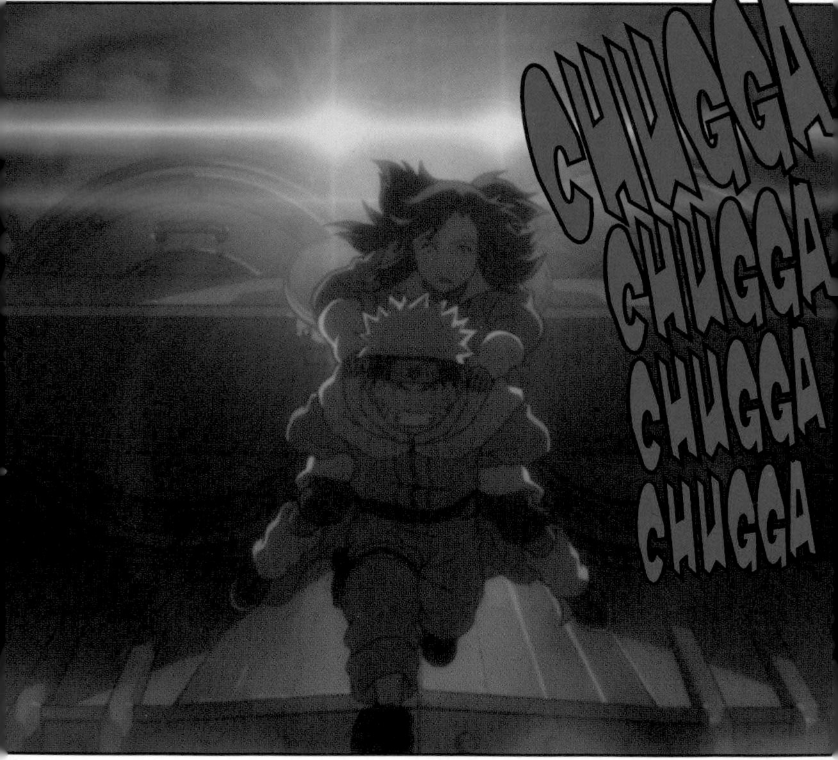
CHUGGA CHUGGA CHUGGA CHUGGA

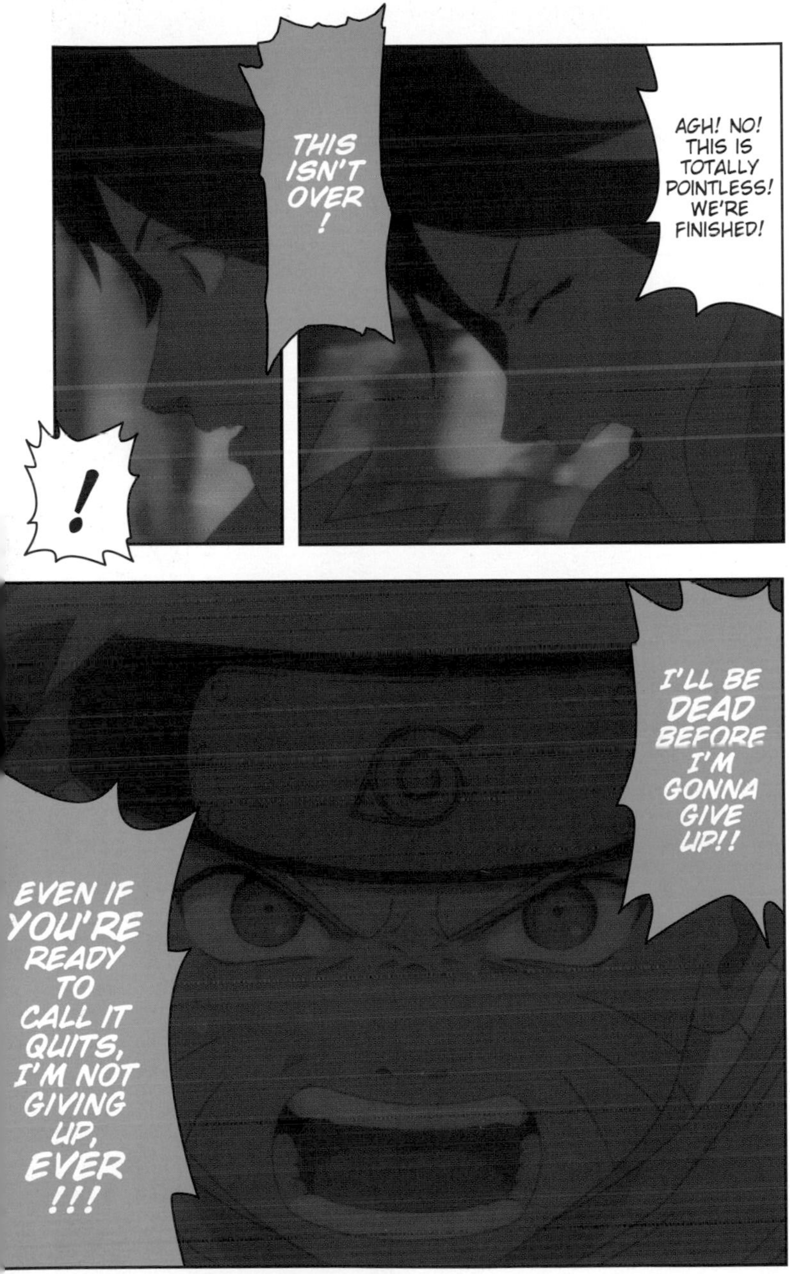
AGH! NO! THIS IS TOTALLY POINTLESS! WE'RE FINISHED!
THIS ISN'T OVER!
!
I'LL BE DEAD BEFORE I'M GONNA GIVE UP!!
EVEN IF YOU'RE READY TO CALL IT QUITS, I'M NOT GIVING UP, EVER!!!

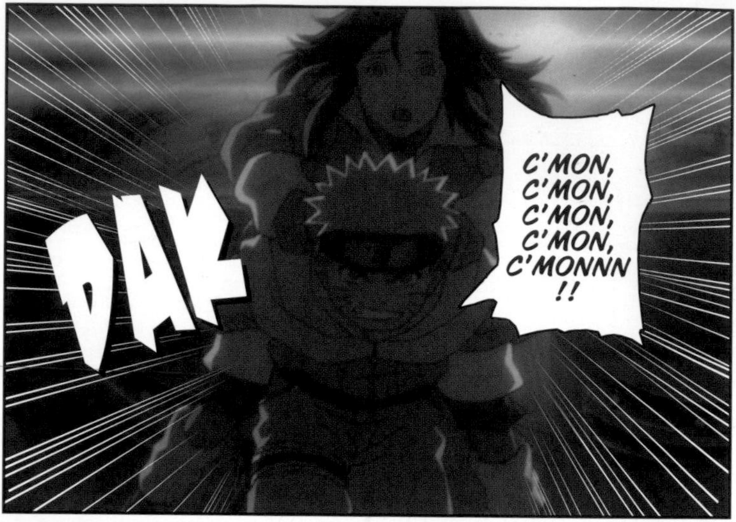
C'MON, C'MON, C'MON, C'MON, C'MONNN !!
DAK

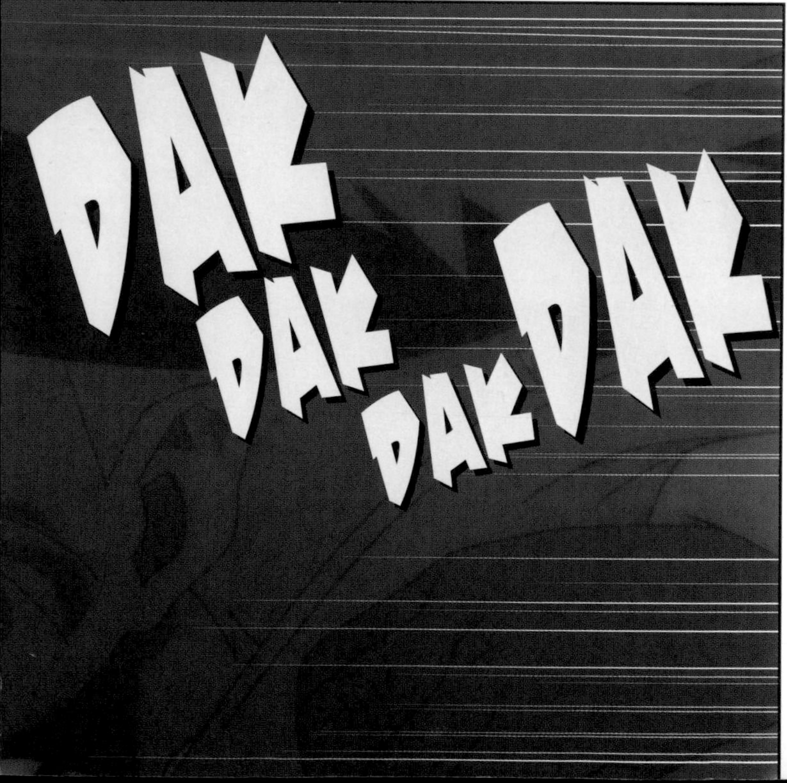
DAK
DAK
DAK
DAK

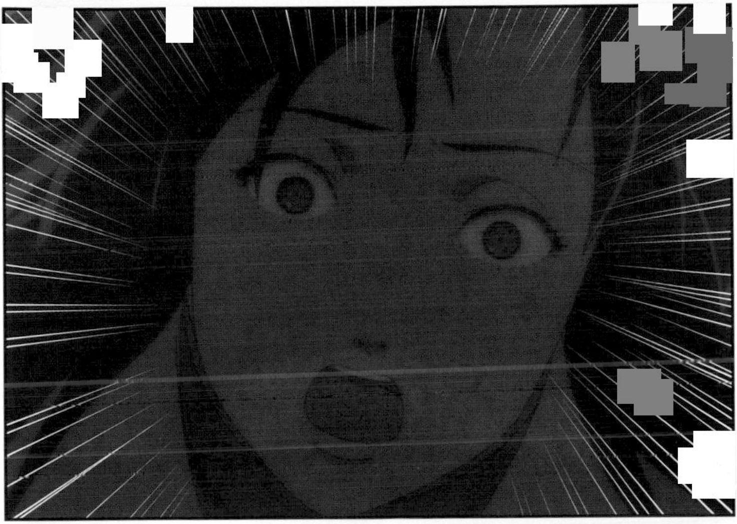

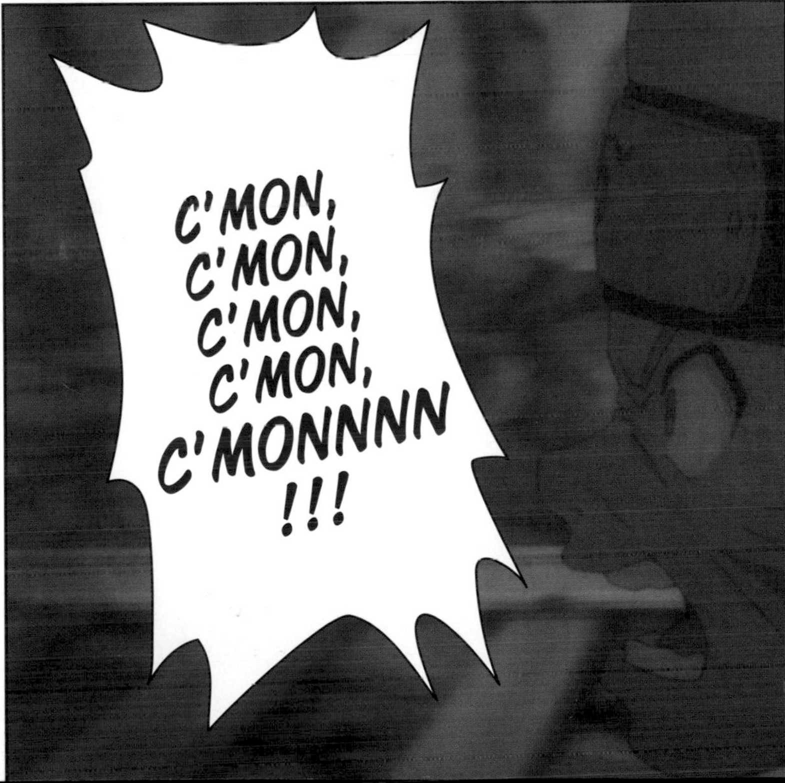
C'MON, C'MON, C'MON, C'MON, C'MONNNN !!!

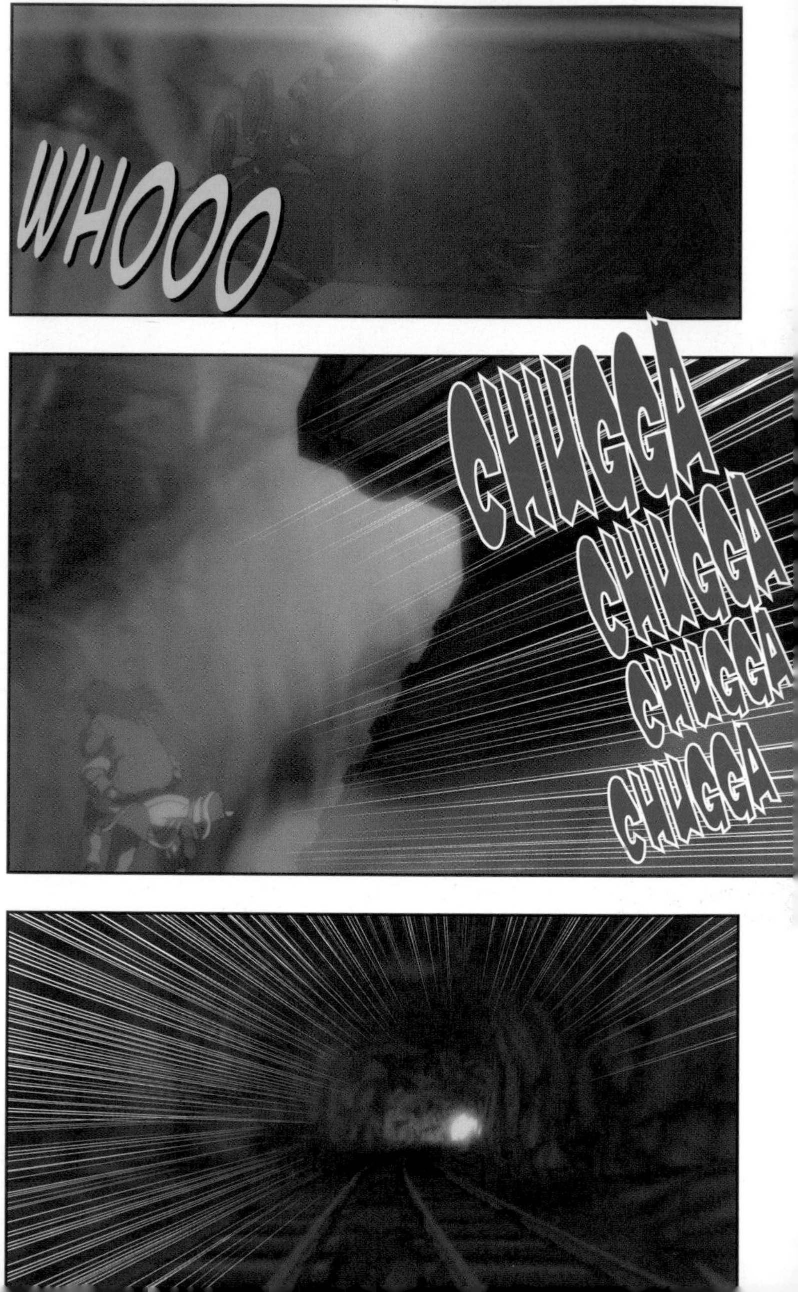
WHOOO
CHUGGA
CHUGGA
CHUGGA
CHUGGA

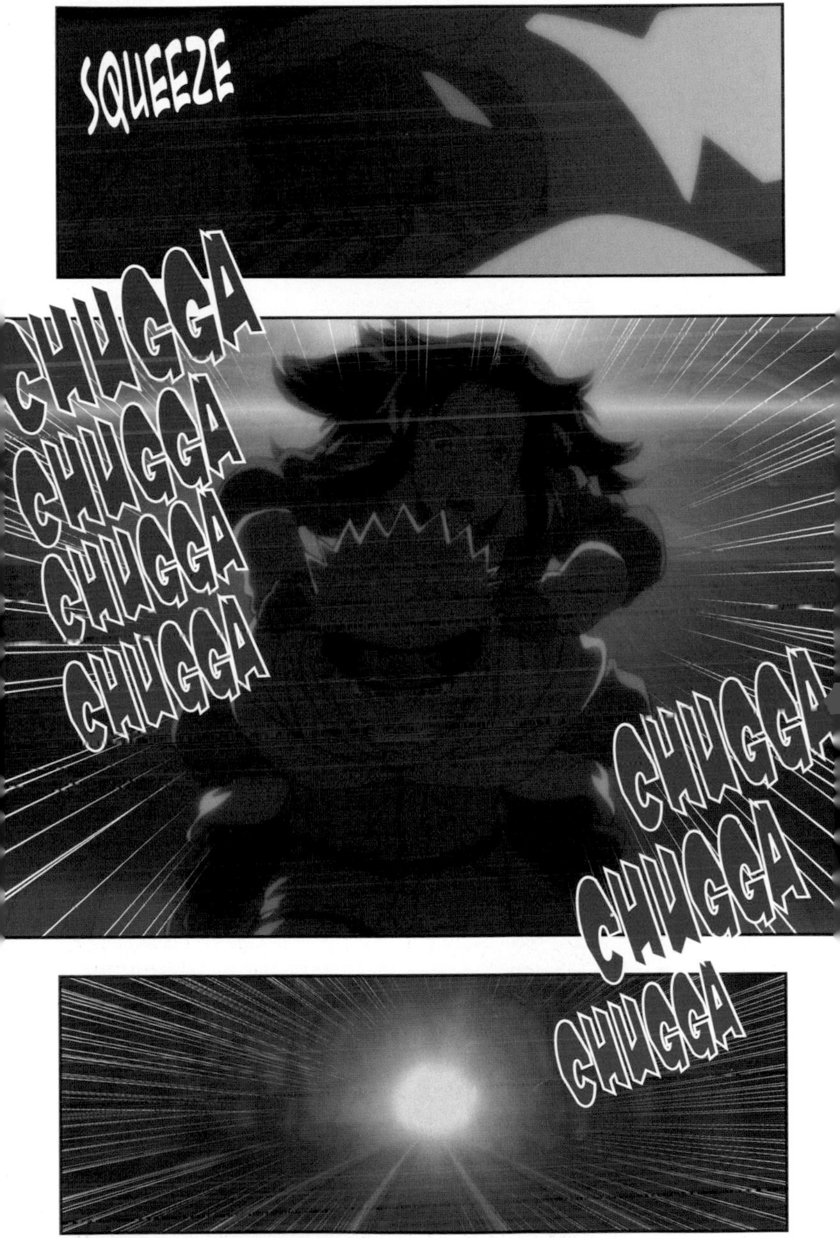
SQUEEZE
CHUGGA
CHUGGA
CHUGGA
CHUGGA
CHUGGA
CHUGGA
CHUGGA

CHUGGA CHUGGA CHUGGA CHUGGA

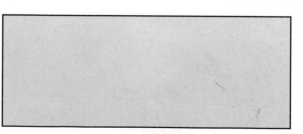

Chapter 4: Don't Waste Tears

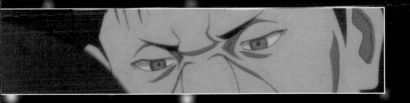

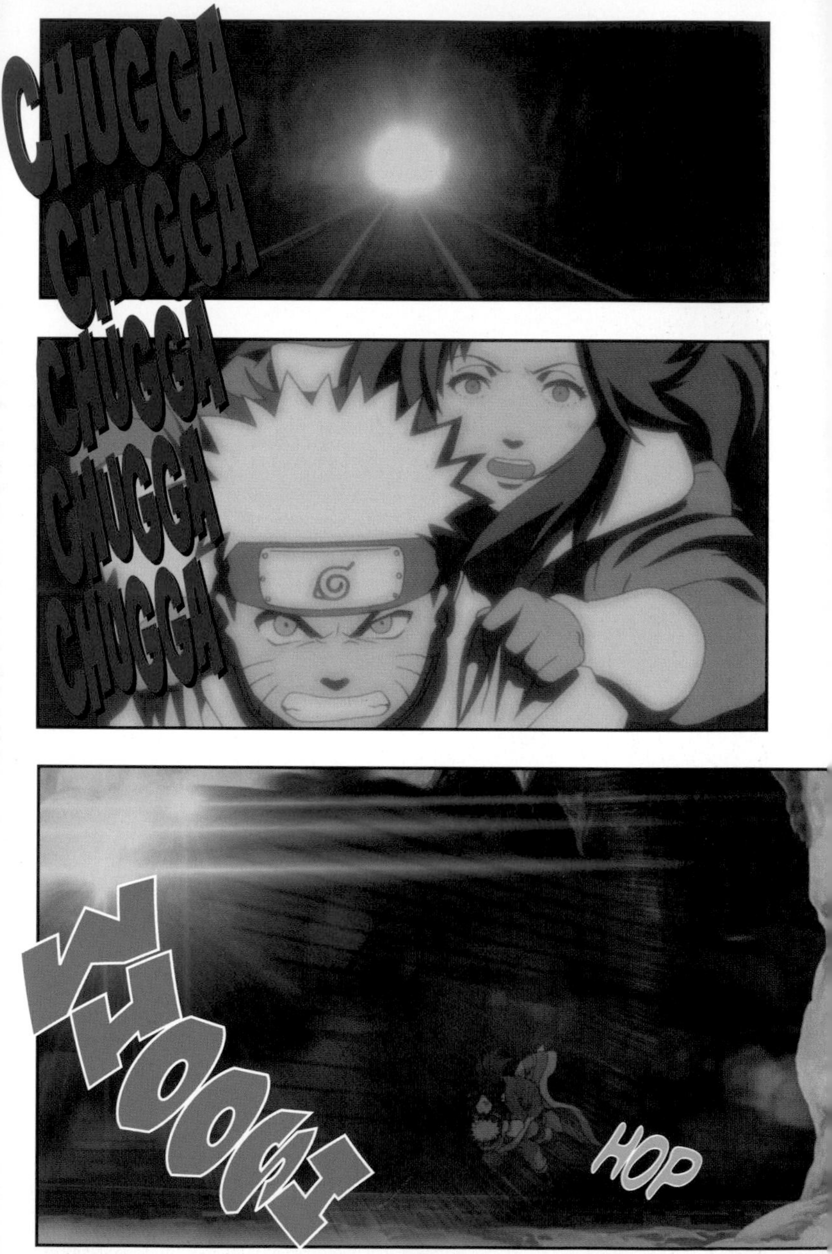
CHUGGA
CHUGGA
CHUGGA
CHUGGA
CHUGGA
HOP
WHOOSH

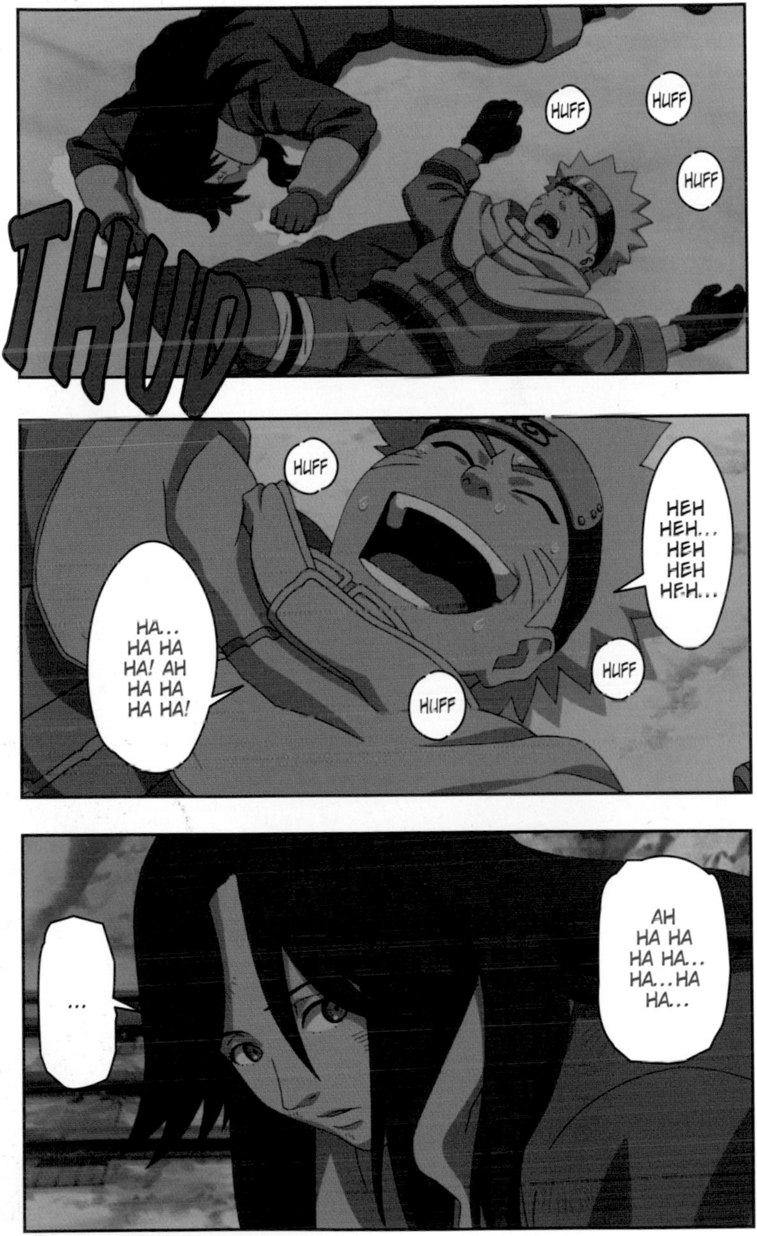
HUFF
HUFF
HUFF
THUD
HEH HEH... HEH HEH HEH...
HUFF
HUFF
HUFF
HA... HA HA HA! AH HA HA HA HA!
AH HA HA HA HA... HA...HA HA...
...

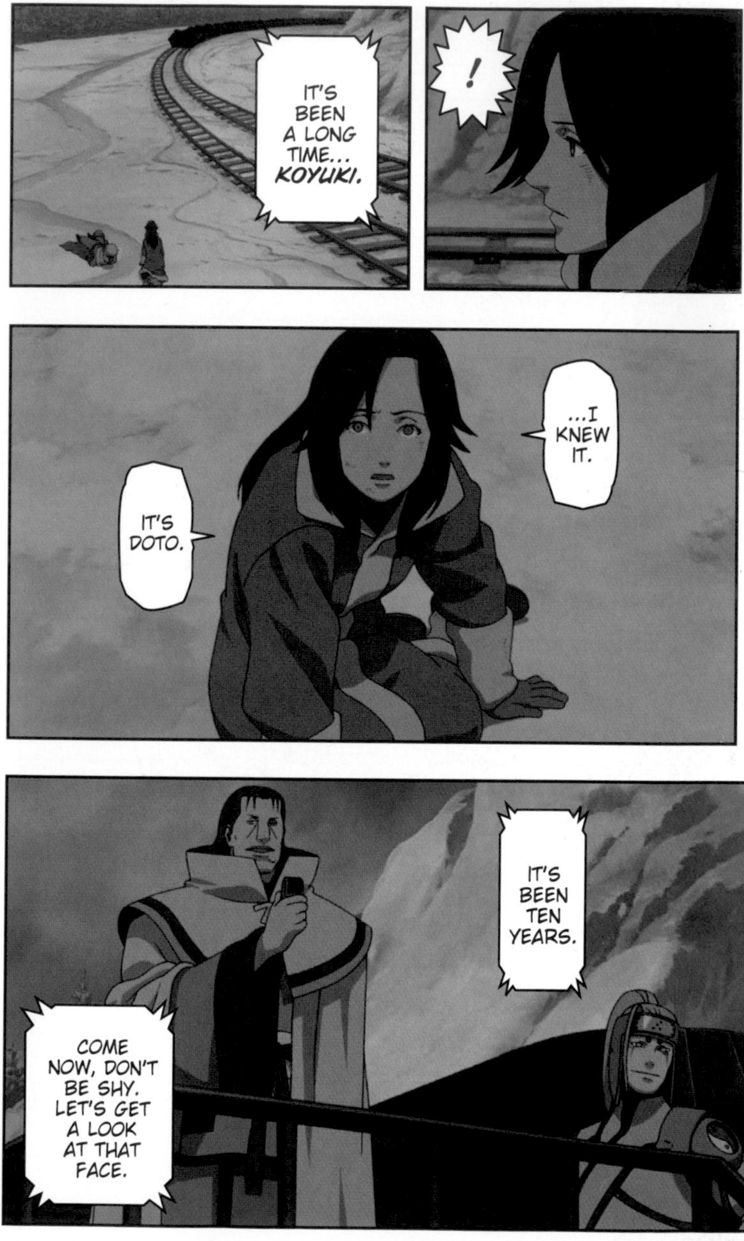
!
IT'S BEEN A LONG TIME... KOYUKI.
...I KNEW IT.
IT'S DOTO.
IT'S BEEN TEN YEARS.
COME NOW, DON'T BE SHY. LET'S GET A LOOK AT THAT FACE.

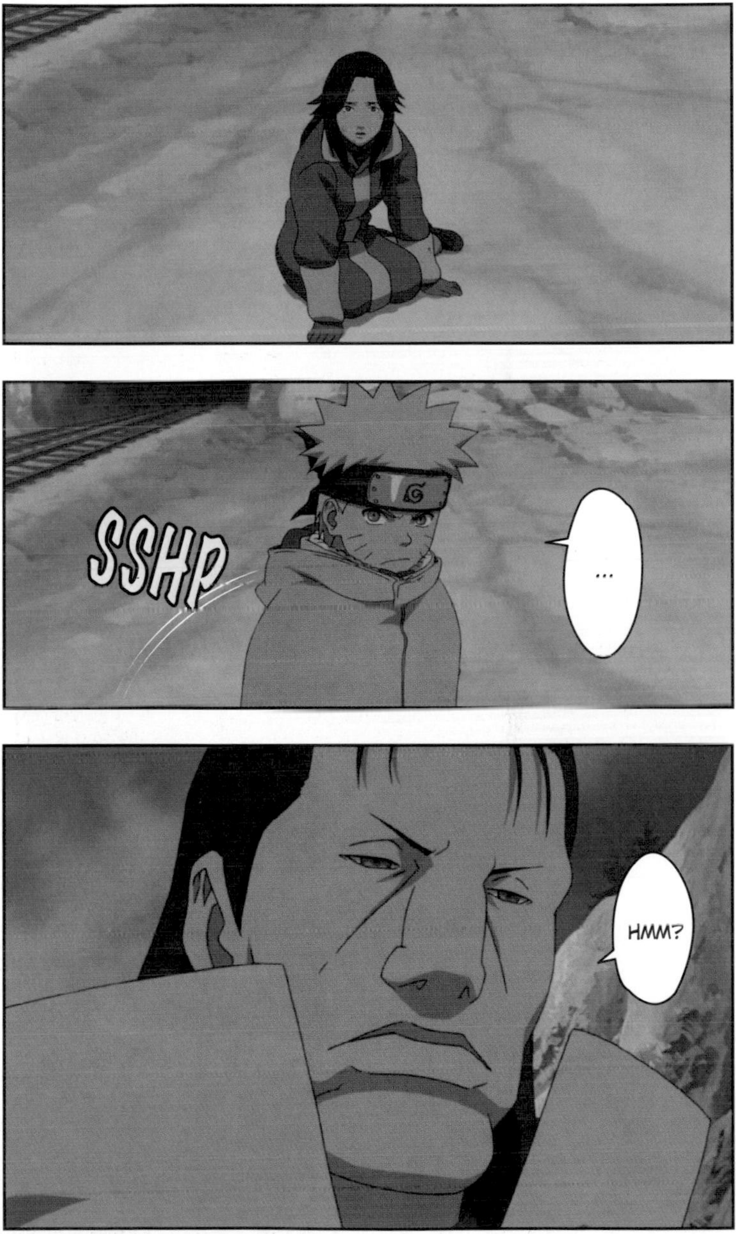
...
SSHP
HMM?

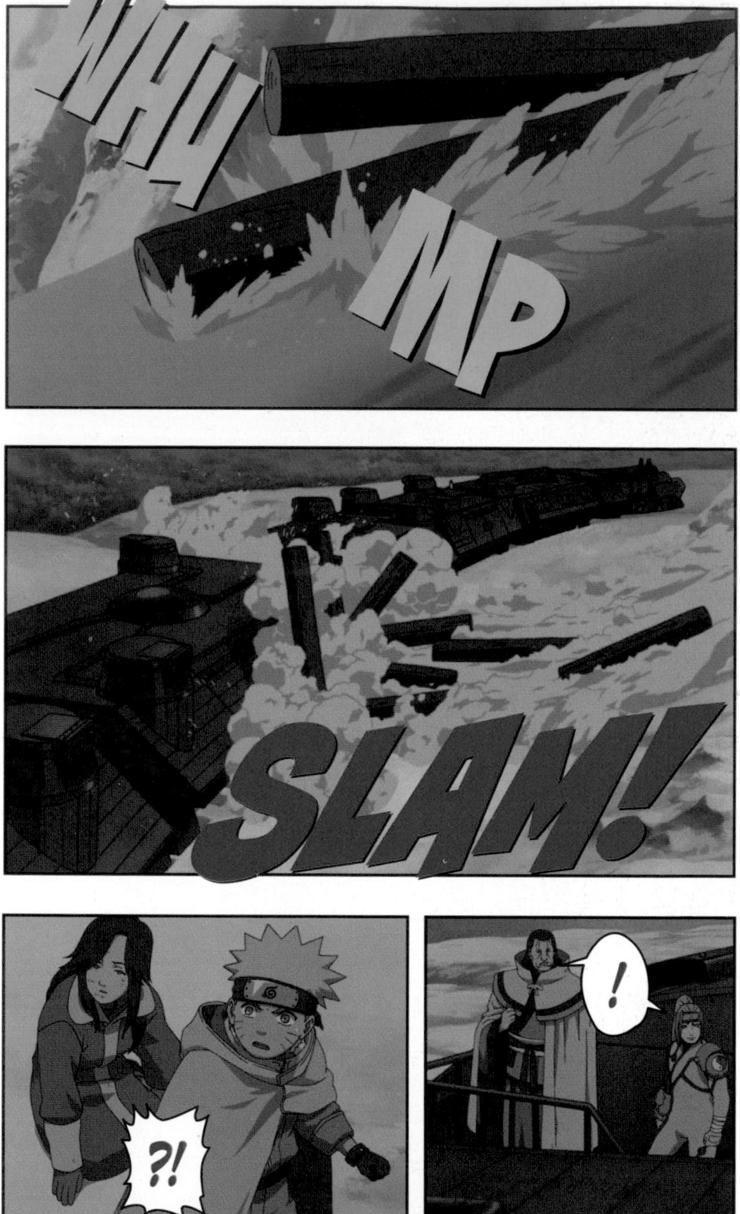
WHUMP
SLAM!
!
?!

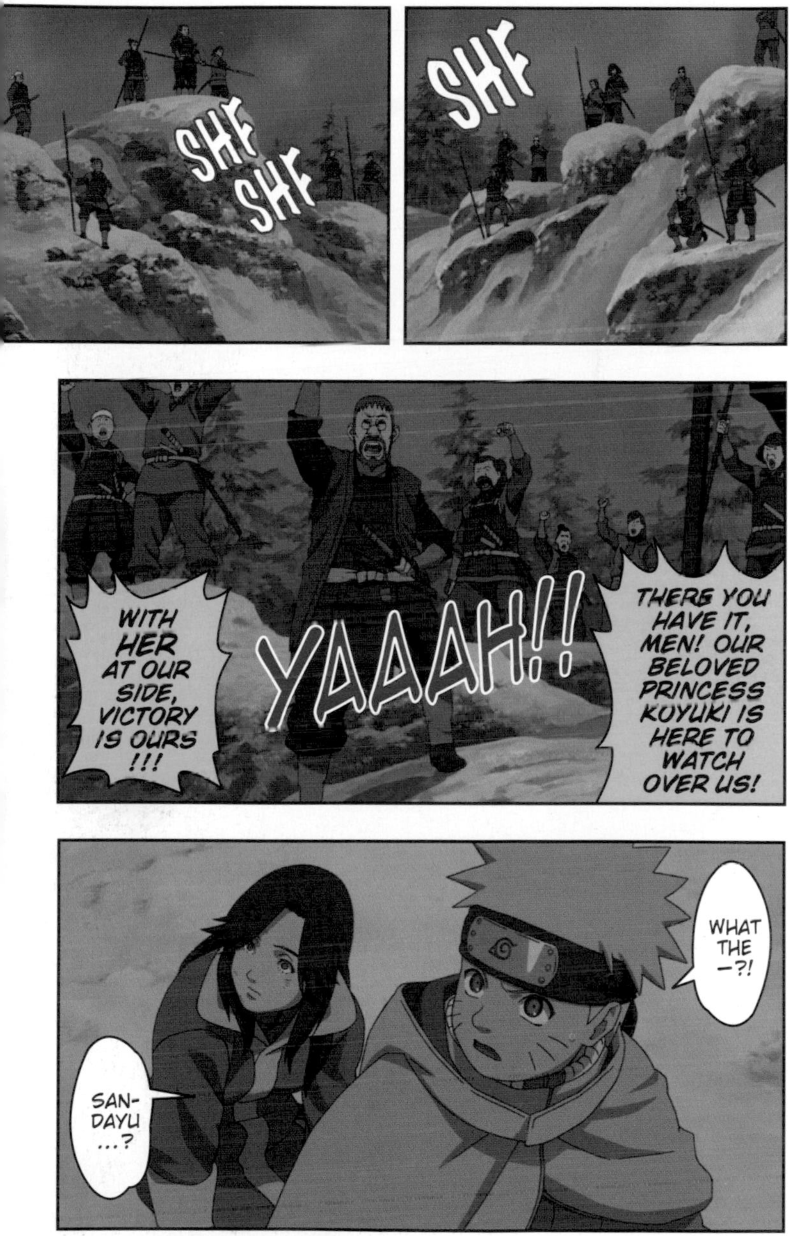
SHF
SHF
SHF
THERE YOU HAVE IT, MEN! OUR BELOVED PRINCESS KOYUKI IS HERE TO WATCH OVER US!
YAAAH!!
WITH HER AT OUR SIDE, VICTORY IS OURS!!!
WHAT THE—?!
SAN-DAYU...?

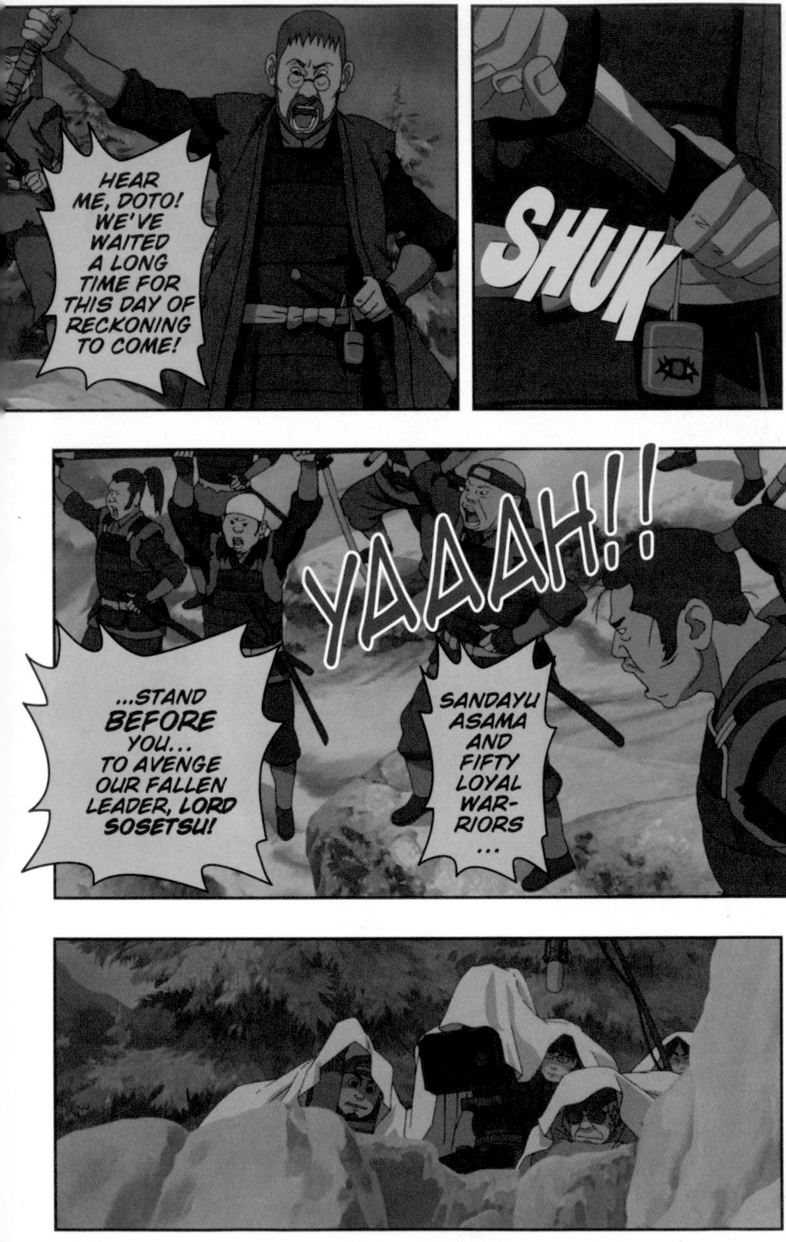
SHUK
HEAR ME, DOTO! WE'VE WAITED A LONG TIME FOR THIS DAY OF RECKONING TO COME!
YAAAH!!
SANDAYU ASAMA AND FIFTY LOYAL WAR-RIORS ...
...STAND **BEFORE** YOU... TO AVENGE OUR FALLEN LEADER, LORD SOSETSU!

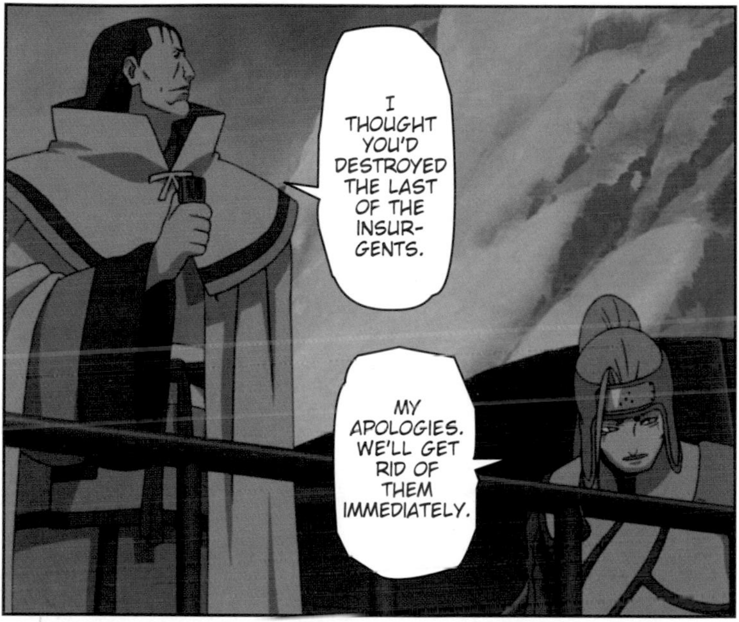
I THOUGHT YOU'D DESTROYED THE LAST OF THE INSURGENTS.
MY APOLOGIES. WE'LL GET RID OF THEM IMMEDIATELY.

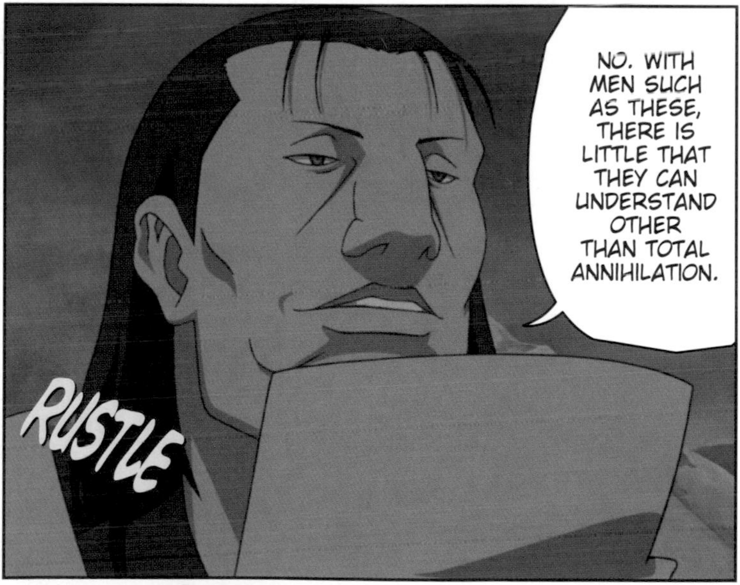
NO. WITH MEN SUCH AS THESE, THERE IS LITTLE THAT THEY CAN UNDERSTAND OTHER THAN TOTAL ANNIHILATION.
RUSTLE

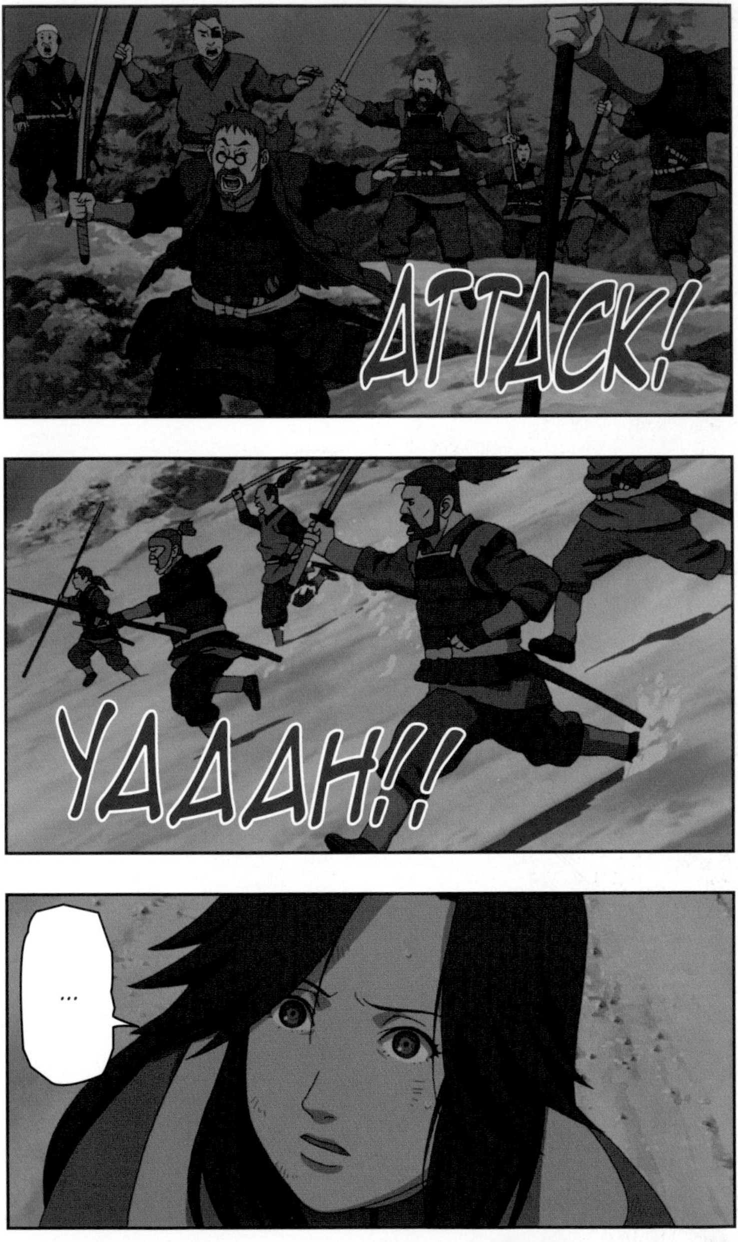
ATTACK!
YAAAH!!
...

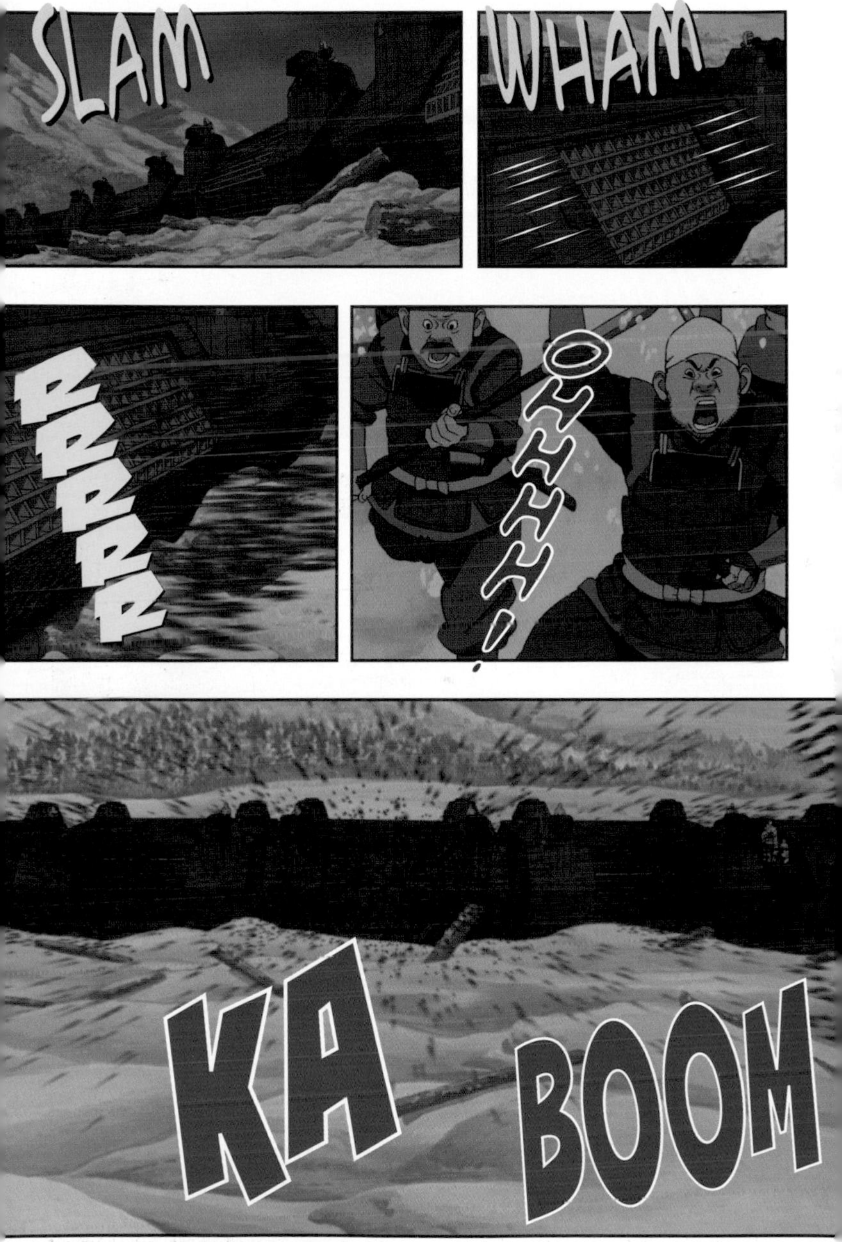
WHAM
SLAM
OHHHH!
RRRRR
KA
BOOM

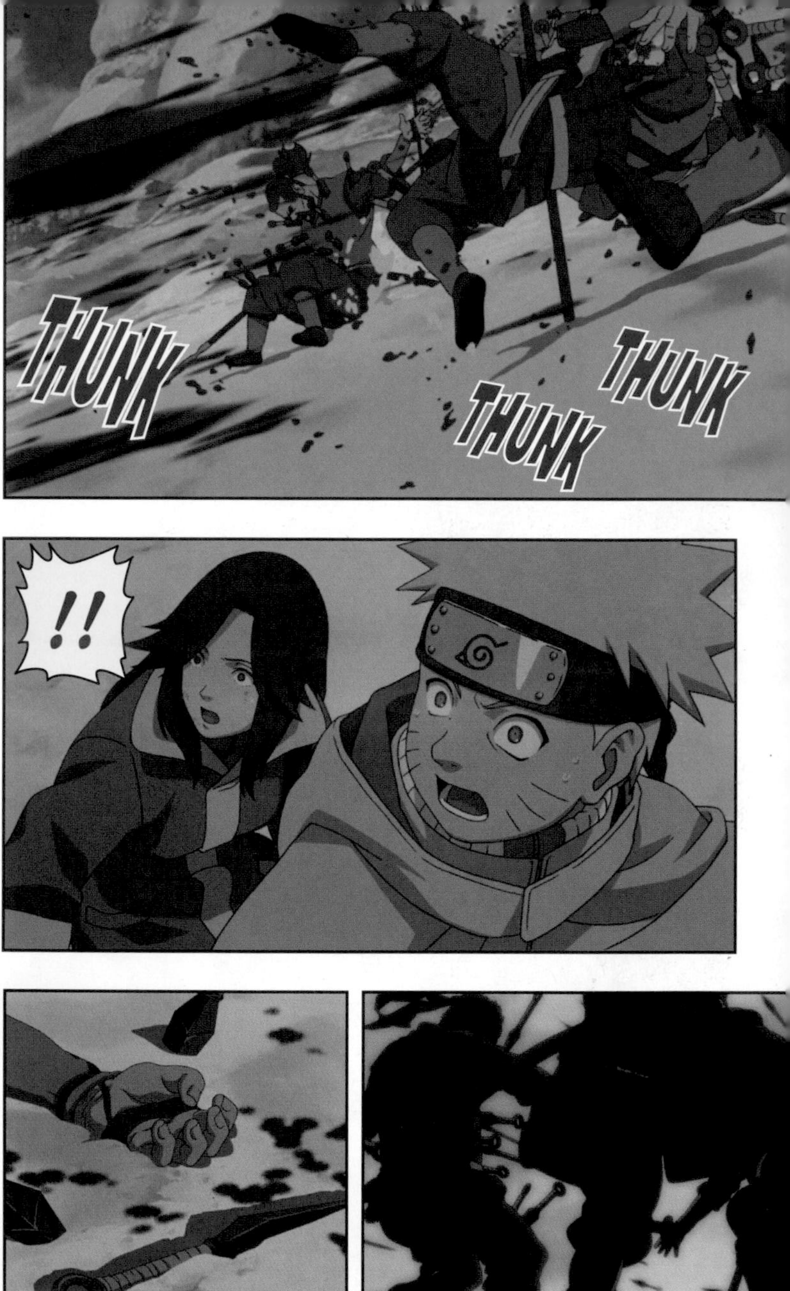
THUNK
THUNK
THUNK
!!

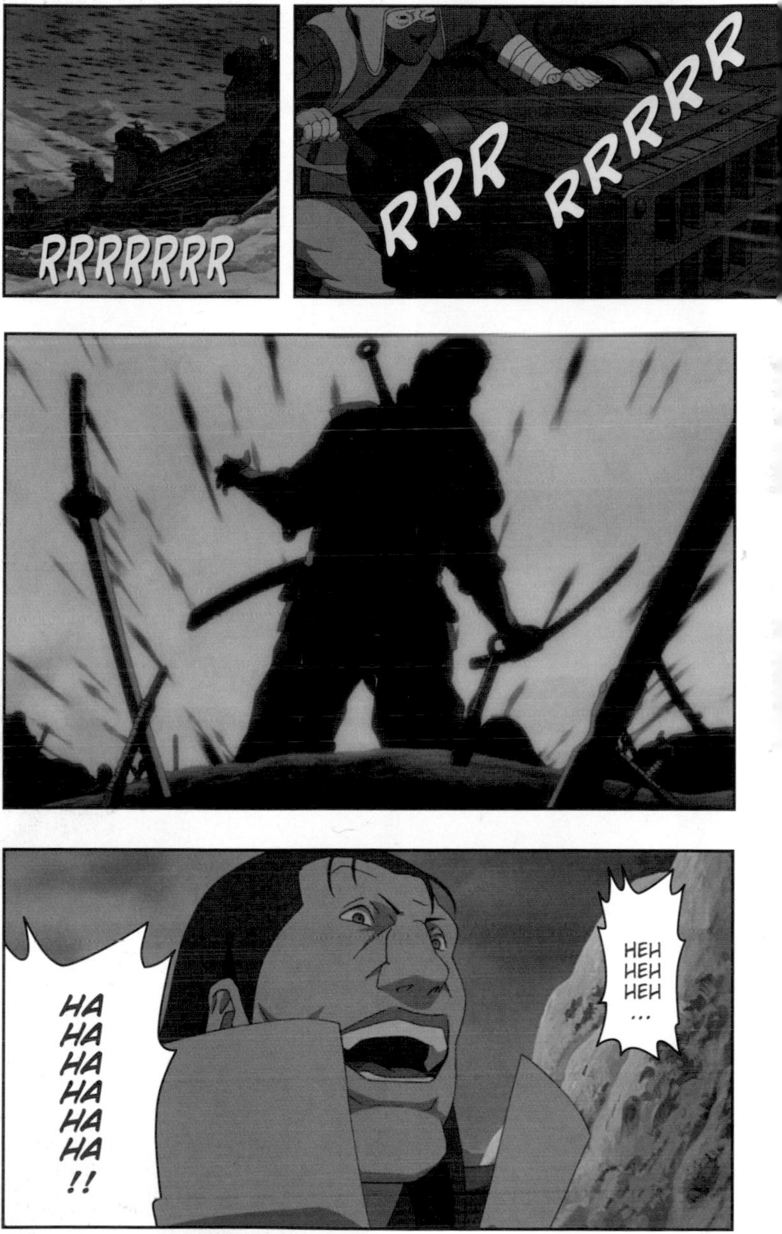
RRR
RRRRRR
RRRRRRR
HEH HEH HEH ...
HA HA HA HA HA HA !!

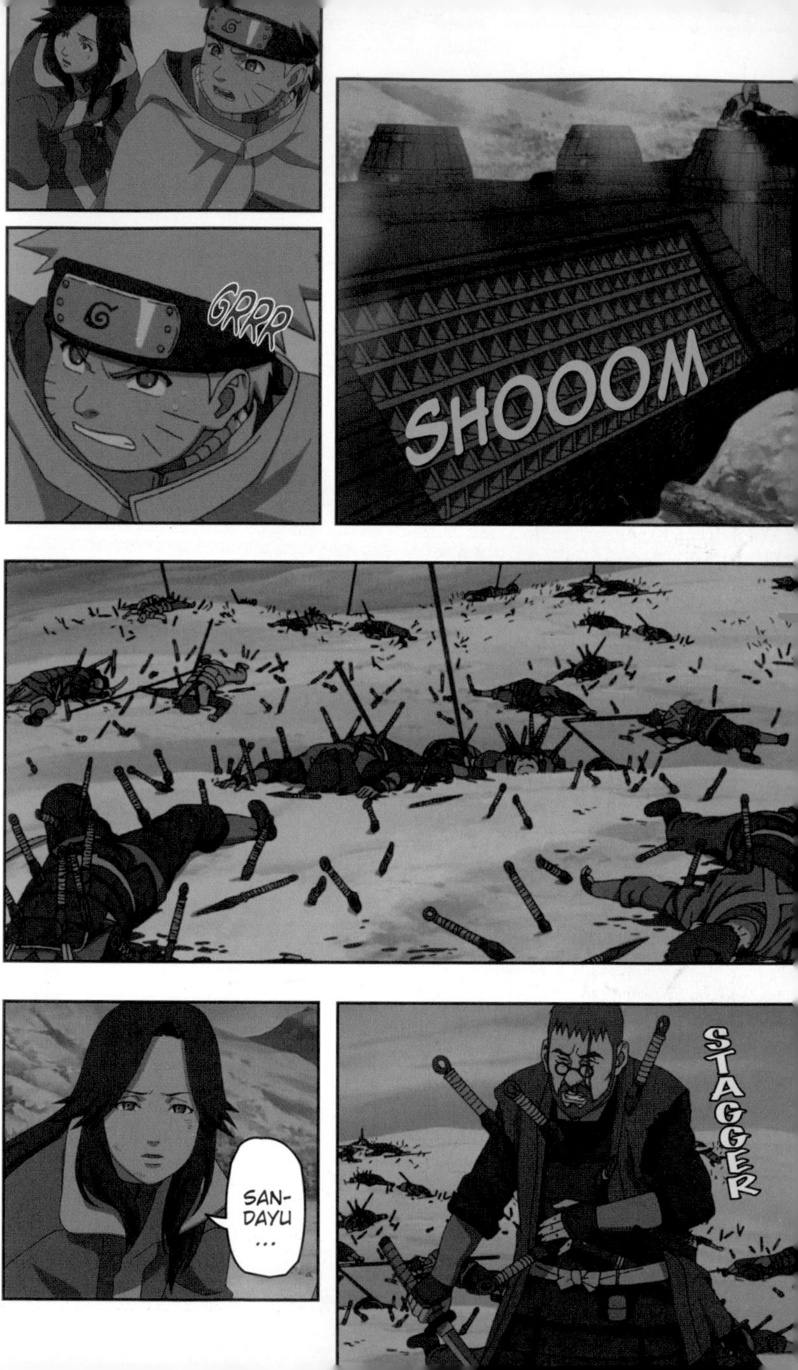
SHOOOM
GRRR
STAGGER
SAN-
DAYU
...

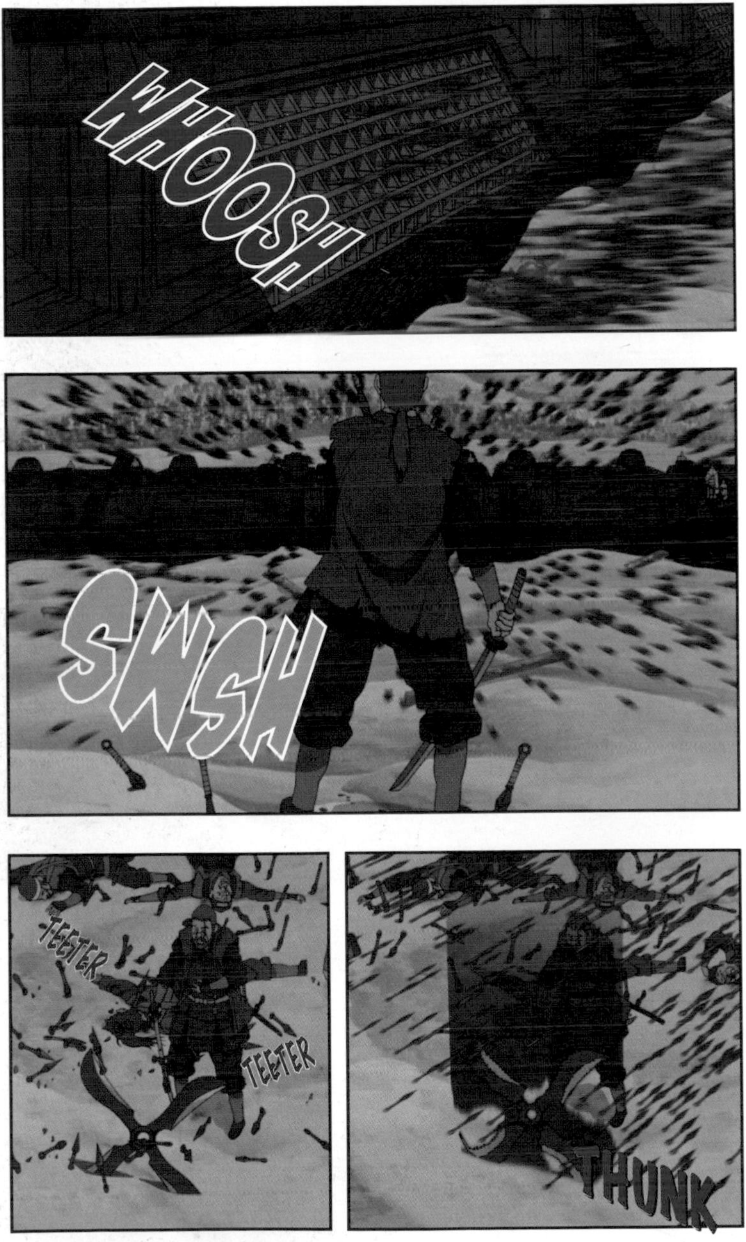
WHOOSH
SWSH
THUNK
TEETER
TEETER

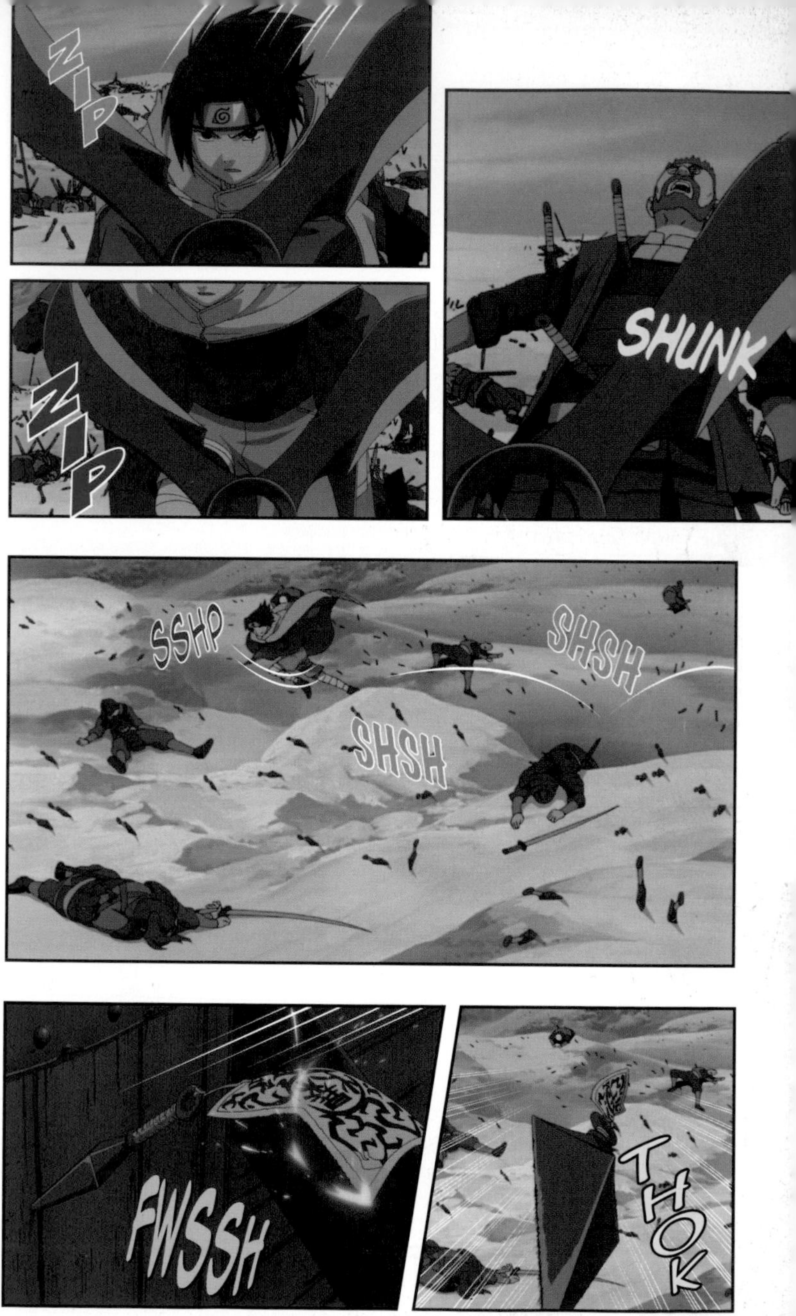
SHUNK
ZIP
ZIP
SHSH
SSHP
SHSH
THOK
FWSSH

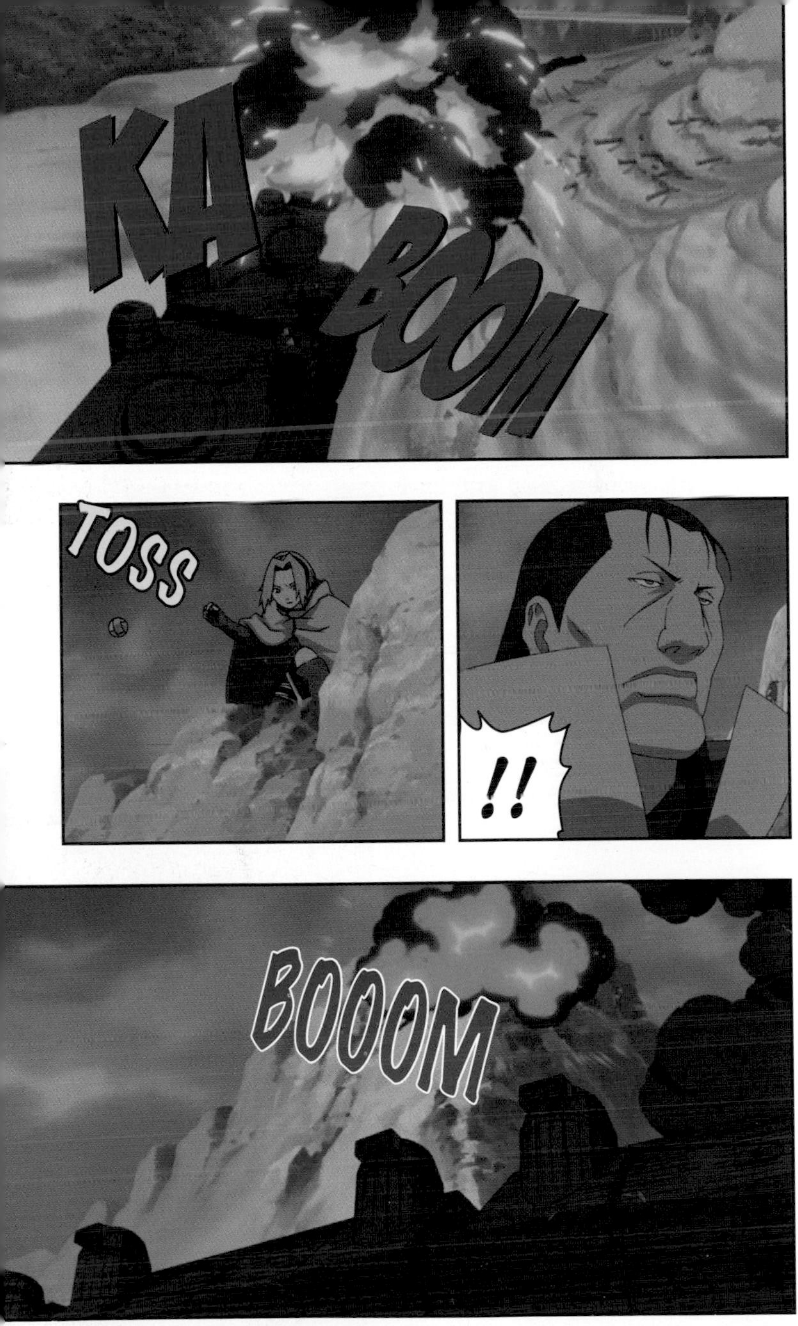
KA
BOOM
!!
TOSS
BOOOM

RMBL
RMBL
RMBL

WHSH

RMBL
RMBL
RMBL

BOOOM

WHSH

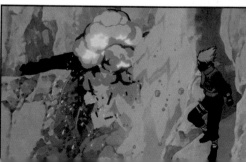

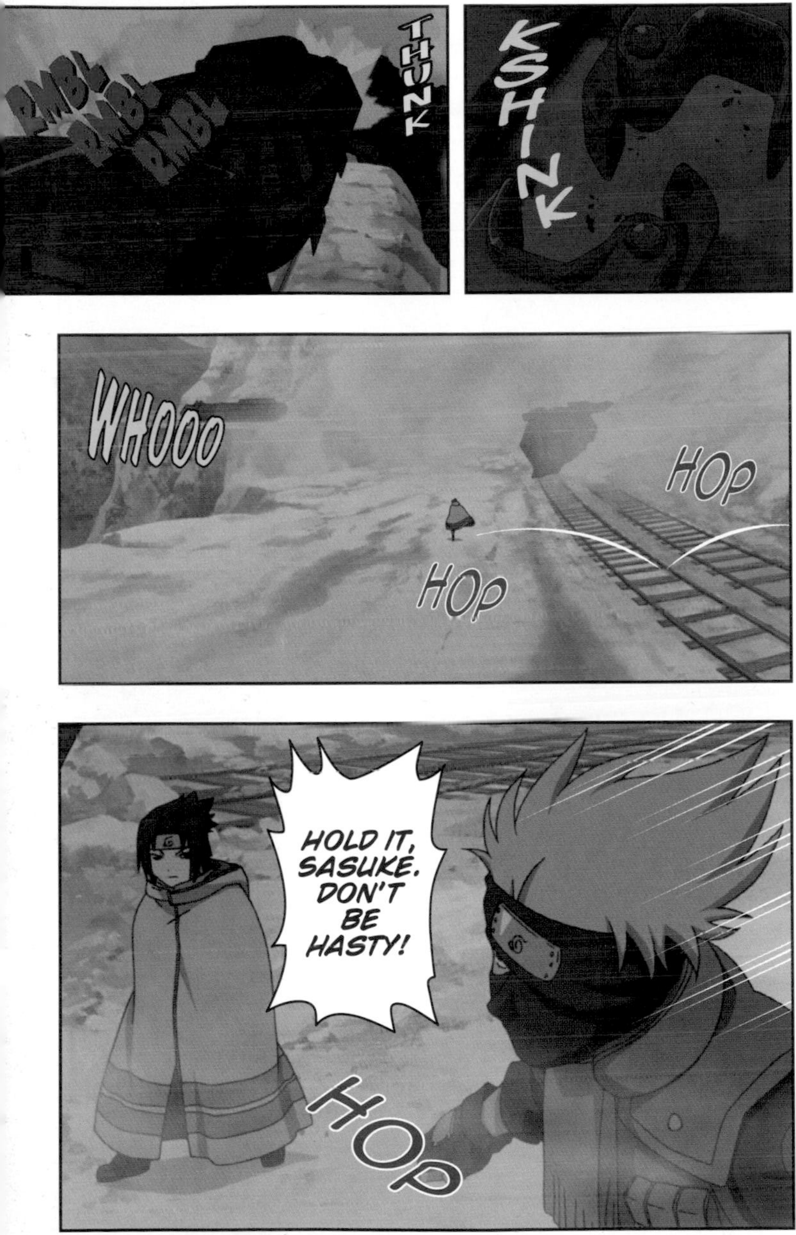
KSHINK
THUNK
RMBL RMBL RMBL
HOP
WHOOO
HOP
HOLD IT, SASUKE. DON'T BE HASTY!
HOP

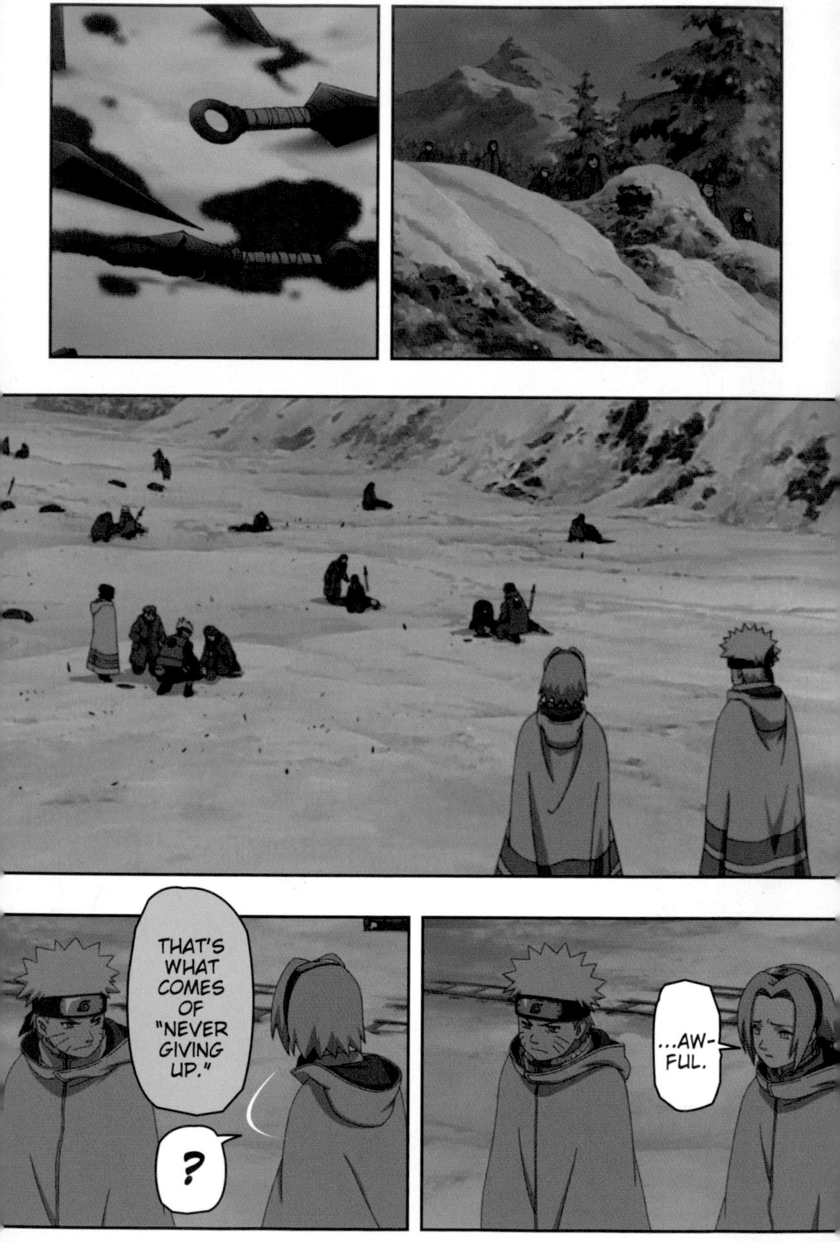
...AW-FUL.
THAT'S WHAT COMES OF "NEVER GIVING UP."
?

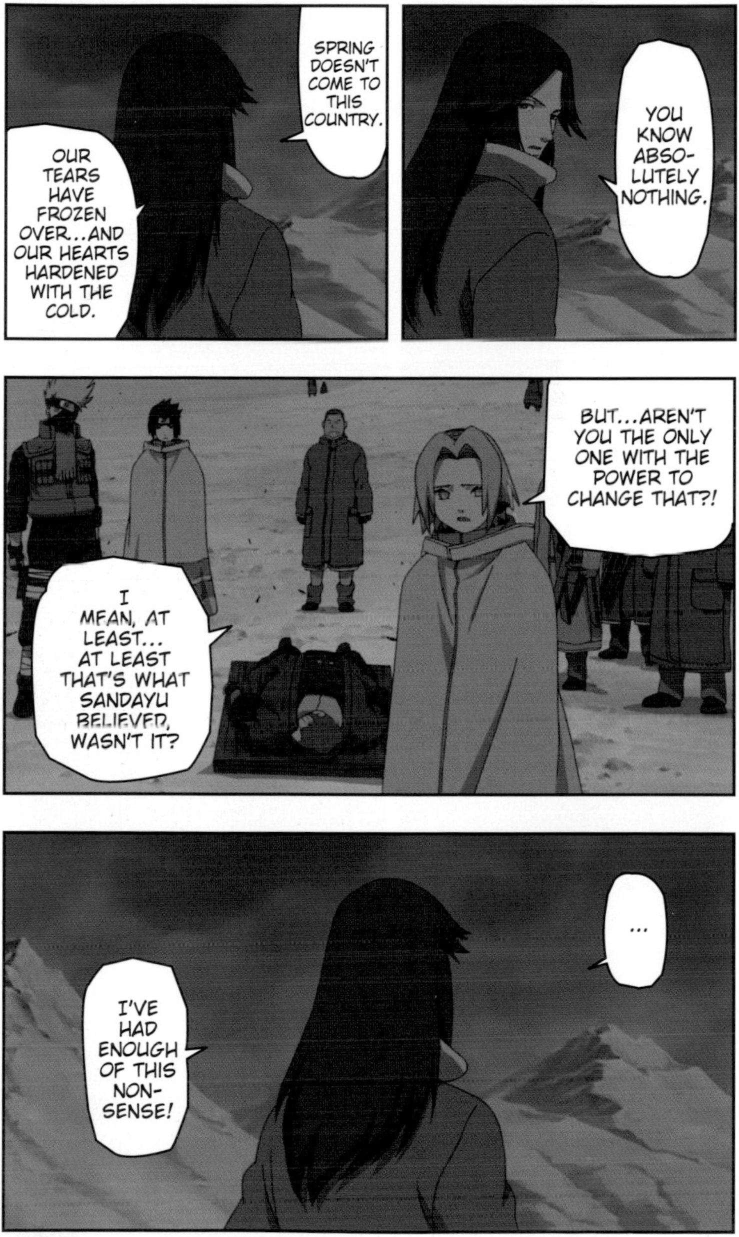
YOU KNOW ABSOLUTELY NOTHING.
SPRING DOESN'T COME TO THIS COUNTRY.
OUR TEARS HAVE FROZEN OVER...AND OUR HEARTS HARDENED WITH THE COLD.
BUT...AREN'T YOU THE ONLY ONE WITH THE POWER TO CHANGE THAT?!
I MEAN, AT LEAST... AT LEAST THAT'S WHAT SANDAYU BELIEVED, WASN'T IT?
...
I'VE HAD ENOUGH OF THIS NONSENSE!

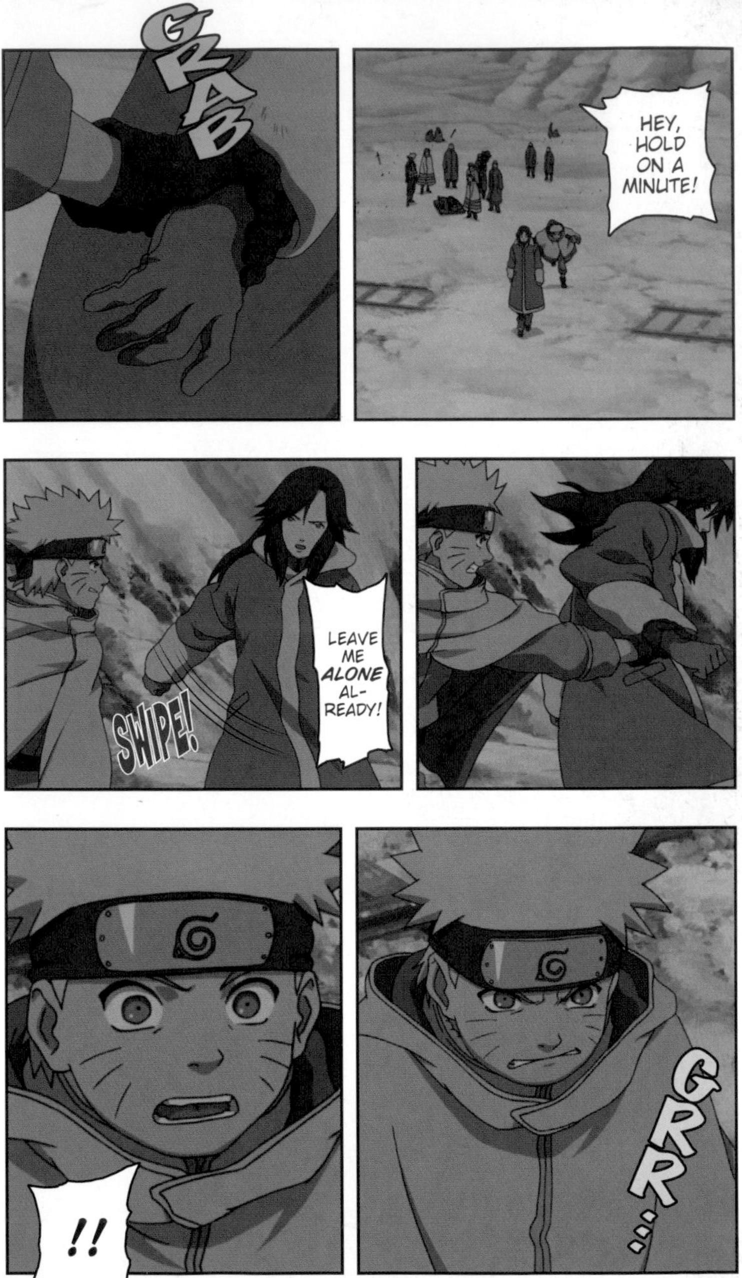
HEY, HOLD ON A MINUTE!
GRAB
LEAVE ME ALONE AL-READY!
SWIPE!
GRR...
!!

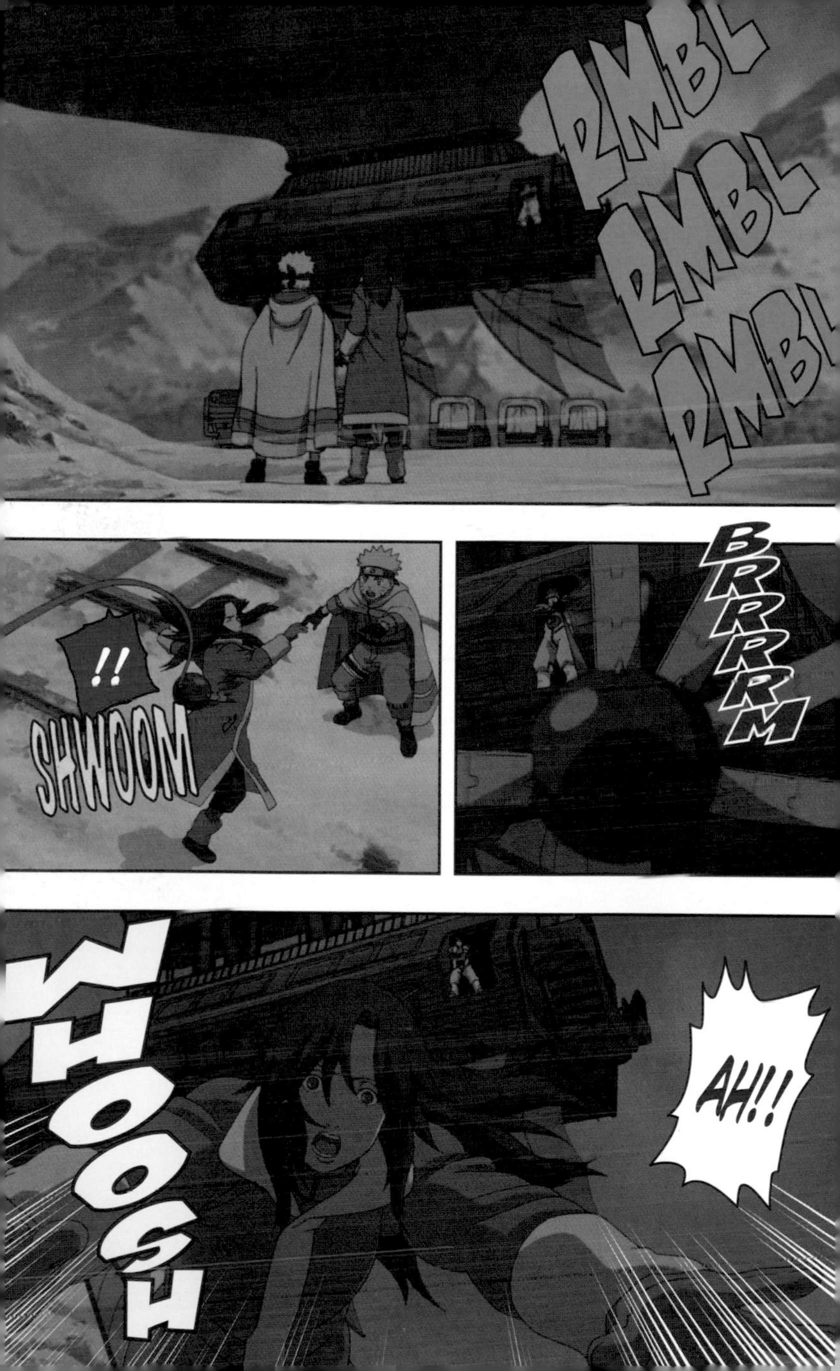
RMBL
RMBL
RMBL
BRRRRRM
!!
SHWOOM
AH!!
WHOOOSH

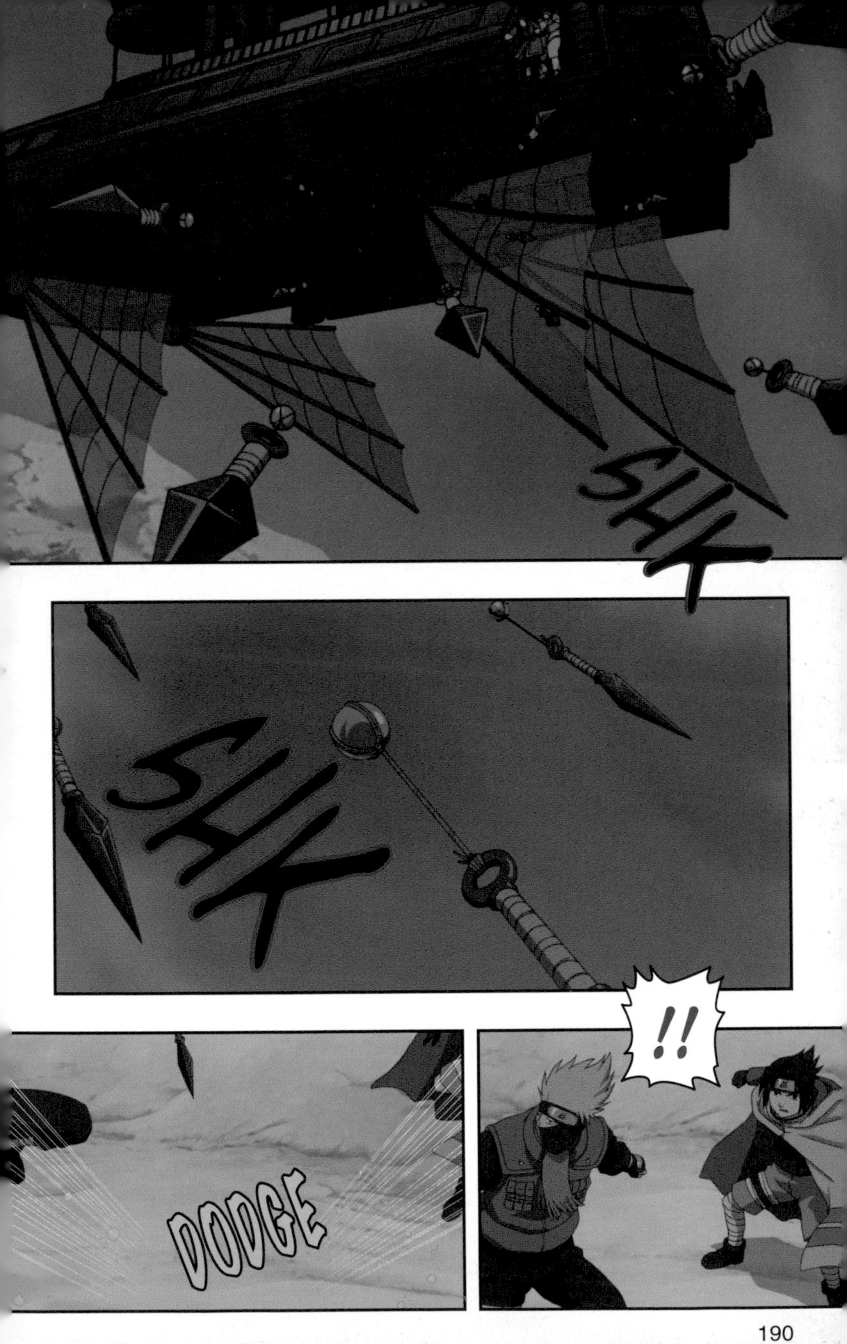
SHK
SHK
!!
DODGE

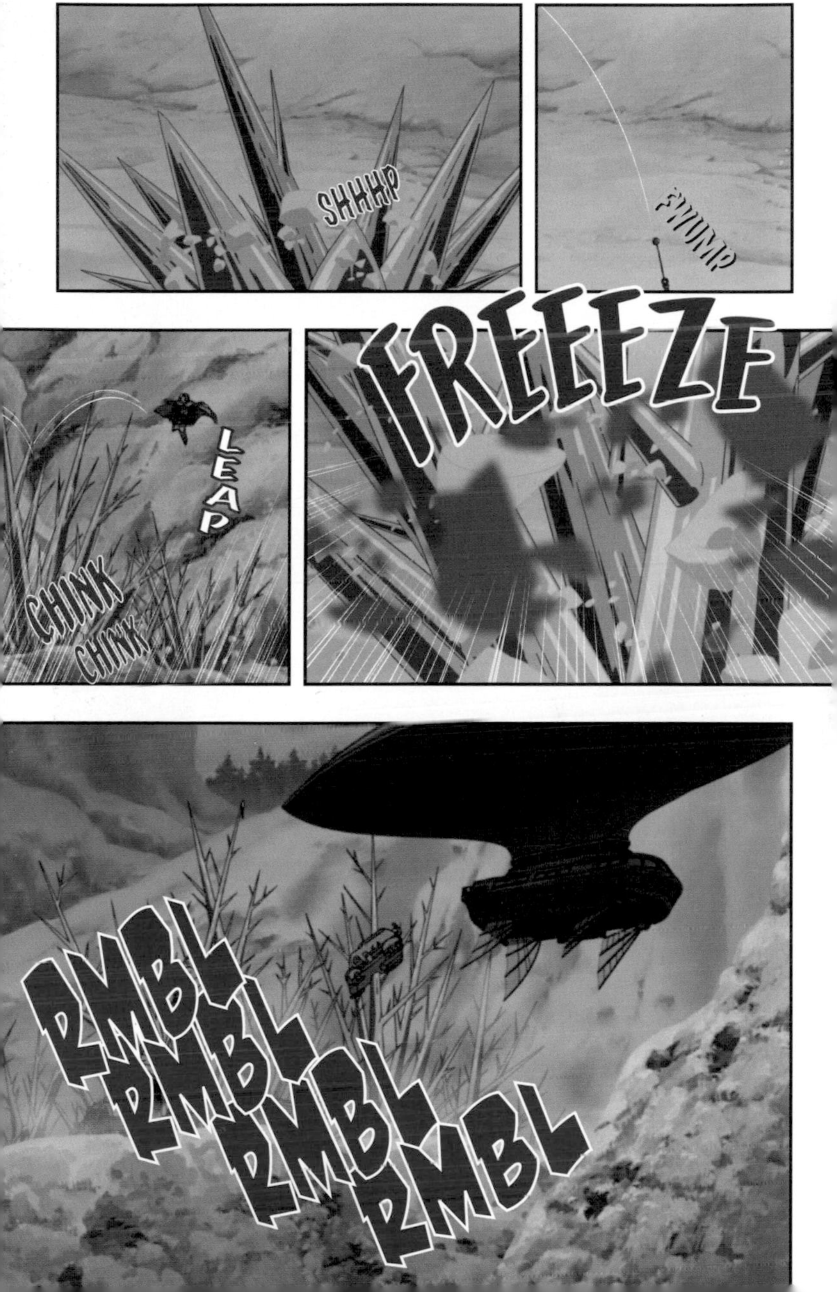
FWUMP
SHHHP
FREEEZE
LEAP
CHINK
CHINK
RMBL
RMBL
RMBL
RMBL

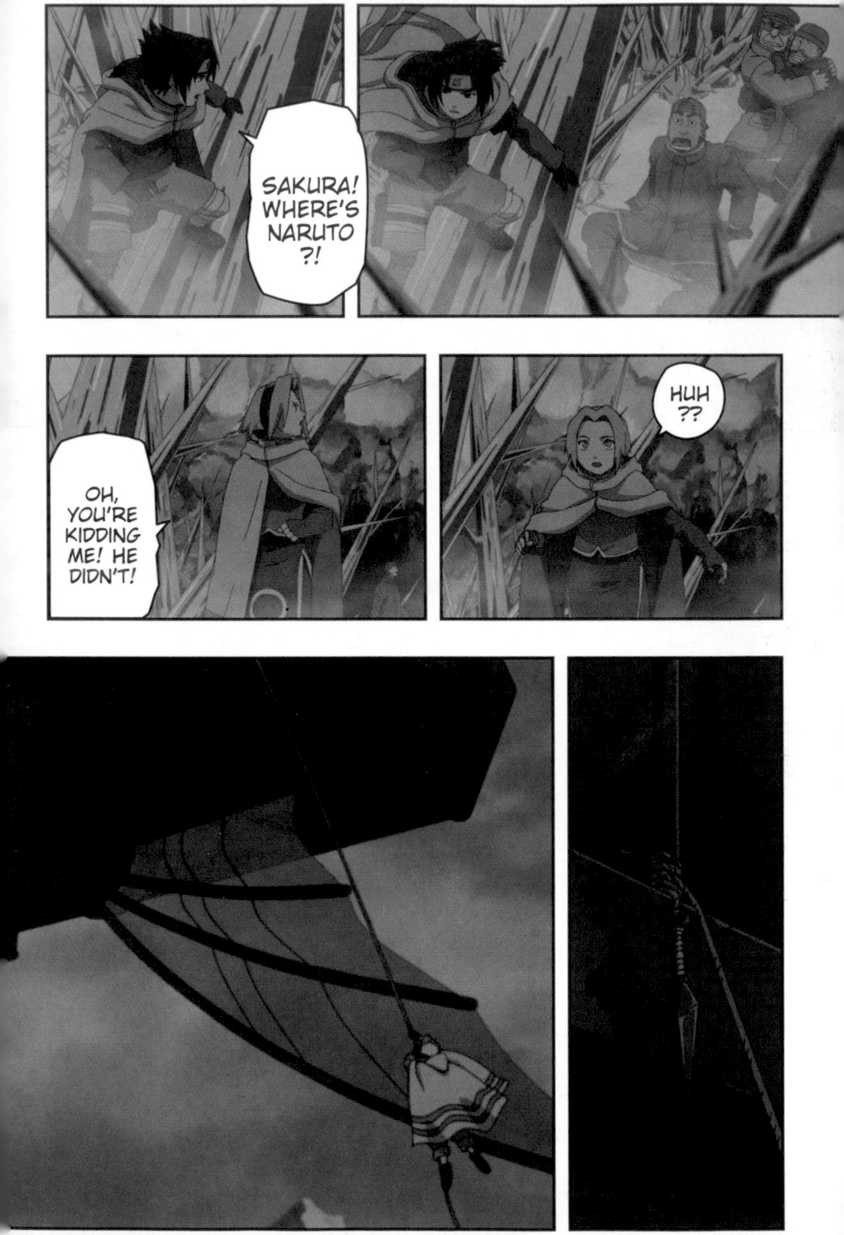
SAKURA! WHERE'S NARUTO ?!
HUH ??
OH, YOU'RE KIDDING ME! HE DIDN'T!

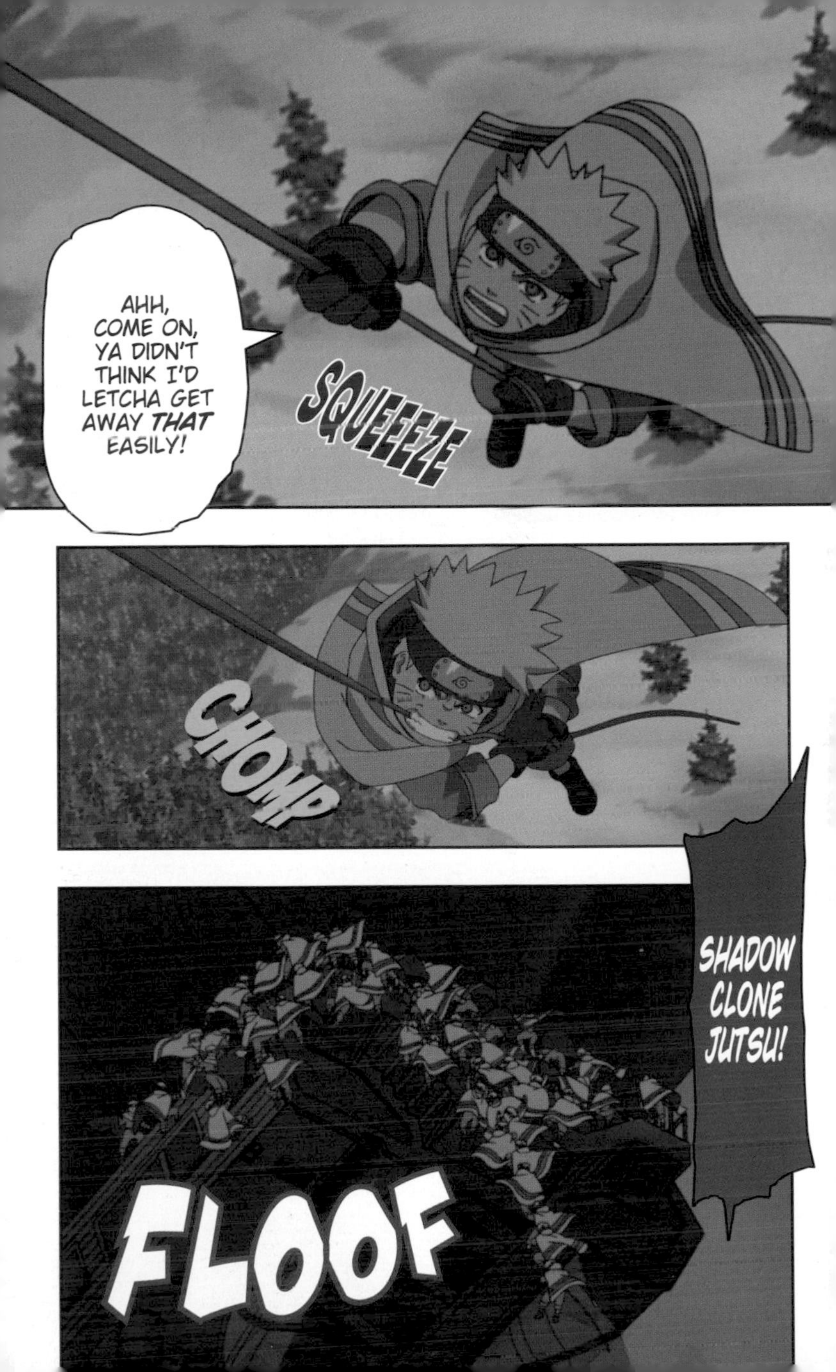
AHH, COME ON, YA DIDN'T THINK I'D LETCHA GET AWAY *THAT* EASILY!
SQUEEEZE
CHOMP
SHADOW CLONE JUTSU!
FLOOF

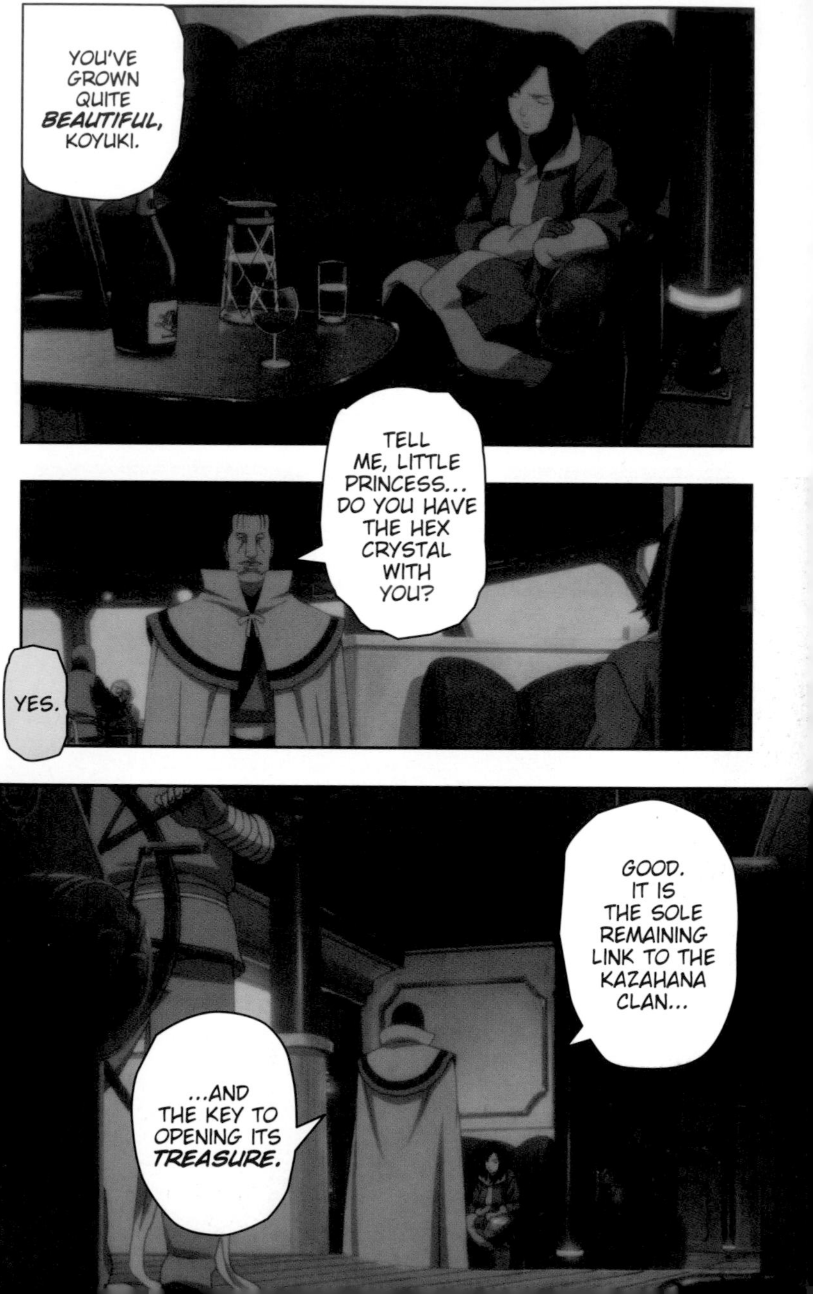
YOU'VE GROWN QUITE BEAUTIFUL, KOYUKI.
TELL ME, LITTLE PRINCESS... DO YOU HAVE THE HEX CRYSTAL WITH YOU?
YES.
GOOD. IT IS THE SOLE REMAINING LINK TO THE KAZAHANA CLAN...
...AND THE KEY TO OPENING ITS TREASURE.

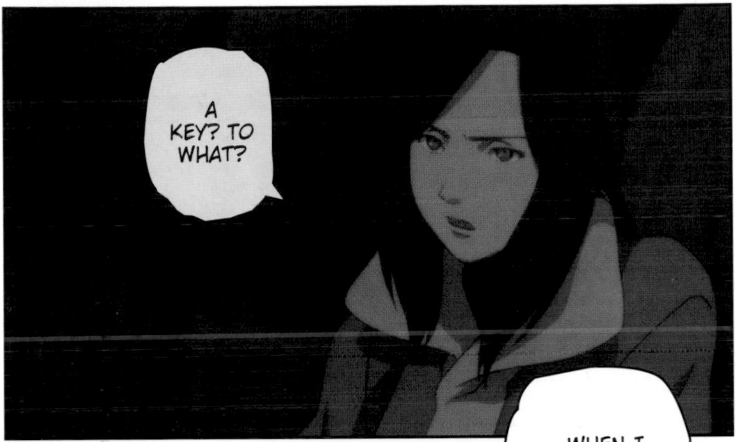
A KEY? TO WHAT?

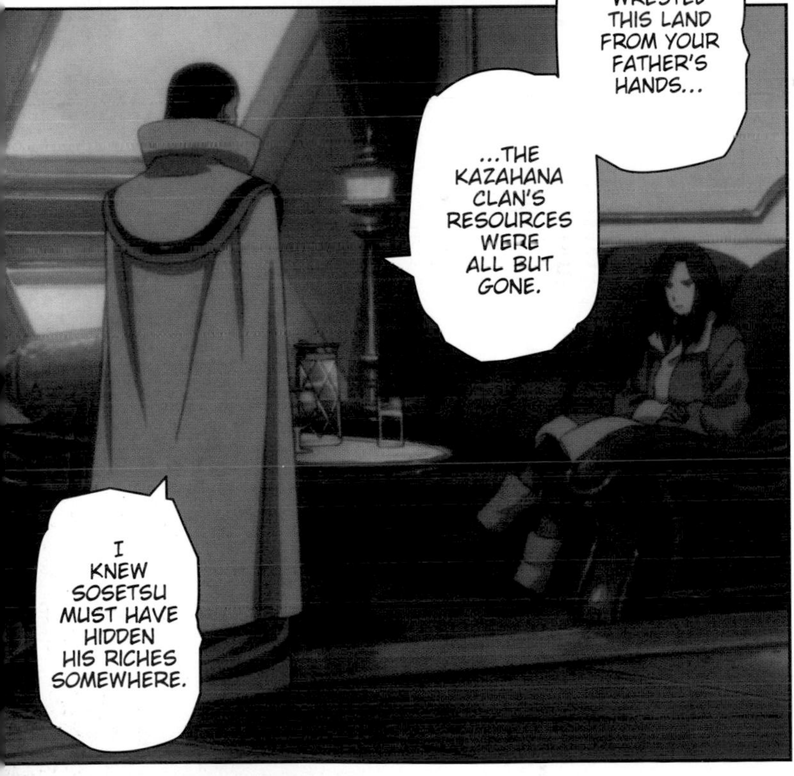
WHEN I WRESTED THIS LAND FROM YOUR FATHER'S HANDS...
...THE KAZAHANA CLAN'S RESOURCES WERE ALL BUT GONE.
I KNEW SOSETSU MUST HAVE HIDDEN HIS RICHES SOMEWHERE.

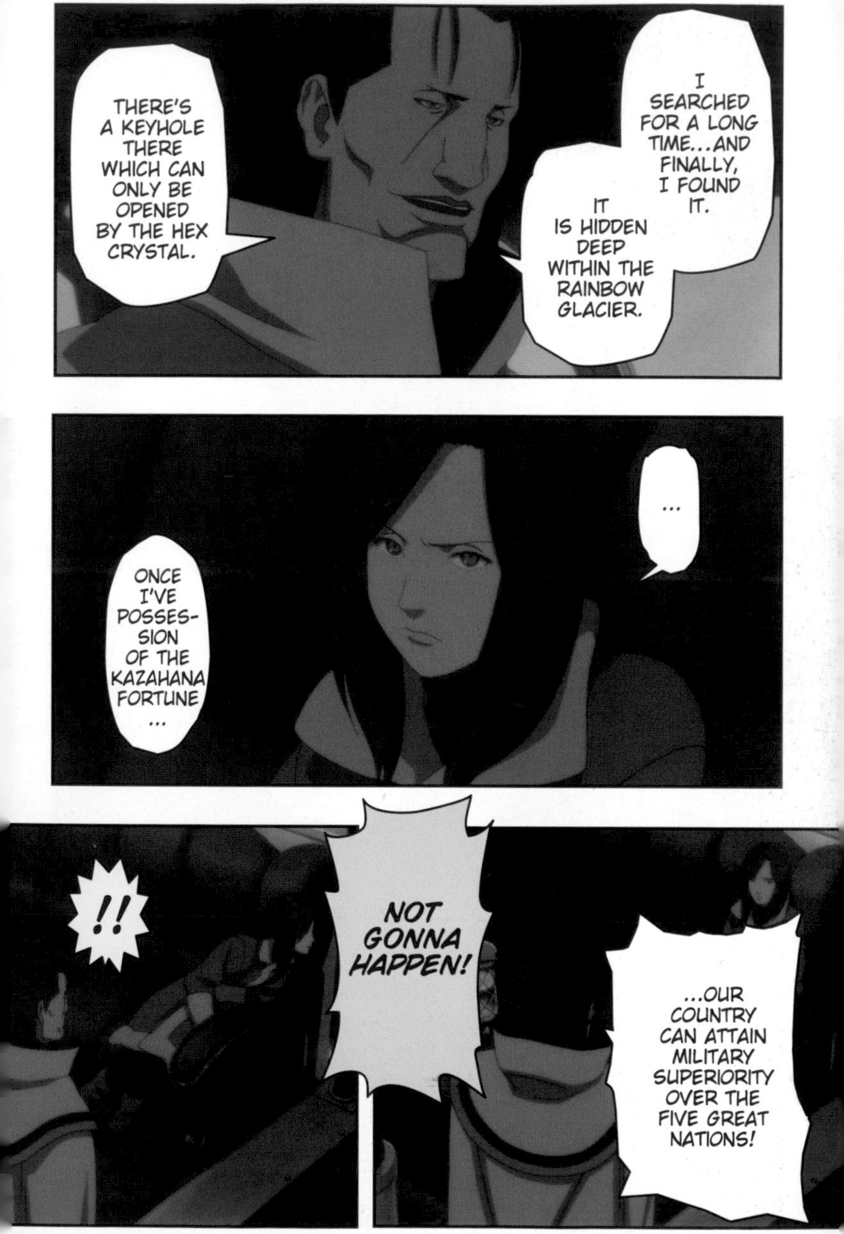
I SEARCHED FOR A LONG TIME...AND FINALLY, I FOUND IT.
IT IS HIDDEN DEEP WITHIN THE RAINBOW GLACIER.
THERE'S A KEYHOLE THERE WHICH CAN ONLY BE OPENED BY THE HEX CRYSTAL.
...
ONCE I'VE POSSESSION OF THE KAZAHANA FORTUNE...
...OUR COUNTRY CAN ATTAIN MILITARY SUPERIORITY OVER THE FIVE GREAT NATIONS!
NOT GONNA HAPPEN!
!!

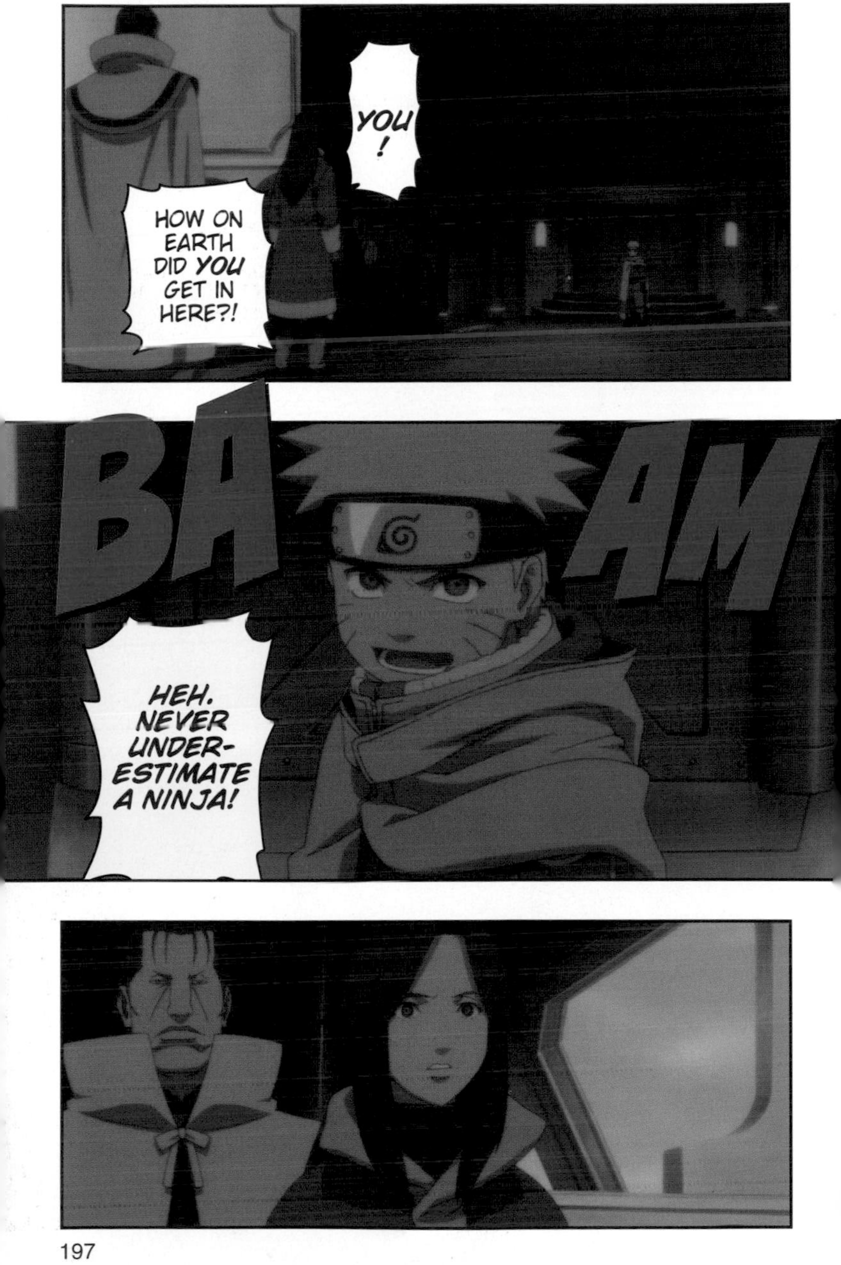
YOU!
HOW ON EARTH DID YOU GET IN HERE?!
BAAM
HEH. NEVER UNDER-ESTIMATE A NINJA!

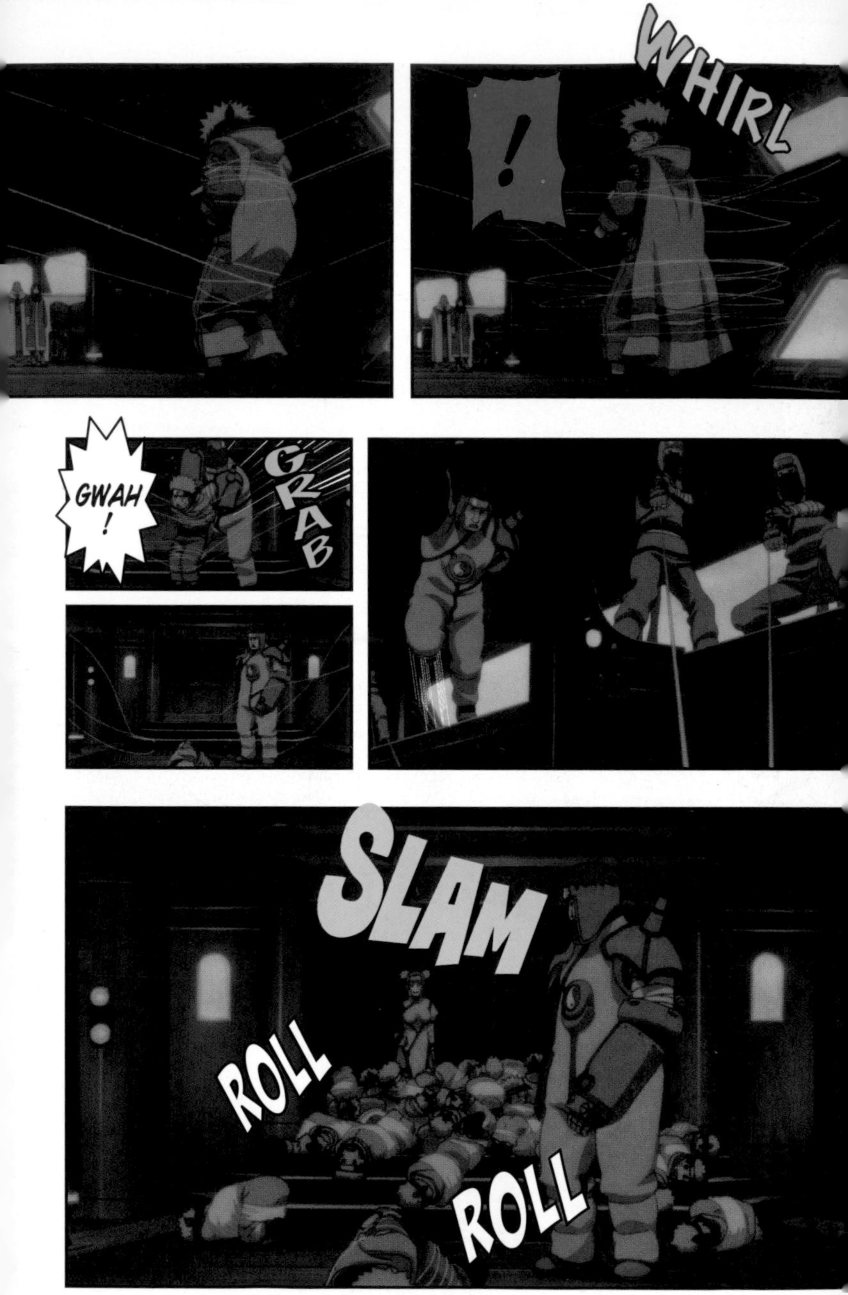
WHIRL
!
GRAB
GWAH!
SLAM
ROLL
ROLL

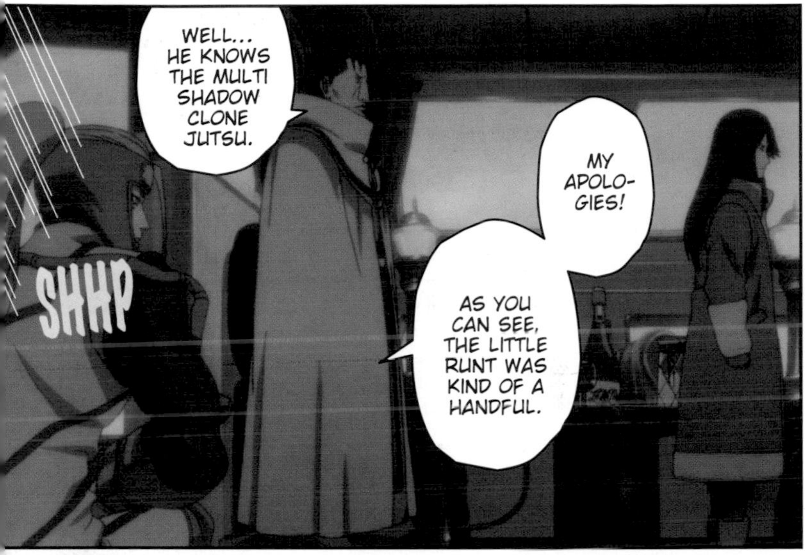
MY APOLOGIES!
AS YOU CAN SEE, THE LITTLE RUNT WAS KIND OF A HANDFUL.
WELL... HE KNOWS THE MULTI SHADOW CLONE JUTSU.
SHHP

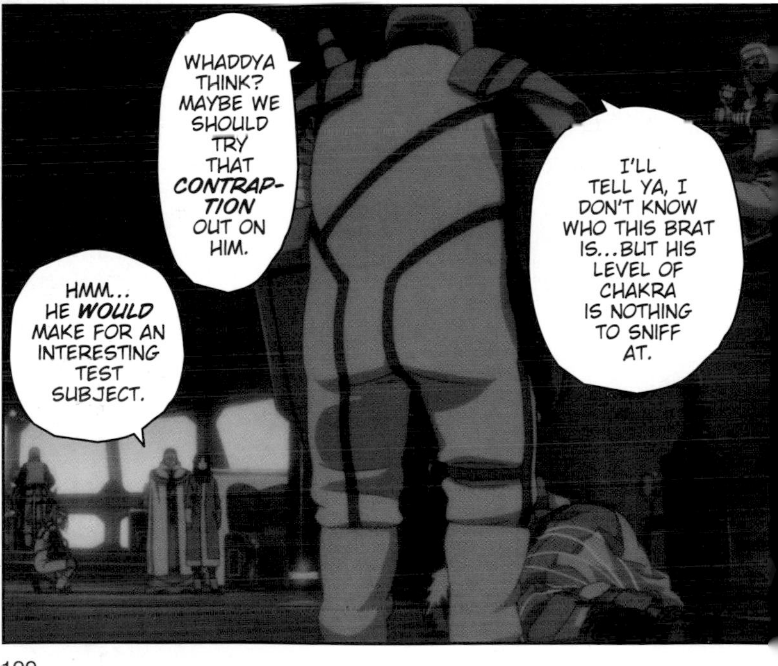
I'LL TELL YA, I DON'T KNOW WHO THIS BRAT IS...BUT HIS LEVEL OF CHAKRA IS NOTHING TO SNIFF AT.
WHADDYA THINK? MAYBE WE SHOULD TRY THAT ***CONTRAPTION*** OUT ON HIM.
HMM... HE ***WOULD*** MAKE FOR AN INTERESTING TEST SUBJECT.

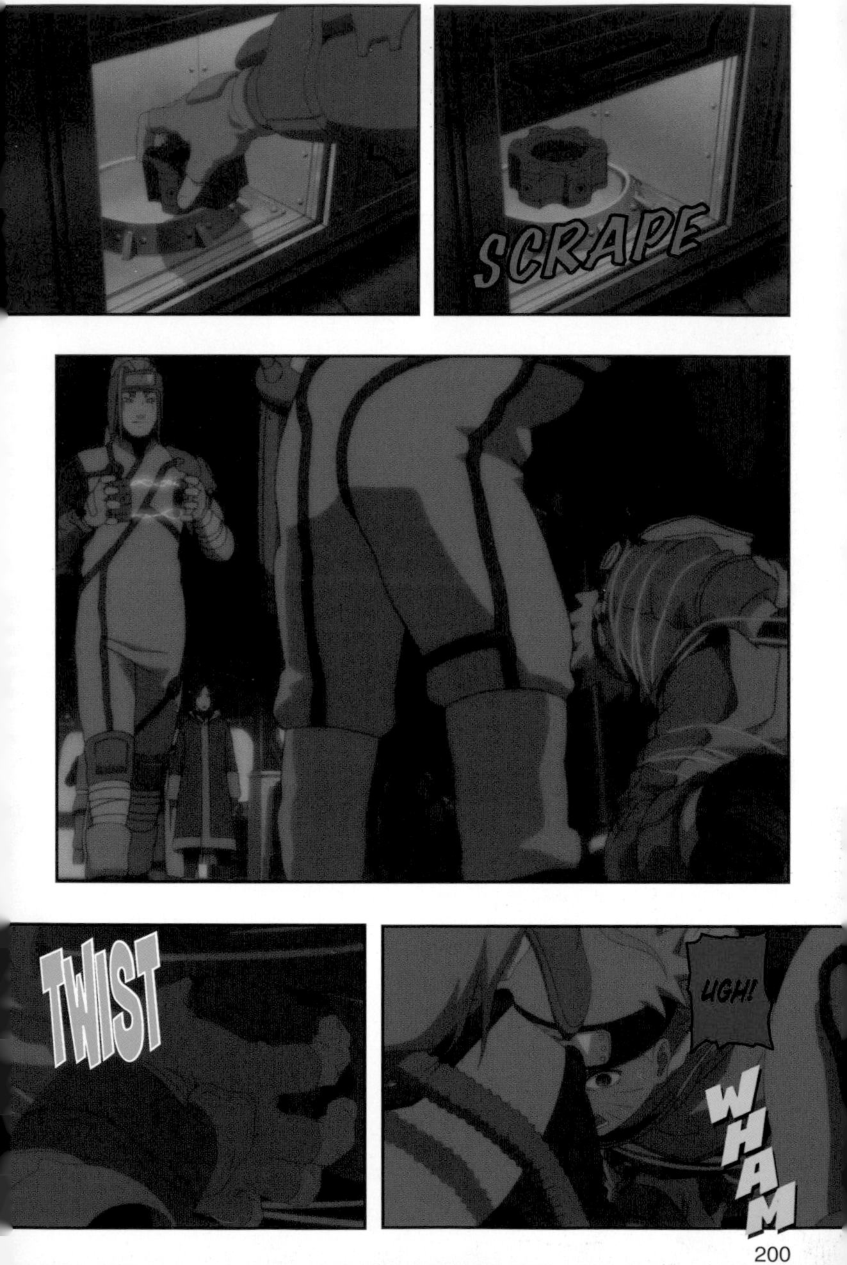
SCRAPE
UGH!
WHAM
TWIST

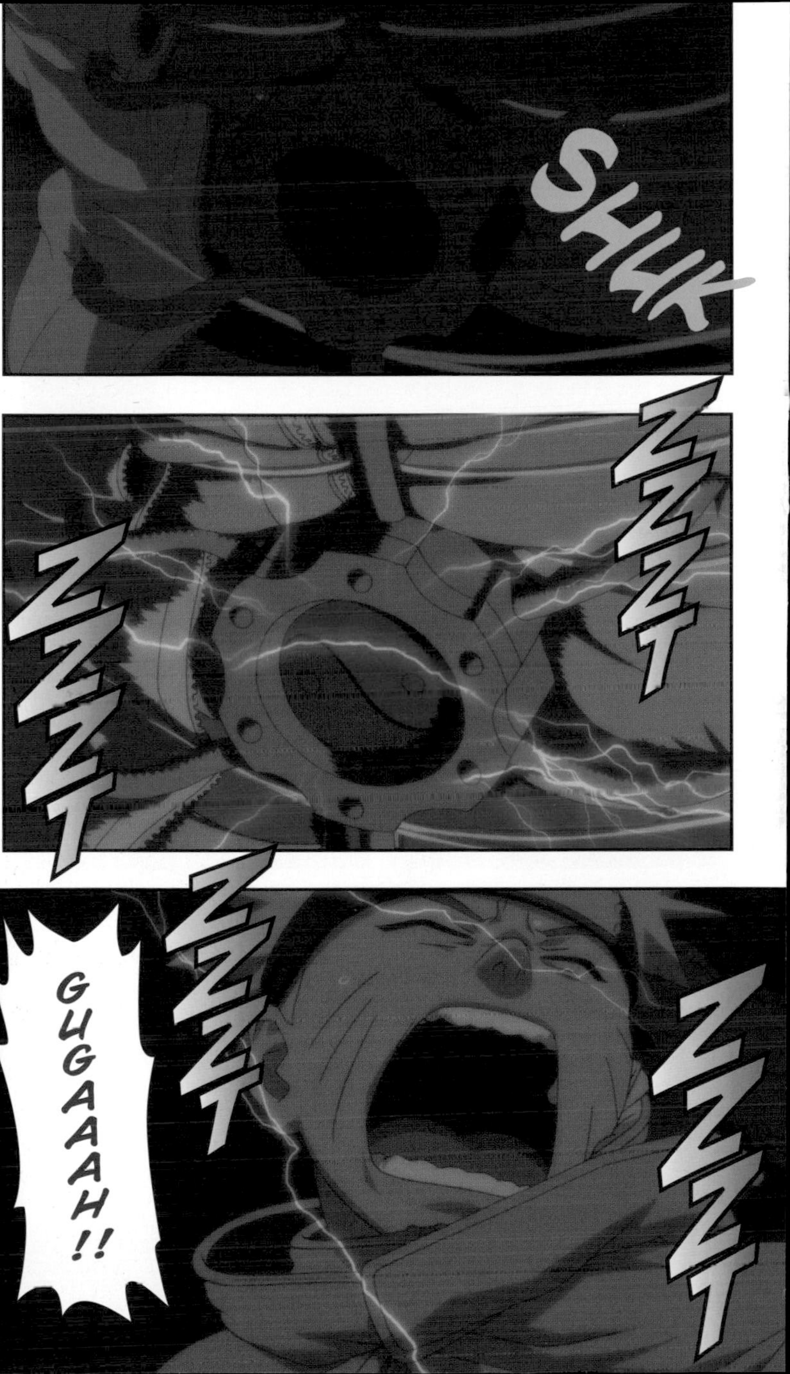
SHUK
ZZZZT
ZZZZT
ZZZZT
ZZZZT
GUGAAAH!!

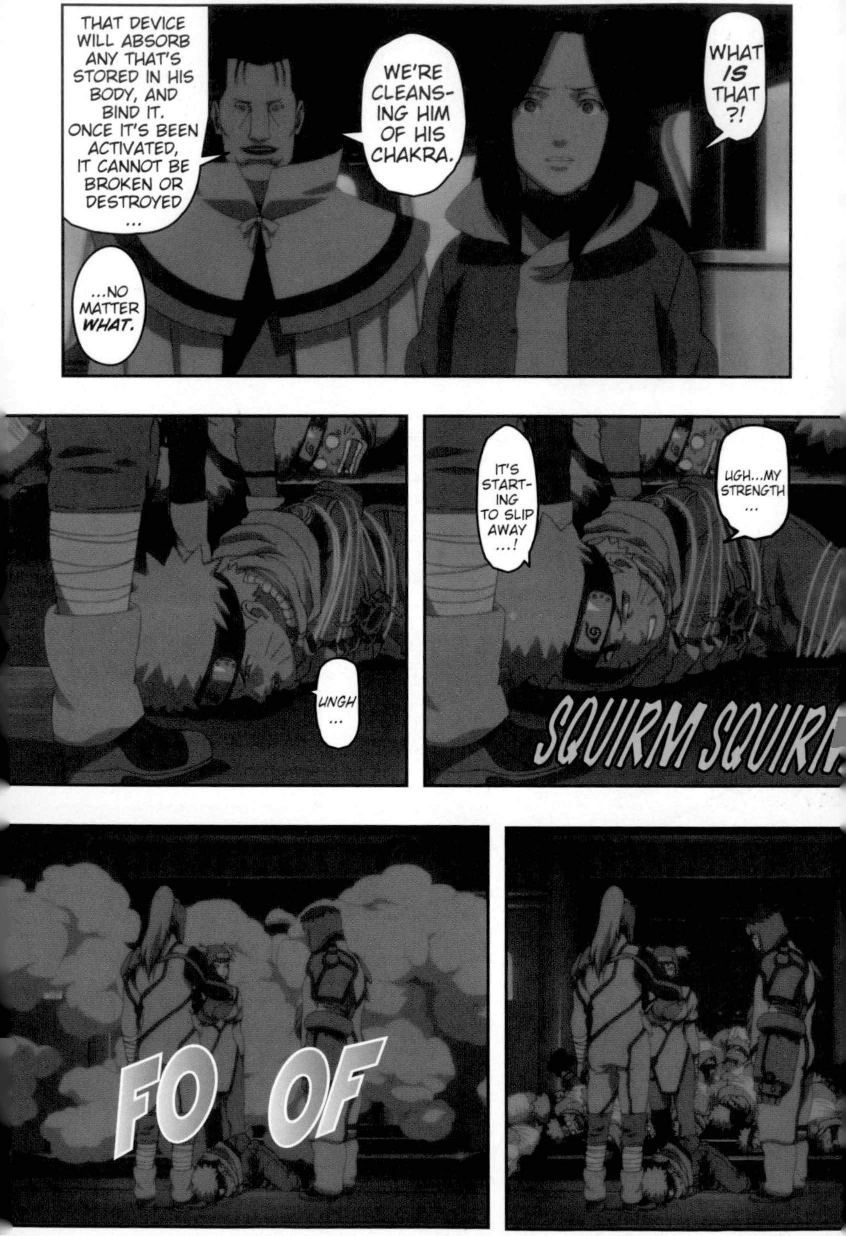
WHAT *IS* THAT?!
WE'RE CLEANSING HIM OF HIS CHAKRA.
THAT DEVICE WILL ABSORB ANY THAT'S STORED IN HIS BODY, AND BIND IT. ONCE IT'S BEEN ACTIVATED, IT CANNOT BE BROKEN OR DESTROYED...
...NO MATTER ***WHAT.***
UGH...MY STRENGTH...
IT'S STARTING TO SLIP AWAY...!
SQUIRM SQUIR
UNGH...
FO OF

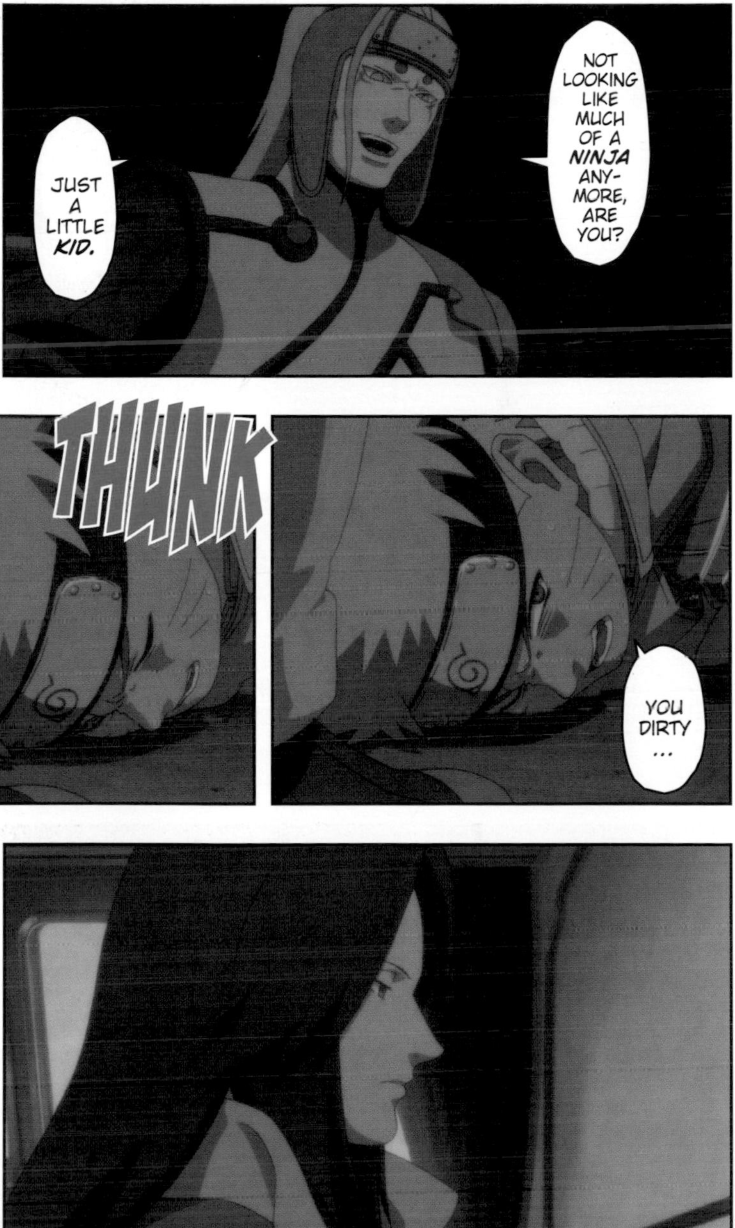
NOT LOOKING LIKE MUCH OF A *NINJA* ANY-MORE, ARE YOU?
JUST A LITTLE *KID.*
YOU DIRTY ...
THUNK

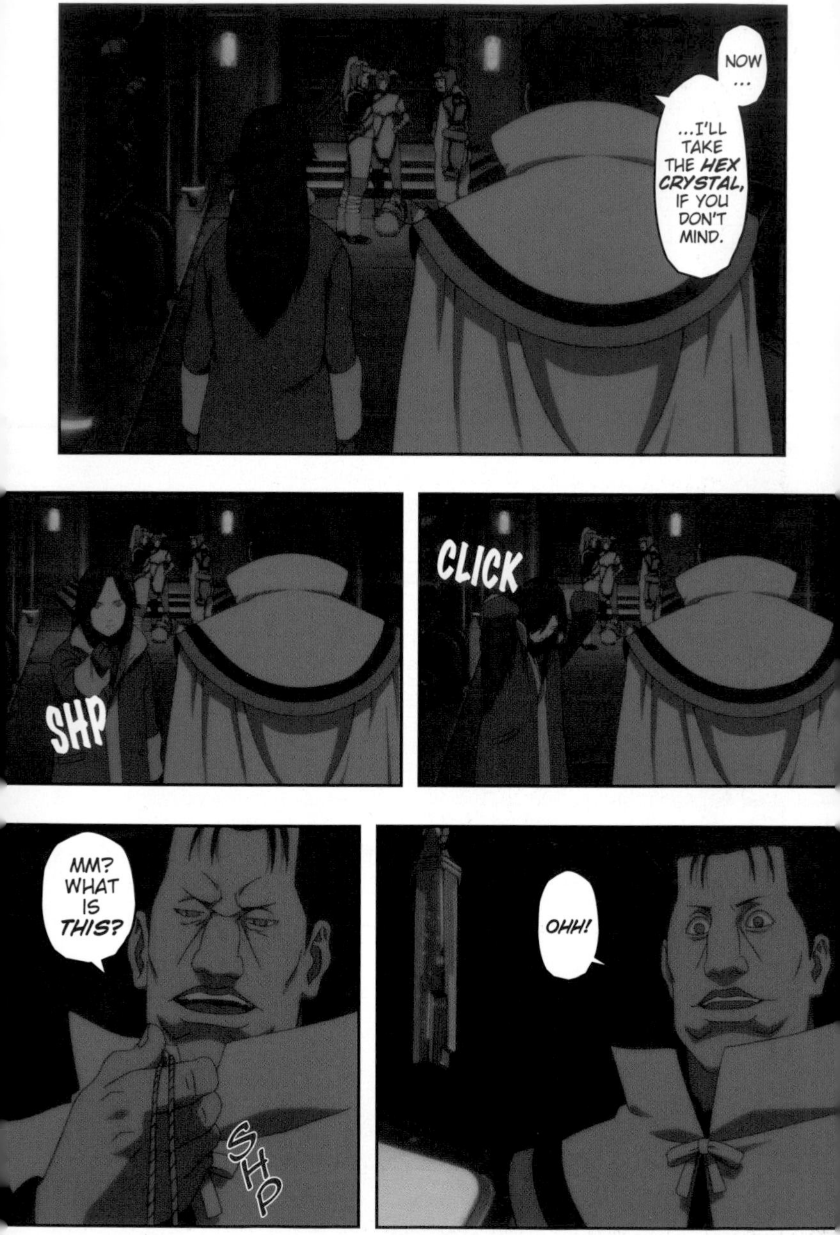
NOW...
...I'LL TAKE THE HEX CRYSTAL, IF YOU DON'T MIND.
CLICK
SHP
OHH!
MM? WHAT IS THIS?
SHP

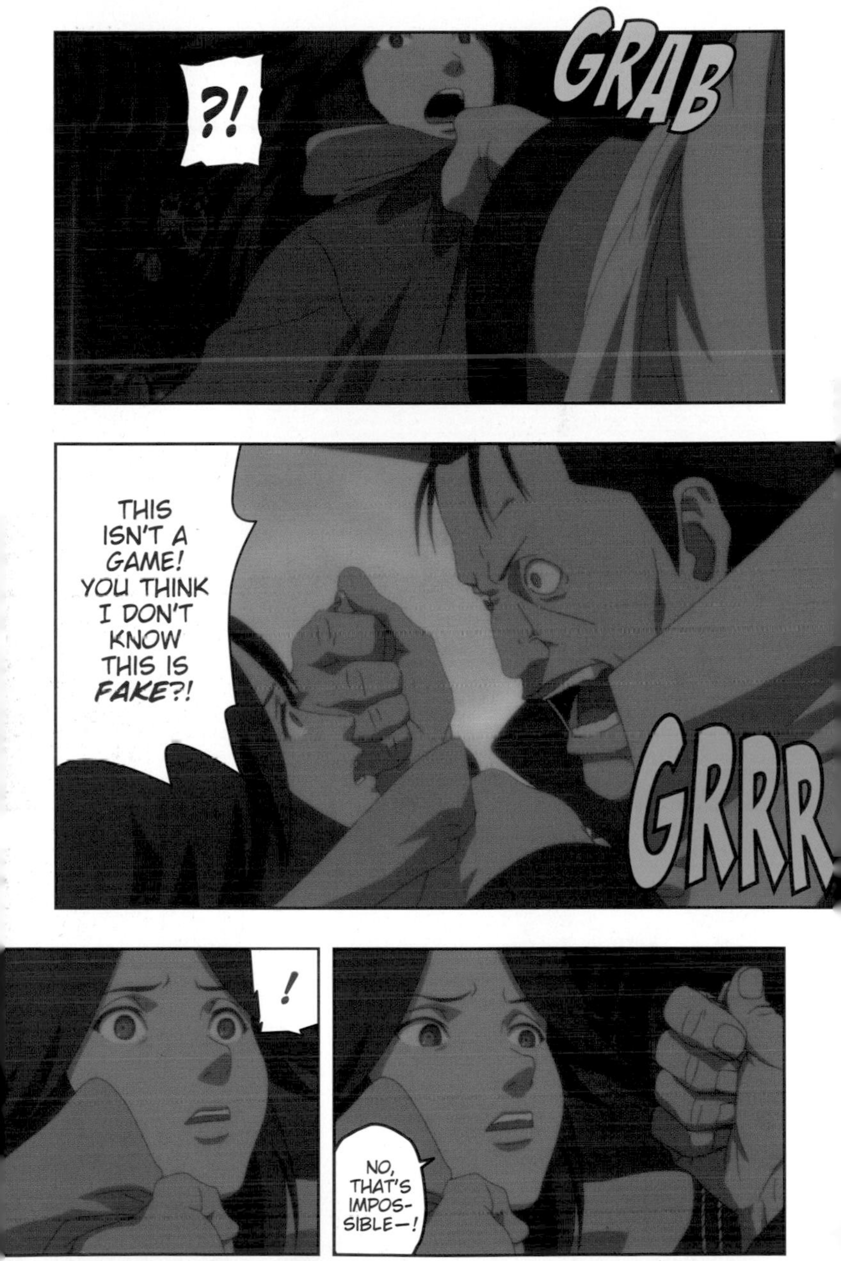
GRAB
?!
THIS ISN'T A GAME! YOU THINK I DON'T KNOW THIS IS **FAKE**?!
GRRR
NO, THAT'S IMPOS-SIBLE—!
!

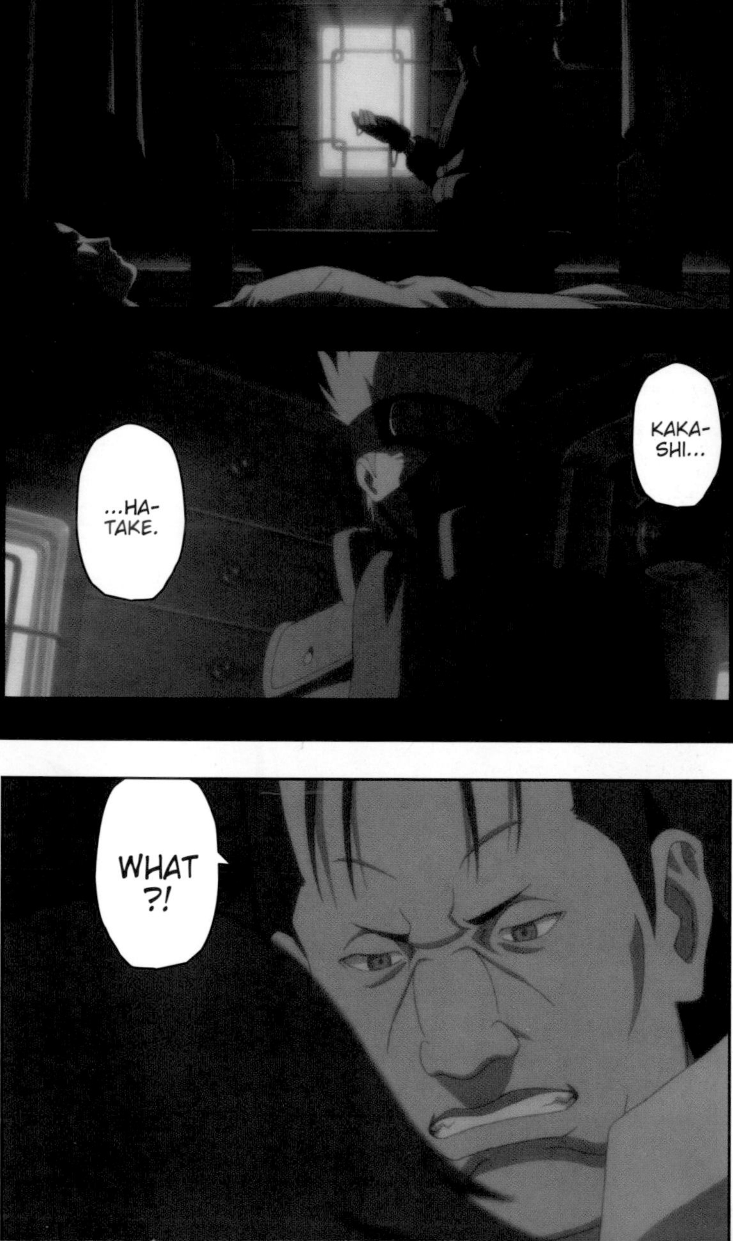
KAKA-SHI...
...HA-TAKE.
WHAT ?!

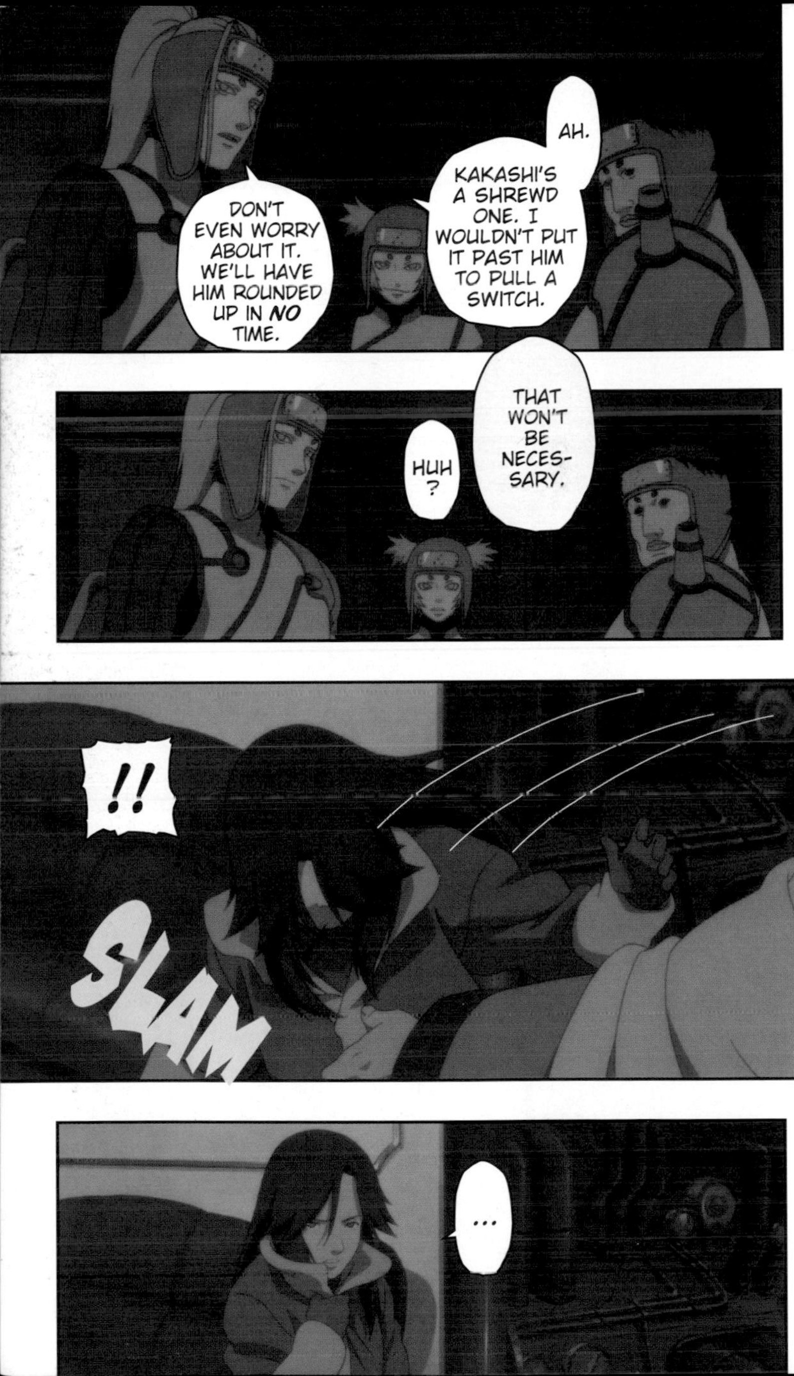
AH.
KAKASHI'S A SHREWD ONE. I WOULDN'T PUT IT PAST HIM TO PULL A SWITCH.
DON'T EVEN WORRY ABOUT IT. WE'LL HAVE HIM ROUNDED UP IN *NO* TIME.
THAT WON'T BE NECES-SARY.
HUH?
!!
SLAM
...

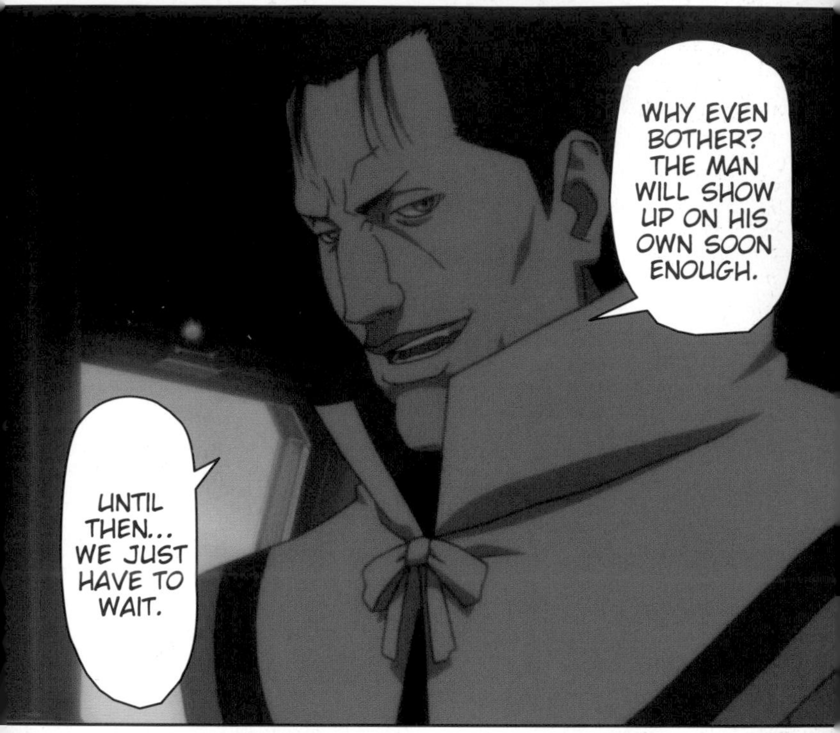
WHY EVEN BOTHER? THE MAN WILL SHOW UP ON HIS OWN SOON ENOUGH.
UNTIL THEN... WE JUST HAVE TO WAIT.
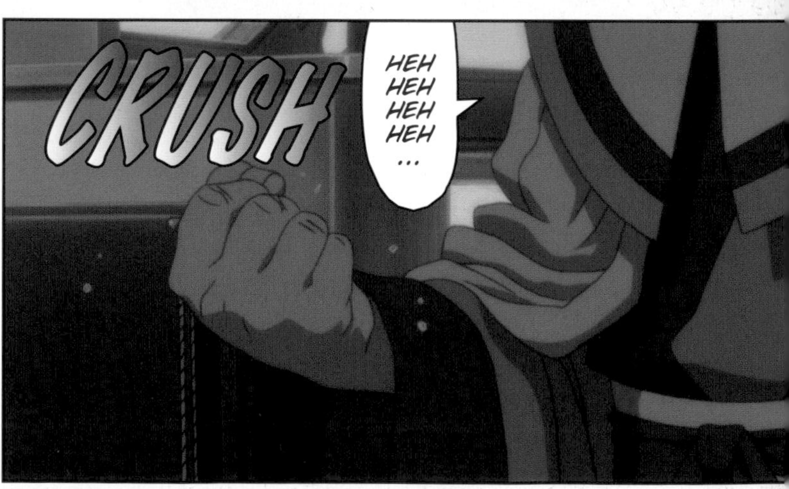
HEH HEH HEH HEH ...
CRUSH

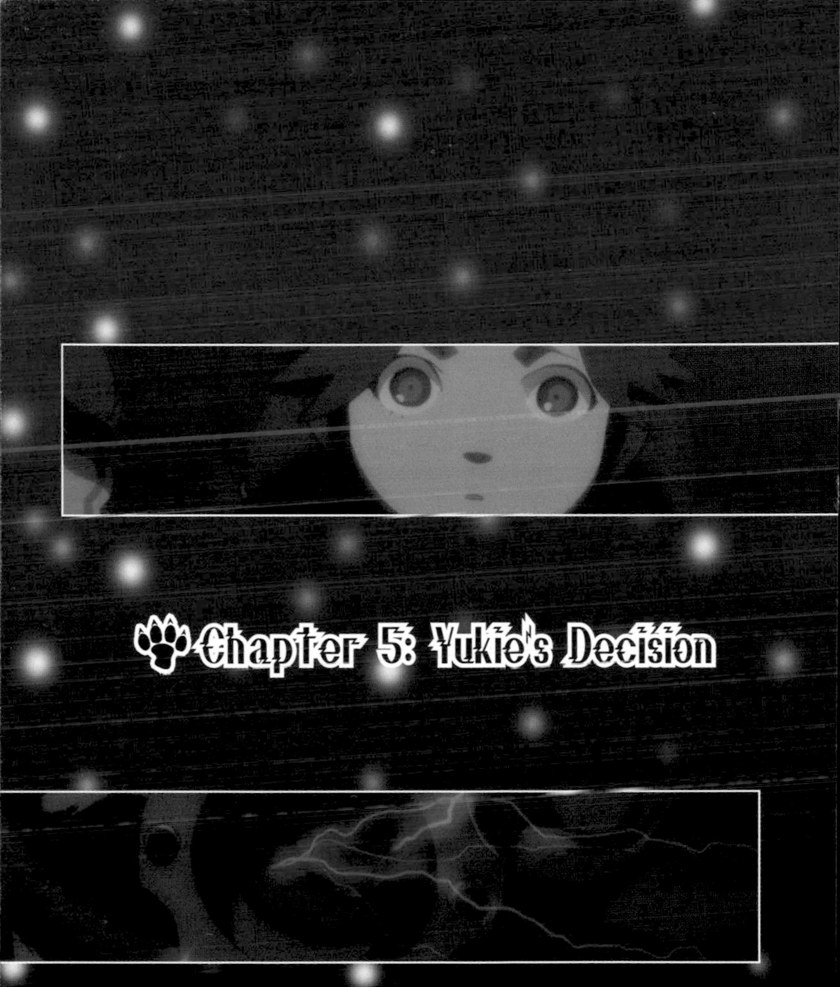
Chapter 5: Yukie's Decision

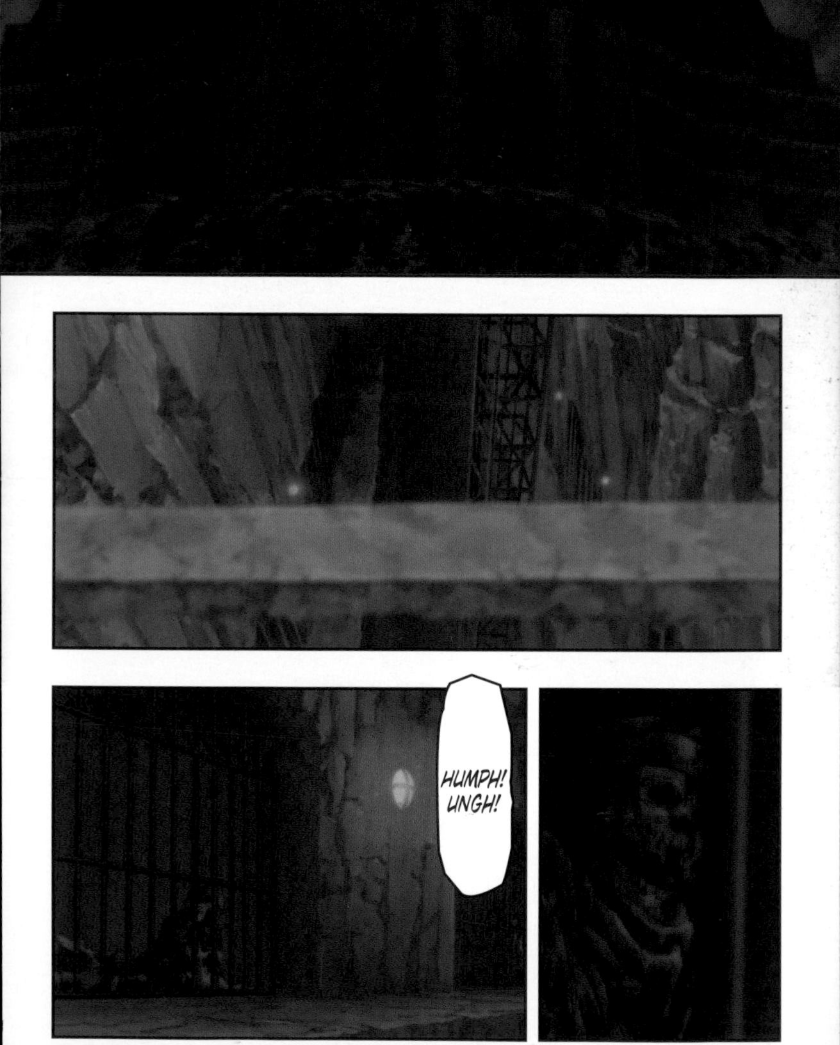
HUMPH! UNGH!

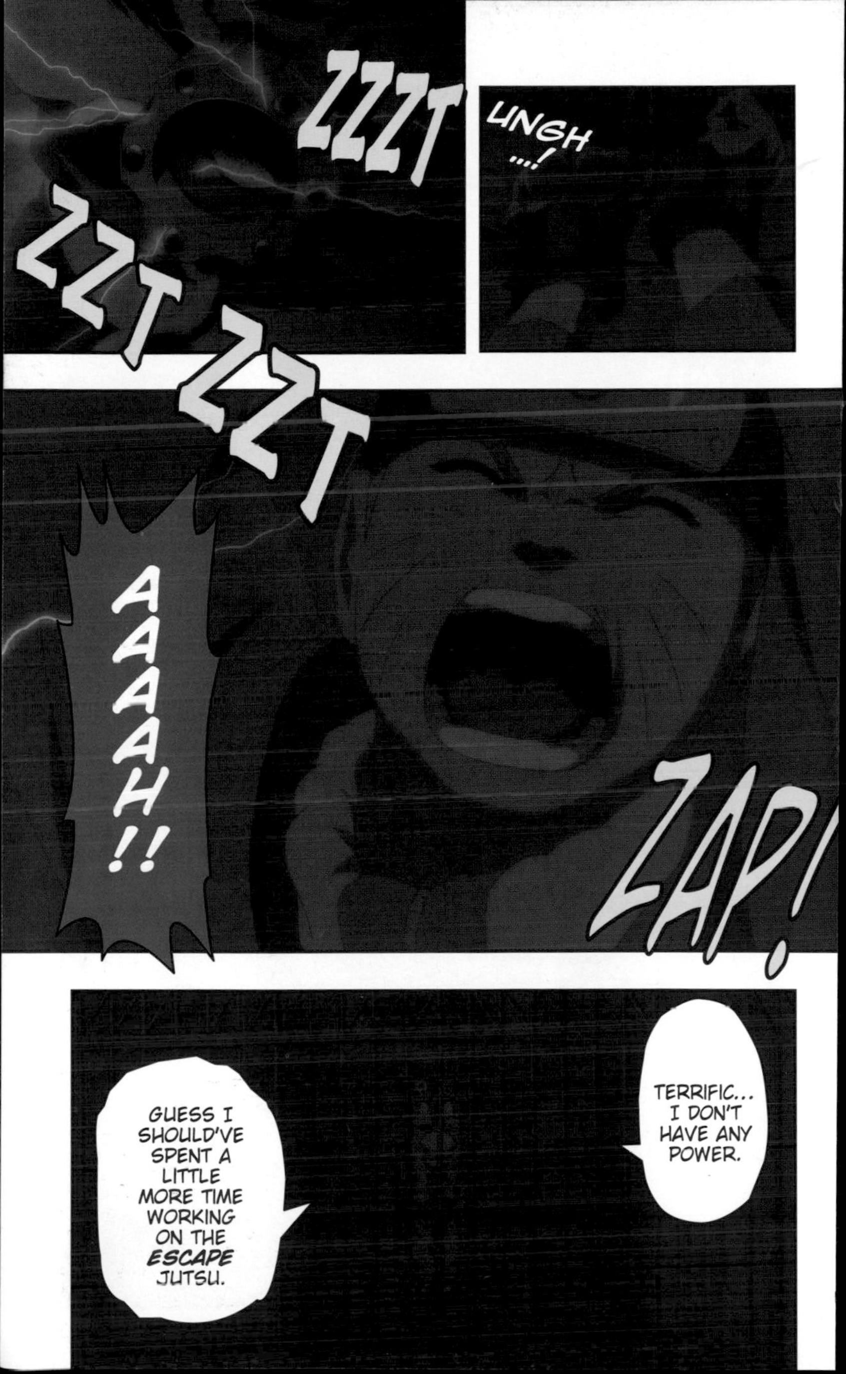
UNGH ...!
ZZZT
ZZZT
ZZZT
AAAAAH!!
ZAP!
TERRIFIC... I DON'T HAVE ANY POWER.
GUESS I SHOULD'VE SPENT A LITTLE MORE TIME WORKING ON THE ESCAPE JUTSU.

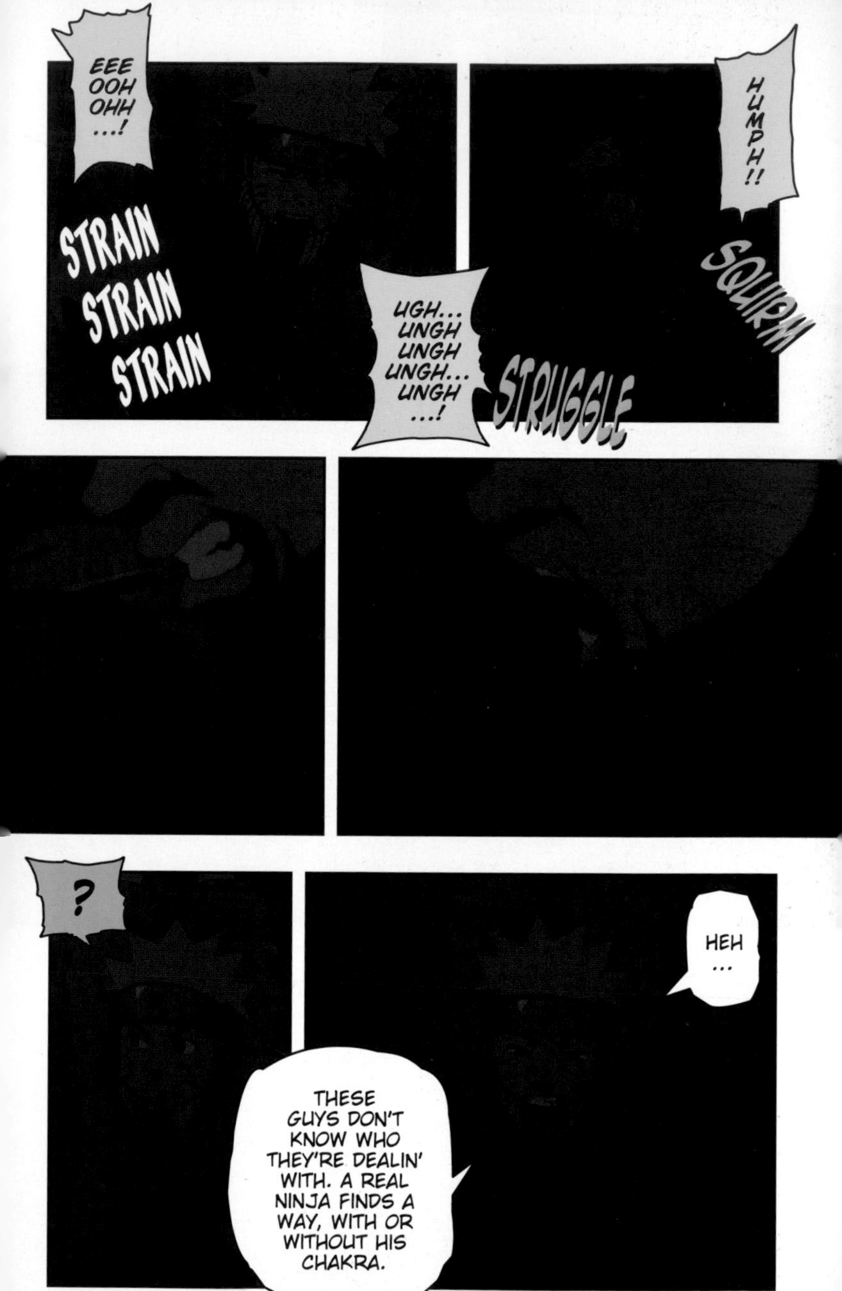
HUMPH!!
SQUIRM
UGH... UNGH UNGH UNGH... UNGH ...!
STRUGGLE
EEE OOH OHH ...!
STRAIN STRAIN STRAIN
HEH ...
THESE GUYS DON'T KNOW WHO THEY'RE DEALIN' WITH. A REAL NINJA FINDS A WAY, WITH OR WITHOUT HIS CHAKRA.
?

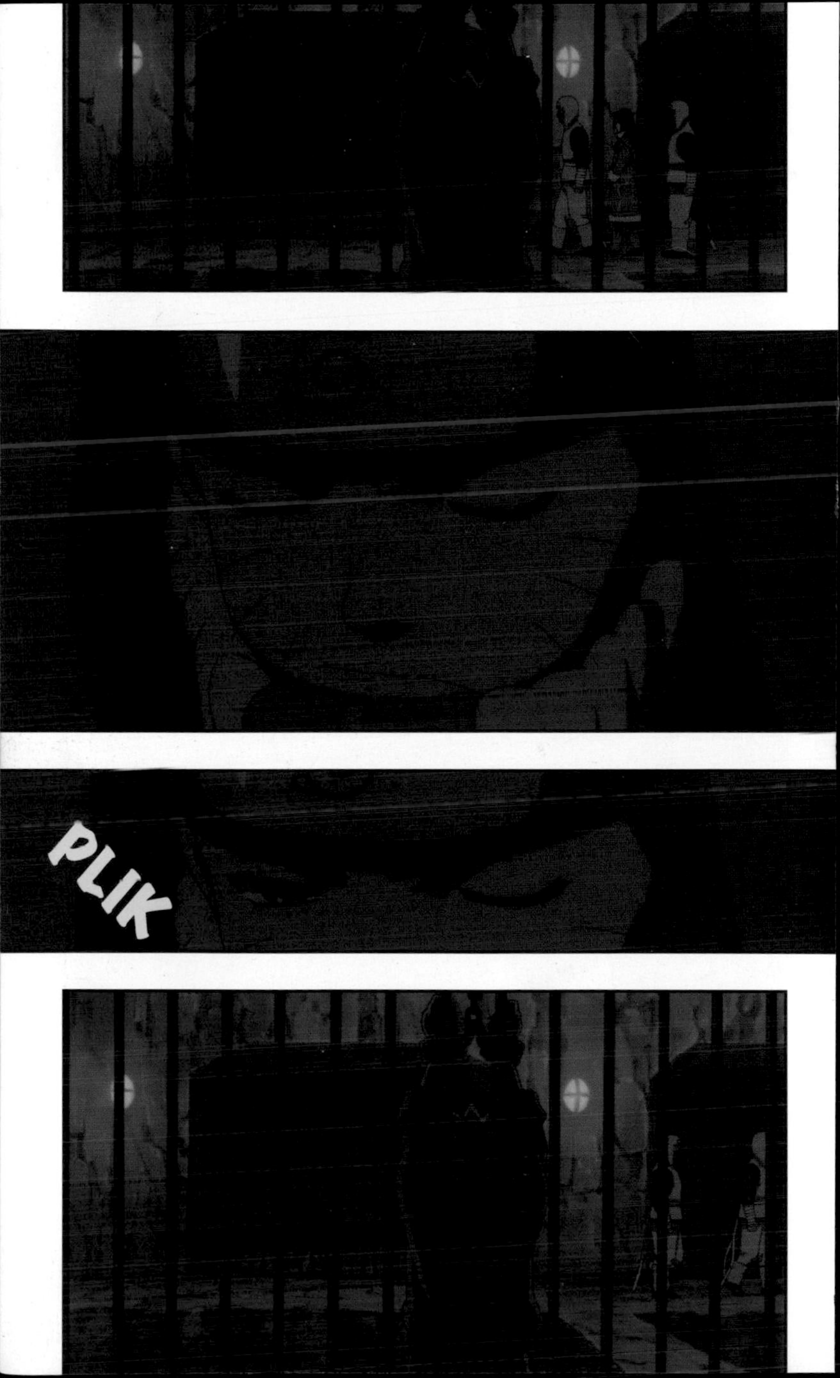
PLIK

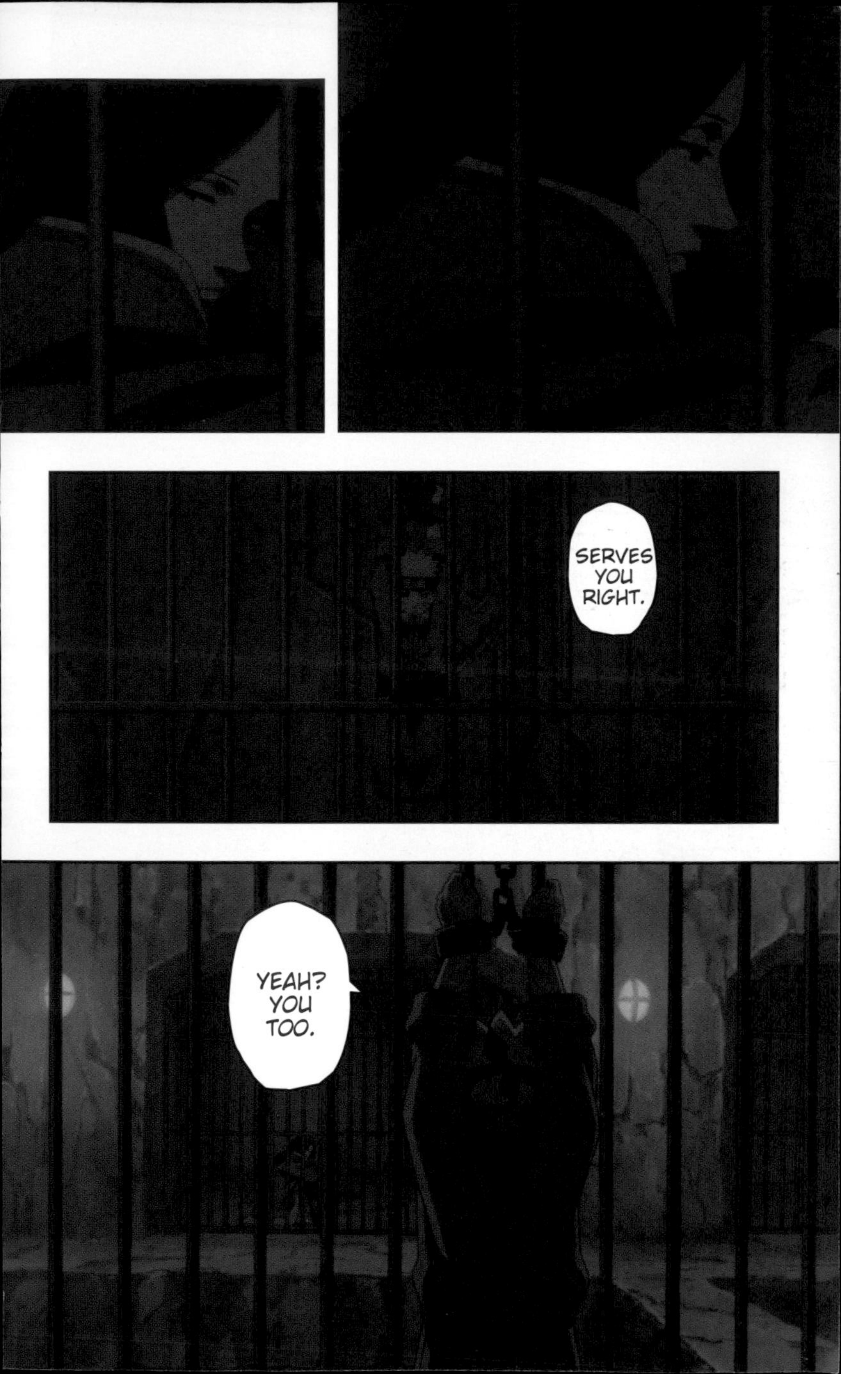
SERVES YOU RIGHT.
YEAH? YOU TOO.

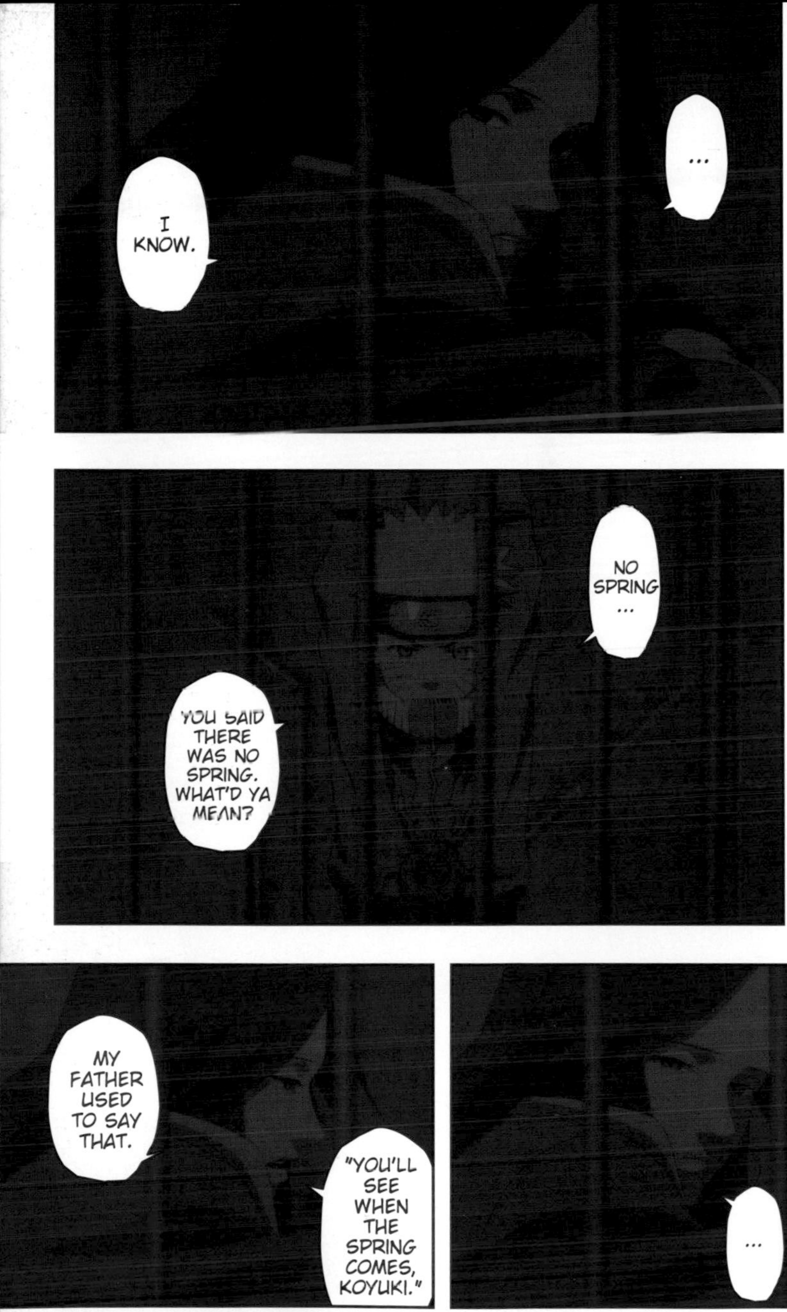
...
I KNOW.
NO SPRING...
YOU SAID THERE WAS NO SPRING. WHAT'D YA MEAN?
...
MY FATHER USED TO SAY THAT.
"YOU'LL SEE WHEN THE SPRING COMES, KOYUKI."

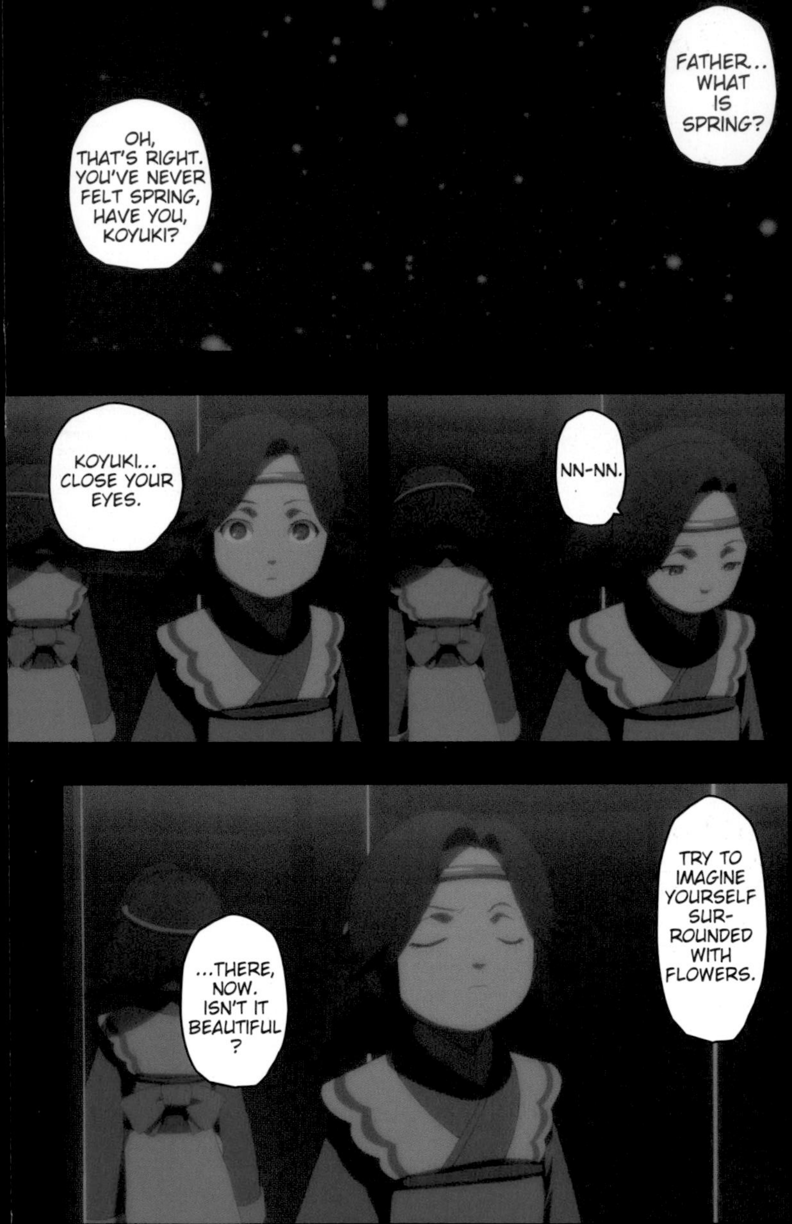
FATHER... WHAT IS SPRING?
OH, THAT'S RIGHT. YOU'VE NEVER FELT SPRING, HAVE YOU, KOYUKI?
NN-NN.
KOYUKI... CLOSE YOUR EYES.
TRY TO IMAGINE YOURSELF SUR-ROUNDED WITH FLOWERS.
...THERE, NOW. ISN'T IT BEAUTIFUL?

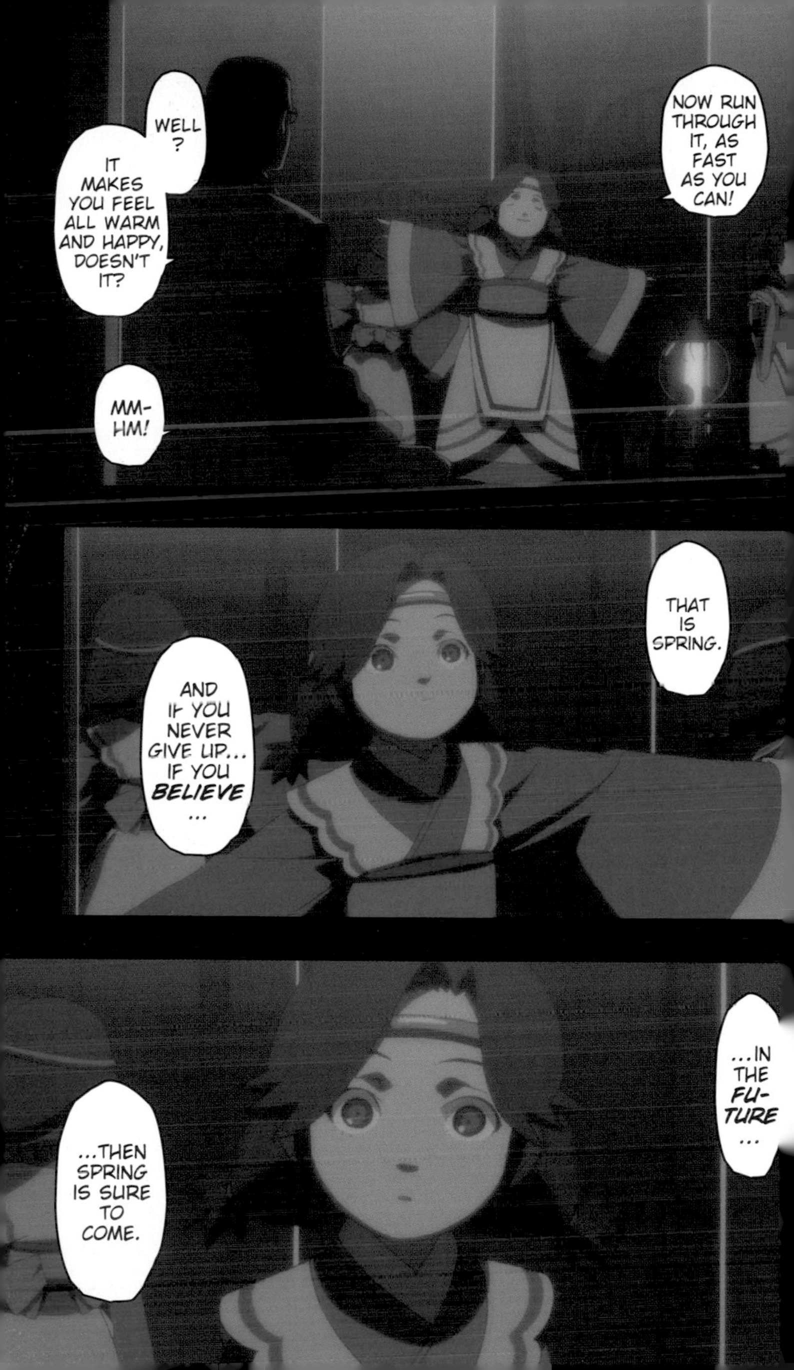
NOW RUN THROUGH IT, AS FAST AS YOU CAN!
WELL?
IT MAKES YOU FEEL ALL WARM AND HAPPY, DOESN'T IT?
MM-HM!
THAT IS SPRING.
AND IF YOU NEVER GIVE UP... IF YOU *BELIEVE*...
...IN THE *FUTURE*...
...THEN SPRING IS SURE TO COME.

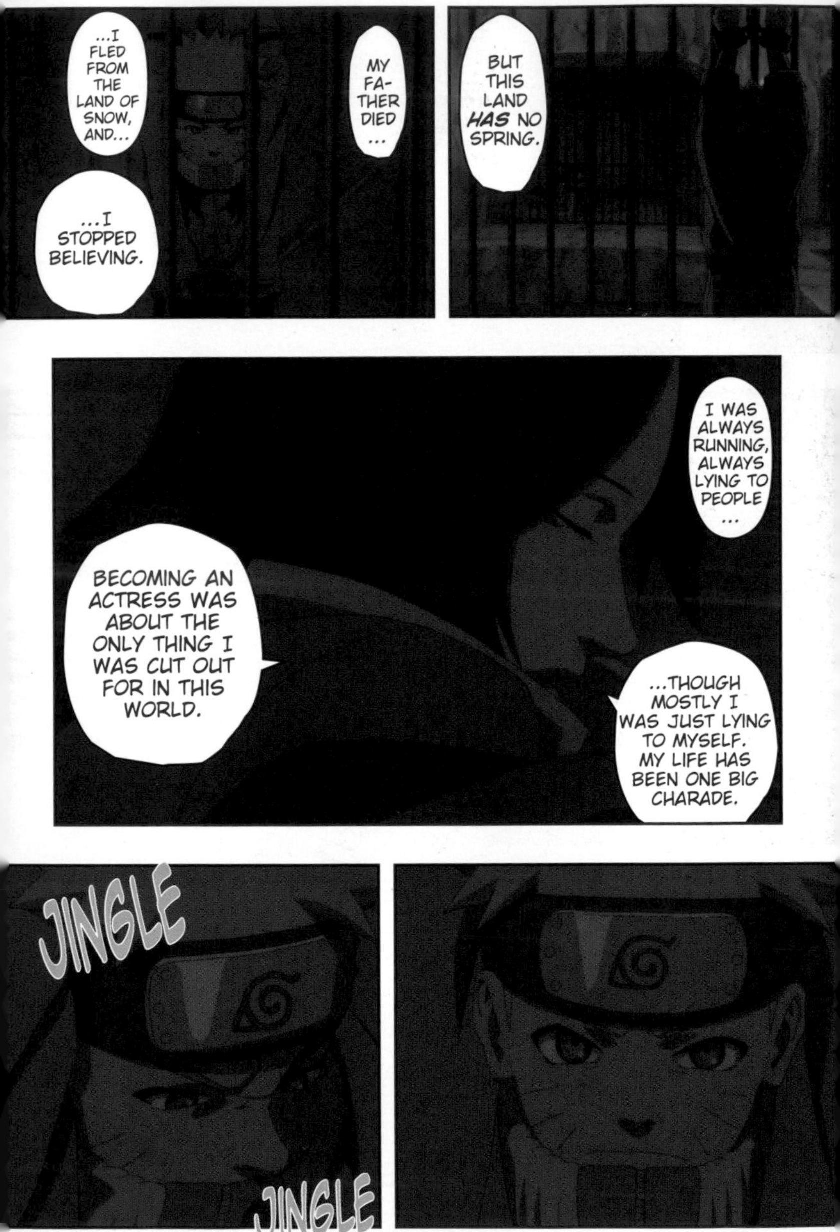
BUT THIS LAND HAS NO SPRING.
MY FATHER DIED...
...I FLED FROM THE LAND OF SNOW, AND...
...I STOPPED BELIEVING.
I WAS ALWAYS RUNNING, ALWAYS LYING TO PEOPLE...
...THOUGH MOSTLY I WAS JUST LYING TO MYSELF. MY LIFE HAS BEEN ONE BIG CHARADE.
BECOMING AN ACTRESS WAS ABOUT THE ONLY THING I WAS CUT OUT FOR IN THIS WORLD.
JINGLE
JINGLE

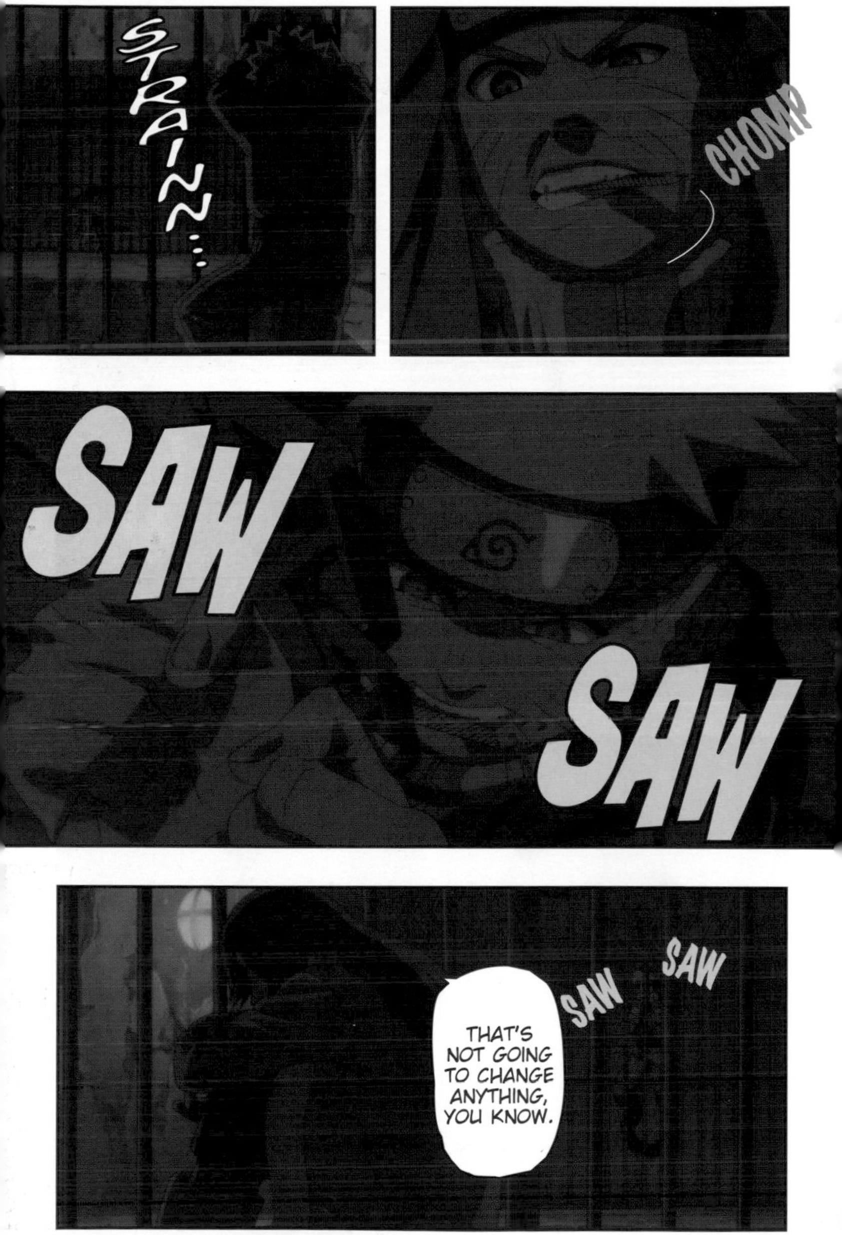
CHOMP
STRAINN...
SAW
SAW
SAW SAW
THAT'S NOT GOING TO CHANGE ANYTHING, YOU KNOW.

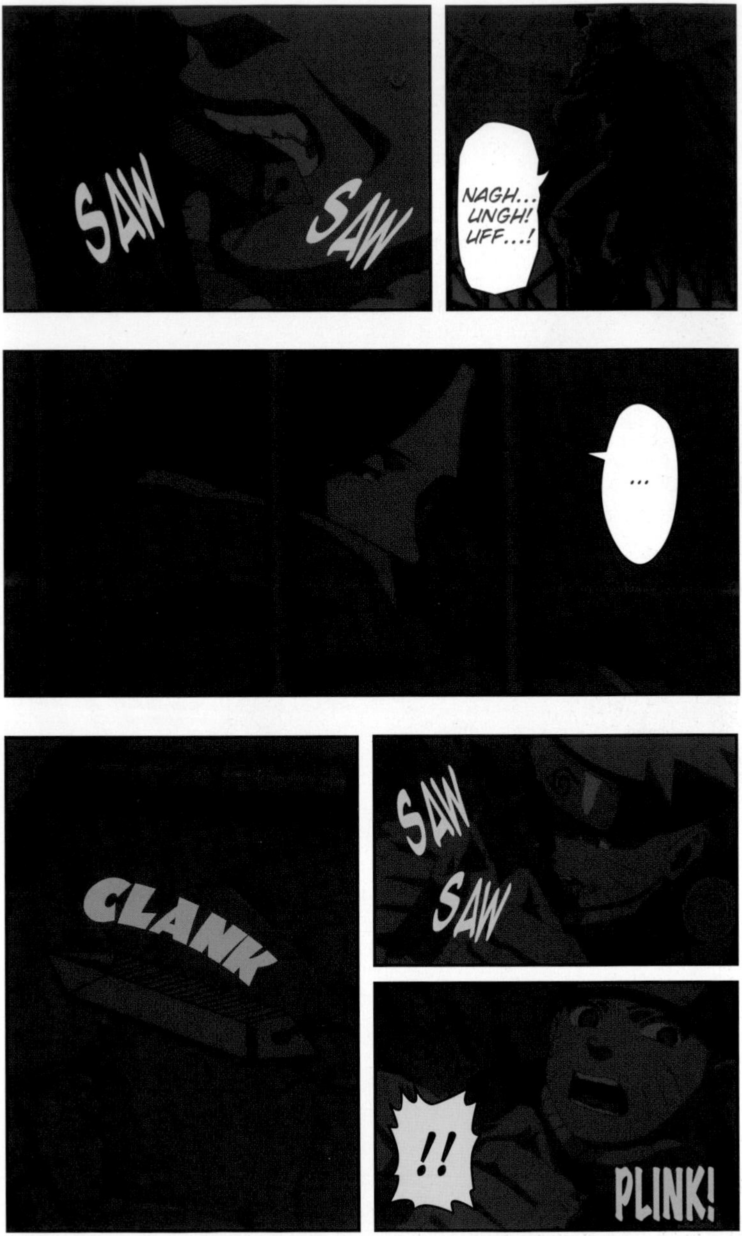
NAGH... UNGH! UFF...!
SAW
SAW
...
SAW
SAW
!!
PLINK!
CLANK

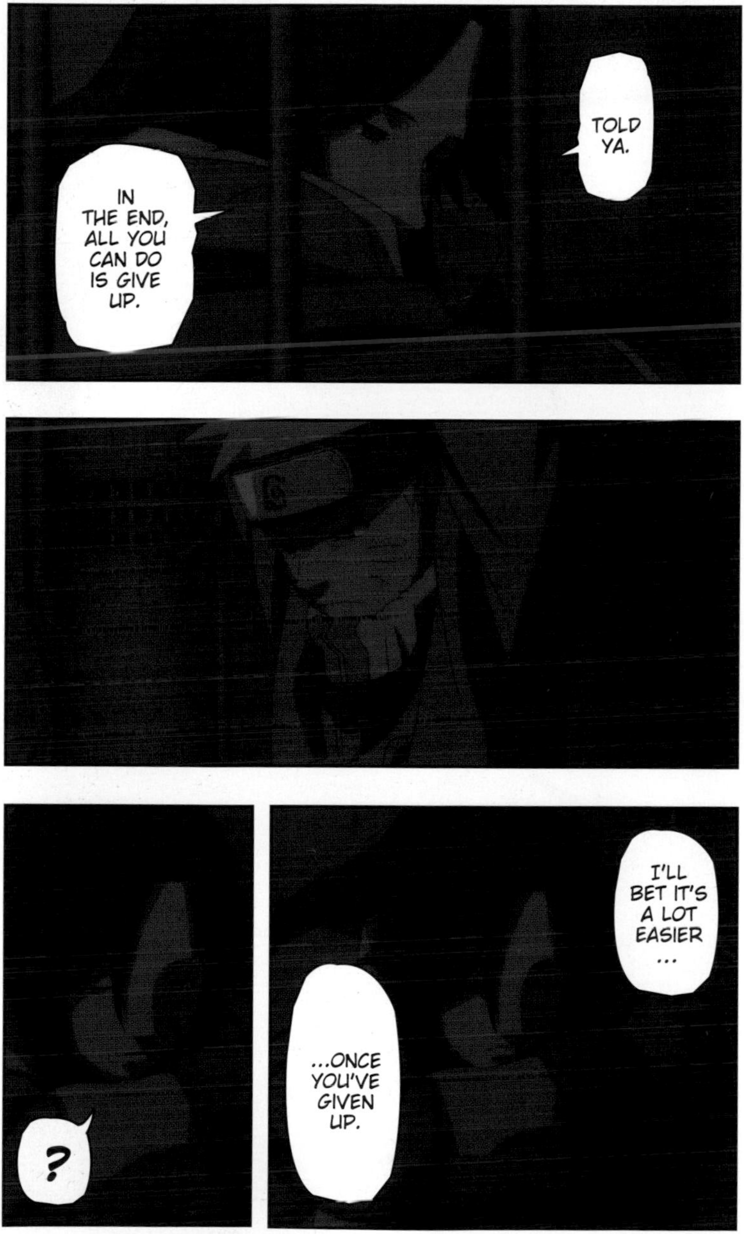
TOLD YA.
IN THE END, ALL YOU CAN DO IS GIVE UP.
I'LL BET IT'S A LOT EASIER...
...ONCE YOU'VE GIVEN UP.
?

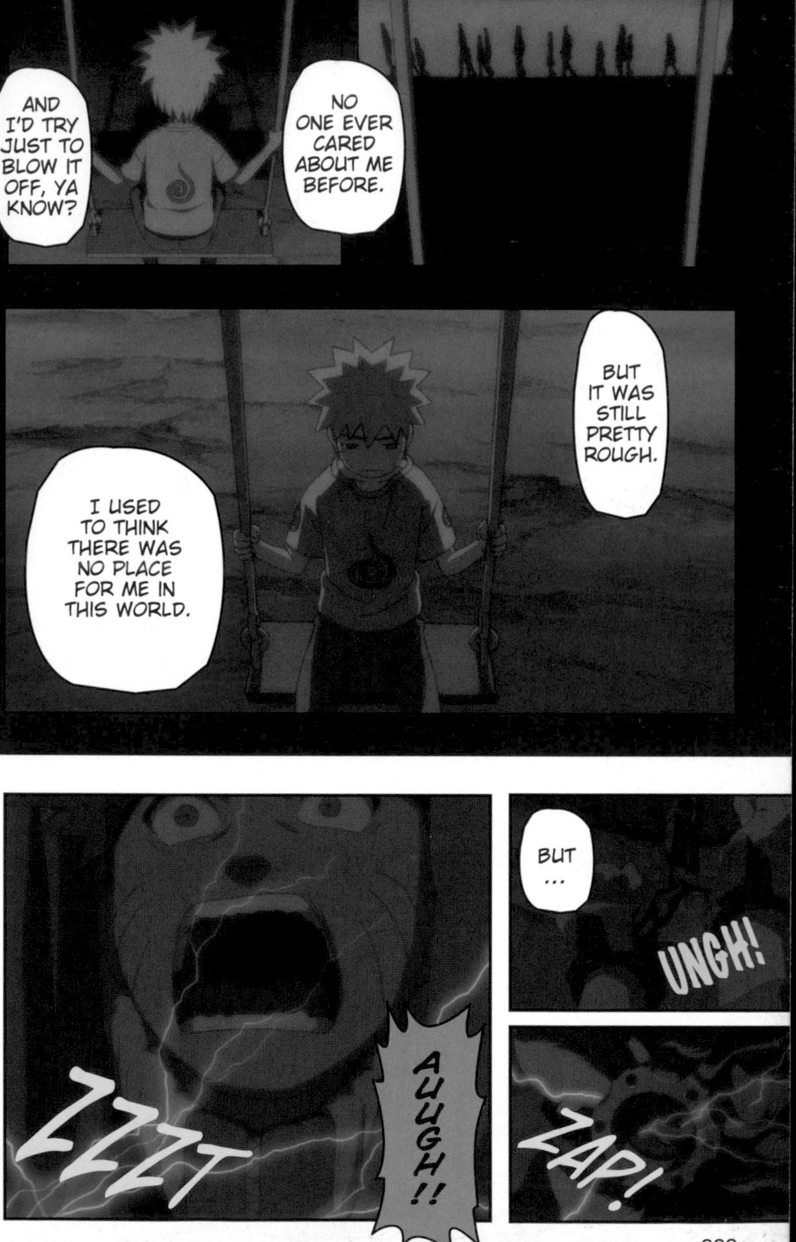
NO ONE EVER CARED ABOUT ME BEFORE.
AND I'D TRY JUST TO BLOW IT OFF, YA KNOW?
BUT IT WAS STILL PRETTY ROUGH.
I USED TO THINK THERE WAS NO PLACE FOR ME IN THIS WORLD.
BUT ...
UNGH!
ZAP!
AUUGH!!
ZZZT

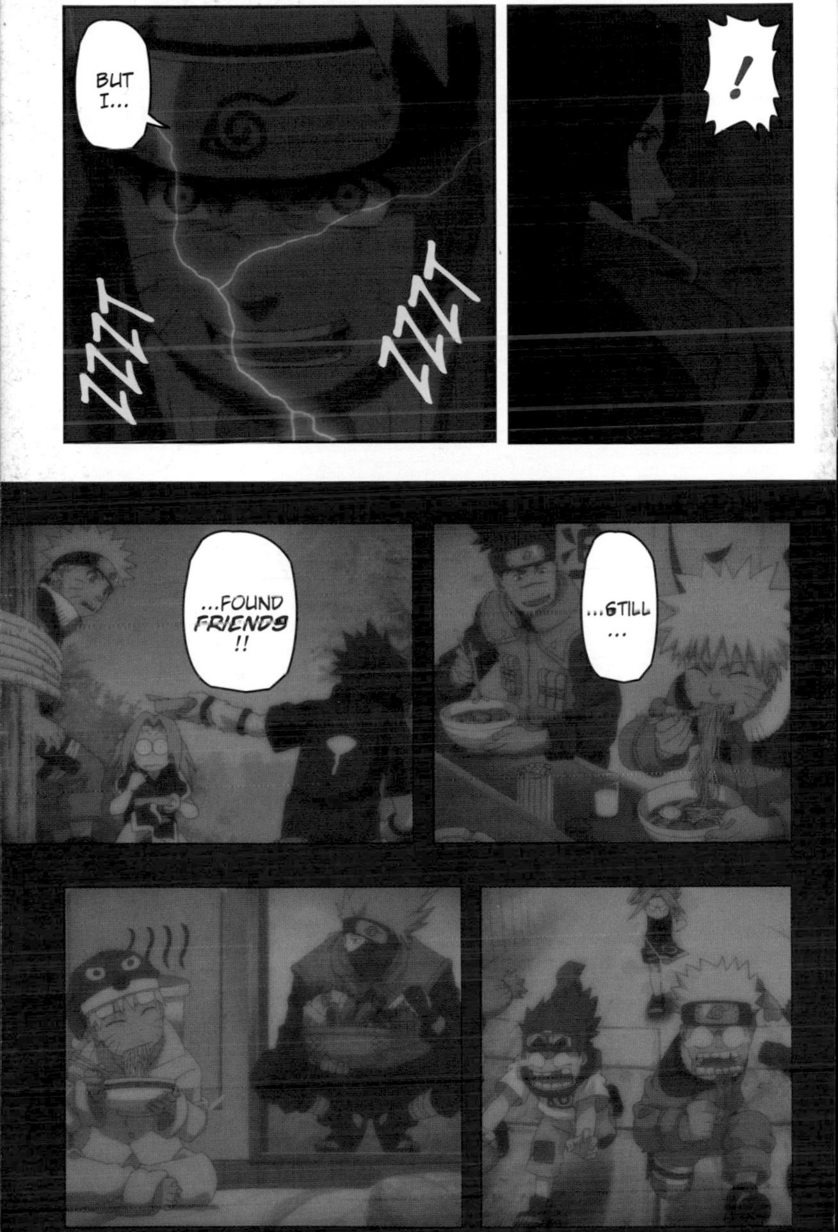
!
BUT I...
ZZZT
ZZZT
...STILL ...
...FOUND FRIENDS !!

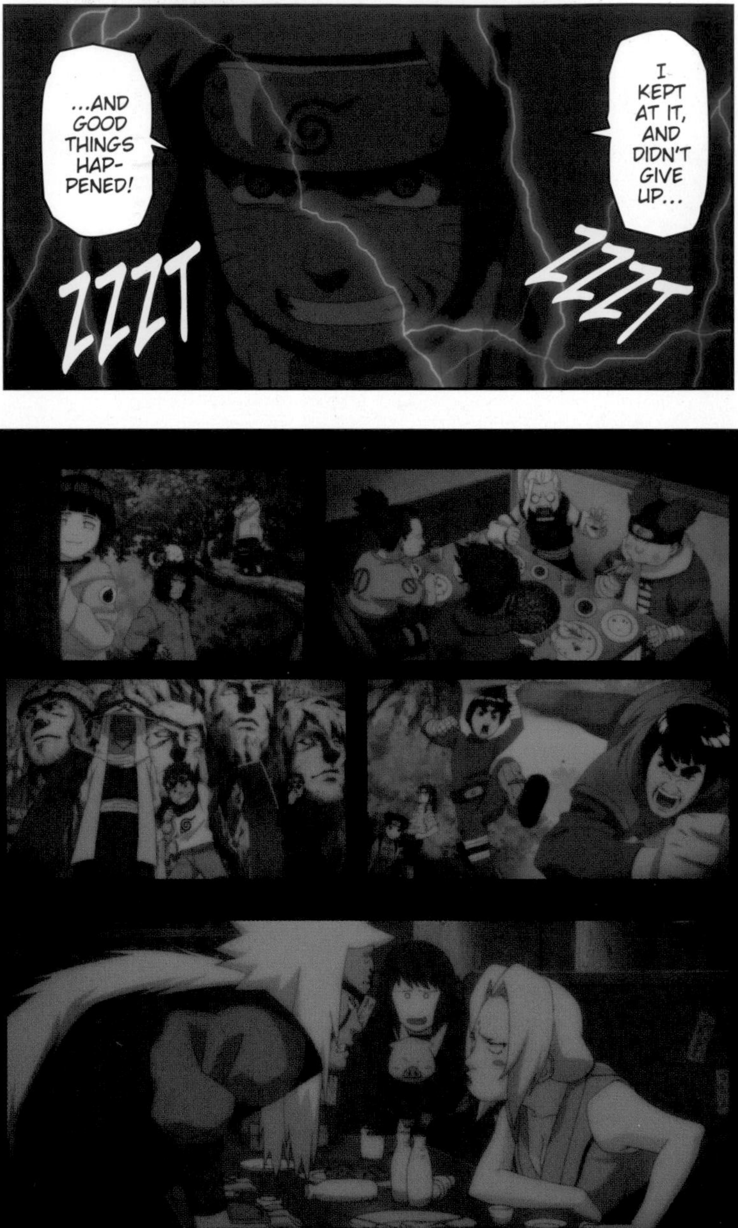
I KEPT AT IT, AND DIDN'T GIVE UP...
ZZZT
...AND GOOD THINGS HAP-PENED!
ZZZT

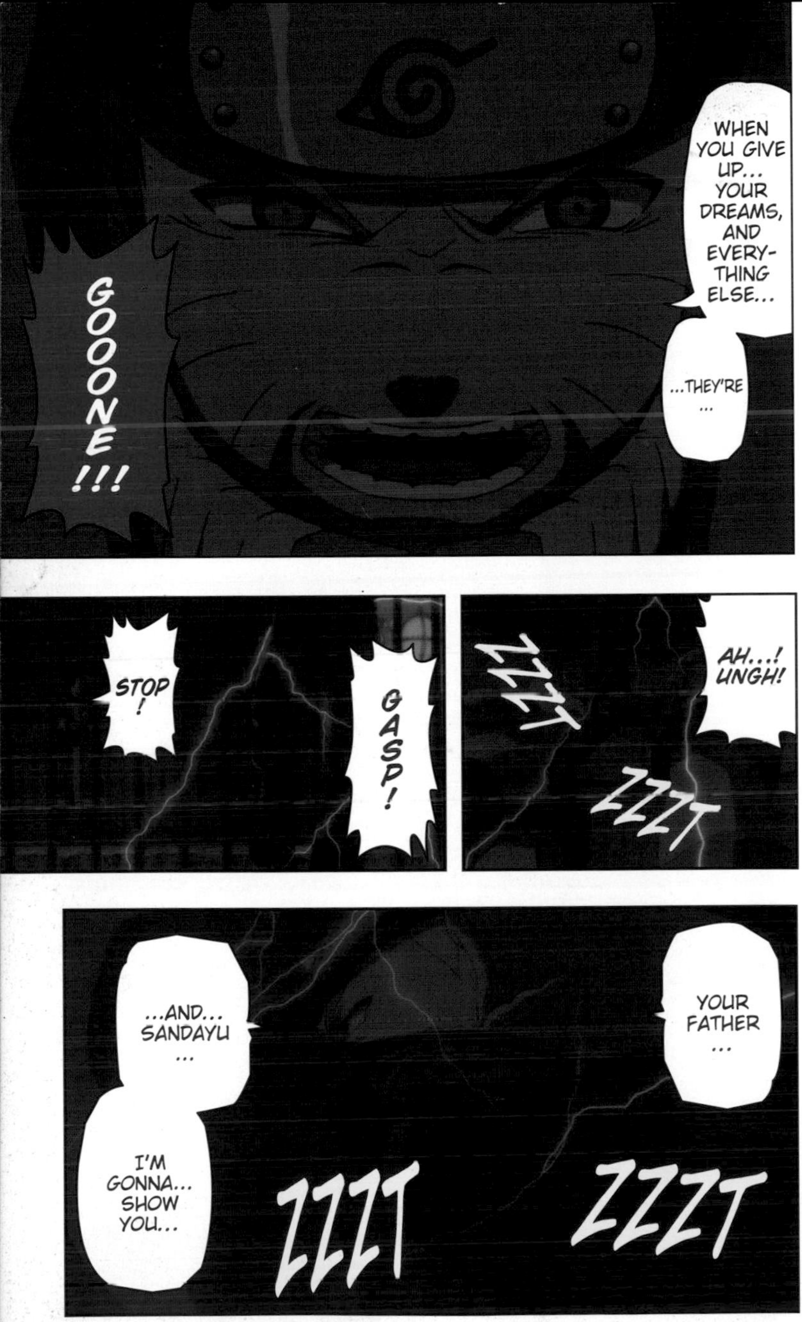
WHEN YOU GIVE UP... YOUR DREAMS, AND EVERY-THING ELSE...
...THEY'RE ...
GOOOONE!!!
AH...! UNGH!
ZZZT
ZZZT
GASP!
STOP!
YOUR FATHER ...
...AND... SANDAYU ...
ZZZT
ZZZT
I'M GONNA... SHOW YOU...

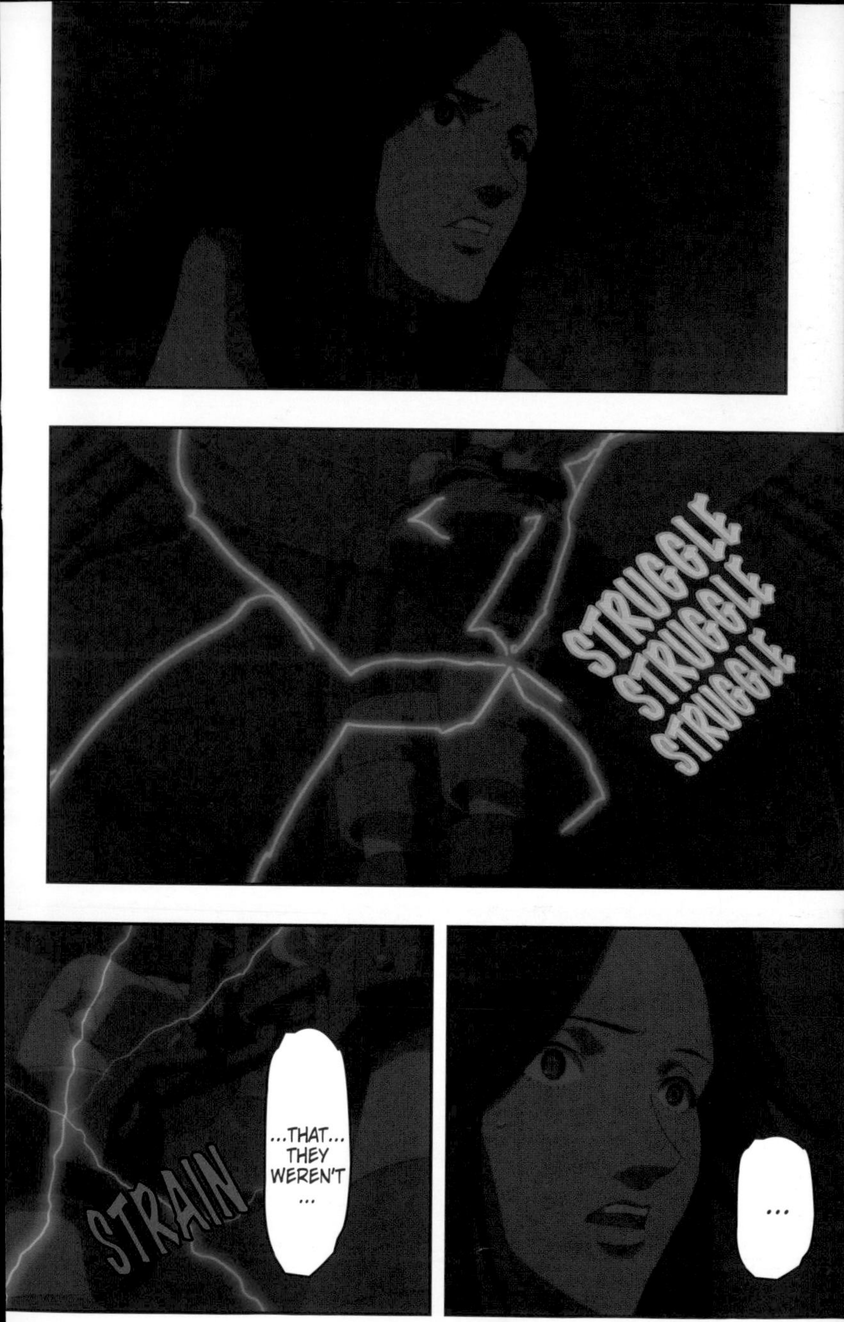
STRUGGLE STRUGGLE STRUGGLE
...
...THAT... THEY WEREN'T ...
STRAIN

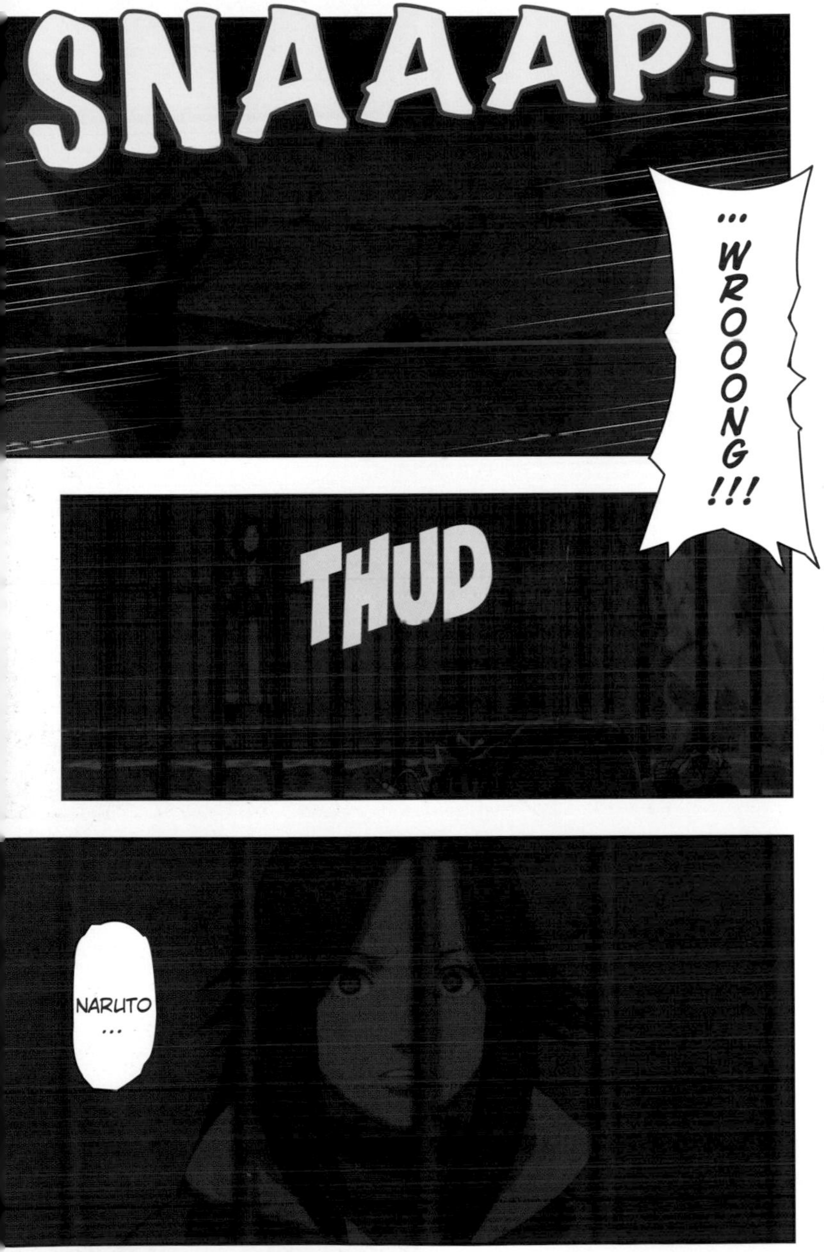
SNAAAP!
...WROOOONG!!!
THUD
NARUTO ...

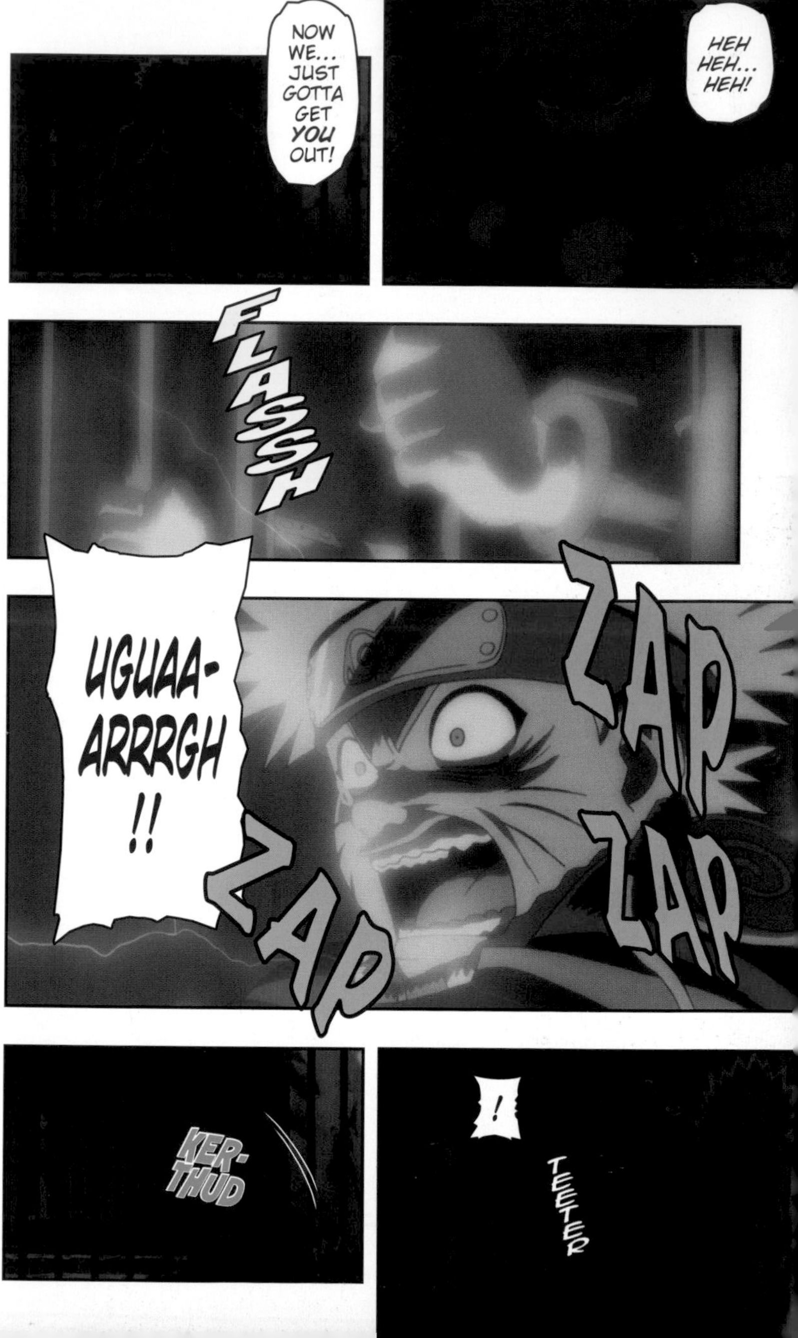
HEH HEH... HEH!
NOW WE... JUST GOTTA GET YOU OUT!
FLASSH
ZAP
ZAP
UGUAA-ARRRGH!!
ZAP
!
TEETER
KER-THUD

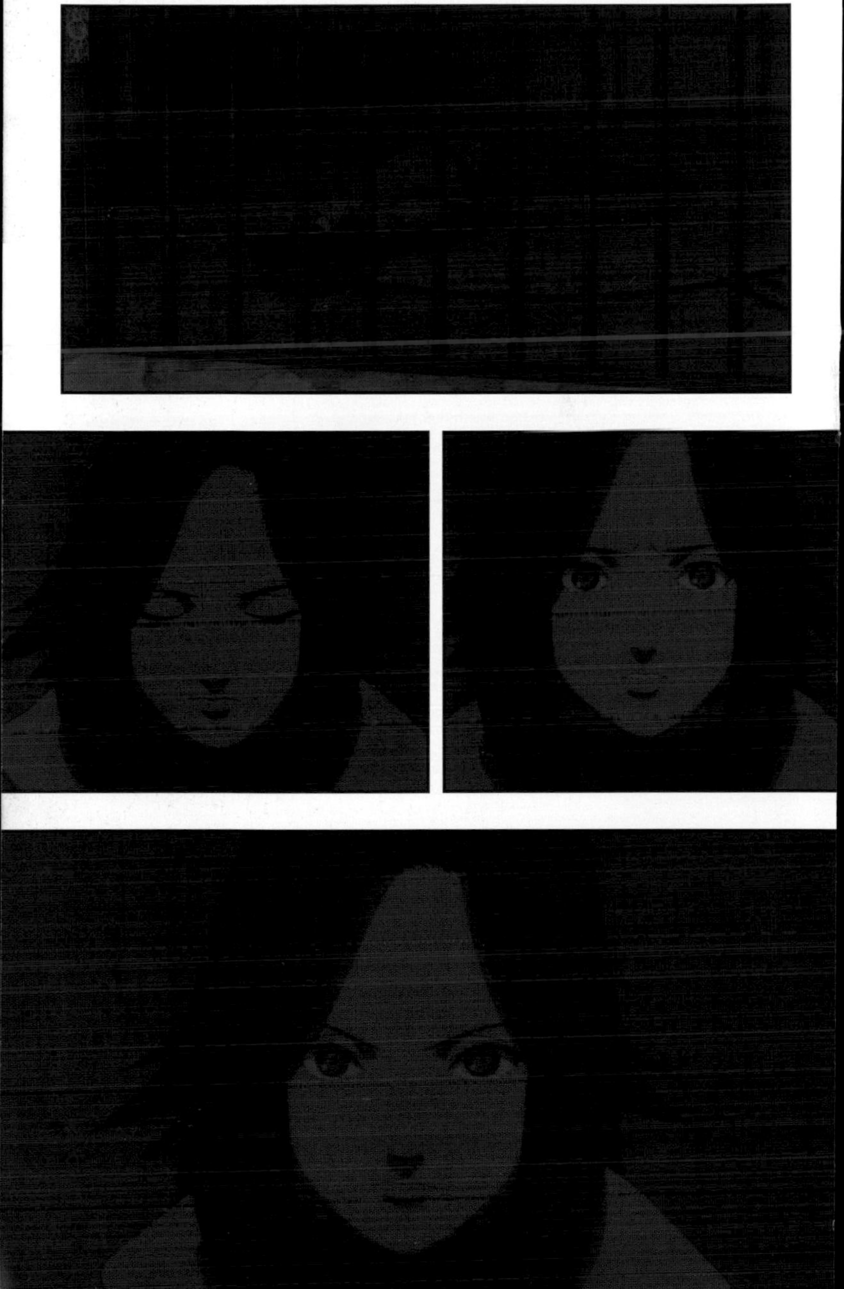

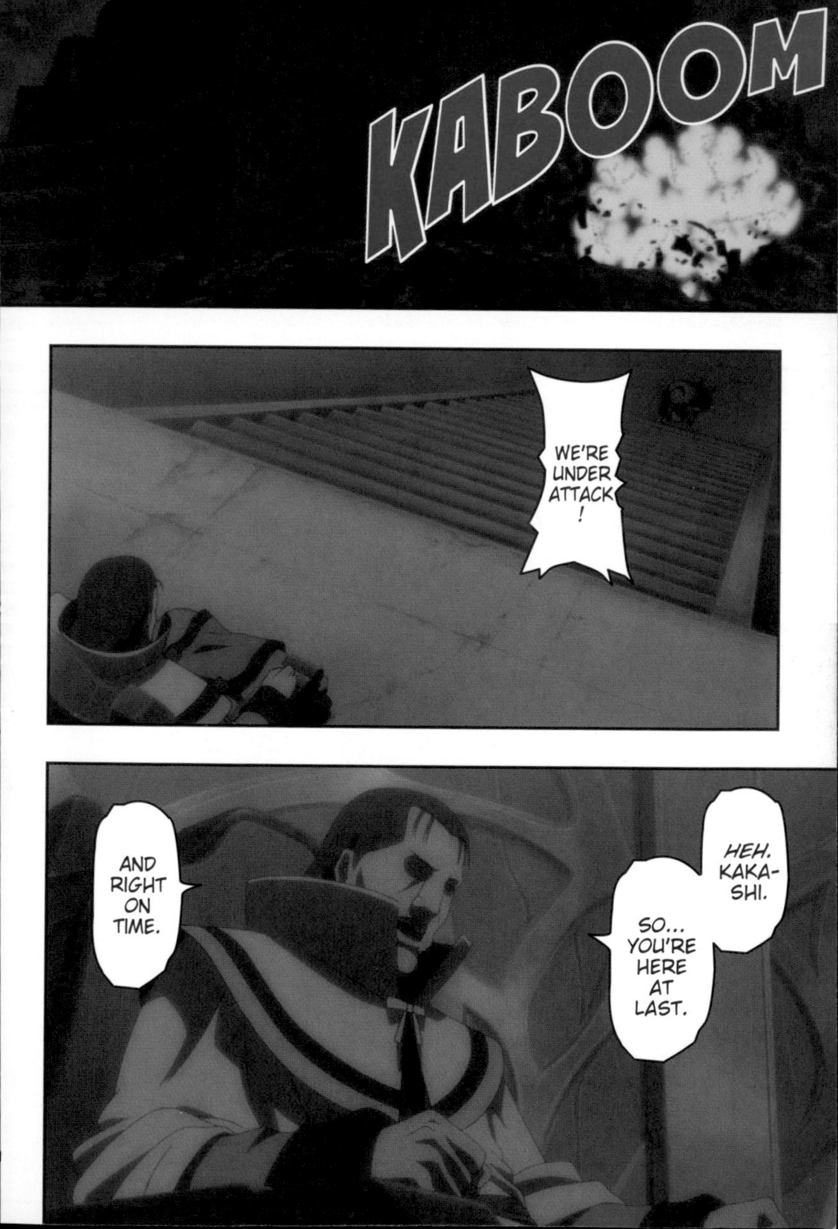
KABOOM
WE'RE UNDER ATTACK!
HEH. KAKA-SHI.
SO... YOU'RE HERE AT LAST.
AND RIGHT ON TIME.

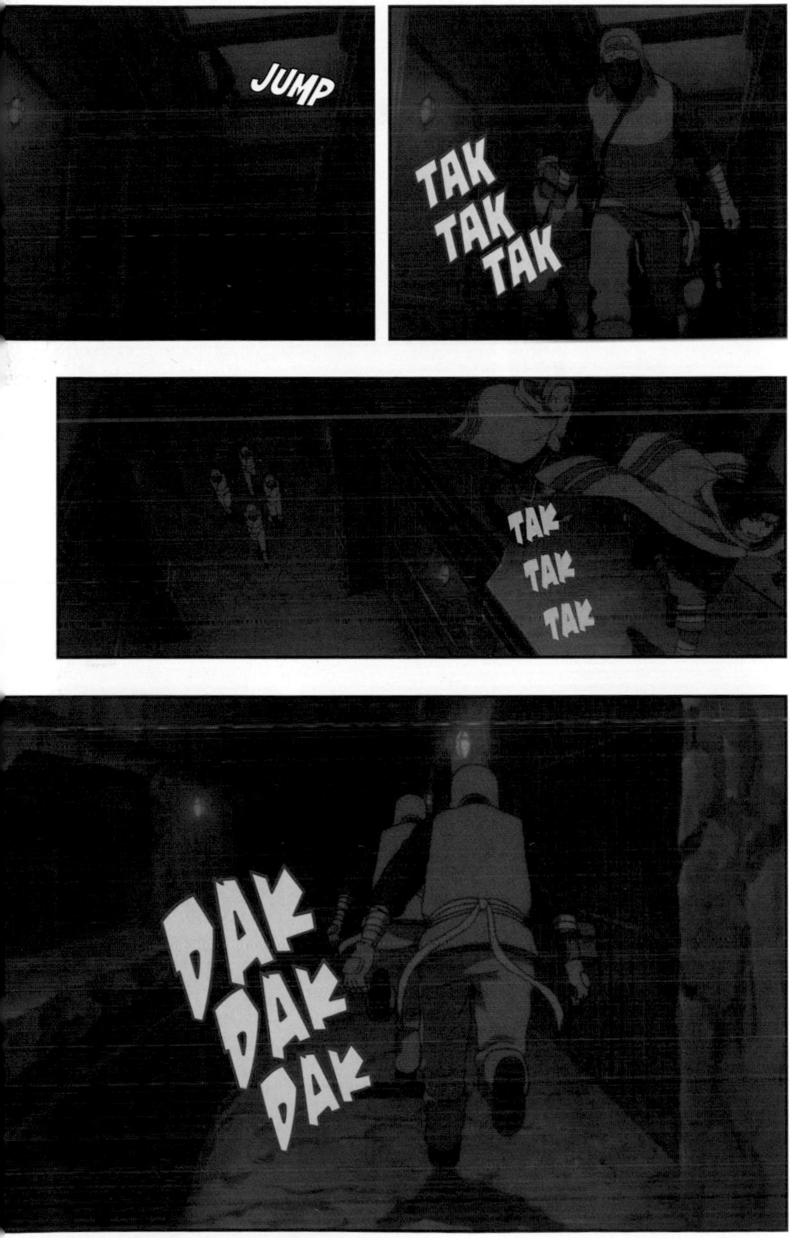
TAK
TAK
TAK
JUMP
TAK
TAK
TAK
DAK
DAK
DAK

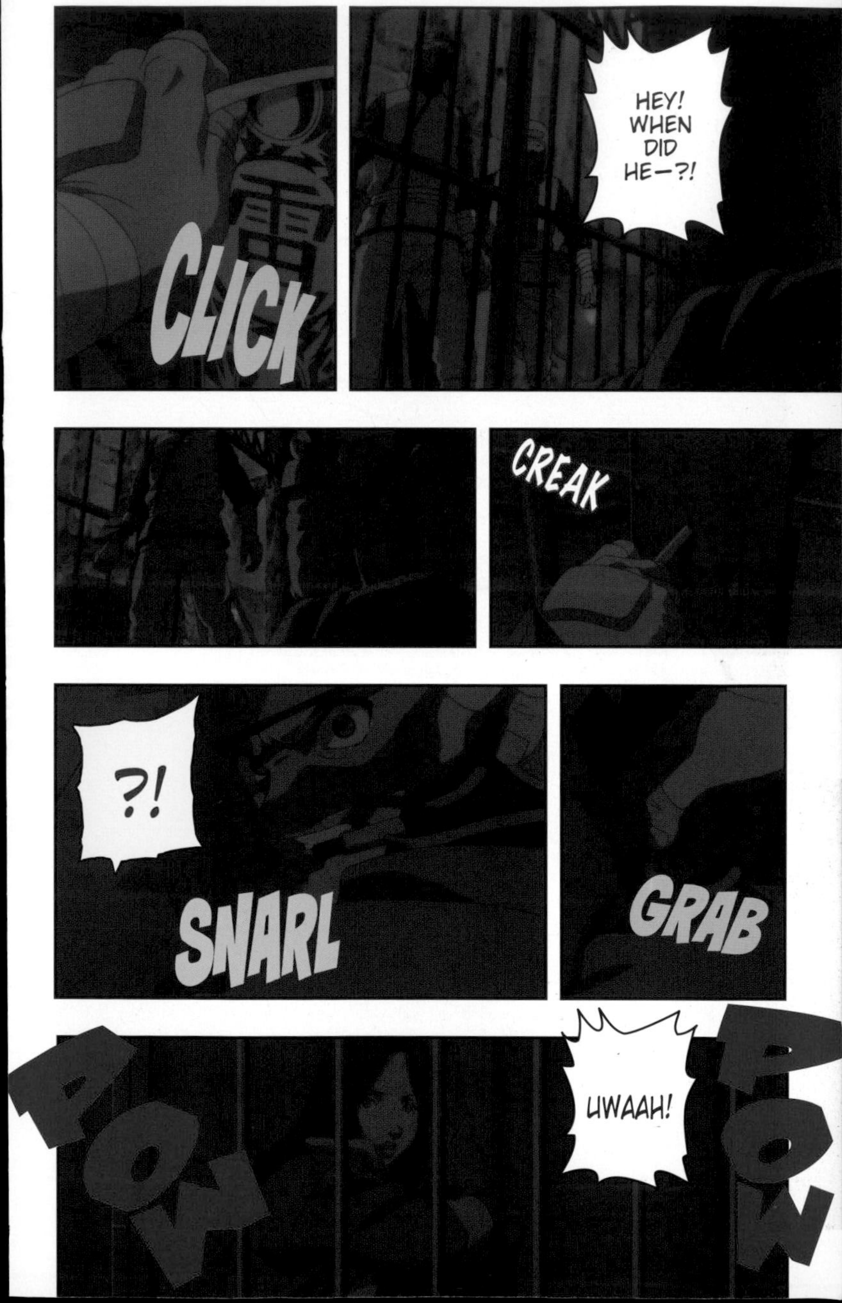

HEY! WHEN DID HE—?!
CLICK
CREAK
GRAB
?!
SNARL
POW
UWAAH!
POW

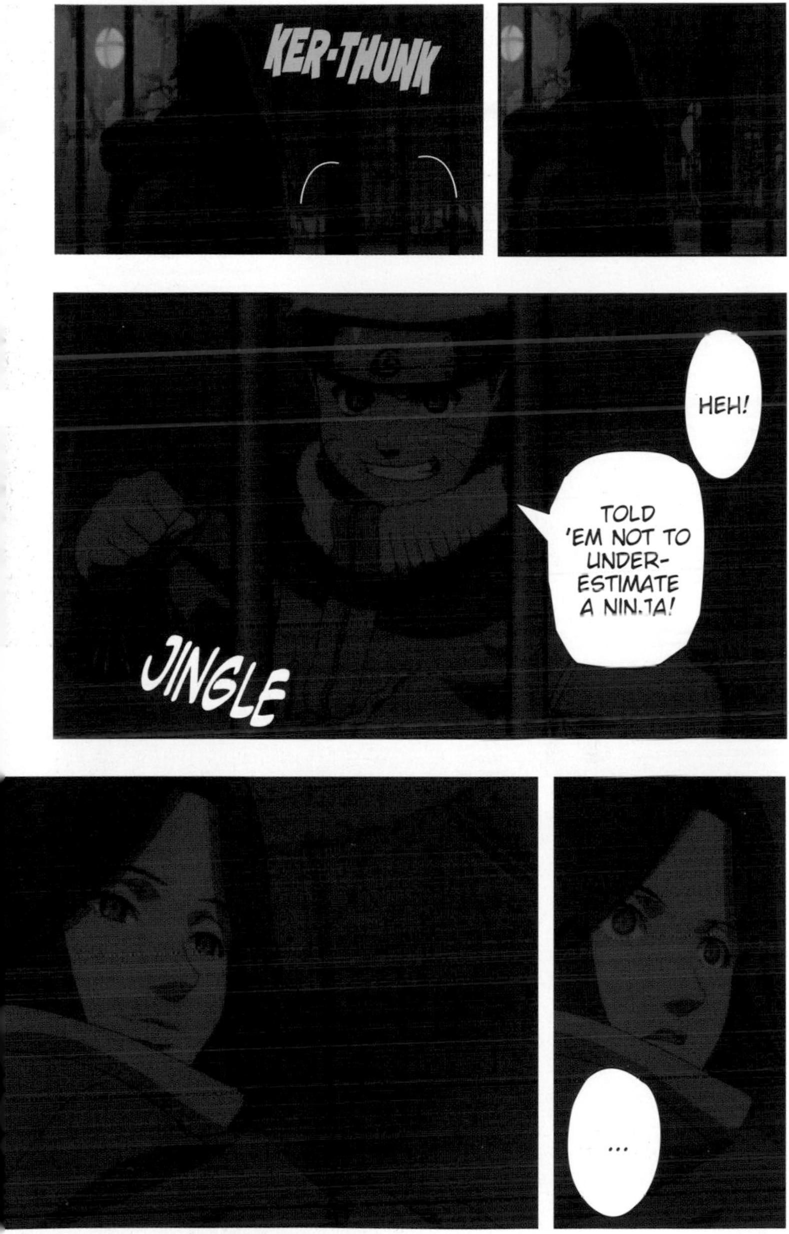
KER-THUNK
HEH!
TOLD 'EM NOT TO UNDER-ESTIMATE A NINJA!
JINGLE
...

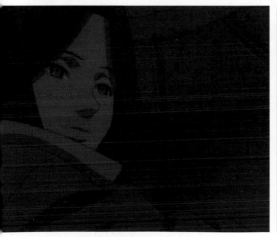

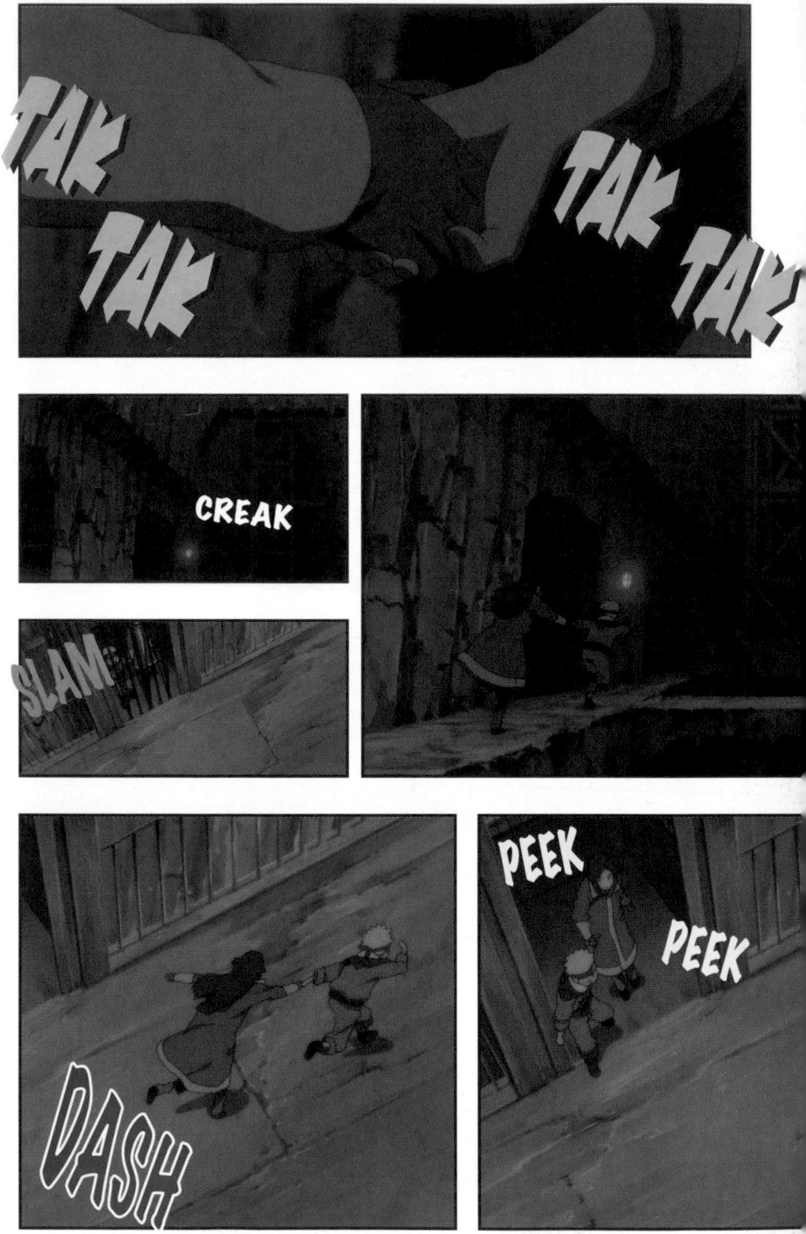
TAK
TAK
TAK
TAK
CREAK
SLAM
PEEK
PEEK
DASH

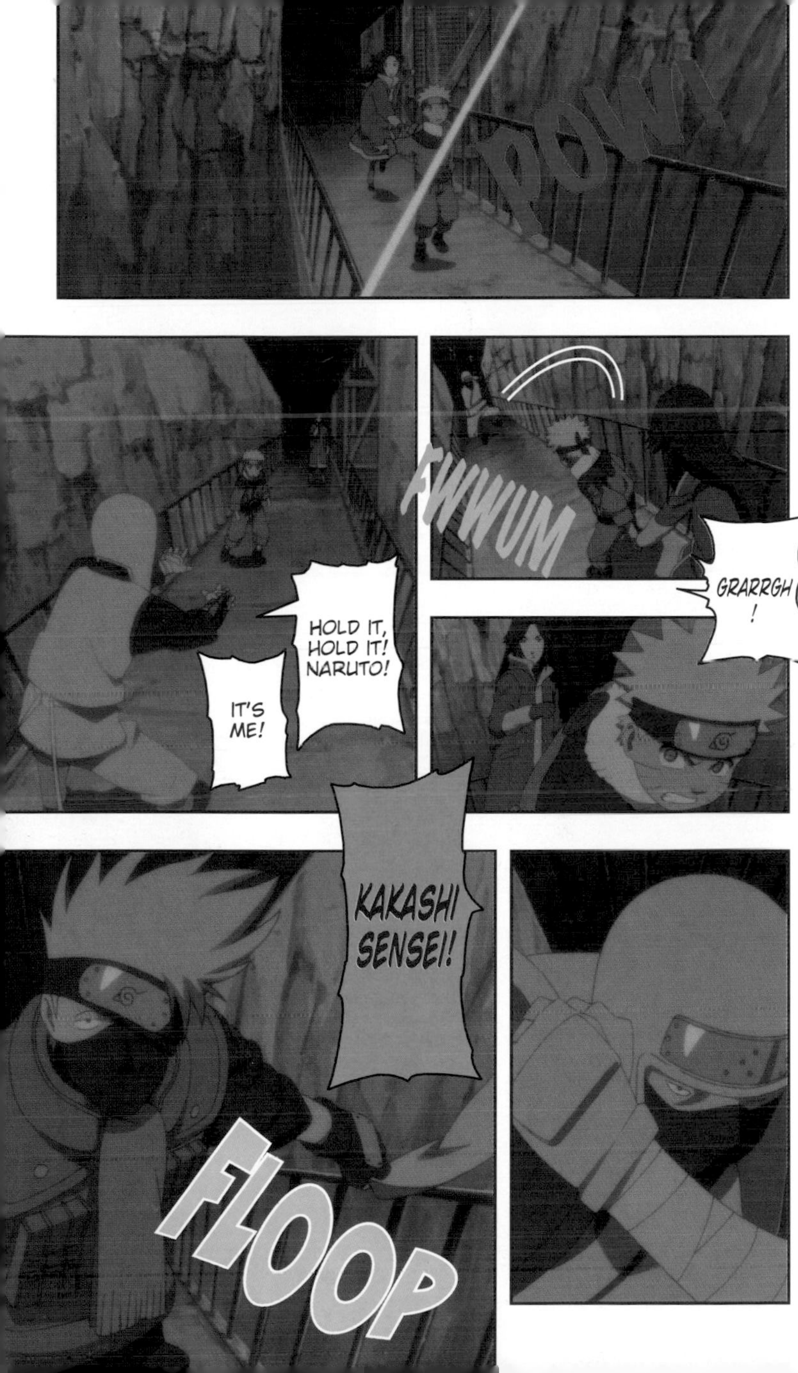
POW!
FWWUM
GRARRGH!
HOLD IT, HOLD IT! NARUTO!
IT'S ME!
KAKASHI SENSEI!
FLOOP

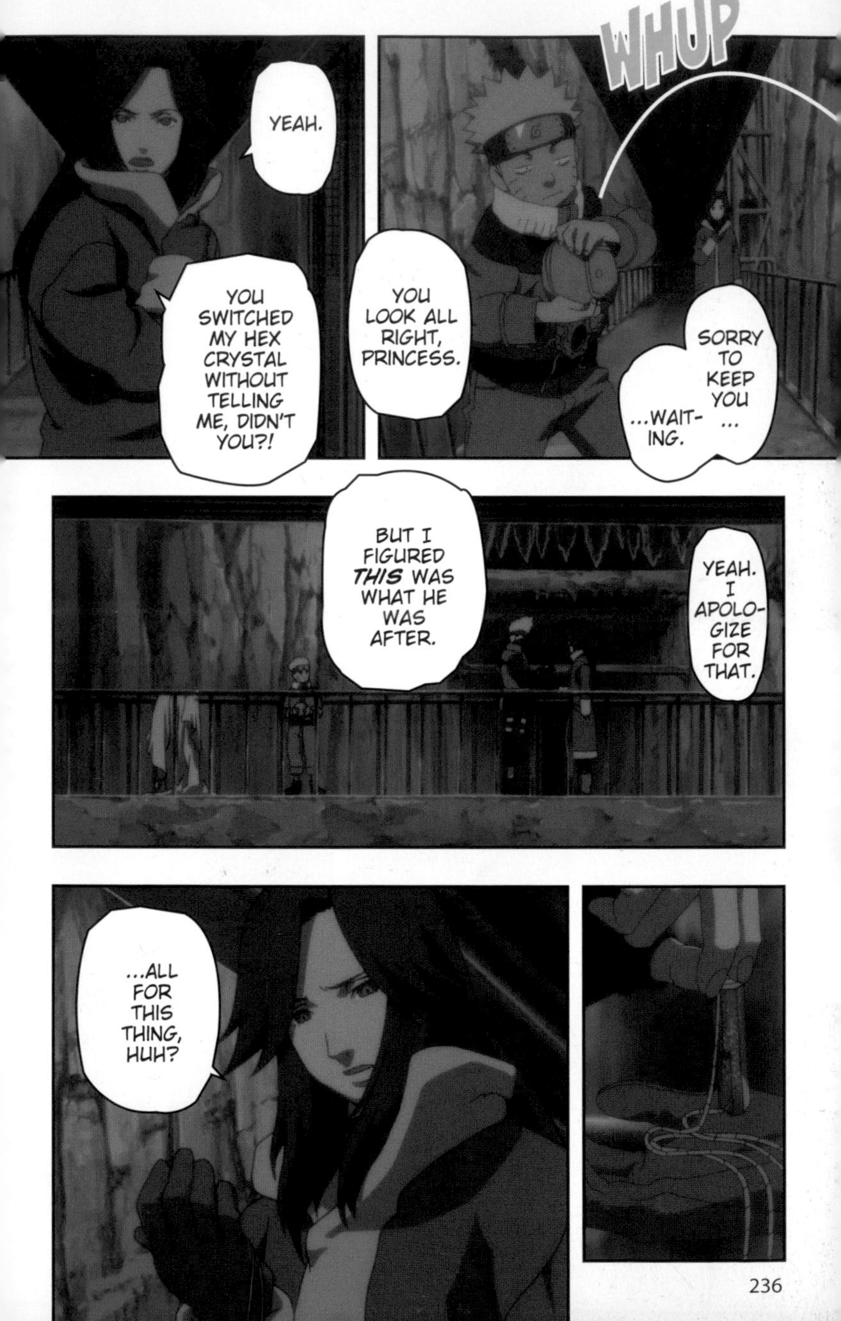
WHUP
SORRY TO KEEP YOU... ...WAIT-ING.
YOU LOOK ALL RIGHT, PRINCESS.
YEAH.
YOU SWITCHED MY HEX CRYSTAL WITHOUT TELLING ME, DIDN'T YOU?!
YEAH. I APOLO-GIZE FOR THAT.
BUT I FIGURED *THIS* WAS WHAT HE WAS AFTER.
...ALL FOR THIS THING, HUH?

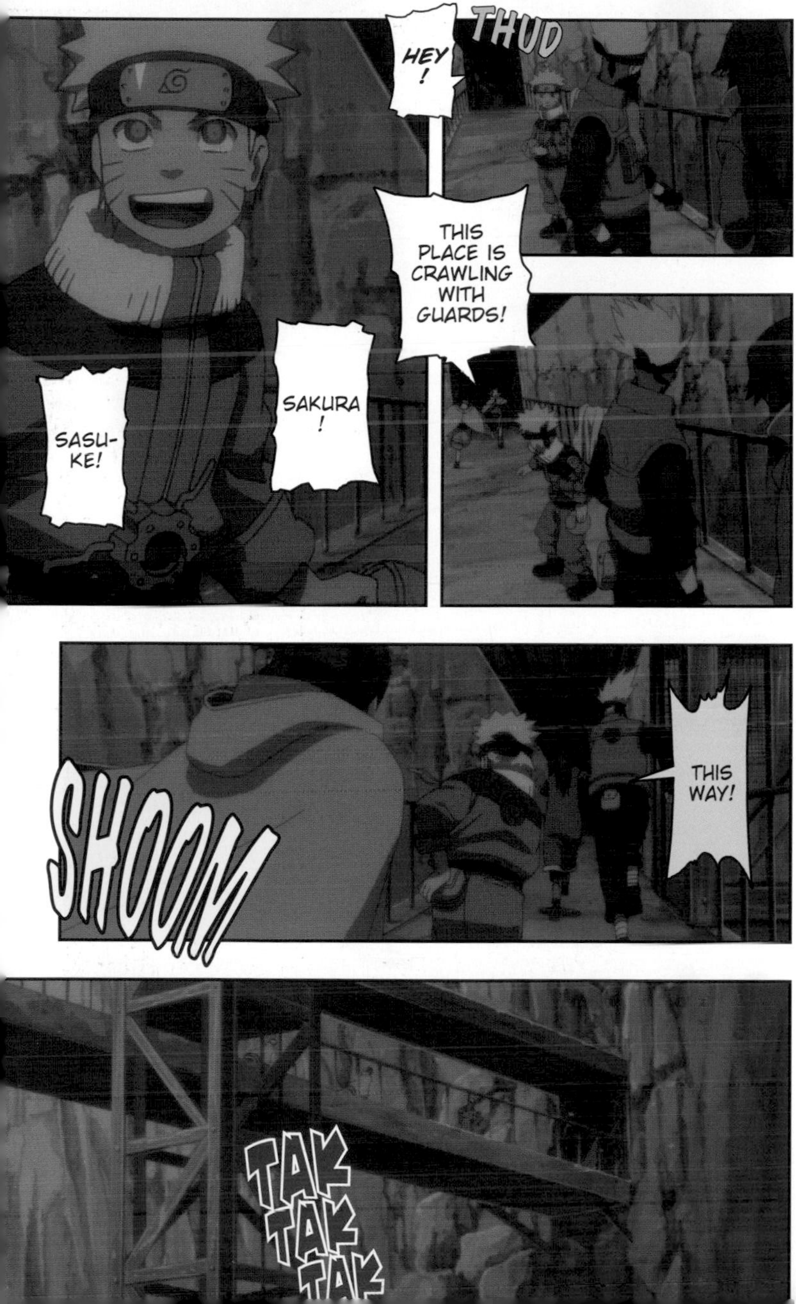
THUD
HEY!
THIS PLACE IS CRAWLING WITH GUARDS!
SAKURA!
SASUKE!
THIS WAY!
SHOOM
TAK TAK TAK

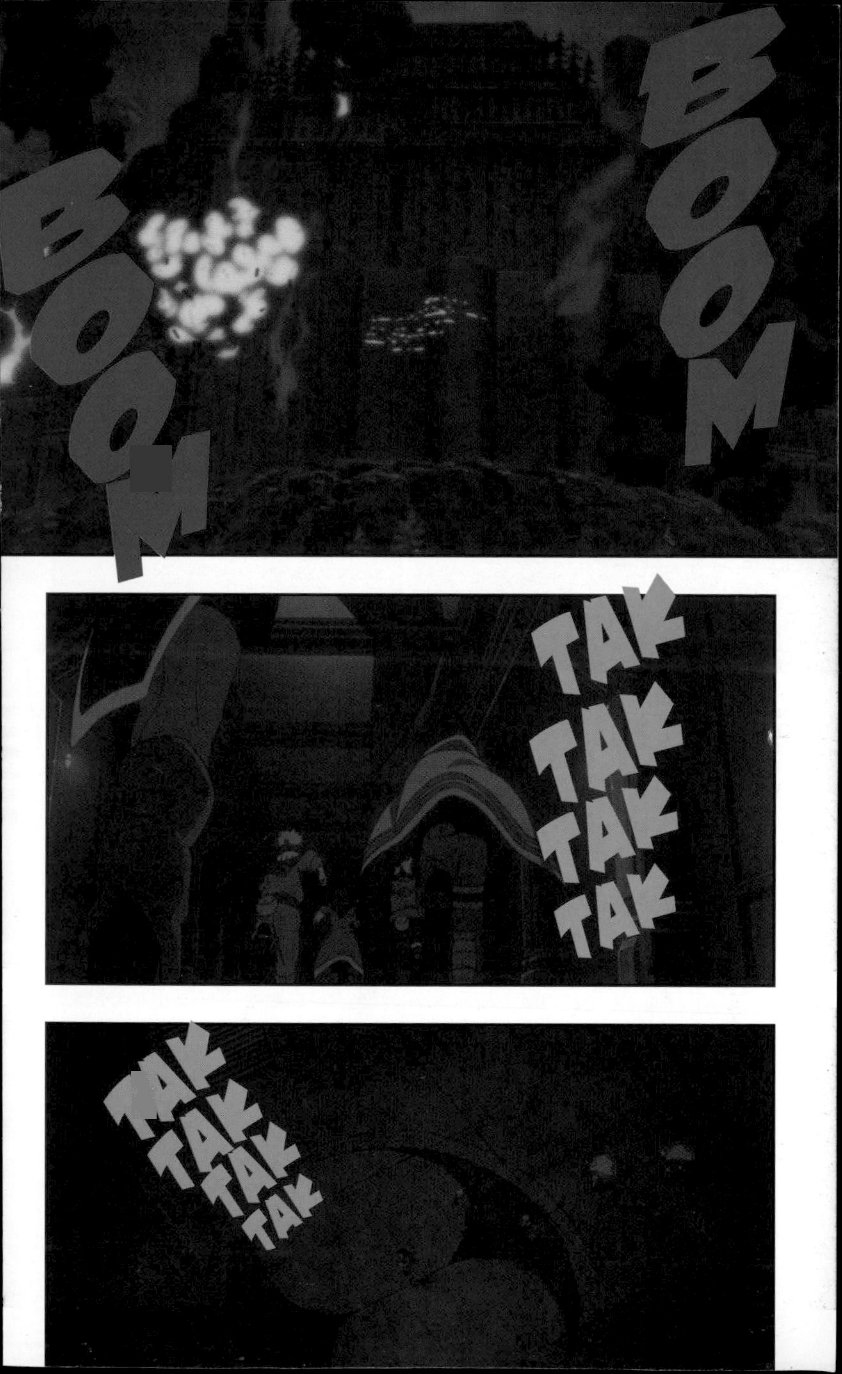
BOOM
BOOM
TAK TAK TAK TAK
TAK TAK TAK TAK

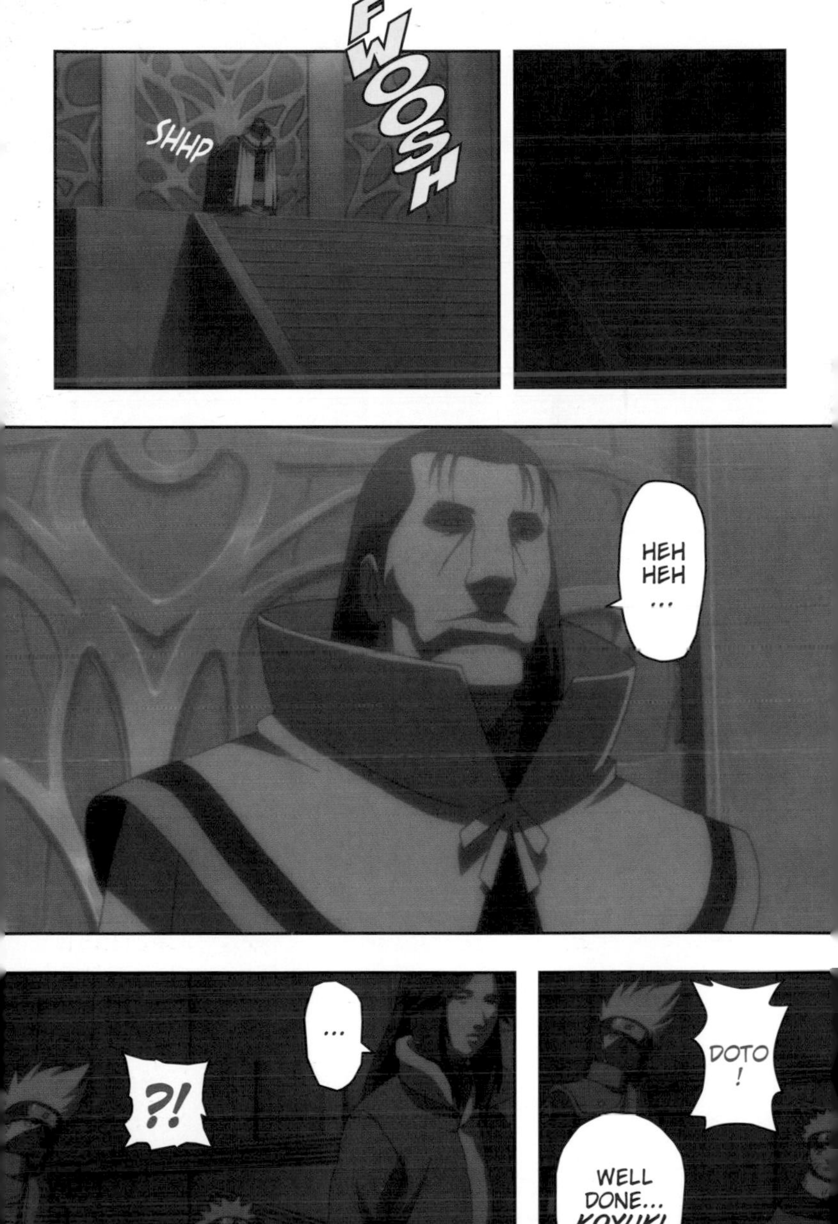
FWOOSH
SHHP
HEH HEH...
DOTO!
WELL DONE... KOYUKI.
...
?!

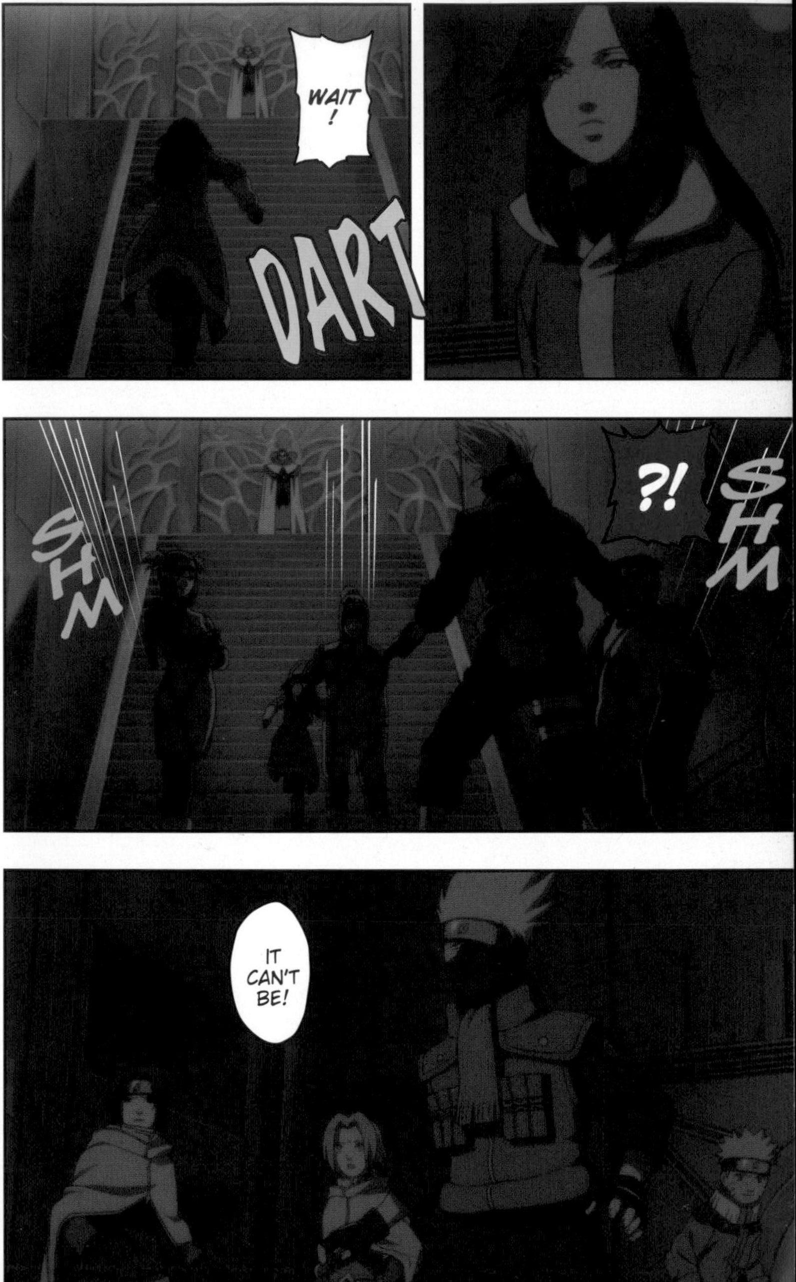
WAIT!
DART
SHM
?!
SHM
IT CAN'T BE!

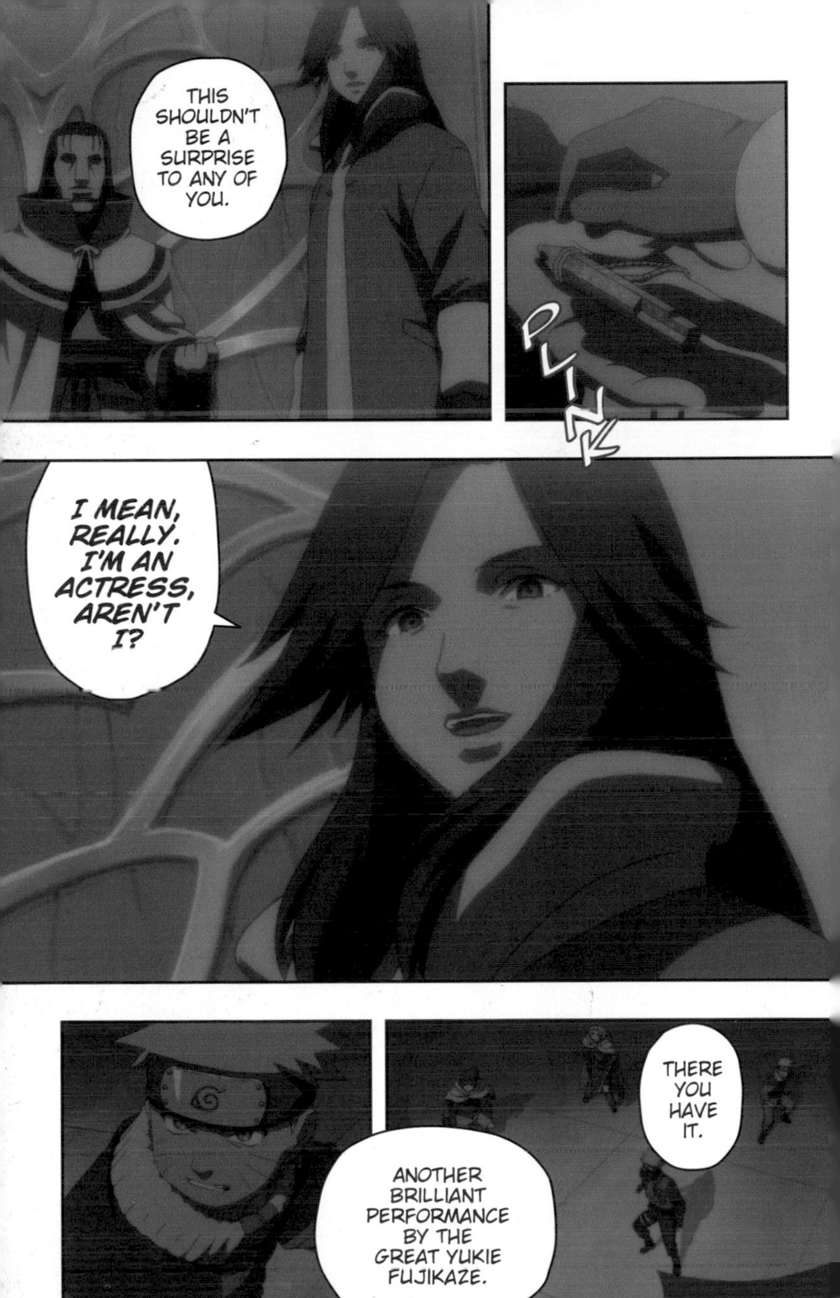
PLINK
THIS SHOULDN'T BE A SURPRISE TO ANY OF YOU.
I MEAN, REALLY. I'M AN ACTRESS, AREN'T I?
THERE YOU HAVE IT.
ANOTHER BRILLIANT PERFORMANCE BY THE GREAT YUKIE FUJIKAZE.

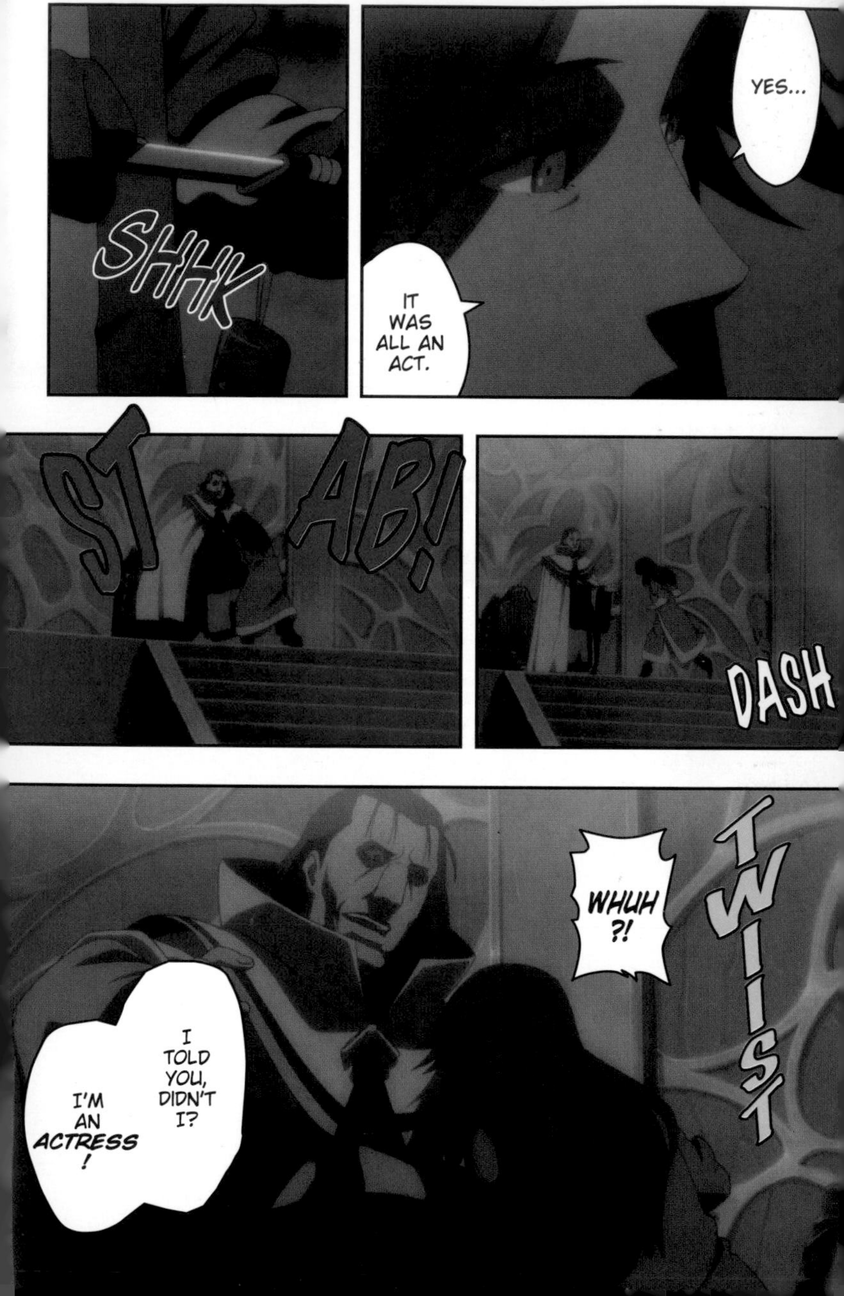
YES...
IT WAS ALL AN ACT.
SHHK
DASH
STAB!
TWIST
WHUH?!
I TOLD YOU, DIDN'T I?
I'M AN ACTRESS!

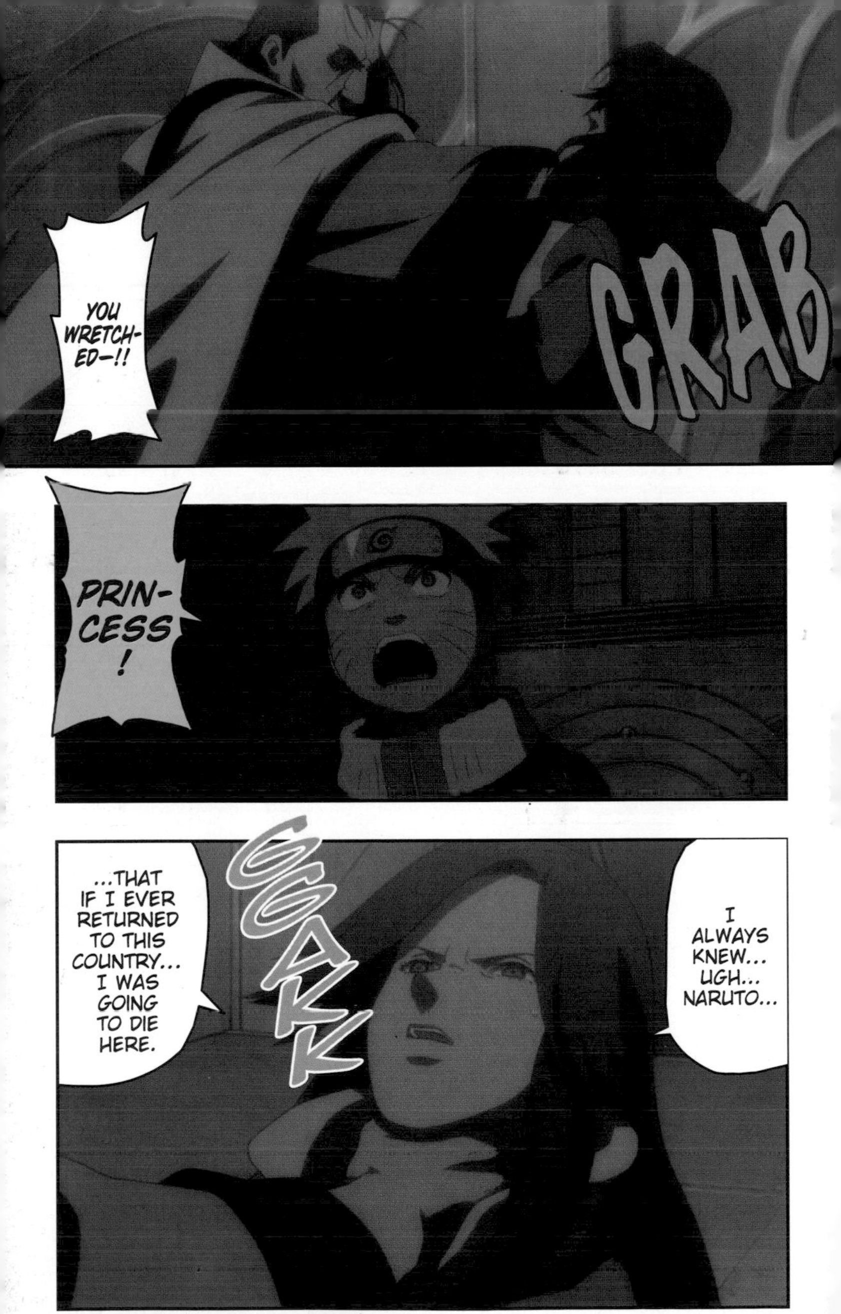
GRAB
YOU WRETCHED-!!
PRINCESS!
I ALWAYS KNEW... UGH... NARUTO...
GGAKK
...THAT IF I EVER RETURNED TO THIS COUNTRY... I WAS GOING TO DIE HERE.

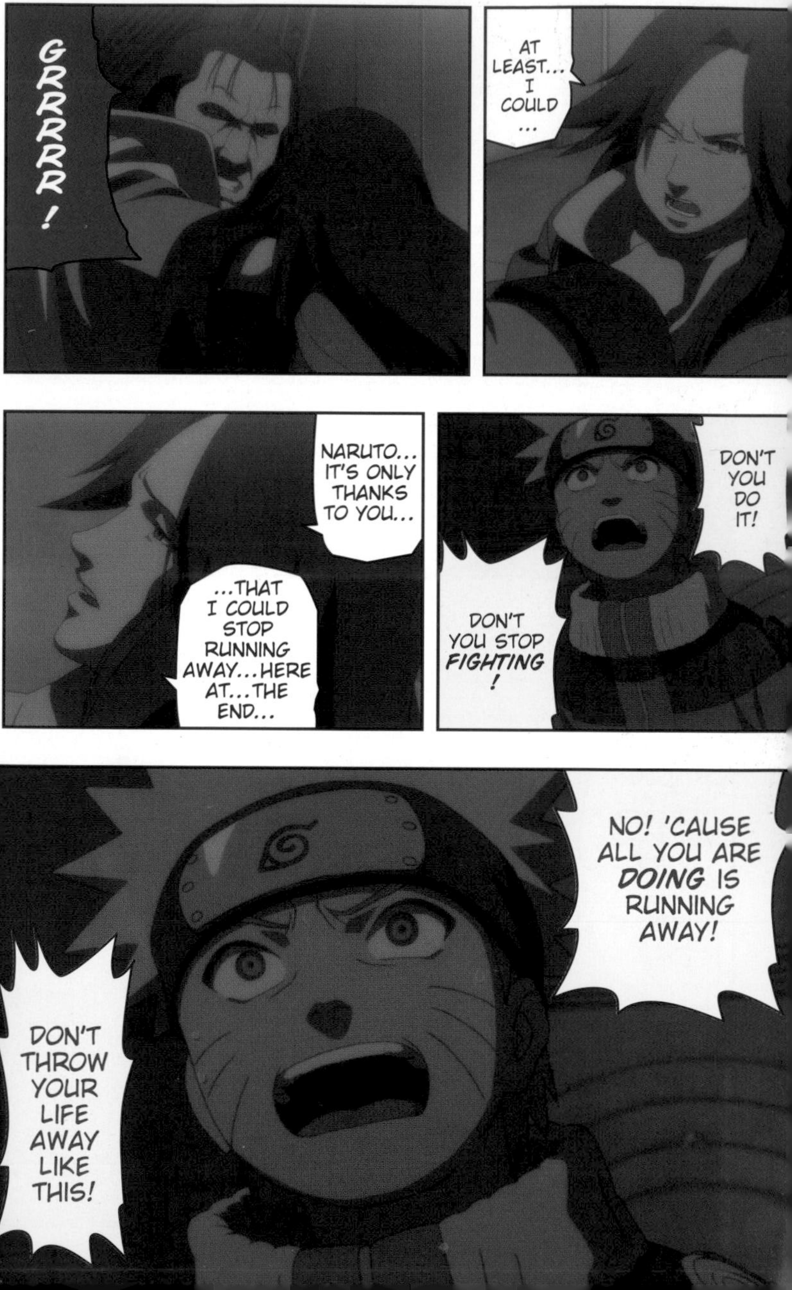
AT LEAST... I COULD ...
GRRRRR!
DON'T YOU DO IT!
DON'T YOU STOP FIGHTING!
NARUTO... IT'S ONLY THANKS TO YOU...
...THAT I COULD STOP RUNNING AWAY...HERE AT...THE END...
NO! 'CAUSE ALL YOU ARE DOING IS RUNNING AWAY!
DON'T THROW YOUR LIFE AWAY LIKE THIS!

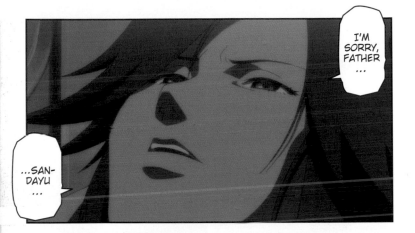

I'M SORRY, FATHER ...

...SAN-DAYU ...

PLUNGE...

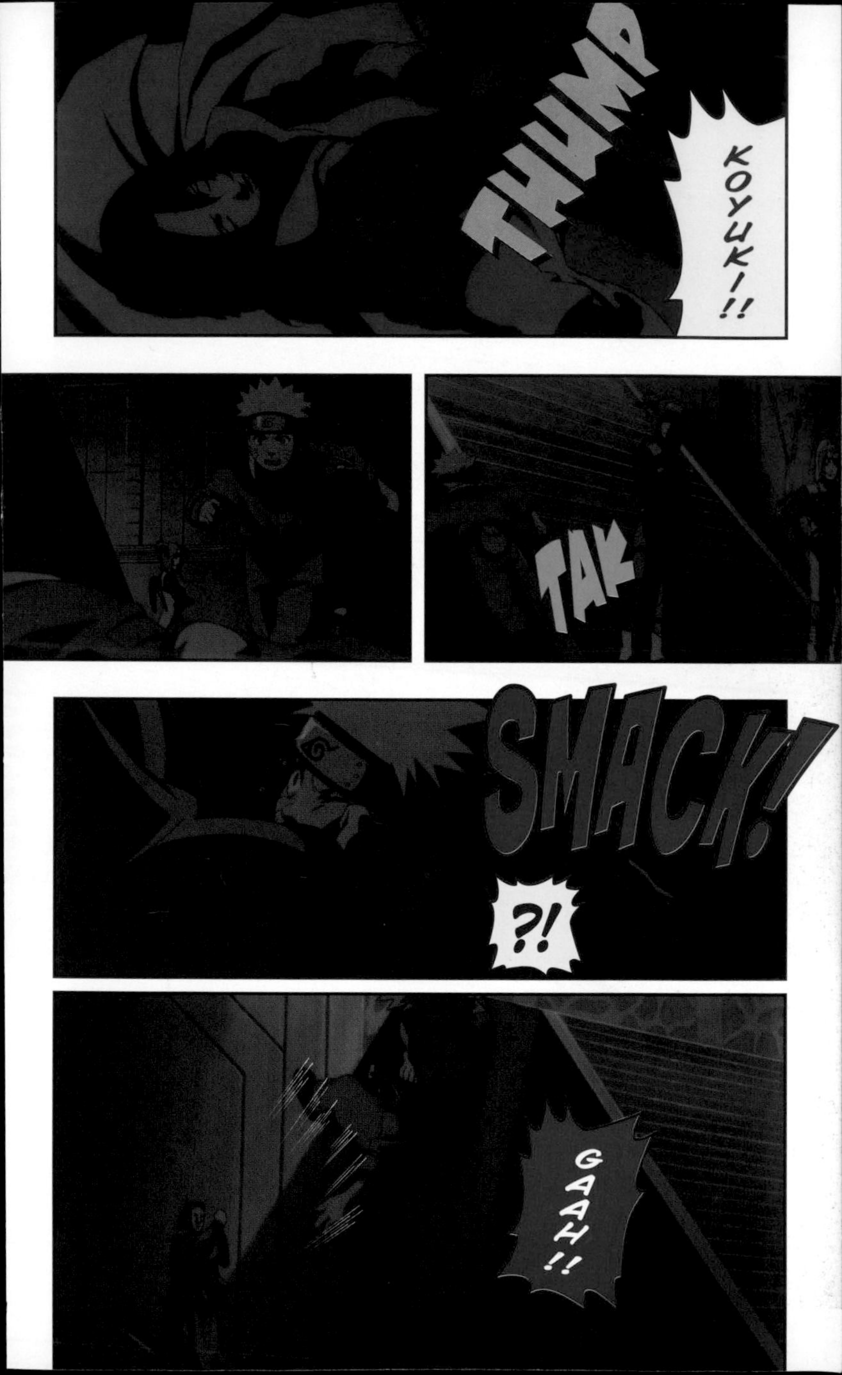
THUMP
KOYUKI!!
TAK
SMACK!
?!
GAAH!!

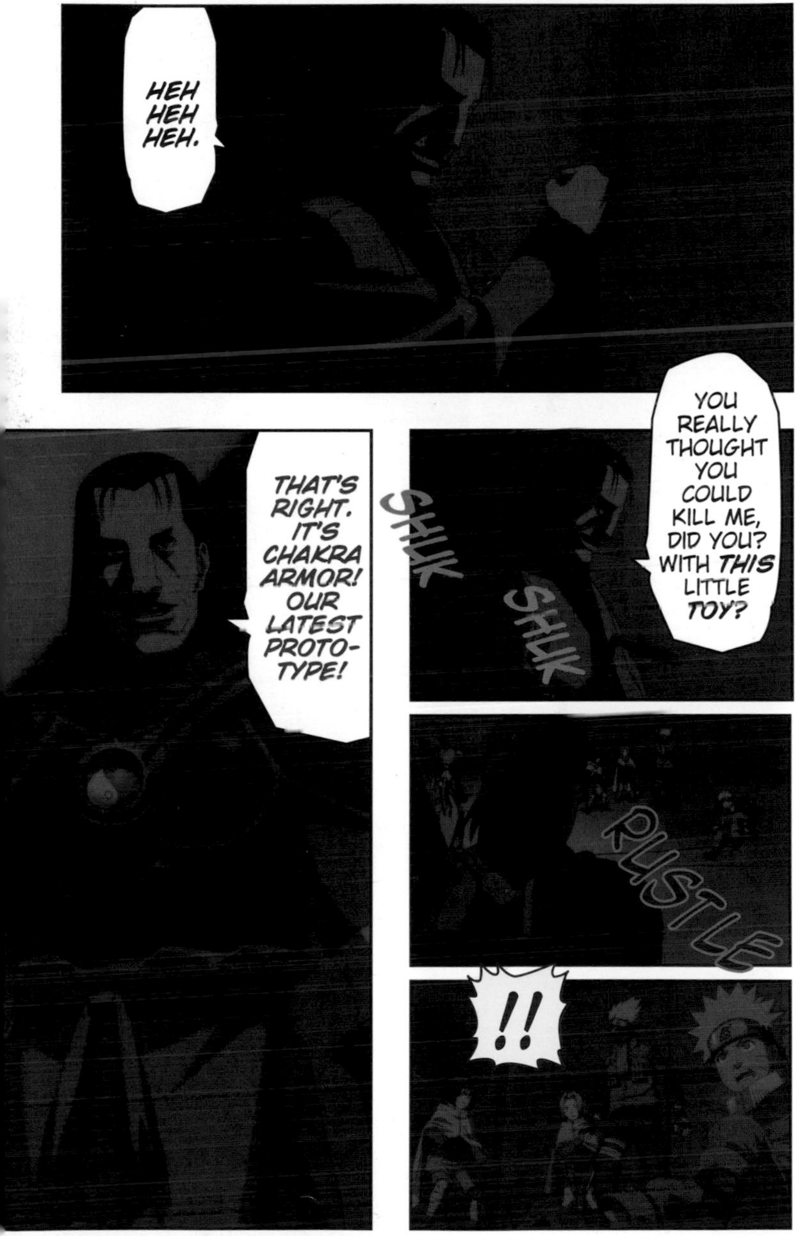
HEH HEH HEH.
YOU REALLY THOUGHT YOU COULD KILL ME, DID YOU? WITH *THIS* LITTLE *TOY?*
SHUK
SHUK
RUSTLE
!!
THAT'S RIGHT. IT'S CHAKRA ARMOR! OUR LATEST PROTO-TYPE!

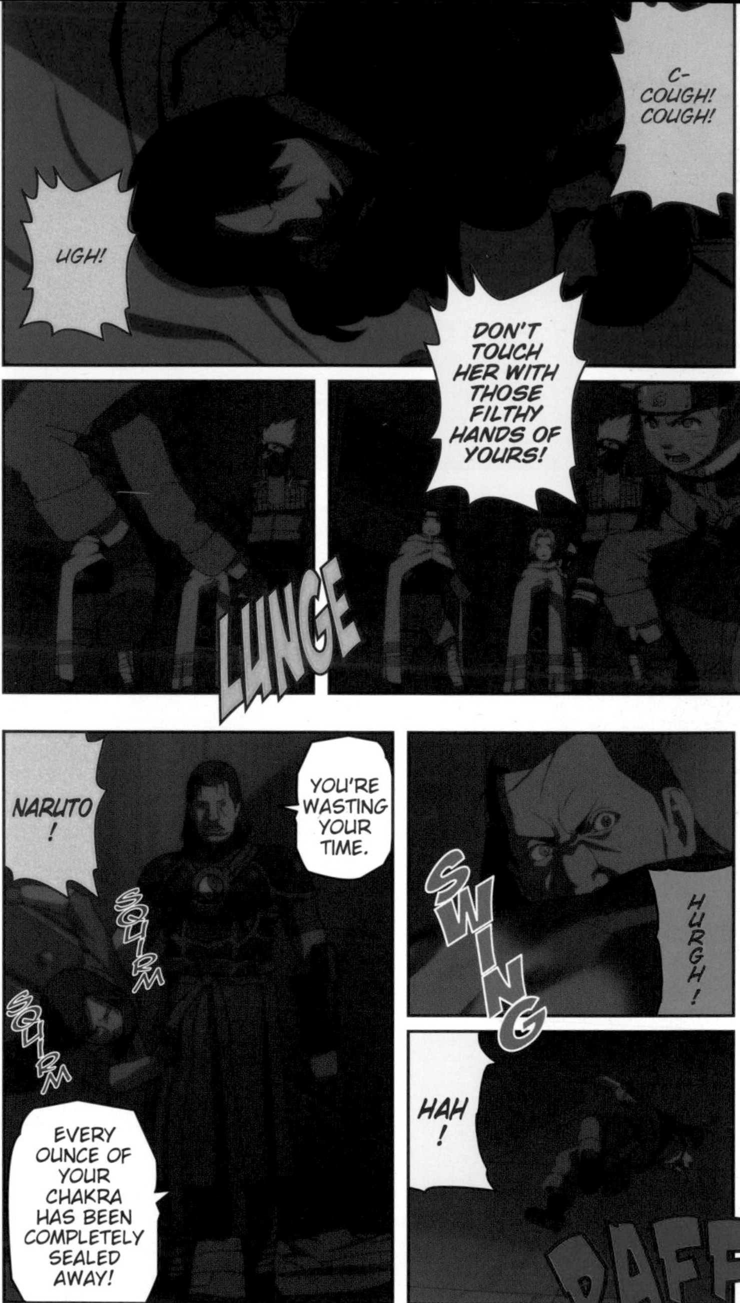
C-COUGH! COUGH!
UGH!
DON'T TOUCH HER WITH THOSE FILTHY HANDS OF YOURS!
LUNGE
SWING
HURGH!
HAH!
PAFF
YOU'RE WASTING YOUR TIME.
NARUTO!
SQUIRM
SQUIRM
EVERY OUNCE OF YOUR CHAKRA HAS BEEN COMPLETELY SEALED AWAY!

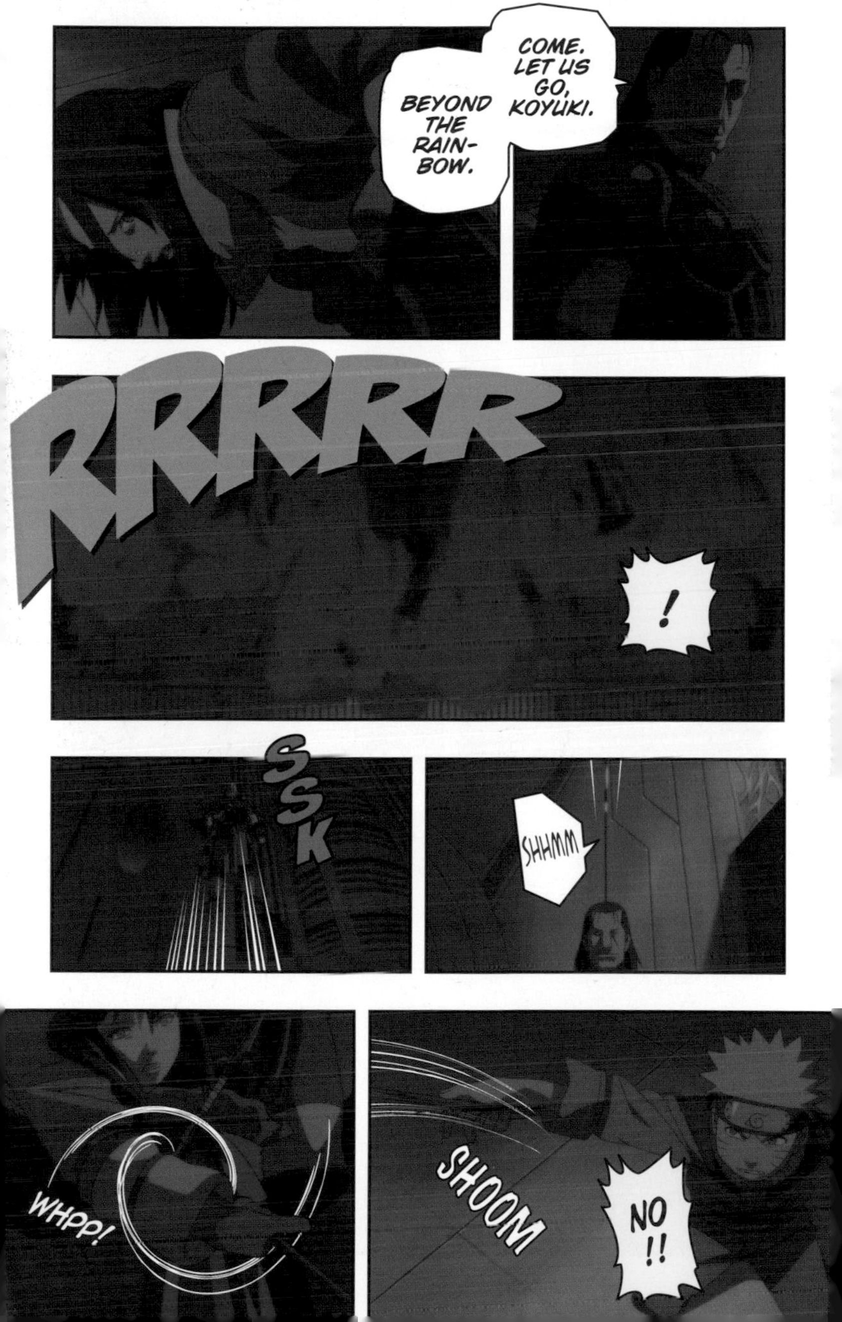
COME. LET US GO, KOYUKI.
BEYOND THE RAIN-BOW.
RRRRR
!
SHHMM
SSK
SHOOM
NO!!
WHPP!

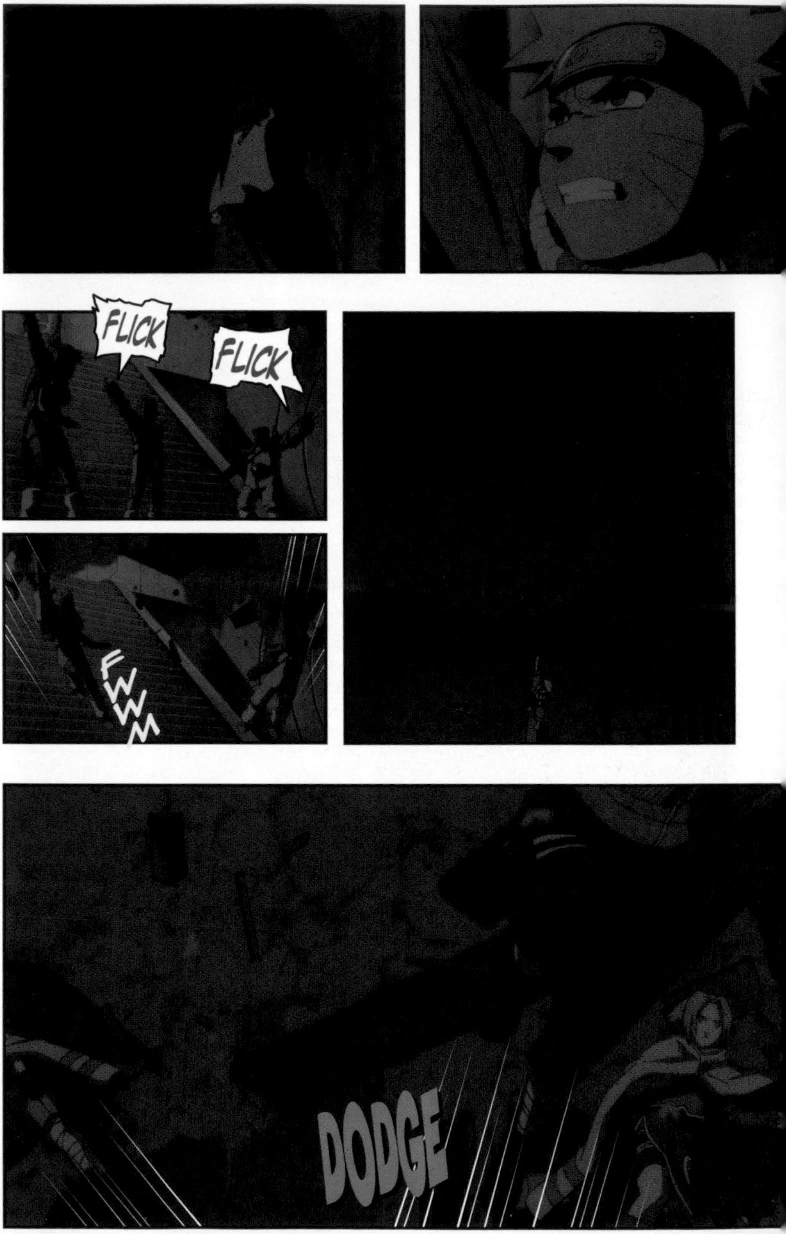
FLICK
FLICK
FWWM
DODGE

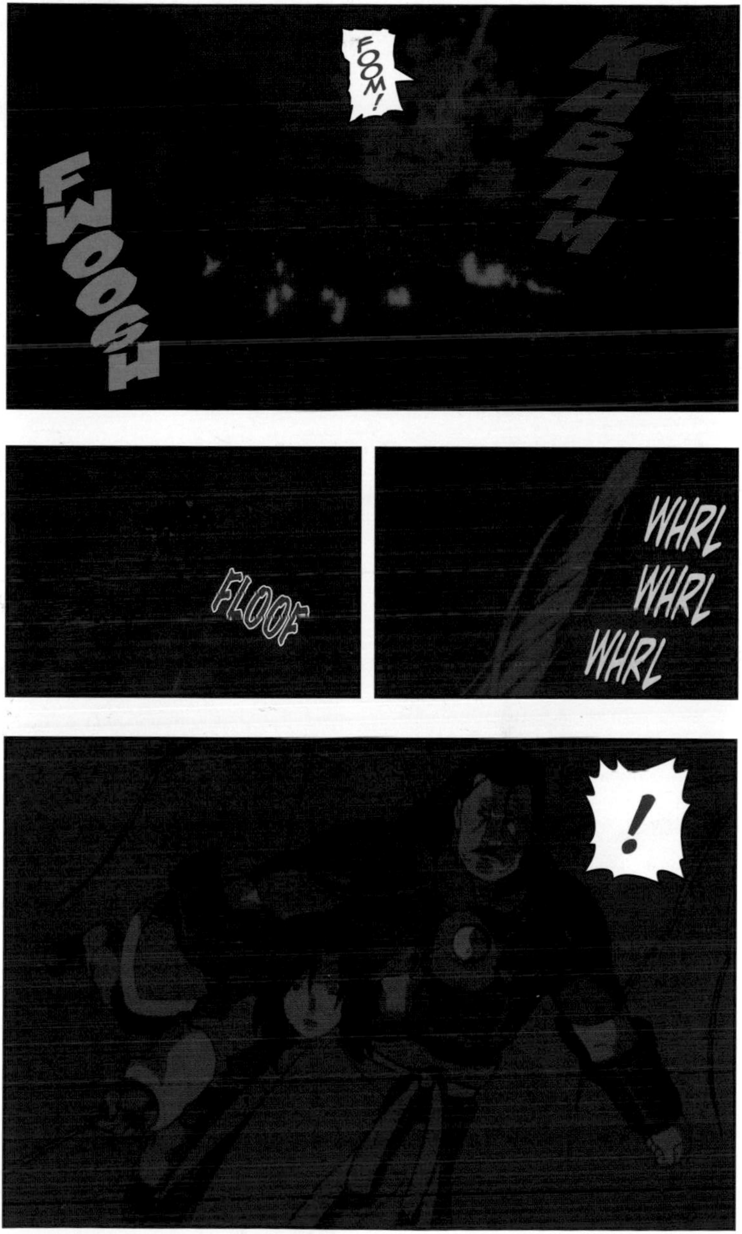
KABAM
FOOM!
FWOOSH
WHRL
WHRL
WHRL
FLOOF
!

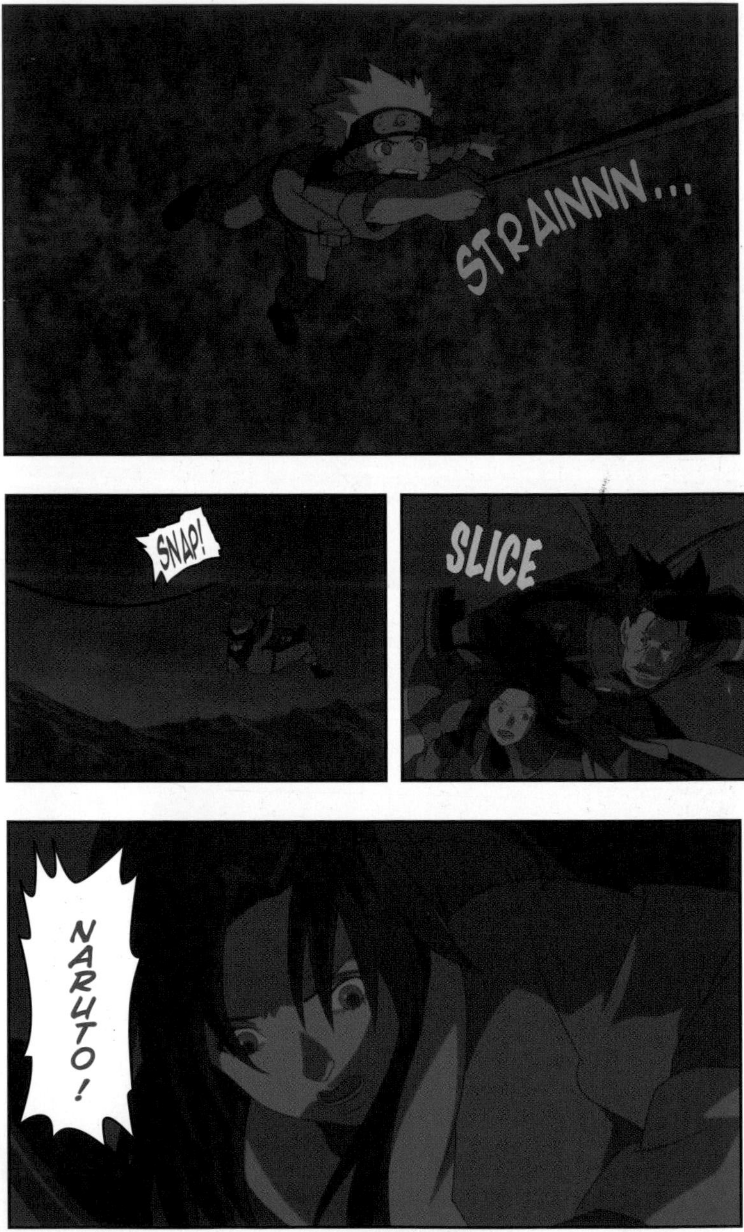
STRAINNN...
SLICE
SNAP!
NARUTO!

HMPH!

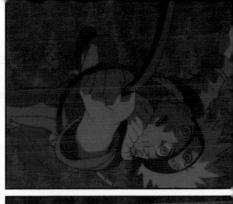

WHOOSH

AH HA HA HA HA !!

SHF SHF SHF SHF

CRACKLE CRACKLE

STAGGER

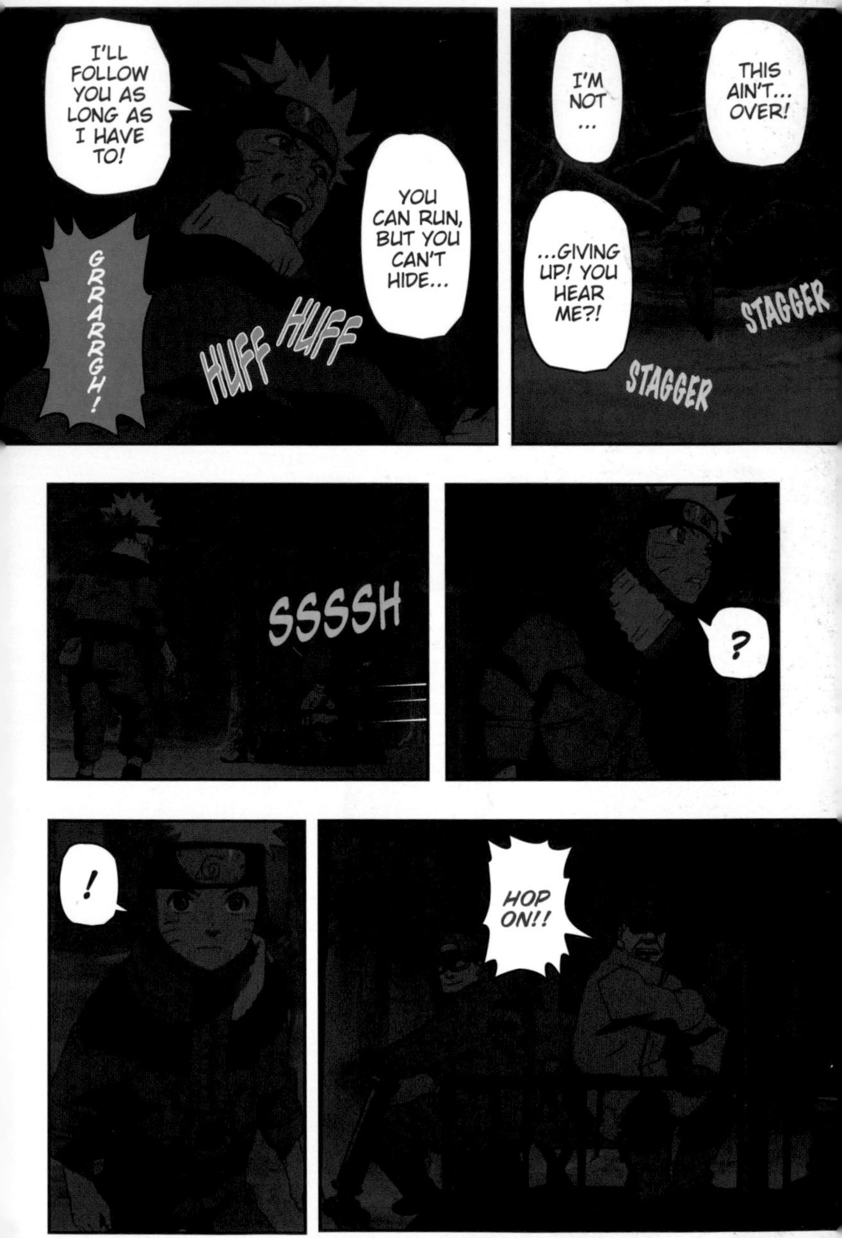
THIS AIN'T... OVER!
I'M NOT ...
...GIVING UP! YOU HEAR ME?!
STAGGER
STAGGER
YOU CAN RUN, BUT YOU CAN'T HIDE...
I'LL FOLLOW YOU AS LONG AS I HAVE TO!
HUFF HUFF
GRRARRGH!
?
SSSSH
HOP ON!!
!

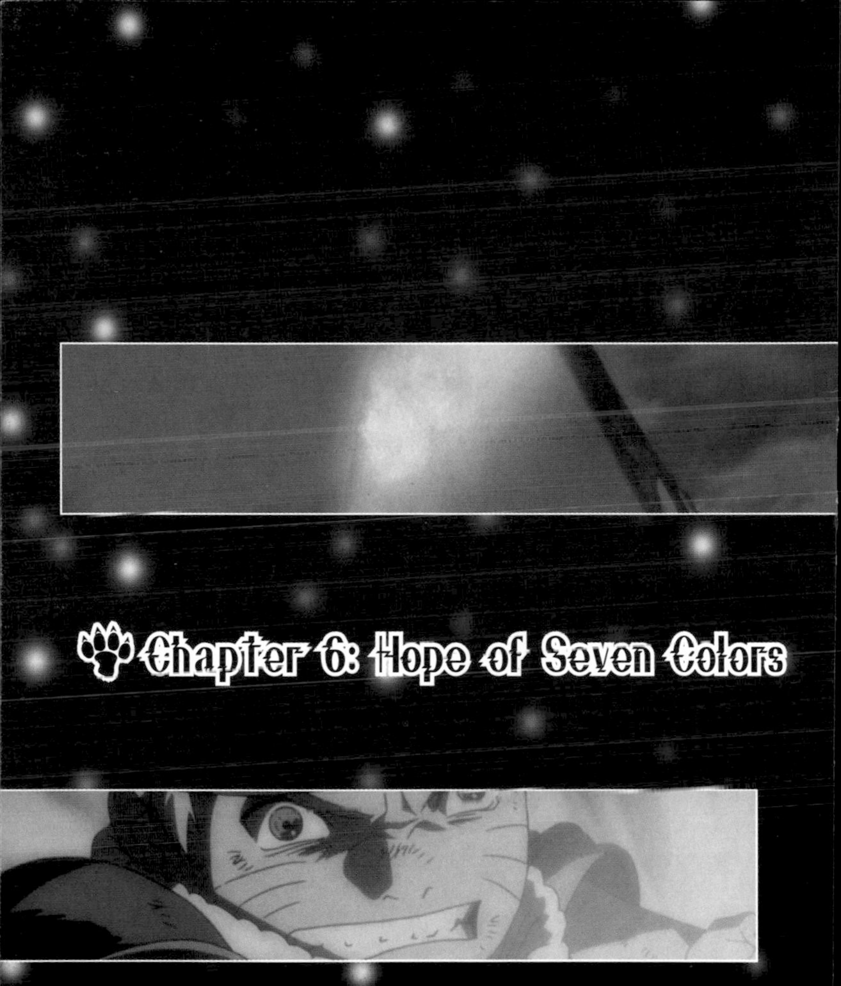
Chapter 6: Hope of Seven Colors

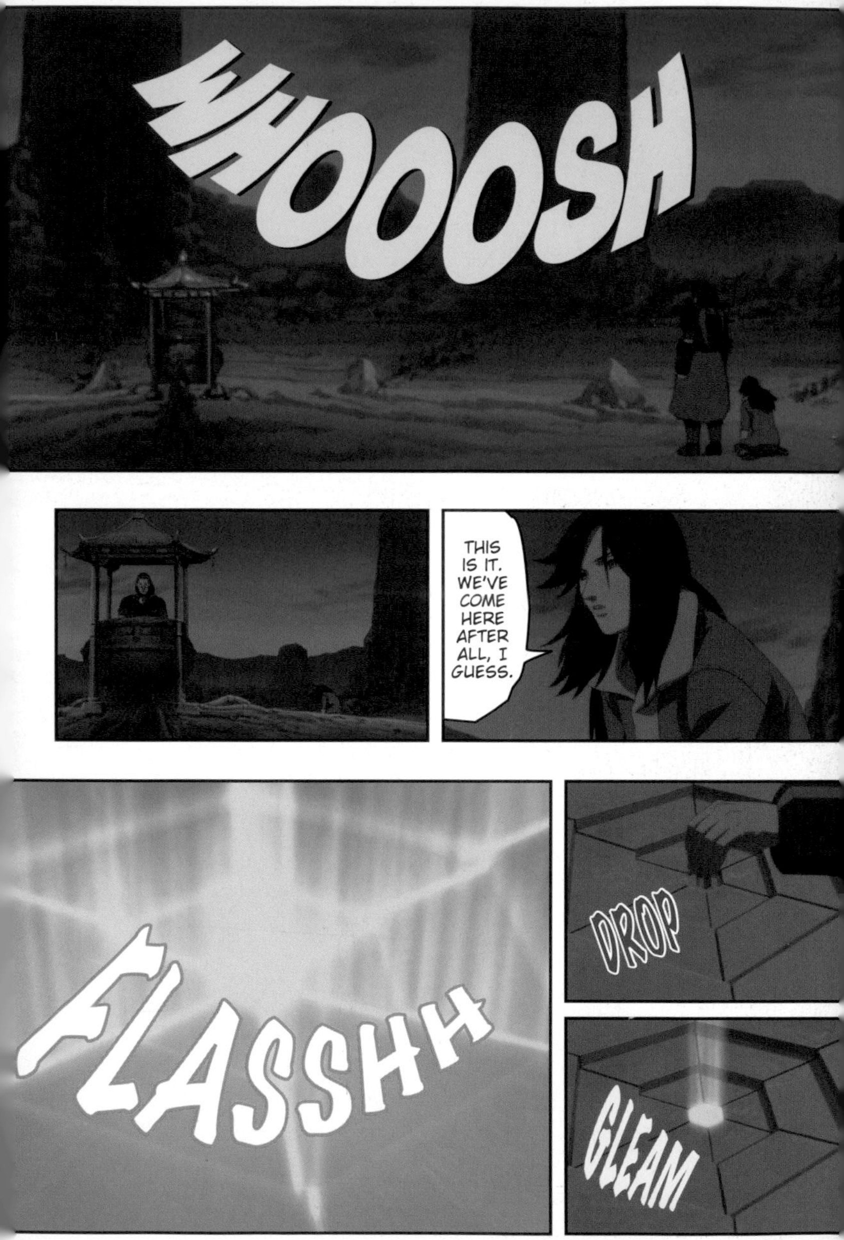
WHOOOSH
THIS IS IT. WE'VE COME HERE AFTER ALL, I GUESS.
DROP
GLEAM
FLASHH

SHIMMER

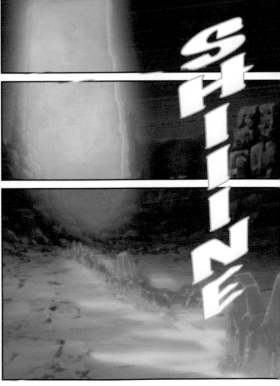

SHIIINE

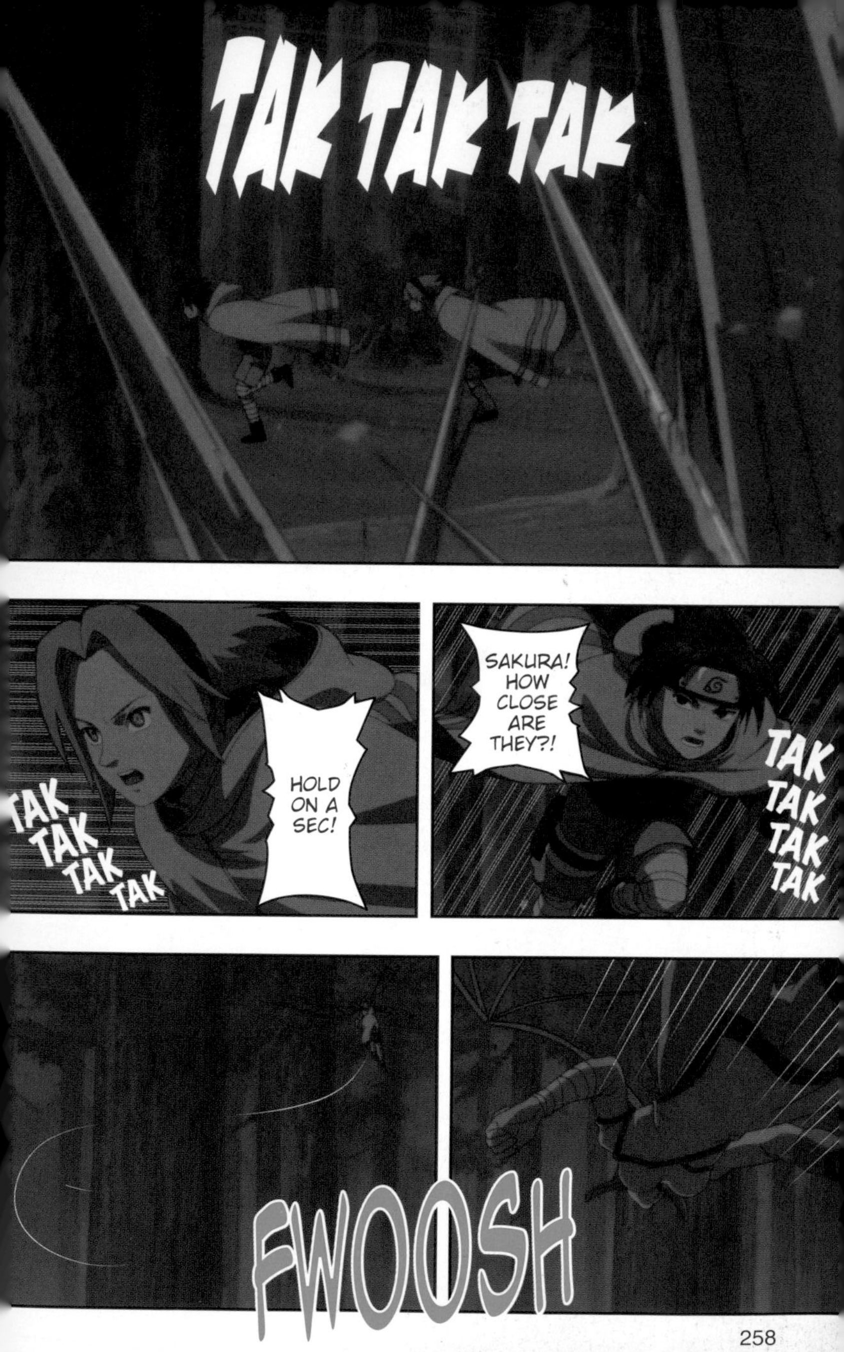
TAK TAK TAK
SAKURA! HOW CLOSE ARE THEY?!
TAK TAK TAK TAK
HOLD ON A SEC!
TAK TAK TAK TAK
FWOOSH

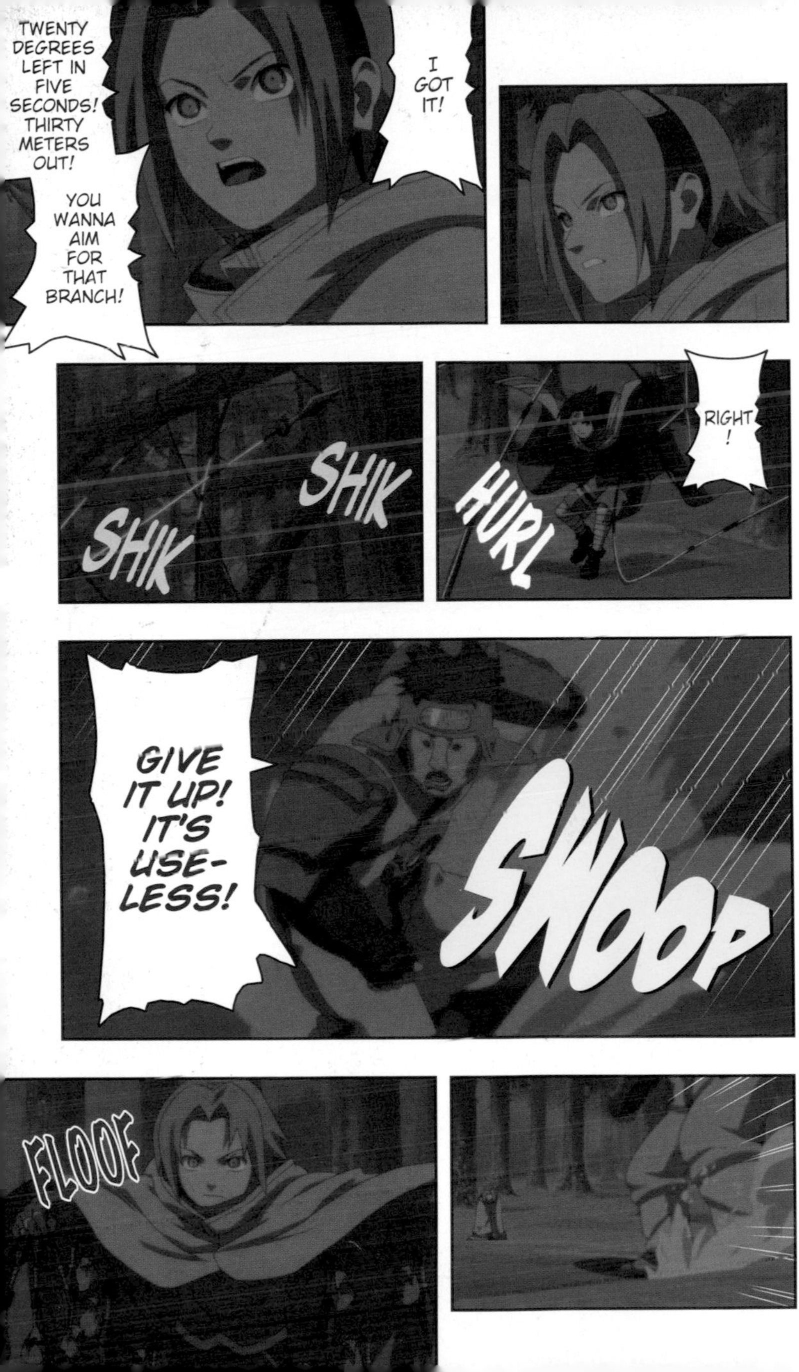

TWENTY DEGREES LEFT IN FIVE SECONDS! THIRTY METERS OUT!
YOU WANNA AIM FOR THAT BRANCH!
I GOT IT!
RIGHT!
HURL
SHIK
SHIK
GIVE IT UP! IT'S USE-LESS!
SHOOP
FLOOF

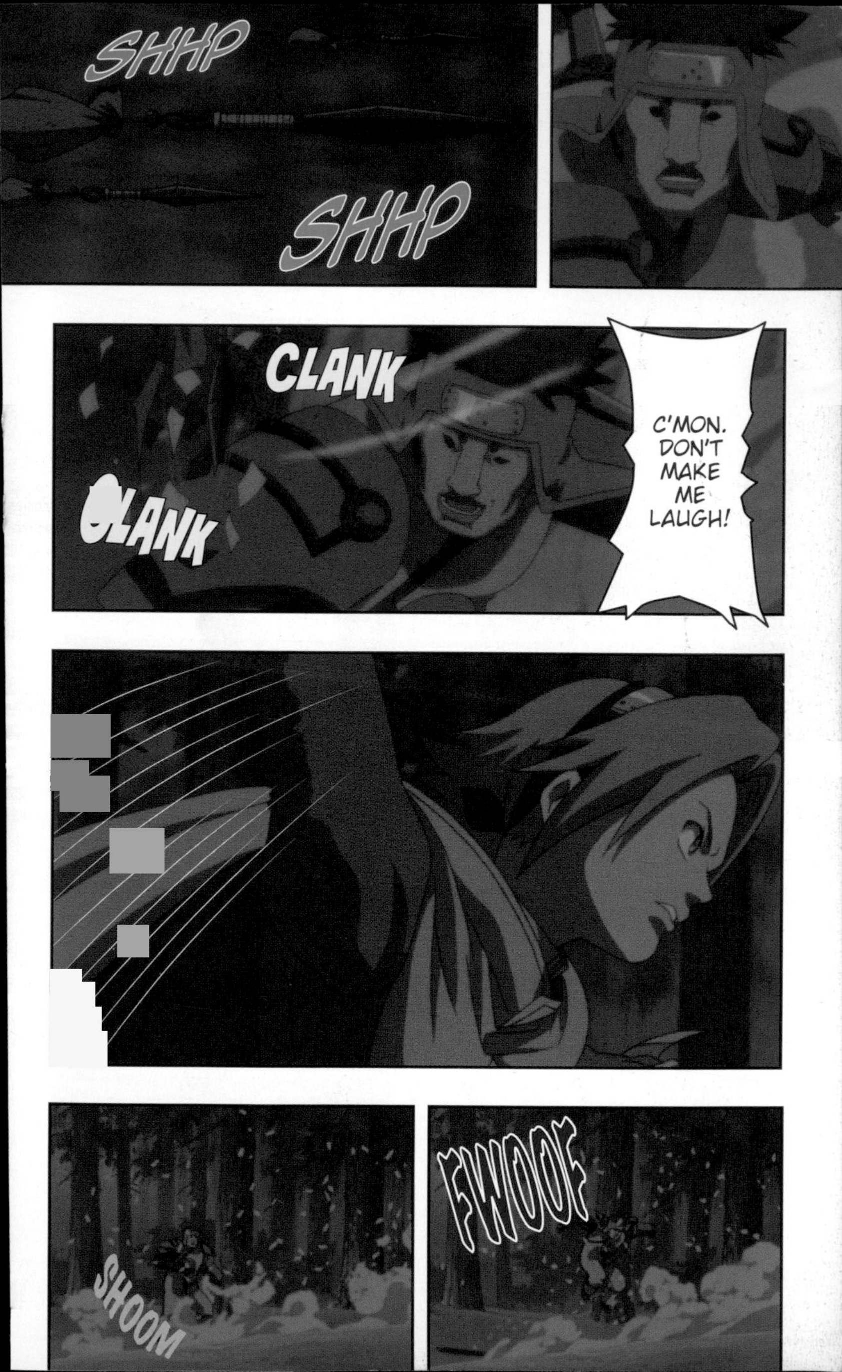
SHHP
SHHP
C'MON. DON'T MAKE ME LAUGH!
CLANK
LANK
FWOOF
SHOOM

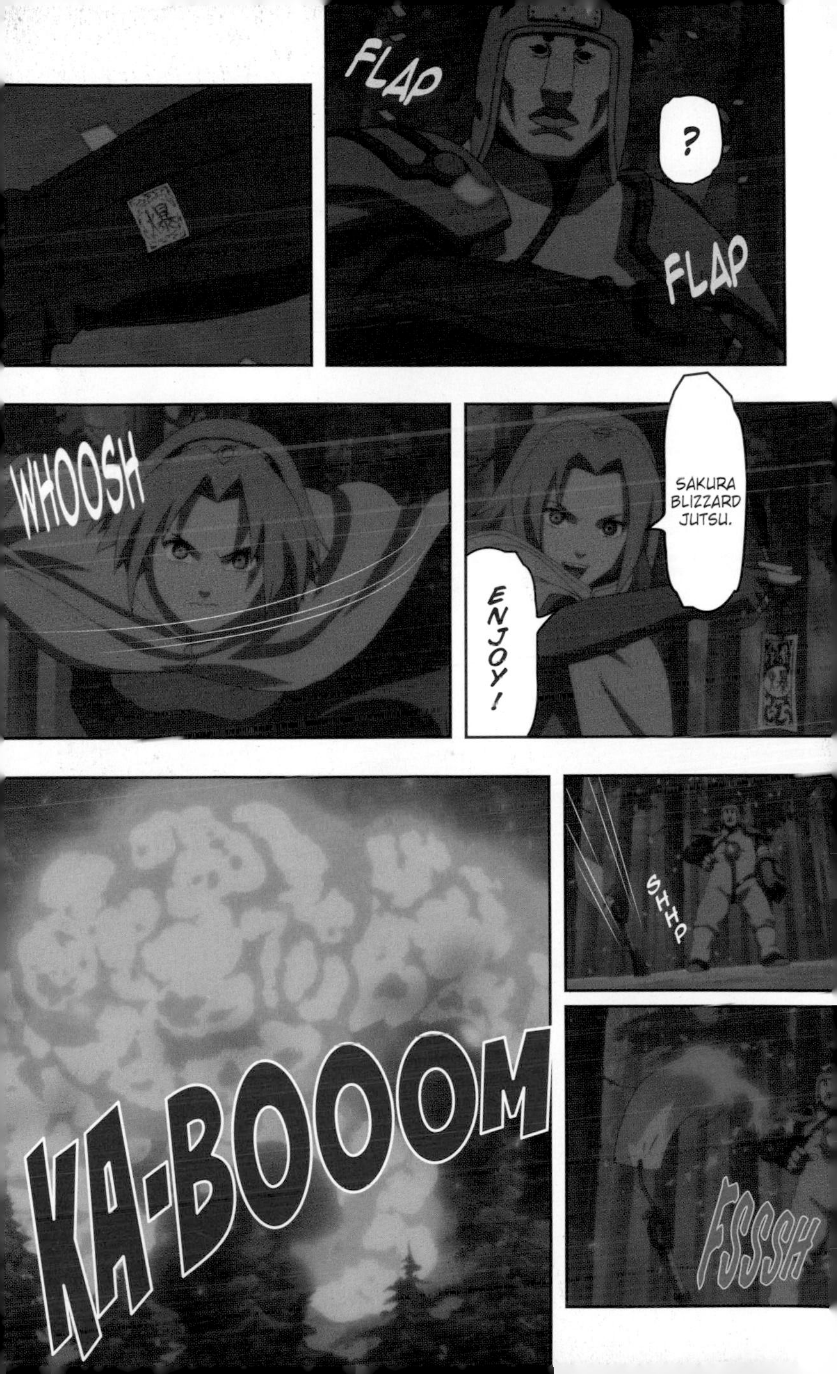
FLAP
?
FLAP
SAKURA BLIZZARD JUTSU.
ENJOY!
WHOOSH
SHHP
FSSSH
KA-BOOOM

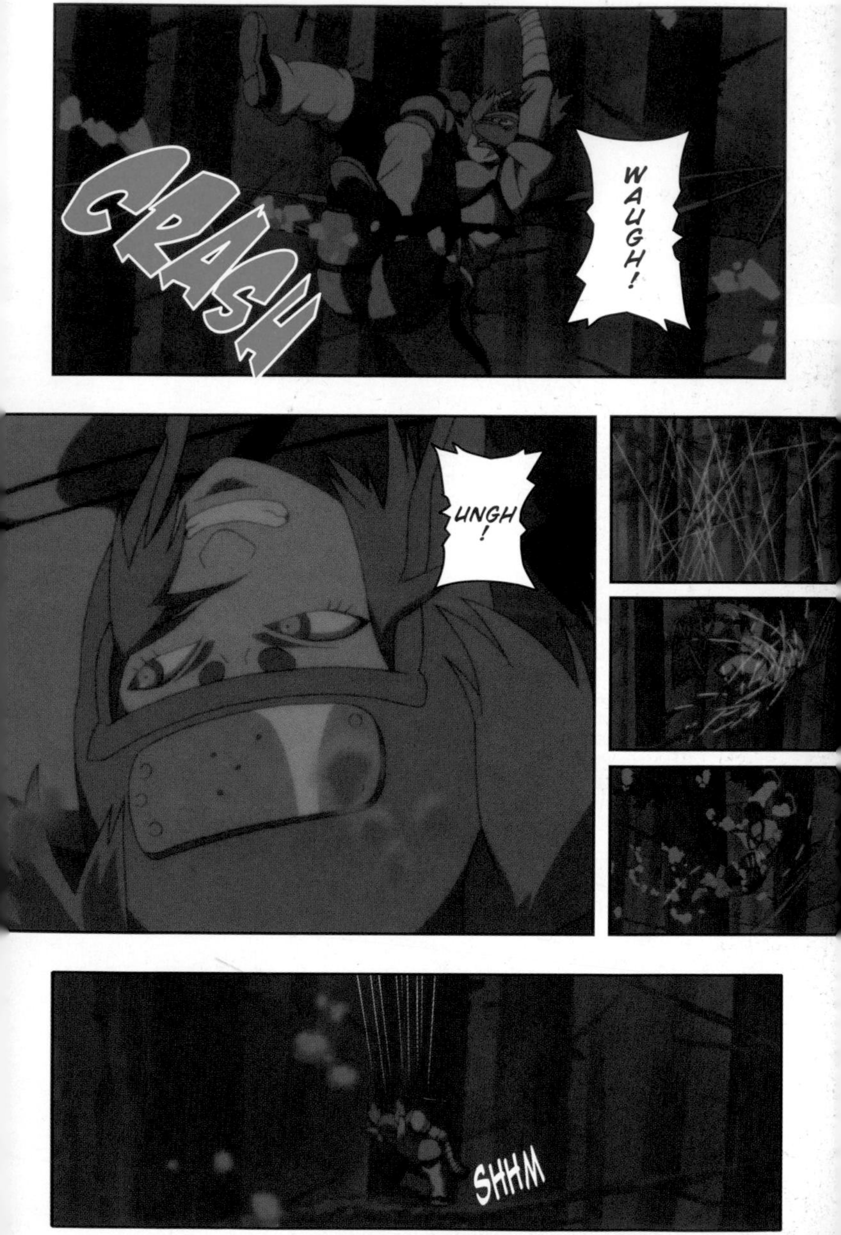
WAUGH!
CRASH
UNGH!
SHHM

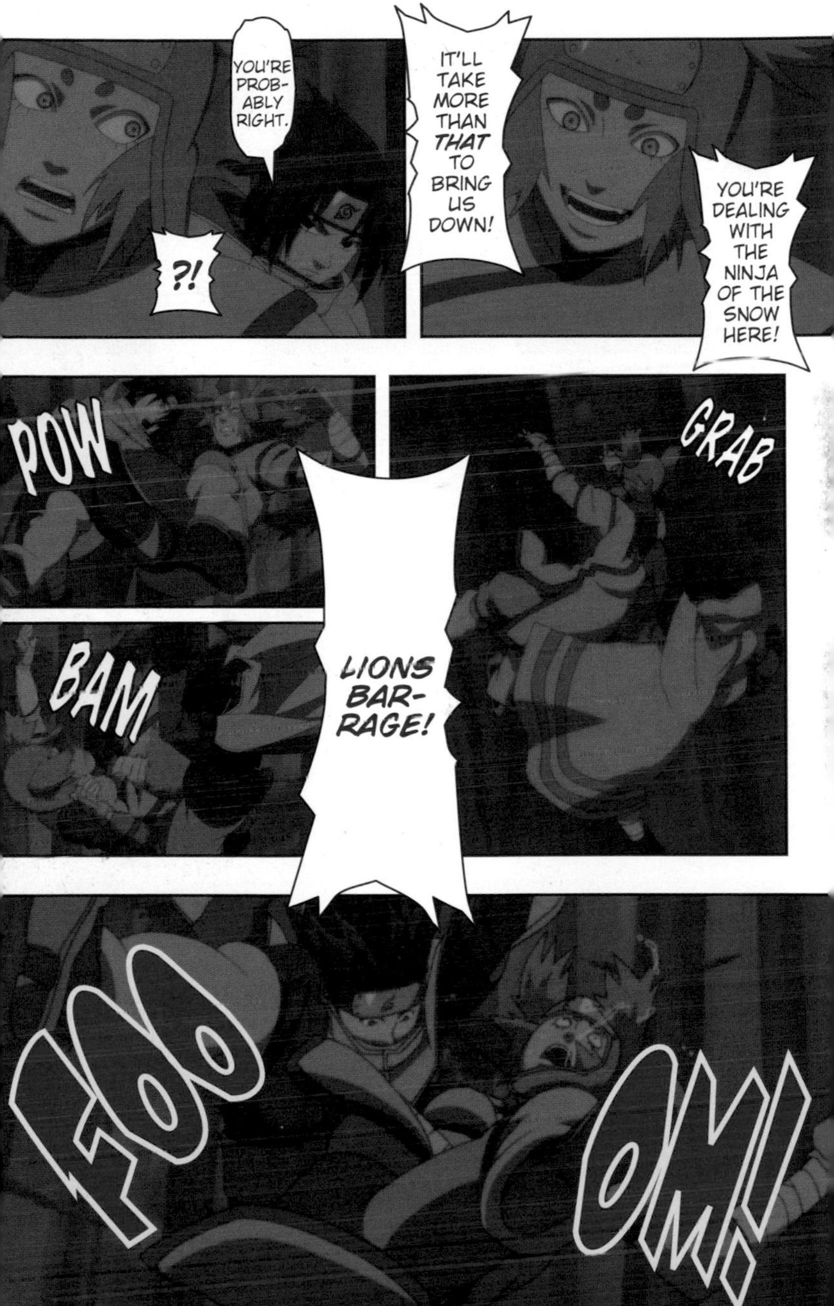
IT'LL TAKE MORE THAN *THAT* TO BRING US DOWN!
YOU'RE DEALING WITH THE NINJA OF THE SNOW HERE!
YOU'RE PROBABLY RIGHT.
?!
GRAB
POW
BAM
LIONS BARRAGE!
FOOOM!

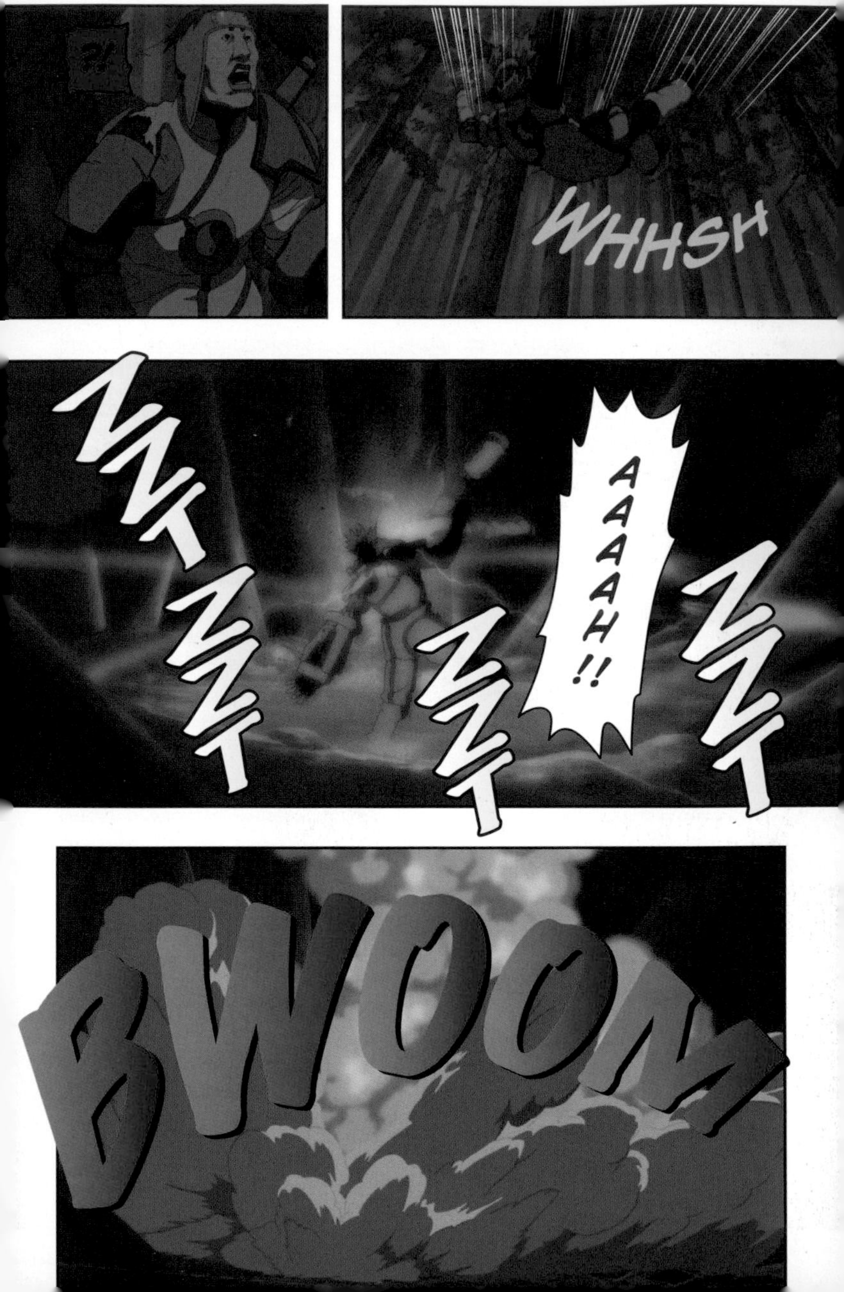
WHHSH
?!
AAAAAH!!
BWOOM

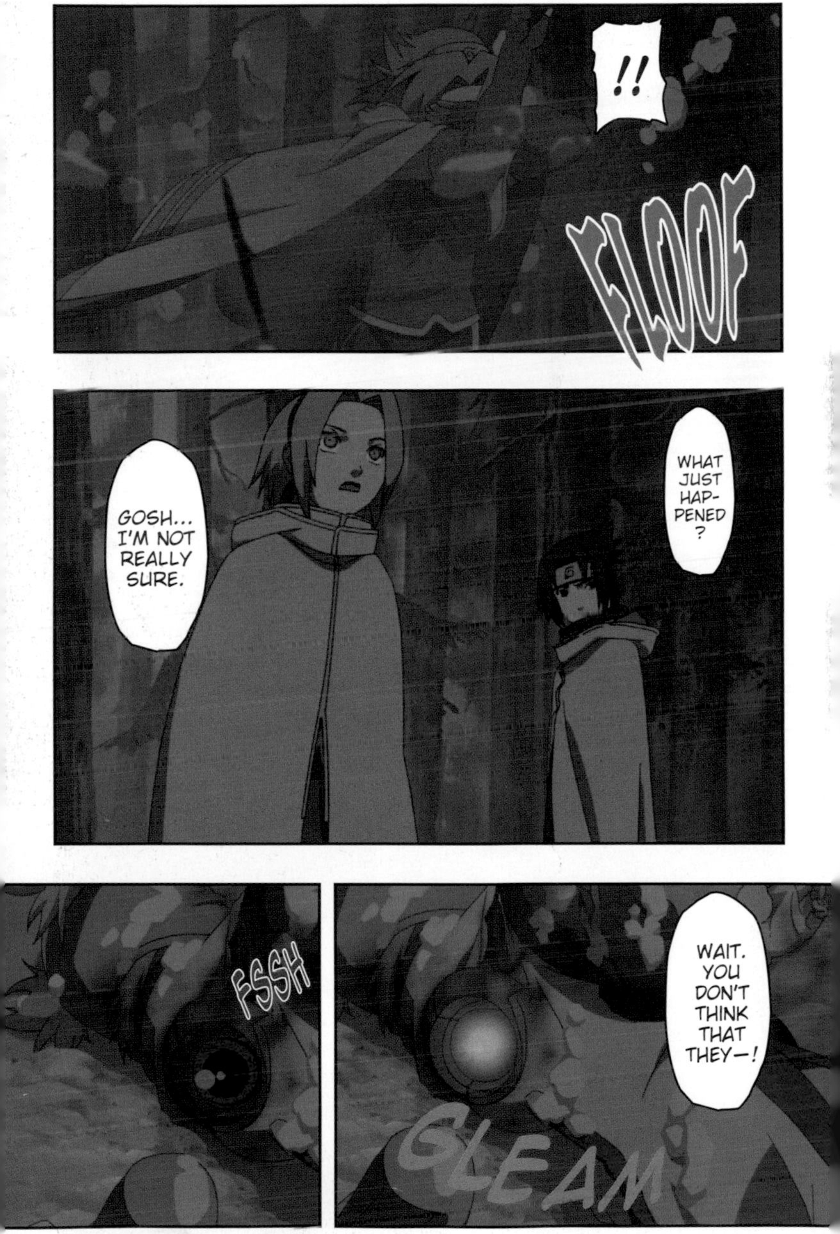
!!
FLOOF
WHAT JUST HAP-PENED?
GOSH... I'M NOT REALLY SURE.
WAIT. YOU DON'T THINK THAT THEY—!
GLEAM
FSSH

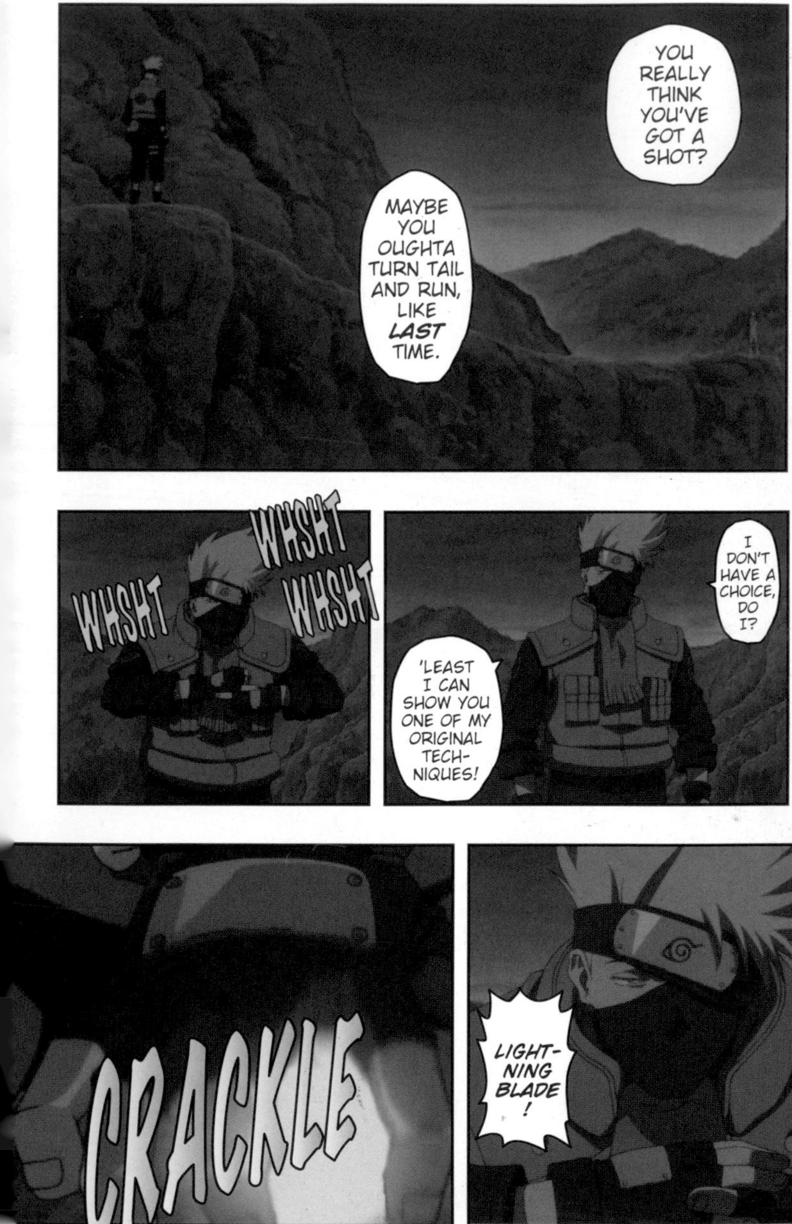
YOU REALLY THINK YOU'VE GOT A SHOT?
MAYBE YOU OUGHTA TURN TAIL AND RUN, LIKE ***LAST*** TIME.
I DON'T HAVE A CHOICE, DO I?
'LEAST I CAN SHOW YOU ONE OF MY ORIGINAL TECHNIQUES!
WHSHT
WHSHT
WHSHT
LIGHTNING BLADE!
CRACKLE

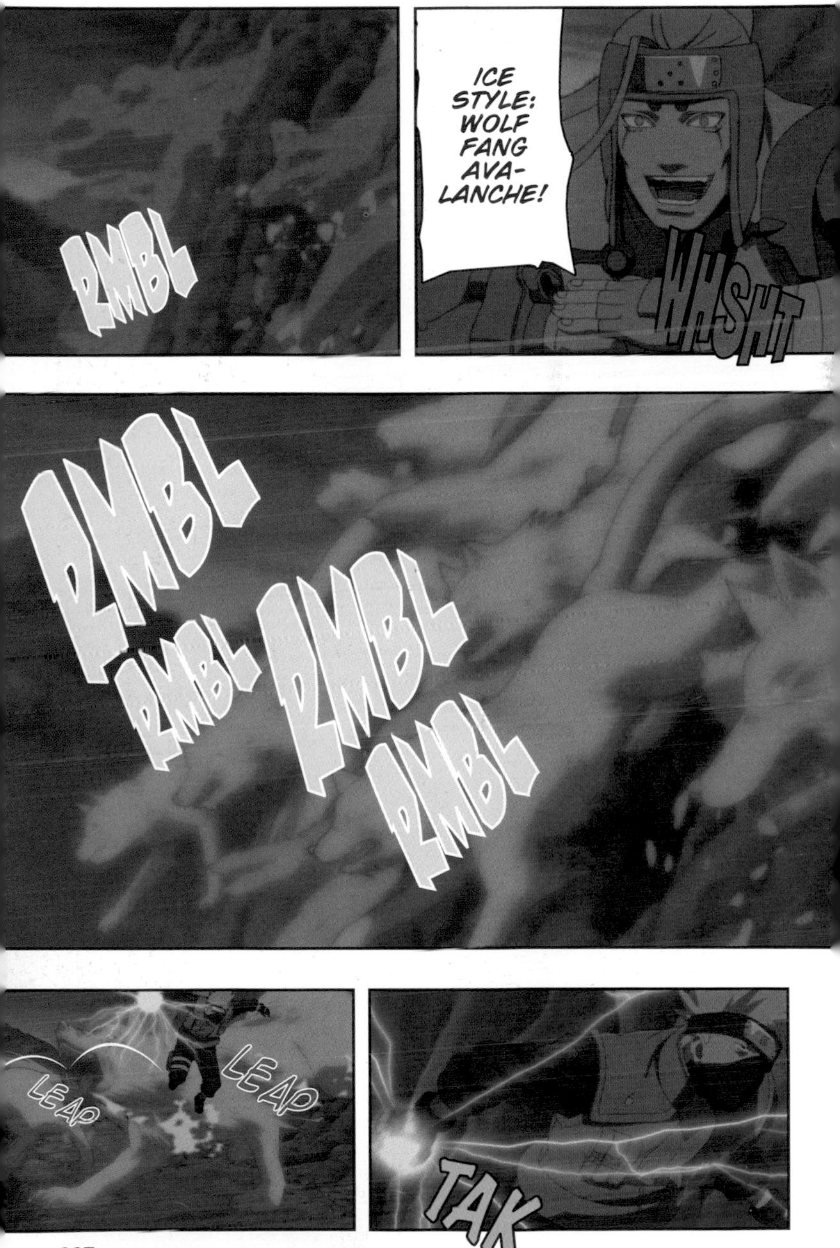

ICE STYLE: WOLF FANG AVA-LANCHE!
WHSHT
RMBL
RMBL
RMBL
RMBL
RMBL
TAK
LEAP
LEAP

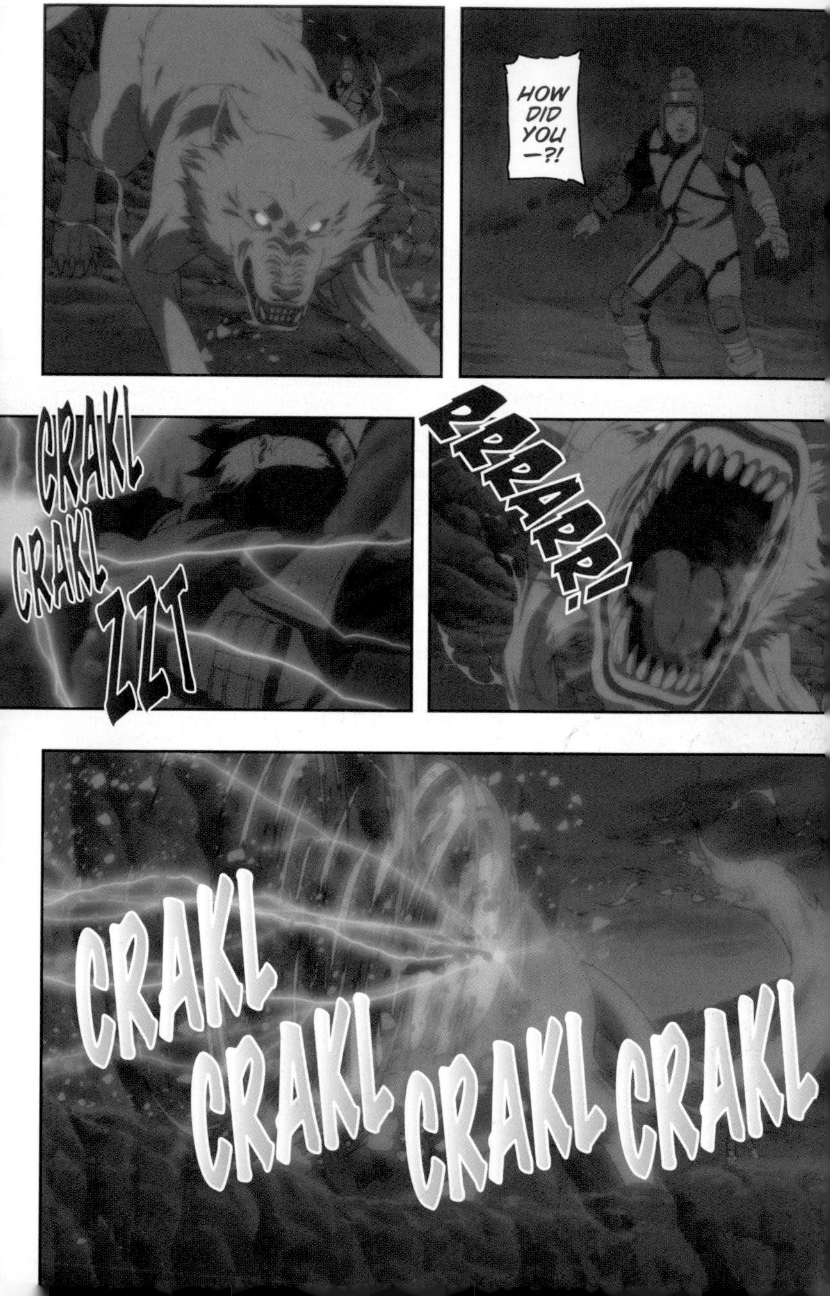
HOW DID YOU—?!
RRRARR!
CRAKL
CRAKL
ZZT
CRAKL
CRAKL
CRAKL
CRAKL

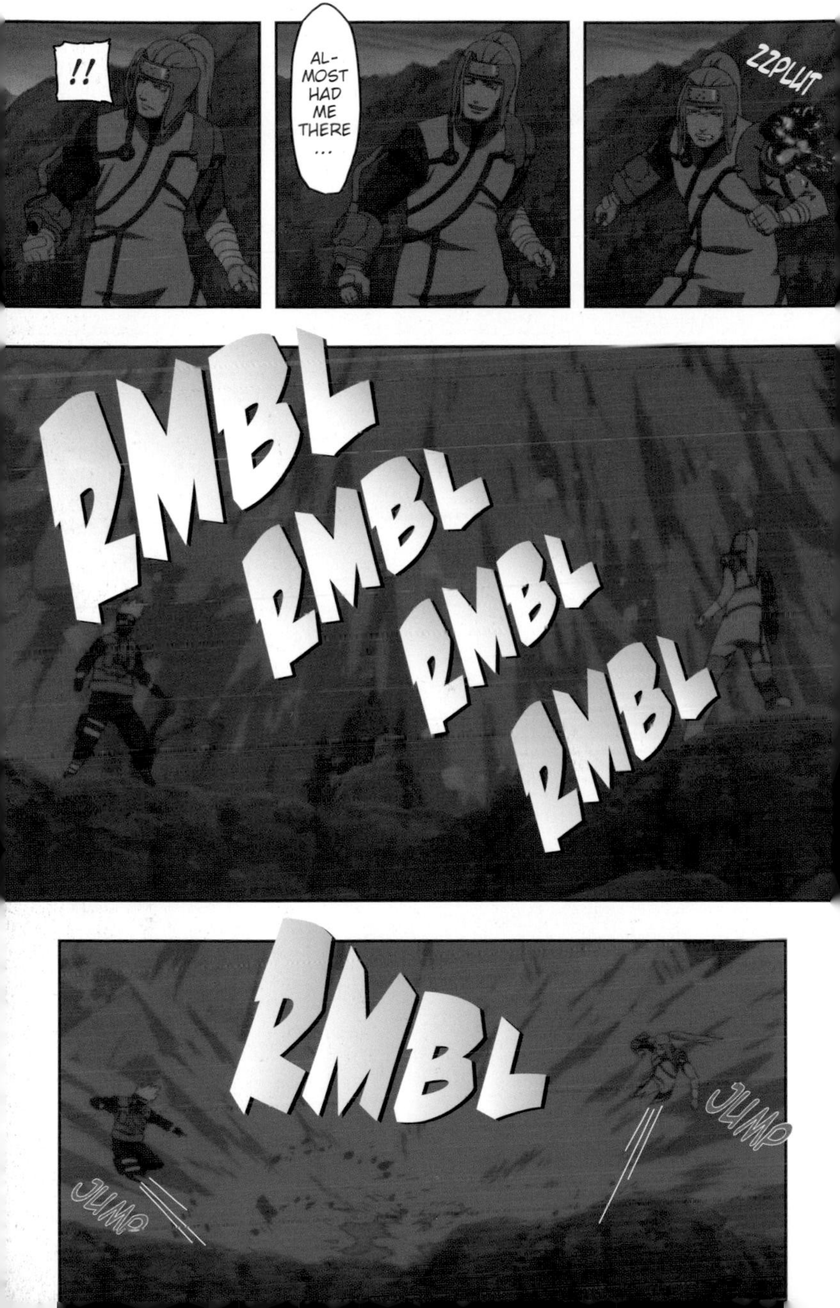
ZZPLUT
AL-MOST HAD ME THERE …
!!
RMBL
RMBL
RMBL
RMBL
RMBL
JUMP
JUMP

SMACK

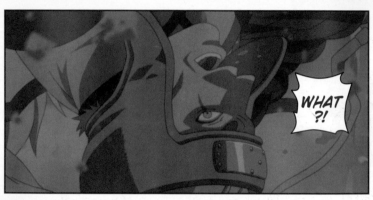

WHAT ?!

EVEN WITHOUT NINJUTSU AND GENJUTSU...

...A NINJA ALWAYS HAS *TAIJUTSU*!

YOU RELY TOO MUCH ON THIS *ARMOR*!

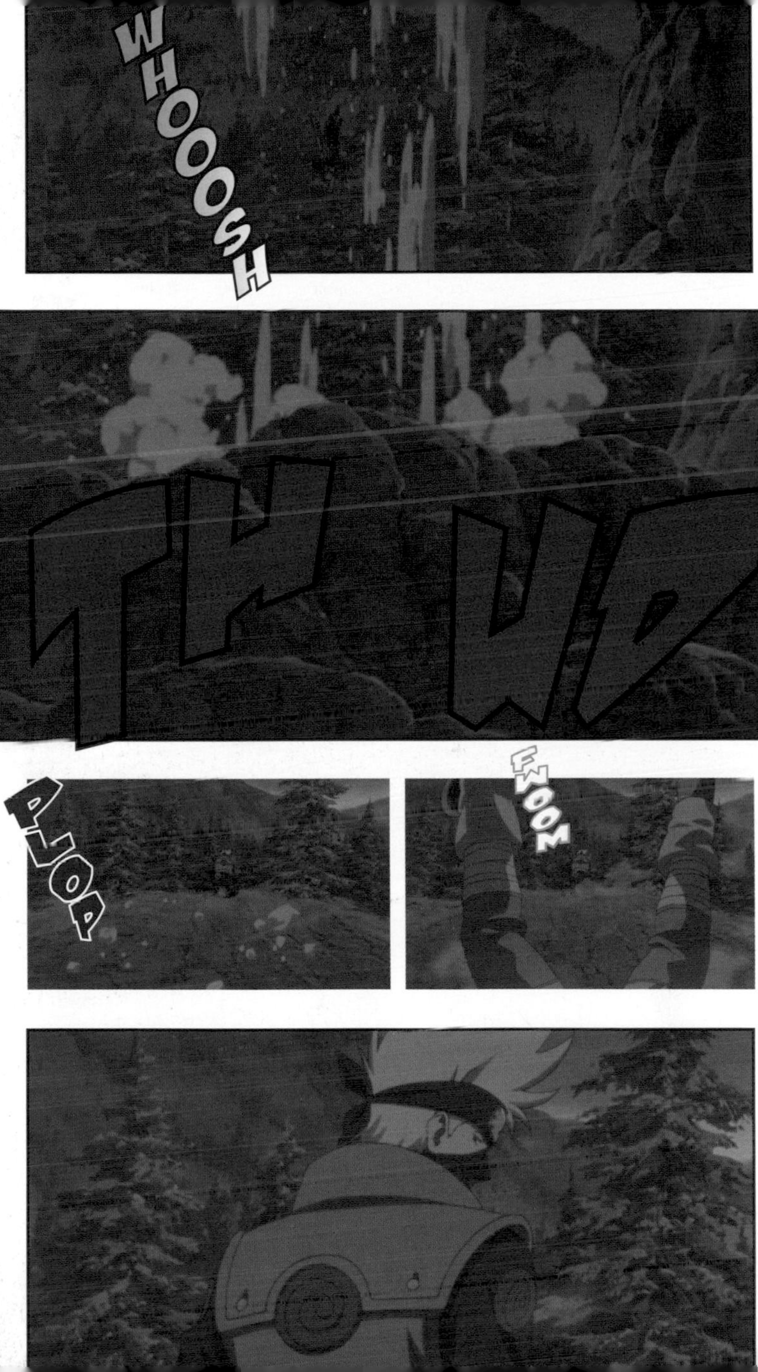
WHOOOSH
THUD
FWOOM
PLOP

GL OW...

THE TREASURE, WHERE IS IT?!

TURN

I DON'T SEE IT!

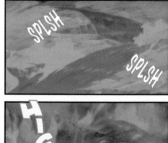

SPLSH

SPLSH

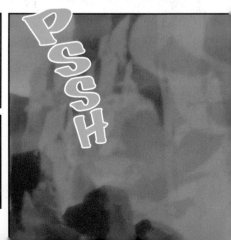

PSSH

HISSSS

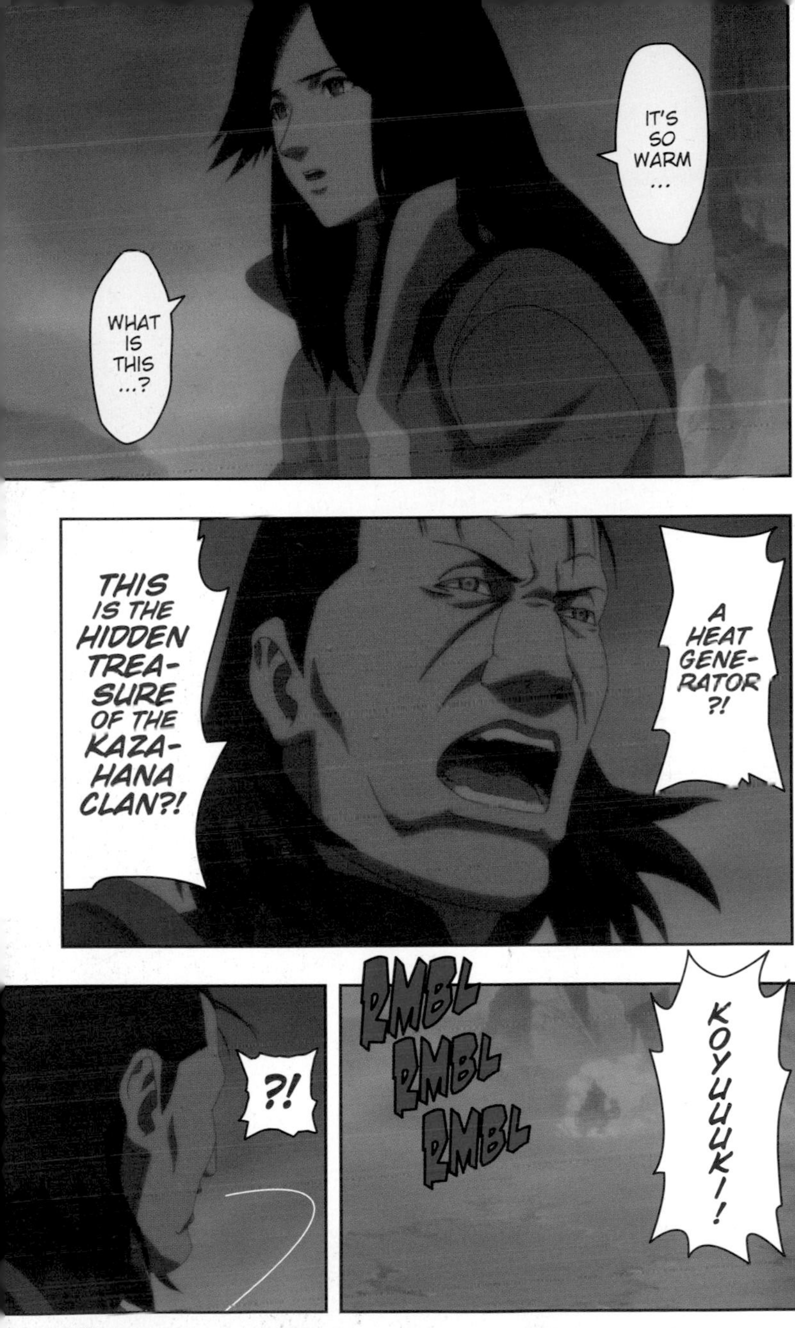
IT'S SO WARM ...
WHAT IS THIS ...?
A HEAT GENERATOR?!
THIS IS THE HIDDEN TREASURE OF THE KAZAHANA CLAN?!
KOYUUUK!!
RMBL RMBL RMBL
?!

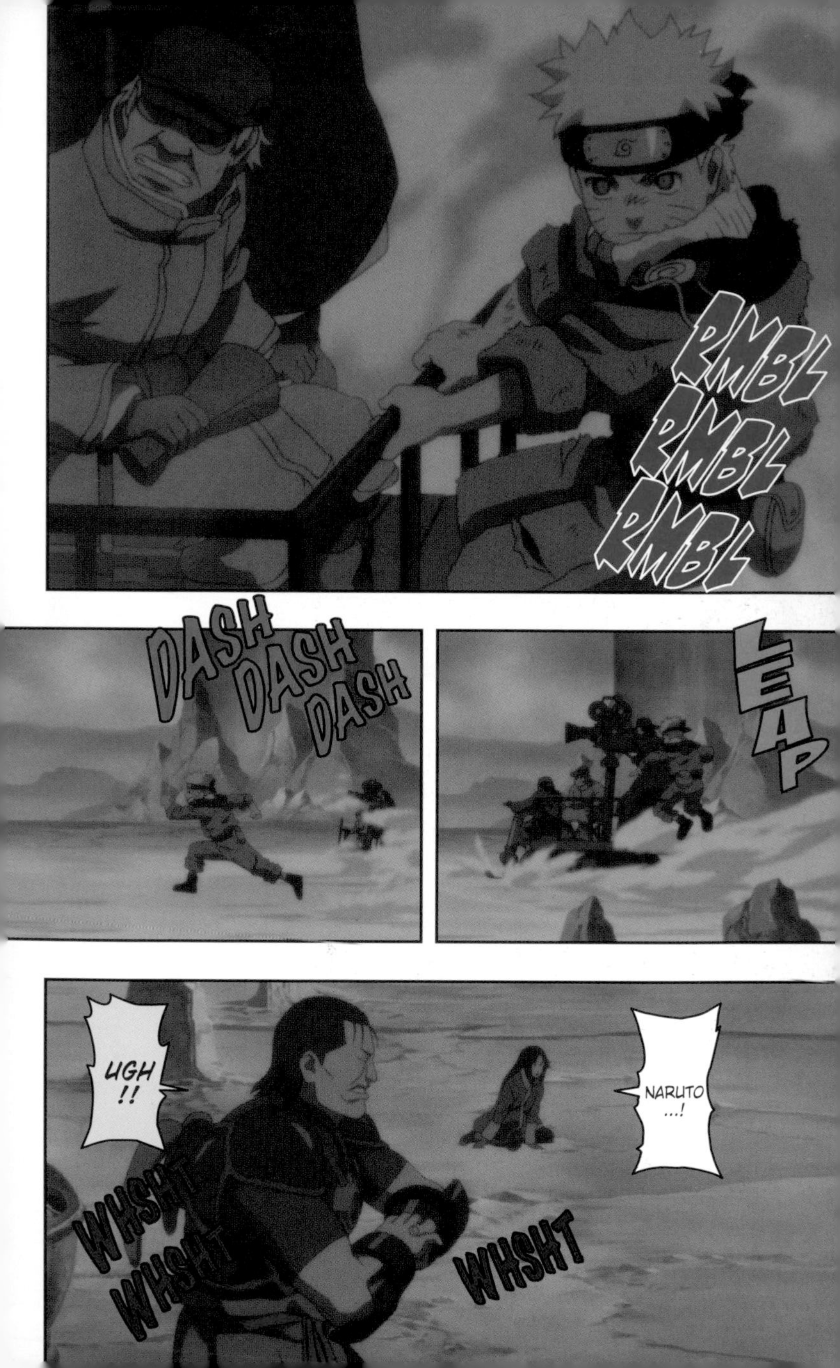
RMBL RMBL RMBL
LEAP
DASH DASH DASH
NARUTO ...!
UGH !!
WHSHT
WHSHT WHSHT

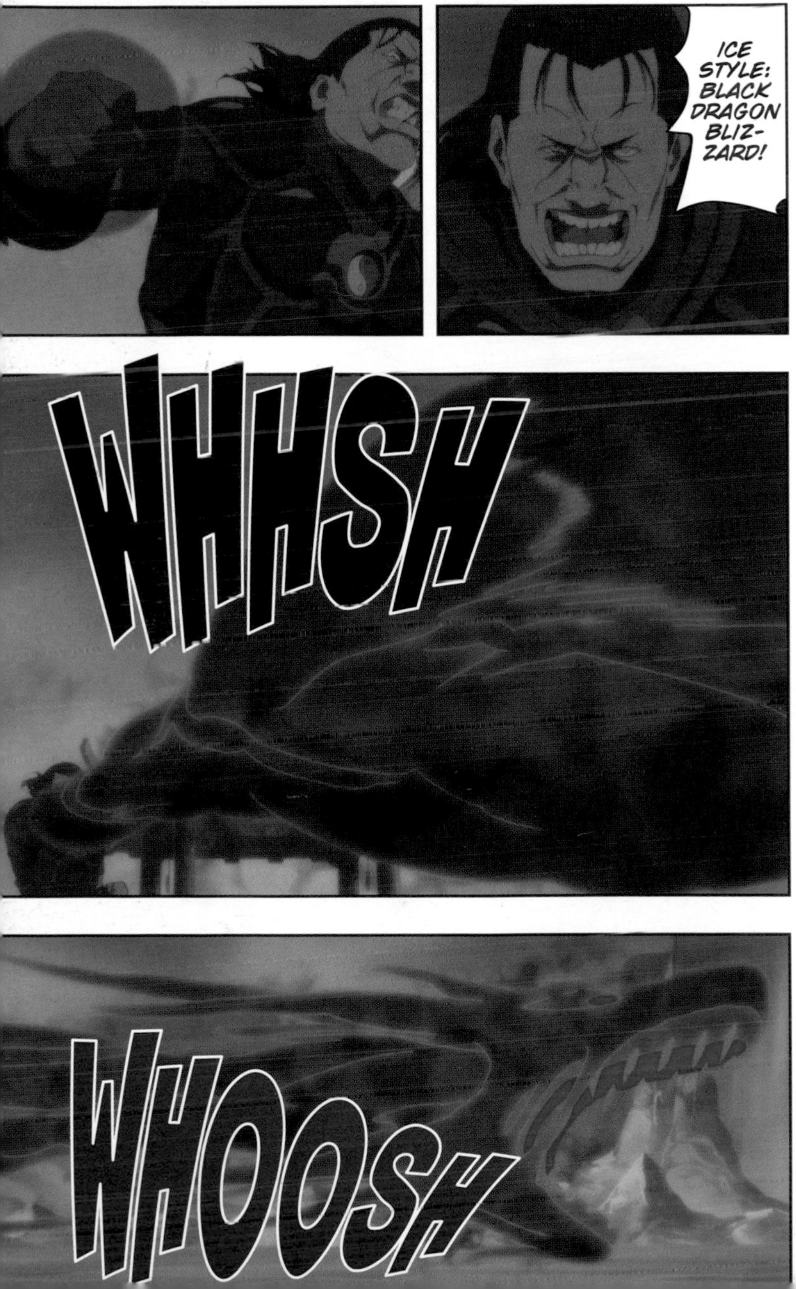
ICE STYLE: BLACK DRAGON BLIZ-ZARD!
WHHSH
WHOOSH

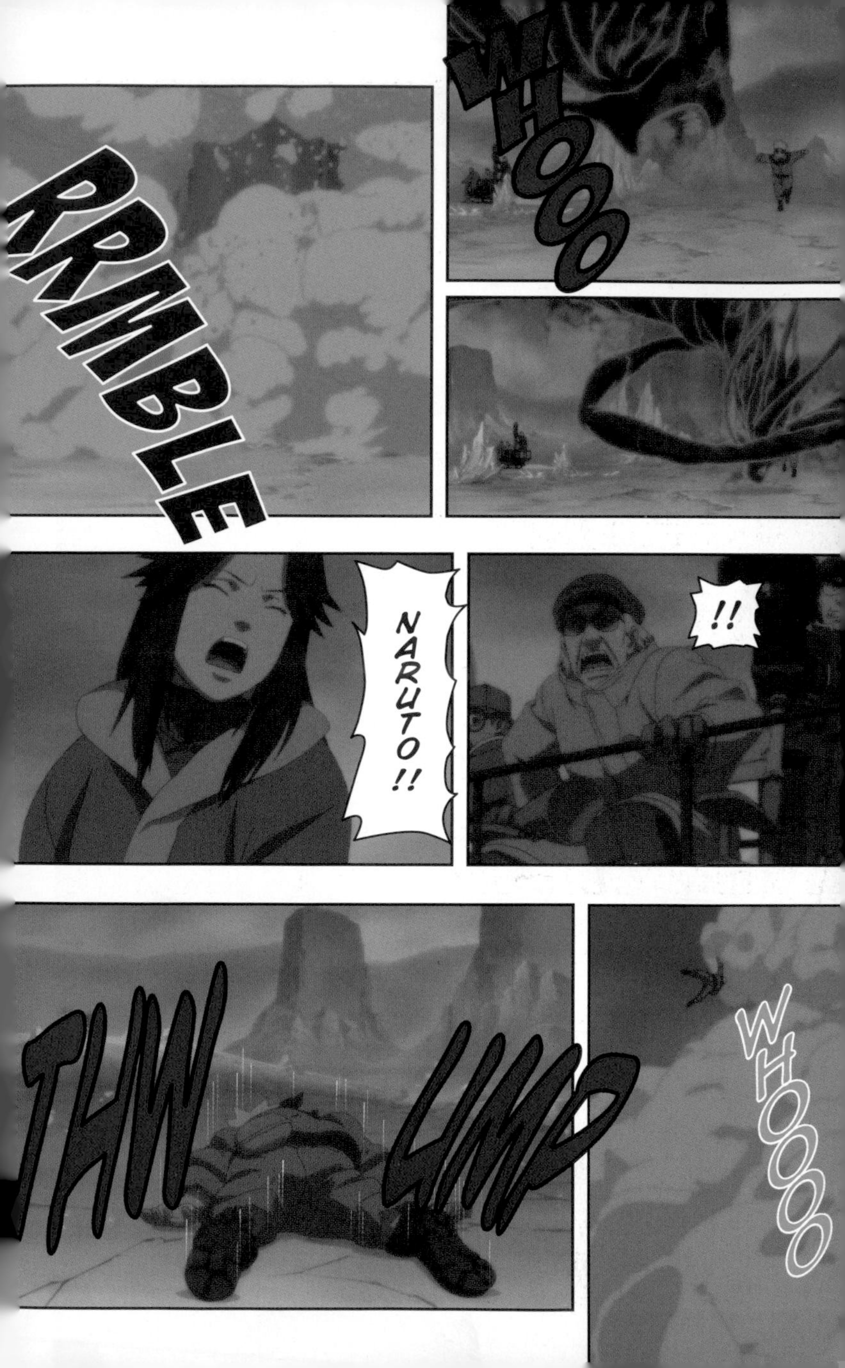
WHOOO
RRMBLE
!!
NARUTO!!
WHOOOO
THWUMP

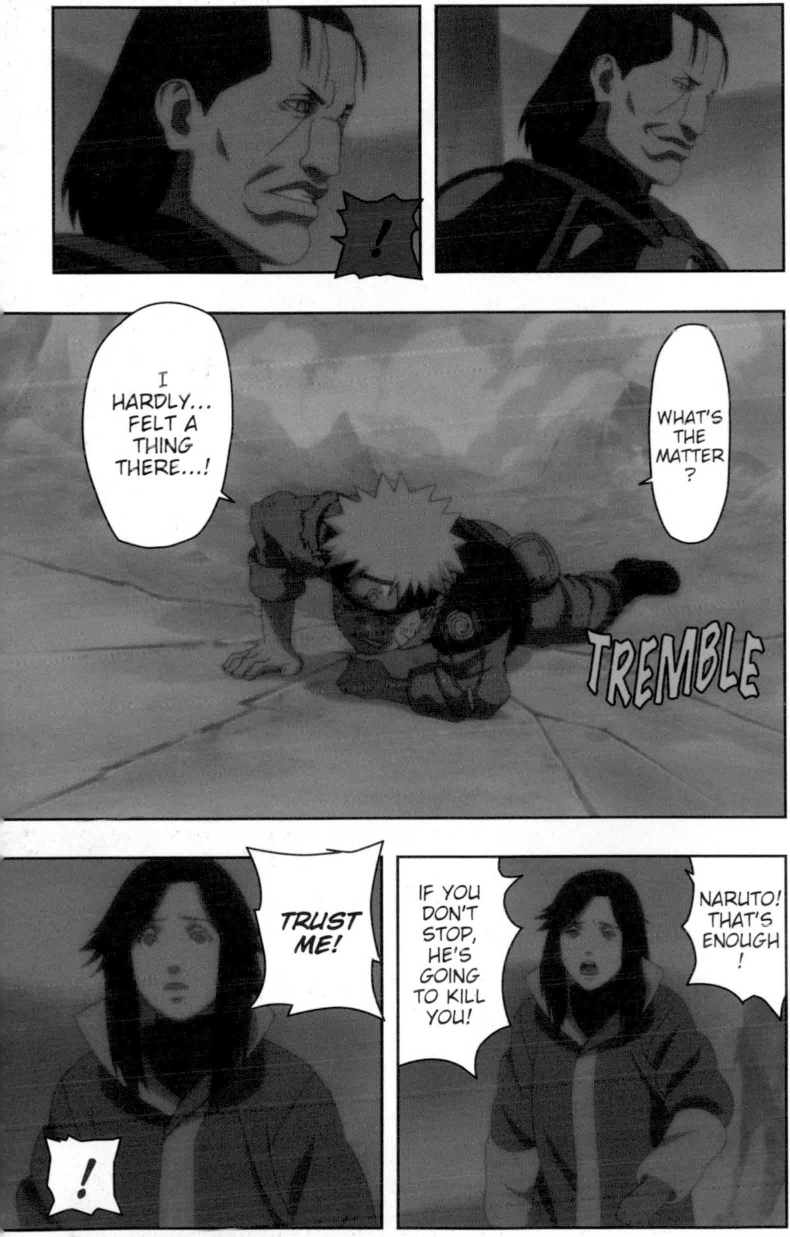
!
WHAT'S THE MATTER?
I HARDLY... FELT A THING THERE...!
TREMBLE
NARUTO! THAT'S ENOUGH!
IF YOU DON'T STOP, HE'S GOING TO KILL YOU!
TRUST ME!
!

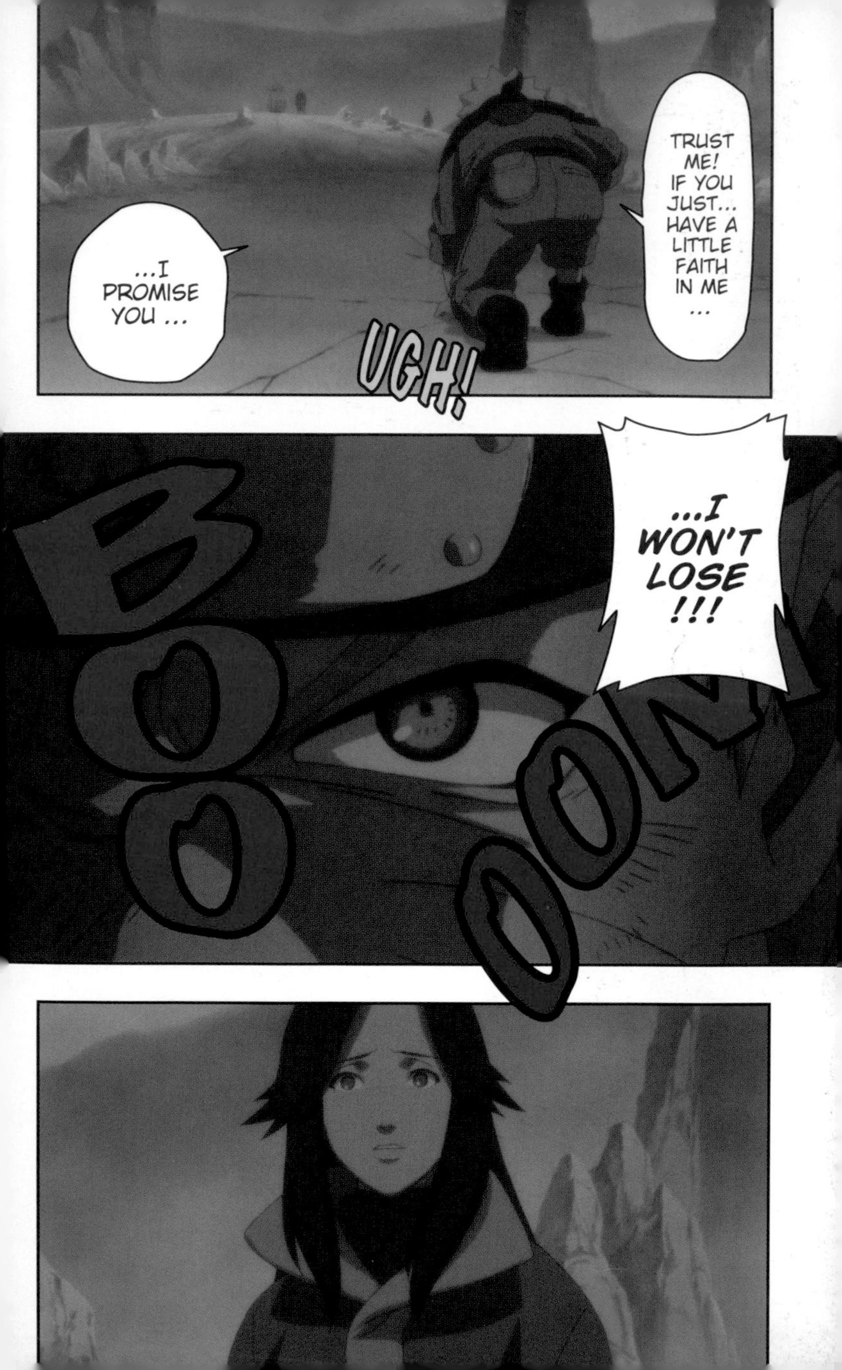
TRUST ME! IF YOU JUST... HAVE A LITTLE FAITH IN ME ...
...I PROMISE YOU ...
UGH!
...I WON'T LOSE !!!
BOOOOOM!

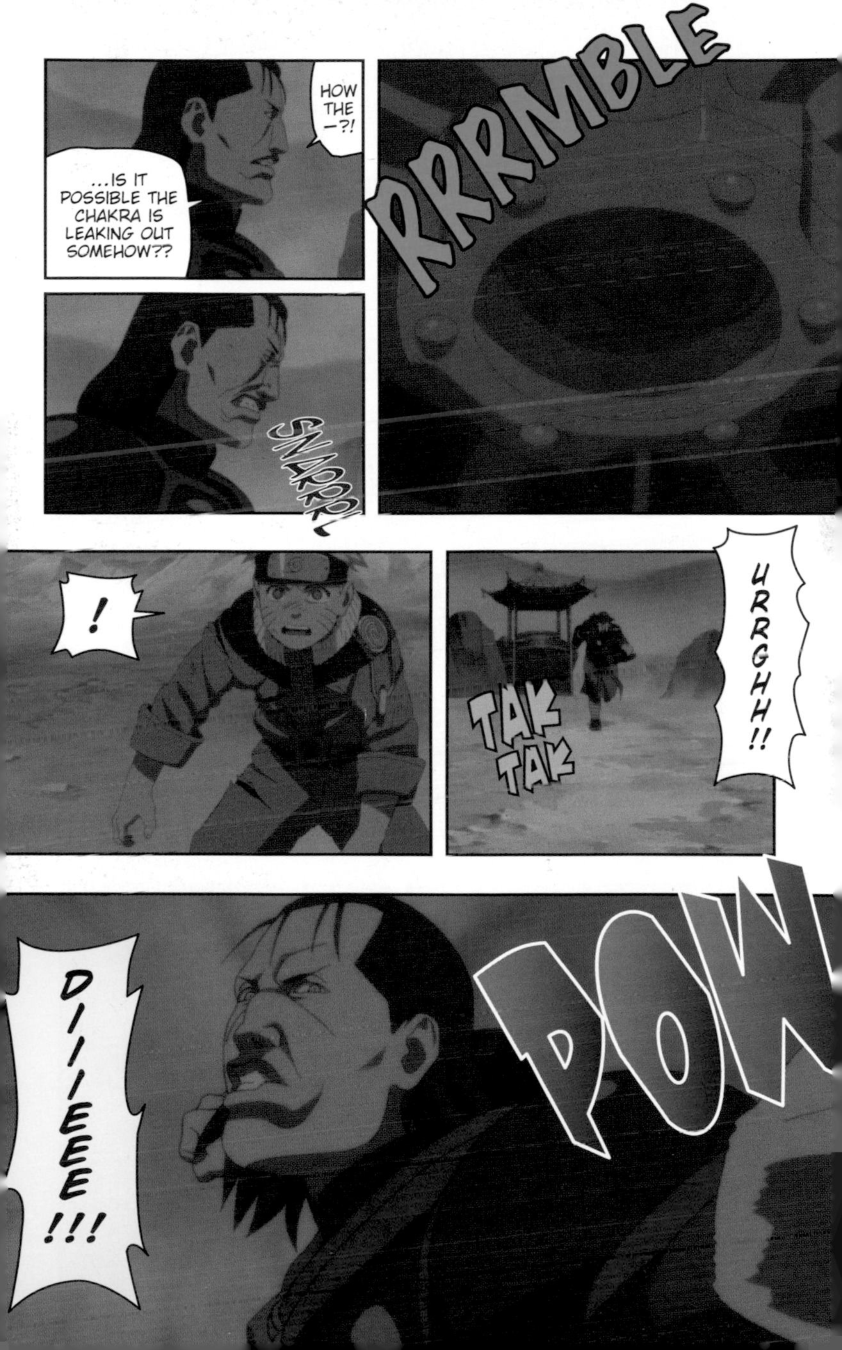
RRRMBLE
HOW THE—?!
...IS IT POSSIBLE THE CHAKRA IS LEAKING OUT SOMEHOW??
SNARRRL
URRGHH!!
TAK TAK
!
POW
DIIIEEE!!!

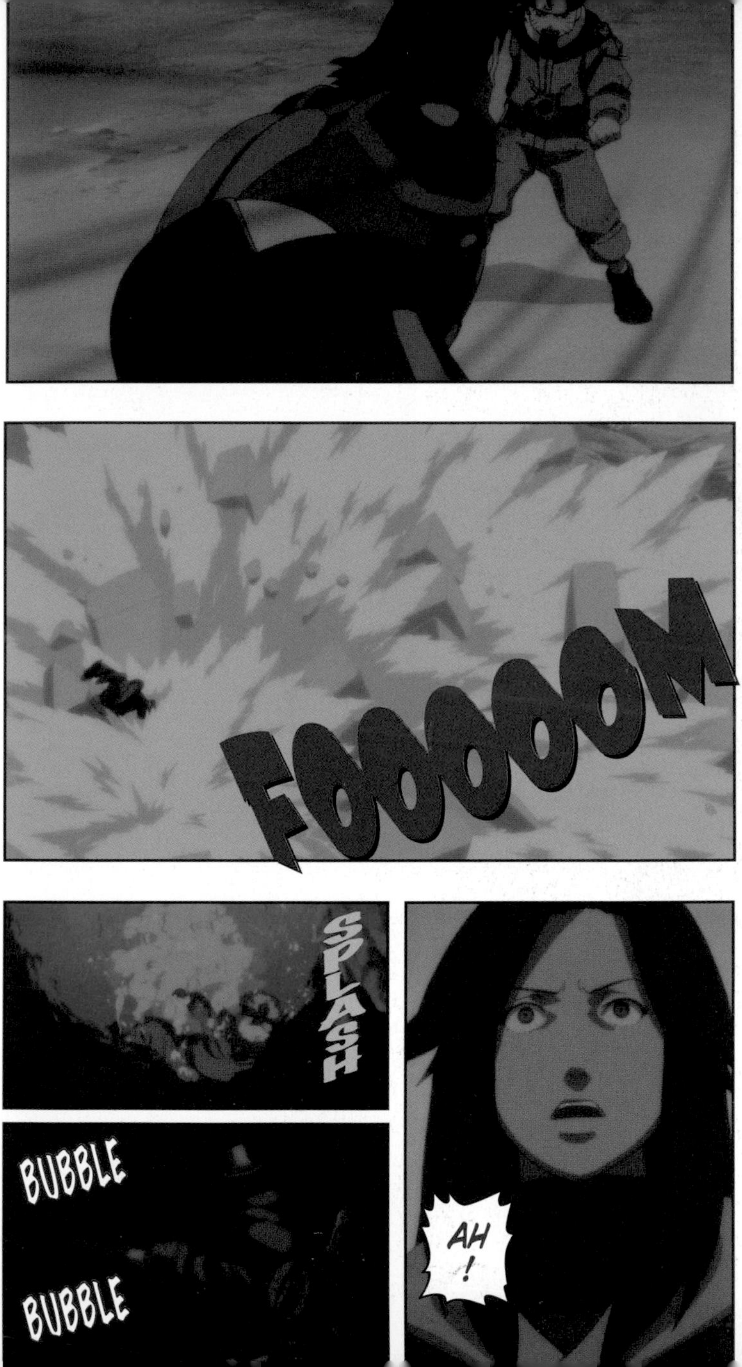
FOOOOOM
AH!
SPLASH
BUBBLE
BUBBLE

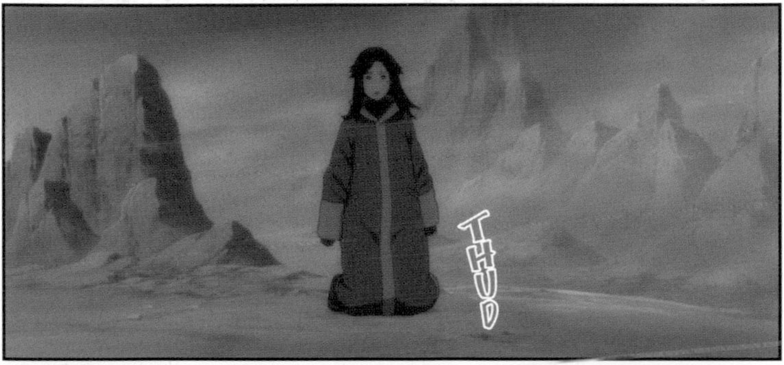
THUD
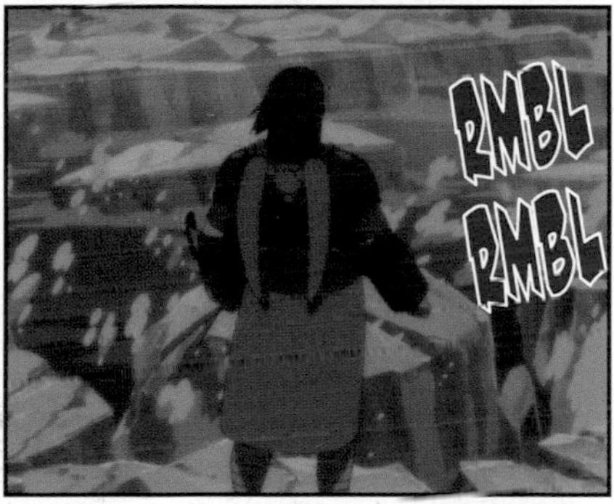
RMBL
RMBL
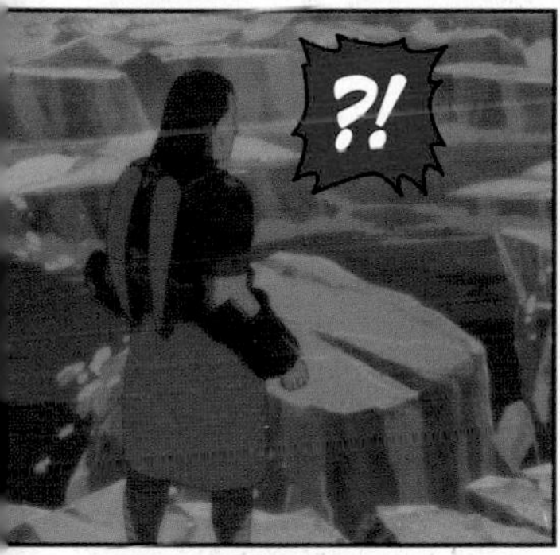
?!
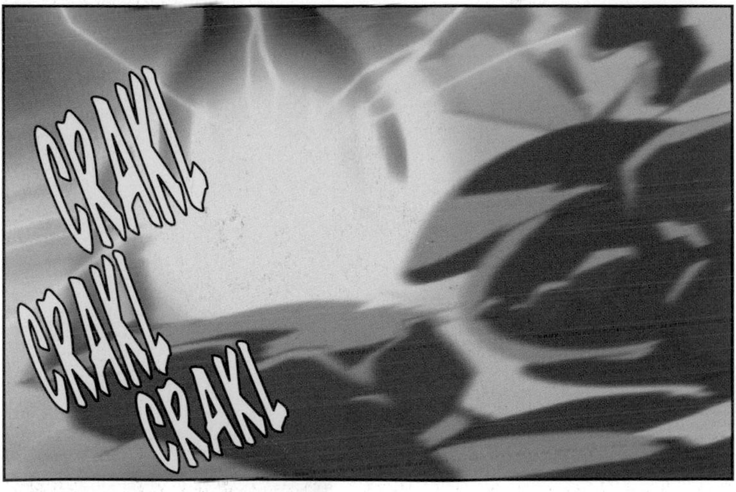
CRAKL
CRAKL
CRAKL

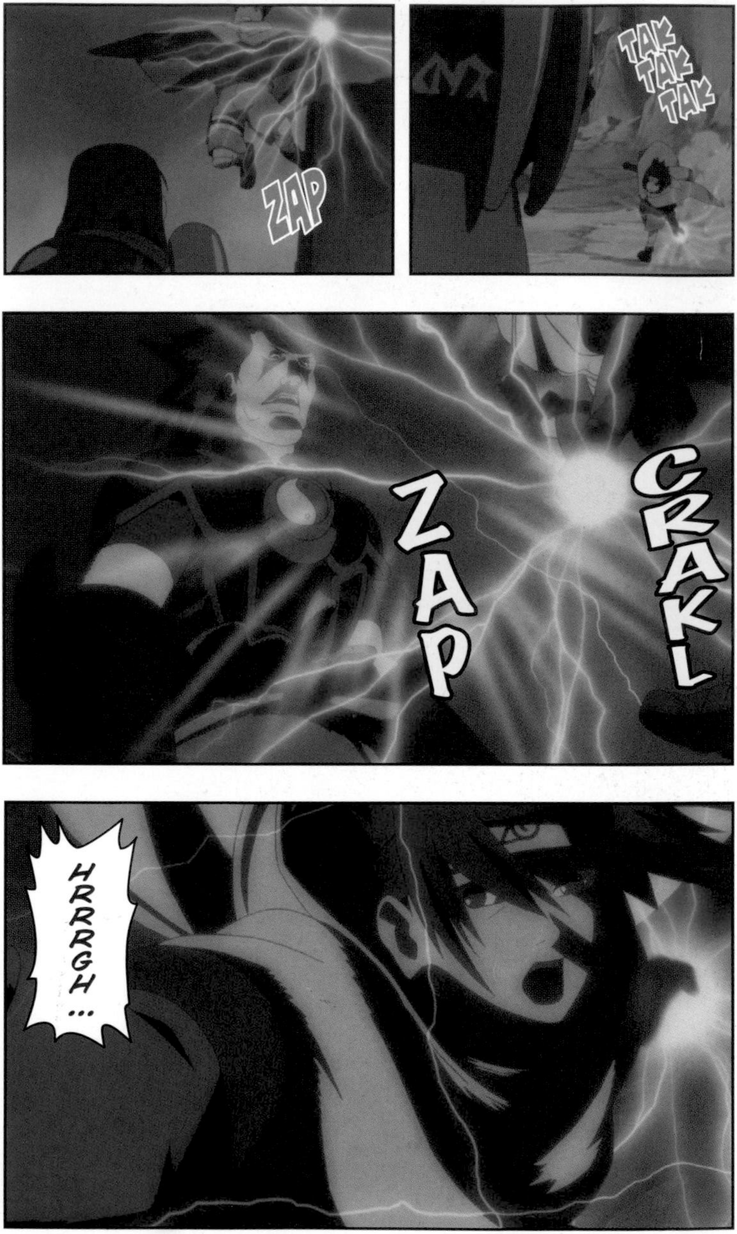
TAK TAK TAK
ZAP
CRAKL
ZAP
HRRRGH...

CHIDO-RIIII!!
CRAKL
CRACK
HMPH!

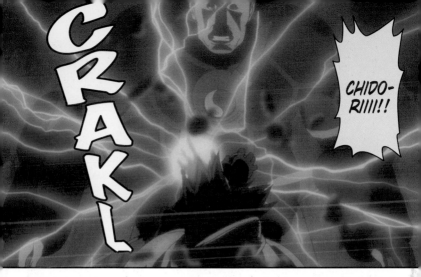

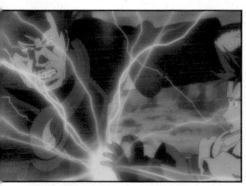

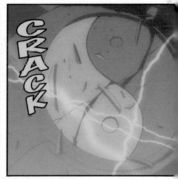

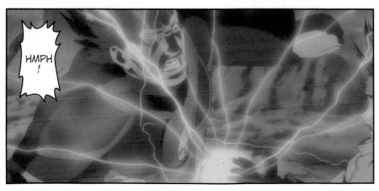

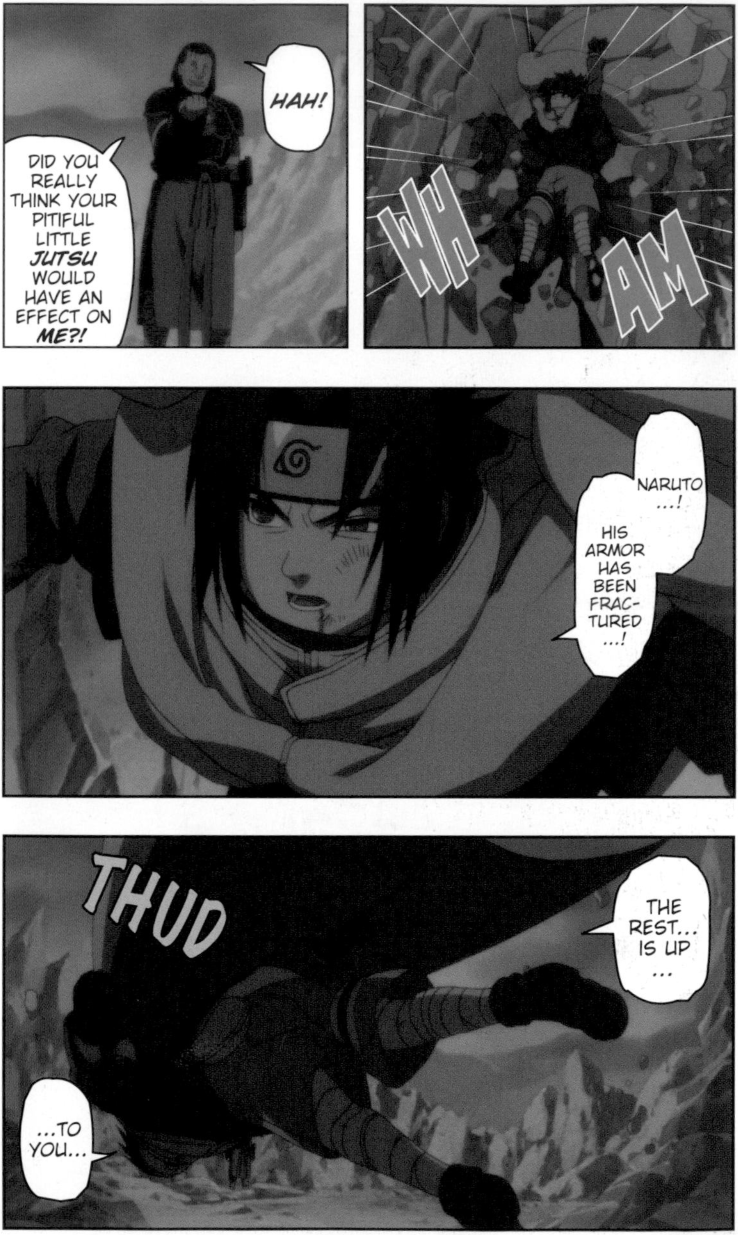
WHAM
HAH!
DID YOU REALLY THINK YOUR PITIFUL LITTLE JUTSU WOULD HAVE AN EFFECT ON ME?!
NARUTO ...!
HIS ARMOR HAS BEEN FRAC- TURED ...!
THE REST... IS UP ...
THUD
...TO YOU...

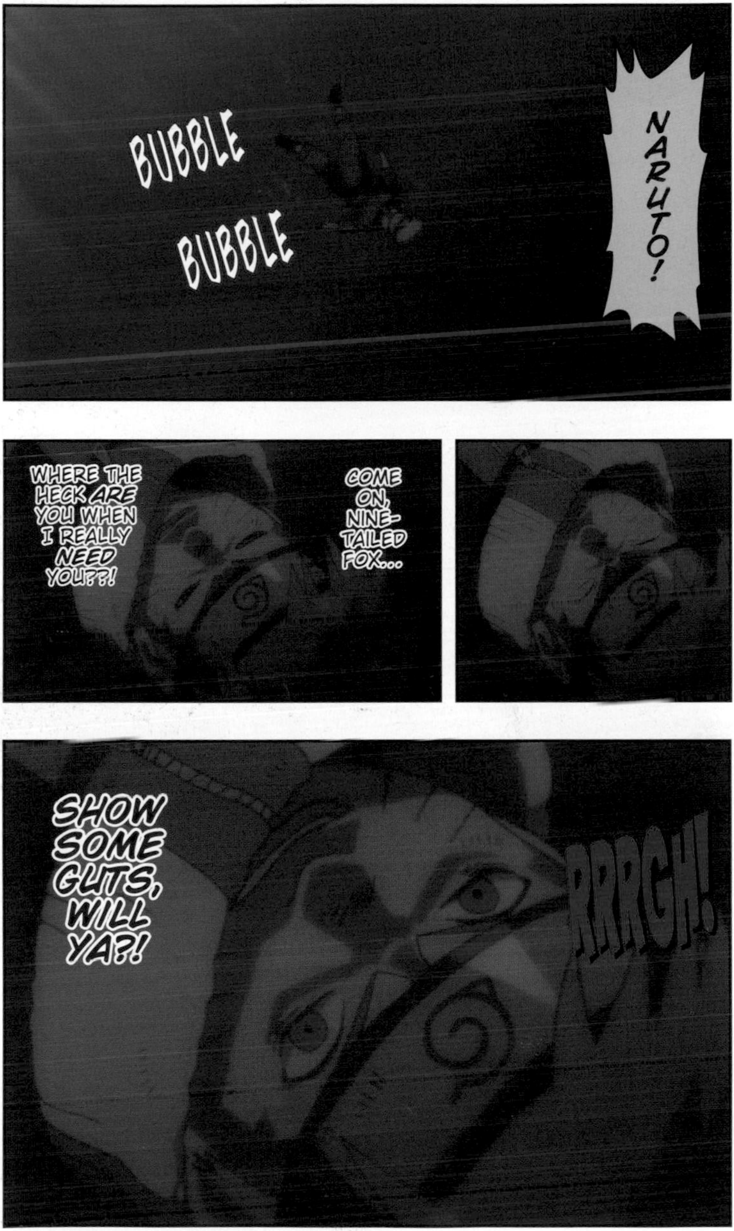
NARUTO!
BUBBLE
BUBBLE
COME ON, NINE-TAILED FOX...
WHERE THE HECK ARE YOU WHEN I REALLY NEED YOU?!?
RRRGH!
SHOW SOME GUTS, WILL YA?!

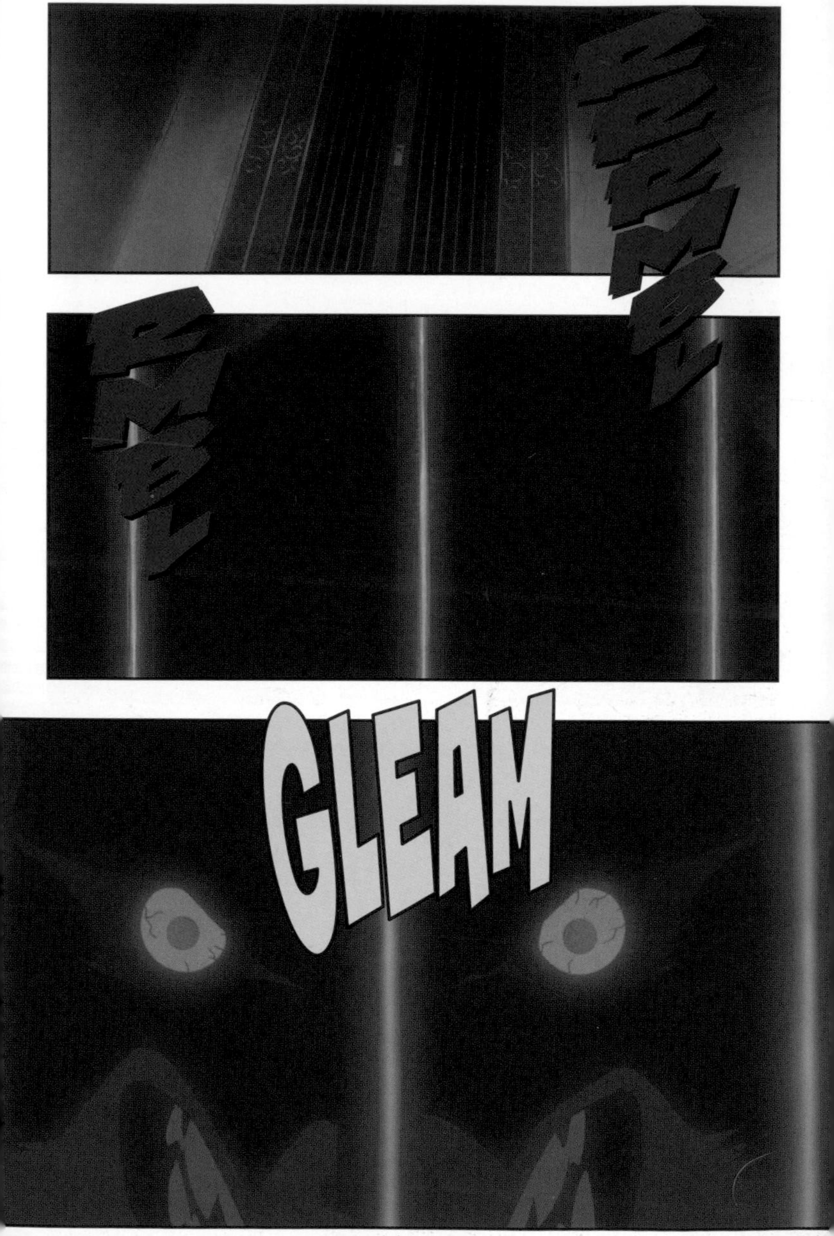
GLEAM

FLICKER

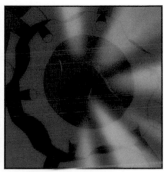

HUH? WHAT IS THAT ?!

RMBL RMBL RMBL

RRMBL RMBL RMBL

SHO

OOM

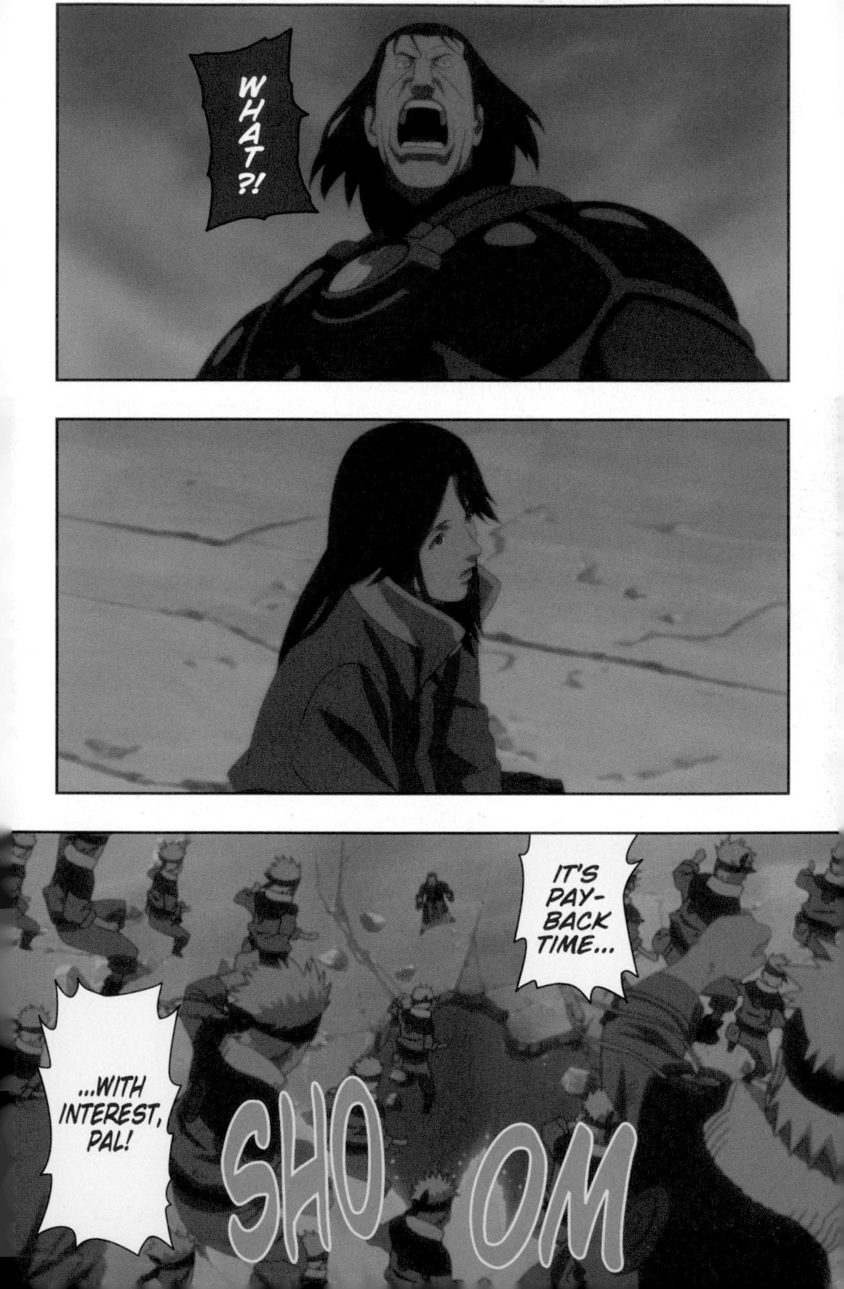
WHAT?!
IT'S PAY-BACK TIME...
...WITH INTEREST, PAL!
SHO OM

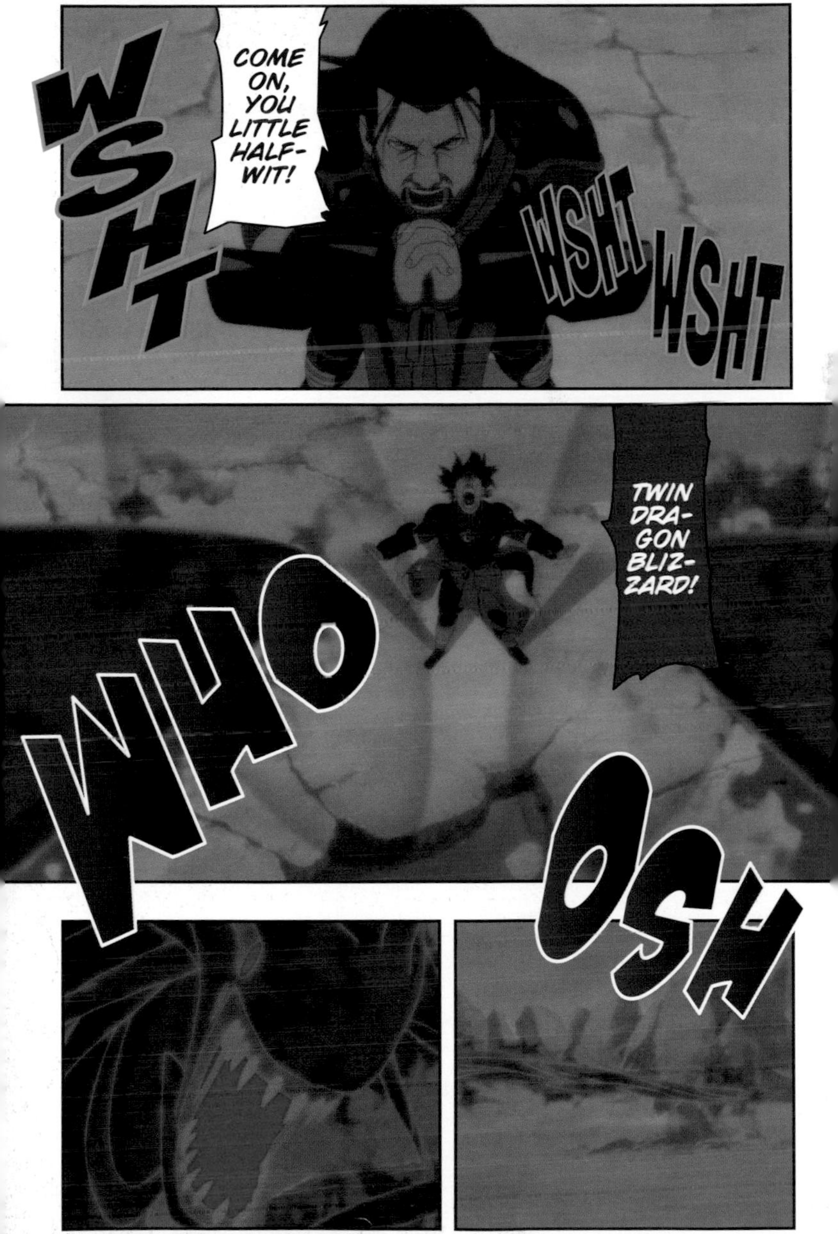
COME ON, YOU LITTLE HALF-WIT!
WSHT
WSHT
WSHT
TWIN DRAGON BLIZZARD!
WHOOSH

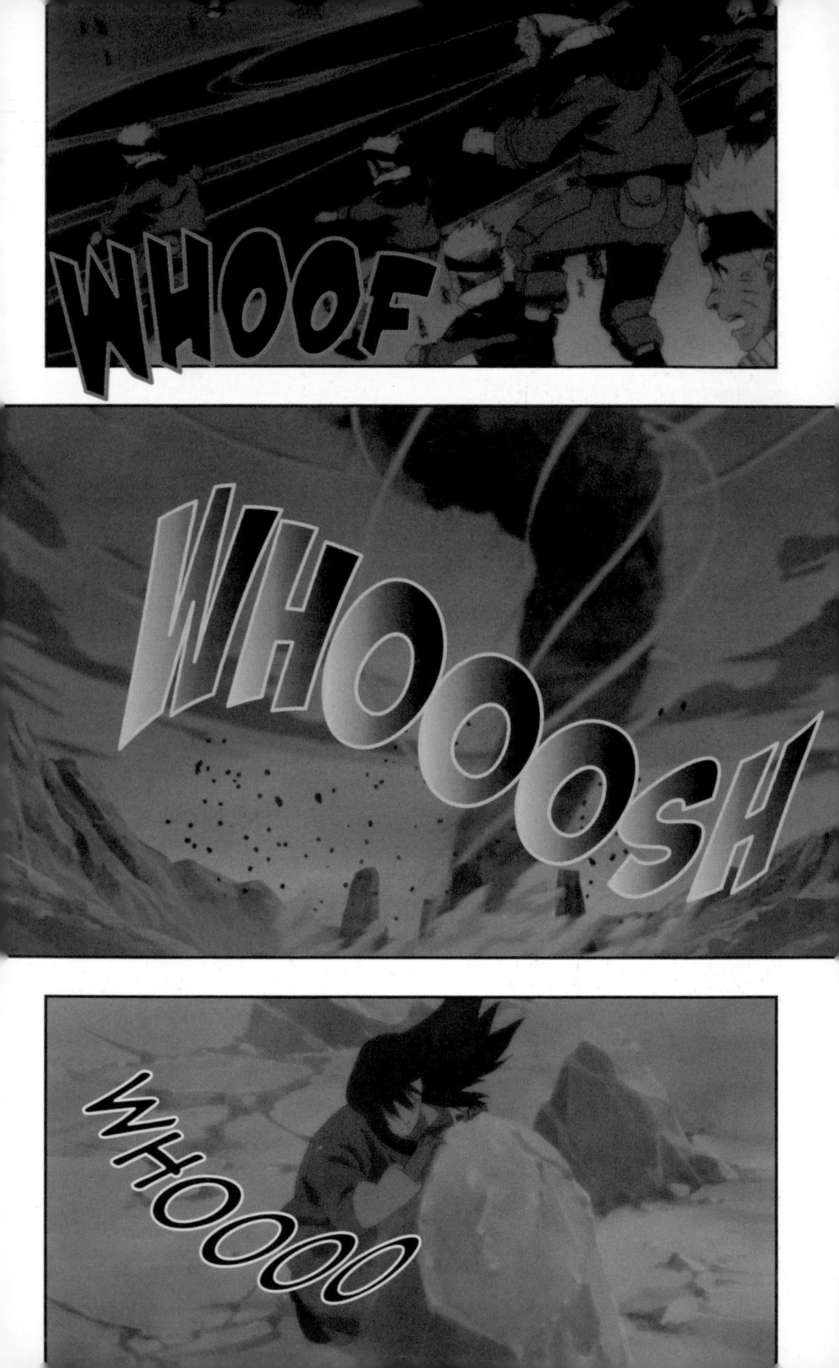
WHOOF
WHOOOSH
WHOOOO

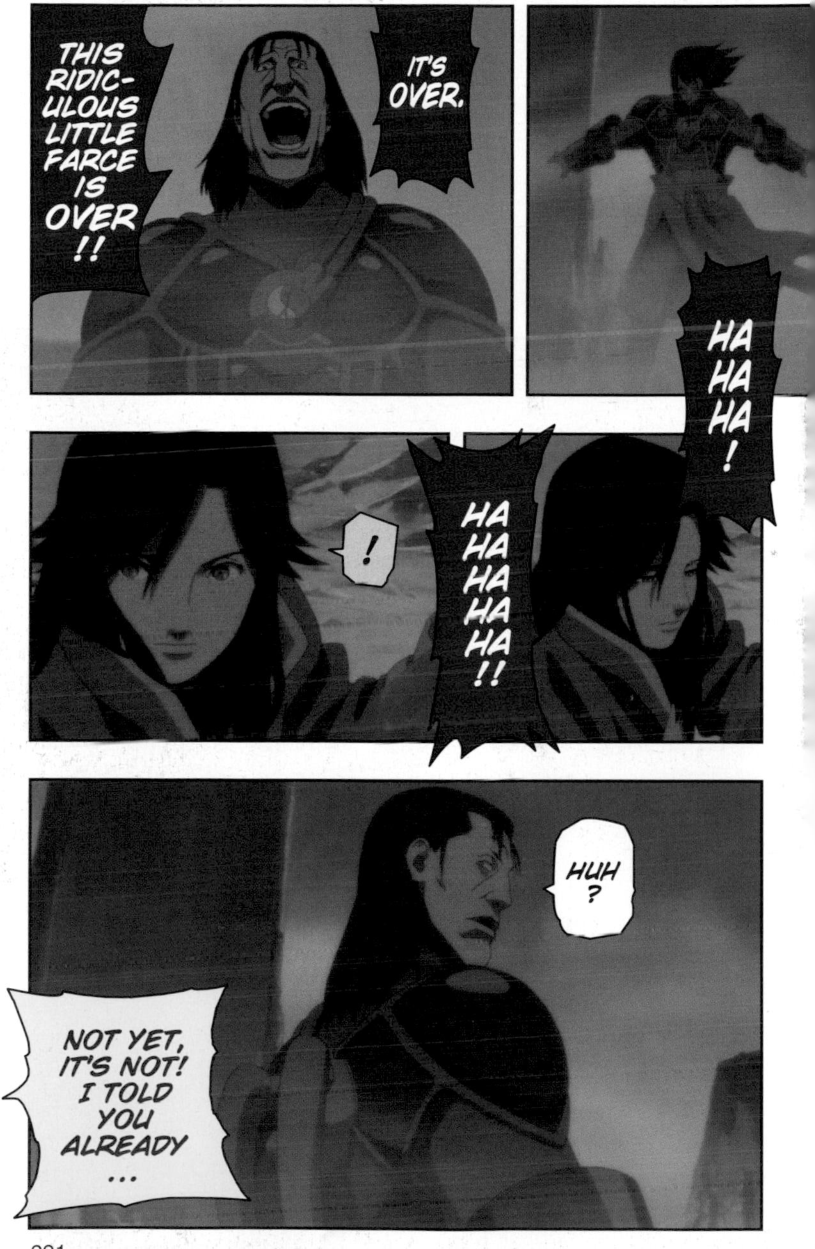
HA HA HA!
IT'S OVER.
THIS RIDICULOUS LITTLE FARCE IS OVER!!
HA HA HA HA HA!!
!
HUH?
NOT YET, IT'S NOT! I TOLD YOU ALREADY...

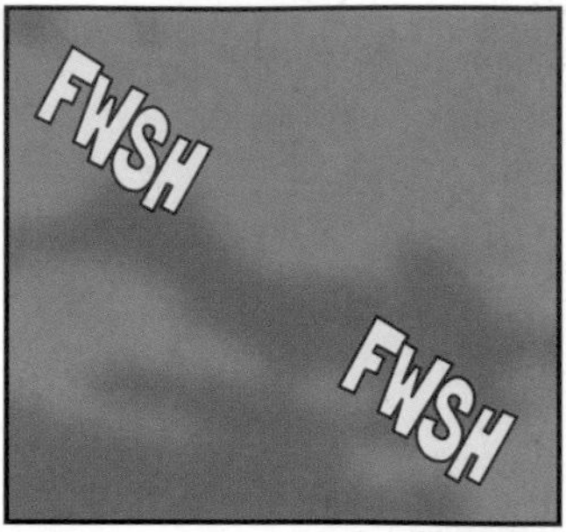
FWSH
FWSH

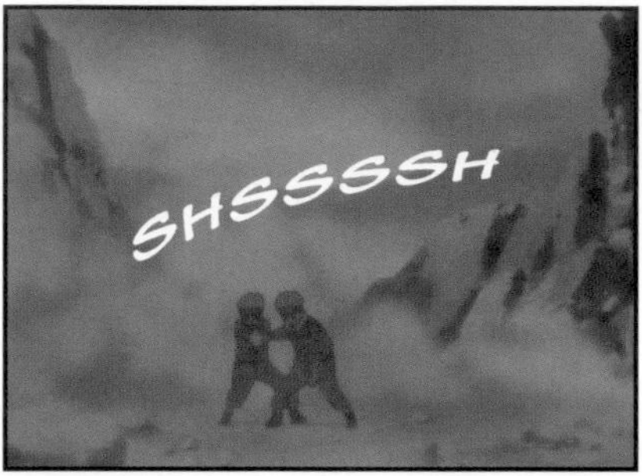
SHSSSSH

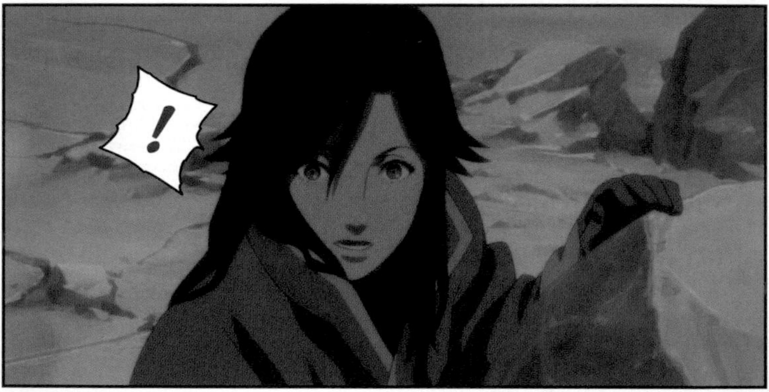
!

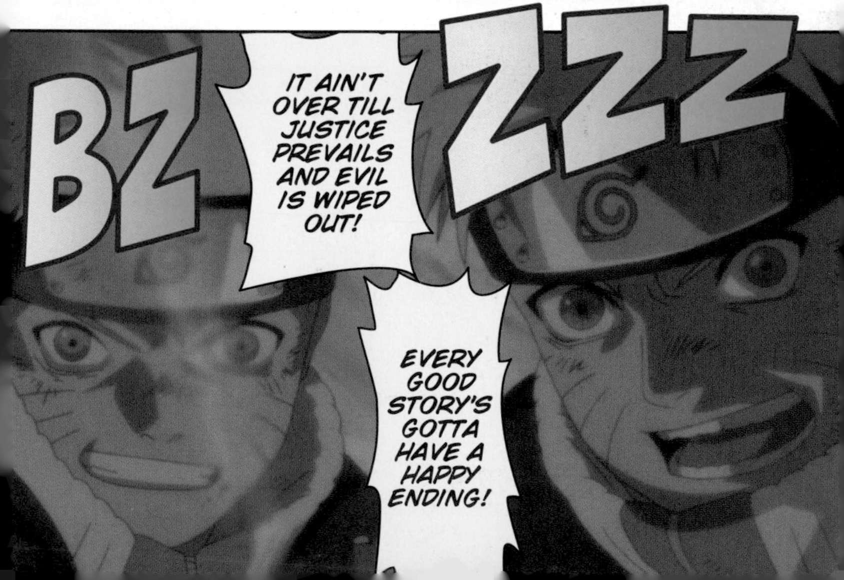
BZZZZ
IT AIN'T OVER TILL JUSTICE PREVAILS AND EVIL IS WIPED OUT!
EVERY GOOD STORY'S GOTTA HAVE A HAPPY ENDING!

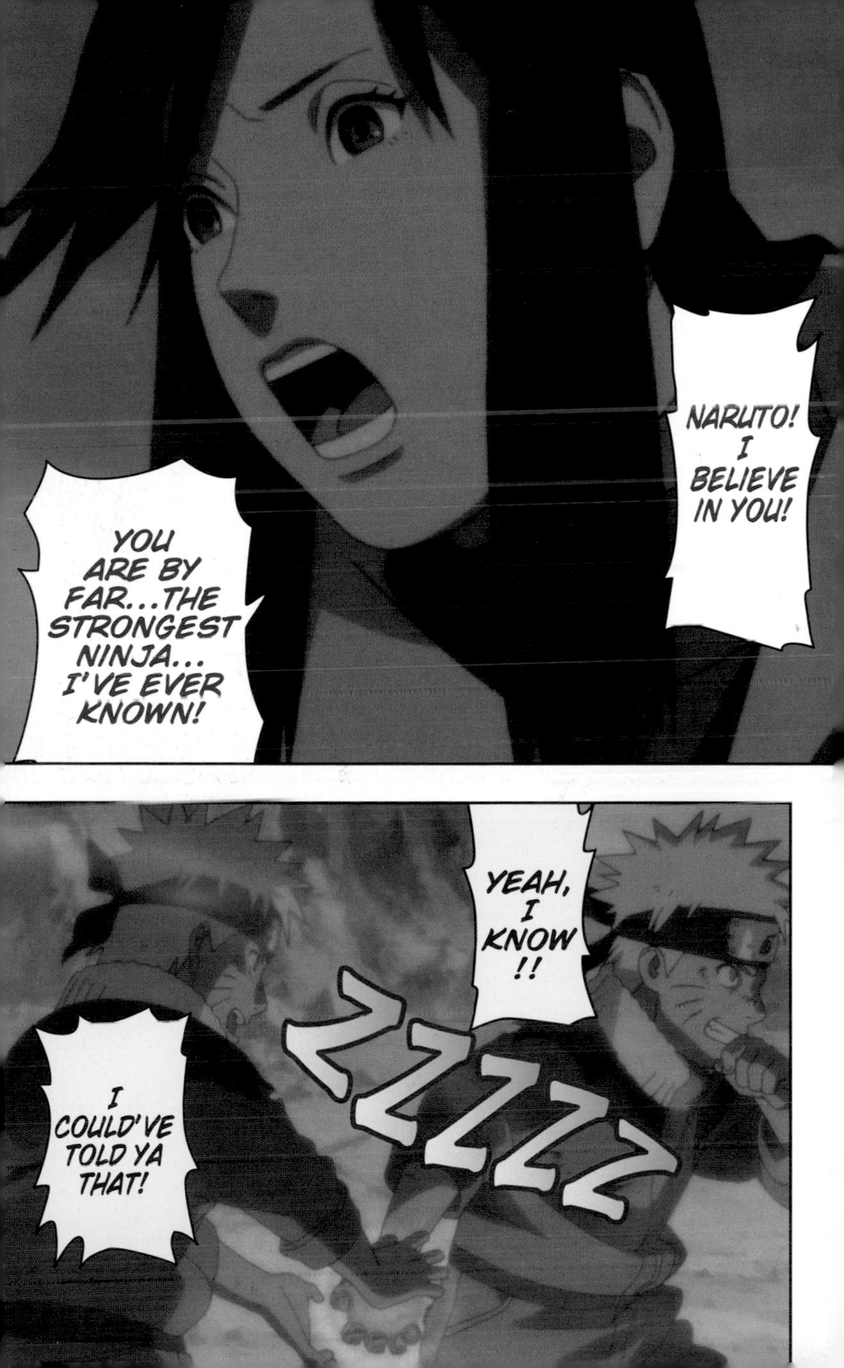
NARUTO! I BELIEVE IN YOU!
YOU ARE BY FAR...THE STRONGEST NINJA... I'VE EVER KNOWN!
YEAH, I KNOW!!
ZZZZ
I COULD'VE TOLD YA THAT!

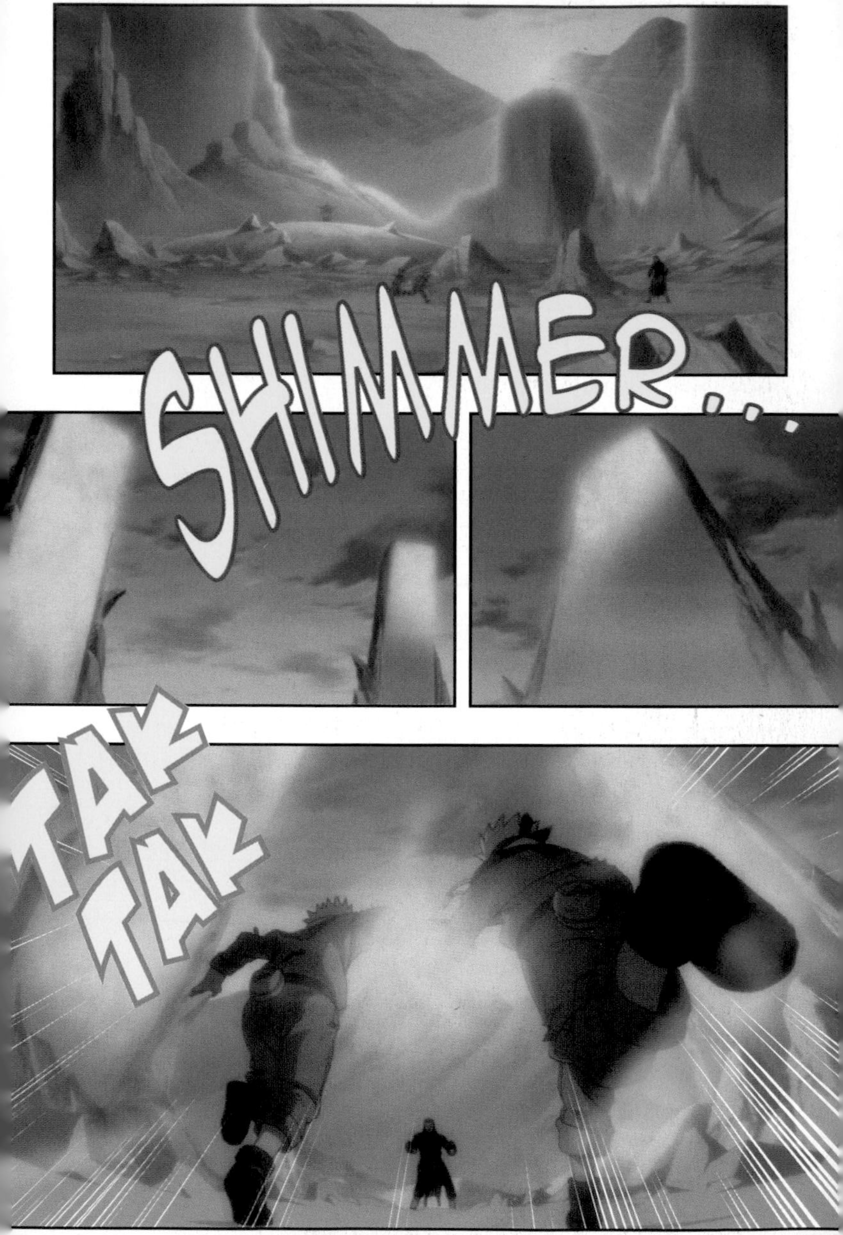
SHIMMER...
TAK TAK

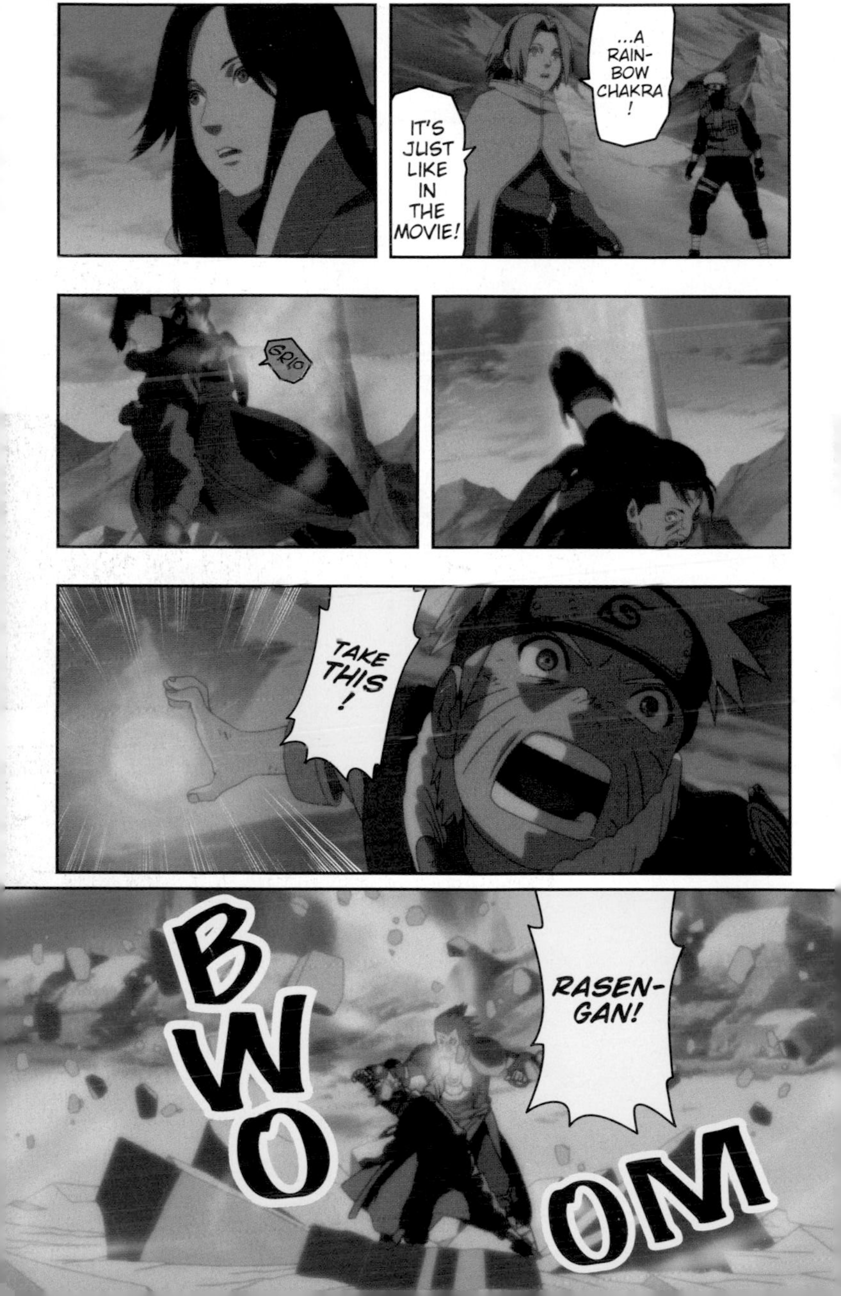
...A RAIN-BOW CHAKRA!
IT'S JUST LIKE IN THE MOVIE!
GRIP
TAKE THIS!
RASEN-GAN!
BWOOM

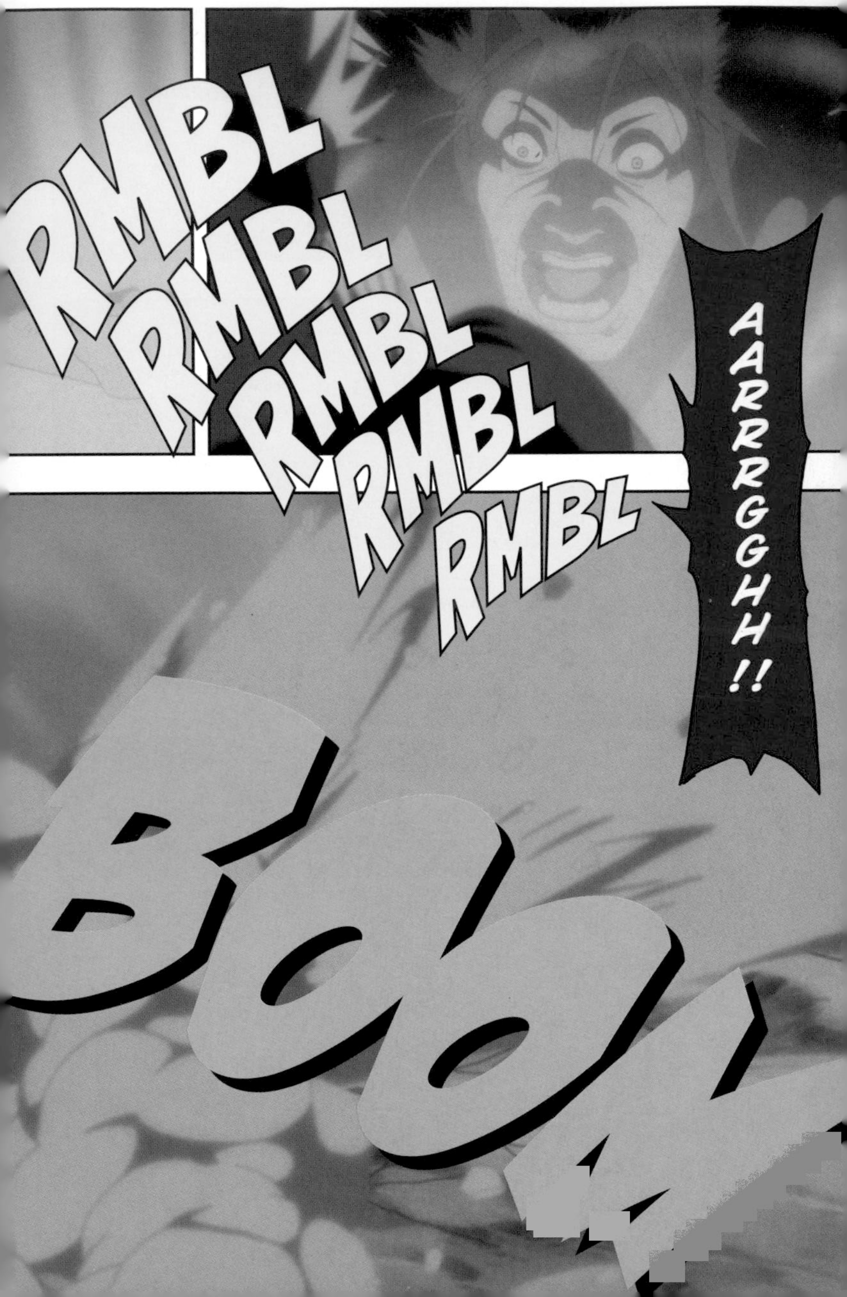
RMBL
RMBL
RMBL
RMBL
RMBL
RMBL
AARRRGGHH!!
BOO

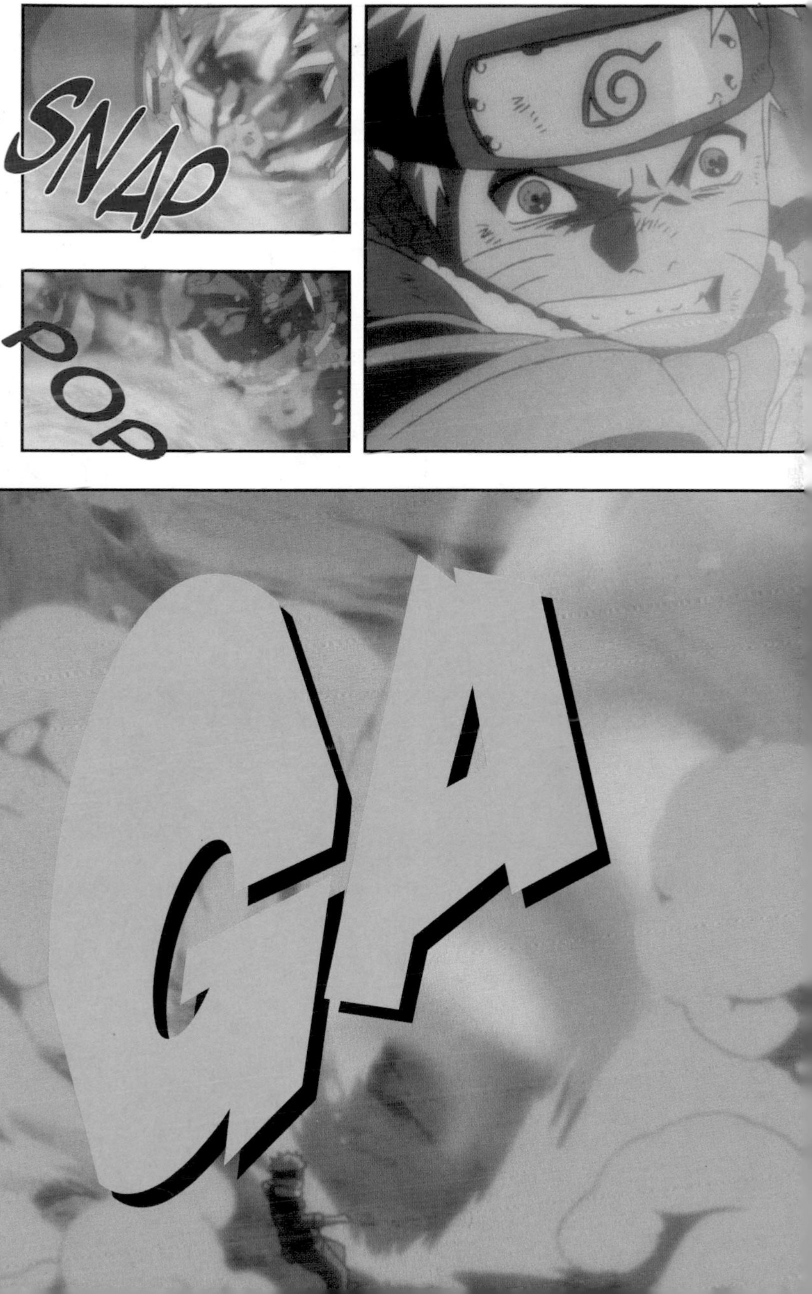
SNAP
POP
GA

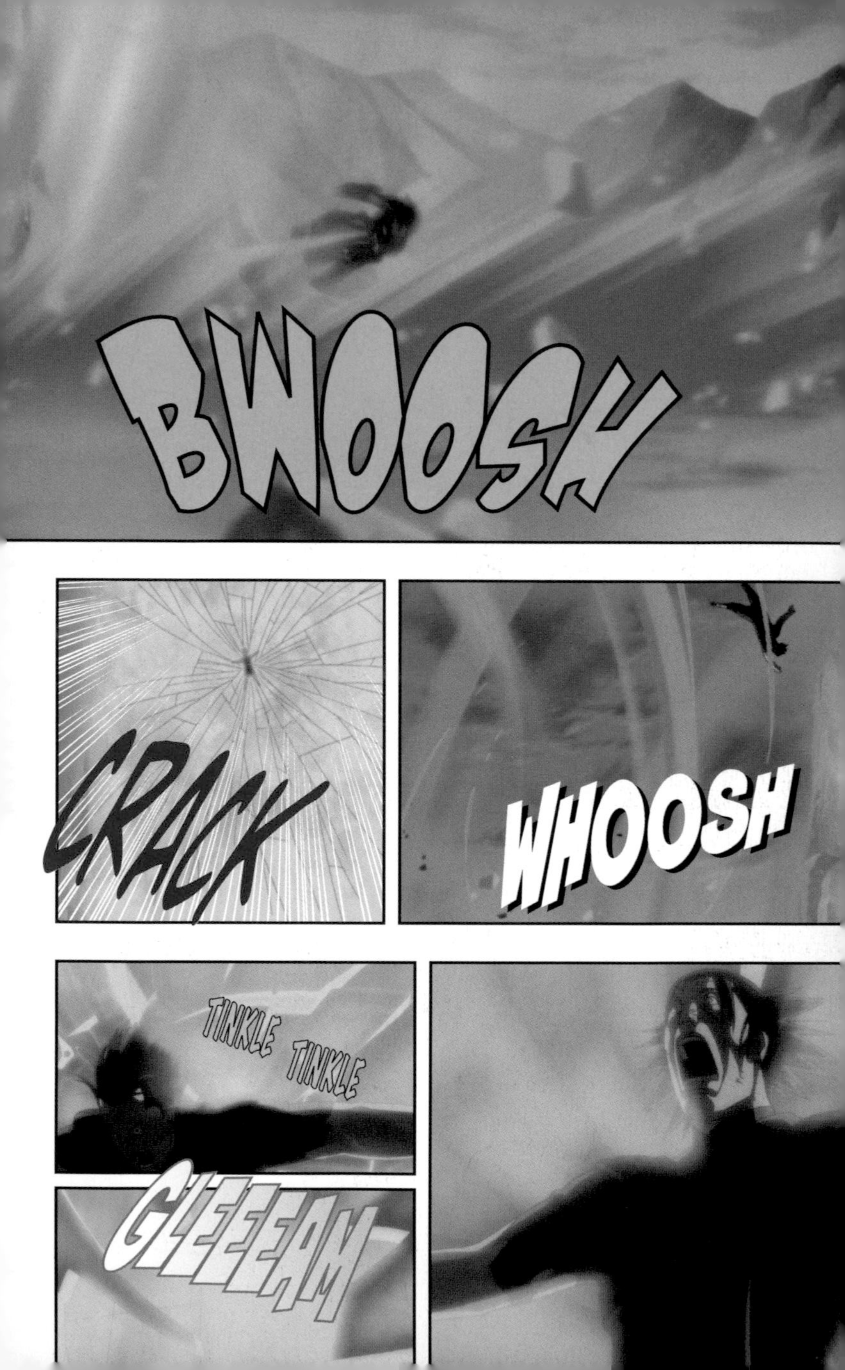
BWOOSH
WHOOSH
CRACK
TINKLE TINKLE
GLEEEAM

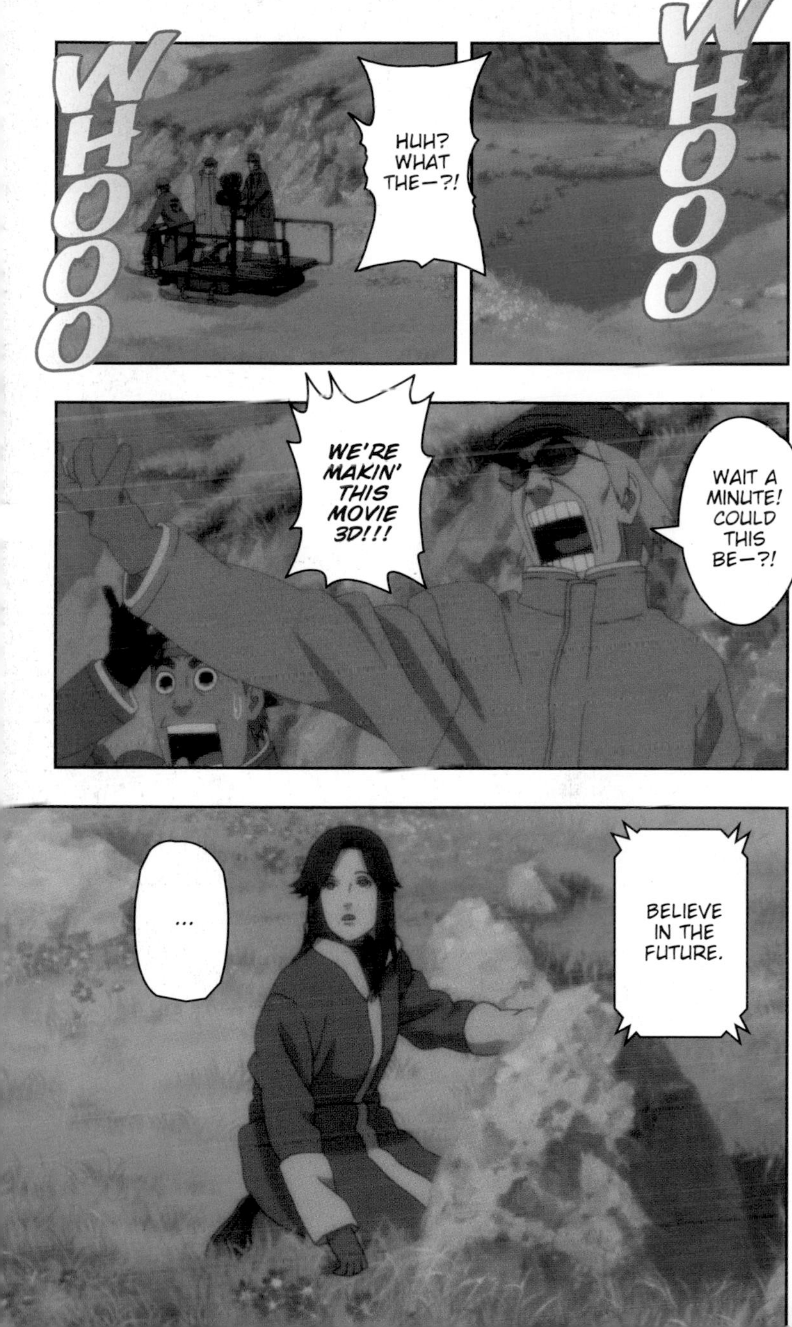
WHOOO
HUH? WHAT THE—?!
WHOOO
WAIT A MINUTE! COULD THIS BE—?!
WE'RE MAKIN' THIS MOVIE 3D!!!
BELIEVE IN THE FUTURE.
...

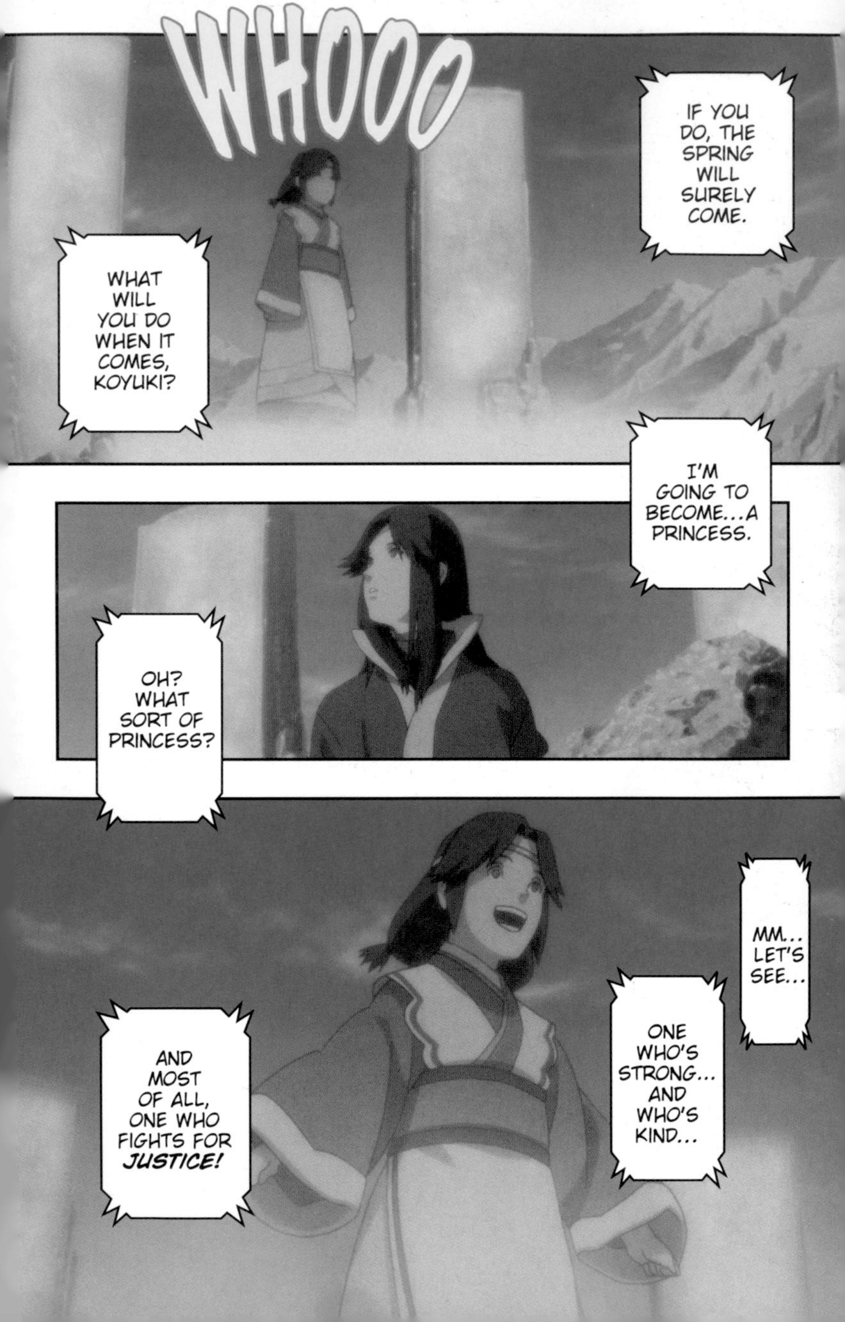
IF YOU DO, THE SPRING WILL SURELY COME.
WHOOO
WHAT WILL YOU DO WHEN IT COMES, KOYUKI?
I'M GOING TO BECOME...A PRINCESS.
OH? WHAT SORT OF PRINCESS?
MM... LET'S SEE...
ONE WHO'S STRONG... AND WHO'S KIND...
AND MOST OF ALL, ONE WHO FIGHTS FOR ***JUSTICE!***

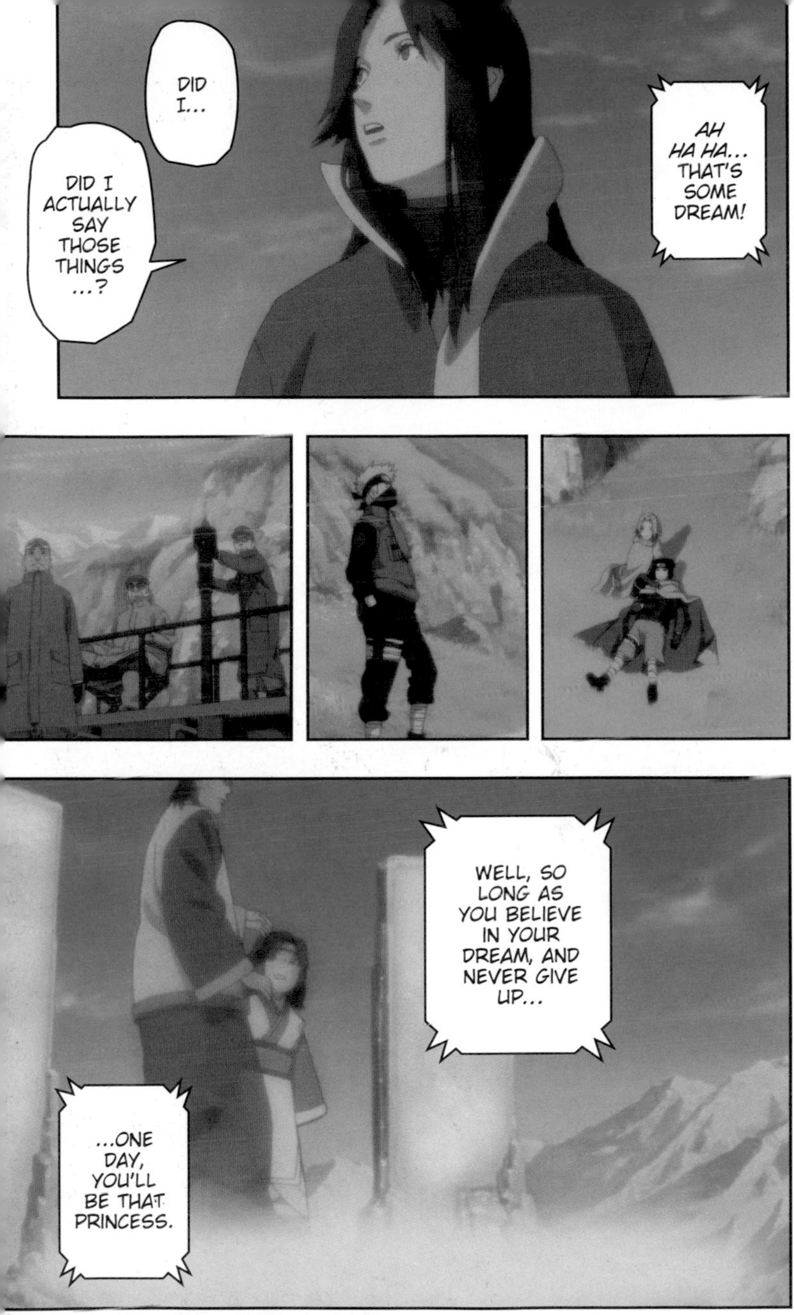
AH HA HA... THAT'S SOME DREAM!
DID I...
DID I ACTUALLY SAY THOSE THINGS ...?
WELL, SO LONG AS YOU BELIEVE IN YOUR DREAM, AND NEVER GIVE UP...
...ONE DAY, YOU'LL BE THAT PRINCESS.

YOU CAN SEE HER, CAN'T YOU?

THERE'S A BEAUTIFUL PRINCESS STANDING RIGHT THERE IN FRONT OF YOU.

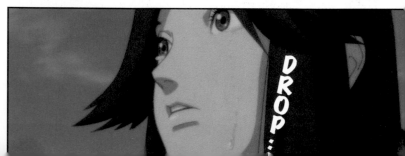

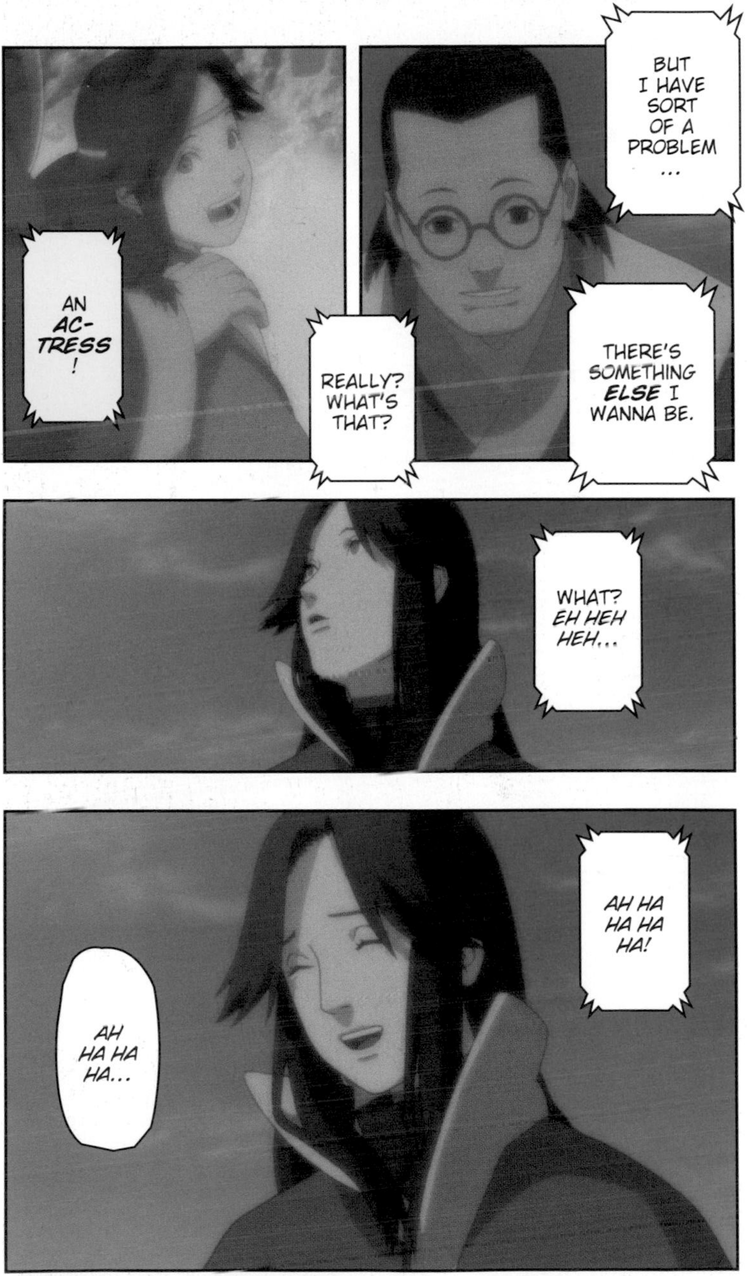
BUT I HAVE SORT OF A PROBLEM ...
THERE'S SOMETHING *ELSE* I WANNA BE.
REALLY? WHAT'S THAT?
AN *AC-TRESS* !
WHAT? *EH HEH HEH...*
AH HA HA HA HA!
AH HA HA HA...

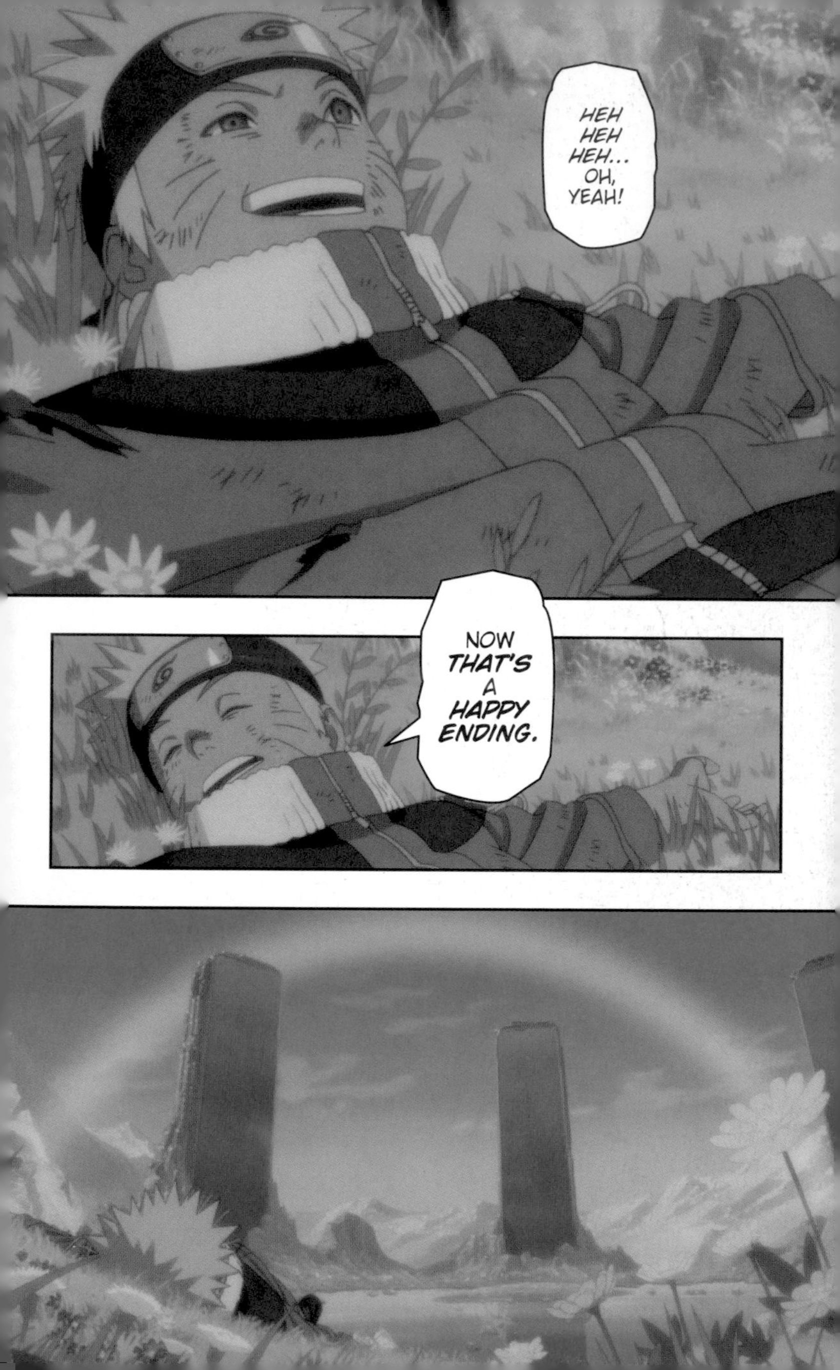
HEH HEH HEH... OH, YEAH!
NOW THAT'S A HAPPY ENDING.

🐾 Chapter 7: Epilogue - Spring

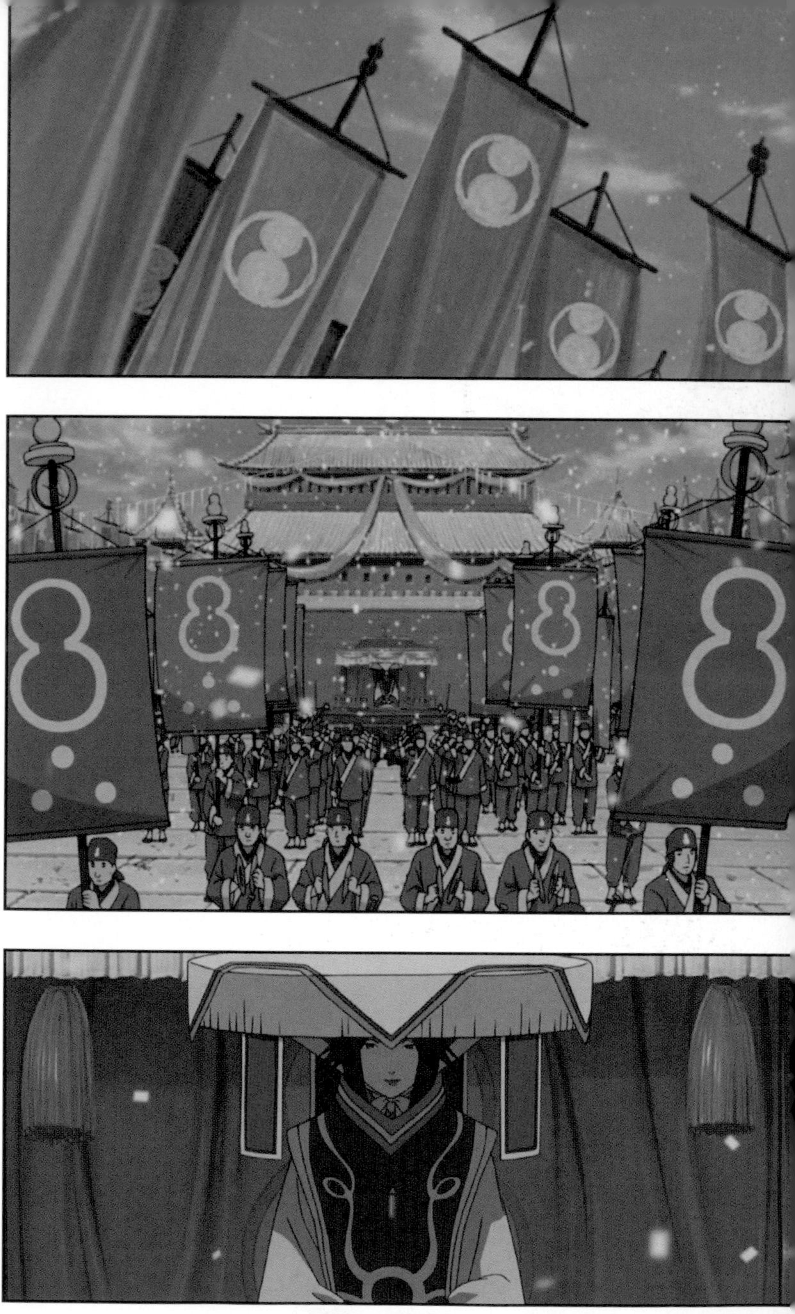

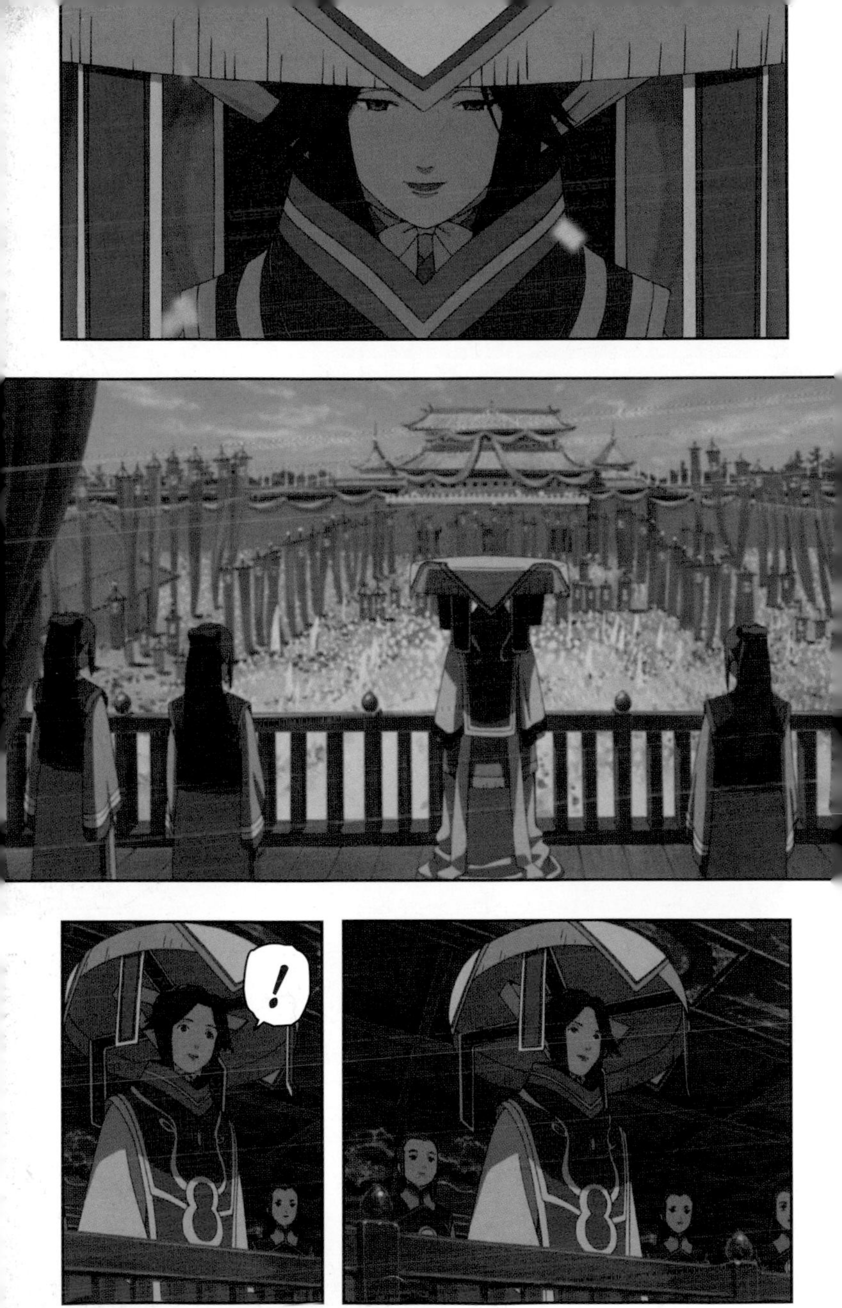
!

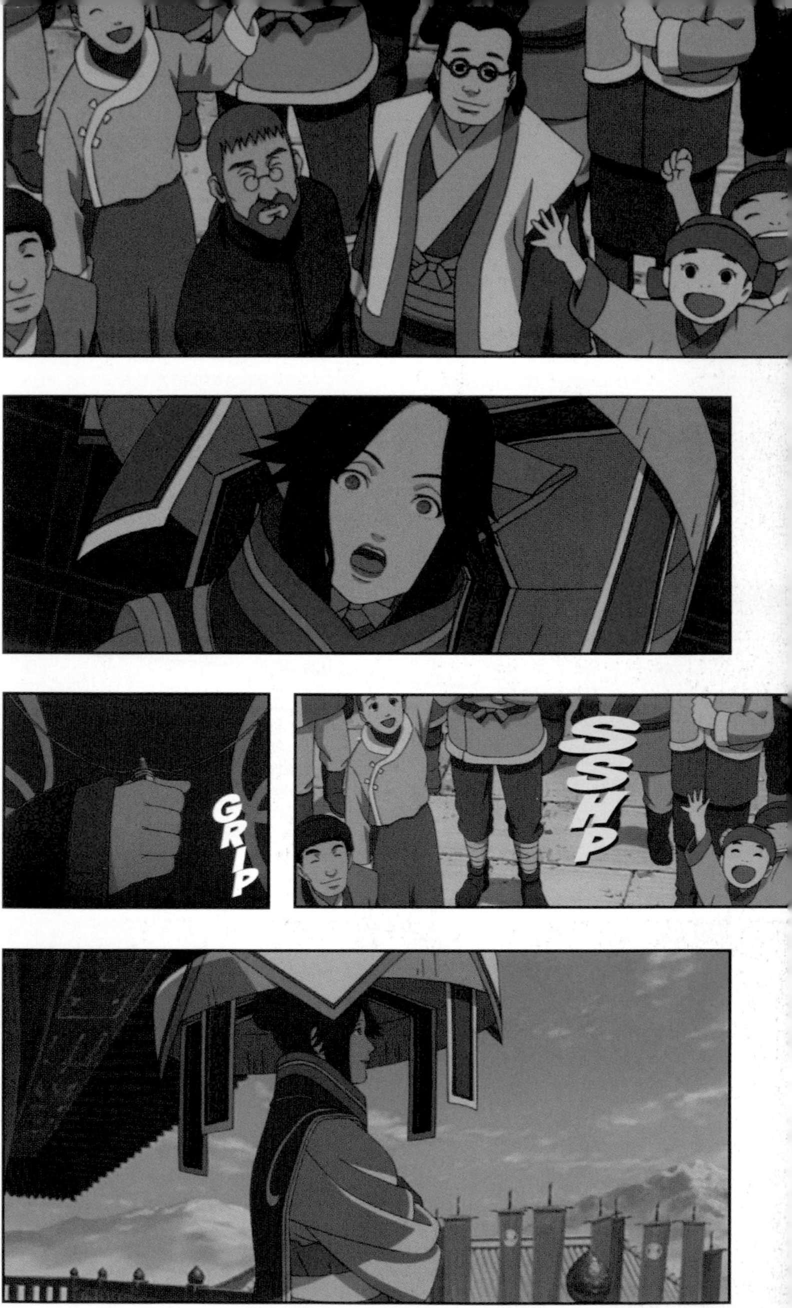
SSHP
GRIP

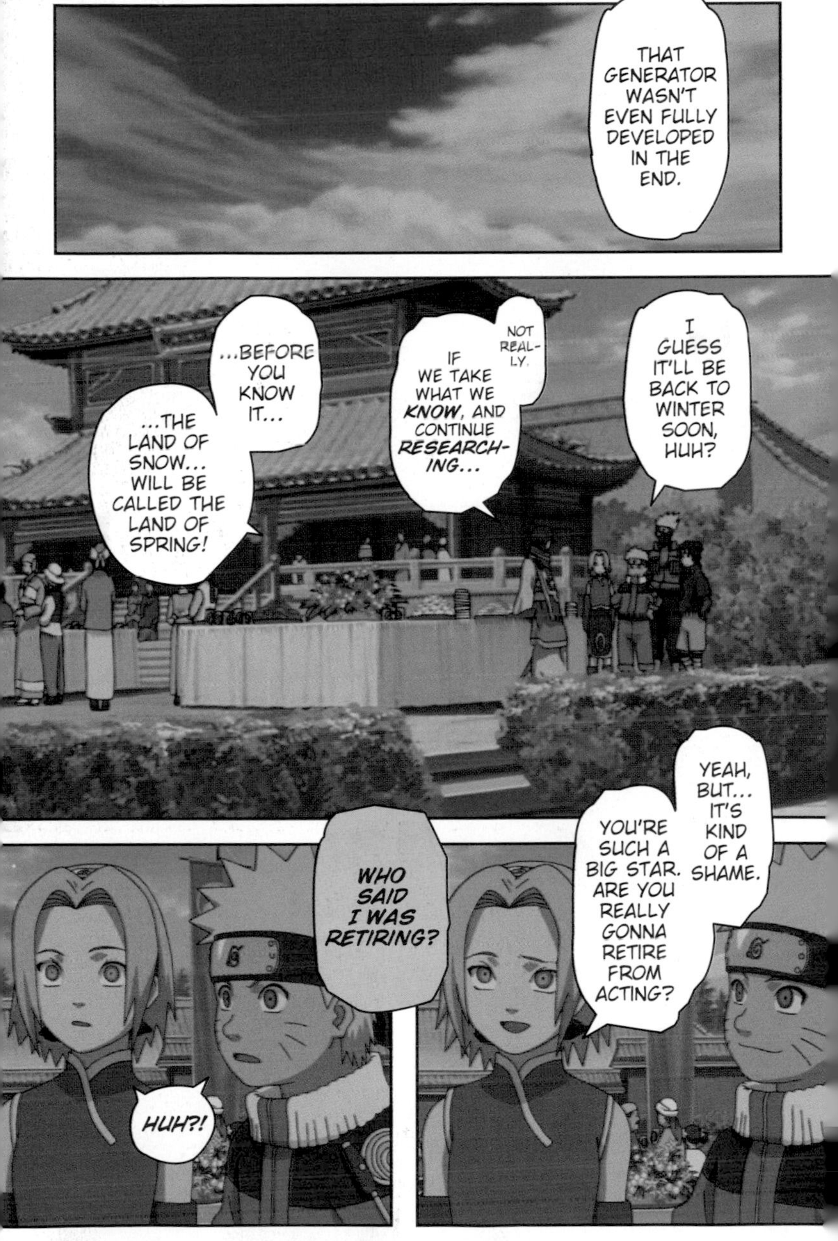
THAT GENERATOR WASN'T EVEN FULLY DEVELOPED IN THE END.
I GUESS IT'LL BE BACK TO WINTER SOON, HUH?
NOT REAL-LY.
IF WE TAKE WHAT WE *KNOW*, AND CONTINUE *RESEARCH-ING*...
...BEFORE YOU KNOW IT...
...THE LAND OF SNOW... WILL BE CALLED THE LAND OF SPRING!
YEAH, BUT... IT'S KIND OF A SHAME.
YOU'RE SUCH A BIG STAR. ARE YOU REALLY GONNA RETIRE FROM ACTING?
WHO SAID I WAS RETIRING?
HUH?!

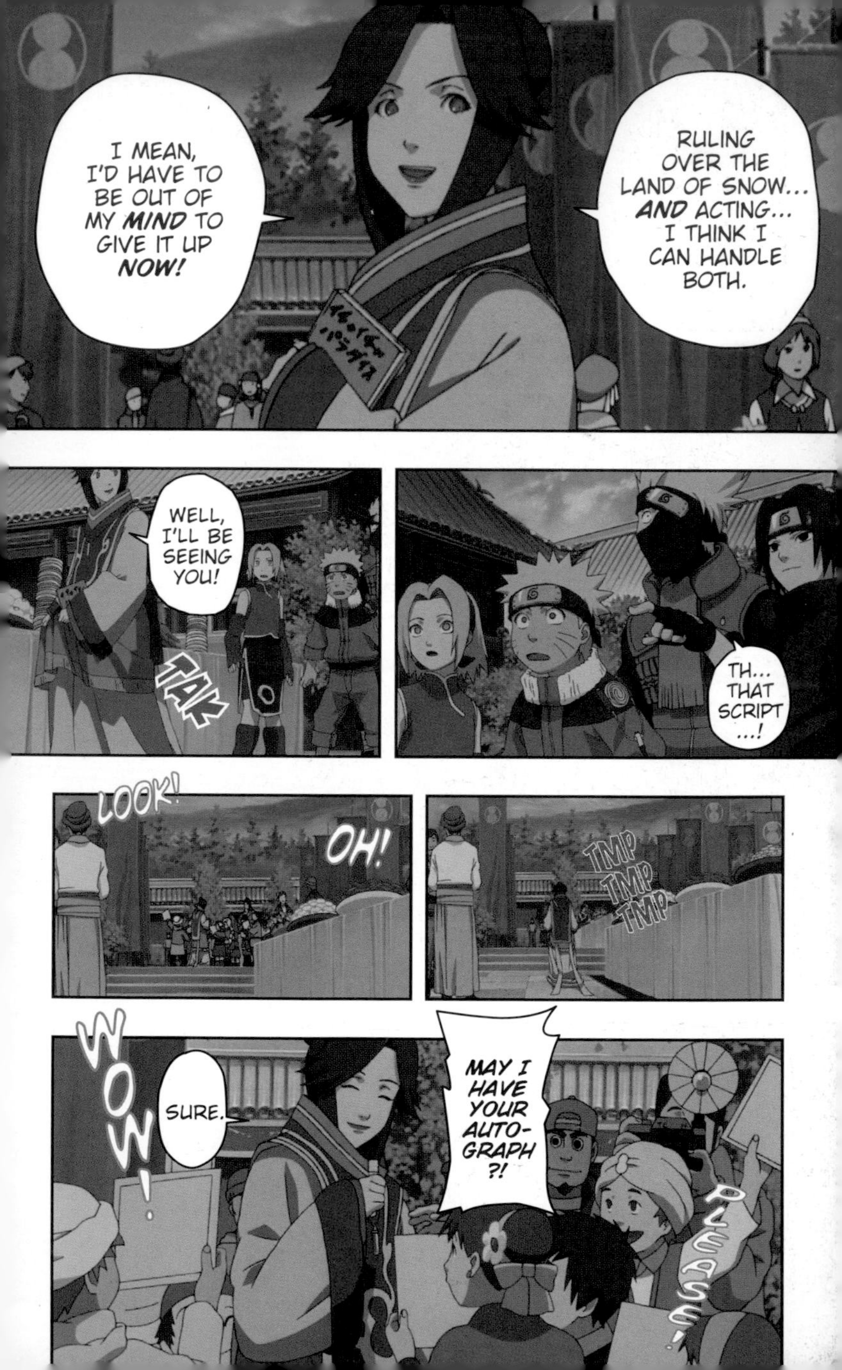
RULING OVER THE LAND OF SNOW… AND ACTING… I THINK I CAN HANDLE BOTH.
I MEAN, I'D HAVE TO BE OUT OF MY MIND TO GIVE IT UP NOW!
TH… THAT SCRIPT …!
WELL, I'LL BE SEEING YOU!
TAK
TMP TMP TMP
OH!
LOOK!
MAY I HAVE YOUR AUTO-GRAPH?!
PLEASE!
SURE.
WOW!

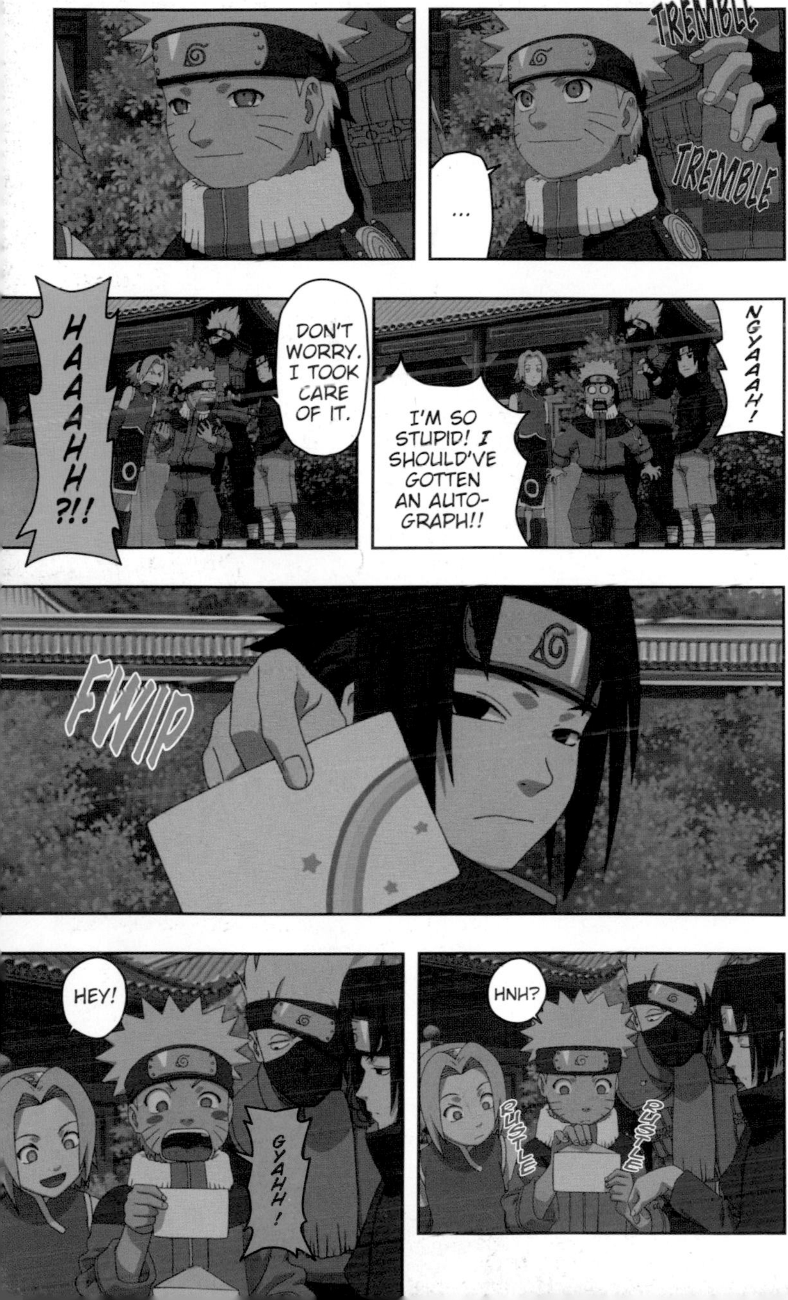
TREMBLE
TREMBLE
...
NGYAAAAH!
I'M SO STUPID! I SHOULD'VE GOTTEN AN AUTO-GRAPH!!
DON'T WORRY. I TOOK CARE OF IT.
HAAAAHH?!!
FWIP
HNH?
RUSTLE
RUSTLE
HEY!
GYAHH!

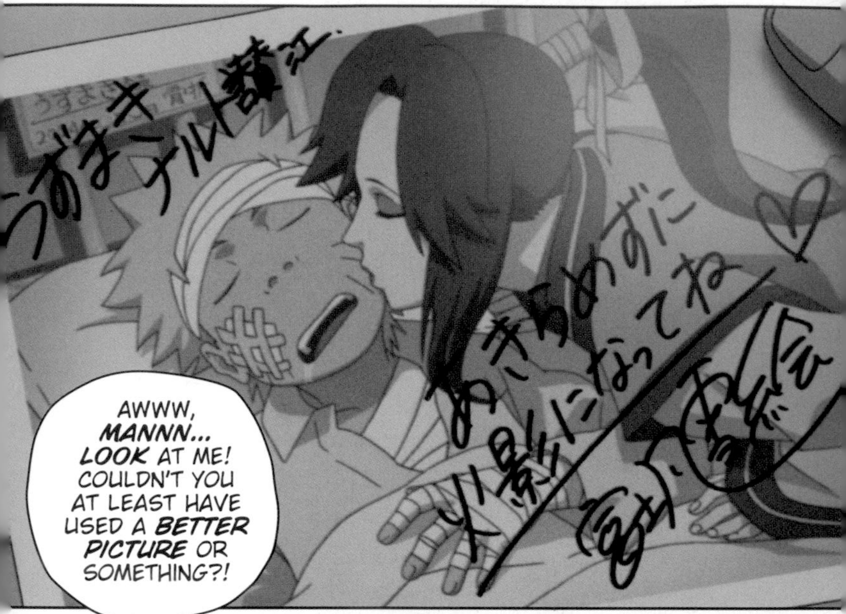
うずまき ナルト
あきらめずに
火影になってね
AWWW, MANNN... LOOK AT ME! COULDN'T YOU AT LEAST HAVE USED A BETTER PICTURE OR SOMETHING?!

*TO NARUTO UZUMAKI: NEVER GIVE UP! BECOME HOKAGE! ♥ —YUKIE FUJIKAZE

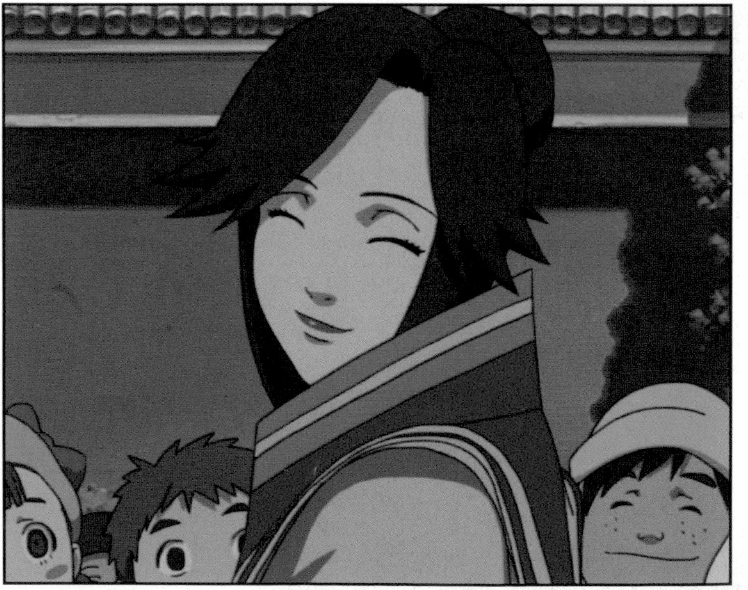

The End

SHONEN JUMP™ NARUTO™ THE MOVIE
Ninja Clash in the Land of Snow

Film Concept Art

設定資料集

Never-before-seen character and
costume designs from the movie!

Film Concept Art

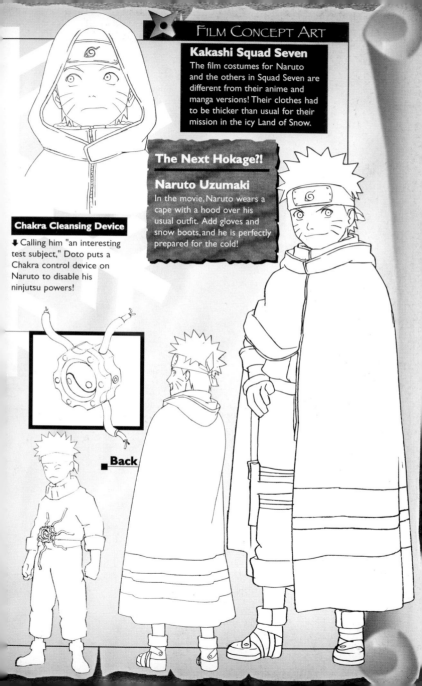

Kakashi Squad Seven

The film costumes for Naruto and the others in Squad Seven are different from their anime and manga versions! Their clothes had to be thicker than usual for their mission in the icy Land of Snow.

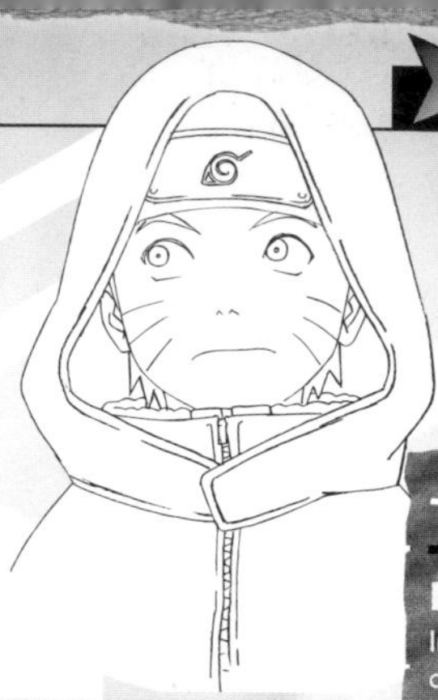

The Next Hokage?!

Naruto Uzumaki

In the movie, Naruto wears a cape with a hood over his usual outfit. Add gloves and snow boots, and he is perfectly prepared for the cold!

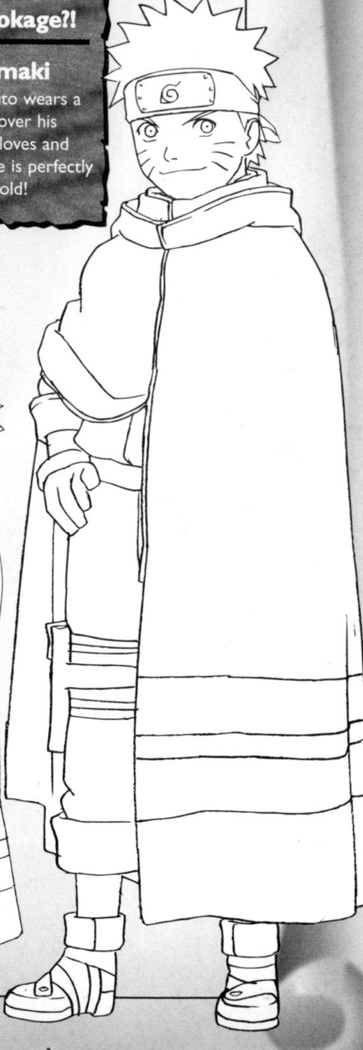

Chakra Cleansing Device

⬇ Calling him "an interesting test subject," Doto puts a Chakra control device on Naruto to disable his ninjutsu powers!

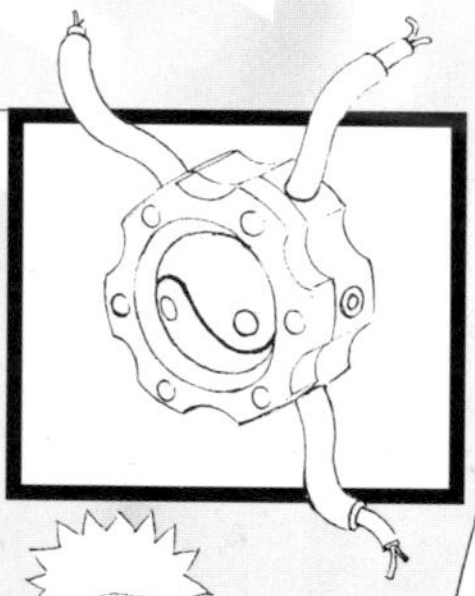

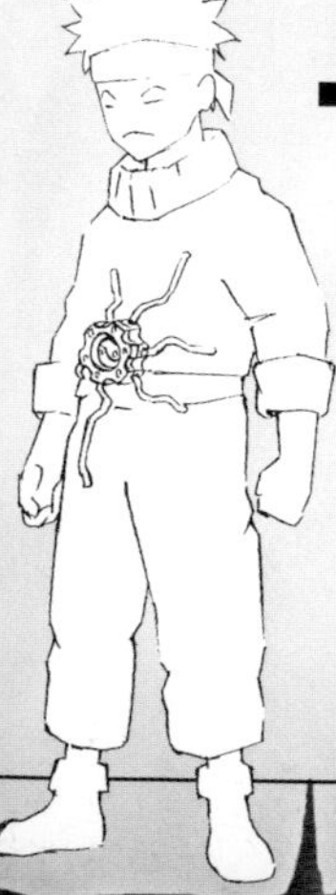

■ **Back**

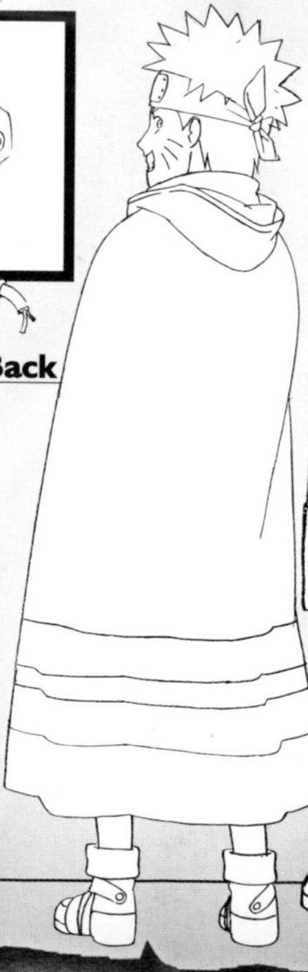

Naruto's Rival!!

Sasuke Uchiha

Sasuke's costume is simple: just a cape over his usual outfit. His legs, visible under his cloak, are wrapped in bandages for protection.

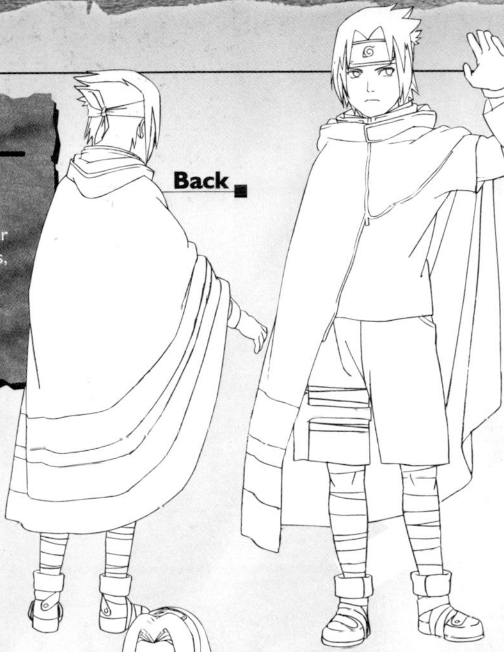
Back

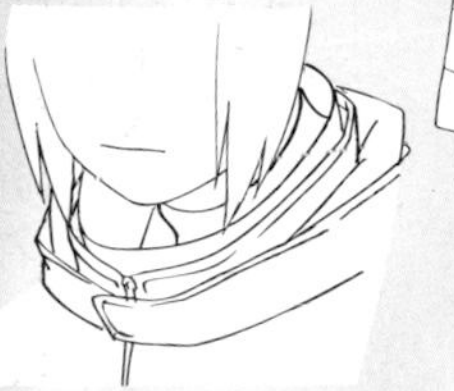

Squad Seven's only girl!

Sakura Haruno

Unlike in the anime version, Sakura wears a sleeveless two-piece garment in the film. Her outfit features leg warmers and fingerless gloves that end above the elbow.

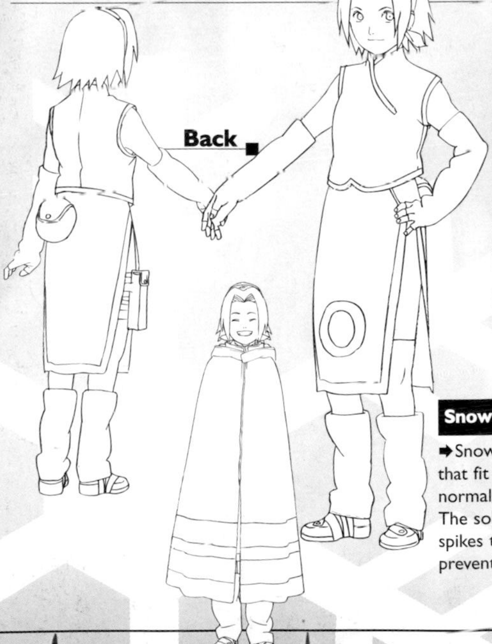
Back

Snow boots

➡Snow boots that fit over her normal shoes. The soles have spikes to prevent slippage.

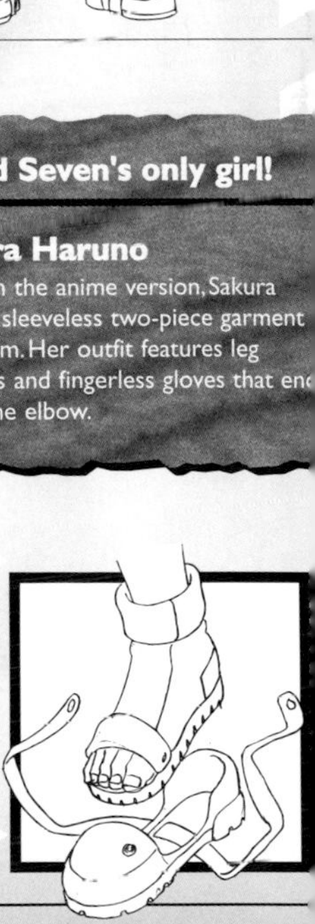

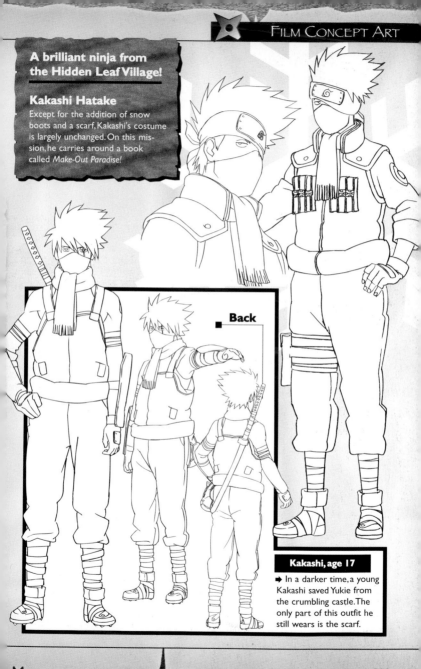

A brilliant ninja from the Hidden Leaf Village!

Kakashi Hatake

Except for the addition of snow boots and a scarf, Kakashi's costume is largely unchanged. On this mission, he carries around a book called *Make-Out Paradise!*

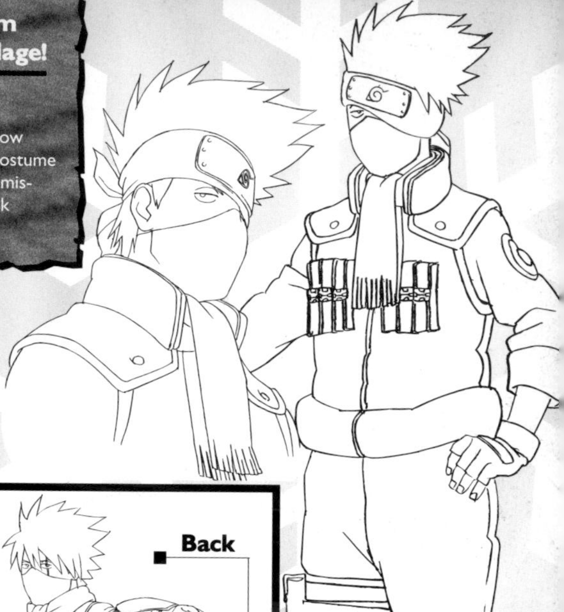

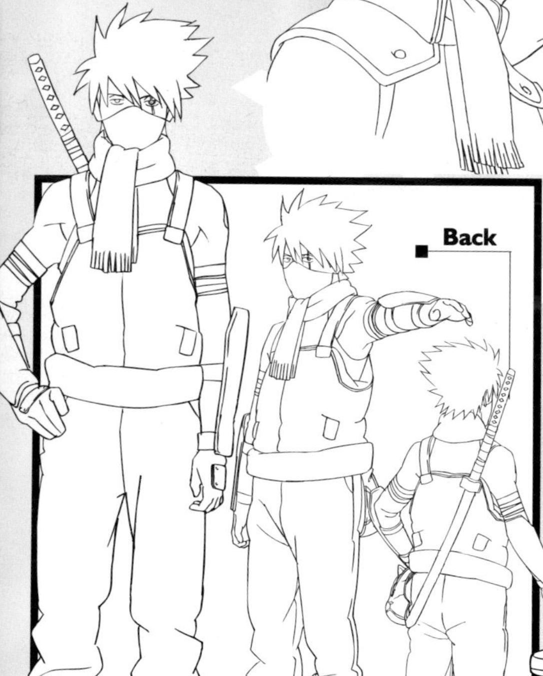
Back

Kakashi, age 17

➡ In a darker time, a young Kakashi saved Yukie from the crumbling castle. The only part of this outfit he still wears is the scarf.

Characters created just for the movie!

The very first versions of characters and costumes drawn especially for the movie! Some of these concepts never even made it into the film, but here they are in full detail!

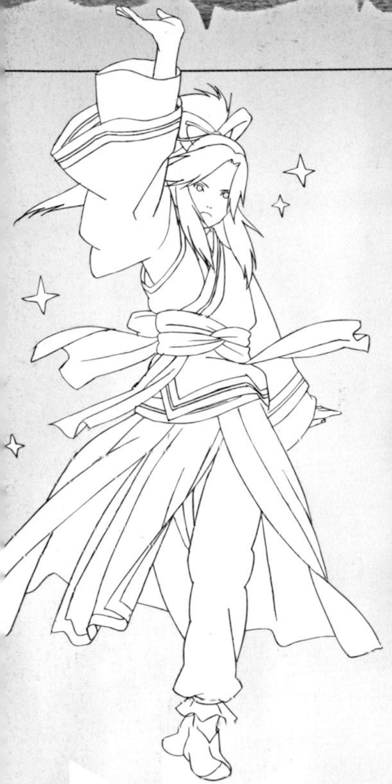

Princess Gale's costume

⬅Yukie's costume for the movie she is filming, *The Adventures of Princess Gale.* She wears this when Naruto and the others see her for the first time.

An Adored Actress!

Yukie Fujikaze (Koyuki Kazahana)

Yukie Fujikaze is the self-centered movie star who plays Princess Gale in Naruto's favorite movie series. When the cameras start to roll, she mesmerizes everyone with her brilliant performances.

Hex Crystal

➡Yukie's father gave this to her when she was small. Doto believes it to be the key to the treasure of the Land of Snow, and will stop at nothing to get it.

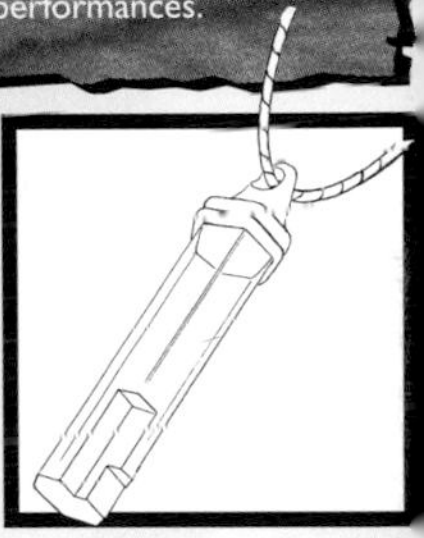

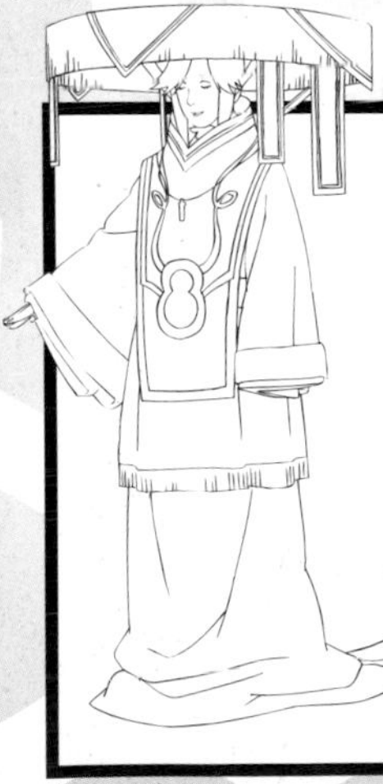

Coronation attire

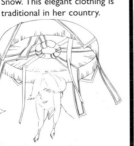

⬅⬇Yukie's outfit when she becomes ruler of the Land of Snow. This elegant clothing is traditional in her country.

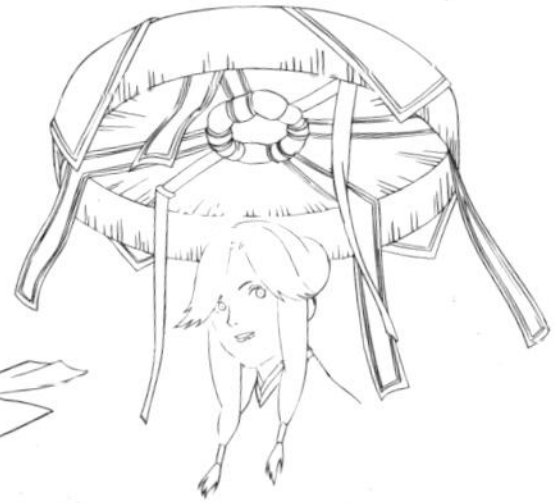

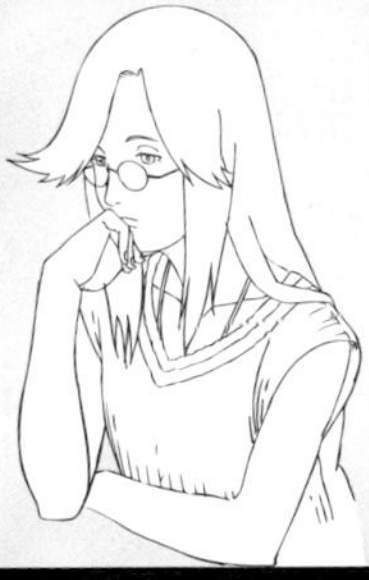

Civilian clothes

⬆Yukie wears plain clothing and sunglasses to avoid being noticed by her fans. She always keeps the Hex Crystal with her, hanging around her neck.

Assistant Director

The assistant director performs various duties as the director's right hand man. With the enthusiasm of a cheerleader, he has the energy needed to hold Makino's team together.

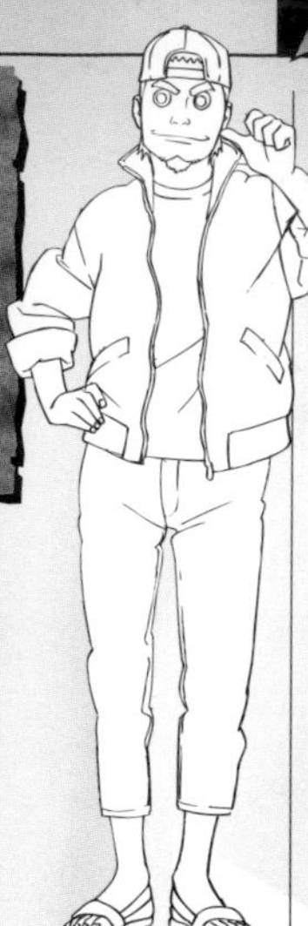

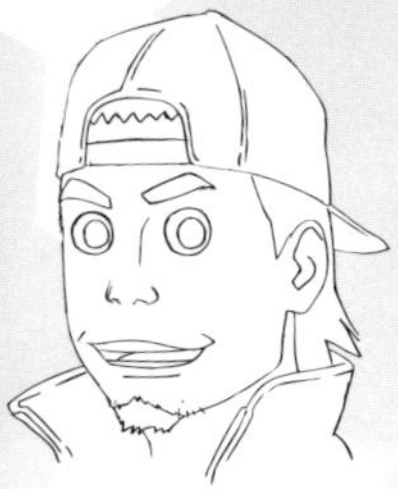

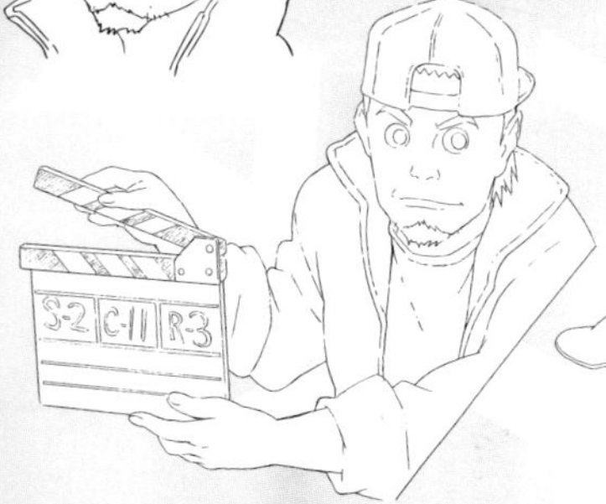
S-2 C-11 R-3

Director Makino

The famous director of *The Adventures of Princess Gale.* He appears stubborn at first, but really overflows with warmth and caring. Of course, he has his own special director's chair.

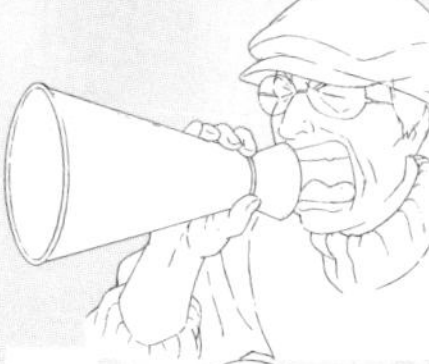

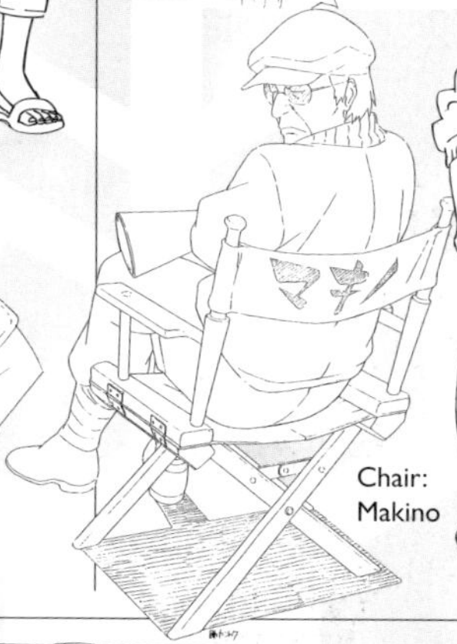

Chair: Makino

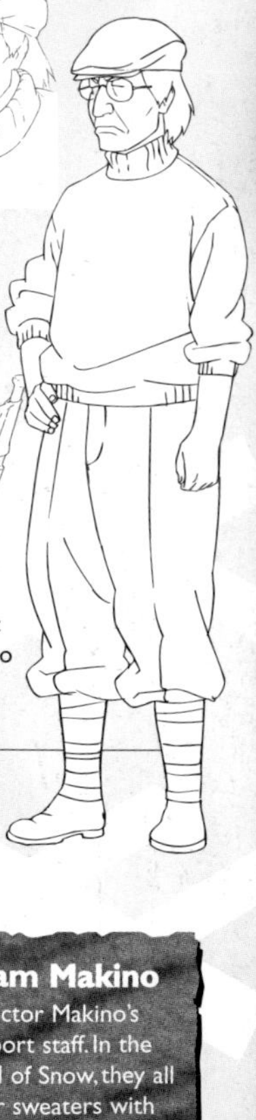

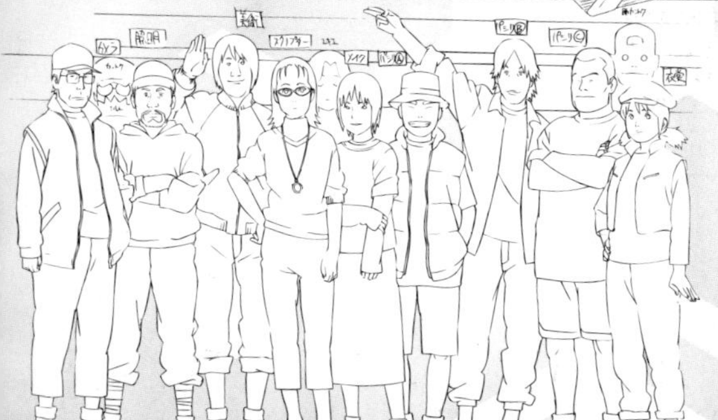

Team Makino

Director Makino's support staff. In the Land of Snow, they all wear sweaters with the character "Ma" (short for Makino) on the back.

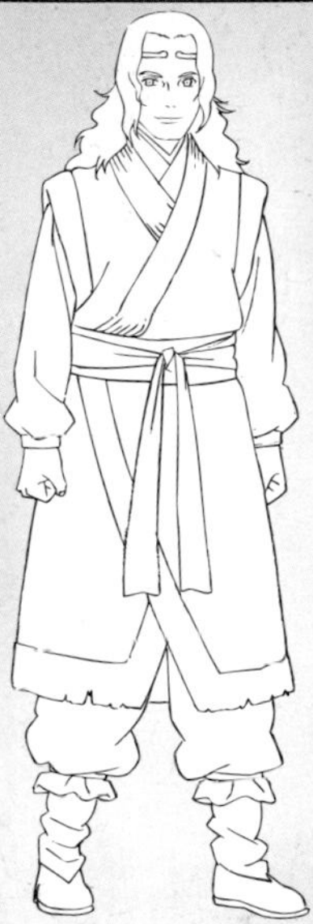

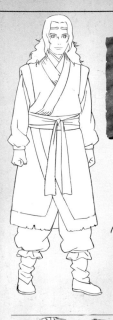

Sukeakuro

Another actor in *The Adventures of Princess Gale.* He has a pretty face, and his nickname is "Mitchi." Sakura's nuts about him.

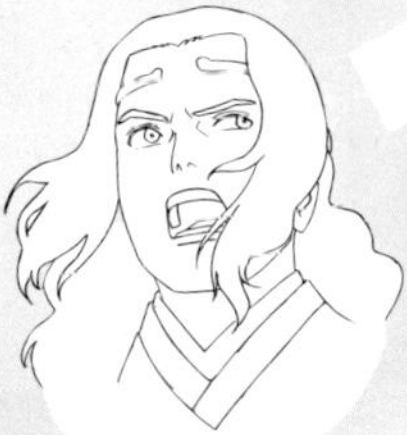

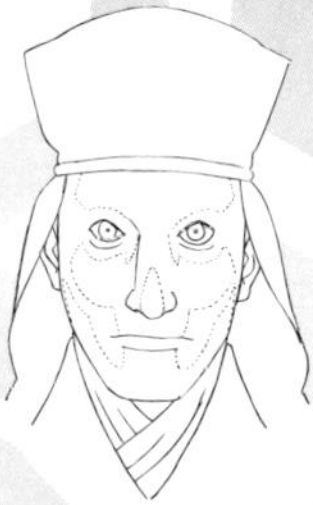

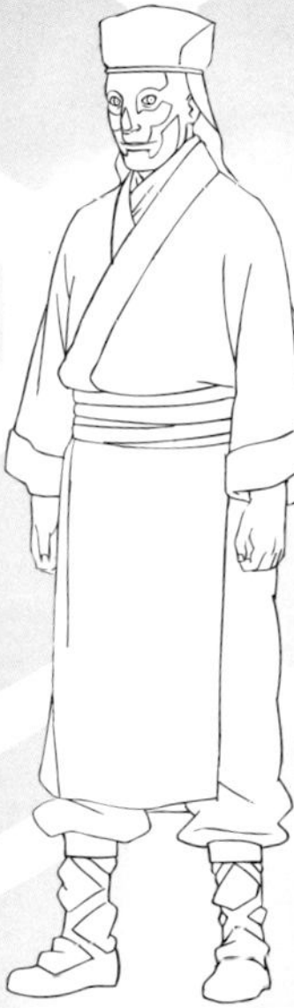

Burikinto

An actor from *The Adventures of Princess Gale:* the movie within the movie! His nick-name is "Ken."

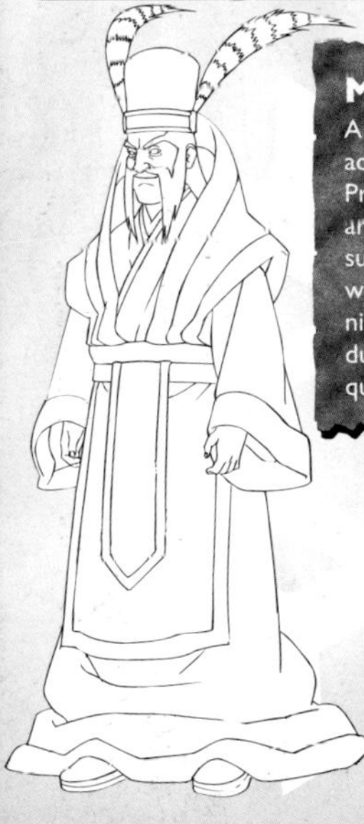

Mao Ozu

A scary-looking actor who plays Princess Gale's archenemy. The surprise on his face when the Snow ninja appeared during filming was quite dramatic!

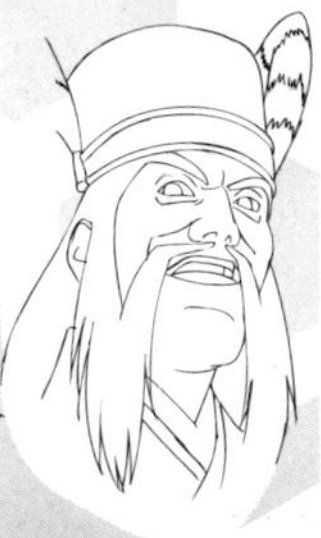

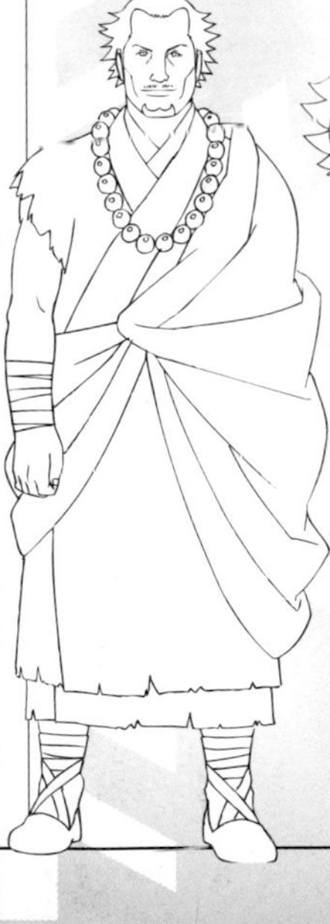

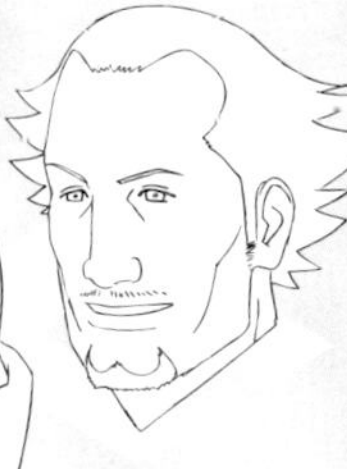

Shishimaru

Another actor in *The Adventures of Princess Gale.* His nickname is Hidero. He's quite friendly.

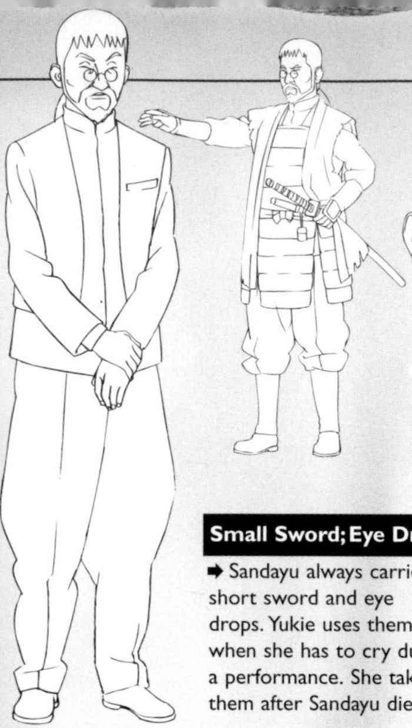

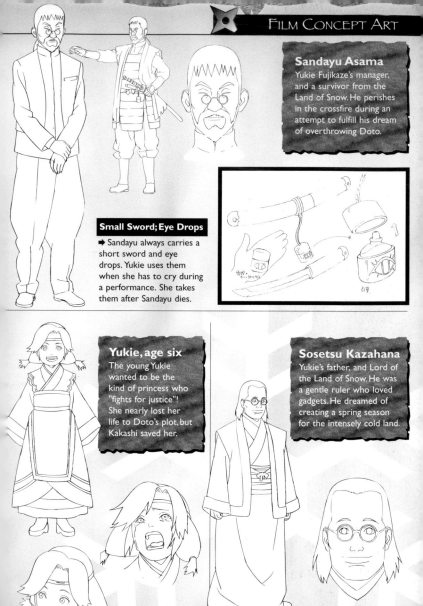

Sandayu Asama

Yukie Fujikaze's manager, and a survivor from the Land of Snow. He perishes in the crossfire during an attempt to fulfill his dream of overthrowing Doto.

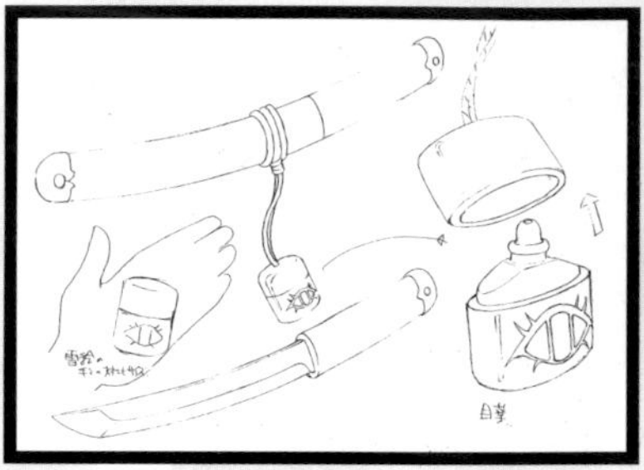

Small Sword; Eye Drops

➡ Sandayu always carries a short sword and eye drops. Yukie uses them when she has to cry during a performance. She takes them after Sandayu dies.

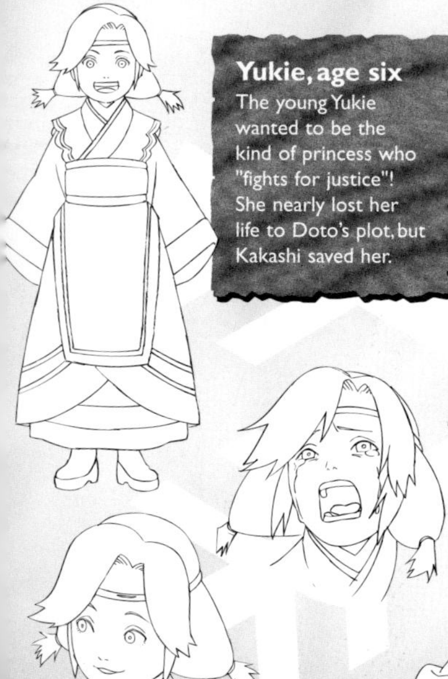

Yukie, age six

The young Yukie wanted to be the kind of princess who "fights for justice"! She nearly lost her life to Doto's plot, but Kakashi saved her.

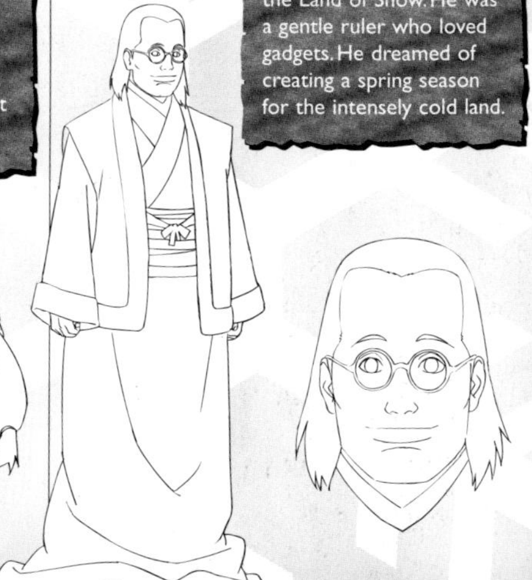

Sosetsu Kazahana

Yukie's father, and Lord of the Land of Snow. He was a gentle ruler who loved gadgets. He dreamed of creating a spring season for the intensely cold land.

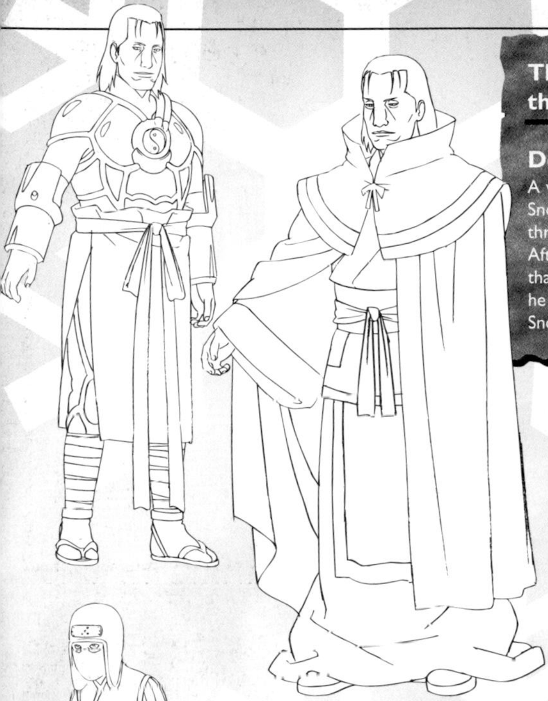

The villains who control the Land of Snow!

Doto Kazahana

A villain who took over the Land of Snow when he betrayed and overthrew his older brother Sosetsu. After creating a special dark armor that can absorb and amplify chakra, he schemed to make the Land of Snow into a military superpower.

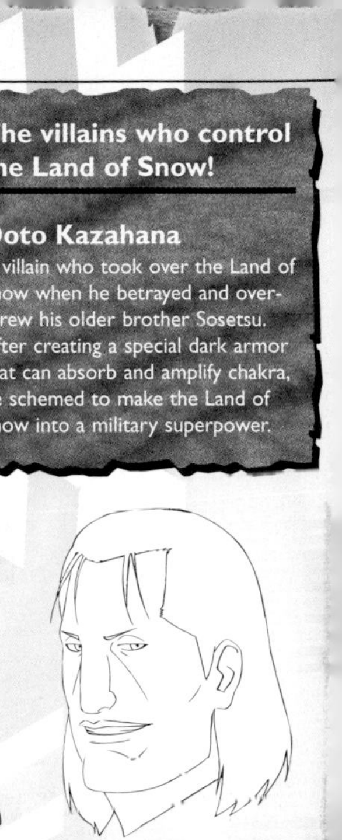

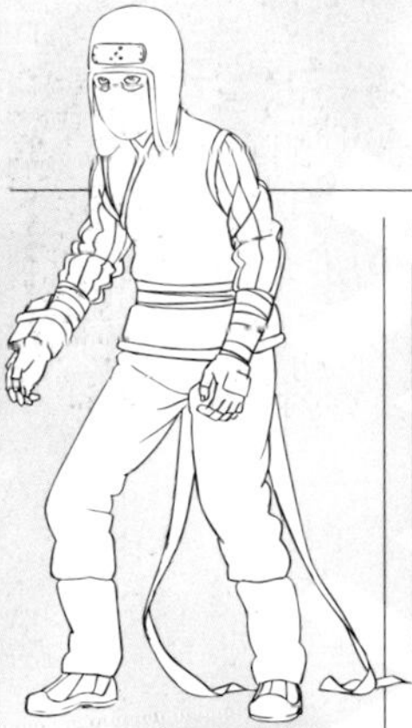

Snow Ninja

⬆ These ninja are hired by Doto, but are not particularly powerful. Kakashi also dresses up as a Snow ninja to get inside the castle.

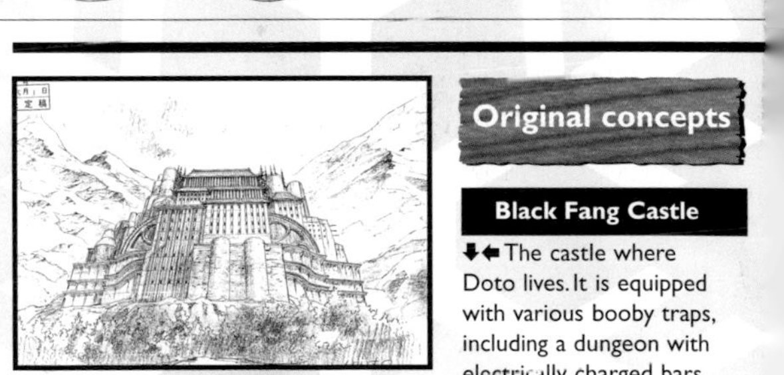

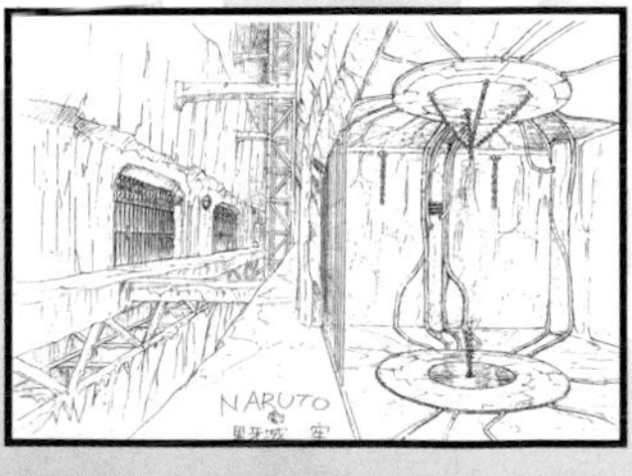
NARUTO

Original concepts

Black Fang Castle

⬇⬅ The castle where Doto lives. It is equipped with various booby traps, including a dungeon with electrically charged bars. When Doto captures them, Naruto and the princess are imprisoned in one of these cells.

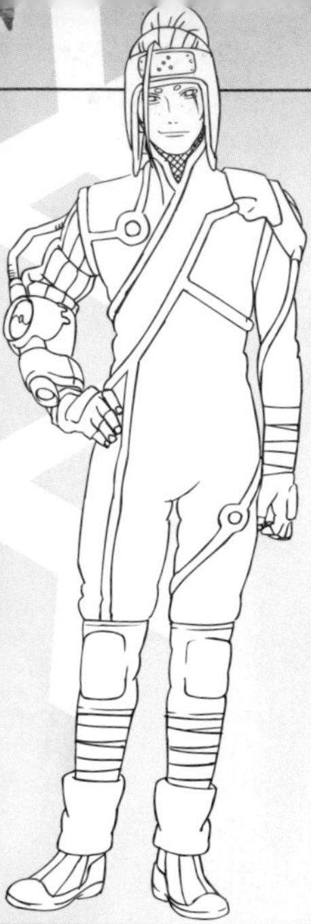

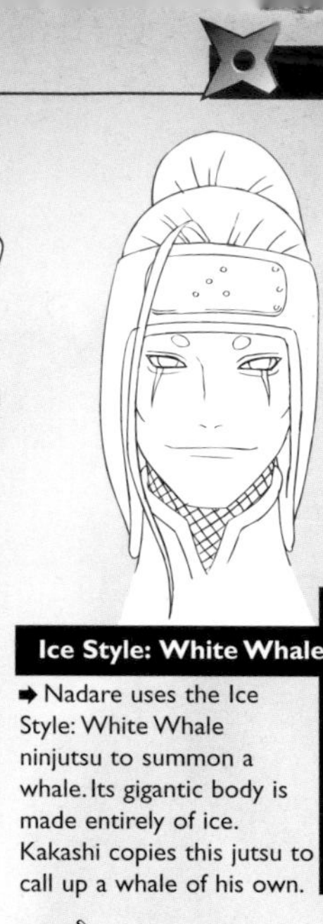

Nadare Roga

The leader of a group of three Snow ninja that have fought against Kakashi before. He has amassed an unusual amount of power by using the Chakra armor that Doto invented.

Ice Style: White Whale

➡ Nadare uses the Ice Style: White Whale ninjutsu to summon a whale. Its gigantic body is made entirely of ice. Kakashi copies this jutsu to call up a whale of his own.

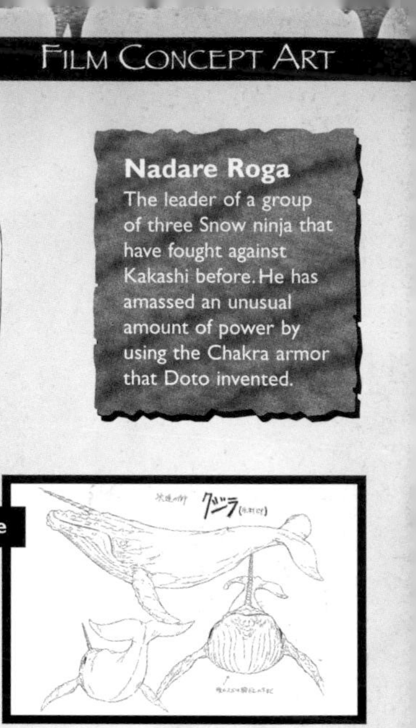

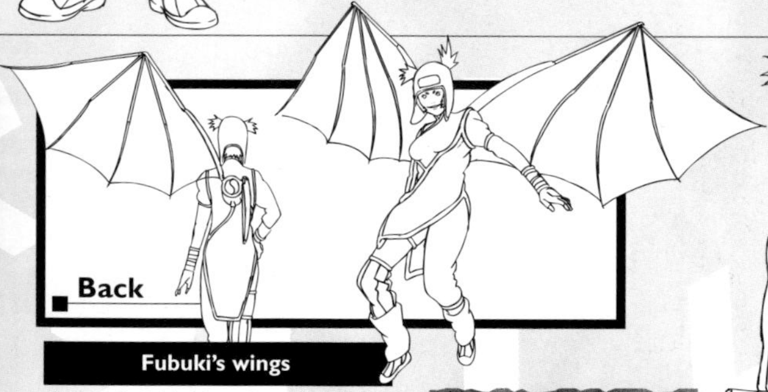
Back

Fubuki's wings

⬆ Usually folded, but she can spread them and fly at will. Doto is equipped with the same mechanism.

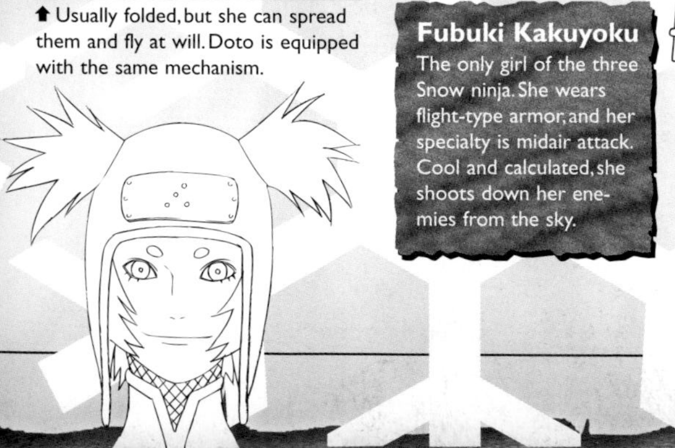

Fubuki Kakuyoku

The only girl of the three Snow ninja. She wears flight-type armor, and her specialty is midair attack. Cool and calculated, she shoots down her enemies from the sky.

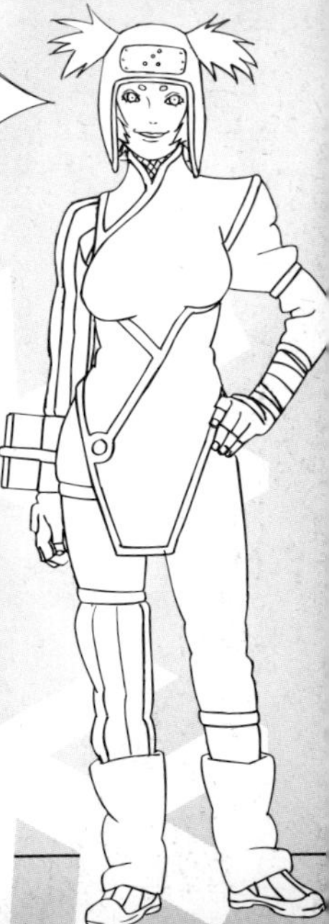

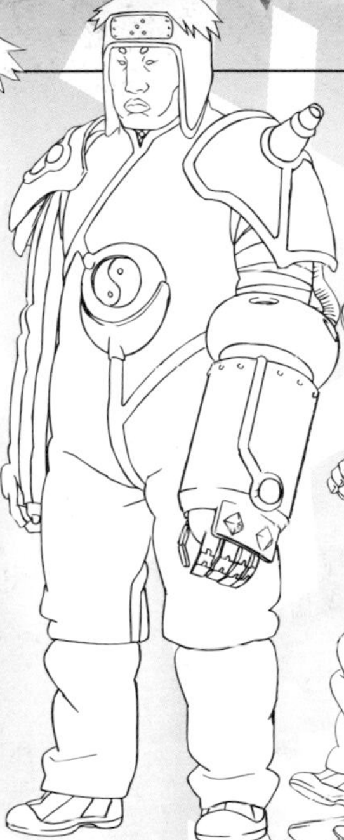

Mizore's Snowboard

⬇ Mizore rides his snowboard with grace and style. It runs on chakra power, which enables it to make high-speed moves.

Mizore Fuyuguma

One of the three Snow ninja, he too wears high-powered armor. At first glance he looks slow and stupid, but his combination of power and speed make him a formidable enemy.

Engine

➡ The engine of the armored train that nearly ran over Naruto and the princess as they followed the tracks. It runs on four rails.

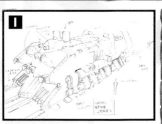

Armored train

Here's a concept sketch of the armored train that Doto used to look for Yukie and the Hex Crystal. This magnificent machine can convert from a train to a tank to an airship.

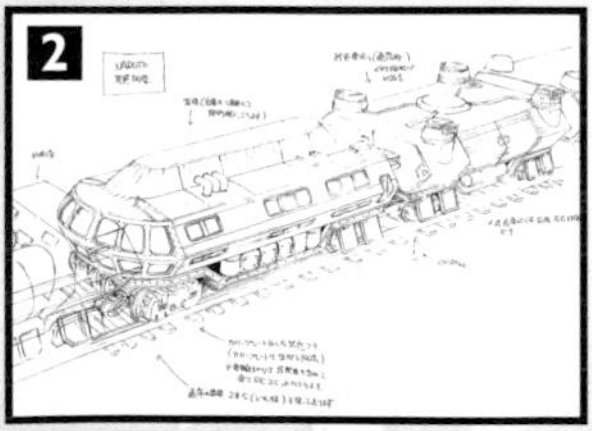

Armored train

⬅ The rest of the train is made up of passenger cars and armored freight cars. The armored cars shoot large quantities of kunai knives.

Dirigible

⬆ This passenger car detaches from the engine and armored cars to form an airship. It can fly extremely high.

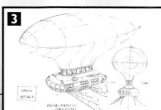

HD24P Editing
Sony PCL
YUKA YAMAGISHI
DAISUKE
TSUKIOKA

HD Conversion
Sony PCL
NORIO TADA
HIKARU OOTSUKI
KAZUMI IHARA

HD Coordination
Sony PCL
HIDEKI ITO

Film Recording
TOKYO
LABORATORY LTD.

FilmsKodak

Recording Director
CHIHARU KAMIO

Sound Director
YASUNORI EBINA

Sound Effects
TAKUYA
HASEGAWA
(SOUND BOX)

TOKYO
TELEVISION
CENTER
SO TAKAGI
KEIICHIRO
MORIMOTO
FUTOSHI UEDA

Sound Engineer
AKIRA NOGUCHI
(sound team * DON
JUAN)

MA Studio
KSS STUDIO
STUDIO GONG
TOKYO
TELEVISION
CENTER

Sound Production
RAKUONSHA

Sound Producer
MASAHIRO
TSUKADA

Digital Recording
Engineer
NOBORU NISHIO

Music Producers
HIDEO
KATSUMATA
HIDEICHI KURITA

Music
TOSHIO MASUDA
& MUSASHI
PROJECT
Music Director
MASAYUKI
WATANABE
Recording Engineers
HITOSHI
HASHIMOTO

AKIKO
NAKAMURA

Mixing Engineers
HITOSHI
HASHIMOTO
AKIKO
NAKAMURA
JUNICHIRO OJIMA

Assistant Mixing
Engineers
HIROMI SHINJOH
TETSUYA
KANESHIGE
JUNICHIRO OJIMA
TOSHIHIKO KASAI

Assistant Music
Director
MITSURU
YAMAMOTO

MUSASHI Members:

Music Producers
KATSUNOSUKE
KOBARI
EMIKO OOIWA

Japanese Drums
TAKARA
OOTSUKA

Shamisen Guitar
HAJIME NISHI

Guitar
MASAAKI IIZUKA

Drums
TAKEKI MIYAUCHI

Shakuhachi, Noukan,
Flute
YASUO SATOH

6 String Bass Guitar
ISAMU TAKITA

Keyboards
YASUHARU
TAKANASHI

Music Cooperation
TV TOKYO MUSIC

Production Chief
SHIGEHIRO SUZUKI

Floor Coordinator
KUNIYUKI AOKI

Production
Coordinators
YOSHIKAZU
TAKAHASHI
KOICHI
MACHIYAMA
TAKAHIRO
NATORI
SAYOKO
NUMASAWA
MIKI KUROSAKA
SYUICHI IWASE
YUTA KIMURA
NAOHIKO
MATSUZAWA

Script/Scenic
Character Design
Editor
YUKA MIYATA

Creative Associates
HIROTSUGU
KAWASAKI
MASAAKI ENDO

Production
Cooperation
SYOJI MATSUI
HIROSHI OGAWA
KAZUYOSHI
OZAWA
KAZUKI
HIRAKAWA
TOMOHIRO
TAKAHASHI

MADHOUSE
MASAO
MOROSAWA
AI MURAYAMA
MASATO
YAMAMOTO

JEONG HAENG
GUEON
ANDY SONG
JOUNG SE KWON
GUEY JY HWANG
JEONG GYUN
JEONG

Animation Supervisor
HAYATO DATE

Production
SYOHEI IZAWA
SHIGEKAZU
TAKEUCHI
HIDEKI YAMASHITA
SOUICHI AKIYAMA
YUJI NUNOKAWA
ATSUSHI
TAKEUCHI
YOSHISHIGE
SHIMATANI

Planning Cooperation
KEISUKE IWATA
KAZUHIKO
TORISHIMA
MICHIYUKI
HONMA
KEN HAGINO

Producers
TOMOKO
GUSHIMA
KAZUTERU
OSHIKIRI

Project Cooperation
SHUEISHA/SHONE
N JUMP
MASAHIKO
IBARAKI
MASANA
TAKAHASHI
KOSUKE YAHAGI

Associate Producers
YUKAKO
MATSUSAKO
MASATO TAKAMI
TAKASHI HARADA

KAZUMICHI UEDA
TAKUYUKI HIROBE
TAIHEI YAMANISHI

Marketing Producer
MASAKI
NAKAYAMA

Marketing
Coordinators
TOMOHIKO EGAMI
AKITO TAKAHASHI
SAYAKA ONO

Naruto Movie
Project
TV TOKYO
TETSUO NAKAO
NORIKO
KOBAYASHI

SHUEISHA
SEIICHI SHIMIZU
KIYOTSUGU
TAKEHANA
KENICHIRO USHIKI

PIERROT
MIKIO IGARASHI
KOTA KITAMURA
EMIKO YAKAME

TOHO
KAZUHIKO SETA
GENKI
KAWAMURA

Aniplex
YUUKI HOSHIJIMA
ATSUHIRO
IWAGAMI
AI ABE
MASAE MINAMI

dentsu
TOICHIRO
SHIRAISHI
TETSUYA
WATANABE
YUKIO
YOSHIMURA

BANDAI
KEISUKE
FURUSAWA
CHUYA ISHIDA

Sponsored by
TOMY
SHUNJI KAMIO
TOSHIHIRO
MORIOKA
SUGURU YOKOTA

Amada Printing MFG
KOICHI SOMEYA
HIRONOBU
KAMADA

SHOWA NOTE
SHIGERU
KATAGISHI
TOMIO HIGANO

BANPRESTO
YASUHIKO
YAMAURA
KAZUNORI GOKA

Cooperation
TOKYO METRO
FAMILYMART
PLENUS
MOVIC

Animation
Production
PIERROT

Produced by
Naruto Movie
Project
TV TOKYO
SHUEISHA
PIERROT
TOHO
Aniplex
dentsu
BANDAI

Director
TENSAI OKAMURA

English Production By
VIZ Media, LLC

Executive Producers
HIDEMI FUKUHARA
AKIRA FUJITA

Producer
JAMIE SIMONE

English Adaptations
by
ARDWIGHT
CHAMBERLIN
LIAM O'BRIEN

Production
Supervisor
WILLIAM GERMAIN

Co-Producers
JASON
BERGENFELD
MIKI MACALUSO

Production Associate
MITSUKO KITAJIMA

Music Coordinator
WILLIAM GERMAIN

Casting
JAMIE SIMONE

Voice Director
MARY ELIZABETH
McGLYNN

Cast
MAILE FLANAGAN
YURI LOWENTHAL
KATE HIGGINS
DAVE
WITTENBERG
KARI WAHLGREN
CAMERON CLARKE
CRISPIN FREEMAN
KYLE HEBERT
DAVID JEREMIAH
LEX LANG
MICHAEL
MCCONNOHIE
DARAN NORRIS
LIAM O'BRIEN
JAMIESON K. PRICE

SAM BRENT RIEGAL
CINDY ROBINSON
DOUG STONE
JAMIE SIMONE

Music Composed and
Performed by
JEREMY A. SWEET
AND MICHAEL
WHITTAKER

"Never Give Up"
(Closing Theme)
COMPOSED BY
JEREMY A. SWEET
PERFORMED BY
JEREMY A. SWEET
AND IAN C.
NICKUS

Post Production
Supervisor
DENNY
DENSMORE

Video Editor
TERRY MARLIN

Assistant Video
Editor
LINDSEY MYERS

Recording Engineers
DAVID W. BARR
MICHAEL CLARK
ERIC LEWIS

Re-Recording Mixer
MARK ETTEL

Production
Coordinator
JESSICA RENSLOW

Production
Accountant
LAURA LOPEZ

Production Assistant
SEAN KELLEY

Produced at
STUDIOPOLIS, INC.
STUDIO CITY, CA
USA

Distributed By
VIZ Media, LLC

Original Author
MASASHI
KISHIMOTO
(SHUEISHA/
SHONEN JUMP)

Screenplay
KATSUYUKI
SUMISAWA

Character Design
TETSUYA NISHIO

Mechanic Design
SHINJI ARAMAKI

Concept Design
MASAAKI ENDO

Chief Animation
Director
HIROTO TANAKA

Art Director
SHIGENORI
TAKADA

Color Design
NOBUKO MIZUTA

Director of
Cinematography
ATSUHO
MATSUMOTO

Editor
SEIJI MORITA

Continuity
TENSAI OKAMURA
HIROTSUGU
KAWASAKI

Voice Director
AYAKO TERUI

Animation Directors
SHIGEO AKAHORI
OSAMU
KOBAYASHI
TSUGUYUKI KUBO
TSUTOMU AWADA
MAMORU SASAKI

Effect Animation
Director
TAKASHI
HASHIMOTO

Helper
MASAAKI ENDO

Assistant Animation
Directors
YASUYUKI SHIMIZU
HIROHUMI
MASUDA
MICHIO MIHARA
HIROOMI
YAMAKAWA
HIDETSUGU ITO
SACHIKO SUGINO
SYUICHI KANEKO
SHIGERU KIMIJIMA

Key Animation
TATSUYA TOMARU
TAKASHI
HASHIMOTO
HIDETSUGU ITO
MAMORU SASAKI
KENJI HACHIZAKI
HIROHUMI
MASUDA
TETSUYA
KUMAGAI
TAKASHI
TOMIOKA
SHINYA
TAKAHASHI
KEIKO SHIMIZU
HIDEKI ITO
ATSUKO OTANI
SHIGEO AKAHORI
HIROTSUGU
KAWASAKI
MICHIO MIHARA
SYUICHI KANEKO
TSUTOMU AWADA
SACHIKO SUGINO
AKIKO
YAMAGUCHI
TOSHIHIKO
MASUDA
YUZO SATO
ATSUSHI HASEBE
TADASHI FUKUDA
AKIKO SEKI
KATSUYA YAMADA
MASAAKI ENDO
HISASHI EGUCHI
YASUYUKI SHIMIZU
TAKAO MAKI
KAZUYOSHI
YAGINUMA
HIROOMI
YAMAKAWA
SHIGERU KIMIJIMA
HIROYUKI
HORIUCHI
TADASHI
MATSUZAKI
HISASHI SAITO
TOSHIHARU SUGIE
MIWA SASAKI
TSUTOMU SUZUKI
KAZUYOSHI
TAKEUCHI
NORIMOTO
TOKURA
MASAHIKO SASAKI
SYUICHI
SHIMAMURA
HIROMI NIIOKA
YOSHIMI ITAZU
TOSHIYUKI
KANNO
YO MORIYAMA
TAKESHI HORI
ATSUSHI KOMORI
KAZUNOBU HOSHI
EI INOUE
KOICHI ARAI
ATSUSHI OGATA
EITARO ABE
YUICHI ENDO
HIROFUMI SUZUKI
KAN SAITO
MASAHIRO NERIKI
TOKUYUKI
MATSUTAKE
TETSUYA NISHIO
TAKESHI HONDA

Backgrounds
Studio Wyeth
SHINOBU
TAKAHASHI
MICHIKO
TANIGUCHI
MOMOKO
TAKATSU
SHINJI SUGIYAMA
RIEKO OOIWA
IZUMI WADA

Studio LOFT
KAZUHIKO SUZUKI
MEGUMI NAKADA
TSUYOSHI
FUKUMOTO
TOSHIKO ABE
JUNJI OOZEKI

SEOUL-LOFT

DR MOVIE
PARK YONG IL
KIM HYUN SOO
YOU CHOONG
HYUN
CHO HAN MO

STUDIO SALLIM
SHIN OG CHUL
PARK SUN YOUNG
KIM MI KYUNG
SONG YUN JUN

In-between
Animation
PIERROT
RYUTA YANAGI
MASAYUKI KOUDA
AIKA KAWASAKI
MEGUMI HATTA
MASAYUKI KATO
ERIKO MURAKAMI
KUMIKO
KAWASHIMA
RINAKO
NISHIHARA
JUNICHI
TAKADATE
MIKA NAIKI

PIERROT
FUKUOKA
MIFUMI TOMITA
KIM BOMIN
MIKA OOKUBO
EMI KIRIKIHIRA
ETSUKO KIMURA

MITSUE AKIYAMA

OH PRODUCTION
MISUZU ICHINOSE
YOSHIE FUJIWARA
MINAKO SEKIHARA
MARIKO ITO
YASUYUKI
KITAZAWA

NARA ANIMATION
STUDIO
HWANG JI NA
LEE HO SOO
PARK EUN JOO
HAN SUENG JIN
KIM JI EUN
GO YE JA
ORK MI YOUNG
CHOI DO YOUNG
CHOI HEE EUN
LEE SUN ME
SEONG BO YANG
HAENG
PARK EUN A
SONG HYUN JOO
KIM MYUNG MI
LIM GAB SOOK

DR MOVIE
HWANG SOON HA
KIM EUN SUN
PARK YOUNG AE
PYUN EUN ME
CHOUNG YOON
HEE
HWANG SU JIN
YOUN MYUNG HEE
BYUN EUN SOON
PARK HYUN AH
HEO YOUNG JIN
JO JEONG HWA
AN KYU HWAN
JEONG YOUN HEE
BYUN HYE SOON
YOON MI
KYOUNG
GO JI SUN
CHO HYE JUNG
AN MI KYOUNG
LYU JI HE
LEE JEONG EUN
RYU SONG I
HEO PIL WON
OH HYUN
KYOUNG

MADHOUSE
DOGA KOBO
Triple A
STUDIO MAT
STUDIO GHIBLI
FAR EASTERN
ANIMATION
LIMITED
ANIME
TOROTORO

Color Correction
NOBUKO MIZUTA
YUKI KASE
MAYUMI
NAGASHIMA

Animation Inspection
MITSUKO
TOSHIMA
HIDETO TANAKA
MANABU NII
AKIRA YAMAUCHI
HIROKO TEZUKA
OTOHIKO IIKURA

Digital Painting
PIERROT
FUKUOKA
YUKIE MATSUZAKI
HITOMI
SHIMOGANNA
YUKIKO
TANISHIMA
MAMI YARIWAKE
SHINNOSUKE
NAGARE

YOSHIKO
TAKIGUCHI

STUDIO KILLY
TOSHIKO IWAKIRI
MEGUMI MATSUI
SAYURI TAKAGI
MIYOKO YOSHIDA
KAORI ISHIKAWA
MICHIKO
IKUSHIMA
NAOMI
TAKAHASHI

STUDIO TARGE
AYA SHIRAISHI
JIN WADA
NATSUKO
INOHARA
KAZUMI
HOSOKAWA
SAYURI MISEZAKI
KUMIKO AKAHORI
HISASHI
KOYANAGI
IKUYO MORITA
RYUSUKE MINAMI
TOSHIYUKI ITO

SEONG BO YANG
HAENG
KWON OH SOOK
SEO KYUNG WHA
HWANG CHONG
SHIL
KIM JEONG HWAN
KOOK KWI SUN
SONG JEONG HAN

NARA ANIMATION
STUDIO
CHO SEOUNG SUK
OH YOUNG SUK
PARK KUYUNG
SUK
SON EUN SUK
LIM HO YOUNG
LEE MI JOUNG
JEONG JI HYUN
LEE GA EUL

DR MOVIE
LEE YOUNG SHIM
SHIN HYE MI
PARK YONG
KYOUNG
JEONG EUN SOOK
CHOI SU RA
HAN JIN YOUNG
CHOI SOON LEE
SEO SAENG HOE
CHOI HYEON OK
LEE JEONG EUN
LEE MI YEUN
LIM MEA IL
PARK YUN HEE
JUN JUNG SUK
AN HYUN JI
LEE KUN HEE
SONG SEUNG HEE
NA YONG SUK
CHOI KI JEONG
YIM JEONG AH
PARK JEONG AH
CHOI BO RA
NA MOON HEE

MADHOUSE
TANTO
Triple A
FAR EASTERN
ANIMATION
LIMITED
SHAFT
STUDIO LAGOON
T2studio

Filming
KAORI
KAWASHIMA
NOBUO KIMURA
MAI UEMATSU
TOSHIO KAIDO
HISAKO TAMADA
ANNA TORII
YUKA NAKAYA
SAEKO YUYAMA

Filming Cooperation
STUDIO COSMOS
DIGITAL FACTORY

Paint Inspection
YOSHIKO SHIMIZU
YUKIE MATSUZAKI
TOMOE IMAMURA
HITOMI
SHIMOGANNA
IZUMI MURASAKI
MAMI YARIWAKE

Background
Retouching
YURI SHIMIZU
KAORU
NAGASAWA
RURIKO IKEJIRI
MAKIKO
YAGIHASHI
KUMIKO KIMURA
KAORI SAKAMOTO
KIMIKO KOJIMA
TOMOE
MURAMATSU

CG Effects
SHINJI YAGINUMA
KENJI IKEDA
NAOMI WADA
KAZUKO
OYANAGI

3D Effect
Cooperation
DIGITAL FRONTIER
Inc.

CG Producer
YUSAKU
TOYOSHIMA

CG Director
YASUHIRO
OHTSUKA

CG Designers
TAKASHI CHIBA
LIN HSUAN FU
KATSURA SATO
YUKINOBU
FUJIMATSU

Production Manager
KUMIKO OGURI

System
TADAHIKO
KURACHI

Production Desk
AI KIKUCHI

Editing
SEIJI MORITA
Assistant Editor
YUKIE OIKAWA

A Few Words from Masashi Kishimoto

Ah, Naruto's big screen debut! It happened in 2004 – a year in which my dreams got so close to reality, it was scary.

I must confess that this anime fan cried unmanly tears (grin) at the special advance screening of the film for the people who were involved in its creation.

I also cried in front of the production staff when I met them, out of sheer gratitude...and here I had thought my tears had all dried up (wait – I'm not the heroine of this movie)!

Anyway, I was so embarrassed. But I was also very grateful for the opportunity to become acquainted with these animators, whom I had respected for such a long time – not to mention the director and the rest of his staff.

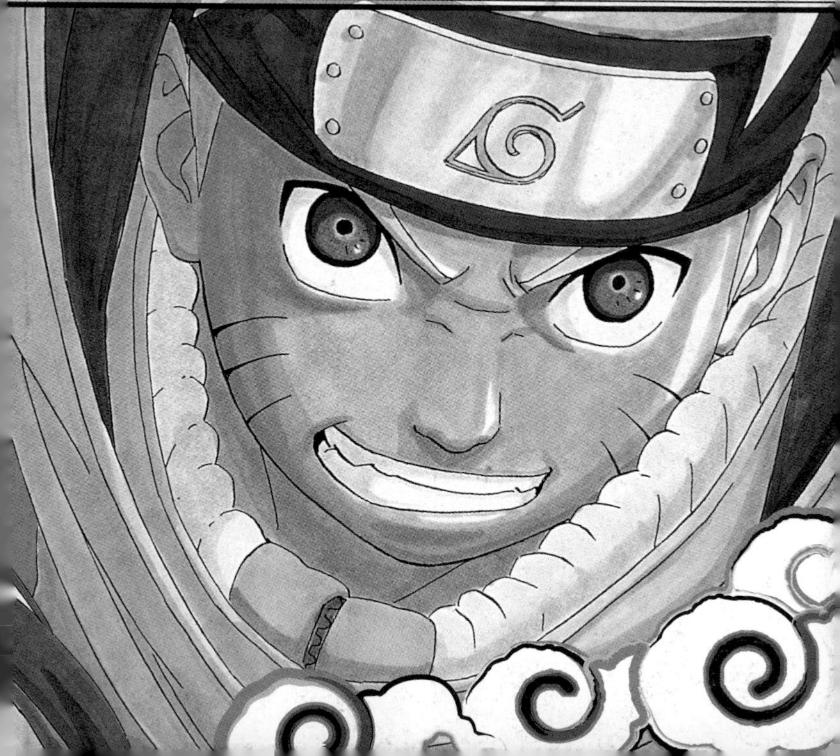

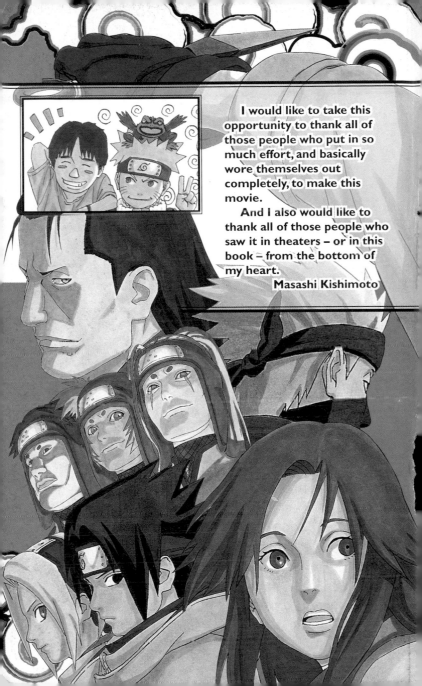

I would like to take this opportunity to thank all of those people who put in so much effort, and basically wore themselves out completely, to make this movie.

And I also would like to thank all of those people who saw it in theaters – or in this book – from the bottom of my heart.

Masashi Kishimoto